Introduction to Homeland Security

Introduction to Homeland Security

Jane A. Bullock

George D. Haddow

Damon Coppola

Erdem Ergin

Lissa Westerman

Sarp Yeletaysi

ELSEVIER
BUTTERWORTH
HEINEMANN

Amsterdam • Boston • Heidelberg • London • New York • Oxford
Paris • San Diego • San Francisco • Singapore • Sydney • Tokyo

Acquisitions Editor: Mark Listewnik
Associate Acquisitions Editor: Jennifer Soucy
Developmental Editor: Pamela Chester
Project Manager: Kyle Sarofeen
Marketing Manager: Christian Nolin
Cover Design: Eric DeCicco
Printer: HING YIP Printing Co., Ltd.

Elsevier Butterworth–Heinemann
200 Wheeler Road, Burlington, MA 01803, USA
Linacre House, Jordan Hill, Oxford OX2 8DP, UK

∞ Recognizing the importance of preserving what has been written, Elsevier-Science prints its books on acid-free paper whenever possible.

Library of Congress Cataloging-in-Publication Data
Introduction to homeland security / by Jane A. Bullock . . . [et al.].
    p. cm
  Includes bibliographical references and index.
  ISBN 0-7506-7787-2
    1. Terrorism—Prevention—Government policy—United States. 2. National security—United States. 3. Civil defense—United States. 4. Emergency management—United States. I. Bullock, Jane A.
HV6432.I58 2004
363.32′0973—dc22   2004016807

British Library Cataloguing-in-Publication Data
A catalogue record for this book is available from the British Library.
ISBN: 0-7506-7787-2

For information on all Butterworth-Heinemann/Elsevier publications visit our web site at: books.elsevier.com/security

05 06 07 08 09 10 10 9 8 7 6 5 4 3 2
Typeset by Newgen Imaging Systems (P) Ltd., Chennai, India
Printed in China

Table of Contents

CHAPTER 3   ORGANIZATIONAL ACTIONS

CHAPTER 4   HAZARDS

CHAPTER 8 **COMMUNICATIONS**

Acknowledgments

The authors of this book would like to express their appreciation for the continued support and encouragement we have received from Dr. Jack Harrald and Dr. Joseph Barbera, codirectors of the Institute for Crisis, Disaster and Risk Management at George Washington University. These two individuals provide outstanding leadership to institutions and governments in designing and implementing homeland security projects. Greg Shaw, also part of the institute, contributed a large dose of practical advice and humor. We would like to acknowledge the many individuals whose research, analysis, and opinions helped to shape the content of this volume.

We would also like to thank Mark Listewnik and Jennifer Soucy at Elsevier for their assistance in conceiving this book and their patience and faith in us.

Finally, we recognize the thousands of professionals and volunteers who, through their daily pursuits, are giving form and substance to creating a more secure and safe homeland.

Introduction

Since the events of September 11 and the subsequent anthrax mailings to the U.S. Congress, governments, organizations, and individuals have engaged in programs and activities to improve the security and safety of our nation. The most comprehensive reorganization of the federal government yet undertaken resulted in the creation of the Department of Homeland Security. Congress passed new laws, including the Patriot Act, which provides the attorney general of the United States with significant new authorities relative to civil liberties to fight the war on terrorism. Thousands of citizens have volunteered to participate in making our communities more secure.

Public safety officials, particularly emergency managers, are in the forefront of preparing for and responding to the potential threat of terrorism. The intent of this book is to provide a primer on homeland security for emergency managers and related disciplines.

FM-1 New York, NY, September 16, 2001—Military and rescue workers stand amid the wreckage of the World Trade Center. Photo by Andrea Booher/FEMA News Photo.

The federal government defines homeland security as follows:

Homeland security is a concerted national effort to prevent terrorist attacks within the United States, reduce America's vulnerability to terrorism, and minimize the damage and recover from attacks that do occur.

Starting with this definition, the early chapters provide a historic perspective on the threat of terrorism, before and after September 11, with detailed descriptions of the extraordinary legislative and organizational actions that were taken in reaction to September 11 and in support of preventing future attacks. The book continues with complete descriptions and fact sheets on the types of hazards and risks that make up the potential vulnerabilities in any future terrorist events. This section is followed by chapters that describe the programs and actions being undertaken by government agencies, organizations, and the private sector to reduce or minimize the threat. We have focused on the areas of security (intelligence, border and transportation, infrastructure and information/cyberspace); preparedness and mitigation (planning, initiatives, community and volunteers, private sector, best practices); communications (threat advisory system, public health strategies, public education); and new technologies (communications, information management, protective equipment).

FM-2   Arlington, VA, September 17, 2001—Work continues throughout the night at the site of the Pentagon terrorist attack. Photo by Jocelyn Augustino/FEMA News Photo.

A significant section is devoted to response and recovery, as these responsibilities are a primary focus of emergency managers. In this chapter we describe the current state of the art in first responder applications and discuss the major changes that are under way within the national response system network. Case studies are included to demonstrate practical application to the materials being presented. In addition, we have included full texts of critical guidance documents for use and reference. Wherever possible, budget and resource charts show past allocations and future projections through 2004. The volume concludes with a chapter that examines future issues that public safety, emergency management, and other types of professionals may confront as we meet the challenges of establishing a secure homeland.

Please note that throughout this book we make constant reference to the Federal Emergency Management Agency (FEMA). Prior to becoming the Emergency Preparedness and Response Directorate (EP&R) in the Department of Homeland Security (DHS), FEMA was an executive branch agency that reported directly to the president of the United States. Recently it was announced that FEMA would retain its name within DHS. So, to keep things simple, the authors refer to FEMA as FEMA and not as EP&R throughout this book.

Homeland security is a new, still-evolving discipline. This book was written at a particular point in time, and changes to programs, activities, and even organizations occur regularly. For that reason we have included online references wherever possible so the reader will have access to information sites that can provide up-to-date information on program or organization changes, new initiatives, or simply more detail on specific issues.

Out of the tragic events of September 11 comes an enormous opportunity for improving the social and economic sustainability of our communities from all threats and disasters, not just terrorism. Public safety officials and emergency managers champion the concept of an all-hazards approach, and despite some unique characteristics, terrorism can be incorporated into that approach as well. With the increased funding being provided, we should have better-trained and better-equipped first responders; a stronger, less vulnerable national infrastructure; and an enhanced delivery system for public health and new technologies to improve and safeguard our information and communications networks.

These improvements will enhance our protection from hurricanes, energy and power outages, and fires. A new focus on research and development should lead to significant advances in the diverse fields included in the homeland security umbrella.

It is too early to ascertain if the actions taken in response to the events of September 11 are having an impact in our communities. The authors' goal in writing this book was to provide as complete a source of practical information, programs, references, and best practices so that any emergency manager, public safety official, community leader or individual could engage in actions to help make their communities safer and more secure. In the end, achieving homeland security will not be accomplished by the federal government but by each individual, each organization, each business, and each community working together to make a difference.

1

Historic Overview of the Terrorist Threat

INTRODUCTION

Harry Truman once said, "The only thing new is the history we don't know." For many Americans the rush of activities by the government in the aftermath of the September 11 attacks in passing new laws, reorganizing government institutions, and allocating vast sums of money appeared to be unprecedented. The reality is that many of the actions taken have precedent in the past, and these past experiences offer insight into the future success or failure of the actions taken after September 11.

The purpose of this chapter is to provide a historic perspective of the evolution of emergency management policies, statutes, and practices in the United States and to examine the chronology of events and actions leading to and beyond September 11. This perspective will help frame the issues to be discussed in subsequent chapters of this book, which will detail the legislative, organizational, and operational underpinnings of America's homeland security structure.

This chapter will provide summaries of the tragic events of September 11 including updated statistics, first responder anecdotes and perspective, timelines, and review of after-action reporters. Additional information is provided for three other major terrorist incidents: the

1993 World Trade Center bombing, the 1995 Oklahoma City bombing of the Murrah Federal Office Building, and the 2001 anthrax incidents in Washington, DC.

EMERGENCY MANAGEMENT IN THE UNITED STATES

The purpose of this section is to discuss the historical, organizational, and legislative history of modern emergency management in the United States. We will review some of the significant events and people that have shaped the emergency management discipline over the years.

Understanding the history and evolution of emergency management is important because at different times the concepts of emergency management have been applied differently. The definition of emergency management can be extremely broad and all-encompassing. Unlike other more structured disciplines, it has expanded and contracted in response to events, the desires of Congress, and leadership styles.

A simple definition is that emergency management is the discipline dealing with risk and risk avoidance. Risk represents a broad range of issues and includes an equally diverse set of players. The range of situations that could possibly involve emergency management or the emergency management system is extensive. This fact supports the premise that emergency management is integral to the security of our daily lives and should be integrated into our daily decisions and not just called on when we think of disasters.

Emergency management is an essential role of government. The Constitution entrusts the states with responsibility for public health and safety—hence, responsibility for public risks—and assigns the federal government to a secondary role. The federal role is to help when the state, local, or individual entity is overwhelmed. This fundamental philosophy continues to guide the government function of emergency management.

Based on this strong foundation, the validity of emergency management as a government function has never been in question. Entities and organizations fulfilling the emergency management function existed at the state and local level long before the federal government became involved. But as events occurred, political philosophies changed, and the nation developed, the federal role in emergency management steadily increased.

EARLY HISTORY—1800–1950

In 1803 a Congressional act was passed to provide financial assistance to a New Hampshire town devastated by fire. This is the first example of the federal government becoming involved in a local disaster. Not until the administration of Franklin Roosevelt began to use government as a tool to stimulate the economy did we see a significant investment in emergency management functions in the federal government.

During the 1930s the Reconstruction Finance Corporation and the Bureau of Public Roads were both granted the authority to make disaster loans available for repair and reconstruction of certain public facilities after disasters. The Tennessee Valley Authority (TVA) was created during this time to produce hydroelectric power and, as a secondary purpose, to reduce flooding in the region.

A significant piece of emergency management legislation was passed during this time. The Flood Control Act of 1934 gave the U.S. Army Corps of Engineers increased authority to design and build flood control projects. This act has had a significant and long-lasting impact on emergency management in this country. The Flood Control Act reflected the philosophy that man could control nature, thereby eliminating the risk of floods. Although this program would promote economic and population growth patterns along the nation's rivers, history has proved this attempt at emergency management to be shortsighted and costly.

THE COLD WAR AND THE RISE OF CIVIL DEFENSE—1950s

The next notable time frame for the evolution of emergency management occurs during the 1950s. The Cold War era presented the principal disaster risk as the potential for nuclear war and nuclear fallout. Civil defense programs proliferated across communities during this time. Individuals and communities were encouraged to build bomb shelters to protect themselves and their families from a nuclear attack by the Soviet Union.

Almost every community had a civil defense director, and most states had someone who represented civil defense in their state government hierarchy. These individuals were usually retired military personnel, and their operations received little political or financial support from their state or local governments. Equally often the civil defense responsibility was an addition to other duties.

Federal support for these activities was vested in the Federal Civil Defense Administration (FCDA), an organization with little staff or financial resources whose main role was to provide technical assistance. In reality, the local and state civil defense directors were the first recognized face of emergency management in the United States.

A companion office to the FCDA, the Office of Defense Mobilization was established in the Department of Defense (DoD). The primary functions of this office were to allow for the quick mobilization of materials and the production and stockpiling of critical materials in the event of a war. It included a function called *emergency preparedness*. In 1958 these two offices were merged into the Office of Civil and Defense Mobilization.

The 1950s were a quiet time for large-scale natural disasters. Hurricane Hazel, a Category 4 hurricane, inflicted significant damage in Virginia and North Carolina in 1954. Hurricane Diane hit several mid-Atlantic and northeastern states in 1955, and Hurricane Audrey, the most damaging of the three storms, struck Louisiana and north Texas in 1957. Congressional response to these disasters followed a familiar pattern of ad hoc legislation to provide increased disaster assistance funds to the affected areas.

As the 1960s began, three major natural disaster events occurred. In a sparsely populated area of Montana, the Hebgen Lake earthquake, measuring 7.3 on the Richter scale, brought attention to the fact that the nation's earthquake risk went beyond the California borders. Also in 1960, Hurricane Donna hit the west coast of Florida and Hurricane Carla blew into Texas in 1961. The incoming Kennedy administration decided to make a change to the federal approach. In 1961 it created the Office of Emergency Preparedness inside the White House to deal with natural disasters. Civil defense responsibilities remained in the Office of Civil Defense within DoD.

NATURAL DISASTERS BRING CHANGES TO EMERGENCY MANAGEMENT—1960s

As the 1960s progressed, the United States would be struck by a series of major natural disasters. The Ash Wednesday storm in 1962 devastated over 620 miles of shoreline on the East Coast, producing over $300 million in damages. In 1964, in Prince William Sound, Alaska, an earthquake measuring 9.2 on the Richter scale became front-page news throughout America and the world. This Easter quake killed 123 people and generated a tsunami that affected beaches as far down the Pacific Coast as California. Hurricane

Betsy struck in 1965, and Hurricane Camille in 1969, killing and injuring hundreds and causing hundreds of millions of dollars in damage along the Gulf Coast.

The response, as with previous disasters, was the passage of ad hoc legislation for funds. However, the financial losses resulting from Hurricane Betsy's path across Florida and Louisiana engendered a discussion of insurance as a protection against future floods and a potential method to reduce continued government assistance after disasters. The unavailability of flood protection insurance on the standard homeowner policy, and the prohibitive cost of such insurance where it was available, prompted Congressional interest. These discussions eventually led to the passage of the National Flood Insurance Act of 1968 that created the National Flood Insurance Program (NFIP).

It is important to note how local and state governments choose to administer this flood risk program. Civil defense departments usually were responsible for dealing with risks and disasters. Although the NFIP dealt with risk and risk avoidance, responsibilities for the NFIP were sent to local planning departments and state Departments of Natural Resources. This is one illustration of the fragmented and piecemeal approach to emergency management that evolved during the 1960s and 1970s.

THE CALL FOR A NATIONAL FOCUS TO EMERGENCY MANAGEMENT—1970s

In the 1970s responsibility for emergency management functions were evident in more than five federal departments and agencies, including the Department of Commerce (weather, warning, and fire protection), the General Services Administration (continuity of government, stockpiling, federal preparedness), the Treasury Department (import investigation), the Nuclear Regulatory Commission (power plants), and the Department of Housing and Urban Development (flood insurance and disaster relief).

With the passage of the Disaster Relief Act of 1974, prompted by the previously mentioned hurricanes and the San Fernando earthquake of 1971, the Department of Housing and Urban Development (HUD) possessed the most significant authority for natural disaster response and recovery through the National Flood Insurance Program (NFIP) under the Federal Insurance Administration (FIA) and the Federal Disaster Assistance Administration (disaster response, temporary housing, and assistance). On the military side, there existed the Defense Civil Preparedness Agency (nuclear attack) and the U.S. Army Corps of Engineers (flood control). However, when one looked at the broad range of risks and potential disasters, more than 100 federal agencies were involved in some aspect of risk and disasters.

This pattern continued down to the state and, to a lesser extent, local levels. Parallel organizations and programs added to confusion and turf wars, especially during disaster response efforts. The states and the governors grew increasingly frustrated over this fragmentation. In the absence of one clear federal lead agency in emergency management, a group of state civil defense directors led by Lacy Suiter of Tennessee and Erie Jones of Illinois launched an effort through the National Governor's Association (NGA) to consolidate federal emergency management activities in one agency.

With the election of Jimmy Carter, a former fellow governor from Georgia, the effort gained steam. President Carter came to Washington committed to streamlining all government agencies and seeking more control over key administrative processes. The state directors lobbied the NGA and Congress for a consolidation of federal emergency management functions. When the Carter administration proposed such an action, it met with a receptive audience in the Senate. Congress had already expressed concerns about the lack of a coherent federal policy and the inability of states to know where to turn in the event of an emergency.

In the midst of these discussions, an accident occurred at the Three Mile Island nuclear power plant in Pennsylvania, which galvanized the consolidation effort. This accident brought national media attention to the lack of adequate off-site preparedness around commercial nuclear power plants and the role of the federal government in responding to such an event.

On June 19, 1978, President Carter transmitted to the Congress the Reorganization Plan Number 3 (3 CFR 1978, 5 U.S. Code 903).

The intent of this plan was to consolidate emergency preparedness, mitigation, and response activities into one federal emergency management organization. The president stated that the plan would provide for the establishment of the Federal Emergency Management Agency (FEMA) and that the FEMA director would report directly to the president.

Reorganization Plan No.3 transferred the following agencies or functions to FEMA: National Fire Prevention Control Administration (Department of Commerce); Federal Insurance Administration (HUD); Federal Broadcast System (Executive Office of the President); Defense Civil Preparedness Agency (DoD); Federal Disaster Assistance Administration (HUD); and the Federal Preparedness Agency (GSA).

Additional transfers of emergency preparedness and mitigation functions to FEMA were as follows: oversight of the Earthquake Hazards Reduction Program (Office of Science and Technology Policy); coordination of dam safety (Office of Science and Technology Policy); assistance to communities in the development of readiness plans for severe weather-related emergencies; coordination of natural and nuclear disaster warning systems; and coordination of preparedness and planning to reduce the consequences of major terrorist incidents.

The plan articulated several fundamental organizational principles:

> First, federal authorities to anticipate, prepare for, and respond to major civil emergencies should be supervised by one official responsible to the president and given attention by other officials at the highest levels. Second, an effective civil defense system requires the most efficient use of all available resources. Third, whenever possible, emergency responsibilities should be extensions of federal agencies. Fourth, federal hazard mitigation activities should be closely linked with emergency preparedness and response functions. (Reorganization Plan Number 3 3CFR 1978; 5 U.S. code 903)

After Congressional review and concurrence, the Federal Emergency Management Agency was officially established by Executive Order 12127 of March 31, 1979 (44 FR 19367, 3 CFR, Comp., p.376). A second executive order, Executive Order 12148, mandated reassignment of agencies, programs, and personnel into the new entity FEMA.

Creating the new organization made sense. Integrating the diverse programs, operations, policies, and people into a cohesive operation was a much bigger task than most people realized when the consolidation began. It would take extraordinary leadership and a common vision. It also created immediate political problems. By consolidating these programs and the legislation that created them, the new agency would have to answer to 23 committees and subcommittees in Congress with oversight of its programs. Unlike most other federal agencies, it would have no organic legislation to support its operations and no clear champions to look to during the Congressional appropriations process.

John Macy became the first director of FEMA, and his task was to unify an organization that was not only physically separated—parts of the agency were in located in five different buildings around Washington — but also philosophically separate. Programs focused on nuclear war preparations were combined with programs focused on a new consciousness of the environment and floodplain management.

Macy focused his efforts by emphasizing the similarities between natural hazards preparedness and civil defense by developing a new concept called the Integrated Emergency Management System (IEMS). This system was an all-hazards approach that included direction, control, and warning as functions common to all emergencies from small isolated events to the ultimate emergency of nuclear attack.

For all of Macy's good efforts, FEMA continued to operate as individual entities pursuing their own interests and answering to their different Congressional bosses. It was a period of few major disasters, so virtually no one noticed this problem of disjointedness.

CIVIL DEFENSE REAPPEARS AS NUCLEAR ATTACK PLANNING—1980s

The early and middle 1980s saw FEMA facing many challenges, but no significant natural disasters.

The absence of the need for a coherent federal response to disasters, as was called for by Congress when it approved the establishment of FEMA, allowed FEMA to continue to exist as an organization of many parts.

In 1982 President Ronald Reagan appointed Louis O. Guiffrida as Director of FEMA. Mr. Guiffrida, a California friend of Ed Meese, one of the President's closest advisors, had a background in training and terrorism preparedness at the state government level.

General Guiffrida proceeded to reorganize FEMA consistent with administration policies and his own background. Top priority was placed on government preparedness for a nuclear attack. Resources within the agency were realigned, and additional budget authority was sought to enhance and elevate the national security responsibilities of the agency. With no real role for the states in these national security activities, the state directors who had lobbied for the creation of FEMA saw their authority and federal funding declining.

Because of Congressional questions about the agency's operations, the Department of Justice and a grand jury began investigations of senior political officials at FEMA. These inquiries led to the resignation of Guiffrida and top aides in response to a variety of charges, including misuse of government funds.

President Reagan then selected General Julius Becton to be the director of FEMA. General Becton was a retired military general and had been the director of the Office of Foreign Disaster Assistance in the State Department. From a policy standpoint, he continued to emphasize the programs of his predecessor, but in a less visible manner. Becton himself expanded the duties of FEMA when he was asked by DoD to take over the program dealing with the off-site cleanup of chemical stockpiles on DoD bases. This program was fraught with problems, and bad feelings existed between the communities and the bases over the funds available to the communities for the cleanup. FEMA had minimal technical expertise to administer this program and depended on DoD/Army for the funding. This situation led to political problems for the agency and did not lead to significant advancements in local emergency management operations as promised by DoD.

AN AGENCY IN TROUBLE—1989–1992

As Congress debated, and finally passed, major reform of federal disaster policy as part of the Stewart McKinney-Robert Stafford Act, the promise of FEMA and its ability to support a national emergency management system remained in doubt.

As the 1980s closed, FEMA was an agency in trouble. It suffered from severe morale problems, disparate leadership, and conflicts with its partners at the state and local levels over agency spending and priorities. In 1989 two devastating natural disasters called into question the continued existence of FEMA. In September, Hurricane Hugo slammed into North Carolina and South Carolina after first hitting Puerto Rico and the Virgin Islands. It was the worst hurricane in a decade, with over $15 billion in damages and 85 deaths. FEMA was slow to respond, waiting for the process to work and for the governors to decide what to do. Sen. Ernest Hollings (D-SC) personally called the FEMA director and asked for help, but the agency moved slowly. Hollings went on national television to berate FEMA in some of the most colorful language ever, calling the agency the "sorriest bunch of bureaucratic jackasses."

Less than a month later, the Bay Area of California was rocked by the Loma Prieta earthquake as the 1989 World Series got under way in Oakland Stadium.

FEMA was not prepared to respond, but it was lucky. While FEMA had spent the last decade focused on nuclear attack planning, FEMA's state partners in emergency management, especially in California, had been preparing for a more realistic risk, an earthquake. Although damages were high, few lives were lost. This was a testament to good mitigation practices in building codes and construction that were adopted in California and some good luck relative to the time the earthquake hit.

In 1992, FEMA was not so lucky. In August 1992, Hurricane Andrew struck Florida and Louisiana and Hurricane Iniki struck Hawaii within months of each other (Figure 1-1).

FEMA wasn't ready, and neither were FEMA's partners at the state level. The agency's failure to respond was witnessed by Americans all across the country as major news organizations followed the crisis. The efficacy of FEMA as the national emergency response agency was in doubt. After dispatching then-Secretary of Transportation Andrew Card to take over the response operation, President George H.W. Bush sent in the military.

It was not just FEMA that failed during Hurricane Andrew; it was the process and the system. In Hurricane Andrew, FEMA recognized the need to apply all of its resources to the response and began to use its national security assets for the first time in a natural disaster response. But it was too late. Starting with Hurricane Hugo, public concern over natural disasters was high. People wanted and expected government to be there to help in their time of need. FEMA seemed incapable of carrying out the essential government function of emergency management.

In the aftermath of Hurricanes Andrew and Iniki, there were calls to abolish FEMA. Investigations by the General Accounting Office (GAO) and other governmental and nongovernmental watchdog groups called for major reforms. None of this was lost on the incoming Clinton administration.

THE WITT REVOLUTION—1993–2001

When President William Jefferson Clinton appointed James Lee Witt to be director of FEMA, he breathed life back into FEMA and brought a new style of leadership to the troubled agency. Witt was the first director with emergency management experience. He was from a constituency that had played a major role in creating FEMA but had been forgotten, the state directors. With Witt, President Clinton had a politician with skill and credibility and, more important, an understanding of the importance of building partnerships and serving the customer.

Witt came in with a mandate to restore the trust of the American people that their government would be there for them during times of crisis. He initiated sweeping reforms inside and outside the agency. Inside FEMA, he reached out to all employees, implemented customer service training, and reorganized the agency to

FIGURE 1-1   Hurricane Andrew, FL, August 24, 1992—Many houses, businesses, and personal effects suffered extensive damage from one of the most destructive hurricanes ever recorded in America. One million people were evacuated, and 54 died in this hurricane. FEMA News Photo.

break down stovepipes. He supported the application of new technologies to the delivery of disaster services and emphasized mitigation and risk avoidance. Outside of the agency, he strengthened the relationships with state and local emergency managers and built new ones with Congress, within the administration and with the media. One of the hallmarks of the Witt years at FEMA was open communication, both internally and externally.

Throughout the next several years, FEMA and its state and local partners would face every possible natural hazard, including killer tornadoes, ice storms, hurricanes, floods, wildfires, and drought.

When President Clinton elevated Witt to the position of Director of FEMA and he became a member of

Clinton's cabinet, the value and importance of emergency management were recognized. Witt used this newfound respect as an opportunity to lobby the nation's governors to include their state emergency management directors in their cabinets.

The Oklahoma City bombing in April 1995 represented a new phase in the evolution of emergency management. This event, which followed the first bombing of the World Trade Center in New York City in 1993, raised the issue of our nation's preparedness for terrorism events (Figure 1-2). As emergency management responsibilities are defined by risks and the consequences of those risks, responding to terrorist threats was included. The Oklahoma City bombing

FIGURE 1-2 Oklahoma City, OK, April 26, 1995—A scene of the devastated Murrah Federal Office Building after the Oklahoma City bombing. FEMA News Photo.

tested this thesis and set the stage for interagency disagreements over which agency would be in charge of terrorism.

The Nunn-Lugar legislation of 1995 left open the question as to who would be the lead agency in terrorism. Many fault FEMA leadership for not quickly claiming that role, and the late 1990s were marked by several different agencies and departments assuming various roles in terrorism planning. The question of who should first respond to a terrorism incident—fire or police department, emergency management or emergency medical personnel—was closely examined, but no clear answers emerged. The state directors looked to FEMA to claim the leadership role. In an uncharacteristic way, the leadership of FEMA vacillated on this issue. Terrorism was certainly part of the all-hazards approach to emergency management

championed by FEMA, but the resources and technologies needed to address specific issues, such as weapons of mass destruction and the consequences of a chem-bio attack, seemed well beyond the reach of the current emergency management structure.

While this debate continued, FEMA took an important step in its commitment to disaster mitigation by launching a national initiative to promote a new community-based approach called Project Impact. Project Impact: Building Disaster Resistant Communities was designed to mainstream emergency management and mitigation practices into every community in America. The goal of Project Impact was to incorporate decisions about risk and risk avoidance into the community's everyday decision-making processes. By building a disaster-resistant community, its members would promote sustainable economic development, protect and enhance their natural resources, and ensure a better quality of life for all citizens. As the decade ended without any major technological glitches from Y2K, FEMA was recognized as the preeminent emergency management system in the world. It was emulated in other countries, and Witt became an Ambassador for emergency management overseas. Hurricane Mitch saw a change in American foreign policy toward promoting and supporting community-based mitigation projects. State and local emergency management programs had grown, and their value was recognized and supported by society. Private sector and business continuity programs were flourishing.

The role and responsibility of emergency management had significantly increased, as had the partnerships supporting it. Its budget and stature had grown. Good emergency management became a way to get economic environmental issues onto the table; it became a staple of discussion relative to a community's quality of life.

The profession of emergency management was attracting a different type of public servant. Political and management skills were critical, and candidates for state, local, and private emergency management positions were now being judged on the basis of their training and experience rather than their political connections.

Undergraduate and advance degree programs in emergency management were flourishing at over 65 national colleges and universities. It was now a respected, challenging, and sought-after profession.

TERRORISM BECOMES MAJOR FOCUS—2001

Before September 11 the Nunn-Lugar legislation provided the primary authority and focus for domestic federal preparedness activities for terrorism. Several agencies, including the Federal Emergency Management Agency (FEMA), Department of Justice (DOJ), Department of Health and Human Resources (HHS), Department of Defense (DoD), and the National Guard, were involved, all jockeying for leadership on the terrorism issue. There were some attempts at coordination but, in general, agencies pursued their own

agendas. The biggest difference among the agencies was the level of funding available, with DoD and DOJ controlling the most funds. State and local governments were confused and unprepared and complained of the need to address their vulnerability and needs should a terrorist event happen. The TOPOFF exercise, held in 1999, reinforced these concerns and vividly demonstrated the problems that could arise in a real event.

With the election of George W. Bush, a new FEMA director, Joe Allbaugh, was named to head the agency. As a former chief of staff to Governor Bush in Texas and President Bush's campaign manager in the 2000 presidential race, Allbaugh has a close personal relationship with the president. As demonstrated by Witt and Clinton, such alliances are viewed as assets for the agency. Allbaugh's lack of emergency management background was not an issue during his confirmation hearings.

As part of a major reorganization of the agency, Allbaugh recreated the Office of National Preparedness (ONP). This office was first established in the 1980s, during the Guiffrida reign, to plan for World War III; Witt eliminated it in 1992. This action raised some concerns among FEMA's constituents and FEMA staff. However, this time the mission of the office focuses on terrorism.

In a September 10, 2001 speech, Director Allbaugh listed his priorities as firefighters, disaster mitigation, and catastrophic preparedness. These topics seem prophetic in light of the events of September 11. As the events of that day unfolded, FEMA activated the Federal Response Plan and response operations proceeded as expected in New York and in Virginia. Most of the agency's senior leaders, including the director, were in Montana, attending the annual meeting of the National Emergency Management Association (NEMA), which represents state emergency management directors. The strength of the system was proven as hundreds of response personnel initiated operations within minutes of the events.

THE FUTURE—2002 AND BEYOND

In the aftermath of the terrorist attacks on September 11, FEMA and the newly formed Department of Homeland Security (DHS), together with their partners in emergency management, fire, police, and public health at the state and local government levels, have been charged with expanding and enhancing our nation's emergency management system to achieve a safe and secure homeland. In the coming years, billions of dollars will be allocated from the federal government to state and local governments in order to expand existing programs and establish new ones designed to meet the new terrorism threat.

As the environment of emergency management has grown, the quality, skill base, technical demands and caliber of its practitioners have increased (see Figure 1-3). Terrorism provides another opportunity to expand the

FIGURE 1-3 New York, NY, October 13, 2001—New York firefighters at the site of the World Trade Center. Photo by Andrea Booher/FEMA News Photo.

base. The goal of this textbook is to provide you with the background and working knowledge of disciplines, players, and organizations that are a part of this nation's homeland security efforts.

As with previous defining events, the environment for emergency management will absorb the event and evolve to reflect its impact. If history repeats itself, the field of emergency management will shift its focus to a national approach to the problem and emphasize preparedness through training and equipment. The resiliency of the system allows for these midstream corrections. The long-term viability and measure of the influence of emergency management will continue to depend on its value to all citizens in all communities, every day and not just during times of crisis.

A summary of which is as follows:

1993 WORLD TRADE CENTER BOMBING

On February 23, 1993, a massive explosion occurred in the parking basement of the World Trade Center in New York City. The bomb, which weighed more than 1,000 pounds, caused extensive damage on seven floors, six of which were below grade. The blast crater measured 130 feet wide by 150 feet long. Over 50,000 people were evacuated, including 25,000 from the twin towers of the Trade Center. The evacuation took approximately 11 hours to complete (Fusco 1993). At the time, the response to the bombing was described as "the largest incident ever handled in the City of New York Fire Department's 128-year history. In terms of the number of fire units that responded, it was the equivalent of a 16-alarm fire" (Fusco 1993). The following provides a summary of relevant data from the bombing event:

- Deaths: 6
- Injuries: 1,042
- Firefighter injuries: 85 (one requiring hospitalization)
- Police officers injured: 35
- EMS workers injured: 1
- Firefighter, police, and EMS deaths: 0

- Number of people evacuated from WTC complex: approximately 50,000
- FDNY engine companies responding: 84
- FDNY truck companies responding: 60
- FDNY special units responding: 26
- FDNY personnel responding: 28 battalion chiefs, 9 deputy chiefs
- Percentage of FDNY on duty staff responding: 45%

Source: Fusco 1993

1995 MURRAH FEDERAL BUILDING BOMBING

On April 19, 1995, a massive truck bomb exploded outside of the Alfred P. Murrah Federal Building in downtown Oklahoma City. All told, 168 died, including 19 children attending a day care program in the building. A total of 674 people were injured. The Murrah building was destroyed, 25 other buildings in the downtown area were severely damaged or destroyed, and another 300 buildings were damaged by the blast. The ensuing rescue and recovery effort over the next 16 days involved 11 FEMA urban search-and-rescue teams (Sidebar 1-1) dispatched

---

SIDEBAR 1-1   FEMA Urban and Search and Rescue at Murrah Building Bombing in Oklahoma City, 1995

At 9:02 A.M. on the morning of April 19, 1995, a bomb exploded from inside a Ryder truck under the Alfred P. Murrah Federal Building in Oklahoma City. The blast caused a partial collapse of all nine floors of the 20-year-old building, and 168 people died.

Rescuers from the Oklahoma City Fire Department entered the building unsure of whether or not the building would continue to support its own weight. Most of the steel support system had been blown out.

Within five hours of the blast the first FEMA urban search-and-rescue task force was deployed. By 6 P.M. the task force was in the building, searching for victims. One of the first assignments was to search the second floor nursery for victims.

Teams with search-and-rescue dogs began the search in the nursery. The dogs are trained to bark when they find live victims. No dogs barked that night.

Eleven of FEMA's 27 USAR task forces worked in the building, with representation from virtually every task force in the country. The FEMA teams coordinated with local fire departments, police departments, and military and federal agencies during the search-and-rescue effort.

The rescue effort involved extensive stabilization of the fragmented building, rescuing of people trapped within tight spaces, rescues from high angles, breaking through concrete, and hazardous materials analysis and removal.

An innovative plan was developed to help rescuers deal with the psychological and emotional trauma of such a grisly scene. The plan allowed workers to be briefed in advance and prepared for what they were to experience; extensive debriefing sessions were also included.

Source: FEMA, www.fema.gov

FIGURE 1-4 Oklahoma City, OK, April 26, 1995—Search-and-rescue crews work to save those trapped beneath the debris after the Oklahoma City bombing. FEMA News Photo.

from across the country to assist local and state officials search first for survivors and, ultimately, for the bodies of the victims (Figure 1-4). (The City of Oklahoma City, 1996.)

SEPTEMBER 11 ATTACKS ON THE WORLD TRADE CENTER AND THE PENTAGON

On September 11, 2001, terrorist hijacked four planes and crashed them into the twin towers of the World Trade Center in New York City, the Pentagon in Washington, DC, and a field in Pennsylvania (see "September 11 Timeline"). These actions resulted in the collapse of the twin towers and a section of the Pentagon and unprecedented deaths and injury:

- Total deaths for all 911 attacks: 3,030
- Total injured for all 911 attacks: 2,337
- Total deaths at World Trade Center: 2,792
- Total injured at World Trade Center: 2,261
- Total firefighter deaths at World Trade Center: 343
- Total police deaths at World Trade Center: 75
- Total deaths at Pentagon: 124
- Total injured at Pentagon: 76
- Total deaths American Flight 77 Pentagon: 64
- Total deaths United Airlines Flight 93 Pennsylvania: 40
- Total deaths American Airlines Flight 11 WTC North Tower: 92
- Total deaths United Airlines Flight 175 WTC South Tower: 65

Source: http://www.september11news.com/911Art.htm

September 11 Timeline

September 11, 2001 Terrorist Attacks Timeline for the Day of the Attacks

All times in New York Time (EDT). This is four hours before GMT.

Tuesday, September 11, 2001

7:58 A.M.: American Airlines Flight 11, a fully fueled Boeing 767 carrying 81 passengers and 11 crew members departs from Boston Logan airport, bound for Los Angeles, California.

8:00 A.M.: United Airlines Flight 175, another fully fueled Boeing 767, carrying 56 passengers and nine crew members, departs from Boston's Logan airport, bound for Los Angeles, California.

8:10 A.M.: American Airlines Flight 77, a Boeing 757 with 58 passengers and six crew members, departs from Washington's Dulles airport for Los Angeles, California.

8:40 A.M.: The FAA notifies NORAD about the suspected hijacking of American Airlines Flight 11.

8:42 A.M.: On United Airlines Flight 93, a Boeing 757 takes off with 37 passengers and seven crew members from Newark airport bound for San Francisco, following a 40-minute delay caused by congested runways. Its flight path initially takes it close to the World Trade Center.

8:43 A.M.: The FAA notifies NORAD about the suspected hijacking of United Airlines Flight 175.

8:46:26 A.M.: American Airlines Flight 11 crashes with a speed of roughly 490 miles per hour into the north side of the north tower of the World Trade Center, between floors 94 and 98. (Many accounts have given times that range between 8:45 A.M. and 8:50 A.M.) The building's structural type, pioneered in the late 1960s to maximize rentable floor space and featuring lightweight tubular design with no masonry elements in the facade, allows the jetliner to literally enter the tower, mostly intact. It plows to the building core, severing all three gypsum-encased stairwells and dragging combustibles with it. A massive shock wave travels down to the ground and up again. The combustibles, as well as the remnants of the aircraft, are ignited by the burning fuel. Because the building lacks a traditional full-cage frame and depends almost entirely on the strength of a narrow structural core running up the center, the fire at the center of the impact zone is in a position to compromise the integrity of all internal columns. People below the severed stairwells in the north tower start to evacuate. Officials in the south tower tell people shortly afterwards by megaphone and office announcements that they are safe and can return to their offices. Some don't hear it; some ignore it and evacuate anyway; others congregate in common areas such as the 78th-floor sky lobby to discuss their options.

9:02:54 A.M.: United Airlines Flight 175 crashes with a speed of about 590 miles per hour into the south side of the south tower, banked between floors 78 and 84 in full view of media cameras. Parts of the plane leave the building at its east and north sides, falling to the ground six blocks away. A passenger on the plane, Peter Hanson, had called his father earlier from the plane reporting that hijackers were stabbing flight attendants in order to force the crew to open the cockpit doors.

8:46 A.M. to 10:29 A.M.: At least twenty people, primarily in the north tower, trapped by fire and smoke in the upper floors, jump to their deaths. There is some evidence that large central portions of the floor near the impact zone in the north tower collapsed soon after the plane hit, perhaps convincing some people that total collapse was imminent. One person at street level, firefighter Daniel Thomas Suhr, is hit by a jumper and dies. No form of airborne evacuation is attempted because the smoke is too dense for a successful landing on the roof of either tower, and New York City lacks helicopters specialized for horizontal rescue.

9:04 A.M. (approximately): The FAA's air route traffic control center in Boston stops all departures from airports in its jurisdiction (New England and eastern New York State).

Continued

FIGURE 1-5   New York, NY, October 5, 2001—Rescue workers continue their efforts at the World Trade Center. Photo by Andrea Booher/FEMA News Photo.

Continued

9:06 A.M.: The FAA bans takeoffs of all flights bound to or through the airspace of New York center from airports in that center and the three adjacent centers—Boston, Cleveland, and Washington. This is referred to as a first-tier groundstop and covers the Northeast from North Carolina north and as far west as eastern Michigan.

9:08 A.M.: The FAA bans all takeoffs nationwide for flights going to or through New York Center airspace.

9:24 A.M.: President George W. Bush is interrupted with the news of the second crash as he participates in a class filled with Florida schoolchildren. He waits out the lesson then rushes into another classroom commandeered by the Secret Service. Within minutes he makes a short statement, calling the developments "a national tragedy," and is hurried aboard Air Force One.

9:24 A.M.: The FAA notifies NORAD's Northeast Air Defense Sector about the suspected hijacking of American Airlines Flight 77. The FAA and NORAD establish an open line to discuss American Airlines Flight 77 and United Airlines Flight 93.

9:26 A.M.: The FAA bans takeoffs of all civilian aircraft regardless of destination—a national groundstop.

9:37 A.M.: American Airlines Flight 77 crashes into the western side of the Pentagon and starts a violent fire. The section of the Pentagon hit consists mainly of newly renovated, unoccupied offices. Passenger Barbara K. Olson had called her husband, Solicitor General Theodore Olson, at the Justice Department twice from the plane to tell him about the hijacking and to report that the passengers and pilots were held in the back of the plane. As bright flames and dark smoke envelope the west side of America's military nerve center, all doubts about the terrorist nature of the attacks are gone.

9:45 A.M.: United States airspace is shut down. No civilian aircraft are allowed to lift off, and all aircraft in flight are ordered to land at the nearest airport as soon as practical. All air traffic headed for the United States is redirected to Canada. Later, the FAA announces that civilian flights are suspended until at least noon, September 12. The groundings last until September 14, but there are exemptions for Saudi families who fear retribution if they stay in the United States. Military and medical flights continue. This is the fourth time all commercial flights in the United States have been stopped, and the first time a suspension was unplanned. All previous suspensions were military-related (Sky Shield I-III) and took place from 1960 to 1962.

9:45 A.M.: The White House and the Capitol are closed.

9:50 A.M. (approximately): The Associated Press reports that American Airlines Flight 11 was apparently hijacked after departure from Boston's Logan Airport. Within an hour, this report is confirmed for both Flight 11 and United Airlines Flight 175.

9:57 A.M.: President Bush is moved from Florida.

9:59:04 A.M.: The south tower of the World Trade Center collapses. A vast TV and radio audience reacts primarily with horrified astonishment. It is later widely reported that the collapse was not directly caused by the jetliner's impact but that the intense sustained heat of the fuel fire was mostly or wholly responsible for the loss of structural integrity. Later, a growing number of structural engineers assert that the fire alone would not have caused the collapse. Both towers made use of external load-bearing mini columns, and on one face of each building approximately 40 of these were severed by the jetliners. Had they been intact to efficiently distribute the increasing gravity load as the bunched core columns and joist trusses weakened in the fires, the towers might have stood far longer or perhaps indefinitely. Concrete in the towers' facades might have prevented most of the debris and fuel from reaching the building core. Investigations that may radically change skyscraper design (or result in a radical retreat to full-cage construction with high concrete-to-steel ratios as in pre-1960s skyscrapers) are ongoing.

10:03 A.M.: United Airlines Flight 93 crashes southeast of Pittsburgh in Somerset county, Pennsylvania. Other reports say 10:06 or 10:10. According to seismographic data readings, the time of impact was 10:06:05. The first reports from the police indicate that

Continued

no one on board survived. Later reports indicate that passengers speaking on cell phones had learned about the World Trade Center and Pentagon crashes and at least three were planning on resisting the hijackers. It is likely that the resistance led to the plane crashing before it reached its intended target. Reports stated that an eyewitness saw a white plane resembling a fighter jet circling the site minutes after the crash. These reports have limited credibility, although fighter jets had been scrambled to defend the Washington, DC, region earlier. These jets, however, stayed within the immediate DC area.

10:10 A.M.: Part of the Pentagon collapses.

10:13 A.M.: Thousands are involved in an evacuation of the United Nations complex in New York.

10:15 A.M. (approximately): The Democratic Front for the Liberation of Palestine is reported to have taken responsibility for the crashes, but this is denied by a senior officer of the group soon after.

10:28:31 A.M.: The north tower of the World Trade Center collapses from the top down, as if being peeled apart. Probably as a result of the destruction of the gypsum-encased stairwells on the impact floors (most skyscraper stairwells are encased in reinforced concrete), no one above the impact zone in the north tower survives. The fact that the north tower stood much longer than the south one is later attributed to three facts: The region of impact was higher (which meant that the gravity load on the most damaged area was lighter), the speed of the airplane was lower, and the affected floors had their fireproofing partially upgraded. Also, the hottest part of the fire in the south tower burned in a corner of the structure, perhaps leading to a more concentrated failure of columns or joist trusses, or both. The Marriott Hotel, located at the base of the two towers, is also destroyed.

10:35 A.M. (approximately): Police are reportedly alerted about a bomb in a car outside the State Department in Washington, DC. Later reports claim that nothing happened at the State Department.

10:39 A.M.: Another hijacked jumbo jet is claimed to be headed for Washington, DC. F-15s are scrambled and patrol the airspace above Washington, DC while other fighter jets sweep the airspace above New York City. They have orders, first issued by Vice President Cheney and later confirmed by President Bush, to shoot down any potentially dangerous planes that do not comply with orders given to them via radio.

10:45 A.M.: CNN reports that a mass evacuation of Washington, DC and New York has been initiated. The UN headquarters are already empty. A few minutes later, New York's mayor orders an evacuation of lower Manhattan.

10:50 A.M.: Five stories of part of the Pentagon collapse as a result of the fire.

10:53 A.M.: New York's primary elections are canceled.

11:15 A.M. (approximately): Reports surfaced that the F-15s over Washington had shot something down. There was no later confirmation of these reports.

11:16 A.M.: American Airlines confirms the loss of its two airplanes.

11:17 A.M.: United Airlines confirms the loss of Flight 93 and states that it is "deeply concerned" about Flight 175.

11:53 A.M.: United Airlines confirms the loss of its two airplanes.

11:55 A.M.: The border between the United States and Mexico is on highest alert, but has not been closed.

12:00 P.M. (approximately): President Bush arrives at Barksdale Air Force Base in Louisiana. He was on a trip in Sarasota, Florida, to speak about education but is now presumed to be returning to the Capitol. He makes a brief and informal initial statement to the effect that terrorism on U.S. soil will not be tolerated, stating that "freedom itself has been attacked and freedom will be protected."

12:02 P.M.: The Taliban government of Afghanistan denounces the attacks.

12:04 P.M.: Los Angeles International Airport, the intended destination of Flight 11, Flight 77, and Flight 175 is shut down.

12:15 P.M.: San Francisco International Airport, the intended destination of United Airlines Flight 93, is shut down.

Continued

12:15 P.M. (approximately): The airspace over the 48 contiguous United States is clear of all commercial and private flights.

1:00 P.M. (approximately): At the Pentagon, fire crews are still fighting fires. The early response to the attack had been coordinated from the National Military Command Center, but that location had to be evacuated when it began to fill with smoke.

1:04 P.M.: President Bush puts the U.S. military on high alert worldwide. He speaks from Barksdale Air Force Base and leaves for Strategic Air Command bunker in Nebraska.

1:27 P.M.: Mayor Anthony A. Williams of Washington, DC, declares a state of emergency; the DC National Guard arrives on-site.

2:30 P.M.: Senator John McCain characterizes the attack as an "act of war."

2:49 P.M.: At a press conference New York, Mayor Rudy Giuliani is asked to estimate the number of casualties at the World Trade Center. He replies, "More than any of us can bear."

4:00 P.M.: National news outlets report that high officials in the federal intelligence community are stating that Osama bin Laden is the primary suspect in the attacks.

4:25 P.M.: The New York Stock Exchange, NASDAQ, and the American Stock Exchange report that they will remain closed on Wednesday, September 12.

5:20 P.M.: Salomon Brothers 7, commonly referred to as "7 World Trade Center," a 47-story building that had sustained what was originally thought to be light damage in the fall of the twin towers and was earlier reported on fire, collapses. Structural engineers are puzzled, and the investigation continues. The building was not designed by the same team responsible for the twin towers. The building contained New York's special emergency center, which may well have been intended for such a disaster as September 11.

6:00 P.M.: Explosions and tracer fire are reported in Kabul, the capital of Afghanistan, by CNN and the BBC. The Northern Alliance, involved in a civil war with the Taliban government, is later reported to have attacked Kabul's airport with helicopter gunships.

6:00 P.M.: Iraq announces the attacks are the fruit of "U.S. crimes against humanity" in an official announcement on state television.

6:54 P.M.: President Bush finally arrives at the White House. Executive authority through much of the day had rested with Vice President Cheney.

7:00 P.M.: Frantic efforts to locate survivors in the rubble that had been the twin towers continue. Fleets of ambulances have been lined up to transport the injured to nearby hospitals. They stand empty. "Ground Zero" is the exclusive domain of the FDNY and NYPD, despite volunteer steel and construction workers who stand ready to move large quantities of debris quickly. Relatives and friends displaying enlarged photographs of the missing printed on home computer printers are flooding downtown. The New York Armory, at Lexington Avenue and 26th Street, and Union Square Park, at 14th Street, become centers of vigil.

7:30 P.M.: The U.S. government denies any responsibility for reported explosions in Kabul.

8:30 P.M.: President Bush addresses the nation from the White House. Among his remarks: "Terrorist attacks can shake the foundations of our biggest buildings, but they cannot touch the foundation of America. These acts shatter steel, but they cannot dent the steel of American resolve." For a full transcript, see this White House web page at www.whitehouse.gov.

9:00 P.M.: President Bush meets with his full National Security Council, followed roughly half an hour later by a meeting with a smaller group of key advisers. Bush and his advisers have evidence that Osama bin Laden is behind the attacks.

11:00 P.M.: There are reports of survivors buried in the rubble in New York making cell phone calls. These rumors were later proved to be wrong.

Source: www.wikipedia.com

The response to these attacks by fire, police, and emergency medical teams was immediate, and their combined efforts saved hundreds if not thousands of lives, especially at the World Trade Center.

- Year the World Trade Center was built: 1970
- Number of companies housed in the WTC: 430
- Number working in World Trade Center on average working day before 11 September: 50,000
- Average number of daily visitors: 140,000
- Number killed in attack on New York, in the twin towers and in aircraft that crashed into them: 2,823
- Maximum heat of fires, in degrees Fahrenheit, at World Trade Center site: 2,300
- Number of days underground fires at World Trade Center continued to burn: 69
- Number of days that workers dug up debris at Ground Zero, searching for body parts: 230
- Number of body parts collected: 19,500
- Number of bodies discovered intact: 291
- Number of victims identified by New York medical examiner: 1,102
- Number of death certificates issued without a body at request of victims' families: 1,616
- Number of people still classified as missing from the World Trade Center that day: 105
- Number of survivors rescued from Ground Zero: 0

Source: http://observer.guardian.co.uk/waronterrorism/story/0,1373,776451,00.html

The addition of another stairway in each tower, the widening of existing stairways, and regular evacuation drills, actions implemented in the aftermath of the 1993 World Trade Center bombing, are credited with facilitating the evacuation of thousands of office workers in the towers before they collapsed. Federal, state and nongovernmental groups (e.g., Red Cross, Salvation Army) also responded quickly, establishing relief centers and dispensing critical services to victims and first responders.

- Cases opened: 55,494
- Mental health contacts made: 240,417
- Health services contacts made: 133,035
- Service delivery sites opened: 101
- Shelters opened: 60
- Shelter population: 3,554
- Meals/snacks served: 14,113,185
- Response vehicles assigned: 292
- Disaster workers assigned: 57,434
  Information as of 31 October 2002

Source: http://www.redcrossalbq.org/04a_911statistics.html

In addition to the stunning loss of life and the physical destruction caused by the attacks, two other losses are significant for their size and impact. First, 343 New York City firefighters and 75 New York City police officers were lost in the World Trade Center when the towers collapsed. So many first responders had never before been lost in a single disaster event in the United States, and their untimely deaths brought extraordinary attention to America's courageous and professional firefighters, police officers, and emergency medical technicians. They became the heroes of September 11, and this increased attention has resulted in increased funding for government programs that provide equipment and training for first responders. It has also resulted in a reexamination of protocols and procedures in light of the new terrorist threat. The examination of the after-action reports from the World Trade Center and the Pentagon in the next section of this chapter provide insight into the issues currently being addressed by the first responder community.

The second significant aspect of the September 11 attacks is the magnitude and the scope of the losses resulting from the attacks. The total economic impact on New York City alone is estimated to be between $82.8 and $94.8 billion. This estimate includes $21.8 billion in lost buildings, infrastructure, and tenant assets; $8.7 billion in the future earnings of those who died; and $52.3–$664.3 billion gross city product (Thompson 2002). The economic impact of the attacks were felt throughout the United States and the world, causing jobs to be lost and businesses to fail in communities hundreds and thousands of miles from Ground Zero.

- Value of U.S. economy: $11 trillion
- Estimated cost of attacks to United States based solely on property losses and insurance costs: $21 billion
- Estimated total losses to the world insurance market from the World Trade Center: £25 billion–£50 billion
- Amount of office space lost, in square feet: 13.5 million
- Estimated number of jobs lost in lower Manhattan area following 9/11: 100,000
- Number of jobs it has been estimated will be lost in the United States as a result of the attacks by the end of 2002: 1.8 million

- Number of jobs lost in U.S. travel industry in the last 5 months of 2001: 237,000
- Amount it has been estimated that U.S. commercial insurance premiums will rise to cover the potential cost of future terrorism between 2002 and 2004: 50%
- Amount allocated by Congress for emergency assistance to airline industry in September 2001: $15 billion

Source: http://observer.guardian.co.uk/waronterrorism/story/0,1373,776451,00.html

The federal government costs were extraordinary, and spending by the Federal Emergency Management Agency (FEMA) on these events easily exceeds its spending on past natural disasters (Table 1-1).

TABLE 1-1 **Top Ten Natural Disasters (Ranked By FEMA Relief Costs)**

Event	Year	FEMA Funding*
World Trade Center attack (NY)	2001	$9.0 billion (projected)
Northridge earthquake (CA)	1994	$6.999 billion
Hurricane Georges (AL, FL, LA, MS, PR, VI)	1998	$2.254 billion
Hurricane Andrew (FL, LA)	1992	$1.848 billion
Hurricane Hugo (NC, SC, PR, VI)	1989	$1.307 billion
Midwest floods (IL, IA, KS, MN, MO, NE, ND, SD, WI)	1993	$1.141 billion
Hurricane Floyd (CT, DE, FL, ME, MD, NH, NJ, NY, NC, PA, SC, VT, VA)	1999	$1.186 billion
Tropical Storm Allison (FL, LA, MS, PA, TX)	2001	$970 million
Loma Prieta earthquake (CA)	1989	$865.7 million
Red River Valley floods (MN, ND, SD)	1997	$740.1 million
Hurricane Fran (MD,NC, PA,VA, WV)	1996	$621.8 million

*Amount obligated from the President's Disaster Relief Fund for FEMA's assistance programs, hazard mitigation grants, federal mission assignments, contractual services, and administrative costs as of July 31, 2003. Figures do not include funding provided by other participating federal agencies, such as the disaster loan programs of the Small Business Administration and the Agriculture Department's Farm Service Agency. Note: Funding amounts are stated in nominal dollars, unadjusted for inflation.

Source: Federal Emergency Management Agency. *A Nation Remembers, A Nation Mourns*. Washington, DC: FEMA, September 2003.

- Direct emergency assistance from FEMA: $297 million
- Aid to individuals and families: $255 million
- Direct housing: 8,957 applications processed, 5,287 applications approved (59%)
- Mortgage and rental assistance: 11,818 applications processed, 6,187 applications approved (14%)
- Individual and family grant program: 43,660 applications processed, 6,139 applications approved (14%)
- Disaster unemployment: 6,657 claims processed, 3,210 claims approved (48%)
- Crisis counseling: $166 million
- Aid to government and nonprofits: $4.49 billion
- Debris removal: 437 million
- Overtime for New York Police Department: $295.4 million
- Overtime for Fire Department New York: $105.6 million

Source: Federal Emergency Management Agency. *A Nation Remembers, A Nation Mourns.* Washington, DC: FEMA, September 2003

In addition, the insurance losses resulting from these events exceed all worldwide records for the 30-year period prior to September 11 and for any disaster event in U.S. history (Table 1-2 and Table 1-3).

- Amount of federal aid New York received within two months: $9.5 billion
- Amount collected by the September 11th Fund: $501 million
- Percentage of fund used for cash assistance and services such as grief counseling for families of victims and survivors: 89
- Quantity, in pounds, of food and supplies supplied by 11 September Fund at Ground Zero: 4.3 million
- Number of hot meals served to rescue workers by 11 September Fund: 343,000

- Number of displaced workers receiving job referrals: 5,000
- Amount of compensation sought by the families of civilian casualties of U.S. bombing in Afghanistan from the U.S. government: $10,000
- Amount of compensation sought for reckless misconduct and negligence from American Airlines by husband of September 11 victim: $50 million

Source: http://observer.guardian.co.uk/waronterrorism/story/0,1373,776451,00.html

Additional information concerning these attacks and their impacts are discussed in subsequent chapters of the book.

FIRST RESPONDER ISSUES

In July and August 2002, two September 11–related after-action reports were released: "Improving NYPD Emergency Preparedness and Response," prepared by McKinsey & Company for the New York City Police Department, and "Arlington County After-Action Report on the Response to the September 11 Terrorist Attack on the Pentagon," prepared for Arlington County, Virginia, by Titan Systems Corporation. Both reports are based on hundreds of interviews with event participants and reviews of organizational plans. These reports provide lessons learned and present hundreds of recommendations.

The NYPD report did not pass judgment on the success or failure of the NYPD on September 11 but rather assessed the NYPD's response objectives and instruments in order to identify 20 "improvement opportunities" for the NYPD, six of which merited immediate action:

- Clearer delineation of roles and responsibilities of NYPD leaders
- Better clarity in the chain of command

TABLE 1-2   The Ten Most Costly World Insurance Losses, 1970–2001 (1) ($ millions)

Date	Country	Event	Insured loss in 2001 U.S. dollars (2)
Sept. 11, 2001	U.S.	Terrorist attack on WTC, Pentagon, and other buildings.	$20,346 (3)
Aug. 23, 1992	U.S., Bahamas	Hurricane Andrew	20,185
Jan. 17, 1994	U.S.	Northridge earthquake	16,720
Sep. 27, 1991	Japan	Typhoon Mireille	7,338
Jan. 25, 1990	France, UK, et al.	Winterstorm Daria	6,221
Dec. 25, 1999	France, Switzerland, et al.	Winterstorm Lothar	6,164
Sep. 15, 1989	Puerto Rico, U.S., et al.	Hurricane Hugo	5,990
Oct. 15, 1987	France, UK, et al.	Storm and floods	4,674
Feb. 25, 1990	Western/Central Europe	Winterstorm Vivian	4,323
Sep. 22, 1999	Japan	Typhoon Bart	4,293

(1) Excluding liability. (2) Adjusted to 2001 dollars by Swiss Re. (3) Preliminary estimate for insured property damage and related coverages only.

Sources: Swiss Re, sigma, No. 1/2002. Insured losses for natural catastrophes in the United States from Insurance Services Office, Inc.
http://www.disasterinformation.org/stats.htm

TABLE 1-3   The Ten Most Costly Catastrophes, United States

Date	Peril	Insured loss ($ millions) Dollars when occurred	In 2001 dollars (1)
Sep. 2001	World Trade Center (2)	$40,000.0	$40,000.0
Aug. 1992	Hurricane Andrew	15,500.0	19,565.6
Jan. 1994	Northridge, CA earthquake	12,500.0	14,937.6
Sep. 1989	Hurricane Hugo	4,195.0	5,991.4
Sep. 1998	Hurricane Georges	2,900.0	3,150.9
Jun. 2001	Tropical Storm Allison	2,500.0	2,500.0
Oct. 1995	Hurricane Opal	2,100.0	2,440.4
Sep. 1999	Hurricane Floyd	1,960.0	2,083.5
Mar. 1993	20-state winter storm	1,750.0	2,144.8
Oct. 1991	Oakland, CA, fire	1,700.0	2,210.5

1. Adjusted to 2001 dollars by the Insurance Information Institute. 2. Insurance Information Institute estimate of total losses.

Sources: Insurance Services Office, Inc., Insurance Information Institute.
http://www.disasterinformation.org/stats.htm

- Radio communications protocols and procedures that optimize information flow
- More effective mobilization of members of the service
- More efficient provisioning and distribution of emergency and donated equipment
- A comprehensive disaster response plan, with a significant counterterrorism component

Source: McKinsey & Company 2002

The Arlington County after-action report declared the response by the county and others to the Pentagon terrorist attack a success that "can be attributed to the efforts of ordinary men and women performing in extraordinary fashion" (Titan Systems Corporation, 2002). The terrorist attack on the Pentagon sorely tested the plans and skills of responders from Arlington County, Virginia; other jurisdictions, and the federal government. Appendix 1-1 presents some facts about September 11 at the Pentagon that were compiled in the report.

The Arlington County report contains 235 recommendations and lessons learned. Of these many recommendations, the report highlights examples of lessons learned in two categories: things that worked well and contributed to the overall success of the response and challenges encountered and overcome by responders that could serve as examples for other jurisdictions in the future. These lessons learned are presented in Appendix 1-2.

FIGURE 1-6 Arlington, VA, March 7, 2002—A view of the Pentagon building shows the progress made in the reconstruction of the area damaged by the terrorist attack on the Pentagon on September 11, 2001. Photo by Jocelyn Augustino/FEMA News Photo.

The events at the World Trade Center and the Pentagon vary significantly in size and impact, but from a responder's perspective, they are similar in terms of surprise and challenges. There are striking similarities between the "improvement opportunities" listed in the NYPD report and the "lessons learned" in the Arlington County report.

While the specifics vary, both responses identified issues in five key areas:

- Command
- Communications
- Coordination
- Planning
- Dispatching Personnel

Many of the actions taken after September 11 by government officials and emergency managers at the federal, state, and local levels reflect the need for changes in order to prepare for the next terrorist event.

CONCLUSION

The terrorist attacks of September 11 have changed America. This was truly the first national disaster since Pearl Harbor. It seemed that everyone in America knew someone or knew of someone who perished in the attacks. Every American felt the economic impact in the form of lost jobs, lost business, and an immediate reduction in the value of their kids' college funds and their retirement savings in the stock market. Moreover, the perception that anyone could be the victim of a terrorist attack spread across the country in the days and weeks after September 11. This perception of risk was only heightened in the wake of the October 2001 anthrax incidents and the sniper attacks in the Washington, DC, metropolitan area on October 2002.

The terrorism threat has created a new set of hazards (e.g., biological, chemical, radiological, and nuclear) that must be studied and understood to best prepare both our first responders and our citizens (see Chapter 4). New laws and executive orders that have been established to address the terrorism threat must strike a balance between our sense of security and our civil rights (see Chapter 2). A new and very large federal government agency, the Department of Homeland Security, has been formed from the parts of 22 other agencies and programs to coordinate and guide our nation's efforts in fighting terrorism on the domestic front (see Chapter 3). New funding programs have been established and there is a new focus for the nation's first responders.

These are significant changes not only in the daily lives of the American people but also in the function of the country's emergency management system. Will this new focus on terrorism reduce the system's capabilities at all levels of government and in the nongovernmental community to mitigate, prepare for, respond to, and recover from natural disasters?

It is important to recall that FEMA, as noted earlier in this chapter, has been down this road before, when its focus was shifted from all-hazards to nuclear attack planning in the 1980s—with disastrous results for the agency and the victims of Hurricane Hugo, the Loma Prieta earthquake, and Hurricane Andrew. Is the Department of Homeland Security (DHS) following the same path as FEMA? Will it take 14 years for DHS to become a functioning agency as it took for FEMA? Will the all-hazards approach be abandoned in favor of an exclusive focus on terrorism, and will this result in future Hurricane Andrews?

As America's emergency management system adapts to the new terrorism risk, these will be the critical questions that must be addressed to ensure that the system can effectively reduce the impact of all future disasters and mount a timely response when these events occur.

REVIEW QUESTIONS

1. Identify the role the U.S. Constitution defines for Federal, State, and local governments in the area of emergency management and public safety?
2. Which President established the Federal Emergency Management Agency (FEMA) and on what date? Which President established the Department of Homeland Security (DHS) and on what date?
3. Why did the National Governor's Association and its members push the Federal government to create FEMA? Why was DHS established?
4. After reviewing the difficulties that FEMA encountered in becoming a functioning emergency management agency, what issues do you anticipate DHS will encounter in its evolution into a functioning government agency? Identify some lessons learned in the FEMA experience that could guide DHS actions in the future. Will history repeat itself as DHS matures as a government agency?
5. Throughout the history of emergency management in the United States, the priorities set for government emergency management agencies have been driven by the most widely perceived threat or hazard. How do you think the new threat of terrorism and the hazards associated with terrorism will impact the practice of emergency management in the United States at all levels of government (federal, state, and local) and in the business sector?

REFERENCES

Federal Emergency Management Agency. 2003. "A Nation Remembers, A Nation Mourns." September 2003.

Fusco, A. L. 1993. "The World Trade Center Bombing: Report and Analysis. U.S. Fire Administration.

McKinsey & Company. 2002. "Improving NYPD Emergency Preparedness and Response," August 19, 2002.

The City of Oklahoma. "Alfred P. Murrah Federal Building Bombing April 19, 1995." Fire Protection Publications. Stillwater, OK: Oklahoma State University, 1993.

APPENDIX 1-1
Notable Facts about September 11 at the Pentagon

- The first Arlington County emergency response unit arrived at the crash site less than three minutes after impact.
- Lieut. Robert Medarios was the first Arlington County Police Department command-level official on-site. He made a verbal agreement with a representative of the Defense Protective Service that Arlington County would lead the rescue efforts of all local and federal agencies.
- Over 30 urban search-and-rescue teams, police departments, fire departments, and federal agencies assisted Arlington's police and fire departments in the rescue. Some of these important partners included the Federal Bureau of Investigation, the Federal Emergency Management Agency, U.S. Park Police, Defense Protective Service, the Military District of Washington, the Metropolitan Washington Airport Authority, the Virginia Department of Emergency Management, and USAR teams from Albuquerque, NM, Fairfax County, VA, Montgomery County, MD, and Memphis, TN.
- Captain Dennis Gilroy and the team on Foam Unit 161 from the Fort Meyer Fire Station were on-site at the Pentagon when Flight 77 crashed into the building. Firefighters Mark Skipper and Alan Wallace, who were next to the unit, received burns and lacerations but immediately began helping Pentagon employees, who were trying to escape from harm's way, out of the first-floor windows.
- Captain Steve McCoy and the crew of Engine 101 were on their way to fire staff training in Crystal City when they saw the plane flying low overhead and an explosion from the vicinity of the Pentagon. McCoy was the first person to call Arlington County's emergency communications center to report the plane crash.
- The Arlington County American Red Cross Chapter coordinated support from the Red Cross. The chapter had 80 trained volunteers at the time of the attack, but the organization's mutual-aid arrangements with other chapters garnered nearly 1,500 volunteers who helped support the emergency services personnel, victims, and their families.
- Business supporters set up temporary food service on the Pentagon parking lot for rescue workers. More than 187,940 meals were served to emergency workers. Many other businesses brought phones for rescuers to call home, building materials, and other vital necessities.
- Over 112 surgeries on nine burn victims were performed in three weeks. One of the nine burn victims died after having over 60 percent of her body burned. There were 106 patients that reported to area hospitals with various injuries.
- 189 people died at the Pentagon—184 victims and 5 terrorists.
- On the morning of September 11, 1941, the original construction on the Pentagon began.

Source: Arlington County (UA) "Arlington County After-Action Report on the Response to the September 11 Terrorist." Titan Systems Inc. Washington, DC July 2002

APPENDIX 1-2
Lessons Learned at the Pentagon

The Arlington County after-action report contains 235 recommendations and lessons learned, each of which must be understood within the context and setting of the Pentagon response. Some specifically apply to a particular response element or activity. Others address overarching issues that apply to Arlington County and other jurisdictions, particularly those in large metropolitan areas. They have not been weighted or prioritized. This is a task best left to those with operational responsibilities and budgetary authority.

Capabilities Others Should Emulate

1. Incident Command System and Unified Command: The primary response participants understood the ICS, implemented it effectively, and complied with its provisions. The Arlington County Fire Department, an experienced ICS practitioner, established its command presence literally within minutes of the attack. Other supporting jurisdictions and agencies, with few exceptions, operated seamlessly within the ICS framework. For those organizations and individuals unfamiliar with the ICS and Unified Command, particularly the military, which has its own clearly defined command and control mechanisms, the incident commander provided explicit information and guidance early during the response and elicited their full cooperation.

2. Mutual aid and outside support: The management and integration of mutual-aid assets and the coordination and cooperation of agencies at all government echelons, volunteer organizations, and private businesses were outstanding. Public safety organizations and chief administrative officers (CAOs) of nearby jurisdictions lent their support to Arlington County. The response to the Pentagon attack revealed the total scope and magnitude of support available throughout the Washington metropolitan area and across the nation.

3. Arlington County CEMP (Community Emergency Management Plan): The CEMP proved to be what its title implies. It was well thought out, properly maintained, frequently practiced, and effectively implemented. Government leaders were able to quickly marshal the substantial resources of Arlington County in support of the first responders, without interfering with tactical operations. County board members worked with counterparts in neighboring jurisdictions and elected federal and state officials to ensure a rapid economic recovery, and they engaged in frequent dialogue with the citizens of Arlington County.

4. Employee Assistance Program (EAP): At the time of the Pentagon attack, Arlington County already had in place an aggressive, well-established EAP offering critical incident stress management (CISM) services to public safety and other county employees. In particular, the ACFD embraced the concept and encouraged all of its members to use EAP services. Thus it is not surprising that the members of the EAP staff were well received when they arrived at the incident site within 3 hours of the attack. During the incident response and in follow-up sessions weeks afterward, the EAP proved invaluable to first responders, their families, and the entire county support network. This is a valuable resource that must be incorporated in response plans.

5. Training, exercises, and shared experiences: The ACED has long recognized the possibility of a terrorist attack using weapons of mass destruction (WMD) in the Washington metropolitan area and has pursued an aggressive preparedness program for such an event, including its pioneering work associated with the MMRS. In preparation for anticipated problems associated with the arrival of Y2K, Arlington County government thoroughly exercised the CEMP. In 1998 the FBI's Washington Field Office (WFO) established a fire liaison position to work specifically with area fire departments. Public safety organizations in the Washington metropolitan area routinely work together on events of national prominence and shared jurisdictional interests, such as presidential inaugural celebrations, visits by heads of state, international

conferences such as the periodic International Monetary Fund (IMF) conference, and others. These organizations also regularly participate in training exercises, including those hosted by the Pentagon and MDW. All this and more contributed to the successful Pentagon response.

Challenges That Must Be Met

1. Self-dispatching: Organizations, response units, and individuals proceeding on their own initiative directly to an incident site, without the knowledge and permission of the host jurisdiction and the incident commander, complicate the exercise of command, increase the risks faced by bona fide responders, and exacerbate the challenge of accountability. WMD terrorist event response plans should designate preselected and well-marked staging areas. Dispatch instructions should be clear. Law enforcement agencies should be familiar with deployment plans and quickly establish incident site-access controls. When identified, self-dispatched resources should be immediately released from the scene, unless incorporated into the incident commander's response plan.

2. Fixed and mobile command and control facilities: Arlington County does not have a facility specifically designed and equipped to support the emergency management functions specified in the CEMP. The conference room currently used as the EOC does not have adequate space and is not configured or properly equipped for that role. The notification and recall capabilities of the emergency communications center are constrained by equipment limitations, and there are no protected telephone lines for outside calls when the 9-1-1 lines are saturated. The ACED does not have a mobile command vehicle and relied on the use of vehicles belonging to other organizations and jurisdictions. The ACPD mobile command unit needs to be replaced or extensively modernized.

3. Communications: Almost all aspects of communications continue to be problematic, from initial notification to tactical operations. Cellular telephones were of little value in the first few hours, and cellular priority access service (CPAS) is not provided to emergency responders. Radio channels were initially oversaturated, and interoperability problems among jurisdic-

tions and agencies persist. Even portable radios that are otherwise compatible were sometimes preprogrammed in a fashion that precluded interoperability. Pagers seemed to be the most reliable means of notification when available and used, but most firefighters are not issued pagers. The Arlington County EOC does not have an installed radio capacity and relied on portable radios coincidentally assigned to staff members assigned duties at the EOC.

4. Logistics: Arlington County, like most other jurisdictions, was not logistically prepared for an operation of the duration and magnitude of the Pentagon attack. The ACED did not have an established logistics function, a centralized supply system, or experience in long-term logistics support. Stock levels of personal protective equipment (PPE), critical high-demand items (such as batteries and breathing apparatus), equipment for reserve vehicles, and medical supplies for EMS units were insufficient for sustained operations. These challenges were overcome at the Pentagon with the aid of the more experienced Fairfax County Fire and Rescue Department logistics staff. A stronger standing capacity, however, is needed for a jurisdiction the size of Arlington County.

5. Hospital coordination: Communications and coordination between EMS control at the incident site and area hospitals receiving injured victims were deficient. The coordination difficulties were not simple equipment failures. They represent flaws in the system present on September 11. Regional hospital disaster plans no longer require a clearinghouse hospital or other designated communications focal point for the dissemination of patient disposition and treatment information. Thus hospitals first learned of en route victims when contacted by transporting EMS units, and EMS control reconstructed much of the disposition information by contacting hospitals after the fact. Although the number of victims of the Pentagon attack were fewer than many anticipated, they were not insignificant. An incident with more casualties would have seriously strained the system.

Source: "Arlington County After-Action Report on the Response to the September 11 Terrorist Attack on the Pentagon" prepared for Arlington County, Virginia by Titan Systems Corporation.

Statutory Authority

INTRODUCTION

The purpose of this chapter is to trace the series of statutes, presidential directives, and executive orders that have been issued and implemented since 1994 to establish the authorities and the infrastructure within the federal government to fight the domestic war on terrorism. The core purpose of many of these legislative actions is to authorize responses by federal agencies to the terrorism threat and to sort out which federal agency was responsible for preventing a given act of terrorism and managing the consequences of terrorist attacks.

A legislative timeline has been created to track terrorism-related legislation, presidential directives, and executive orders. More detailed analysis is provided for two significant pieces of legislation: the U.S.A. Patriot Act of 2001 and the Homeland Security Act of 2002. The Patriot Act placed new authority in the hands of the U.S. Justice Department to assist their efforts to identify and detain suspected terrorists operating in the United States. The Homeland Security Act initiated the largest government reorganization since 1947 and established the Department of Homeland Security.

The chapter includes a review of Homeland Security Presidential Directive/HSPD-5, an analysis of the fiscal year 2004 budget for the Department of Homeland Security, and an analysis of the ongoing struggle by public officials to balance the need for increased security in the domestic war on terrorism and the need to protect the civil liberties of all Americans.

LEGISLATIVE, PRESIDENTIAL DIRECTIVE, AND EXECUTIVE ORDER TIMELINE

The information provided in this timeline was excerpted from "Historical Chronology of FEMA Consequence Management, Preparedness and Response to Terrorism" prepared by Dr. Thomas E. Baldwin, Argonne National Laboratory, Argonne, Illinois. Additional information was obtained from the "Terrorism Time Line: Major Focusing Events and U.S. Outcomes (1993–2002)" prepared by Claire B. Rubin, M.A., William R. Cummings, J.D., and Irmak Renda-Tanali, D.Sc.

Abbreviations to note: EO, executive order; PDD, presidential decision directive; HSPD, homeland security presidential directive; PL—Public Law.

November 18, 1988—Executive Order 12656— Assignment of Emergency Preparedness Responsibilities. This executive order defines a national security emergency as any occurrence that seriously degrades or threatens the national security of the United States. Terrorist incidents were not specifically mentioned except for Department of Justice (DOJ) responsibilities. The National Security Council is assigned responsibility for developing and administering this policy. The director of FEMA shall assist in the implementation of and management of national security emergency management preparedness policy by coordinating with other federal departments. FEMA is responsible for coordinating, supporting, developing, and implementing the following: civil national security emergency preparedness and response programs, continuity of government functions, and civil-military support. This EO was in draft and coordination for five years.

November 18, 1988—EO 12657—FEMA Assistance in Emergency Preparedness Planning at Commercial Nuclear Power Plants Responsibilities. This EO allows FEMA to initially respond in coordinating federal response activities when advance state and local commitments (e.g., response planning) are absent or inadequate off-site at commercial nuclear power plants. FEMA is authorized to assume any necessary command and control function, or delegate such function to another federal agency, in the event that no competent state and local authority is available to perform such function.

November 23, 1988—President Reagan signs into law the Robert T. Stafford Disaster Relief and Emergency Assistance Act (PL 100-707) amending the Federal Disaster Relief Act of 1974.

March 23, 1989—EO 12673 delegates Stafford Act authority with some exceptions (principally declarations) to the director of FEMA.

April 1992—Federal Response Plan (FRP) is issued. This plan "established a process and structure for the systematic, coordinated, and effective delivery of federal assistance to address the consequences of any major disaster or emergency declared under the Robert T. Stafford Disaster Relief and Emergency Assistance Act, as amended." Under "Scope" the FRP states

> [I]n some instances, a disaster or emergency may result in a situation, which affects the national security of the United States. For those instances, appropriate national security

authorities and procedures will be utilized to address the national security requirements of the situation.

Law enforcement emergencies are defined under "Policies," and procedures are referenced under which DOJ and Department of Defense (DoD) personnel respond to law enforcement emergencies under 28 CFR part 65 and 10 USC. 331-333.

November 30, 1993—PL 103-160 §1704. Joint Resolution of Congress on FEMA terrorism-preparedness planning provides that

> [I]t is the sense of Congress that the president should strengthen federal interagency emergency planning by the federal emergency management agency and other appropriate federal, state, and local agencies for development of a capability for early detection and warning of and response to (1) potential terrorist use of chemical or biological agents or weapons; and (2) emergencies or natural disasters involving industrial chemicals or the widespread outbreak of disease.

June 3, 1994—EO 12919—National Defense Industrial Resources Preparedness. This EO delegates authorities and addresses national defense industrial resource policies and programs under the Defense Production Act of 1950, as amended, except for the amendments to Title III of the act in the Energy Security Act of 1980 and excludes telecommunication authorities under EO No. 12472. Under this order the FEMA director: (1) serves as an advisor to the National Security Council on issues of national security resource preparedness and on the use of the authorities and functions delegated by this order; (2) provides for the central coordination of the plans and programs incident to authorities and functions delegated under this order, and provides guidance and procedures approved by the assistant to the president for National Security Affairs to the federal departments and agencies under this order; (3) established procedures, in consultation with federal departments and agencies assigned functions under this order, to resolve in a timely and effective manner conflicts and issues that may arise in implementing the authorities and functions delegated under this order; and (4) reports to the president periodically concerning all program activities conducted pursuant to this order.

November 1994—PL 103-337. This law repeals the Federal Civil Defense Act. In new Title VI of the Stafford Act, the policy of the federal government is for FEMA to provide necessary direction, coordination and guidance, and necessary assistance, as authorized in the title so that a comprehensive emergency preparedness system exists for all hazards in the United States FEMA is directed to: (1) prepare federal response plans and programs for the emergency preparedness of the United States and (2) sponsor and direct such plans and programs to coordinate such plans and programs with state efforts. The FEMA director may request such reports on state plans and operations for emergency preparedness as may be necessary to keep the president, Congress, and the states advised of the status of emergency preparedness in the United States. Interstate emergency preparedness compacts are authorized to: (a) assist and encourage the states to negotiate and enter into interstate emergency preparedness compacts; (b) facilitate uniformity between state compacts and consistency with federal emergency response plans and programs; (c) assist and coordinate the activities under state compacts; and (d) aid and assist reciprocal state emergency-preparedness legislation that will permit mutual aid in the event of a hazard that cannot be adequately met or controlled by a state or political subdivision thereof. PL 103-337 amended PL 93-288 as previously amended by PL 100-707.

January 22, 1995—Director of FEMA establishes the office of National Security Coordination, which reports directly to him.

March 19, 1995—Sarin Gas attack on a subway in Tokyo, Japan.

April 19, 1995—The Murrah Federal Office Building in Oklahoma City is bombed. Within 7 hours of the explosion president Clinton signs an emergency declaration. This is the first use of the president's authority under the Stafford Act to "self-initiate" an emergency declaration for emergencies with federal involvement.

June 21, 1995—Presidential Decision Directive 39. This directive states that it is the policy of the United States to use all appropriate means to deter, defeat, and respond to all terrorist attacks on our territory and resources, both people and facilities, wherever they occur. Established DOJ personnel lead responsibility for crisis management, and FEMA personnel lead responsibility for consequence management. FEMA chairs the Senior Interagency Group for Training and Preparedness.

April 24, 1996—Antiterrorism and Effective Death Penalty Act of 1996, PL 104-132 [110 stat.1255]. Congress funds first responder and firefighter training by grants. United States Fire Administration receives funds from DOJ to conduct first responder training.

May 1, 1996—Federal Radiological Emergency Response Plan (FRERP) signed by FEMA Director James L. Witt. The FRERP addresses radiological sabotage and terrorism and states that

> coordinated response to contain or mitigate a threatened or actual release of radioactive material would be essentially the same whether it resulted from an accidental or deliberate act.... Therefore, sabotage and terrorism are not treated as separate types of emergencies rather they are considered a complicating dimension of [radiological emergencies].

July 15, 1996—EO 13010—Critical Infrastructure Protection. This EO establishes the President's Commission on Critical Infrastructure Protection (PCCIP) and the Critical Infrastructure Protection Working Group (CIPWG). Certain national infrastructures are so vital that their incapacity or destruction would have a debilitating impact on the defense or economic security of the United States. It is essential that the government and private sector work together to develop a strategy for protecting them and assuring their continued operation. These infrastructures include telecommunications, transportation, water supply systems, emergency services (including medical, police, fire, and rescue), and continuity of government.

1996—Anti-Terrorism and Effective Death Penalty Act (PL 104-132). The president signs a law authorizing FEMA and the DOJ's Office of Justice Programs to fund and develop an emergency response to terrorism training program for fire, emergency medical service, and public safety personnel. Annual appropriation to DOJ is shared with FEMA through FY 2002. DOJ administers grants through its State and Local Domestic Preparedness Office (SLDPO) in its Office of Justice Assistance (not in the FBI).

September 23, 1996—Defense Against Weapons of Mass Destruction Act (PL 104-201), also called Nunn-Lugar legislation. The president signs a law directing the DoD to lead, for three years, domestic preparedness for responding to and managing the consequences of a terrorist attack using weapons of mass destruction (WMD). The law authorizes transfer of this responsibility to another agency after three years with presidential concurrence.

February 7, 1997—FEMA director adopts the Terrorism Incident Annex (TIA) to Federal Response Plan. This annex provides federal emergency planners with information and a framework to address the consequences of terrorist attacks.

May 22, 1998—Presidential Decision Directives (PDDs) 62 "Combating Terrorism" and 63 "Critical Infrastructure Protection" are signed by President Clinton. The president designates a national coordinator for security, infrastructure protection, and counterterrorism (Richard Clarke of NSC staff) who is not to direct agencies' activities but is to integrate the government's policies and programs on unconventional threats to the homeland and Americans abroad, including terrorism. The national coordinator oversees the broad variety of relevant polices and programs including counterterrorism, protection of critical infrastructure, preparedness, and consequence management for weapons of mass destruction. The national coordinator works within the National Security Council process and reports to the president through the assistant to the president for National Security Affairs and produces an annual security preparedness report. The national coordinator will also provide advice regarding budgets for counterterror programs and lead in the development of guidelines that might be needed for crisis management.

August 7, 1998—Bombings of the U.S. embassies in Nairobi, Kenya, and Dares Salaam, Tanzania.

April 1999—The Federal Response Plan is revised after full interagency coordination to incorporate the 11 changes published to the plan since 1992. The FRP was also revised to ensure consistency with current policy guidance; integrate recovery and mitigation functions into the response structure; and describe relationships to other emergency operations plans. The revised FRP as adopted includes four new support annexes (community relations, donations management, logistics management, and occupational safety and health), the terrorism incident annex and two new appendices (FRP changes and revision, and overview of a disaster operation).

May 2000—Congressionally mandated No-Notice Operation TOPOFF Exercise, simulating terrorist attacks in both Denver, Colorado, and Portsmouth, New Hampshire. Communication difficulties and the lack of a lead agency severely hinder operations in both locations. The DOJ assigned executive responsibility for after-action reports.

July 25, 2000—House of Representatives passes HR 4210, which would have established a President's Council on Domestic Terrorism Preparedness composed of the president, directors of FEMA and OMB, the attorney general, the secretary of defense, the assistant to the president for national security affairs, and additional members appointed by the president. Purposes were to (1) improve federal assistance to state and local emergency preparedness and response for domestic terrorist attacks, (2) designates the President's Council to coordinate federal efforts, and (3) updates federal authorities to reflect increased risk of terrorist attacks. Because the Senate did not act, this legislation died in the 106th Congress.

February 8, 2001—Introduction of HR 525, "Preparedness Against Domestic Terrorism Act of 2001." This resolution amends the Stafford Act to include acts of terrorism or other catastrophic events within its definition of "major disaster" for purposes of authorized disaster relief. It requires the president (current law authorizes the director of FEMA) to be responsible for carrying out federal emergency-preparedness plans and programs. It includes into the definition of hazards as covered under the Stafford Act a domestic terrorist attack involving a weapon of mass destruction. It also establishes the President's Council on Domestic Preparedness to eliminate duplication within federal terrorism-preparedness programs. It requires the council to: (1) publish a domestic terrorism-preparedness plan and an annual implementation strategy; (2) designate an entity to assess the risk of terrorist attacks against transportation, energy, and other infrastructure facilities; and (3) establish voluntary minimum guidelines for preparedness programs. Finally, it authorizes the council to attend meetings of the National Security Council pertaining to domestic terrorist-attack preparedness matters, subject to the direction of the president.

March 21 and 29, 2001—The introduction of HR 1158, which establishes a National Homeland Security Agency, and HR 1292 requiring the president to develop and implement a strategy for homeland security. It is anticipated that these bills will be combined with HR 525 addressing preparedness against acts of domestic terrorism.

September 11, 2001—Terrorist attacks on the World Trade Center and the Pentagon. President George W. Bush issues a disaster declaration for New York City within 6 hours after Governor Pataki's state disaster declaration (approximately 6 hours after the initial attack at 8:43 A.M. EDT).

September 14, 2001—President Bush signs a declaration of national emergency as a result of the terrorist attacks at the World Trade Center, the Pentagon, and the continuing and immediate threat of further attacks on the United States.

September 15, 2001—Congress approves a $40 billion expenditure on disaster relief and anti- and counterterrorism (HR 2888).

October 8, 2001—President Bush signs an EO establishing the Office of Homeland Security and the Homeland Security Council, to be headed by the assistant to the president for homeland security. Former Pennsylvania Governor Tom Ridge was sworn in as the first director of Homeland Security. (EO 13228 published at 66 Federal Register 51812–51817.)

November 2002—President Bush signs PL 107–296, establishing Department of Homeland Security effective January 24, 2003.

January 24, 2003. The Department of Homeland Security is activated.

THE PATRIOT ACT OF 2001

The Patriot Act of 2001 (PL 107-56), officially titled "Uniting and Strengthening America by Providing Appropriate Tools Required to Intercept and Obstruct Terrorism (U.S.A. PATRIOT ACT) Act of 2001," was signed into law by President Bush on October 26, 2001. This legislation was introduced in the U.S. House of Representatives by Representative F. James Sensenbrenner, Jr. [WI-9] on October 23, 2001, "to deter and punish terrorist acts in the United States and around the world, to enhance law enforcement investigatory tools, and for other purposes." (Congress.gov 2003)

This legislation, considered to be among the most comprehensive in its impact on civil liberties, is worth describing in detail.

Summaries of the Patriot Act's nine titles are presented in Appendix 2-1 at the end of this chapter. A full summary of the Patriot Act is presented in Appendix 2.

The principal focus of the Patriot Act is to provide authorities to law enforcement agencies to support their efforts to collect information on suspected terrorists, to detain suspected terrorists, to detour terrorists from entering and operating within the borders of the United States, and to further limit the ability of terrorists to engage in money-laundering activities that support terrorist actions.

The major provisions of the Partiot Act are as follows:

- Relaxes restrictions on information-sharing between U.S. law enforcement and intelligence officers on the subject of suspected terrorists.
- Makes it illegal to knowingly harbor a terrorist.
- Authorizes "roving wiretaps," which allows law enforcement officials to get court orders to wiretap any phone a suspected terrorist would use. The provision was needed, advocates said, with the advent of cellular and disposable phones.
- Allows the federal government to detain non-U.S. citizens suspected of terrorism for up to seven days without specific charges. The administration originally wanted to hold these suspects indefinitely.

- Allows law enforcement officials greater subpoena power for e-mail records of terrorist suspects.
- Triples the number of border patrol personnel, customs service inspectors, and Immigration and Naturalization Service inspectors at the northern border of the United States and provides $100 million to improve technology and equipment on the U.S. border with Canada.
- Expands measures against money-laundering by requiring additional record-keeping and reports for certain transactions and requiring identification of account holders.
- Eliminates the statute of limitations for prosecuting the most egregious terrorist acts but maintains the statute of limitation on most crimes at 5 to 8 years.

Source: CNN, www.cnn.com

The Patriot Act has sparked concern among many people and organizations involved in protecting the civil rights and liberties of all Americans. These critics have questioned the constitutionality of some of the provisions of the act and have expressed grave concerns regarding the methods by which some of the act's provisions will be used by law enforcement agencies in their pursuit of terrorists. The U.S. attorney general and the DOJ counter that they need these authorities to more effectively track and detain terrorists. The act has generated lawsuits, resistance from community officials, and concern about the way its provisions may affect everyday Americans. Sidebars 2-1 to 2-3 present three news accounts that provide different perspectives on the Patriot Act.

SIDEBAR 2-1   Patriot Act Perspective—ACLU Files against Patriot Act

From Kevin Bohn, CNN Washington Bureau

WASHINGTON (CNN)—The American Civil Liberties Union Wednesday filed the first lawsuit against the Patriot Act, the antiterrorism law passed after the attacks of September 11, 2001.

The lawsuit claims one section of the law authorizing searches of records, including those of businesses, libraries, and bookstores, is unconstitutional.

"This lawsuit challenges the constitutionality of Section 215 of the U.S.A. Patriot Act, which vastly expands the power of the Federal Bureau of Investigation to obtain records and other 'tangible things' of people not suspected of criminal activity," the lawsuit states.

The ACLU filed the lawsuit in U.S. District Court in Michigan on behalf of six mostly Arab and Muslim-American groups.

The groups claim the provisions of the law allowing the searches violates the Constitution's First, Fourth, and Fifth amendments.

They include the Muslim Community Association of Ann Arbor, Arab Community Center for Economic and Social Services, and the Islamic Center of Portland, Masjed As-Saber.

Without directly commenting on the suit, Justice Department spokeswoman Barbara Comstock defended the act in a written statement, saying it was "a long overdue measure to close gaping holes" in the government's antiterrorism efforts.

She described Section 215 as having "a narrow scope that scrupulously respects First Amendment rights, requires a court order to obtain any business records, and is subject to congressional reporting and oversight on a regular basis."

Justice Department officials say the section can be used only in a narrow set of circumstances, including to obtain foreign intelligence information about people who are neither American citizens nor lawful permanent residents, and to defend the United States against foreign spies or international terrorists.

"Section 215 cannot be used to investigate garden-variety crimes, or even domestic terrorism," Comstock said in her statement.

Those bringing the lawsuit contend it is too easy to get approval for a search under Section 215.

"To obtain a Section 215 order, the FBI need only assert that the records or personal belongings are 'sought for' an ongoing foreign intelligence, counterintelligence, or international terrorism investigation," the lawsuit says.

"The FBI is not required to show probable cause—or any reason—to believe that the target of the order is a criminal suspect or foreign agent."

Previously, such broad powers were permitted only in investigations of suspected agents of foreign powers. Section 215 expanded the type of information that can be subpoenaed and broadened the scope to add probes into al Qaeda and other terrorism suspects.

Another controversial element of the Patriot Act involves what are called "sneak and peek" searches of homes and other locations in which the owners are informed only after the search has been conducted.

Last week, the House of Representatives voted to bar the Justice Department from executing such searches under the act.

In a letter last week to House Speaker Rep. Dennis Hastert, R-Illinois, the department said the idea of delaying notification of such searches is "to prevent tipping off terrorists in the war on terror" and is a "long-existing, crime-fighting tool."

In February, the ACLU and a coalition of other civil liberties groups asked the U.S. Supreme Court to overturn new, more lenient standards for wiretaps in foreign intelligence investigations.

Before the Patriot Act, foreign intelligence had to be a "primary" purpose of the investigation. Now, foreign intelligence has to be a "significant" purpose. The court overseeing the issuance of wiretaps had ruled against that interpretation last year, saying it was too broad.

Source: CNN, www.cnn.com

SIDEBAR 2-2   Patriot Act Perspective—How the New Antiterrorism Bill Could Affect You

By Lance Gay, Scripps Howard News Service (published 10/26/2001)

WASHINGTON—Do you use your local library's computers or a cyber-cafe to surf the Internet? If a suspected terrorist used the computer before you, the FBI can use "sneak and peek " warrants to collect your surfing habits and look at your e-mails.

Do you rent rooms? If that quiet upstairs boarder turns out to be a suspected terrorist, you could be charged with the new crime of "harboring" a terrorist.

Do you make a lot of large cash deposits in the bank? The CIA and other intelligence agencies will be alerted to find out if you are involved in money laundering.

Those are just a few of the sweeping changes that will affect Americans under the antiterrorism bill that Congress sent to President Bush on Thursday. It vastly expands the powers of the FBI and CIA to monitor Internet surfing, intercept e-mails, and look at bank transactions and other

personal records of Americans just on mere suspicion that someone is involved in terrorist activities.

Congressional leaders say the new law—dubbed the Uniting and Strengthening America by Providing the Appropriate Tools Required to Intercept and Obstruct Terrorism, or U.S.A. Patriot Act—closes loopholes that have allowed terrorists to operate cells in the United States like those involved in the Sept. 11 attacks.

Critics, ranging from the Electronic Privacy Information Center, the Gun Owners of America, and the American Civil Liberties Union, says the U.S.A. Patriot Act is so broadly drafted it could disrupt the lives of ordinary Americans.

Lawmakers admitted the powers they are giving the government are extraordinary and sought to dampen civil liberties concerns by including "sunset" provisions in the legislation, allowing many to exist only until Dec. 31, 2005.

Some even admitted they expect the new law will cause problems. "There will be some abuses, and if there are abuses we can reverse it. It sunsets in four years," said Sen. Paul Wellstone, D-Minn.

In most cases, federal agents will have to get advance wiretap approval from the Foreign Intelligence Surveillance Court. About the only thing known publicly about the seven-member panel created in 1978 that sits secretly in the basement of the Justice Department is that it has never rejected an FBI request for a secret warrant. Open warrants, much more common, get approval in regular federal courts.

Here's how the U.S.A. Patriot Act could affect your life:

- The FBI is given new authority for Internet searches and can ask the secret court for a warrant to monitor Internet activities of anyone suspected of terrorism. If that involves use of Internet connections at libraries or cyber-cafes, the FBI can collect all the e-mails and information on Internet sites visited but would have to get another warrant to read e-mail texts of those who aren't targets of the investigation. "The net is cast so broadly, a lot of innocent communications are caught up," said David Sobel, general counsel of the Electronic Privacy Information Center.
- The FBI is authorized to investigate anyone believed linked either to international terrorism or someone involved in "domestic terrorism." Although not thought to be directly involved in terrorism themselves, these people could be charged with "harboring" a suspected terrorist or "providing material support" to a suspect. Anyone involved in providing assistance to a suspected terrorist, no matter how minor, is affected.
- Make a deposit that a bank clerk thinks is suspicious or in violation of some state or federal law, or that involves more than $10,000, and the reports will be turned over to federal intelligence agencies, including the CIA, without

any notification to you. Under a 1992 law, banks file such reports only with the Treasury Department. The U.S.A. Patriot Act allows intelligence agencies to obtain this information to track money-laundering activities.
- Credit, medical, and student records can be retrieved secretly by federal agencies on anyone suspected of involvement in terrorism, after approval by the secret court, regardless of state privacy laws.
- The U.S.A. Patriot Act defines domestic terrorism as "an attempt to intimidate or coerce a civilian population" or change "the policy of the government by intimidation or coercion." The American Civil Liberties Union says that definition is so broad it could cover political dissent by activists involved in protests against world trade, animal rights, or environmental concerns if police conclude their activities endanger human lives.
- Using a secret warrant, the FBI can break into offices or homes to conduct secret searches. Agents don't need probable cause, just a suspicion of involvement in a crime. Laura Murphy, director of the Washington office of the American Civil Liberties Union, said that poses major Fourth Amendment search-and-seizure concerns. There would be no notification of what was found in the secret searches.
- Immigrants and noncitizens could be detained for up to 7 days before charges are filed. Those charged with immigration violations, including overstaying visas, can be deported. If their home countries refuse to take them back, they can be held indefinitely.
- Information collected during grand jury proceedings could be shared by the FBI with the CIA, giving the CIA domestic information it has been restricted in the past from receiving.

William Webster, a former director of both the FBI and the CIA, said that while Congress is granting very broad powers to federal agencies, there's a check requiring federal judges to review what federal agents are doing.

"I'm comfortable as long as the courts have a role to play," said Webster, a former judge.

John Velleco, director of federal affairs for Gun Owners of America, said the government already has sufficient powers to investigate and deal with terrorists.

Jeff Kerr, general counsel for People for the Ethical Treatment of Animals, said his organization is concerned that police could use the new domestic terrorism provisions against social activists.

"There's a fine line that has to be guarded very carefully here," he said. "Something that is educational to one person may be coercive to someone else—a boycott, for example, against any industry. Is that intimidating and coercive?"

Source: *Star Tribune*, www.startribune.com

SIDEBAR 2-3 Patriot Act Perspective: Communities Shun Patriot Act

By Gus Taylor, *The Washington Times*

About 165 communities nationwide have passed resolutions condemning the U.S.A. Patriot Act. But one little city in northern California has taken its opposition a step further, making it a misdemeanor for city employees to cooperate in enforcing the federal antiterrorism measure.

In March, Arcata officials set down a $57 fine for those who don't "promptly notify the city manager" if federal law-enforcement authorities contact them seeking help in an investigation, interrogation, or arrest under the provisions of the act.

But a city fine would be nothing compared with the penalties an Arcata official faces for obstructing a federal probe, a Justice Department spokesman said.

"Obviously, the folks [in Arcata] who voted for this ordinance haven't read the law," said Justice Department spokesman Mark C. Corallo.

"This is not the FBI or the Justice Department acting unilaterally," Mr. Corallo said. "Just like any other criminal investigation, these are tools that are not just legal, but they are constitutional and they are tools that have been available for law-enforcement authorities for decades."

The Patriot Act's most-criticized provision, for so-called roving wiretaps, merely allows investigators to "track a terrorist, instead of having to get multiple warrants for every phone the guy uses," Mr. Corallo explained.

Still, critics say, the reason so many communities are denouncing the Patriot Act is because they believe the measure passed in the wake of the September 11 attacks vastly expands the power of federal investigators, not only for investigating terrorism suspects but also for probing into the lives of ordinary Americans.

Most of the resolutions being signed against the 340-page act (the acronym stands for "Uniting and Strengthening America by Providing Appropriate Tools Required to Intercept and Obstruct Terrorism") condemn its provisions that compel libraries and bookstores to assist federal investigators in monitoring the reading habits of suspects.

Timothy H. Edgar, the legislative counsel for the American Civil Liberties Union, said that a far more frightening provision of the Patriot Act is one that "allows investigators to sneak into your house with a warrant and conduct a search and not notify you until much later, if at all."

Further, according to a report issued earlier this month by the ACLU, the act gives the FBI "access to highly personal 'business records' including financial, medical, mental health, library, and student records with no meaningful judicial oversight."

The report continues: "Federal officials actually can obtain a court order for records of the books you borrow from libraries or buy from bookstores, without showing probable cause of criminal activity or intent, and the librarian or bookseller cannot even tell you that the government is investigating what you read."

Justice Department officials say such criticisms are arbitrary, noting that investigators still are required to get permission from a federal judge to obtain records about the reading habits of suspects. Mr. Corallo said the wave of objections to the Patriot Act has done little more than illustrate some Americans' "incredible ignorance of federal law."

But Arcata officials aren't second-guessing themselves; they take pride in their city's stance. "A lot of people are becoming more aware of the problems with the Patriot Act," says Arcata Mayor Bob Ornelas.

"We were the first to put it in our municipal code," he said. "It's one thing to have a proclamation; we have an ordinance saying you can't engage in the Patriot Act where it violates people's constitutional rights."

Arcata, a town of about 16,000 nearly 300 miles north of San Francisco, made headlines as a haven of liberalism in the early 1990s when its city council became first in the country with a Green Party majority. But Mr. Ornales and others point out that liberals aren't the only ones objecting to the Patriot Act.

"From the NAACP to the NRA, people are working together on these resolutions," says ACLU spokesman Damon Moglin, in reference to the National Association for the Advancement of Colored People and the National Rifle Association. "We see this as being a true grass-roots response."

The ACLU's July 3 report says "more than 16 million people in 26 states have passed resolutions" condemning the Patriot Act and that among them are some "traditionally conservative locales, such as Oklahoma City, … Alaska, Hawaii, and Vermont."

The Washington Times, http://www.washingtontimes.com

HOMELAND SECURITY ACT OF 2002

The Homeland Security of 2002 (PL 107-296) was signed into law by President Bush on November 25, 2002. This legislation was introduced in the U.S. House of Representatives by Representative Richard K. Armey [TX-26] on June 24, 2003, "to establish the Department of Homeland Security, and for other purposes" (Congress.gov 2003). A summary of selected sections under each of the act's titles is presented in Appendix 2-2.

As noted in this summary, the Homeland Security Act provides authorization for the establishment of the Department of Homeland Security (DHS). The act establishes DHS as an executive branch agency with the DHS secretary reporting directly to the president.

The act outlines the DHS management structure, identifies those agencies and programs to be migrated to DHS, and details the roles and responsibilities of the five directorates that make up DHS—Information Analysis and Infrastructure Protection, Science and Technology, Border and Transportation Security, Emergency Preparedness, and Response and Management. The act calls for the migration of the Secret Service and the Coast Guard to DHS and transfers the Bureau of Alcohol, Tobacco, Firearms, and Explosives from the Treasury Department to the Department of Justice. The act establishes within the executive office of the president the Homeland Security Council to advise the president on homeland security matters and the Office for State and Local Coordination reporting to the DHS secretary.

HOMELAND SECURITY PRESIDENTIAL DIRECTIVE/HSPD-5

On February 28, 2003, the White House released Homeland Security Presidential Directive/HSPD-5. As noted in the White House press release, the purpose of HSPD-5 is "to enhance the ability of the United States to manage domestic incidents by establishing a single, comprehensive national incident management system" (office of the press secretary 2003). HSPD-5 tasks the secretary of the Department of Homeland Security (DHS) to develop and administer a National Incident Management System (NIMS) and a National Response Plan (NRP). Draft versions of NIMS and NRP are to be submitted to the Homeland Security Council for review. HSPD-5 sets a time frame for the development of initial versions of these documents, consultation with other federal agencies, and adoption by state and local departments and agencies. The full text of HSPD-5 is presented in Sidebar 2-4.

The Congress has set the fiscal year 2004 budget for DHS at $29.4 billion. This represents a very slight (1.8%) increase from FY 2003. Highlights of the appropriations conference report are presented in Sidebar 2-5.

The FY 2004 budget includes funding in these principal areas:

- $4.2 billion   Issuing state and local first responders
- $9 billion   Border protection and related activities
- $5.2 billion   Transportation security administration (TSA)

- $918 million   Science and technology
- $839 million   Critical infrastructure protection
- $2.6 billion   Coast Guard
- $1.14 billion   U.S. Selective Service
- $.1.8 billion   Disaster relief

FUTURE LEGISLATION

Numerous considerations exist for future legislation and executive action concerning homeland security. One area currently under discussion in Congress is how communities, families, and individuals can become better prepared to respond to terrorism attacks. In September 2003, congressional members of the House Select Committee on Homeland Security proposed the Preparing America to Respond Effectively (PREPARE) Act of 2003, "a comprehensive approach to prepare the nation to respond to acts of terrorism." The major elements of the PREPARE Act are as follows:

- Meeting the needs of first responders
- Making sense of threat alerts
- Improving information sharing
- Providing interoperable communications and equipment
- Encouraging participation of "second responders"
- Educating schoolchildren to be prepared

A bill summary of the PREPARE Act is presented as Appendix 2-3.

SIDEBAR 2-4   Homeland Security Presidential Directive/HSPD-5
Subject: Management of Domestic Incidents

Purpose

(1) To enhance the ability of the United States to manage domestic incidents by establishing a single, comprehensive national incident management system.

Definitions

(2) In this directive:

(a) the term "secretary" means the secretary of Homeland Security.

(b) the term "federal departments and agencies" means those executive departments enumerated in 5 U.S.C. 101, together with the Department of Homeland Security; independent establishments as defined by 5 U.S.C. 104(1); government corporations as defined by 5 U.S.C. 103(1); and the United States Postal Service.

(c) the terms "state," "local," and the "United States," when it is used in a geographical sense, have the same meanings as used in the Homeland Security Act of 2002, PL 107-296.

Policy

(3) To prevent, prepare for, respond to, and recover from terrorist attacks, major disasters, and other emergencies, the United States government shall establish a single, comprehensive approach to domestic incident management. The objective of the United States government is to ensure that all levels of government across the nation have the capability to work efficiently and effectively together, using a national approach to domestic incident management. In these efforts, with regard to domestic incidents, the United States government treats crisis management and consequence management as a single, integrated function, rather than as two separate functions.

(4) The secretary of Homeland Security is the principal federal official for domestic incident management. Pursuant to the Homeland Security Act of 2002, the secretary is responsible for coordinating federal operations within the United States to prepare for, respond to, and recover from terrorist attacks, major disasters, and other emergencies. The secretary shall coordinate the federal government's resources utilized in response to or recovery from terrorist attacks, major disasters, or other emergencies if and when any one of the following four conditions applies: (1) a federal department or agency acting under its own authority has requested the assistance of the secretary; (2) the resources of state and local authorities are overwhelmed and federal assistance has been requested by the appropriate state and local authorities; (3) more than one federal department or agency has become substantially involved in responding to the incident; or (4) the secretary has been directed to assume responsibility for managing the domestic incident by the president.

(5) Nothing in this directive alters, or impedes the ability to carry out, the authorities of federal departments and agencies to perform their responsibilities under law. All federal departments and agencies shall cooperate with the secretary in the secretary's domestic incident management role.

(6) The federal government recognizes the roles and responsibilities of state and local authorities in domestic incident management. Initial responsibility for managing domestic incidents generally falls on state and local authorities. The federal government will assist state and local authorities when their resources are overwhelmed, or when federal interests are involved. The secretary will coordinate with state and local governments to ensure adequate planning, equipment, training, and exercise activities. The secretary will also provide assistance to state and local governments to develop all-hazards plans and capabilities, including those of greatest importance to the security of the United States, and will ensure that state, local, and federal plans are compatible.

(7) The federal government recognizes the role that the private and nongovernmental sectors play in preventing, preparing for, responding to, and recovering from terrorist attacks, major disasters, and other emergencies. The secretary will coordinate with the private and nongovernmental sectors to ensure adequate planning, equipment, training, and exercise activities and to promote partnerships to address incident management capabilities.

(8) The attorney general has lead responsibility for criminal investigations of terrorist acts or terrorist threats by individuals or groups inside the United States, or directed at United States citizens or institutions abroad, where such acts are within the federal criminal jurisdiction of the United States, as well as for related intelligence collection activities within the United States, subject to the National Security Act of 1947 and other applicable law, EO 12333, and attorney general–approved procedures pursuant to that executive order. Generally acting through the Federal Bureau of Investigation, the attorney general, in cooperation with other federal departments and agencies engaged in activities to protect our national security, shall also coordinate the activities of the other members of the law enforcement community to detect, prevent, preempt, and disrupt terrorist attacks against the United States. Following a terrorist threat or an actual incident that falls within the criminal jurisdiction of the United States, the full capabilities of the United States shall be dedicated, consistent with United States law and with activities of other federal departments and agencies to protect our national security, to assisting the attorney general to identify the perpetrators and bring them to justice. The attorney general and the secretary shall establish appropriate relationships and mechanisms for cooperation and coordination between their two departments.

(9) Nothing in this directive impairs or otherwise affects the authority of the secretary of defense over the Department of Defense, including the chain of command for military forces from the president as commander in chief, to the secretary of defense, to the commander of military forces, or military command and control procedures. The secretary of defense shall provide military support to civil authorities for domestic incidents as directed by the president or when consistent with military readiness and appropriate under the circumstances and the law. The secretary of defense shall retain command of military forces providing civil support. The secretary of defense and the secretary shall establish appropriate relationships and mechanisms for cooperation and coordination between their two departments.

(10) The secretary of state has the responsibility, consistent with other United States government activities to protect our national security, to coordinate international activities related to the prevention, preparation, response, and recovery from a domestic incident, and for the protection of United States citizens and United States interests overseas. The secretary of state and the secretary shall establish appropriate relationships and mechanisms for cooperation and coordination between their two departments.

(11) The assistant to the president for Homeland Security and the assistant to the president for National Security Affairs shall be responsible for interagency policy coordination on domestic and international incident management, respectively, as directed by the president. The assistant to the president for Homeland Security and the assistant to the president for National Security Affairs shall work together to ensure that the United States' domestic and international incident management efforts are seamlessly united.

(12) The secretary shall ensure that, as appropriate, information related to domestic incidents is gathered and provided to the public, the private sector, state and local authorities, federal departments and agencies, and, generally through the assistant to the president for Homeland Security, to the president. The secretary shall provide standardized, quantitative reports to the assistant to the president for Homeland Security on

the readiness and preparedness of the nation—at all levels of government—to prevent, prepare for, respond to, and recover from domestic incidents.

(13) Nothing in this directive shall be construed to grant to any assistant to the president any authority to issue orders to federal departments and agencies, their officers, or their employees.

Tasking

(14) The heads of all federal departments and agencies are directed to provide their full and prompt cooperation, resources, and support, as appropriate and consistent with their own responsibilities for protecting our national security, to the secretary, the attorney general, the secretary of defense, and the secretary of state in the exercise of the individual leadership responsibilities and missions assigned in paragraphs (4), (8), (9), and (10), respectively, above.

(15) The secretary shall develop, submit for review to the Homeland Security Council, and administer a National Incident Management System (NIMS). This system will provide a consistent nationwide approach for federal, state, and local governments to work effectively and efficiently together to prepare for, respond to, and recover from domestic incidents, regardless of cause, size, or complexity. To provide for interoperability and compatibility among federal, state, and local capabilities, the NIMS will include a core set of concepts, principles, terminology, and technologies covering the incident command system; multiagency coordination systems; unified command; training; identification and management of resources (including systems for classifying types of resources); qualifications and certification; and the collection, tracking, and reporting of incident information and incident resources.

(16) The secretary shall develop, submit for review to the Homeland Security Council, and administer a National Response Plan (NRP). The secretary shall consult with appropriate assistants to the president (including the assistant to the president for Economic Policy) and the director of the office of Science and Technology Policy, and other such federal officials as may be appropriate, in developing and implementing the NRP. This plan shall integrate federal government domestic prevention, preparedness, response, and recovery plans into one all-discipline, all-hazards plan. The NRP shall be unclassified. If certain operational aspects require classification, they shall be included in classified annexes to the NRP.

(a) The NRP, using the NIMS, shall, with regard to response to domestic incidents, provide the structure and mechanisms for national level policy and operational direction for federal support to state and local incident managers and for exercising direct federal authorities and responsibilities, as appropriate.

(b) The NRP will include protocols for operating under different threats or threat levels; incorporation of existing federal emergency and incident management plans (with appropriate modifications and revisions) as either integrated components of the NRP or as supporting operational plans; and additional operational plans or annexes, as appropriate, including public affairs and intergovernmental communications.

(c) The NRP will include a consistent approach to reporting incidents, providing assessments, and making recommendations to the president, the secretary, and the Homeland Security Council.

(d) The NRP will include rigorous requirements for continuous improvements from testing, exercising, experience with incidents, and new information and technologies.

(17) The secretary shall:

(a) By April 1, 2003, (1) develop and publish an initial version of the NRP, in consultation with other federal departments and agencies; and (2) provide the assistant to the president for Homeland Security with a plan for full development and implementation of the NRP.

(b) By June 1, 2003, (1) in consultation with federal departments and agencies and with state and local governments, develop a national system of standards, guidelines, and protocols to implement the NIMS; and (2) establish a mechanism for ensuring ongoing management and maintenance of the NIMS, including regular consultation with other federal departments and agencies and with state and local governments.

(c) By September 1, 2003, in consultation with federal departments and agencies and the assistant to the president for Homeland Security, review existing authorities and regulations and prepare recommendations for the president on revisions necessary to implement fully the NRP.

(18) The heads of federal departments and agencies shall adopt the NIMS within their departments and agencies and shall provide support and assistance to the secretary in the development and maintenance of the NIMS. All federal departments and agencies will use the NIMS in their domestic incident management and emergency prevention, preparedness, response, recovery, and mitigation activities, as well as those actions taken in support of state or local entities. The heads of federal departments and agencies shall participate in the NRP, shall assist and support the secretary in the development and maintenance of the NRP, and shall participate in and use domestic incident reporting systems and protocols established by the secretary.

(19) The head of each federal department and agency shall:

(a) By June 1, 2003, make initial revisions to existing plans in accordance with the initial version of the NRP.

(b) By August 1, 2003, submit a plan to adopt and implement the NIMS to the secretary and the assistant to the president for Homeland Security. The assistant to the president for Homeland Security shall advise the president on whether such plans effectively implement the NIMS.

(20) Beginning in fiscal year 2005, federal departments and agencies shall make adoption of the NIMS a requirement, to the extent permitted by law, for providing federal preparedness assistance through grants, contracts, or other activities. The secretary shall develop standards and guidelines for determining whether a state or local entity has adopted the NIMS.

Technical and Conforming Amendments to National Security Presidential Directive-1 (NSPD-1)

(21) NSPD-1 ("Organization of the National Security Council System") is amended by replacing the fifth sentence of the third paragraph on the first page with the following: "The attorney general, the secretary of Homeland Security, and the director of the office of Management and Budget shall be invited to attend meetings pertaining to their responsibilities."

Technical and Conforming Amendments to National Security Presidential Directive-8 (NSPD-8)

(22) NSPD-8 ("National Director and Deputy National Security Advisor for Combating Terrorism") is amended by striking "and the office of Homeland Security," on page 4, and inserting "the Department of Homeland Security, and the Homeland Security Council" in lieu thereof.

Technical and Conforming Amendments to Homeland Security Presidential Directive-2 (HSPD-2)

(23) HSPD-2 ("Combating Terrorism Through Immigration Policies") is amended as follows:

(a) striking "the commissioner of the Immigration and Naturalization Service (INS)" in the second sentence of the second paragraph in section 1, and inserting "the secretary of Homeland Security" in lieu thereof ;

(b) striking "the INS," in the third paragraph in section 1, and inserting "the Department of Homeland Security" in lieu thereof;

(c) inserting "the secretary of Homeland Security," after "The attorney general" in the fourth paragraph in section 1;

(d) inserting "the secretary of Homeland Security," after "the attorney general" in the fifth paragraph in section 1;

(e) striking "the INS and the customs service" in the first sentence of the first paragraph of section 2, and inserting "the Department of Homeland Security" in lieu thereof;

(f) striking "customs and INS" in the first sentence of the second paragraph of section 2, and inserting "the Department of Homeland Security" in lieu thereof;

(g) striking "the two agencies" in the second sentence of the second paragraph of section 2, and inserting "the Department of Homeland Security" in lieu thereof;

(h) striking "the secretary of the Treasury" wherever it appears in section 2, and inserting "the secretary of Homeland Security" in lieu thereof;

(i) inserting ", the secretary of Homeland Security," after "the secretary of state" wherever the latter appears in section 3;

(j) inserting ", the Department of Homeland Security," after "the Department of state," in the second sentence in the third paragraph in section 3;

(k) inserting "the secretary of Homeland Security," after "the secretary of state," in the first sentence of the fifth paragraph of section 3;

(l) striking "INS" in the first sentence of the sixth paragraph of section 3, and inserting "Department of Homeland Security" in lieu thereof;

(m) striking "the Treasury" wherever it appears in section 4 and inserting "Homeland Security" in lieu thereof;

(n) inserting ", the secretary of Homeland Security," after "the attorney general" in the first sentence in section 5; and

(o) inserting ", Homeland Security" after "State" in the first sentence of section 6.

Technical and Conforming Amendments to Homeland Security Presidential Directive-3 (HSPD-3)

(24) The Homeland Security Act of 2002 assigned the responsibility for administering the Homeland Security Advisory System to the secretary of Homeland Security. Accordingly, HSPD-3 of March 11, 2002 ("Homeland Security Advisory System") is amended as follows:

(a) replacing the third sentence of the second paragraph entitled "Homeland Security Advisory System" with "Except in exigent circumstances, the secretary of Homeland Security shall seek the views of the attorney general, and any other federal agency heads the secretary deems appropriate, including other members of the Homeland Security Council, on the threat condition to be assigned."

(b) inserting "At the request of the secretary of Homeland Security, the Department of Justice shall permit and facilitate the use of delivery systems administered or managed by the Department of Justice for the purposes of delivering threat information pursuant to the Homeland Security Advisory System." as a new paragraph after the fifth paragraph of the section entitled "Homeland Security Advisory System."

(c) inserting ", the secretary of Homeland Security" after "The director of Central Intelligence" in the first sentence of the seventh paragraph of the section entitled "Homeland Security Advisory System."

(d) striking "attorney general" wherever it appears (except in the sentences referred to in subsections (a) and (c) above), and inserting "the secretary of Homeland Security" in lieu thereof; and

(e) striking the section entitled "Comment and Review Periods."

GEORGE W. BUSH

Source: Office of the press secretary, the White House

SIDEBAR 2-5   **Highlights of FY 2004 Homeland Security Appropriations Conference Agreement, September 17, 2003**

The conference agreement provides $29.4 billion for operations and activities of the Department of Homeland Security (DHS) in fiscal year 2004, an increase of $535.8 million (1.8 percent) above the fiscal year 2003 enacted levels, and $1 billion (3.7 percent) above the President's request.

The conference agreement recognizes that, while the Department of Homeland Security has the lead in *developing* our national homeland security strategy, *implementing* the strategy requires the active participation of state and local governments and the private sector. It also recognizes that many of the agencies that merged into DHS on March 1, 2003, have traditional missions that must continue in concert with the newly established priorities for homeland security. The bill strikes a balance between these missions and supports partnerships with state and local governments and the private sector as we seek ways to protect our country from future terrorist attacks.

Supporting State and Local First Responders

The bill provides $4.2 billion for the Office for Domestic Preparedness (ODP), firefighters, and emergency management; this is $541 million above the amounts proposed by the president. Since September 11th, 2001, and including grants funded outside the jurisdiction of the Homeland Security Subcommittee, this brings total support of first responders to $20.5 billion. Specifically, the bill includes the following:

- $1.7 billion for ODP basic formula grants;
- $500 million for state and local law enforcement terrorism prevention grants;
- $725 million for high-threat, high-density urban areas;
- $750 million for firefighter grants;
- $180 million for Emergency Management Performance grants;

- $60 million for Urban Search and Rescue;
- $50 million for the Metropolitan Medical Response System;
- $60 million for competitive training grants;
- $135 million for the National Domestic Preparedness Consortium; and
- $80 million for technical assistance, and national exercises.

Protecting Our Nation's Borders

The bill provides $9 billion for border protection and related activities, an increase of $400 million over fiscal year 2003 enacted levels (excluding Liberty Shield Coast Guard port security operations). This includes $2 billion for U.S. Coast Guard homeland security activities. Specific initiatives and efforts for border security include the following:

- $125 million for TSA port security grants, bringing the total to $513 million since September 11th;
- $125 million for inspection technologies and operations for vehicles and cargo;
- $61.7 million for the Container Security Initiative;
- $14.1 million for the Customs-Trade Partnership Against Terrorism;
- $215.6 million for Air and Marine Interdiction for border and airspace security, including $40.6 million for a new Northern Border Air Wing; and
- $668 million for the U.S. Coast Guard's "Deepwater" capital acquisition program.

Enhancing Transportation Security

The bill includes $5.2 billion for TSA and the Federal Air Marshal Program, $405 million above the amounts requested by the president (including port security grants), providing funding for both aviation and nonaviation security:

- $1.8 billion for passenger screening;
- $1.3 billion for baggage screening efforts, including $250 million to install in-line explosive detection systems, and $150 million to procure additional systems;
- $85 million for air cargo security;
- $10 million for intercity bus security;
- $22 million for trucking security;
- $7 million for hazardous materials security; and
- $17 million for Operation Safe Commerce.

Using Science and Technology to Protect Our Nation

The bill includes $918 million for science and technology, $115 million above amounts requested by the president. Funds are targeted to research, development, and deployment of innovative technologies, including those proposed by universities, national laboratories, not-for-profit organizations, and private companies:

- $455 million to develop radiological, nuclear, chemical, biological, and high explosives countermeasures;
- $88 million to initiate construction of the National Biodefense Analysis and Countermeasures Center;
- $75 million for rapid development and prototyping of homeland security technologies;
- $60 million for research, development, and testing of antimissile devices for commercial aircraft;
- $40 million to deploy sensors to detect aerosolized biothreats in large metropolitan areas; and
- $70 million for university-based centers of excellence.

Protecting the Nation's Critical Infrastructure

The bill includes $839 million for protecting the nation's critical infrastructure and key assets, an increase of $10 million above amounts requested by the president.

- $81 million for intelligence and warnings to develop timely, integrated, and accurate assessments of terrorist threats;
- $570 million for reducing the nation's vulnerability to physical and cyber attacks, minimizing damage, and assisting in recovery from terrorist acts; and
- $188 million for management and administration and outreach activities with federal, state, and local governments, and with the private sector, which owns and operates 85 percent of the nation's infrastructure.

Supporting Traditional Missions Such as Immigration, Disaster Mitigation and Relief, Drug Interdiction, Law Enforcement, Maritime Safety and Security, and Trade

- $811 million to modernize border, customs, and immigration information technology, including $330 million for the U.S. VISIT program and $318 million for the Automated Commercial Environment;
- $2.6 billion for traditional Coast Guard operating activities, including maritime safety, drug interdiction, and fisheries, and environmental and humanitarian missions;
- $1.14 billion for the U.S. Secret Service;
- $1.8 billion for Disaster Relief;
- $21 million to enforce laws related to forced child labor, intellectual property rights, and textile transshipment;
- $7 million to support investigations related to missing and exploited children; and
- $236 million for immigration services.

Other Provisions

- Includes bill language regarding air cargo security screening and inspections;
- Includes bill language prohibiting the use of funds to deploy or implement CAPPSII until the General Accounting Office completes a report evaluating the system;

CONCLUSION

The issue of terrorism and the methods by which the federal government should prepare for and respond to this threat did not suddenly appear after the devastating events of September 11. As this chapter has shown, concerns about potential threats to the United States have been recognized and actions taken to address them since the early 1980s. Precipitating events, such as the earlier bombing of the World Trade Center in 1992 and attacks on U.S. embassies and installations abroad, brought attention to the problems at the highest levels of Congress and the White House. The domestic terrorist bombing of the Murrah Federal Office Building in Oklahoma City vividly pointed out conflicts as to who was in charge of these events within the federal government. As Congress passed legislation it thought would address the problems, conflicts, competition, and a lack of resources at the federal level failed to address the concerns and needs of first responders at the state and local levels. The federal response worked surprisingly well on September 11, but the enormous loss of lives among civilians and the first responder community demanded and produced a flurry of activity to ensure that this tragedy would not be repeated. Two of the most far-reaching pieces of legislation, the Patriot Act and the Homeland Security Act, dramatically changed the power, organization, and functions of the federal government. The Patriot Act gave the attorney general and the DOJ unsurpassed authority over the civil rights and liberties of individuals. Combining 22 federal entities with a mandate to establish a safe and secure homeland, the Homeland Security Act represents the largest single reorganization of the federal government since World War II.

Whether these actions have created a safer, more secure homeland is yet to be determined. As the federal government consolidates programs and responsibilities, authorized funding is making its way to the states, but localities complain about being left out of the equation. Funding for the very first line of first responders, local government, is slow in coming. The volunteer effort, championed as a way to help at the local level, has received minimal funds and is still looking for strong support from the leadership.

All the authorities are there; all the legislation has been passed. Future historians will assess the effectiveness of these authorities and whether their implementation has accomplished the goals of a safe and secure homeland.

- $5.6 billion over 10 years to encourage commercial development and production of medical countermeasures against bioterrorism (Bioshield), $890 million of which is available in fiscal year 2004; and

- Transfers the federal air marshals to the bureau of Immigration and Customs Enforcement from the Transportation Security Administration, as recommended by the Administration.

Source: Appropriations Committee, U.S. House of Representatives

REVIEW QUESTIONS

1. What are the two principal purposes for establishing legislation to support government homeland security activities and programs?
2. What are the principal functions of the Patriot Act, the Homeland Security Act, and Homeland Security Presidential Directive/ HSPD-5?
3. What issues have been raised concerning some of the authorities granted government agencies in the Patriot Act?
4. If you were a member of Congress, what types of standards would you propose to measure the effectiveness of the spending that is occurring for homeland security? How would you propose to determine if the spending has raised individual, community, and private sector preparedness for the new terrorist threat? How would these measurements be enforced and by what government agency(s) at what level of government (federal, state, and/or local)?
5. What additional statutory authorities and resources do you think emergency managers require in order to function effectively in homeland security? Should certain preparedness and mitigation actions and activities be made mandatory like building codes and seat belt use? Should greater emphasis be placed on enforcement of current and future restrictions and requirements? Should additional resources become part of a regular annual appropriation at all levels of government? How would the impact of the new authorities and resources be measured to ensure that they are successfully applied?

REFERENCES

Appropriations Committee. 2002. United States House of Representatives

Baldwin, Dr. T.E. "Historical Chronology of FEMA Consequence Management, Preparedness and Response to Terrorism." Argonne, IL: Argonne National Laboratory.

Bohn, K. 2003. "ACLU Files against Patriot Act." Cable News Network. July 30, 2003. www.cnn.com.

Gay, L. 2001. "How the New Antiterrorism Bill Could Affect You." Scripps Howard News Service. October 26, 2001. www.startribune.com.

Office of the Press Secretary. 2003. The White House. www.whitehouse.gov.

Rubin, C.B., William R. Cummings, and Irmak Renda-Tanali. 2003. "Terrorism Time Line: Major Focusing Events and U.S. Outcomes (1993–2002)." May 2003.

Taylor, G. 2003. "Communities Share Patriot Act." *The Washington Times*.

Washington, DC. July 21, 2003. www.washington-times.com. www.congress.gov. 2003. The Library of Congress. Washington, DC.

APPENDIX 2-1
Patriot Act of 2001—Summary of Titles

Title I: Enhancing Domestic Security against Terrorism—Establishes in the treasury the counter-terrorism fund.

Title II: Enhanced Surveillance Procedures—Amends the federal criminal code to authorize the interception of wire, oral, and electronic communications for the production of evidence of: (1) specified chemical weapons or terrorism offenses; and (2) computer fraud and abuse.

Title III: International Money-Laundering Abatement and Anti-Terrorist Financing Act of 2001; International Money-Laundering Abatement and Financial Anti-Terrorism Act of 2001—Sunsets this act after the first day of FY 2005 if Congress enacts a specified joint resolution to that effect.

Subtitle A: International Counter Money Laundering and Related Measures—Amends federal law governing monetary transactions to prescribe procedural guidelines under which the secretary of the Treasury (the secretary) may require domestic financial institutions and agencies to take specified measures if the secretary finds that reasonable grounds exist for concluding that jurisdictions, financial institutions, types of accounts, or transactions operating outside or within the United States, are of primary money laundering concern. Includes mandatory disclosure of specified information relating to certain correspondent accounts.

Subtitle B: Bank Secrecy Act Amendments and Related Improvements—Amends federal law known as the Bank Secrecy Act to revise requirements for civil liability immunity for voluntary financial institution disclosure of suspicious activities. Authorizes the inclusion of suspicions of illegal activity in written employment references.

Subtitle C: Currency Crimes—Establishes as a bulk cash smuggling felony the knowing concealment and attempted transport (or transfer) across U.S.

borders of currency and monetary instruments in excess of $10,000, with intent to evade specified currency reporting requirements.

Title IV: Protecting the Border

Subtitle A: Protecting the Northern Border—Authorizes the attorney general to waive certain Immigration and Naturalization Service (INS) personnel caps with respect to ensuring security needs on the northern border.

Subtitle B: Enhanced Immigration Provisions—Amends the Immigration and Nationality Act to broaden the scope of aliens ineligible for admission or deportable due to terrorist activities to include an alien who: (1) is a representative of a political, social, or similar group whose political endorsement of terrorist acts undermines U.S. antiterrorist efforts; (2) has used a position of prominence to endorse terrorist activity or to persuade others to support such activity in a way that undermines U.S. antiterrorist efforts (or the child or spouse of such an alien under specified circumstances); or (3) has been associated with a terrorist organization and intends to engage in threatening activities while in the United States.

Subtitle C: Preservation of Immigration Benefits for Victims of Terrorism—Authorizes the attorney general to provide permanent resident status through the special immigrant program to an alien (and spouse, child, or grandparent under specified circumstances) who was the beneficiary of a petition filed on or before September 11, 2001, to grant the alien permanent residence as an employer-sponsored immigrant or of an application for labor certification if the petition or application was rendered null because of the disability of the beneficiary or loss of employment due to physical damage to, or destruction of, the business of the petitioner or applicant as a direct result of the terrorist attacks on September 11, 2001 (September attacks) or because of the death of the petitioner or applicant as a direct result of such attacks.

Title V: Removing Obstacles to Investigating Terrorism—Authorizes the attorney general to pay rewards from available funds pursuant to public advertisements for assistance to the DOJ to combat terrorism and defend the nation against terrorist acts, in accordance with procedures and regulations established or issued by the attorney general, subject to specified conditions, including a prohibition against any such reward of $250,000 or more from being made or offered without the personal approval of either the attorney general or the president.

Title VI: Providing for Victims of Terrorism, Public Safety Officers, and Their Families

Subtitle A: Aid to Families of Public Safety Officers—Provides for expedited payments for: (1) public safety officers involved in the prevention, investigation, rescue, or recovery efforts related to a terrorist attack; and (2) heroic public safety officers. Increases Public Safety Officers Benefit Program payments.

Subtitle B: Amendments to the Victims of Crime Act of 1984—Amends the Victims of Crime Act of 1984 to: (1) revise provisions regarding the allocation of funds for compensation and assistance, location of compensable crime, and the relationship of crime victim compensation to means-tested federal benefit programs and to the September 11th victim compensation fund; and (2) establish an antiterrorism emergency reserve in the Victims of Crime Fund.

Title VII: Increased Information Sharing for Critical Infrastructure Protection—Amends the Omnibus Crime Control and Safe Streets Act of 1968 to extend Bureau of Justice Assistance regional information-sharing-system grants to systems that enhance the investigation and prosecution abilities of participating federal, state, and local law enforcement agencies in addressing multi-jurisdictional terrorist conspiracies and activities. Authorizes appropriations.

Title VIII: Strengthening the Criminal Laws Against Terrorism—Amends the federal criminal code to prohibit specific terrorist acts or otherwise destructive, disruptive, or violent acts against mass transportation vehicles, ferries, providers, employees, passengers, or operating systems.

Title IX: Improved Intelligence—Amends the National Security Act of 1947 to require the director of Central Intelligence (DCI) to establish requirements and priorities for foreign intelligence collected under the Foreign Intelligence Surveillance Act of 1978 and to provide assistance to the attorney general (AG) to ensure that information derived from electronic surveillance or physical searches is disseminated for efficient and effective foreign intelligence purposes. Requires the inclusion of international terrorist activities within the scope of foreign intelligence under such act.

Title X: Miscellaneous—Directs the inspector general of the Department of Justice to designate one official to review allegations of abuse of civil rights, civil liberties, and racial and ethnic profiling by government employees and officials.

Source: www.congress.gov

APPENDIX 2-2
Homeland Security Act of 2002: Summary of Title I

Title I: Department of Homeland Security (Sec. 101)—Establishes a Department of Homeland Security (DHS) as an executive department of the United States, headed by a secretary of Homeland Security (secretary) appointed by the president, by and with the advice and consent of the Senate, to: (1) prevent terrorist attacks within the United States; (2) reduce the vulnerability of the United States to terrorism; (3) minimize the damage, and assist in the recovery, from terrorist attacks that occur within the United States; (4) carry out all functions of entities transferred to DHS; (5) ensure that the functions of the agencies and subdivisions within DHS that are not related directly to securing the homeland are not diminished or neglected except by a specific act of Congress; (6) ensure that the overall economic security of the United States is not diminished by efforts, activities, and programs aimed at securing the homeland; and (7) monitor connections between illegal drug trafficking and terrorism, coordinate efforts to sever such connections, and otherwise contribute to efforts to interdict illegal drug trafficking. Vests primary responsibility for investigating and prosecuting acts of terrorism in federal, state, and local law enforcement agencies with proper jurisdiction except as specifically provided by law with respect to entities transferred to DHS under this act.

(Sec. 102)—Directs the secretary to appoint a special assistant to carry out specified homeland security liaison activities between DHS and the private sector.

(Sec. 103)—Creates the following: (1) a deputy secretary of Homeland Security; (2) an undersecretary for Information Analysis and Infrastructure Protection; (3) an undersecretary for Science and Technology; (4) an undersecretary for Border and Transportation Security; (5) an undersecretary for Emergency Preparedness and Response; (6) a director of the Bureau of Citizenship and Immigration Services; (7) an undersecretary for Management; (8) not more than 12 assistant secretaries;

and (9) a general counsel. Establishes an inspector general (to be appointed under the Inspector General Act of 1978). Requires the following individuals to assist the secretary in the performance of the secretary's functions: (1) the commandant of the Coast Guard; (2) the director of the Secret Service; (3) a chief information officer; (4) a chief human capital officer; (5) a chief financial officer; and (6) an officer for Civil Rights and Civil Liberties.

Source: www.congress.gov

Homeland Security Act of 2002: Summary of Title II

Title II: Information Analysis and Infrastructure Protection—Subtitle A: Directorate for Information Analysis and Infrastructure Protection; Access to Information (Sec. 201)—Establishes in the department: (1) a directorate for Information Analysis and Infrastructure Protection, headed by an undersecretary for Information Analysis and Infrastructure Protection; (2) an assistant secretary for Information Analysis; and (3) an assistant secretary for Infrastructure Protection.

Requires the undersecretary to: (1) access, receive, and analyze law enforcement and intelligence information from federal, state, and local agencies and the private sector to identify the nature, scope, and identity of terrorist threats to the United States, as well as potential U.S. vulnerabilities; (2) carry out comprehensive assessments of vulnerabilities of key U.S. resources and critical infrastructures; (3) integrate relevant information, analyses, and vulnerability assessments to identify protection priorities; (4) ensure timely and efficient department access to necessary information for discharging responsibilities; (5) develop a comprehensive national plan for securing key U.S. resources and critical infrastructures; (6) recommend necessary measures to protect such resources and infrastructure in coordination with other entities; (7) administer the Homeland Security Advisory System; (8) review, analyze, and make recommendations for improvements in policies and procedures governing the sharing of law enforcement, intelligence, and intelligence-related information and other information related to homeland security within the federal government and between the federal government and state and local government agencies and authorities; (9) disseminate department homeland security information to other appropriate federal, state, and local agencies; (10) consult with the director of Central Intelligence (DCI) and other appropriate federal intelligence, law enforcement, or other elements to establish collection priorities and strategies for information relating to the terrorism threats; (11) consult with state and local governments and private entities to ensure appropriate exchanges of information relating to such threats; (12) ensure the protection from unauthorized disclosure of homeland security and intelligence information; (13) request additional information from appropriate entities relating to threats of terrorism in the United States; (14) establish and utilize a secure communications and information technology infrastructure for receiving and analyzing data; (15) ensure the compatibility and privacy protection of shared information databases and analytical tools; (16) coordinate training and other support to facilitate the identification and sharing of information; (17) coordinate activities with elements of the intelligence community, federal, state, and local law enforcement agencies, and the private sector; and (18) provide intelligence and information analysis and support to other elements of the department. Provides for: (1) staffing, including the use of private sector analysts; and (2) cooperative agreements for the detail of appropriate personnel.

Transfers to the secretary the functions, personnel, assets, and liabilities of the following entities: (1) the National Infrastructure Protection Center of the Federal Bureau of Investigation (other than the Computer Investigations and Operations Section); (2) the National Communications System of the Department of Defense; (3) the Critical Infrastructure Assurance Offices of the Department of Commerce; (4) the National Infrastructure Simulation and Analysis Center of the Department of Energy and its energy security and assurance program; and (5) the Federal Computer Incident Response Center of the General Services Administration.

Amends the National Security Act of 1947 to include as elements of the intelligence community the department elements concerned with analyses of foreign intelligence information.

Subtitle B: Critical Infrastructure Information—Critical Infrastructure Information Act of 2002 (Sec. 213)—allows a critical infrastructure protection program to be so designated by either the president or the secretary.

Subtitle C: Information Security—(Sec. 221)—requires the secretary to establish procedures on the use of shared information that: (1) limit its redissemination to ensure it is not used for an unauthorized purpose; (2) ensure its security and confidentiality; (3) protect the constitutional and statutory rights of individuals who are subjects of such information; and (4) provide data integrity through the timely removal and destruction of obsolete or erroneous names and information.

Subtitle D: Office of Science and Technology—(Sec. 231)—establishes within the Department of Justice (DOJ) an Office of Science and Technology whose mission is to: (1) serve as the national focal point for work on law enforcement technology (investigative and forensic technologies, corrections technologies, and technologies that support the judicial process); and (2) carry out programs that improve the safety and effectiveness of such technology and improve technology access by federal, state, and local law enforcement agencies. Sets forth office duties, including: (1) establishing and maintaining technology advisory groups and performance standards; (2) carrying out research, development, testing, evaluation, and cost-benefit analyses for improving the safety, effectiveness, and efficiency of technologies used by federal, state, and local law enforcement agencies; and (3) operating the regional National Law Enforcement and Corrections Technology Centers (established under this subtitle) and establishing additional centers.

Requires the office director to report annually on office activities.

Source: www.congress.gov

Homeland Security Act of 2002:
Summary of Title III

Title III: Science and Technology in Support of Homeland Security—(Sec. 301)—establishes in DHS a directorate of Science and Technology, headed by an undersecretary for Science and Technology to be responsible for: (1) advising the secretary regarding research and development (R&D) efforts and priorities in support of DHS missions; (2) developing a national policy and strategic plan for identifying priorities, goals, objectives, and policies for, and coordinating the federal government's civilian efforts to identify and develop countermeasures to chemical, biological, radiological, nuclear, and other emerging terrorist threats; (3) supporting the undersecretary for Information Analysis and Infrastructure Protection by assessing and testing homeland security vulnerabilities and possible threats; (4) conducting basic and applied R&D activities relevant to DHS elements, provided that such responsibility does not extend to human health-related R&D activities; (5) establishing priorities for directing, funding, and conducting national R&D and procurement of technology systems for preventing the importation of chemical, biological, radiological, nuclear, and related weapons and material and for detecting, preventing, protecting against, and responding to terrorist attacks; (6) establishing a system for transferring homeland security developments or technologies to federal, state, and local government and private sector entities; (7) entering into agreements with the Department of Energy (DOE) regarding the use of the national laboratories or sites and support of the science and technology base at those facilities; (8) collaborating with the secretary of agriculture and the attorney general in the regulation of certain biological agents and toxins as provided in the Agricultural Bioterrorism Protection Act of 2002; (9) collaborating with the secretary of health and human services and the attorney general in determining new biological agents and toxins that shall be listed as select agents in the Code of Federal Regulations; (10) supporting U.S. leadership in science and technology; (11) establishing and administering the primary R&D activities of DHS; (12) coordinating and integrating all DHS R&D activities; (13) coordinating with other appropriate executive agencies in developing and carrying out the science and technology agenda of DHS to reduce duplication and identify unmet needs; and (14) developing and overseeing the administration of guidelines for merit review of R&D projects throughout DHS and for the dissemination of DHS research.

Source: www.congress.gov

Homeland Security Act of 2002:
Summary of Title IV

Title IV: Directorate of Border and Transportation Security—Subtitle A: Undersecretary for Border and Transportation Security—(Sec. 401)—establishes in DHS a directorate of Border and Transportation Security to be headed by an undersecretary for Border and Transportation Security. Makes the secretary, acting through the undersecretary for Border and Transportation Security, responsible for: (1) preventing the entry of terrorists and the instruments of terrorism into the United States; (2) securing the borders, territorial waters, ports, terminals, waterways, and air, land, and sea transportation systems of the United States; (3) carrying out the immigration enforcement functions vested by statute in, or performed by, the commissioner of Immigration and Naturalization immediately before their transfer to the undersecretary; (4) establishing and administering rules governing the granting of visas or other forms of permission to enter the United States to individuals who are not citizens or aliens lawfully admitted for permanent residence in the United States; (5) establishing national immigration enforcement policies and priorities; (6) administering the customs laws of the United States (with certain exceptions); (7) conducting the inspection and related administrative functions of the Department of Agriculture transferred to the secretary; and (8) ensuring the speedy, orderly, and efficient flow of lawful traffic and commerce in carrying out the foregoing responsibilities.

(Sec. 403)—Transfers to the secretary the functions, personnel, assets, and liabilities of: (1) the U.S. Customs Service; (2) the Transportation Security Administration; (3) the Federal Protective Service of the General Services Administration (GSA); (4) the Federal Law Enforcement Training Center of the Department of the Treasury; and (5) the Office for Domestic Preparedness of the Office of Justice Programs of the Department of Justice (DOJ).

Subtitle B: United States Customs Service—(Sec. 411)—establishes in DHS the U.S. Customs Service (transferred from the Department of the Treasury but with certain customs-revenue functions remaining with the secretary of the Treasury). Authorizes the secretary of the Treasury to appoint up to 20 new personnel to work with DHS personnel in performing customs revenue functions.

Subtitle C: Miscellaneous Provisions—(Sec. 421)—transfers to the secretary the functions of the secretary of Agriculture relating to agricultural import and entry inspection activities under specified animal and plant protection laws. Requires the secretary of agriculture and the secretary to enter into an agreement to effectuate such transfer and to transfer periodically funds collected pursuant to fee authorities under the Food, Agriculture, Conservation, and Trade Act of 1990 to the secretary for activities carried out by the secretary for which such fees were collected. Directs the secretary of agriculture to transfer to the secretary not more than 3,200 full-time equivalent positions of the Department of Agriculture.

Subtitle D: Immigration Enforcement Functions—(Sec. 441)—transfers from the commissioner of Immigration and Naturalization to the undersecretary for Border and Transportation Security all functions performed under the following programs and all personnel, assets, and liabilities pertaining to such programs, immediately before such transfer occurs: (1) the border patrol program; (2) the detention and removal program; (3) the intelligence program; (4) the

investigations program; and (5) the inspections program.

Subtitle E: Citizenship and Immigration Services—(Sec. 451)—establishes in DHS a Bureau of Citizenship and Immigration Services, headed by the director of the Bureau of Citizenship and Immigration Services, who shall: (1) establish the policies for performing and administering transferred functions; (2) establish national immigration services policies and priorities; and (3) implement a managerial rotation program. Authorizes the director to implement pilot initiatives to eliminate the backlog of immigration benefit applications. Transfers all Immigration and Naturalization Service (INS) adjudications and related personnel and funding to the director. Establishes for the bureau positions of: (1) chief of Policy and Strategy; (2) legal adviser; (3) budget officer; and (4) chief of the Office of Citizenship to promote citizenship instruction and training for aliens interested in becoming naturalized U.S. citizens.

Subtitle F: General Immigration Provisions—(Sec. 471)—abolishes INS upon completion of all transfers from it as provided for by this act.

Source: www.congress.gov

Homeland Security Act of 2002: Summary of Title V

Title V: Emergency Preparedness and Response—(Sec. 501)—establishes in DHS a directorate of Emergency Preparedness and Response, headed by an undersecretary.

(Sec. 502)—requires the responsibilities of the secretary, acting through the undersecretary, to include: (1) helping to ensure the effectiveness of emergency response providers to terrorist attacks, major disasters, and other emergencies; (2) with respect to the Nuclear Incident Response Team, establishing and certifying compliance with standards, conducting joint and other exercises and training, and providing funds to the Department of Energy and the Environmental Protection Agency for homeland security planning, training, and equipment; (3) providing the federal government's response to terrorist attacks and major disasters; (4) aiding recovery from terrorist attacks and major disasters; (5) building a comprehensive national incident management system with federal, state, and local governments to respond to such attacks and disasters; (6) consolidating existing federal government emergency response plans into a single, coordinated national response plan; and (7) developing comprehensive programs for developing interoperative communications technology and helping to ensure that emergency response providers acquire such technology.

(Sec. 503)—transfers to the secretary the functions, personnel, assets, and liabilities of: (1) the Federal Emergency Management Agency (FEMA); (2) the Integrated Hazard Information System of the National Oceanic and Atmospheric Administration, which shall be renamed FIRESAT; (3) the National Domestic Preparedness Office of the FBI; (4) the Domestic Emergency Support Teams of DOJ; (5) the Office of Emergency Preparedness, the National Disaster Medical System, and the Metropolitan Medical Response System of HHS; and (6) the Strategic National Stockpile of HHS.

Source: www.congress.gov

Homeland Security Act of 2002: Summary of Title VI

Title VI: Management—(Sec. 701)—Makes the secretary, acting through the undersecretary for Management, responsible for the management and administration of DHS. Details certain responsibilities of the undersecretary with respect to immigration statistics. Transfers to the undersecretary functions previously performed by the Statistics Branch of the Office of Policy and Planning of the Immigration and Naturalization Service (INS) with respect to: (1) the border patrol program; (2) the detention and removal program; (3) the intelligence program; (4) the investigations program; (5) the inspections program; and (6) INS adjudications.

Source: www.congress.gov

Homeland Security Act of 2002: Summary of Title VII

Title VII: Coordination with Non-Federal Entities; Inspector General; United States Secret Service; Coast Guard; General Provisions—Subtitle A: Coordination with Non-Federal Entities—(Sec. 801)—Establishes within the office of the secretary the office for State and Local Government Coordination to oversee and coordinate department homeland security programs for and relationships with state and local governments.

Subtitle C: United States Secret Service—(Sec. 821)—Transfers to the secretary the functions of the United States Secret Service, which shall be maintained as a distinct entity within DHS.

Subtitle F: Federal Emergency Procurement Flexibility—(Sec. 852)—Provides that the simplified acquisition threshold to be applied for any executive agency in the procurement of property or services that are to be used to facilitate the defense against or recovery from terrorism or nuclear, biological, chemical, or radiological attack and that are carried out in support of a humanitarian or peacekeeping operation or a contingency operation shall be: (1) $200,000 for a contract to be awarded and performed, or a purchase to be made, inside the United States; or (2) $300,000 for a contract to be awarded and performed, or a purchase to be made, outside the United States.

Subtitle I: Information Sharing—Homeland Security Information Sharing Act—(Sec. 891)—Expresses the sense of Congress that federal, state, and local entities should share homeland security information to the maximum extent practicable, with special emphasis on hard-to-reach urban and rural communities.

Source: www.congress.gov

Homeland Security Act of 2002: Summary of Titles IX to XI and XIV to XV

Miscellaneous Titles

Title IX: National Homeland Security Council—(Sec. 901)—Establishes within the executive office of the president the Homeland Security Council to advise the president on homeland security matters. (Sec. 903)—Includes as members of the council: (1) the president; (2) the vice president; (3) the secretary; (4) the attorney general; and (5) the secretary of defense. (Sec. 904)—Requires the council to: (1) assess the objectives, commitments, and risks of the United States in the interest of homeland security and make recommendations to the president; and (2) oversee and review federal homeland security policies and make policy recommendations to the president.

Title X: Information Security—Federal Information Security Management Act of 2002—(Sec. 1001)—Revises government information security requirements. Requires the head of each agency operating or exercising control of a national security system to ensure that the agency: (1) provides information security protections commensurate with the risk and magnitude of the harm resulting from the unauthorized access, use, disclosure, disruption, modification, or destruction of the information; and (2) implements information security policies and practices as required by standards and guidelines for national security systems. Authorizes appropriations for FY 2003 through 2007.

Title XI: Subtitle B: Transfer of the Bureau of Alcohol, Tobacco, and Firearms to the Department of Justice—(Sec. 1111)—Establishes within DOJ, under the attorney general's authority, the Bureau of Alcohol, Tobacco, Firearms, and Explosives (the bureau). Transfers to DOJ the authorities, functions, personnel, and assets of the Bureau of Alcohol, Tobacco and Firearms (BATF), which shall be maintained as a distinct entity within DOJ, including the related functions of the secretary of the Treasury.

Title XIV: Arming Pilots Against Terrorism—Arming Pilots Against Terrorism Act—(Sec. 1402)—Amends federal law to direct the undersecretary of transportation for security (in the Transportation Security Administration) to establish a two-year pilot program to: (1) deputize volunteer pilots of air carriers as federal law enforcement officers to defend the flight decks of aircraft against acts of criminal violence or air piracy (federal flight deck officers); and (2) provide training, supervision, and equipment for such officers. Requires the undersecretary to begin the process of training and deputizing qualified pilots to be federal flight deck officers under the program. Allows the undersecretary to request another federal agency to deputize such officers.

Title XV: Transition—Subtitle A: Reorganization Plan—(Sec. 1502)—Requires the president, within 60 days after enactment of this act, to transmit to the appropriate congressional committees a reorganization plan regarding: (1) the transfer of agencies, personnel, assets, and obligations to DHS pursuant to this act; and (2) any consolidation, reorganization, or streamlining of agencies transferred to DHS pursuant to this Act. (Sec. 1503)—Expresses the sense of Congress that each House of Congress should review its committee structure in light of the reorganization of responsibilities within the executive branch by the establishment of DHS.

Source: www.congress.gov

APPENDIX 2-3
Bill Summary: Preparing America to Respond Effectively (PREPARE) Act of 2003

PREPARING AMERICA TO RESPOND EFFEC-
TIVELY (PREPARE) ACT OF 2003, H.R. 3158:
BILL SUMMARY
September 24, 2003

The Preparing America to Respond Effectively Act
(PREPARE Act) is a comprehensive approach to prepare the nation to respond to acts of terrorism. The
legislation improves the first responder funding system; bolsters information sharing, threat warnings,
communications, and equipment interoperability;
integrates private companies and the public into
response plans; and provides grants to educate schoolchildren to be prepared. Major elements of the legislation include the following:

Meeting the Needs of First Responders

The PREPARE Act moves beyond the current
debate over the first responder grant system by
creating a method to identify and provide what cities,
counties, and states need in order to be prepared to
handle a terrorist attack. As the Council on Foreign
Relations Task Force recently stated, "The absence of
a functioning methodology to determine national
requirements for emergency preparedness constitutes
a public policy crisis. Establishing national standards
that define levels of preparedness is a critical first step
toward determining the nature and extent of additional
requirements and the human and financial resources
needed to fulfill them." The Gilmore commission's
most recent report to Congress states, "…without a
comprehensive approach to measuring how well we
are doing with the resources being applied at any point
in time, there will be very little prospect for answering
the question 'How well prepared are we?'."

The PREPARE Act addresses these findings by creating a task force on standards for terrorism preparedness, which will develop a methodology for local and
state governments to use to determine what resources
(e.g., personnel, equipment, training, etc.) are needed
to be prepared for a terrorist attack. For the first time,

we will know how prepared we are and where more
preparation is needed.

The act then creates PREPARE grants to provide
every jurisdiction with what it needs to be prepared to
defend against terrorist attack, meeting the highest priority needs first. Currently, there is no way to establish
priorities. The act consolidates all terrorism preparedness grants in one DHS office in order to streamline
interaction with state and local officials.

Making Sense of Threat Alerts

The PREPARE Act requires the Department of
Homeland Security (DHS) to reform the threat advisory
system so it can issue alerts to the affected geographic
area or industry sector. The act mandates that DHS will
notify Congress before issuing threat advisories, provide threat information, and recommend actions at the
state and local level, for the general public and the private sector, as appropriate. In addition, the act requires
the department to reimburse personnel costs incurred
by local and state governments when the threat level is
increased.

Improving Information Sharing

The PREPARE Act requires the Administration
to clarify DHS's responsibilities for sharing and receiving information with local and state governments. The
act provides support for obtaining security clearances
and equipment that local and state law enforcement
officials need to receive and use classified intelligence.

Providing Interoperable Communications and Equipment

The PREPARE Act requires DHS, with other agencies, to ensure that first responder equipment and
training standards are developed and that such equipment is interoperable within the first responder communities. The act authorizes $20 million to give every
state and major metropolitan area the immediate
capability to connect radios of different responder
agencies.

Encouraging Participation of "Second Responders"

The PREPARE Act recognizes that local and state emergency officials are the first to respond to a terrorist attack. The act, however, also takes into account the public volunteers, the private companies, and other groups that play important roles in the longer term response. The PREPARE Act stresses the importance of public training and education, and expands current programs to link company resources with emergency response.

Educating Schoolchildren to Be Prepared

The PREPARE Act authorizes a three-year grant program for public elementary and secondary schools to develop and implement instruction regarding age-appropriate skills to prepare for and respond to a man-made emergency or a natural disaster.

3

Organizational Actions

INTRODUCTION

Before September 11 the Nunn-Lugar legislation provided the primary authority and focus for domestic federal preparedness activities for terrorism. Several agencies—the Federal Emergency Management Agency (FEMA), Department of Justice (DOJ), Department of Health and Human Resources (HHS), Department of Defense (DoD), and the National Guard—were involved, all jockeying for leadership of the terrorism issue. There were some attempts at coordination, but in general, agencies pursued their own agendas. The biggest difference among the agencies was the level of funding available, with DoD and DOJ controlling the most funds. State and local governments were confused, felt unprepared, and complained of the need to recognize their vulnerability and needs should an event happen. The TOPOFF exercise, held in 1999, reinforced these concerns and vividly demonstrated the problems that could arise in a real event.

The events of September 11, unfortunately, validated their concerns and visibly demonstrated the need for changes in the federal approach to terrorism.

There are five groups that must be fully engaged in the nation's war on terrorism: the diplomats, the intelligence community, the military, law enforcement, and emergency management. The principal goal of the diplomats, intelligence community, the military, and law enforcement is to reduce, if not eliminate, the possibility of future terrorist attacks on American citizens inside our borders and abroad.

The goal of emergency management should be to be prepared and to reduce the future impact in terms of loss of life, injuries, property damage, and economic disruption caused by the next terrorist attack. As President George W. Bush and many of his advisors have repeatedly informed the nation, it is not a question of if, but rather when, the next terrorist attack occurs. It is therefore incumbent upon emergency managers to apply the same diligence to preparing for the next bombing or biochemical event as they do for the next hurricane or flood or tornado. The focus of emergency management in the war on terrorism must be on reducing the danger to first responders, the general public, the business community, the economy, and our way of life from future terrorist attacks.

The creation of the Department of Homeland Security (DHS) represents a landmark change for the federal community, especially for emergency management. The consolidation of all federal agencies involved in fighting the war on terrorism follows the same logic that first established FEMA in 1979. At that time, then President Jimmy Carter, at the request and suggestion of the nation's governors, consolidated all the federal agencies and programs involved in federal disaster relief, preparedness, and mitigation into one single federal agency, FEMA.

The director of the new agency, FEMA, reported directly to the president as will the DHS secretary. However, when FEMA was absorbed into DHS, the FEMA director no longer reported directly to the president but rather to the DHS secretary. This change could have a significant impact on FEMA and its state and local partners in managing natural and other technological disasters in the future.

At the request of President Bush, FEMA established the Office of National Preparedness in 2001 to focus attention on the then undeclared terrorist threat and other national security issues. This was the first step in the refocusing of FEMA's mission and attention from an all-hazards approach to emergency management embraced by the Clinton Administration. The shift in focus was accelerated by the events of September 11 and has been embraced by state and local emergency management operations across the country. A similar shift of focus in FEMA occurred in 1981 at the beginning of the Reagan Administration. Then the shift of focus was from disaster management to planning for a nuclear war. For the remaining years of the Reagan Administration and the four years of President George H. W. Bush's administration, FEMA resources and personnel focused their attention of ensuring continuity of government operations in the event of a nuclear attack. Little attention was paid to natural hazard management, and FEMA was left unprepared to deal with a series of catastrophic natural disasters starting with Hurricane Hugo in 1989 and culminating with Hurricane Andrew in 1992.

If history repeats itself, the current change in focus away from the all-hazard approach of the 1990s could result in a weakening of FEMA's natural disaster management capabilities in the future.

In the remaining sections of this chapter we will discuss how these changes are affecting emergency management organizations at the federal, state, and local levels. A summary of the response and recovery efforts to the World Trade Center and Pentagon attacks may provide a perspective on why such dramatic actions are being proposed.

THE DEPARTMENT OF HOMELAND SECURITY (DHS)

On November 25, 2002, President Bush signed into law the Homeland Security Act of 2002 (Public Law 107-296; referred to as "HS Act" herein), and announced that former Pennsylvania governor Tom Ridge would be secretary of a new Department of Homeland Security (DHS) that was to be created. This act, which authorizes the greatest federal government reorganization since President Harry Truman joined the various branches of the armed forces under the Department of Defense, is charged with a threefold mission of protecting the United States from further terrorist attacks, reducing the nation's vulnerability to terrorism, and minimizing the damage from potential terrorist attacks and natural disasters (Sidebar 3-1).

A sweeping reorganization into the new department, which officially opened its doors on January 24, 2003, joined together more than 179,000 federal employees from twenty-two existing federal agencies under the umbrella of a single, cabinet-level organization. Additionally, several changes occurred within federal agencies that are only remotely or not at all affiliated with DHS, as defined in the HS Act.

The creation of DHS is the culmination of an evolutionary legislative process that began largely in response to criticism that increased federal intelligence and inter-agency cooperation could have prevented the September 11th terrorist attacks. Just nine days after those attacks, President Bush created the Office of Homeland Security (by executive order), with Tom Ridge as director, but the small office became widely viewed as ineffective (Brookings 2003). Both the White House and Congress recognized that a Homeland Security czar would require both a staff and a large budget in order to succeed, and thus began deliberations to create a new cabinet-level

SIDEBAR 3-1 Homeland Security Timeline

- September 11, 2001—Terrorists attacks occur in Washington, DC, New York, and Pennsylvania.
- September 20, 2001—In an address to congress, President Bush announces the creation of the Office of Homeland Security (DHS) and the appointment of Tom Ridge as director.
- October 8, 2001—President swears in Tom Ridge as assistant to the president for Homeland Security and issues an executive order creating DHS.
- October 9, 2001—President swears in General Wayne Downing as director of the Office of Combating Terrorism (OCT) and issues an executive order creating OCT.
- October 16, 2001—President Bush issues an executive order establishing the president's Critical Infrastructure Protection Board to coordinate and have cognizance of federal efforts and programs that relate to protection of information systems.
- October 26, 2001—President Bush signs the U.S.A. Patriot Act.
- October 29, 2001—President Bush chairs the first meeting of the Homeland Security Council (HSC) and issues Homeland Security Presidential Directive-1 (HSPD-1), establishing the organization and operation of the HSC, and HSPD-2, establishing the Foreign Terrorist Tracking Task Force and increasing immigration vigilance.
- November 8, 2001—President Bush announces that the Corporation for National and Community Service (CNCS) will support homeland security, "mobilizing more than 20,000 Senior Corps and AmeriCorps participants."
- November 8, 2001—President Bush creates the Presidential Task Force on Citizen Preparedness in the War Against Terrorism to "help prepare Americans in their homes, neighborhoods, schools, workplaces, places of worship and public places from the potential consequences of terrorist attacks."
- November 15, 2001—FEMA announces Individual and Family Grant program for disaster assistance.
- January 30, 2002—President Bush issues an executive order establishing the U.S.A. Freedom Corps, encouraging all Americans to serve their country for the equivalent of at least 2 years (4,000 hours) over their lifetimes.
- February 4, 2002—President Bush submits the president's budget for FY 2003 to Congress, directing $37.7 billion to homeland security (up from $19.5 billion in FY 2002).
- March 12, 2002—President Bush establishes the Homeland Security Advisory System (HSPD-3).
- March 19, 2002—President Bush issues an executive order establishing the President's Homeland Security Advisory Council.
- November 25, 2002—President Bush signs the Homeland Security Act of 2002 (HR 5005) as Public Law 107-296. Tom Ridge is announced as secretary, Navy Secretary Gordon England is nominated as deputy secretary of DHS, and DEA Administrator Asa Hutchinson is nominated as the undersecretary of border and transportation security.
- January 24, 2003—60 days after it was signed, the Homeland Security Act becomes effective.
- March 1, 2003—Most affected federal agencies are incorporated into DHS.
- June 1, 2003—All remaining affected federal agencies are incorporated into DHS.

Source: Compiled from multiple sources by Damon Coppola, January 2003

department that would fuse many of the security-related agencies dispersed throughout the federal government.

For several months during the second half of 2002, Congress jockeyed between different versions of the Homeland Security bill in an effort to establish legislation that was passable yet effective. Lawmakers were particularly mired on the issue of the rights of employees (the final legislation explicitly states that no agency or agency subdivision transferred to DHS can be excluded from coverage of federal civil service labor-management relations law unless the agency's mission and responsibilities materially change *and* a majority of the employees within the agency have as their primary duty intelligence, counterintelligence, or investigative work directly related to terrorism investigation).

Furthermore, the White House ultimately failed in its attempt to incorporate many of the intelligence-gathering and investigative law enforcement agencies, namely the National Security Agency (NSA), the Federal Bureau of Investigation (FBI), and the Central Intelligence Agency (CIA). Despite these delays and setbacks, the Republican seats gained in both the House and Senate gave the president the leverage he needed to pass the bill without further deliberation (HR, 299-121 on November 13, 2002; Senate, 90-9 on November 19, 2002). While the passage of this act represented a significant milestone, it can be assumed that the coming implementation phase will present the greatest challenge, a view expressed by several leaders of agencies to be absorbed. On November 25, 2002 President Bush submitted his reorganization plan (as required by the legislation), which maps out the schedule, methodology, and budget for the monumental task that lies ahead.

By March 1, 2003 almost all of the federal agencies (and their respective employees) named in the act began their move, whether literally or symbolically, into the new department. Those remaining followed on June 1, 2003, with all incidental transfers completed by September 1, 2003. While a handful of these agencies remained intact after the move, most were incorporated into one of four new directorates: Border and Transportation Security (BTS), Information Analysis and Infrastructure Protection (IAIP),

Emergency Preparedness and Response (EP&R), and Science and Technology (S&T). A fifth directorate, Management, will not incorporate any existing federal agencies.

Secretary Ridge has exactly one year to develop a comprehensive structural framework for DHS and to name new leadership for all five directorates and other offices created under the legislation. The DHS Transition Planning Office (TPO), established June of 2002, has created a comprehensive team that is working to ensure a successful changeover of the more than 179,000 employees into the new department. This so-called "team of teams," which includes representatives from the 22 incorporated agencies, the Office of Personnel Management (OPM), the Office of Management and Budget (OMB), and the White House, has been created to "[map] out logistical options and reorganization details for the incoming DHS leadership who will ultimately make the substantive policy decisions on these issues," with a goal to "make the reorganization a collaborative effort with the tapped agencies, employees, unions, Congress, state and local entities, and the private sector." (White House web site www.whitehouse.gov)

On January 24, 2003, Ridge and a small initial staff commenced work at the Nebraska Avenue Center (NAC) headquarters, a facility shared with the U.S. Navy in northwest Washington, DC, that had previously been used by the Office of Homeland Security. Eight days later, when the Space Shuttle Challenger tragically exploded over Texas, the department was tasked with its first disaster response. One week later, in reaction to information gathered by intelligence agencies, President Bush raised the color-coded terrorist threat index from yellow (elevated) to orange (high) after consulting with the Homeland Security Council.

ORGANIZATION AND FUNCTIONS OF THE DEPARTMENT OF HOMELAND SECURITY

The following pages describe the organizational structure of the new Department of Homeland Security (please refer to the DHS organizational chart found in Figure 3-1). While this structure is expected to change slightly as the 22 existing agencies are incorporated and the new divisions are created, it should remain fundamentally intact.

THE OFFICE OF THE SECRETARY

The secretary of Homeland Security, a cabinet-level official within the executive branch, leads the new department. Former Pennsylvania Governor Tom Ridge, having been confirmed by Congress, is the first to hold this post. Secretary Ridge's initial charge as secretary, as stipulated in the HS Act, will be to reorganize the department by allocating and reallocating the functions vested within it and by transferring funds between the functional units. Ridge must complete these reorganization efforts within his first year of service. Other specific tasks the secretary must complete during this time, as outlined in the HS Act, include the following:

- Appoint a Senior Privacy Officer to assume primary responsibility for privacy policy.
- Appoint an Officer for Civil Rights and Civil Liberties to assess alleged abuses of civil rights, civil liberties, and racial and ethnic profiling by DHS employees and officials.
- Appoint a Counternarcotics Officer to coordinate policy within DHS and between DHS and other federal agencies with respect to blocking the entry of illegal drugs into the United States, and tracking connections between illegal drug trafficking and terrorism.
- Establish procedures for sharing information both within DHS and between other federal, state, and local agencies, and other public and private entities.
- Establish a Homeland Security Institute
- Establish an Office of International Affairs and an Office for National Capitol Region (the HS Act requires the secretary to work in cooperation with the mayor of Washington, DC, in order to further integrate the city government into the planning, coordination, and execution of federal government domestic preparedness actions).

- Establish a Joint Interagency Homeland Security Task Force, composed of both military and civilian representatives, that will work to "anticipate terrorist threats and prevent terrorist attacks against the U.S."
- Enable the "Support Anti-Terrorism by Fostering Effective Technologies Act of 2002" (SAFETY Act), incorporated into HS Act of 2002, which authorizes the secretary to designate antiterrorism technologies that qualify for protection to sellers from claims that arise following the use of such technologies during the defense against or response or recovery from terrorism.

Several existing agencies that are being transferred into the Department of Homeland Security intact, and others that are to be newly created, report directly to the office of the secretary. Most notable of these agencies are the U.S. Coast Guard, the U.S. Secret Service, the Office of the Inspector General, the Office of State and Local Government Coordination, and the Office of the Deputy Secretary. These five are described individually below:

U.S. Coast Guard

The U.S. Coast Guard, under the direction of Commandant Thomas H. Collins, will be transferred to DHS as an intact agency on March 1st of 2003. The primary function of the Coast Guard will remain consistent with its historic mission, as identified in the following five functional areas:

- Maritime safety
- National defense
- Maritime security
- Mobility
- Protection of natural resources

The Coast Guard is expected to receive a substantial boost in funding upon its move into the new department (11 percent over 2002 spending), to be used primarily to update a fleet of ships and aircraft that is considered outdated (in relation to the other armed services of the United States) and to hire more people. Several lawmakers have voiced concerns that

The United States Department

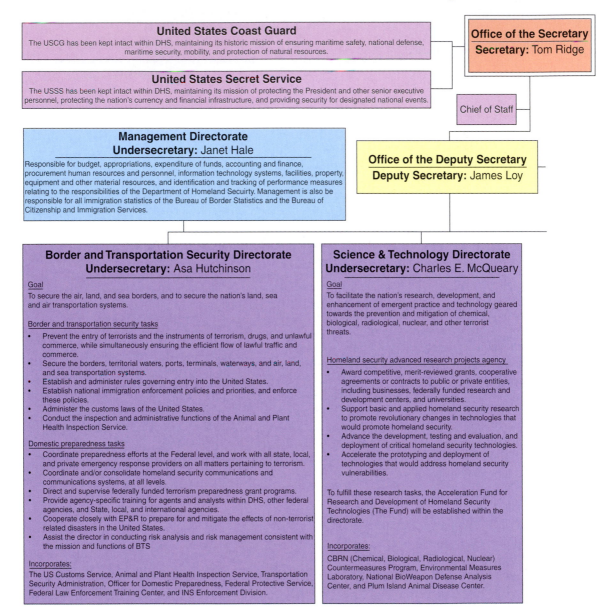

United States Coast Guard
The USCG has been kept intact within DHS, maintaining its historic mission of ensuring maritime safety, national defense, maritime security, mobility, and protection of natural resources.

Office of the Secretary
Secretary: Tom Ridge

United States Secret Service
The USSS has been kept intact within DHS, maintaining its mission of protecting the President and other senior executive personnel, protecting the nation's currency and financial infrastructure, and providing security for designated national events.

Chief of Staff

Management Directorate
Undersecretary: Janet Hale
Responsible for budget, appropriations, expenditure of funds, accounting and finance, procurement human resources and personnel, information technology systems, facilities, property, equipment and other material resources, and identification and tracking of performance measures relating to the responsibilities of the Department of Homeland Secuirty. Management is also be responsible for all immigration statistics of the Bureau of Border Statistics and the Bureau of Citizenship and Immigration Services.

Office of the Deputy Secretary
Deputy Secretary: James Loy

Border and Transportation Security Directorate
Undersecretary: Asa Hutchinson

Goal
To secure the air, land, and sea borders, and to secure the nation's land, sea and air transportation systems.

Border and transportation security tasks
- Prevent the entry of terrorists and the instruments of terrorism, drugs, and unlawful commerce, while simultaneously ensuring the efficient flow of lawful traffic and commerce.
- Secure the borders, territorial waters, ports, terminals, waterways, and air, land, and sea transportation systems.
- Establish and administer rules governing entry into the United States.
- Establish national immigration enforcement policies and priorities, and enforce these policies.
- Administer the customs laws of the United States.
- Conduct the inspection and administrative functions of the Animal and Plant Health Inspection Service.

Domestic preparedness tasks
- Coordinate preparedness efforts at the Federal level, and work with all state, local, and private emergency response providers on all matters pertaining to terrorism.
- Coordinate and/or consolidate homeland security communications and communications systems, at all levels.
- Direct and supervise federally funded terrorism preparedness grant programs.
- Provide agency-specific training for agents and analysts within DHS, other federal agencies, and State, local, and international agencies.
- Cooperate closely with EP&R to prepare for and mitigate the effects of non-terrorist related disasters in the United States.
- Assist the director in conducting risk analysis and risk management consistent with the mission and functions of BTS

Incorporates:
The US Customs Service, Animal and Plant Health Inspection Service, Transportation Security Administration, Officer for Domestic Preparedness, Federal Protective Service, Federal Law Enforcement Training Center, and INS Enforcement Division.

Science & Technology Directorate
Undersecretary: Charles E. McQueary

Goal
To facilitate the nation's research, development, and enhancement of emergent practice and technology geared towards the prevention and mitigation of chemical, biological, radiological, nuclear, and other terrorist threats.

Homeland security advanced research projects agency
- Award competitive, merit-reviewed grants, cooperative agreements or contracts to public or private entities, including businesses, federally funded research and development centers, and universities.
- Support basic and applied homeland security research to promote revolutionary changes in technologies that would promote homeland security.
- Advance the development, testing and evaluation, and deployment of critical homeland security technologies.
- Accelerate the prototyping and deployment of technologies that would address homeland security vulnerabilities.

To fulfill these research tasks, the Acceleration Fund for Research and Development of Homeland Security Technologies (The Fund) will be established within the directorate.

Incorporates:
CBRN (Chemical, Biological, Radiological, Nuclear) Countermeasures Program, Environmental Measures Laboratory, National BioWeapon Defense Analysis Center, and Plum Island Animal Disease Center.

FIGURE 3-1   DHS organizational chart

# of Homeland Security

Office of the Secretary
Secretary: Tom Ridge

Office of State and Local Government Coordination
Office of National Capital Region Coordination
Office for Small and Disadvantaged Businesses
Assistant Secretary for Public Affairs
Special Assistant to the Secretary for the Private Sector
Office of Civil Rights and Civil Liberties

Office of International Affairs
Office of the Inspector General
Office of Legislative Affairs
Office of the Executive Secretary
Office of the General Counsel
Counter Narcotics Office

Bureau of Citizenship and Immigration Services (BCIS)

Will establish new immigration policies, practices, and priorities of DHS, and will administer immigration laws and perform services such as immigrant sponsorship, adjustment of status, work authorization and other permits, naturalization for citizenship, and asylum or refugee processing.

Office of the Citizenship and Immigration Ombudsman

Will assist individuals and employers in resolving problems with the Bureau of Citizenship and Immigration Services, and provide oversight and imporvement recommendations for the administrative practices of that Bureau. This office will essentially be a 'customer service' agent for BCIS, appointing at least one local ombudsmand for each state.

Bureau of Shared Services

Will coordinate the resources required and utilized by the two immigration-related bureaus of DHS (BCIS, and the Bureau of Border Security within the Border and Transportation Security Directorate), which cannot ever be combined or share budgets according to the legislation of the Homeland Securiyt Act of 2002.

Information Analysis & Infrastructure Protection Directorate
Undersecretary: Frank Libutti

Goal

To identify and assess current and future terrorist threats, assess and mitigate risks to the nation's critical infrastructure systems, and disseminate threat information.

Information analysis tasks

- Identify and assess the nature and scope of terrorist threats, and detect such threats. Administer the five-color coded Homeland Security Advisory System.
- Ensure efficient access by DHS to all related information gathered or analyzed, and disseminate relevant homeland security information externally to DHS.
- Establish and utilize a secure but compatible National Security and Emergency Preparedness communications system for the Federal government.
- Conduct Training for Federal, State, and local governments in information identification, analysis, and sharing.

Infrastructure protection tasks

- Conduct a comprehensive risk assessment of US Critical Infrastructure and develop a comprehensive plan for securing its components.
- Work with other agencies at the Federal, state, local, and private levels to recommend protection measures, and provide technical assistance and crisis management support upon request.
- Coordinate with other Federal government agencies to provide specific warning information to State, local, private, public, and other agencies.

Incorporates:

Critical Infrastructure Assurance Office, Federal Computer Incident Response Center, National Communications System, National Infrastructure Protection Center, National Infrastructure Simulation and Analysis Center, and Energy Security and Assurance Program.

Emergency Preparedness and Response Directorate
Undersecretary: Michael Brown

Goal

To prepare for and respond to natural and technological disasters and terrorism.

Emergency preparedness and response tasks

- Coordinate with local and State first responders to manage disasters requiring federal assistance, and to recover from their effects.
- Administer the Disaster Relief Fund.
- Practice a comprehensive, risk-based approach, employing a program of preparedness, prevention, response, and recovery.
- Proactively help communities and citizens avoid becoming victims, utilizing public education and volunteerism to achieve this goal.
- Develop a curriculum for and manage the training and evaluation of local, State, and Federal emergency responders.
- Maintain administration of the National Flood Insurance Program.
- Continue training and research responsibilities of the USFA
- Continue to offer mitigation grant programs, including the Hazards Mitigation Grant Program, the Pre-Disaster Mitigation Program, and the Flood Mitigation Assistance Program.
- Administer the Citizen Corps, Program, which includes:
  - Citizen Corps Councils
  - Community Emergency Response Teams (CERT)
  - Citizen Preparedness Publications
  - Volunteers in Police Service (VIPS)
  - Medical Reserve Corps
  - Neighborhood Watch

Incorporates:

Federal Emergency Management Agency, Strategic National Stockpile, National Disaster Medical System, Nuclear Incident Response Team, Domestic Emergency Support Teams, and National Domestic Preparedness Office.

Designed by Damon Coppola for Bullock & Haddow, funding provided by the Annie E. Casey Foundation LLC October 1, 2003.

the Coast Guard's new role in homeland security could result in a decrease in boater safety and rescue efforts and in fisheries protection.

U.S Secret Service

The U.S. Secret Service, under the leadership of W. Ralph Basham, will be transferred to DHS as an intact agency on March 1st of 2003. The Secret Service will continue its mission of protecting the President and senior executive personnel, in addition to protecting the country's currency and financial infrastructure and providing security for designated national events (the Super Bowl and the Olympics, for instance).

Office of the Inspector General

The office of the inspector general, as stipulated in the Inspector General Act of 1978, will through Inspector General Clark Kent Ervin conduct and supervise audits, investigations, inspections and other activities related to the programs and operations of DHS. This office works to "promote economy, efficiency, and effectiveness" and "prevent and detect fraud, waste, abuse, and mismanagement in programs and operations of DHS."

Office of State and Local Government Coordination

The Office of State and Local Government Coordination works to ensure that close coordination takes place with state and local first responders, emergency services, and governments in all DHS programs and activities. It is important to note that the primary responsibility for investigating and prosecuting acts of terrorism remains in federal, state, and local law enforcement agencies except as specifically transferred to DHS by the Homeland Security Act of 2002. The specific tasks of the office appear in the text of the legislation as follows:

- Coordinate the activities of the department relating to state and local government;
- Assess, and advocate for, the resources needed by state and local government to implement the national strategy for combating terrorism;

- Provide state and local government with regular information, research, and technical support to assist local efforts at securing the homeland; and
- Develop a process for receiving meaningful input from State and local government to assist the development of the national strategy for combating terrorism and other homeland security activities.

The secretary must appoint a chief homeland security liaison officer and appoint for each state no less than one DHS employee who will serve as a state liaison officer. Each state homeland security liaison officer is responsible for the following in his or her respective state:

- Ensure coordination between the department and
  - State, local, and community based law enforcement;
  - fire and rescue agencies; and
  - medical and emergency relief organizations;
- Identify state and local areas requiring additional information, training, resources, and security;
- Provide training, information, and education regarding homeland security for state and local entities;
- Identify homeland security functions in which the federal role is duplicative of the state or local role, and recommend ways to decrease or eliminate inefficiencies;
- Assist state and local entities in priority-setting based on discovered needs of first responder organizations, including law enforcement agencies, fire and rescue agencies, medical providers, emergency service providers, and relief agencies;
- Assist the department to identify and implement state and local homeland security objectives in an efficient and productive manner; and
- Serve as a liaison to the department in representing state and local priorities and concerns regarding homeland security.

Office of the Deputy Secretary

The Office of the Deputy Secretary, which reports directly to the Office of the Secretary, will be in direct charge of three new BHS components, displayed below:

Bureau of Citizenship and Immigration Services (BCIS)

The Bureau of Citizenship and Immigration Services (BCIS), is tasked with establishing the new immigration policies, practices, and priorities of DHS. BCIS administers immigration laws and performs services such as immigrant and nonimmigrant sponsorship, adjustment of status, work authorization and other permits, naturalization for citizenship, and asylum or refugee processing.

Citizenship and Immigration Services Ombudsman

The citizenship and immigration ombudsman, who also reports directly to the deputy secretary, assists individuals and employers in resolving problems with the Bureau of Citizenship and Immigration Services and provides oversight and improvement recommendations for the administrative practices of that bureau. The citizenship and immigration services ombudsman is essentially a "customer service" agent of BCIS, appointing at least one local ombudsman for each state.

The Bureau of Shared Services

The Bureau of Shared Services coordinates the resources required and utilized by the two immigration-related bureaus of DHS (the Bureau of Citizenship and Immigration Services and the Bureau of Border Security), which, according to the legislation behind BHS, cannot share budgets or be combined.

THE FIVE DIRECTORATES

The primary functions of DHS will be divided among five "Directorates," as described below:

BORDER AND TRANSPORTATION SECURITY (BTS) DIRECTORATE

The largest of the five directorates, Border and Transportation Security (BTS) incorporates all of the functions of six former federal agencies: the U.S. Customs Service, the INS Enforcement Division, the Animal and Plant Health Inspection Service, the Transportation Security Administration, the Office for Domestic Preparedness, and the Federal Protective Service. The goal of BTS is to secure the air, land, and sea borders (includes port security and immigration enforcement) and to secure the nation's land, sea, and air transportation systems. Its stated primary goal is "to prevent the entry of terrorists and the instruments of terrorism while simultaneously ensuring the efficient flow of lawful traffic and commerce."

BTS will be administered by the undersecretary for BTS, who is assisted by an assistant secretary for border security and the director of the Office for Domestic Preparedness. Specific BTS tasks will be as follows:

Immigration and Border Security-Related Tasks

- Prevent the entry of terrorists and the instruments of terrorism, drugs, and unlawful commerce, while simultaneously ensuring the efficient flow of lawful traffic and commerce.
- Secure the borders, territorial waters, ports, terminals, waterways, and air, land, and sea transportation systems of the United States.
- Establish and administer rules governing entry into the United States.
- Establish national immigration enforcement policies and priorities, and enforce these policies.
- Administer the customs laws of the United States.
- Conduct the inspection and administrative functions of the (incorporated) USDA Animal and Plant Health Inspection Service.

Domestic Preparedness-Related Tasks

- Coordinate preparedness efforts at the federal level, and work with all state, local, tribal, parish, and private sector emergency response providers on all matters pertaining to terrorism, including training, exercises, and equipment support.
- Coordinate and/or consolidate communications and systems of communications relating to homeland security at all government levels.

- Direct and supervise federally funded terrorism preparedness grant programs.
- Provide agency-specific training for agents and analysts within DHS, other federal agencies, and state, local, and international agencies.
- Cooperate closely with EP&R Directorate to prepare for and mitigate the effects of nonterrorist-related disasters in the United States.
- Assist the director in conducting risk analysis and risk management activities of state, local, and tribal governments consistent with the mission and functions of BTS.

The former Department of Transportation (DOT) Transportation Security Administration (TSA) must be kept intact within BTS. According to the HS Act, BTS was required to deploy explosive detection equipment for checked baggage to all public airports by December 31, 2003. BTS will also keep intact the Office of Domestic Preparedness (ODP—formerly DOJ), which will incorporate from FEMA the terrorism-focused Office of National Preparedness (ONP). ODP's primary function is to prepare the United States for future acts of terrorism.

EMERGENCY PREPAREDNESS AND RESPONSE (EP&R) DIRECTORATE

The Emergency Preparedness and Response (EP&R) Directorate is led by an undersecretary, who also serves as the director of the Federal Emergency

FIGURE 3-2   New York, NY, October 4, 2001—Relief efforts continued day and night at the site of the World Trade Center. Photo by Andrea Booher/FEMA News Photo.

Management Agency (FEMA); this combination of duties took effect after FEMA was incorporated into EP&R on March 1, 2003. FEMA will retain its name within EP&R, and the EP&R undersecretary also serves as the director of FEMA.

EP&R assumes FEMA's responsibilities—namely, preparing for and responding to natural and technological disasters and terrorist attacks. EP&R coordinates with local and state first responders to manage disasters requiring federal government assistance and to recover from their damaging effects. The directorate continues to practice a comprehensive, risk-based approach, employing a program of preparedness, prevention (mitigation), response, and recovery.

Additionally, EP&R hopes to continue FEMA's mission to "proactively help communities and citizens avoid becoming victims" (rather than relying wholly upon response), utilizing public education efforts and volunteerism to achieve this goal. Federal grants to promote the "disaster-resistant communities" concept, partnering public and private actors to reduce risk in disaster-prone areas, will be continued. EP&R continues to develop a curriculum and manage the training and evaluation of local, state, and federal emergency responders.

It is anticipated that EP&R will no longer be using the Federal Response Plan (FRP) as a framework for federal government disaster response. Under the FRP, which is invoked when the president declares a national disaster, various agencies throughout the government are charged with mission-specific tasks related to response and recovery. FEMA was tasked by the FRP with, among other responsibilities, coordinating the response of all federal agencies. While this coordination responsibility will likely remain in the EP&R Directorate after the FRP is replaced with the new "National Response Plan," there are likely to be many changes to the way in which non-DHS agencies become involved. It is important to note that while EP&R will no longer be responsible for the training of first responders for terrorism-related events (whether conventional, biological, chemical, or nuclear), it will be responsible for coordinating the federal government's response to them.

Although it is expected that several procedural changes to these grants may occur, EP&R continues to offer three mitigation grant programs currently managed by FEMA: the Hazards Mitigation Grant Program, the Pre-Disaster Mitigation Program, the Flood Mitigation Assistance Program, and the U.S. Fire Administration Grants.

FEMA's Citizen Corps Program will also continue within the EP&R Directorate. The program is heralded as a "broad network of volunteer efforts [that] will harness the power of the American people by relying on their individual skills and interests to prepare local communities to effectively prevent and respond to the threats of terrorism, crime, or any kind of disaster." Citizen Corps provides funding for the formation and training of local Citizen Corps Councils, which will increase local involvement (in Citizen Corps), develop community action plans, perform threat assessments, identify local resources for homeland security, and locally coordinate the Citizen Corps programs. The existing programs, administered by several federal agencies both internal and external to homeland security, will involve leaders from law enforcement, fire, and emergency medical services, businesses, community-based institutions, schools, places of worship, health care facilities, public works, and other key community sectors.

Current Citizen Corps programs include the following:

- Community Emergency Response Teams (CERT); administered by DHS.
- Volunteers in Police Service (VIPS) program; administered by DOJ.
- Medical Reserve Corps; administered by HHS.
- Neighborhood Watch programs; administered by DOJ.
- Citizen-preparedness publications: Several public education guides that seek to increase individual knowledge and preparedness for crime, terrorism, and disasters at home, in neighborhoods, at places of work, and in public spaces.

Citizen Corps activities are documented in greater detail in Chapter 6 of this book.

INFORMATION ANALYSIS & INFRASTRUCTURE PROTECTION (IAIP) DIRECTORATE

The Information Analysis & Infrastructure Protection Directorate, as its name suggests, is tasked with identifying and assessing current and future terrorist threats to the United States; assessing and mitigating risks to the nation's critical infrastructure systems; and disseminating threat information as appropriate. IAIP must also enforce the nation's "cyber security," both through the transfer of existing subject-specific agencies and by authority of the "Cyber Security Enhancement Act of 2002."

The directorate fully incorporated the functions of the six agencies, including the following: the Critical Infrastructure Assurance Office, the Federal Computer Incident Response Center, the National Communications System, the National Infrastructure Protection Center, the National Infrastructure Simulation and Analysis Center, and the Energy Security and Assurance Program.

The IAIP undersecretary conducts his or her tasks through two assistant secretaries: the assistant secretary for Information Analysis and the assistant secretary for Infrastructure Protection. The divisions these two assistant secretaries are charged with divide the IAIP tasks as follows:

Information Analysis

- Identify and assess the nature and scope of terrorist threats to the nation (relevant to actual and potential vulnerabilities), and detect such threats. Administer the five-color coded Homeland Security Advisory System.
- Identify priorities (in coordination with the assistant secretary for Infrastructure Protection) for infrastructure protection measures by all government, private, and other agencies.

Ensure efficient access by DHS to all related information gathered or analyzed, and disseminate relevant homeland security information to other agencies within the Federal Government and to appropriate State, local and private sector entities.

- Recommend improvement to the collection and sharing of information related to homeland security within the federal government and between federal, state, and local agencies.
- Establish and utilize a secure but fully compatible National Security and Emergency Preparedness (NS/EP) communications system for the federal government, including a secure information technology infrastructure.
- Conduct training for federal, state, and local governments in information identification, analysis, and sharing.

Infrastructure Protection

- Conduct a comprehensive risk assessment of the U.S. critical infrastructure.
- Develop a comprehensive national plan for securing the U.S. critical infrastructure, including systems for power production; generation and distribution; information technology and telecommunications; electronic, financial, and property record storage and transmissions; and emergency preparedness communications, as well as the physical assets that support such systems; and other infrastructure, such as food, water, and health care.
- Work with other agencies at the federal, state, local, and private level to recommend protection measures and provide technical assistance and crisis management support upon request.
- Coordinate with other federal government agencies to provide specific warning information and advice to state, local, private, public, and other agencies.

SCIENCE AND TECHNOLOGY (S&T) DIRECTORATE

The Science and Technology (S&T) Directorate facilitates the nation's research, development, and enhancement of emergent practice and technology geared toward the prevention and mitigation of chemical, biological, radiological, nuclear, and other terrorist threats. To carry out this task, a national policy and strategic plan is being developed to prioritize and enable the funding of projects by the vast resource base of government, private, and academic institutions that have previously conducted national security research or plan to in the future. These research priorities will focus on identifying and reducing areas of national vulnerability to terrorism and enhancing systems of national security throughout the United States.

DHS primarily seeks to utilize this research to avoid catastrophic terrorism or "threats to the security of our homeland that could result in large-scale loss of life and major economic impact." This will include the development and testing to invent new vaccines, antidotes, diagnostics, and therapies against biological and chemical warfare agents.

S&T will be led by an undersecretary. The HS Act effectively abolishes the Office of Science and Technology of the National Institute of Justice (NIJ-DOJ) and transfers all applicable functions to S&T. Within the directorate will be created the Homeland Security Advanced Research Projects Agency (HSARPA) and the Acceleration Fund for Research and Development of Homeland Security Technologies to carry out the mission of S&T. HSARPA will be established to "award competitive, merit-reviewed grants, cooperative agreements or contracts to public or private entities, including businesses, federally funded research and development centers, and universities." The secretary-appointed director of HSARPA will administer the fund to achieve the following goals:

- Support basic and applied homeland security research to promote revolutionary changes in technologies that would promote homeland security;
- Advance the development, testing and evaluation, and deployment of critical homeland security technologies; and
- Accelerate the prototyping and deployment of technologies that would address homeland security vulnerabilities.

The Acceleration Fund for Research and Development of Homeland Security Technologies (the fund) will be administered by the Director of HSARPA. The HS Act stipulates that no less than 10 percent of the fund will be authorized only for the undersecretary, in joint agreement with commandant of the Coast Guard, to "carry out research and development of improved ports, waterways, and coastal security surveillance and perimeter protection capabilities for the purpose of minimizing the possibility that Coast Guard cutters, aircraft, helicopters, and personnel will be diverted from nonhomeland security missions to the ports, waterways, and coastal security mission."

MANAGEMENT DIRECTORATE

The Management Directorate, led by an undersecretary, is responsible for budget, appropriations, expenditure of funds, accounting and finance; procurement, human resources and personnel; information technology systems; facilities, property, equipment, and other material resources; and identification and tracking of performance measurements relating to the responsibilities of the department. Management is also responsible for all immigration statistics of the Bureau of Border Statistics and the Bureau of Citizenship and Immigration Services.

OTHER ACTIONS STIPULATED IN THE HOMELAND SECURITY ACT OF 2002

In addition to the creation of the Department of Homeland Security, the HS Act makes several changes to other federal agencies and their programs and creates several new programs. A list of the most significant is presented below:

- Establishes within the executive office of the president a National Homeland Security Council, which will assess U.S. objectives, commitments, and risks in the interest of homeland security, oversee and review federal homeland security policies, and make recommendations to the president.

FIGURE 3-3   New York, NY, September 20, 2001—A dust-covered office in a building near the World Trade Center. Photo by Andrea Booher/FEMA News Photo.

- Transfers the Bureau of Alcohol, Tobacco, and Firearms (ATF) from the Department of the Treasury to the Department of Justice (DOJ).
- Explicitly prohibits both the creation of a national ID card and the proposed Citizen Corps "Terrorism Information and Prevention System" (Operation TIPS, which encouraged transportation workers, postal workers, and public utility employees to identify and report suspicious activities linked to terrorism and crime). The act also reaffirms the Posse Comitatus Act, prohibiting the use of the armed forces in law enforcement activities except under Constitutional or congressional authority (the Coast Guard is exempt from this act).
- The "Arming Pilots Against Terrorism Act," which was incorporated into the HS Act, allows pilots to defend aircraft cockpits with firearms or other "less-than-lethal weapons" against acts of criminal violence or air piracy and provides antiterrorism training to flight crews.
- The Critical Infrastructure Information Act (2002), also incorporated, exempts certain components of critical infrastructure from Freedom of Information Act (FOIA) regulations.
- The "Johnny Michael Spann Patriot Trusts" will be created to provide support for surviving spouses, children, or dependent parents, grandparents, or siblings of various federal employees who die in the line of duty as a result of terrorist attacks, military operations, intelligence operations, or law enforcements operations.

OTHER AGENCIES PARTICIPATING IN COMMUNITY-LEVEL FUNDING

Several other federal agencies outside of the new Department of Homeland Security have maintained or created programs that fund homeland security–related initiatives at the community level. Many of these programs are either in the transitional or developmental phase but have already begun active funding within a homeland security context.

U.S.A. FREEDOM CORPS

The U.S.A. Freedom Corps is an umbrella organization that includes the Peace Corps, the Corporation for National and Community Service (CNCS), and Citizen Corps. CNCS and Citizen Corps are detailed below.

The Corporation for National and Community Service administers Americorps, Senior Corps, and Learn and Serve America:

- AmeriCorps: A network of national service programs that "engage more than 50,000 Americans each year in intensive service to meet critical needs in education, public safety, health, and the environment." AmeriCorps members serve through more than 2,100 nonprofits, public agencies, and faith-based organizations, tutoring and mentoring youth, building affordable housing, teaching computer skills, cleaning parks and streams, running after-school programs, and helping communities respond to disasters. These programs engage more than 2 million Americans of all ages and backgrounds in service each year.
- Senior Corps: A network of programs that "tap the experience, skills, and talents of older citizens to meet community challenges." It includes three programs: Foster Grandparents, Senior Companions, and the Retired and Senior Volunteer Program (RSVP). More than one half-million Americans age 55 and over assist local nonprofits, public agencies, and faith-based organizations in carrying out their missions.
- Learn and Serve America: "Supports service-learning programs in schools and community organizations that help nearly one million students from kindergarten through college meet community needs, while improving their academic skills and learning the habits of good citizenship."

In July 2002, The Corporation for National and Community Service awarded 43 grants totaling $10.3 million to communities, government agencies, and voluntary organizations to fund volunteer programs activities in homeland security. A list of the grantees and their proposed activities is presented in Appendix 6.

U.S. DEPARTMENT OF AGRICULTURE (USDA)

"The president has made agriculture an important part of his homeland security plan. In his FY 2003 budget, President Bush asked for $146 million in new spending for homeland security efforts through the U.S. Department of Agriculture. And as part of the Defense Supplemental Appropriations Act, signed in January, he also committed $328 million to that goal. These new resources will invest in critical issues: additional inspectors, new computer technologies, X-ray equipment, new dog teams, research and renovations at key laboratories—all to help improve the strong systems that we already have in place."— USDA Secretary Ann Veneman

The following extract is from USDA Homeland Security Efforts; September 2002: USDA formed a Homeland Security Council within the department to develop a department-wide plan and coordinate efforts among all USDA agencies and offices. The efforts have focused on three key areas: food supply and agricultural production, USDA facilities, and USDA staff and emergency preparedness. Highlights include the following:

Protecting U.S. borders from invasive pests and diseases

- USDA increased safeguarding personnel at borders by 50 percent over FY 2000 levels to enhance prevention efforts to keep foreign agricultural pests and diseases from entering the

United States. In addition, 18 new veterinarians have been added to the agricultural quarantine inspection staff at borders and ports of entry and on farms to ensure strong preparedness programs are in place to protect U.S. agriculture. Up to 20 new food import inspectors are being added to port of entry efforts.

- The department has maintained National Forest Service enforcement personnel along the hundreds of miles of continuous Forest Service land along northern and southern borders.
- USDA is purchasing remote sensing/diagnostic equipment to quickly detect possible introduction of foreign pest and animal diseases at ports of entry.
- Protecting the health of farm animals and crops and natural resources and ensuring successful rapid responses to animal and crop disease outbreaks and pest infestations.
- USDA has developed guidance documents for distribution to farmers and ranchers to help remind them of steps they can take to secure their operations. Information was posted on the USDA web site and distributed through the USDA extension system to reach every county in the nation.
- USDA upgraded security efforts at USDA state and county offices, including a web-based tracking system for disaster reporting; maintaining databases of fertilizer, food, feed, and seed listings; and coordinating with state and county emergency boards to assist during an emergency.
- USDA has held and continues to hold ongoing Foreign Animal Disease Awareness Training seminars for federal and state veterinarians from all 50 states to help states better prepare for accidental and intentional introductions of foreign animal diseases and has conducted and continues to conduct emergency preparedness satellite seminars to share vital information among 1,700 federal and state veterinary officials and emergency planners, military representatives, and academics on emergency preparedness.

- A CD-ROM was developed to help practitioners better identify and diagnose animal diseases.
- USDA provided $43 million to states, universities, and tribal lands to increase homeland security prevention, detection, and response efforts.
- USDA developed the National Animal Health Reserve Corps to mobilize close to 300 private veterinarians from around the United States to assist locally during an emergency.
- The department has upgraded its Extension Disaster Education Network systems and web site with homeland security information.
- A department-wide National Incident Command System structure, based on the successful system developed by the U.S. Forest Service, is being implemented. Training and exercises are being conducted across the department.
- USDA is spending $18 million to develop rapid tests for agents that pose the most serious threat to our agricultural system. Some examples are foot-and-mouth disease, rinderpest, and wheat rust.

Assuring a safe food supply

- USDA prepared and distributed food security guidance documents to meat-, poultry-, and egg-products-processing plants and developed information on biosecurity and the food supply for constituents and processors.
- USDA coordinated with other government food agencies to develop prevention, detection, and response procedures to protect the nation's food supply.
- USDA implemented the national Consumer Complaint Monitoring System, a surveillance and sentinel system that monitors and tracks food-related consumers complaints.
- USDA participated in several drills and exercises at the federal and state level to increase response procedures.
- USDA is conducting vulnerability assessments for domestic and imported food, and has developed a food security.

- USDA Plan and conducted training sessions for employees, veterinarians, and inspectors in preparedness activities.
- USDA is conducting threat assessments to ensure the security of food. This includes food purchased by USDA for federal feeding programs as well as shipping procedures and storage.

Protecting and enhancing research and laboratory facilities

- USDA has developed department policies for the sponsorship of noncitizen visiting scientists, including a tracking system for all foreign visitors to USDA facilities. Background checks are being conducted for noncitizen visiting scientists.
- All positions at USDA labs are being examined for personnel reliability clearances beginning with the BSL-3 locations.
- USDA is spending $21.7 million for physical security upgrades at laboratory facilities for security assessments, background investigations, and additional security personnel at facilities.
- Security assessments of all USDA BSL-3 facilities were conducted.

Protecting other infrastructure

- USDA developed a threat advisory system for rural infrastructure and enhanced evacuation procedures for USDA rural development entities.
- USDA completed security assessments of 13 U.S. Forest Service aviation facilities and implemented additional security measures as a result.
- U.S. Forest Service has enhanced efforts to protect forestland and facilities, including dams, reservoirs, pipelines, water treatment plants, power lines, and energy production facilities on government property.

Securing information technology

- USDA reviewed and conducted tests of all USDA network systems to assess threat levels.
- USDA upgraded the security status of key IT personnel and conducted training and planning sessions to strengthen the department's continuity of operations plans.
- The department enhanced its monitoring and surveillance telecommunications network and assisted with off-site facilities enhancement to prepare for emergency.

Continuity of operations

- Full and complete continuity of operations are developed for all USDA agencies and offices. Alternate work places have been upgraded and improved to avoid disruption in the work of USDA. A National Interagency Incident Management System (NIIMS) is being expanded department wide.

Audits and investigations

- USDA launched an aggressive initiative to identify and protect USDA assets, both physical and cyber-based; prevent USDA assets from being used against the United States; and preclude USDA programs from being used to finance terrorism.
- Eleven audit reports have been issued, and 22 audits that affect homeland security are currently in the process of being completed. The audits review existing controls, identify potential vulnerabilities, and recommend additional measures to protect USDA assets and resources. USDA is also participating in interagency audit efforts at the federal level to ensure that government-wide and cross-agency vulnerabilities are addressed.
- USDA has initiated 47 criminal investigations related to counterterrorism and homeland security activities and participates in efforts to target businesses transferring money overseas to terrorists groups.

DEPARTMENT OF COMMERCE

The following excerpt was taken from Commerce Press Release, February 3, 2003: "Commerce Budget Reflects President's Focus on Economic Growth, Homeland Security and Fiscal Responsibility."

One of the key bureaus providing homeland defense is the Bureau of Industry and Security (BIS). BIS is requesting a $2.3 million increase to address vulnerabilities in regulating exports of critical goods and services as well as encouraging growth of exports to maintain U.S. global economic leadership in order to advance national security and foreign policy interests. The increase will enable BIS to strengthen export enforcement with additional agents and capabilities and to enhance the bureau's analysis of U.S. export control regulations to ensure that they reflect the dynamics of 21st century market and technological changes.

The Department of Commerce's budget requests $10.3 million for the National Institute of Standards and Technology (NIST) to provide the measurement infrastructure necessary for stronger homeland security. This includes developing and disseminating standards for safety and security of buildings, for biometric identification systems, and for radiation systems.

To address increased security issues, the National Oceanic and Atmospheric Administration (NOAA) is requesting a program increase of $7.7 million. These funds will facilitate cooperation between the National Weather Service (NWS) and local officials in the development of an All Hazards Weather Radio Warning Network, allowing the dissemination of all types of emergency warnings in addition to warnings for severe weather. NOAA also will use a portion of these funds to upgrade physical security at NWS facilities.

DEPARTMENT OF EDUCATION

The following excerpt was taken from a Department of Education press release, dated September 17, 2002: "Paige Announces Formation of Two New Offices"

U.S. Secretary of Education Rod Paige today announced the formation of two new offices within the Education Department—the Office of Safe and Drug-Free Schools and the Office of Innovation and Improvement.

All activities related to safe schools, crisis response, alcohol and drug prevention, health and well-being of students, and building strong character and citizenship will be located in the safe and drug-free schools office. It will also take the leadership role in the department's homeland security efforts.

The new innovation and improvement office is intended to be a nimble, entrepreneurial arm of the Education Department, making strategic investments in promising practices and widely disseminating their results. It will also lead the movement for greater parental options and information in education and will free other offices to focus on their core missions.

Both offices will be directed by new deputy undersecretaries of education with the programs to form the units coming primarily from the Office of Elementary and Secondary Education and the Office of Educational Research and Improvement.

Former Texas appeals court justice Eric G. Andell, currently senior advisor to Secretary Paige, will lead the safe and drug-free schools office. Heading the innovation and improvement office will be Nina Shokraii Rees, deputy assistant to the vice president for domestic policy. Before joining the White House, Rees served as an education advisor to the Bush campaign, a senior education analyst at the Heritage Foundation, and director of outreach at the Institute for Justice.

Of the new safe and drug-free schools office, Secretary Paige said it will help bring together into a single unit programs that are currently scattered in several offices.

"Folding all programs that deal with safety, health, and citizenship into one office will enable us to better respond to the critical needs of schools in these areas and also help us to develop a broad-based comprehensive strategy," Paige said. "Ensuring that all schools are safe, free of alcohol and drugs, and teach students good citizenship and character is essential if we are to ensure that no child is left behind."

Paige said that school shootings in recent years and the terrorist attacks of 9/11 sent a clear message that schools need to be better prepared to deal with an entirely new class of emerging threats. Schools must be ready to deal with everything from natural disasters such as hurricanes, tornadoes, and earthquakes, to shooting, accidents, and terrorist attacks.

A primary goal of the Office of Safe and Drug-Free Schools will be to assist schools in developing plans to deal with the variety of threats they face and which if not addressed could impede teaching and learning.

Likewise, the Office of Innovation and Improvement will consolidate programs related to parental options and education, including those for charter schools, magnet schools, public school choice, non-public education, and family educational rights.

It will also coordinate with the Office of Elementary and Secondary Education the public school choice and supplemental services provisions of the new No Child Left Behind Act.

Under that landmark act, parents play a crucial role in school improvement. Greater parental options are supported by the law, including expanded public school choice, charter schools, supplemental educational services, and services for children in private schools.

The Office of Innovation and Improvement will also house many of the department's discretionary programs, such as transition to teaching and teaching American history.

"Like today's best entrepreneurial foundations, this office will support promising programs and—working with the Office of Educational Research and Improvement—rigorously evaluate their results," Paige said.

"This office will become the department's expert in leveraging competitive grant programs for maximum learning and maximum impact and will aggressively disseminate findings about what works to the educational field," he said.

Creation of the new offices will result in minimal costs to the department since the funds for the staff and other activities will transfer from their existing offices to the new ones.

Less than 200 of the Education Department's 5,000 employees will be affected by the moves.

The following was taken from a Department of Education press release dated June 6, 2002, titled "Paige Issues Statement on President Bush's Plan for New Department of Homeland Security."

U.S. Secretary of Education Rod Paige today released the following statement on President Bush's plan to create a new Department of Homeland Security:

"President Bush and I are committed to ensuring our children and their teachers are safe in school. Since Sept. 11, we've worked with our state and local education leaders to equip them with the information and resources they need to help plan for and respond to often unthinkable acts of violence and terror. Our efforts will continue.

"Today, I'm proud to applaud the president for his bold action today to transform the patchwork of our government's safety and security activities into a single department whose primary mission is to protect every American. I look forward to our continued work with the president and my new colleague on the cabinet to keep our nation and our citizens safe and secure."

ENVIRONMENTAL PROTECTION AGENCY

Chemical Emergency Preparedness and Prevention Office (CEPPO)

CEPPO's Mission

EPA's Chemical Emergency Preparedness and Prevention Office (CEPPO) provides leadership, builds partnerships, and offers technical assistance to accomplish the following goals: prevent and prepare for chemical emergencies; respond to environmental crises; inform the public about chemical hazards in their community; and share lessons learned about chemical accidents.

The CEPPO Difference

CEPPO created a program with substantial flexibility that emphasizes cooperation with its partners rather than command-and-control approaches. We recognize that the fundamental responsibility for protecting public safety rests with state and local governments and with industry. We believe that emergency planners, with their intimate knowledge of local conditions and the business community, are in the best position to work with facilities to reduce chemical hazards and risks and to take action to prevent incidents.

Local Risk, Local Action, Local Benefit

Prevention, preparedness, and response to accidental releases of hazardous chemicals can be dealt with effectively only at the local level. The Emergency Planning and Community Right-to-Know Act and Risk Management Program regulations under the Clean Air Act reaffirm this local focus.

Experience has shown that emergency preparedness improves when local stakeholders share information and participate in environmental decision making. To that end, CEPPO works with numerous federal, state, local, and tribal governments; industry groups; environmental groups; labor organizations; and community groups to help them better understand the risks posed by chemicals in their communities, to manage and reduce those risks, and to deal with emergencies.

Partnerships to Improve Safety

CEPPO works with its state and local partners to develop new, streamlined approaches to deal with emergency preparedness and accident prevention. CEPPO assists Local Emergency Planning Committees (LEPCs) and State Emergency Response Commissions (SERCs) by providing national leadership, issuing regulations, developing technical guidance, and enabling SERCs and LEPCs to develop their own unique emergency planning systems.

The relationship forged among government, industry, public interest groups, first responders, and the public provides access to information about the presence of hazardous chemicals and for representation in the local decision-making process through their LEPCs.

CEPPO also works closely with the National Response Team to help states and localities better prepare for, respond to, and prevent accidents. The NRT consists of 16 federal agencies with interests and expertise in various aspects of emergency response to pollution incidents.

When a major chemical accident occurs, EPA works with the Occupational Safety and Health Administration and the Chemical Safety and Hazard Investigation Board to determine the causes and the contributing factors associated with chemical accidents and to prevent their recurrence.

Better Customer Service

CEPPO strives to understand and meet our customer and environmental needs. We seek the involvement of our state, regional, local, and industry partners from the time regulations are written through the implementation phase. CEPPO's program development staff writes regulations and provides technical assistance and guidance to community-based emergency planners and industry, while the program implementation and coordination staff ensures that our partners have an opportunity to help shape our programs. Our outreach efforts are designed to educate stakeholders and to keep in close touch with our various partners to gain their valuable input on our programs.

CEPPO's web site links to general information and subject-specific data about the Emergency Planning and Community Right-to-Know Act (EPCRA), the risk management planning requirements of the Clean Air Act, up-to-date information on chemical accidents, as well as publication, regulations, conference listings, and links to other databases to help regulators, SERCs, LEPCs, industry, and the public find out more about chemical emergency preparedness and accident prevention.

Roadmap to the Future

In 1990 the Clean Air Act amendments responded to the public's concern about what could be done to prevent chemical accidents from occurring in their communities. Regulations require industry to tell EPA and states how they manage chemical risks and what they are doing to reduce risk to the community. CEPPO has developed important prevention programs with our partners:

- Risk Management Plans (RMPs)—RMPs, submitted from industry in June 1999, require certain facilities to tell the public and CEPPO what they are doing to prevent accidents, how they plan to operate safely, and manage their chemicals in a responsible way.
- RMP*Info™—Summaries of facility risk-management programs are available to the public via the Internet. The data are useful to environmental groups, state and local agencies, community organizations, and the public in understanding the chemical risks in their communities.
- Counterterrorism—Incidents such as the deliberate chemical release in Tokyo, Japan, have highlighted the need to ensure that local emergency response plans consider this possibility, however slight it may be for any specific community. While the U.S. government has structures and mechanisms in place to address this situation, state and local emergency responders need to be well prepared. CEPPO is working with communities on how local emergency plans can address deliberate chemical releases and provide suggestions for rapid response.

ACTIVITIES BY STATE AND LOCAL ORGANIZATIONS

Understandably, the organizations representative of state and local governments were actively engaged in the debates over the HS Act. State and local governments have expended considerable human and financial resources to secure their jurisdictions from the perceived threat of terrorism, almost entirely without federal compensation. Each time DHS announces an increased level of warning via the Homeland Security Advisory System, local leaders must divert resources from other areas to adequately address the threat.

While large allocations of funding to reimburse these expenditures have repeatedly been promised by Congress and the White House, very little has materialized. The following is an excerpt from a February 3, 2003 statement from the United States Conference of Mayors, addressing the president's 2004 budget request that explicitly states the concerns described above:

"Unfortunately, the administration's proposed budget for fiscal year 2004 fails to address many of our cities' key priorities. At a time when city budgets are severely pinched by the weak economy and significant local homeland security investments, the president's budget contains no general economic assistance for states and cities. Rather than boosting strategic investments in transportation, housing, job training, and brownfields redevelopment, the budget instead recommends very small increases and some large cuts in these and other key programs. While we are pleased that the budget proposes a second installment of $3.5 billion for local homeland security investments, cities continue to wait for the first round of this funding, which was promised more than one year ago. At a time when homeland security needs are only growing, we cannot afford to neglect our first responders. We continue to urge that these funds be provided directly to local governments, where they can be invested in homeland security most quickly and most efficiently."

The states, counties, and cities, through their associations, have addressed both their own need to increase public safety for their constituents and the federal government responsibility to help them to fulfill this mission. The actions of four of these groups, the United States Conference of Mayors (USCM), the National League of Cities (NLC), the National Association of Counties (NACo), and the National Governors Association (NGA), are described in detail in the following sections.

UNITED STATES CONFERENCE OF MAYORS (USCM)

In December 2001, the United States Conference of Mayors released "A National Action Plan for Safety and Security in America's Cities." The document was prepared as part of the Mayors Emergency Safety and Security Summit held in Washington, DC, on October 23–25, 2001. It contains recommendations in four priority areas: transportation security, emergency preparedness, federal-local law enforcement, and economic security (Sidebar 3-2). In this document, the mayors made the following critical point:

"It is important to understand that while the fourth area, economic security, is viewed as the ultimate goal of a nation; it cannot be achieved in the absence of the first three. That is, securing our transportation system, maximizing our emergency response capability, and coordinating our law enforcement response to threats and incidents at all levels are viewed as prerequisites to eliminating the anxiety that has accelerated the nation's economic downturn, and to achieving economic security for the nation."—from "A National Action Plan for Safety and Security in America's Cities," The United States Conference of Mayors, December 2001.

In the section on emergency preparedness, the mayors' plan presents recommendations for action in the following areas:

- Office of Homeland Security
- Reimbursement for heightened security
- Metropolitan emergency management
- Communications technology
- Protective equipment/training—direct local assistance
- Public health system
- Coordination
- Communications
- Training
- Personnel
- Facilities
- Equipment/supplies
- Stadium/arena security
- Water and wastewater security

The principal areas of concern in federal-local law enforcement for the mayors are communications, coordination, and border-city security. In the transportation security section, the mayors' paper presents recommendations concerning security issues in each of the major transportation modes: airport, transit, highway, rail, and port.

USCM leadership has repeatedly expressed concern that a significant amount of funding from the federal government has not reached the cities for

---

SIDEBAR 3-2   Selected U.S. Conference of Mayors' Homeland Security Priorities

Emergency Preparedness

1. "Of the approximately $10 billion federal terrorism budget identified by the OMB, only 4.9 percent is allocated to state and local first response activities. And, of this limited amount, most goes to the states rather than directly to America's cities and major population centers."

2. "In the event of a catastrophic disaster, most communities will run short of critical emergency response resources (e.g., life-saving equipment, PPE, respirators, etc.) in six hours, and federal help won't arrive for 12 hours. Prepositioned equipment pods should be strategically located throughout the United States to resupply local responders. The limited funding now available to the Department of Justice for equipment pods should be increased."

3. "Effective preparedness efforts require an empowered community and the involvement of community representatives in the development of emergency response plans. The public should be educated in basic life-saving techniques so that bystanders can provide assistance to those injured until help arrives.

4. "There must be communication system interoperability to insure clear communication among city departments and federal, regional, state, and other local entities responding to disasters."

5. "The compatibility, security and reliability of federal, state, regional, and local emergency telecommunications systems must be assured."

Economic Security

1. "Unemployment insurance should be expanded to provide benefits to those directly and indirectly affected by disaster-related job loss, and unemployment benefits should be extended from 26 to 78 weeks for all workers. Eligibility requirements should be modified to provide equal benefits to those who lost their jobs as a result of the economic downturn but who are ineligible for regular benefits, such as temporary and part-time workers and former Temporary Assistance to Needy Family (TANF) recipients. This would allow workers to be hired for community service jobs."

2. "Funding of job training programs for dislocated workers, adults, and youth under the Workforce Investment Act (WIA) should be sufficient to enable those who are laid off, especially if they are low-skilled workers, to get upgrade training, basic skills training, and ESL education."

3. "Free or low-cost health insurance should be provided to low-income families affected by the September 11 attack. Federal subsidies for COBRA for individuals who are unemployed due to the economic downturn should be provided."

4. "The rescission in the FY 2001 dislocated workers appropriation should be restored."

5. "It should be recognized that young workers served by WIA, especially those in Youth Opportunity Grant programs, will most likely be the first laid off in a recession and that many of these youth are high-school dropouts who need job training and financial subsidies."

combating terrorism. The mayors expressed that they have been working on initiatives related to homeland security, largely without any federal assistance. Select initiatives, related to communities, that they mentioned include the following: (1) conducting exercises to help prepare for emergencies and improve response capabilities; (2) expanded public information and education efforts; and (3) conducted vulnerability assessments of potential key targets.

NATIONAL LEAGUE OF CITIES (NLC)

The National League of Cities (NLC) has been conducting a letter-writing campaign to the White House and Congress to build support for the first responder funds. NLC proposed a $75.5 billion stimulus package that would include $10 billion for unmet homeland security needs.

In January of 2003, NLC President Karen Anderson appointed a special Working Group on Homeland Security to serve a NLC's front line resource on the subject. That group works to prepare resources to help city officials in carrying out their new roles as the "front line of hometown defense."

The following excerpts were taken from an NLC February 17, 2003 press release:

> City leaders say they are taking appropriate actions to safeguard their communities while the nation remains under a heightened state of alert, but how long they can maintain an elevated state of vigilance is not known.
>
> "I know cities are responding to the orange alert and doing what they believe is necessary, but we're doing it with our own resources, with no help from the federal government. Some states have offered to assist their cities, but that alone will not see us through, especially as we see these alerts may continue for longer than we have expected," said Karen Anderson, mayor of Minnetonka, Minn., and immediate past president of the National League of Cities.
>
> For now, Anderson's city will continue to pay overtime to cover the cost of tighter security, as will other cities. But she and other city leaders believe the time has come for Congress to approve the $3.5 billion in first responder funding that was promised after the Sept. 11, 2001, terrorist attacks on the World Trade Center and Pentagon. They even question if that will be enough to assist cities during a period of heightened alert.

> "This is more important than ever if we are going to be at orange alert or even if the alert status goes higher in the future," said Brenda Barger, mayor of Watertown, S.D., and a member of NLC's Working Group on Homeland Security. "Our cities and our towns want to live up to their responsibilities, but the economic downturn is hurting us. We must have the ability and resources to properly train and equip our first responders, and that costs money."

NLC has developed two publications to assist local governments in participating in homeland security.

- "Homeland Security: Federal Resources for Local Governments" (http://www.nlc.org/nlc_org/site/files/reports/fedlresrc.pdf)
- "Homeland Security: Practical Tools for Local Governments" (http://www.nlc.org/nlc_org/site/files/reports/terrorism.pdf)

NATIONAL ASSOCIATION OF COUNTIES (NACo)

The National Association of Counties (NACo) has created a "Policy Agenda to Secure the People of America's Counties." This policy paper states, "Counties are the first responders to terrorist attacks, natural disasters and major emergencies" (National Association of Counties, 2001). NACo has established a 43-member NACo Homeland Security Task Force that on October 23, 2001, prepared a set of 20 recommendations in four general categories concerning homeland security issues. The four general areas are public health, local law enforcement and intelligence, infrastructure security, and emergency planning and public safety. The titles of each of the 20 NACO recommendations are presented in Sidebar 3-3.

NATIONAL GOVERNOR'S ASSOCIATION (NGA)

In August 2002, the Center for Best Practices of the National Governors Association (NGA) released "States' Homeland Security Priorities." A list of 10 "major priorities and issues" was identified by the NGA center through a survey of states and territories state homeland security offices (NGA Center for Best

Practices, 2002). A list of these priorities as presented are as follows:

- Coordination must involve all levels of government;
- The federal government must disseminate timely intelligence information to the states;
- The states must work with local governments to develop interoperable communications between first responders, and adequate wireless spectrum must be set aside to do the job;
- State and local governments need help and technical assistance to identify and protect critical infrastructure;
- Both the states and federal government must focus on enhancing bioterrorism preparedness

and rebuilding the nation's public health system to address 21st century threats;
- The federal government should provide adequate federal funding and support to ensure that homeland security needs are met;
- The federal government should work with states to protect sensitive security information, including restricting access to information available through "freedom of information" requests;
- An effective system must be developed that secures points of entry at borders, airports, and seaports without placing an undue burden on commerce;
- The National Guard has proven itself to be an effective force during emergencies and crises. The mission of the National Guard should

---

SIDEBAR 3-3   Recommendations for Counties and Homeland Security Prepared by the National Association of Counties (NACo) Homeland Security Task Force

Public Health

1. Fund the Public Health Threats and Emergencies Act
2. Improve the health alert network
3. Ensure an adequate supply of vaccines and antibiotics
4. Develop a national policy to prioritize medical treatment
5. Train health personnel
6. Ensure that adequate medical surge capacity exists

Local Law Enforcement and Intelligence

7. Authorize a local antiterrorism block grant
8. Include counties in antiterrorism task forces
9. Balance heightened border security with economic activity

Infrastructure Security

10. Reimburse counties for airport security costs
11. Assist ports and transit systems in financing security measures

12. Help localities secure public utilities and a safe water supply
13. Include security in infrastructure development
14. Reimburse counties for costs incurred on behalf of the federal government
15. Assist counties to develop evacuation capacity

Emergency Planning and Public Safety

16. Train county officials to prepare for and respond to acts of terror
17. Assist public safety communications interoperability and interference issues
18. Establish a public communication network
19. Urge the release of federal research to assist counties
20. Provide immunity to encourage mutual aid and support

Source: "Policy Agenda to Secure the People of America's Counties," National Association of Counties, October 2001

remain flexible, and Guard units should primarily remain under the control of the governor during times of crises;

- Federal agencies should integrate their command systems into existing state and local incident command systems (ICS) rather than requiring state and local agencies to adapt to federal command systems.

Source: NGA Center for Best Practices, Issue Brief, August 19, 2002

Coordination, command, information sharing, funding support, and interoperability of communications are some of the critical issues identified by the NGA. Use of the National Guard, resource dispatch issues, support for bioterrorism preparedness, and the rebuilding of the public health system are also critical issues.

TERRORISM-RELATED ACTIVITY AMONG STATE EMERGENCY MANAGERS

A good way to understand state government activities in terrorism is to examine the priorities set by the nation's emergency managers. A survey of state homeland security structures by the National Emergency Management Agency (NEMA) conducted June 2002 found that all 50 states maintain primary point of contact for antiterrorism/homeland security efforts:

- Governor's office—12 states
- Military/adjutant general—12 states
- Emergency management—10 states
- Public safety—9 states
- Law enforcement—3 states
- Attorney general—2 states
- Lieutenant governor—2 states
- Land commissioner—1 state

(National Emergency Management Association 2002)

On October 1, 2001, the NEMA released a "White Paper on Domestic Preparedness" that was supported by the Adjutants Generals Association of the United States, the International Association of Emergency Managers (which represents local emergency management officials), and the National Guard Association of America. The document states that "NEMA thinks it critical that the following enhancements be incorporated into a nationwide strategy for catastrophic disaster preparedness" (National Emergency Management Association, 2001). A total of 22 enhancements were presented in the white paper in three general categories: emergency preparedness and response, health and medical, and additional WMD (weapons of mass destruction) recommendations. A partial list of these enhancements is presented in Sidebar 3-4.

The NEMA White Paper presents "enhancements" that address coordination, communications, command, information sharing, funding, technology, and public health system and preparedness issues. Also included were the use of National Guard assets and increasing the capabilities of state-local Urban Search and Rescue. Expanding the FEMA fire grant program and establishment of standardized national donations protocol was included in the paper.

Many states are moving ahead in terrorism and homeland security planning and other activities. A report compiled by the White House Office of Homeland Security found activities in many states, cities, and counties in the following four general areas (White House Office of Homeland Security 2002):

- Developing plans
- Information sharing
- Responding to biological threats
- Protecting critical infrastructure

LOCAL GOVERNMENT TERRORISM ACTIVITIES

Emergency preparedness, mitigation, response, and recovery all occur at the local community level. It is at the local level that the critical planning, communications, technology, coordination, command, and spending decisions matter the most. The priorities of groups such as the National Conference of Mayors and the

SIDEBAR 3-4 **Partial List of Enhancements Presented in the NEMA Paper on Domestic Preparedness**

Emergency Preparedness and Response

- Congress should provide to the states immediate federal funding for full-time catastrophic disaster coordinators in moderate and high-risk local jurisdictions of the United States.
- States need financial assistance to improve catastrophic response and Continuity of Operations Plans (COOP) and Continuity of Government (COG) for states.
- Interstate and intrastate mutual assistance must be recognized and supported by the federal government as an expedient, cost-effective approach to disaster response and recovery.
- FEMA, state, and local emergency managers must implement renewed emphasis on family and community preparedness to ensure Americans have the skills necessary to survive a catastrophic disaster.
- A standardized national donations management protocol is needed to address the outpouring of food, clothing, supplies, and other items that are commonly sent to impacted states localities following a disaster.

Health and Medical

- The medical surge capacity must be strengthened. The emergency management, medical, and public health professions must work with lawmakers to ensure each region of our nation has a certain minimum surge capacity to deal with mass casualty events.
- State-local disaster medical assistance teams should be developed across the country, with standardized equipment, personnel, and training.

Additional WMD Recommendations

- The Department of Justice should immediately release the FY00 and FY01 equipment funds in order to begin implementation of these recommendations and then require a basic statewide strategy in order to receive FY02 funds; and further, provide funding to states to administer the equipment program.
- Congress and the Department of Defense should authorize homeland defense as a key federal defense mission tasking for the National Guard.

State and local Urban Search and Rescue capabilities should be developed across the country, with the standardized equipment, personnel, and training.

- National interagency and intergovernmental information management protocols are needed to support information sharing (i.e., damage/situation reports, warning/intelligence reports, resource coordination).
- Better federal interagency coordination is needed to assist states in identifying and accessing the full range of federal resources and assistance available to them.
- FEMA's fire grant program should be expanded and modified to strengthen regional and national, not just local, fire protection capabilities to respond to catastrophic disasters.
- There is a need for technology transfer from the federal government and technology contractors to state and local governments to support an automated decision support system.

Source: National Emergency Management Association, White Paper of Domestic Preparedness, October 1, 2001

National Associations of Counties represent what matters at the local community level in the fight against terrorism. The fight against terrorism has spawned a series of new requirements in preparedness and mitigation planning at the local level.

Both the NACo and the mayors' policy papers identify issues in the areas of command, coordination, communications, funding and equipment, training, and mutual aid. These two papers also raise concerns about critical community infrastructure, including the public health system, which is maintained and secured at the local level of government.

The events of September 11 established the security of community infrastructure as a potential target for terrorist attacks. Community infrastructure has always been vulnerable to natural and other technological disaster events—so much so that FEMA's largest disaster assistance program, Public Assistance, is designed to fund the rebuilding of community infrastructure damaged by a disaster event. Local government officials and local emergency managers must now increase the attention they give to protecting and securing community infrastructure from a terrorist attack. They must also include in these preparedness efforts the local public health system. The following is a checklist designed for the City of Boone (NC) as part of a technological annex developed for the town's All-Hazards Planning and Operations Manual in March 2002:

- Identify the types of events that might occur in the community.
- Plan emergency activities in advance to ensure a coordinated response.
- Build capabilities necessary to response effectively to the consequences of terrorism.
- Identify the type or nature of an event when it does happen.
- Implement the planned response quickly and efficiently.
- Recover from the incident.

The response to terrorism is similar in many ways to that of other natural or man-made disasters for which Boone has already prepared. With additions and modifications, the development of a completely separate system can be avoided. Training and public education are vital, and understanding the conditions for obtaining available federal assistance will drastically increase local capacity before and during a terrorist attack.

The following are the general types of activities that Boone must undertake to meet the above-mentioned objectives:

- Strengthen information and communications technology
- Establish a well-defined incident command structure that includes the FBI
- Strengthen local working relationships and communications
- Educate health-care and emergency-response community about identification of bioterrorist attacks and agents
- Educate health-care and emergency-response community about medical treatment and prophylaxis for possible biological agents
- Educate local health department about state and federal requirements and assistance
- Maintain locally accessible supply of medications, vaccines, and supplies
- Address health-care-worker safety issues
- Designate a spokesperson to maintain contact with the public
- Develop comprehensive evacuation plans
- Become familiar with state and local laws relating to isolation/quarantine
- Develop or enhance local capability to prosecute crimes involving weapons of mass destruction or the planning of terrorism events
- Develop, maintain, and practice an infectious diseases emergency response plan
- Practice with surrounding jurisdictions to strengthen mutual agreement plans
- Outline the roles of federal agency assistance in planning and response
- Educate the public in recognizing events and ways to respond as individuals
- Stay current

(Source: Town of Boone All-Hazards Planning and Operations Manual, Technological Hazards Annex, March 2002)

Local officials must also understand how to work with federal law enforcement officials should a terror-ist incident occur in the community. Sidebar 3-5 pre-sents information from the Boone Technological Hazards Annex on the process of transitioning from fire to law enforcement to FBI as part of the incident command system.

SIDEBAR 3-5   Incident Command System Structure: Process of Transitioning from Fire to Law Enforcement to FBI

Local FBI personnel should be the first contacted after an attack. That call will lead to the DoD, DOJ, HHS, DOE, FEMA, EPA, and many others. The FBI will set up a Strategic Information Operations Center (SIOC) to provide constant direction in the attack response. If other agencies are involved, then the duties of the SIOC will be expanded into a Joint Operations Center (JOC). This will address the areas of command, operations, support, and conse-quence management and will include a Joint Information Center (JIC) to provide information to the media and the public.

FEMA will contact the governor and the presi-dent to determine if federal assistance is necessary. They will establish a Regional Operations Center (ROC), for a deployed Emergency Support Team (EST).

The local government is responsible for the first consequence management. This includes measures to protect public health and safety, restore essential government services, and provide emergency relief to governments, businesses, and individuals affected by the consequences of terrorism. The log-ical steps in coordination and command that should be followed are detailed below:

- When the Fire Department is in command, during the initial response, law enforcement (LE) follows the principles for assisting with a mass casualty incident.
- When command passes to LE, the officer in charge will set the goals for the operation and begin the preliminary criminal investigation.

- When fire begins to wind down, the fire and LE commanders will agree when the incident command passes to LE. When this occurs, simultaneous broadcasts should be made on both fire and LE channels so that all personnel understand the pass of command.
- The specific location for the LE command post should be repeated via radio so there is no mis-taking the location.
- It is essential that a command-level fire official remain in the command post to ensure continu-ity of information and to provide an officer who can direct fire resources if needed at this time.
- It is important to remember that, until the call is made that the incident is an act of domestic or foreign terrorism, the event is the local jurisdiction's homicide, assault, vandalism, bombing, etc.

The FBI will usually dispatch an initial special agent as soon as the incident occurs, as a direct result of just being in your town and monitoring radio fre-quencies. If there is even a slight suspicion of terror-ism, the FBI needs to be contacted. The time for the special agent to arrive is from minutes to several hours. It is better to have FBI employees on the scene as soon as possible because they speed up the inves-tigation if it turns out to be actual terrorism and sim-ply act as additional highly trained officials if it is just a homicide. FBI also provides technical support and resources not normally found at the local level.

When the FBI team is assembled and in place, it assumes command. The FBI has its own policies

CONCLUSION

Emergency management in the United States was changed forever by the events of September 11. New focus, new funding, new partners, and new concerns associated with the fight against terrorism are changing the way emergency management functions in this country every day. At the federal government level, the new Department of Homeland Security includes FEMA and all of the federal government disaster management programs. How traditional disaster response recovery and mitigation programs will fare in this new structure is uncertain. At the state level, governors and state emergency management directors are calling for better coordination, new communications technologies, and always more and more funding. For local governments, terrorism is a new threat that greatly expands their facility security requirements, one that must be added to a long list of needs and priorities. But the threat of terrorism is one that can't be ignored. Issues of coordination, communications, and funding concern local governments as well.

The United States has taken its typical response to a new problem. It has reorganized and committed huge amounts of funding to reducing the problem. The ability of the Department of Homeland Security to achieve an enhanced level of coordination, communication, and readiness remains uncertain. DHS' transportation and border security functions join the intelligence community, the military, diplomatic corps, and law enforcement in the effort to prevent future terrorism attacks within the United States. DHS is also involved in supporting a better prepared and better equipped first responder cadre and enhanced and effective emergency management programs.

about evidence collection, so if terrorism is suspected, it is best to seal the area and let the FBI evidence technicians collect the evidence when they arrive to prevent a later chain of custody issue of evidence. If some evidence needs to be preserved immediately, this should be done for later transfer to FBI custody.

The FBI will still need continued support and assistance from the local LE and Fire Departments. The FBI personnel need help with traffic control, body and evidence recovery, scene security, and a host of other critical tasks. They will create a Joint Operations Center to coordinate the federal response to the event, similar to the EOC. All federal agencies will report to and act out of this office. If possible, the FBI team members will try to colocate the JOC and EOC. At a minimum, they will try to provide a command-level officer to stay in the local agency EOC to facilitate direct communication between the groups involved in the unified command and to facilitate sharing of information resources and personnel.

It is best to work out of one central EOC. The FBI's JOC is based on the large number of agencies and support staff that may be called in. If the event is a large one, the incident commander should seek an area large enough to accommodate these priorities so that both facilities can be at the same location.

As the local agencies' activities wind down, fewer staff members will be necessary, until the JOC will become the only coordination point for the incident. When on-scene activity ceases, all follow-up investigative activity will be responsibility of the FBI.

This is the triangle issue of FBI, LE, and FIRE, and during each of the phases the three move around the triangle, sharing concerns and information in the unified command concept.

Source: Town of Boone All-Hazards Planning and Operations Manual, Technological Hazards Annex, March 2002

But how long will it take for DHS to operate as a cohesive organization? In the rush to demonstrate action, both the Bush Administration and Congress have failed to look carefully at the longer-term implications of these decisions. A massive natural disaster is as likely to occur as another terrorism event. Will the DHS focus on terrorism erode our progress in natural hazards risk reduction, and will we be ready for the next major hurricane or earthquake? An American leader once quipped that if we fail to learn from our mistakes, we are destined to repeat them. Let's hope that history doesn't repeat itself. A timeline of Homeland Security Actions since September 11 is presented in Sidebar 3-1.

SIDEBAR 3-6   Select Web Sites for Additional Information

- Americorps: www.americorps.org
- Animal and Plant Health Inspection Service: www.aphis.usda.gov
- Citizen Corps: www.citizencorps.gov
- Corporation for National and Community Service: www.nationalservice.org
- Department of Homeland Security: www.dhs.gov
- Federal Emergency Management Agency: www.fema.gov
- Immigration and Nationalization Service: www.ins.gov
- Medical Reserve Corps: www.medicalreservecorps.gov
- Office for Domestic Preparedness: www.ojp.usdoj.gov/odp
- Office for National Preparedness: www.fema.gov/onp
- National Association of Counties: www.naco.org
- National Governors Association: www.nga.org
- National League of Cities: www.nlc.org
- Neighborhood Watch: www.usaonwatch.org
- Senior Corps: www.seniorcorps.org
- Transportation Security Administration: www.tsa.dot.gov
- United States Coast Guard: www.uscg.mil
- United States Conference of Mayors: www.usmayors.org
- United States Customs Service: www.customs.ustreas.gov
- United States Secret Service: www.ustreas.gov/usss/
- USA Freedom Corps: www.usafreedomcorps.gov
- Volunteers in Police Service: www.policevolunteers.org

REVIEW QUESTIONS

1. What is the principal role of emergency management in homeland security? Identify the other major players and their roles in homeland security.
2. Identify the five principal directorates of the Department of Homeland Security and discuss their respective missions?
3. Discuss the role of other federal agencies in homeland security.
4. Make the case for retaining an all-hazards approach to emergency management that includes terrorism and its associated hazards as one of many hazards? Discuss the pros and cons of such an approach as it relates to all four phases of emergency management—mitigation, preparedness, response, and recovery.

5. If you had been in charge of establishing the Department of Homeland Security (DHS), would you have included the Federal Emergency Management Agency (FEMA) in DHS or would you have retained it as an independent Executive Branch agency reporting directly to the President? Discuss the possible ramifications of moving FEMA into DHS in terms of FEMA's mission, programs, and reporting structure? The Director of FEMA no longer reports directly to the President, will this be a problem in future natural and terrorist related disasters? What will be the impact of FEMA's inclusion in DHS be on the nation's emergency management system?

REFERENCES

National Association of Counties (NACo). 2002. "Counties and Homeland Security: Policy Agenda to Secure the People of America's Counties," August 2002. <http://www.naco.org/programs/homesecurity?policyplan.cfm>

National Emergency Management Association (NEMA), 2002. "NEMA Reports on State Homeland Security Structures," June 2002. <http://www.nemaweb.org/ShowExtendedNewscfm?ID=171>

The United States Conference of Mayors, 2001. "A National Action Plan for Safety and Security in America's Cities," December 2001. <http://www.usmayors.org/uscm/home.asp>

4

Hazards

INTRODUCTION

The threat or risk posed by terrorism has introduced an expanded and, in some cases, a new set of hazards. These new hazards fall in four principal categories: explosives, chemical, biological, and nuclear/radiological. These new hazards join the numerous traditional natural and technological hazards such as hurricanes, tornados, floods, earthquakes, fires, hazardous materials transportation and storage accidents, power outages, and releases at nuclear power plants.

There are two significant differences between the new hazards and the traditional hazards. First, much is known about the traditional hazards as a result of years of research, actual occurrence, and response and recovery from these hazards. We can now predict fairly accurately the track of a hurricane. We know enough about the destructive force of a tornado to design and build safe rooms. We have spent the better part of a century trying, with some success, to control flooding. We have developed building codes and standards that protect structures from earthquakes, fires, and wind damage. We have enough experience in responding to disaster events caused by these hazards to ensure that our first responders have effective protective gear and are trained and exercised in the best response protocols and practices.

While research is ongoing and new practices continue to be discovered, the emergency management community in this country is well trained and experienced in dealing with the long list of traditional hazard events. This is not the case with the new hazards presented by the terrorist threat. Knowledge of properties and the destructive qualities of the various chemical and biological threats is limited at best, even in the agencies charged with knowing the most about these hazards. The first responder community, the state and local emergency managers, and the general public are almost completely uninformed about these hazards as are community and national leaders and the media.

It took decades of research and experience for all parties to become fluent in the traditional mix of natural and technological disasters. Not surprisingly, it will take time, maybe not decades but years, before we all can reach a comfort level with our knowledge of the new hazards.

The second significant difference between the traditional and new terrorism hazards is the way we come to encounter the new hazards. Traditional hazards occur as an act of nature or weather or by accident or negligence. Hurricanes, tornados, and earthquakes are natural events that have occurred for centuries. Releases at nuclear plant and hazardous materials spills caused by train and truck accidents have traditionally been just that, accidents. The new hazards raised by the terrorist threat differ in that they will be intentionally used to cause death and destruction. These hazards will be weaponized and used to advance political, ideological, or religious agendas. No hurricane or earthquake has ever advanced a human agenda (Sidebar 4-1).

STUDY PREDICTING TERROR ATTACKS PLACES UNITED STATES AS NUMBER THREE

The United States ranks fourth among the top five countries most likely to be targeted for a terrorist attack within the next 12 months, according to a risk index published on August 18, 2003 by the World Markets Research Center (WMRC), a business intelligence firm based in London. The index also predicted that "another September 11-style terrorist attack in the United States is highly likely." Colombia, Israel, and Pakistan ranked in the top three positions, respectively. After the United States, the Philippines, Afghanistan, Indonesia, Iraq, India, and Britain, which tied with Sri Lanka, rounded out the top ten, respectively. North Korea ranked as the least likely country to experience a terrorist attack within the next year. The index assessed the risk of terrorism to some 186 countries and their interests based on five criteria: "motivation of terrorists; the presence of terror groups; the scale and frequency of past attacks; efficacy of the groups in carrying out attacks; and how many attacks were thwarted by the country." Explaining the U.S. ranking, the index stated that while the presence of militant Islamic networks within the United States is less extensive than in Western Europe, "U.S.-led military action in Afghanistan and Iraq has exacerbated anti-U.S. sentiment." (Source: Homeland Security Monitor, 8/19/2003)

This fact makes issues such as detection, containment, control, quarantine, and vaccination—to name just a few—significant factors in developing new response and recovery practices for first responders. Political affairs and events across the globe must now figure into efforts to prepare the population and to mitigate the impacts of these new hazards on our population, our critical infrastructure, our communities, our economy, and our way of life.

The lack of knowledge of these new hazards and the fact that they will be used deliberately to attack us has resulted in the perception by nearly all Americans that they are potential terrorist victims. Unlike hurricanes or tornados, the terrorist threat and the new hazards must be considered national risks. People in Montana do not worry about hurricanes, and it rarely floods in the desert of Nevada. There have been few if any tornados reported in Maine. But all people consider

---

SIDEBAR 4-1   Where Will Terrorists Strike? Two Theories . . .

HHS Dep. Secy. Says Rural Areas Most Likely Location for Next Terror Attack

While major U.S. cities are considered the most likely targets for terrorist attacks, a senior official said on August 27 that rural America could be the site of the next terror attack, especially a bioterrorism attack, an Associated Press report said. Speaking at a forum on rural health care in Casper, Wyoming, Deputy Secretary of Health and Human Services Claude Allen said, "Some rural communities are among the most vulnerable to attack, simply because of their proximity to a missile silo or to a chemical stockpile. Other rural communities are vulnerable simply because they mistakenly believe that terrorism is an urban problem and they are safe from attack." While Allen said the federal government has increased funding for bioterrorism preparedness, he also noted that rural areas are made even more vulnerable given their "limited infrastructure for public health as well as fewer health care providers and volunteer systems."

Source: Homeland Security Monitor, 8/28/2003

themselves, however remotely, potential victims of terrorism, and the reality of the new hazards only reinforce this risk perception. A list of selected Chemical Biological Radiological Nuclear (CBRN) incidents compiled by the Central Intelligence Agency (CIA) is presented in Sidebar 4-2.

SIDEBAR 4-2   Selected Examples of CBRN Incidents

February 2002: Italian authorities arrested as many as nine Moroccan nationals who may have been plotting to poison the water supply of the U.S. Embassy in Rome. Authorities confiscated a detailed map of Rome's underground water system, highlighting the location of the U.S. Embassy's pipes. The suspects also had 4 kilograms of potassium ferrocyanide in their possession.

December 2001: According to press reporting, the military wing of HAMAS (Palestinian Islamic Resistance Movement) claimed that the bolts and nails packed into explosives detonated by a suicide bomber had been dipped into rat poison.

October 2001: U.S. and international law enforcement authorities stepped up investigations in the United States and abroad to determine the sources of confirmed cases of anthrax exposures in Florida, New York, and Washington, DC. In the past several years, there have been hundreds of hoaxes involving anthrax in the United States In the aftermath of the September 11 terrorist attacks against the United States, these anthrax scares have spread across the globe and have exacerbated international concerns. The confirmed anthrax cases involved letters sent through the mail to the U.S. Congress and several media organizations. More than 50 individuals were exposed to *B. anthracis* spores, including 18 who became infected, and five people died from inhalation anthrax—the first reported cases in the United States in 25 years. U.S. and international health organizations have treated thousands of individuals associated with these incidents.

September 2001: Columbian police accused the Revolutionary Armed Forces of Colombia (FARC) of using improvised grenades filled with poisonous gas during an attack on the city of San Adolfo in the Huila Department. According to media accounts, four policemen died and another six suffered respiratory problems from the attack.

January 2000: According to press reports, a Russian general accused Chechen rebels of delivering poisoned wine and canned fruit to Russian soldiers in Chechnya.

November 1999: Raw materials for making Ricin were seized by law-enforcement authorities during the arrest of a U.S. citizen who threatened to poison two Colorado judges.

June 1998: U.S. law enforcement authorities arrested two members of the violent secessionist group, the Republic of Texas, for planning to construct a device with toxins to kill selected government officials. A U.S. Federal Court convicted them in October 1998 for threatening to use a weapon of mass destruction.

December 1996: Sri Lankan press noted that government authorities warned the military in the northern region not to purchase food or stamps from local vendors, because some stamps had been found laced with cyanide.

July 1995: Four improvised chemical devices (ICDs) were found in restrooms at the Kayaba-cho, Tokyo, and Ginza subway stations and the Japanese railway's Shinjuku station. Each device was slightly different but contained the same chemicals.

May 1995: An improvised chemical device (ICD) was left in Shinjuku station in Tokyo. The device consisted of the two plastic bags, one containing

Sidebar 4.2 continued

The first step in reducing this fear is to better understand these new hazards and how individuals, communities, and countries can deal with them. The purpose of this chapter is to present basic information concerning the four new hazards—explosives, chemical, biological, and nuclear/radiological. Most of this information has been taken from the web sites and reports maintained and prepared by the Centers for Disease Control (CDC) and the Federal Emergency Management Agency (FEMA). In many cases, the authors have reprinted the information provided by the CDC, FEMA, and others in its original form in order to present the most accurate and succinct information for each hazard.

CONVENTIONAL EXPLOSIVES AND SECONDARY DEVICES

An interim planning guide for state and local government entitled "Managing the Emergency Consequences of Terrorist Incidents" was prepared by FEMA in July 2002 and states the following about conventional explosives and secondary devices:

> The easiest to obtain and use of all weapons is still a conventional explosive device, or improvised bomb, which may be used to cause massive local destruction or to disperse chemical, biological, or radiological agents. The components are readily available, as are detailed instructions on constructing such a device.

sodium cyanide and the other sulfuric acid. If the device had not been neutralized, the chemicals would have combined to produce a cyanide gas.

A U.S. citizen acquired three vials of *Yersinia pestis*, the bacteria that causes plague. Law enforcement officials recovered the unopened material and arrested the individual. No delivery system was recovered, and no information indicated the subject's purpose in obtaining the bacteria.

March 20, 1995: Members of the Japanese cult Aum Shinrikyo used ICDs to release sarin nerve gas in the Tokyo subway station. Twelve people died, and thousands of others were hospitalized or required medical treatment.

March 15, 1995: Three briefcases were left at locations in the Kasumigaseki train station in Tokyo. No injuries resulted, but an Aum Shinrikyo member later confessed that this was a failed biological attack with Botulinum toxin.

January 1995: Tajik opposition members laced champagne with cyanide at a New Year's celebration, killing six Russian soldiers and the wife of another soldier, and sickening other revelers.

June 27, 1994: A substance identified as sarin was dispersed using a modified van in a residential area near Matsumoto; seven persons died, and more than 200 people were injured. Reportedly, an Aum

Shinrikyo member confessed that the cult targeted three judges who lived there to prevent them from returning an adverse decision against the cult.

1993: A U.S. citizen was detained by the Canadian Customs Service as he attempted to enter Canada from Alaska. A white powdery substance was confiscated and later identified through laboratory analysis as Ricin. The individual, traveling with a large sum of cash, told officials that he was carrying the poison to protect his money.

1992: Four individuals were convicted by a U.S. federal court for producing Ricin and advocating the violent overthrow of the government. The subjects, who had espoused extremist, antigovernment, antitax ideals, specifically had targeted a deputy U.S. marshal who previously had served papers on one of them for tax violations.

1984: An outbreak of salmonella poisoning that occurred in Oregon during a 2-week period was linked to the salad bars of eight restaurants. More than 700 people were affected, but no fatalities occurred. Investigators of the outbreak determined that two members of the Rajneesh religious sect produced and dispensed salmonella bacteria in the restaurants, in order to influence a local election by incapacitating opposition voters.

Source: CIA, "Terrorism: Guide to Chemical, Biological, Radiological, and Nuclear Weapons Indicators" 2002

Improvised explosive devices are categorized as being explosive or incendiary, employing high- or low-filler explosive materials to explode and/or cause fires. Explosions and fires also can be caused by projectiles and missiles, including aircraft used against high-profile targets such as buildings, monuments, and special events. Bombs and firebombs are cheap and easily constructed, involve low technology, and are the terrorist weapon most likely to be encountered. Large, powerful devices can be outfitted with timed or remotely triggered detonators and can be designed to be activated by light, pressure, movement, or radio transmission.

The potential exists for single or multiple bombing incidents in single or multiple municipalities. Historically, less than 5 percent of actual or attempted bombings were preceded by a threat. Explosive materials can be employed covertly with little signature and are not readily detectable. Secondary explosive devices may also be used as weapons against responders and the public in coincident acts. Other diversionary events or attacks could also be aimed at responders. (Source: FEMA 2002)

CHEMICAL AGENTS

An interim planning guide for state and local government entitled "Managing the Emergency Consequences of Terrorist Incidents" was prepared by FEMA in July 2002 and states the following about chemical agents:

Chemical agents are intended to kill, seriously injure, or incapacitate people through physiological effects. A terrorist incident involving a chemical agent will demand immediate reaction from emergency responders—fire departments, police, hazardous materials (HazMat) teams, emergency medical services (EMS), and emergency room staff—which will need adequate training and equipment.

Hazardous chemicals, including industrial chemicals and agents, can be introduced via aerosol devices (e.g., munitions, sprayers, or aerosol generators), breaking containers, or covert dissemination. Such an attack might involve the release of a chemical warfare agent, such as a nerve or blister agent or an industrial chemical, which may have serious consequences. [Some indicators of the possible use of chemical agents are listed in Sidebar 4-3].

Early in an investigation, it may not be obvious whether an outbreak was caused by an infectious agent or a hazardous chemical; however, most chemical attacks will be localized, and their effects will be evident within a few minutes. There are both persistent and nonpersistent chemical agents. Persistent agents remain in the affected area for hours, days, or weeks. Nonpersistent agents have high evaporation rates, are lighter than air, and disperse rapidly, thereby losing their ability to cause casualties after 10 to 15 minutes, although they may be more persistent in small, unventilated areas. (Source: FEMA 2002)

A list of chemical agents compiled by the Centers for Disease Control (CDC) is presented in Sidebar 4-4.

Facts Sheets compiled from the CDC web site for the following selected chemical agents are presented in the following pages:

- Cyanide
- Sulfur mustard (mustard gas)
- Sarin

SIDEBAR 4-3   General Indicators of Possible Chemical Agent Use

- Stated threat to release a chemical agent
- Unusual occurrence of dead or dying animals
  - For example, lack of insects, dead birds
- Unexplained casualties
  - Multiple victims
  - Surge of similar 911 calls
  - Serious illnesses
  - Nausea, disorientation, difficulty breathing, or convulsions
  - Definite casualty patterns
  - Unusual liquid, spray, vapor, or powder

  - Droplets, oily film
  - Unexplained odor
  - Low-lying clouds/fog unrelated to weather
- Suspicious devices, packages, or letters
  - Unusual metal debris
  - Abandoned spray devices
  - Unexplained munitions

Source: Interim Planning Guide for State and Local Government: Managing the Emergency Consequences of Terrorist Incidents, FEMA, July 2002

- Ricin
- Chlorine.

The new chemical agent hazard raises critical questions about whether individuals and communities should evacuate or seek shelter in place in the event of a chemical agent attack. Guidance developed by the CDC is presented on both evacuation and shelter in place in Chapter 6 "Mitigation and Preparedness."

SIDEBAR 4-4   List of Chemical Agents

Compiled by the Centers for Disease Control

Abrin
Adamsite (DM)
Agent 15
Ammonia
Arsenic
Arsine (SA)
Benzene
Bromobenzylcyanide (CA)
BZ
Cannabinoids
Chlorine (CL)
Chloroacetophenone (CN)
Chlorobenzylidenemalononitrile (CS)
Chloropicrin (PS)
Cyanide
Cyanogen Chloride (CK)
Cyclohexyl Sarin (GF)
Dibenzoxazepine (CR)
Diphenylchloroarsine (DA)
Diphenylcyanoarsine (DC)
Diphosgene (DP)
Distilled Mustard (HD)
Ethyldichloroarsine (ED)
Ethylene Glycol
Fentanyls and Other Opioids
Hydrofluoric Acid
Hydrogen Chloride
Hydrogen Cyanide (AC)
Lewisite (L, L-1, L-2, L-3)
LSD
Mercury
Methyldichloroarsine (MD)
Mustard Gas (H) (Sulfur Mustard)
Mustard/Lewisite (HL)

Mustard/T
Nitrogen Mustard (HN-1, HN-2, HN-3)
Nitrogen Oxide (NO)
Paraquat
Perflurorisobutylene (PHIB)
Phenodichloroarsine (PD)
Phenothiazines
Phosgene (CG)
Phosgene Oxime (CX)
Phosphine
Potassium Cyanide (KCN)
Red Phosphorous (RP)
Ricin
Sarin (GB)
Sesqui Mustard
Sodium Azide
Sodium Cyanide (NaCN)
Soman (GD)
Stibine
Strychnine
Sulfur Mustard (H) (Mustard Gas)
Sulfur Trioxide-Chlorosulfonic Acid (FS)
Super Warfarin
Tabun (GA)
Teflon and Perflurorisobutylene (PHIB)
Thallium
Titanium Tetrachloride (FM)
Unidentified Chemical (http://www.atsdr.cdc.gov/
     MHMI/mmg170.pdf)
VX
White Phosphorus
Zinc Oxide (HC)

Source: http://www.bt.cdc.gov/agent/agentlistchem.asp

FACTS ABOUT CYANIDE

What Cyanide Is

- Cyanide is a rapidly acting, potentially deadly chemical that can exist in various forms.
- Cyanide can be a colorless gas, such as hydrogen cyanide (HCN) or cyanogen chloride (CNCl), or a crystal form such as sodium cyanide (NaCN) or potassium cyanide (KCN).
- Cyanide sometimes is described as having a "bitter almond" smell, but it does not always give off an odor, and not everyone can detect the odor when it does exist.
- Cyanide is also known by the military designations AN (for hydrogen cyanide) and CK (for cyanogen chloride).

Where Cyanide Is Found and How It Is Used

- Hydrogen cyanide, under the name Zyklon B, was used as a genocidal agent by the Germans in World War II.
- Reports have indicated that during the Iran–Iraq War in the 1980s, hydrogen cyanide gas may have been used along with other chemical agents against the inhabitants of the Kurdish city of Halabja in northern Iraq.
- Cyanide is naturally present in some foods and in certain plants such as cassava. Cyanide is contained in cigarette smoke and the combustion products of synthetic materials such as plastics. Combustion products are substances given off when things burn.
- In manufacturing, cyanide is used to make paper, textiles, and plastics. It is present in the chemicals used to develop photographs. Cyanide salts are used in metallurgy for electroplating, metal cleaning, and removing gold from its ore. Cyanide gas is used to exterminate pests and vermin in ships and buildings.
- If accidentally ingested (swallowed), chemicals found in acetonitrile-based products that are used to remove artificial nails can produce cyanide.

How People Can Be Exposed to Cyanide

- People may be exposed to cyanide by breathing air, drinking water, eating food, or touching soil that contains cyanide.
- Cyanide enters water, soil, or air as a result of both natural processes and industrial activities. In air, cyanide is present mainly as gaseous hydrogen cyanide.
- Smoking cigarettes is probably one of the major sources of cyanide exposure for people who do not work in cyanide-related industries.

How Cyanide Works

- Poisoning caused by cyanide depends on the amount of cyanide a person is exposed to, the route of exposure, and the length of time that a person is exposed.
- Breathing cyanide gas causes the most harm, but ingesting cyanide can be toxic as well.
- Cyanide gas is most dangerous in enclosed places where the gas will be trapped.
- Cyanide gas evaporates and disperses quickly in open spaces, making it less harmful outdoors.
- Cyanide gas is less dense than air, so it will rise.
- Cyanide prevents the cells of the body from getting oxygen. When this happens, the cells die.
- Cyanide is more harmful to the heart and brain than to other organs because the heart and brain use a lot of oxygen.

Immediate Signs and Symptoms of Cyanide Exposure

- People exposed to a small amount of cyanide by breathing it, absorbing it through their skin, or eating foods that contain it may have some or all of the following symptoms within minutes:
  - Rapid breathing
  - Restlessness
  - Dizziness
  - Weakness
  - Headache
  - Nausea and vomiting
  - Rapid heart rate
- Exposure to a large amount of cyanide by any route may cause these other health effects as well:
  - Convulsions
  - Low blood pressure
  - Slow heart rate
  - Loss of consciousness
  - Lung injury
  - Respiratory failure leading to death
- Showing these signs and symptoms does not necessarily mean that a person has been exposed to cyanide.

What the Long-Term Health Effects May Be

Survivors of serious cyanide poisoning may develop heart and brain damage.

How People Can Protect Themselves and What They Should Do if They Are Exposed to Cyanide

- First, get fresh air by leaving the area where the cyanide was released. Moving to an area with fresh air is a good way to reduce the possibility of death from exposure to cyanide gas.
  - If the cyanide release was outside, move away from the area where the cyanide was released.
  - If the cyanide release was indoors, get out of the building.
- If leaving the area that was exposed to cyanide is not an option, stay as low to the ground as possible.
- Remove any clothing that has liquid cyanide on it. If possible, seal the clothing in a plastic bag, and then seal that bag inside a second plastic bag. Removing and sealing the clothing in this way will help protect people from any chemicals that might be on their clothes.
- If clothes were placed in plastic bags, inform either the local or state health department or emergency coordinators upon their arrival. Do not handle the plastic bags.
- Rinse the eyes with plain water for 10 to 15 minutes if they are burning or if vision is blurred.
- Wash any liquid cyanide from the skin thoroughly with soap and water.
- If cyanide is known to be ingested (swallowed), do not induce vomiting or give fluids to drink.
- Seek medical attention right away. Dial 911 and explain what has happened.

How Cyanide Poisoning Is Treated

Cyanide poisoning is treated with specific antidotes and supportive medical care in a hospital setting. The most important thing is for victims to seek medical treatment as soon as possible.

How People Can Get More Information About Cyanide

People can contact one of the following:
- Regional poison control center at 1-800-222-1222
- Centers for Disease Control and Prevention
  - Public Response Hotline (CDC)
    - English: 1-888-246-2675
    - Español: 1-888-246-2857
    - TTY: 1-866-874-2646
  - Emergency Preparedness and Response web site: http://www.bt.cdc.gov/
  - E-mail inquiries: cdcresponse@ashastd.org
  - Mail inquiries:
    Public Inquiry c/o BPRP
    Bioterrorism Preparedness and Response Planning
    Centers for Disease Control and Prevention
    Mailstop C-18
    1600 Clifton Road
    Atlanta, GA 30333
- Agency for Toxic Substances and Disease Registry (ATSDR): 1-888-422-8737
  - E-mail inquiries: atsdric@cdc.gov
  - Mail inquiries:
    Agency for Toxic Substances and Disease Registry
    Division of Toxicology
    1600 Clifton Road NE, Mailstop E-29
    Atlanta, GA 30333
- Centers for Disease Control and Prevention (CDC), National Institute for Occupational Safety and Health (NIOSH), Pocket Guide to Chemical Hazards (http://www.cdc.gov/niosh/ npg/npgd0000.html).

Source: www.cdc.gov

FACTS ABOUT SULFUR MUSTARD

What Sulfur Mustard Is
- Sulfur mustard is a type of chemical warfare agent. These kinds of agents are called vesicants, or blistering agents, because they cause blistering of the skin and mucous membranes on contact.
- Sulfur mustard is also known as "mustard gas or mustard agent" or by the military designations H, HD, and HT.
- Sulfur mustard sometimes smells like garlic, onions, or mustard and sometimes has no odor. It can be a vapor (the gaseous form of a liquid), an oily-textured liquid, or a solid.
- Sulfur mustard can be clear to yellow or brown when it is in liquid or solid form.

Where Sulfur Mustard Is Found and How It Is Used
- Sulfur mustard is not found naturally in the environment.
- Sulfur mustard was introduced in World War I as a chemical warfare agent. Until recently, it was available for use in the treatment of a skin condition called psoriasis. Currently, it has no medical use.

How People Can Be Exposed to Sulfur Mustard
- If sulfur mustard is released into the air as a vapor, people can be exposed through skin contact, eye contact, or breathing. Sulfur mustard vapor can be carried long distances by wind.
- If sulfur mustard is released into water, people can be exposed by drinking the contaminated water or getting it on their skin.
- People can be exposed by coming in contact with liquid sulfur mustard.
- Sulfur mustard can last from 1 to 2 days in the environment under average weather conditions and from weeks to months under very cold conditions.
- Sulfur mustard breaks down slowly in the body, so repeated exposure may have a cumulative effect (that is, it can build up in the body).

How Sulfur Mustard Works
- Adverse health effects caused by sulfur mustard depend on the amount to which people are exposed, the route of exposure, and the length of exposure time.
- Sulfur mustard is a powerful irritant and blistering agent that damages the skin, eyes, and respiratory (breathing) tract.

- It damages DNA, a vital component of cells in the body.
- Sulfur mustard vapor is heavier than air, so it will settle in low-lying areas.

Immediate Signs and Symptoms of Sulfur Mustard Exposure
- Exposure to sulfur mustard is usually not fatal. When sulfur mustard was used during World War I, it killed fewer than 5 percent of the people who were exposed and got medical care.
- People may not know right away that they have been exposed because sulfur mustard often has no smell or has a smell that might not cause alarm.
- Typically, signs and symptoms do not occur immediately. Depending on the severity of the exposure, symptoms may not occur for 2 to 24 hours. Some people are more sensitive to sulfur mustard than are other people and may have symptoms sooner.
- Sulfur mustard can have the following effects on specific parts of the body:
  - Skin: Redness and itching of the skin may occur 2 to 48 hours after exposure and change eventually to yellow blistering of the skin.
  - Eyes: Irritation, pain, swelling, and tearing may occur within 3 to 12 hours of a mild to moderate exposure. A severe exposure may cause symptoms within 1 to 2 hours and may include the symptoms of a mild or moderate exposure plus light sensitivity, severe pain, or blindness (lasting up to 10 days).
  - Respiratory tract: Runny nose, sneezing, hoarseness, bloody nose, sinus pain, shortness of breath, and cough may occur within 12 to 24 hours of a mild exposure and within 2 to 4 hours of a severe exposure.
  - Digestive tract: Abdominal pain, diarrhea, fever, nausea, and vomiting may occur.
- Showing these signs and symptoms does not necessarily mean that a person has been exposed to sulfur mustard.

What the Long-Term Health Effects May Be
- Exposure to sulfur mustard liquid is more likely to produce second- and third-degree burns and later scarring than is exposure to sulfur mustard vapor. Extensive skin burning can be fatal.
- Extensive breathing in of the vapors can cause chronic respiratory disease, repeated respiratory infections, or death.

- Extensive eye exposure can cause permanent blindness.
- Exposure to sulfur mustard may increase a person's risk for lung and respiratory cancer.

How People Can Protect Themselves and What They Should Do if They Are Exposed to Sulfur Mustard

- Because no antidote exists for sulfur mustard exposure, the best thing to do is avoid it. Immediately leave the area where the sulfur mustard was released. Try to find higher ground, because sulfur mustard is heavier than air and will settle in low-lying areas.
- If avoiding sulfur mustard exposure is not possible, rapidly remove the sulfur mustard from the body. Getting the sulfur mustard off as soon as possible after exposure is the only effective way to prevent or decrease tissue damage to the body.
- Quickly remove any clothing that has liquid sulfur mustard on it. If possible, seal the clothing in a plastic bag, and then seal that bag inside a second plastic bag.
- Immediately wash any exposed part of the body (eyes, skin, etc.) thoroughly with plain, clean water. Eyes need to be flushed with water for 5 to 10 minutes. Do *not* cover eyes with bandages, but do protect them with dark glasses or goggles.
- If someone has ingested sulfur mustard, do *not* induce vomiting. Give the person milk to drink.
- Seek medical attention right away. Dial 911 and explain what has happened.

How Sulfur Mustard Exposure Is Treated

The most important factor is removing sulfur mustard from the body. Exposure to sulfur mustard is treated by giving the victim supportive medical care to minimize the effects of the exposure. Though no antidote exists for sulfur mustard, exposure is usually not fatal.

Where People Can Get More Information About Sulfur Mustard

For more information about sulfur mustard, people can contact the following:

- Regional poison control center: 1-800-222-1222
- Centers for Disease Control and Prevention
  - Public Response Hotline (CDC)
    - English: 888-246-2675
    - Español: 888-246-2857
    - TTY: 866-874-2646
  - Emergency Preparedness and Response web site
  - E-mail inquiries: cdcresponse@ashastd.org
  - Mail inquiries:
    Public Inquiry c/o BPRP
    Bioterrorism Preparedness and Response Planning
    Centers for Disease Control and Prevention
    Mailstop C-18
    1600 Clifton Road
    Atlanta, GA 30333
- Agency for Toxic Substances and Disease Registry (ATSDR): 1-888-422-8737
  - E-mail inquiries: atsdric@cdc.gov
  - Mail inquiries:
    Agency for Toxic Substances and Disease Registry
    Division of Toxicology
    1600 Clifton Road NE, Mailstop E-29
    Atlanta, GA 30333

Source: www.cdc.gov

FACTS ABOUT SARIN

What Sarin Is

- Sarin is a human-made chemical warfare agent classified as a nerve agent. Nerve agents are the most toxic and rapidly acting of the known chemical warfare agents. They are similar to certain kinds of pesticides (insect killers) called organophosphates in terms of how they work and what kind of harmful effects they cause. However, nerve agents are much more potent than organophosphate pesticides.
- Sarin originally was developed in 1938 in Germany as a pesticide.
- Sarin is a clear, colorless, and tasteless liquid that has no odor in its pure form. However, sarin can evaporate into a vapor (gas) and spread into the environment.
- Sarin is also known as GB.

Where Sarin Is Found and How It Is Used

- Sarin and other nerve agents may have been used in chemical warfare during the Iran–Iraq War in the 1980s.
- Sarin was used in two terrorist attacks in Japan in 1994 and 1995.
- Sarin is not found naturally in the environment.

How People Can Be Exposed to Sarin

- Following release of sarin into the air, people can be exposed through skin contact or eye contact. They can also be exposed by breathing air that contains sarin.
- Sarin mixes easily with water, so it could be used to poison water. Following release of sarin into water, people can be exposed by touching or drinking water that contains sarin.
- After contamination of food with sarin, people can be exposed by eating the contaminated food.
- A person's clothing can release sarin for about 30 minutes after it has come in contact with sarin vapor, which can lead to exposure of other people.
- Because sarin breaks down slowly in the body, people who are repeatedly exposed to sarin may suffer more harmful health effects.
- Because sarin vapor is heavier than air, it will sink to low-lying areas and create a greater exposure hazard there.

How Sarin Works

- The extent of poisoning caused by sarin depends on the amount of sarin to which a person was exposed, the way the person was exposed, and the length of time of the exposure.
- Symptoms will appear within a few seconds after exposure to the vapor form of sarin and within a few minutes up to 18 hours after exposure to the liquid form.
- All the nerve agents cause their toxic effects by preventing the proper operation of the chemical that acts as the body's "off switch" for glands and muscles. Without an "off switch," the glands and muscles are constantly being stimulated. They may tire and no longer be able to sustain breathing function.
- Sarin is the most volatile of the nerve agents, which means that it can easily and quickly evaporate from a liquid into a vapor and spread into the environment. People can be exposed to the vapor even if they do not come in contact with the liquid form of sarin.
- Because it evaporates so quickly, sarin presents an immediate but short-lived threat.

Immediate Signs and Symptoms of Sarin Exposure

- People may not know that they were exposed because sarin has no odor.
- People exposed to a low or moderate dose of sarin by breathing contaminated air, eating contaminated food, drinking contaminated water, or touching contaminated surfaces may experience some or all of the following symptoms within seconds to hours of exposure:
  – Runny nose
  – Watery eyes
  – Small, pinpoint pupils
  – Eye pain
  – Blurred vision
  – Drooling and excessive sweating
  – Cough
  – Chest tightness
  – Rapid breathing
  – Diarrhea
  – Increased urination
  – Confusion
  – Drowsiness
  – Weakness
  – Headache
  – Nausea, vomiting, and/or abdominal pain
  – Slow or fast heart rate
  – Low or high blood pressure

- Even a small drop of sarin on the skin can cause sweating and muscle twitching where sarin touched the skin.
- Exposure to large doses of sarin by any route may result in the following harmful health effects:
  - Loss of consciousness
  - Convulsions
  - Paralysis
  - Respiratory failure possibly leading to death
- Showing these signs and symptoms does not necessarily mean that a person has been exposed to sarin.

What the Long-Term Health Effects Are

Mild or moderately exposed people usually recover completely. Severely exposed people are not likely to survive. Unlike some organophosphate pesticides, nerve agents have not been associated with neurological problems lasting more than 1 to 2 weeks after the exposure.

How People Can Protect Themselves and What They Should Do if They Are Exposed to Sarin

- Recovery from sarin exposure is possible with treatment, but the antidotes available must be used quickly to be effective. Therefore, the best thing to do is avoid exposure:
  - Leave the area where the sarin was released and get to fresh air. Quickly moving to an area where fresh air is available is highly effective in reducing the possibility of death from exposure to sarin vapor.
    - If the sarin release was outdoors, move away from the area where the sarin was released. Go to the highest ground possible because sarin is heavier than air and will sink to low-lying areas.
    - If the sarin release was indoors, get out of the building.
- If people think they may have been exposed, they should remove their clothing, rapidly wash their entire body with soap and water, and get medical care as quickly as possible.
- Removing and disposing of clothing:
  - Quickly take off clothing that has liquid sarin on it. Any clothing that has to be pulled over the head should be cut off the body instead of pulled over the head. If possible, seal the clothing in a plastic bag. Then seal the first plastic bag in a second plastic bag. Removing and sealing the clothing in this way will help protect people from any chemicals that might be on their clothes.
  - If clothes were placed in plastic bags, inform either the local or state health department or emergency personnel upon their arrival. Do not handle the plastic bags.

- If helping other people remove their clothing, try to avoid touching any contaminated areas, and remove the clothing as quickly as possible.
- Washing the body:
  - As quickly as possible, wash any liquid sarin from the skin with large amounts of soap and water. Washing with soap and water will help protect people from any chemicals on their bodies.
  - Rinse the eyes with plain water for 10 to 15 minutes if they are burning or if vision is blurred.
- If sarin has been swallowed, do not induce vomiting or give fluids to drink.
- Seek medical attention immediately. Dial 911 and explain what has happened.

How Sarin Exposure Is Treated

Treatment consists of removing sarin from the body as soon as possible and providing supportive medical care in a hospital setting. Antidotes are available for sarin. They are most useful if given as soon as possible after exposure.

How People Can Get More Information About Sarin

People can contact one of the following:
- Regional poison control center: 1-800-222-1222
- Centers for Disease Control and Prevention
  - Public Response Hotline (CDC)
    - English: 1-888-246-2675
    - Español: 1-888-246-2857
    - TTY: 1-866-874-2646
  - Emergency Preparedness and Response web site: http://www.bt.cdc.gov/
  - E-mail inquiries: cdcresponse@ashastd.org
  - Mail inquiries:
    Public Inquiry c/o BPRP
    Bioterrorism Preparedness and Response Planning
    Centers for Disease Control and Prevention
    Mailstop C-18
    1600 Clifton Road
    Atlanta, GA 30333
- Agency for Toxic Substances and Disease Registry (ATSDR): 1-888-422-8737
  - E-mail inquiries: atsdric@cdc.gov
  - Mail inquiries:
    Agency for Toxic Substances and Disease Registry
    Division of Toxicology
    1600 Clifton Road NE, Mailstop E-29
    Atlanta, GA 30333

Source: www.cdc.gov

FREQUENTLY ASKED QUESTIONS (FAQ) ABOUT RICIN

What Is Ricin?
- Ricin is a poison that can be made from the waste left over from processing castor beans.
- It can be in the form of a powder, a mist, or a pellet, or it can be dissolved in water or weak acid.
- It is a stable substance. For example, it is not affected much by extreme conditions such as very hot or very cold temperatures.

Where Is Ricin Found, and How Is It Used?
- Castor beans are processed throughout the world to make castor oil. Ricin is part of the waste "mash" produced when castor oil is made. Amateurs can make ricin from castor beans.
- Ricin has some potential medical uses, such as in bone marrow transplants and cancer treatment (to kill cancer cells).

How Can People Be Exposed to Ricin?
- It would take a deliberate act to make ricin and use it to poison people. Accidental exposure to ricin is highly unlikely.
- People can breathe in ricin mist or powder and be poisoned.
- Ricin can also get into water or food and then be swallowed.
- Pellets of ricin, or ricin dissolved in a liquid, can be injected into people's bodies.
- Depending on the route of exposure (such as injection), as little as 500 micrograms of ricin could be enough to kill an adult. A 500-microgram dose of ricin would be about the size of the head of a pin. A much greater amount would be needed to kill people if the ricin were inhaled (breathed in) or swallowed.
- Ricin poisoning is not contagious. It cannot be spread from person to person through casual contact.
- In 1978 Georgi Markov, a Bulgarian writer and journalist who was living in London, died after he was attacked by a man with an umbrella. The umbrella had been rigged to inject a poison ricin pellet under Markov's skin.
- Some reports have indicated that ricin may have been used in the Iran–Iraq war during the 1980s and that quantities of ricin were found in al Qaeda caves in Afghanistan.

How Does Ricin Work?
- Ricin works by getting inside the cells of a person's body and preventing the cells from making the proteins they need. Without the proteins, cells die, and eventually the whole body can shut down and die.
- Specific effects of ricin poisoning depend on whether ricin was inhaled, swallowed, or injected.

What Are the Signs and Symptoms of Ricin Exposure?
- Inhalation: Within a few hours of inhaling significant amounts of ricin, the likely symptoms would be coughing, tightness in the chest, difficulty breathing, nausea, and aching muscles. Within the next few hours, the body's airways (such as the lungs) would become severely inflamed (swollen and hot), excess fluid would build up in the lungs, breathing would become even more difficult, and the skin might turn blue. Excess fluid in the lungs would be diagnosed by X-ray or by listening to the chest with a stethoscope.
- Ingestion: If someone swallows a significant amount of ricin, he or she would have internal bleeding of the stomach and intestines that would lead to vomiting and bloody diarrhea. Eventually, the person's liver, spleen, and kidneys might stop working, and the person could die.
- Injection: Injection of a lethal amount of ricin at first would cause the muscles and lymph nodes near the injection site to die. Eventually, the liver, kidneys, and spleen would stop working, and the person would have massive bleeding from the stomach and intestines. The person would die from multiple organ failure.
- Death from ricin poisoning could take place within 36 to 48 hours of exposure, whether by injection, ingestion, or inhalation. If the person lives longer than 5 days without complications, he or she will probably not die.
- Showing these signs and symptoms does not necessarily mean that a person has been exposed to ricin.

How Is Ricin Poisoning Treated?
- No antidote exists for ricin. Ricin poisoning is treated by giving the victim supportive medical care to minimize the effects of the poisoning. The types of supportive medical care would depend on several factors, such as the route by which the victim was poisoned (that is, by inhalation, ingestion, or injection). Care could include such measures as helping the victim breathe and giving him or her intravenous fluids and medications to treat swelling.

How Do We Know for Sure Whether People Have Been Exposed to Ricin?

- If we suspect that people have inhaled ricin, a possible clue would be that a large number of people who had been close to each other suddenly developed fever, cough, and excess fluid in their lungs. These symptoms could be followed by severe breathing problems and possibly death.
- No widely available, reliable test exists to confirm that a person has been exposed to ricin.

What Can People Do If They Think They May Have Been Exposed to Ricin?

Unintentional ricin poisoning is highly unlikely. CDC has no reports of intentional ricin poisoning. If people think they might have been exposed to ricin, however, they should contact the regional poison control center at 1-800-222-1222.

How Can People Get More Information About Ricin?

They can contact one of the following:

- Regional poison control center: 1-800-222-1222
- Centers for Disease Control and Prevention
  - Public response hotline (CDC)
    - English: 888-246-2675
    - Español: 888-246-2857
    - TTY: 866-874-2646
  - Emergency Preparedness and Response web site www.fema.gov
  - E-mail inquiries: cdcresponse@ashastd.org
  - Mail inquiries:
    Public Inquiry c/o BPRP
    Bioterrorism Preparedness and Response Planning
    Centers for Disease Control and Prevention
    Mailstop C-18
    1600 Clifton Road
    Atlanta, GA 30333
- Agency for Toxic Substances and Disease Registry (ATSDR): 1-888-422-8737
  - E-mail inquiries: atsdric@cdc.gov
  - Mail inquiries:
    Agency for Toxic Substances and Disease Registry
    Division of Toxicology
    1600 Clifton Road NE, Mailstop E-29
    Atlanta, GA 30333

Source: www.cdc.gov

FACTS ABOUT CHLORINE

What Chlorine Is
- Chlorine is an element used in industry and found in some household products.
- Chlorine is sometimes in the form of a poisonous gas. Chlorine gas can be pressurized and cooled to change it into a liquid so that it can be shipped and stored. When liquid chlorine is released, it quickly turns into a gas that stays close to the ground and spreads rapidly.
- Chlorine gas can be recognized by its pungent, irritating odor, which is like the odor of bleach. The strong smell may provide an adequate warning to people that they have been exposed.
- Chlorine gas appears to be yellow-green in color.
- Chlorine itself is not flammable, but it can react explosively or form explosive compounds with other chemicals such as turpentine and ammonia.

Where Chlorine Is Found and How It Is Used
- Chlorine was used during World War I as a choking (pulmonary) agent.
- Chlorine is one of the most commonly manufactured chemicals in the United States. Its most important use is as a bleach in the manufacture of paper and cloth, but it is also used to make pesticides (insect killers), rubber, and solvents.
- Chlorine is used in drinking water and swimming pool water to kill harmful bacteria. It is also used as part of the sanitation process for industrial waste and sewage.
- Household chlorine bleach can release chlorine gas if it is mixed with other cleaning agents.

How People Can Be Exposed to Chlorine
- People's risk for exposure depends on how close they are to the place where the chlorine was released.
- If chlorine gas is released into the air, people may be exposed through skin contact or eye contact. They may also be exposed by breathing air that contains chlorine.
- If chlorine liquid is released into water, people may be exposed by touching or drinking water that contains chlorine.
- If chlorine liquid comes into contact with food, people may be exposed by eating the contaminated food.
- Chlorine gas is heavier than air, so it would settle in low-lying areas.

How Chlorine Works
- The extent of poisoning caused by chlorine depends on the amount of chlorine a person is exposed to, how the person was exposed, and the length of time of the exposure.
- When chlorine gas comes into contact with moist tissues such as the eyes, throat, and lungs, an acid is produced that can damage these tissues.

Immediate Signs and Symptoms of Chlorine Exposure
- During or immediately after exposure to dangerous concentrations of chlorine, the following signs and symptoms may develop:
  - Coughing
  - Chest tightness
  - Burning sensation in the nose, throat, and eyes
  - Watery eyes
  - Blurred vision
  - Nausea and vomiting
  - Burning pain, redness, and blisters on the skin if exposed to gas; skin injury similar to frostbite if exposed to liquid chlorine
  - Difficulty breathing or shortness of breath (may appear immediately if high concentrations of chlorine gas are inhaled, or may be delayed if low concentrations of chlorine gas are inhaled)
  - Fluid in the lungs (pulmonary edema) within 2 to 4 hours
- Showing these signs or symptoms does not necessarily mean that a person has been exposed to chlorine.

What the Long-Term Health Effects Are
- Long-term complications from chlorine exposure are not found in people who survive a sudden exposure unless they suffer complications such as pneumonia during therapy. Chronic bronchitis may develop in people who develop pneumonia during therapy.

How People Can Protect Themselves and What They Should Do if They Are Exposed to Chlorine
- Leave the area where the chlorine was released and get to fresh air. Quickly moving to an area where fresh air is available is highly effective in reducing exposure to chlorine.
  - If the chlorine release was outdoors, move away from the area where the chlorine was released. Go

to the highest ground possible, because chlorine is heavier than air and will sink to low-lying areas.
- If the chlorine release was indoors, get out of the building.
- If you think you may have been exposed, remove your clothing, rapidly wash your entire body with soap and water, and get medical care as quickly as possible.
• Removing and disposing of clothing:
- Quickly take off clothing that has liquid chlorine on it. Any clothing that has to be pulled over the head should be cut off the body instead of pulled over the head. If possible, seal the clothing in a plastic bag. Then seal the first plastic bag in a second plastic bag. Removing and sealing the clothing in this way will help protect you and other people from any chemicals that might be on your clothes.
- If you placed your clothes in plastic bags, inform either the local or state health department or emergency personnel upon their arrival. Do not handle the plastic bags.
- If you are helping other people remove their clothing, try to avoid touching any contaminated areas, and remove the clothing as quickly as possible.
• Washing the body:
- As quickly as possible, wash your entire body with large amounts of soap and water. Washing with soap and water will help protect people from any chemicals on their bodies.
- If your eyes are burning or your vision is blurred, rinse your eyes with plain water for 10 to 15 minutes. If you wear contacts, remove them before rinsing your eyes, and place them in the bags with the contaminated clothing. Do not put the contacts back in your eyes. You should dispose of them even if you do not wear disposable contacts. If you wear eyeglasses, wash them with soap and water. You can put the eyeglasses back on after you wash them.
• If you have ingested (swallowed) chlorine, do not induce vomiting or drink fluids.

• Seek medical attention right away. Dial 911 and explain what has happened.

How Chlorine Exposure Is Treated
No antidote exists for chlorine exposure. Treatment consists of removing the chlorine from the body as soon as possible and providing supportive medical care in a hospital setting.

How People Can Get More Information About Chlorine
People can contact one of the following:
• Regional poison control center: 1-800-222-1222
• Centers for Disease Control and Prevention
- Public response hotline (CDC)
• English: 1-888-246-2675
• Español: 1-888-246-2857
• TTY: 1-866-874-2646
- Emergency Preparedness and Response web site. www.fema.gov
- E-mail inquiries: cdcresponse@ashastd.org
- Mail inquiries:
Public Inquiry c/o BPRP
Bioterrorism Preparedness and Response Planning
Centers for Disease Control and Prevention
Mailstop C-18
1600 Clifton Road
Atlanta, GA 30333
• Agency for Toxic Substances and Disease Registry (ATSDR): 1-888-422-8737
- E-mail inquiries: atsdric@cdc.gov
- Mail inquiries:
Agency for Toxic Substances and Disease Registry
Division of Toxicology
1600 Clifton Road NE, Mailstop E-29
Atlanta, GA 30333
- Centers for Disease Control and Prevention (CDC), National Institute for Occupational Safety and Health (NIOSH), Pocket Guide to Chemical Hazards.

Source: www.cdc.gov

BIOLOGICAL AGENTS

An interim planning guide for state and local government entitled "Managing the Emergency Consequences of Terrorist Incidents" was prepared by FEMA in July 2002 and states the following concerning biological agents:

Recognition of a biological hazard can occur through several methods, including identification of a credible threat, discovery of bioterrorism evidence (devices, agent, clandestine lab), diagnosis (identification of a disease caused by an agent identified as a possible bioterrorism agent), and detection (gathering and interpretation of public health surveillance data).

When people are exposed to a pathogen such as anthrax or smallpox, they may not know that they have been exposed, and those who are infected, or subsequently become infected, may not feel sick for some time. This delay between exposure and onset of illness, the incubation period, is characteristic of infectious diseases. The incubation period may range from several hours to a few weeks, depending on the exposure and pathogen. Unlike acute incidents involving explosives or some hazardous chemicals, the initial detection and response to a biological attack on civilians is likely to be made by direct patient care providers and the public health community.

Terrorists could also employ a biological agent that would affect agricultural commodities over a large area (e.g., wheat rust or a virus affecting livestock), potentially devastating the local or even national economy. The response to agricultural bioterrorism should also be considered during the planning process.

Responders should be familiar with the characteristics of the biological agents of greatest concern for use in a bioterrorism event. Unlike victims of exposure to chemical or radiological agents, victims of biological agent attack may serve as carriers of the disease with the capability of infecting others (e.g., smallpox, plague). (Source: FEMA 2002)

Some indicators of biological attack are as follows:

- Stated threat to release a biological agent
- Unusual occurrence of dead or dying animals
- Unusual casualties
  - Unusual illness for region/area
  - Definite pattern inconsistent with natural disease
- Unusual liquid, spray, vapor, or powder
  - Spraying, suspicious devices, packages, or letters

SIDEBAR 4-5 List of Biological Agents
Compiled by the Centers for Disease Control

- Anthrax (*Bacillus anthracis*)
- *Bacillus anthracis* (anthrax)
- Botulism (*Clostridium botulinum* toxin)
- *Brucella species* (brucellosis)
- Brucellosis (*Brucella* species)
- *Burkholderia mallei* (glanders)
- *Burkholderia pseudomallei* (melioidosis)
- *Chlamydia psittaci* (psittacosis)
- Cholera (*Vibrio cholerae*)
- *Clostridium botulinum toxin* (botulism)

- *Clostridium perfringens* (Epsilon toxin)
- *Coxiella burnetii* (Q fever)
- *E. coli* O157:H7 (*Escherichia coli*)
- Emerging infectious diseases such as Nipah virus and hantavirus
- Epsilon toxin of *Clostridium perfringens*
- *Escherichia coli* O157:H7 (E. coli)
- Food safety threats (e.g., Salmonella species, *Escherichia coli* O157:H7, *Shigella*)
- *Francisella tularensis* (tularemia)

(*Source*: Interim Planning Guide for State and Local Government: Managing the Emergency Consequences of Terrorist Incidents, FEMA, July 2002).

A list of biological agents compiled by the Centers for Disease Control (CDC) is presented in Sidebar 4-5.

Facts sheets compiled from the CDC web site for the following selected biological agents are presented in the following pages:

- Anthrax
- Smallpox
- Plague
- Salmonellosis
- Typhoid Fever
- Botulism
- Tularemia

- Glanders (*Burkholderia mallei*)
- Melioidosis (*Burkholderia pseudomallei*)
- Plague (*Yersinia pestis*)
- Psittacosis (*Chlamydia psittaci*)
- Q fever (*Coxiella burnetii*)
- Ricin toxin from *Ricinus communis* (castor beans)
- *Rickettsia prowazekii* (typhus fever)
- *Salmonella species* (salmonellosis)
- *Salmonella Typhi* (typhoid fever)
- Salmonellosis (Salmonella species)
- *Shigella* (shigellosis)
- Shigellosis (*Shigella*)
- Smallpox (variola major)
- Staphylococcal enterotoxin B
- Tularemia (*Francisella tularensis*)

- Typhoid fever (*Salmonella Typhi*)
- Typhus fever (*Rickettsia prowazekii*)
- *Variola major* (smallpox)
- *Vibrio cholerae* (cholera)
- Viral encephalitis (alphaviruses [e.g., Venezuelan equine encephalitis, eastern equine encephalitis, western equine encephalitis])
- Viral hemorrhagic fevers (filoviruses [e.g., Ebola, Marburg] and arenaviruses [e.g., Lassa, Machupo])
- Water safety threats (e.g., *Vibrio cholerae, Cryptosporidium parvum*)
- *Yersinia pestis* (plague).

Source: http://www.bt.cdc.gov/agent/agentlist.asp

ANTHRAX: WHAT YOU NEED TO KNOW

What Is Anthrax?

Anthrax is a serious disease caused by *Bacillus anthracis*, a bacterium that forms spores. A bacterium is a very small organism made up of one cell. Many bacteria can cause disease. A spore is a cell that is dormant (asleep) but may come to life with the right conditions.

There are three types of anthrax:

- Skin (cutaneous)
- Lungs (inhalation)
- Digestive (gastrointestinal)

How Do You Get It?

Anthrax is not known to spread from one person to another.

Humans can become infected with anthrax by handling products from infected animals or by breathing in anthrax spores from infected animal products (like wool, for example). People also can become infected with gastrointestinal anthrax by eating undercooked meat from infected animals.

Anthrax also can be used as a weapon. This happened in the United States in 2001. Anthrax was deliberately spread through the postal system by sending letters with powder containing anthrax. This caused 22 cases of anthrax infection.

How Dangerous Is Anthrax?

The Centers for Disease Control and Prevention classify agents with recognized bioterrorism potential into three priority areas (A, B, and C). Anthrax is classified a Category A agent. Category A agents are those that do the following:

- Pose the greatest possible threat for a bad effect on public health
- May spread across a large area or need public awareness
- Need a great deal of planning to protect the public's health.

In most cases, early treatment with antibiotics can cure cutaneous anthrax. Even if untreated, 80 percent of people who become infected with cutaneous anthrax do not die. Gastrointestinal anthrax is more serious because between one fourth and more than half of cases lead to death. Inhalation anthrax is much more severe. In 2001, about half of the cases of inhalation anthrax ended in death.

What Are the Symptoms?

The symptoms (warning signs) of anthrax are different depending on the type of the disease:

- Cutaneous: The first symptom is a small sore that develops into a blister. The blister then develops into a skin ulcer with a black area in the center. The sore, blister, and ulcer do not hurt.
- Gastrointestinal: The first symptoms are nausea, loss of appetite, bloody diarrhea, and fever, followed by severe stomach pain.
- Inhalation: The first symptoms of inhalation anthrax are like those associated with cold or flu and can include a sore throat, mild fever, and muscle aches. Later symptoms include cough, chest discomfort, shortness of breath, tiredness, and muscle aches. (Caution: Do not assume that just because a person has cold or flu symptoms that they have inhalation anthrax.)

How Soon Do Infected People Get Sick?

Symptoms can appear within 7 days of coming in contact with the bacterium for all three types of anthrax. For inhalation anthrax, symptoms can appear within a week or can take up to 42 days to appear.

How Is Anthrax Treated?

Antibiotics are used to treat all three types of anthrax. Early identification and treatment are important. Treatment is different for a person who is exposed to anthrax but is not yet sick. Health-care providers will use antibiotics (such as ciprofloxacin, doxycycline, or penicillin) combined with the anthrax vaccine to prevent anthrax infection.

Treatment after infection usually calls for a 60-day course of antibiotics. Success depends on the type of anthrax and how soon treatment begins.

Can Anthrax Be Prevented?

There is a vaccine to prevent anthrax, but it is not yet available for the general public. Anyone who may be exposed to anthrax, including certain members of the U.S. armed forces, laboratory workers, and workers who may enter or reenter contaminated areas, may get the vaccine. Also, in the event of an attack using anthrax as a weapon, people exposed would get the vaccine.

What Should I Do if I Think I Have Anthrax?

If you are showing symptoms of anthrax infection, call your health-care provider right away.

What Should I Do if I Think I Have Been Exposed to Anthrax?

Contact local law enforcement immediately if you think that you may have been exposed to anthrax. This includes being exposed to a suspicious package or envelope that contains powder.

What Is CDC Doing to Prepare for a Possible Anthrax Attack?

CDC is working with state and local health authorities to prepare for an anthrax attack. Activities include the following:

- Developing plans and procedures to respond to an attack using anthrax
- Training and equipping emergency response teams to help state and local governments control infection, gather samples, and perform tests; educating health-care providers, media, and the general public about what to do in the event of an attack
- Working closely with health departments, veterinarians, and laboratories to watch for suspected cases of anthrax; developing a national electronic database to track potential cases of anthrax
- Ensuring that there are enough safe laboratories for quick testing of suspected anthrax cases
- Working with hospitals, laboratories, emergency response teams, and health-care providers to make sure they have the supplies they need in case of an attack

Source: www.cdc.gov

SMALLPOX OVERVIEW

The Disease

Smallpox is a serious, contagious, and sometimes fatal infectious disease. There is no specific treatment for smallpox disease, and the only prevention is vaccination. The name *smallpox* is derived from the Latin word for "spotted" and refers to the raised bumps that appear on the face and body of an infected person.

There are two clinical forms of smallpox. *Variola major* is the severe and most common form of smallpox, with a more extensive rash and higher fever. There are four types of *variola major* smallpox: ordinary (the most frequent type, accounting for 90 percent or more of cases); modified (mild and occurring in previously vaccinated persons); flat; and hemorrhagic (both rare and very severe). Historically, *variola major* has an overall fatality rate of about 30 percent; however, flat and hemorrhagic smallpox usually are fatal. *Variola minor* is a less common presentation of smallpox and a much less severe disease, with death rates historically of 1 percent or less.

Smallpox outbreaks have occurred from time to time for thousands of years, but the disease is now eradicated after a successful worldwide vaccination program. The last case of smallpox in the United States was in 1949. The last naturally occurring case in the world was in Somalia in 1977. After the disease was eliminated from the world, routine vaccination against smallpox among the general public was stopped because it was no longer necessary for prevention.

Smallpox Disease

Incubation period (Duration: 7 to 17 days)	Exposure to the virus is followed by an incubation period during which people do not have any symptoms and may feel fine. This incubation period averages about 12 to 14 days but can range from 7 to 17 days.
Not contagious	During this time, people are not contagious.
Initial symptoms (prodrome) (Duration: 2 to 4 days) Sometimes contagious*	The first symptoms of smallpox include fever, malaise, head and body aches, and sometimes vomiting. The fever is usually high, in the range of 101 to 104 degrees Fahrenheit. At this time, people are usually too sick to carry on their normal activities. This is called the prodrome phase and may last for 2 to 4 days.
Early rash (Duration: about 4 days)	A rash emerges first as small red spots on the tongue and in the mouth.
Most contagious	These spots develop into sores that break open and spread large amounts of the virus into the mouth and throat. At this time, the person becomes most contagious.
Rash distribution: 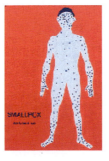	Around the time the sores in the mouth break down, a rash appears on the skin, starting on the face and spreading to the arms and legs and then to the hands and feet. Usually the rash spreads to all parts of the body within 24 hours. As the rash appears, the fever usually falls and the person may start to feel better.

View enlarged image.	By the third day of the rash, the rash becomes raised bumps.
	By the fourth day, the bumps fill with a thick, opaque fluid and often have a depression in the center that looks like a bellybutton. (This is a major distinguishing characteristic of smallpox.)
	Fever often will rise again at this time and remain high until scabs form over the bumps.
Pustular rash (Duration: about 5 days) Contagious	The bumps become pustules—sharply raised, usually round and firm to the touch as if there's a small round object under the skin. People often say the bumps feel like BB pellets embedded in the skin.
Pustules and scabs (Duration: about 5 days) Contagious	The pustules begin to form a crust and then scab. By the end of the second week after the rash appears, most of the sores have scabbed over.
Resolving scabs (Duration: about 6 days) Contagious	The scabs begin to fall off, leaving marks on the skin that eventually become pitted scars. Most scabs will have fallen off three weeks after the rash appears.
	The person is contagious to others until all of the scabs have fallen off.
Scabs resolved Not contagious	Scabs have fallen off. Person is no longer contagious.

* Smallpox may be contagious during the prodrome phase but is most infectious during the first 7 to 10 days after rash onset.

Where Smallpox Comes From

Smallpox is caused by the variola virus that emerged in human populations thousands of years ago. Except for laboratory stockpiles, the variola virus has been eliminated. However, in the aftermath of the events of September and October, 2001, there is heightened concern that the variola virus might be used as an agent of bioterrorism. For this reason, the U.S. government is taking precautions for dealing with a smallpox outbreak.

Transmission

Generally, direct and fairly prolonged face-to-face contact is required to spread smallpox from one person to another.

Smallpox also can be spread through direct contact with infected bodily fluids or contaminated objects such as bedding or clothing. Rarely, smallpox has been spread by virus carried in the air in enclosed settings such as buildings, buses, and trains. Humans are the only natural hosts of variola. Smallpox is not known to be transmitted by insects or animals.

A person with smallpox is sometimes contagious with onset of fever (prodrome phase), but the person becomes most contagious with the onset of rash. At this stage the infected person is usually very sick and not able to move around in the community. The infected person is contagious until the last smallpox scab falls off.

Source: www.cdc.gov

FREQUENTLY ASKED QUESTIONS (FAQ) ABOUT PLAGUE

What Is Plague?

Plague is a disease caused by *Yersinia pestis* (*Y. pestis*), a bacterium found in rodents and their fleas in many areas around the world.

Why Are We Concerned About Pneumonic Plague as a Bioweapon?

Yersinia pestis used in an aerosol attack could cause cases of the pneumonic form of plague. One to six days after becoming infected with the bacteria, people would develop pneumonic plague. Once people have the disease, the bacteria can spread to others who have close contact with them. Because of the delay between being exposed to the bacteria and becoming sick, people could travel over a large area before becoming contagious and possibly infecting others. Controlling the disease would then be more difficult. A bioweapon carrying *Y. pestis* is possible because the bacterium occurs in nature and could be isolated and grown in quantity in a laboratory. Even so, manufacturing an effective weapon using *Y. pestis* would require advanced knowledge and technology.

Is Pneumonic Plague Different from Bubonic Plague?

Yes. Both are caused by *Yersinia pestis*, but they are transmitted differently and their symptoms differ. Pneumonic plague can be transmitted from person to person; bubonic plague cannot. Pneumonic plague affects the lungs and is transmitted when a person breathes in *Y. pestis* particles in the air. Bubonic plague is transmitted through the bite of an infected flea or exposure to infected material through a break in the skin. Symptoms include swollen, tender lymph glands called *buboes*. Buboes are not present in pneumonic plague. If bubonic plague is not treated, however, the bacteria can spread through the bloodstream and infect the lungs, causing a secondary case of pneumonic plague.

What Are the Signs and Symptoms of Pneumonic Plague?

Patients usually have fever, weakness, and rapidly developing pneumonia with shortness of breath, chest pain, cough, and sometimes bloody or watery sputum. Nausea, vomiting, and abdominal pain may also occur. Without early treatment, pneumonic plague usually leads to respiratory failure, shock, and rapid death.

How Do People Become Infected with Pneumonic Plague?

Pneumonic plague occurs when *Yersinia pestis* infects the lungs. Transmission can take place if someone breathes in *Y. pestis* particles, which could happen in an aerosol release during a bioterrorism attack. Pneumonic plague is also transmitted by breathing in *Y. pestis* suspended in respiratory droplets from a person (or animal) with pneumonic plague. Respiratory droplets are spread most readily by coughing or sneezing. Becoming infected in this way usually requires direct and close (within 6 feet) contact with the ill person or animal. Pneumonic plague may also occur if a person with bubonic or septicemic plague is untreated and the bacteria spread to the lungs.

Does Plague Occur Naturally?

Yes. The World Health Organization reports 1,000 to 3,000 cases of plague worldwide every year. An average of 5 to 15 cases occur each year in the western United States. These cases are usually scattered and occur in rural to semirural areas. Most cases are of the bubonic form of the disease. Naturally occurring pneumonic plague is uncommon, although small outbreaks do occur. Both types of plague are readily controlled by standard public health response measures.

Can a Person Exposed to Pneumonic Plague Avoid Becoming Sick?

Yes. People who have had close contact with an infected person can greatly reduce the chance of becoming sick if they begin treatment within 7 days of their exposure. Treatment consists of taking antibiotics for at least 7 days.

How Quickly Would Someone Get Sick if Exposed to Plague Bacteria Through the Air?

Someone exposed to *Yersinia pestis* through the air—either from an intentional aerosol release or from close and direct exposure to someone with plague pneumonia—would become ill within 1 to 6 days.

Can Pneumonic Plague Be Treated?

Yes. To prevent a high risk of death, antibiotics should be given within 24 hours of the first symptoms. Several types of antibiotics are effective for curing the disease and for preventing it. Available oral medications are a tetracycline (such as doxycycline) or a fluoroquinolone (such as ciprofloxacin). For injection or intravenous use, streptomycin or gentamicin antibiotics are used. Early in the response to a bioterrorism attack, these drugs would be tested to determine which is most effective against the particular weapon that was used.

Would Enough Medication Be Available in the Event of a Bioterrorism Attack Involving Pneumonic Plague?

National and state public health officials have large supplies of drugs needed in the event of a bioterrorism attack. These supplies can be sent anywhere in the United States within 12 hours.

What Should People Do if They Suspect They or Others Have Been Exposed to Plague?

Get immediate medical attention: To prevent illness, a person who has been exposed to pneumonic plague must receive antibiotic treatment without delay. If an exposed person becomes ill, antibiotics must be administered within 24 hours of the first symptoms to reduce the risk of death. Notify authorities: Immediately notify local or state health departments so they can begin to investigate and control the problem right away. If bioterrorism is suspected, the health departments will notify the CDC, FBI, and other appropriate authorities.

How Can Someone Reduce the Risk of Getting Pneumonic Plague from Another Person or Giving It to Someone Else?

People having direct and close contact with someone with pneumonic plague should wear tightly fitting disposable surgical masks. Patients with the disease should be isolated and medically supervised for at least the first 48 hours of antibiotic treatment. People who have been exposed to a contagious person can be protected from developing plague by receiving prompt antibiotic treatment.

How Is Plague Diagnosed?

The first step is evaluation by a health worker. If the health worker suspects pneumonic plague, samples of the patient's blood, sputum, or lymph node aspirate are sent to a laboratory for testing. Once the laboratory receives the sample, preliminary results can be ready in less than two hours. Confirmation will take longer, usually 24 to 48 hours.

How Long Can Plague Bacteria Exist in the Environment?

Yersinia pestis is easily destroyed by sunlight and drying. Even so, when released into air, the bacterium will survive for up to one hour, depending on conditions.

Is a Vaccine Available to Prevent Pneumonic Plague?

Currently, no plague vaccine is available in the United States. Research is in progress, but we are not likely to have vaccines for several years or more.

Source: www.cdc.gov

SALMONELLOSIS

Frequently Asked Questions
- What is salmonellosis?
- What sort of germ is *Salmonella*?
- How can *Salmonella* infections be diagnosed?
- How can *Salmonella* infections be treated?
- Are there long-term consequences to a *Salmonella* infection?
- How do people catch *Salmonella*?
- What can a person do to prevent this illness?
- How common is salmonellosis?
- What else can be done to prevent salmonellosis?
- What is the government doing about salmonellosis?
- How can I learn more about this and other public health problems?
- What can I do to prevent salmonellosis?

What Is Salmonellosis?
Salmonellosis is an infection with a bacteria called *Salmonella*. Most persons infected with *Salmonella* develop diarrhea, fever, and abdominal cramps 12 to 72 hours after infection. The illness usually lasts 4 to 7 days, and most persons recover without treatment. However, in some persons the diarrhea may be so severe that the patient needs to be hospitalized. In these patients, the *Salmonella* infection may spread from the intestines to the blood stream and then to other body sites and can cause death unless the person is treated promptly with antibiotics. The elderly, infants, and those with impaired immune systems are more likely to have a severe illness.

What Sort of Germ Is Salmonella?
The *Salmonella* germ is actually a group of bacteria that can cause diarrheal illness in humans. They are microscopic living creatures that pass from the feces of people or animals to other people or other animals. There are many different kinds of *Salmonella* bacteria. Salmonella serotype Typhimurium and *Salmonella* serotype Enteritidis are the most common in the United States. Salmonella has been known to cause illness for over 100 years. They were discovered by a American scientist named Salmon, for whom they are named.

How Can Salmonella Infections Be Diagnosed?
Many different kinds of illnesses can cause diarrhea, fever, or abdominal cramps. Determining that *Salmonella* is the cause of the illness depends on laboratory tests that identify *Salmonella* in the stools of an infected person. These tests are sometimes not performed unless the laboratory is instructed specifically to look for the organism. Once *Salmonella* has been identified, further testing can determine its specific type, and which antibiotics could be used to treat it.

How Can Salmonella Infections Be Treated?
Salmonella infections usually resolve in 5 to 7 days and often do not require treatment unless the patient becomes severely dehydrated or the infection spreads from the intestines. Persons with severe diarrhea may require rehydration, often with intravenous fluids. Antibiotics are not usually necessary unless the infection spreads from the intestines, then it can be treated with ampicillin, gentamicin, trimethoprim/sulfamethoxazole, or ciprofloxacin. Unfortunately, some *Salmonella* bacteria have become resistant to antibiotics, largely as a result of the use of antibiotics to promote the growth of feed animals.

Are There Long-Term Consequences to a Salmonella Infection?
Persons with diarrhea usually recover completely, although it may be several months before their bowel habits are entirely normal. A small number of persons who are infected with *Salmonella*, will go on to develop pains in their joints, irritation of the eyes, and painful urination. This is called *Reiter's syndrome*. It can last for months or years, and can lead to chronic arthritis, which is difficult to treat. Antibiotic treatment does not affect whether the person later develops arthritis.

How Do People Catch Salmonella?
Salmonella live in the intestinal tracts of humans and other animals, including birds. *Salmonella* are usually transmitted to humans by eating foods contaminated with animal feces. Contaminated foods usually look and smell normal. Contaminated foods are often of animal origin, such as beef, poultry, milk, or eggs, but all foods, including vegetables, may become contaminated. Many raw foods of animal origin are frequently contaminated, but, fortunately, thorough cooking kills *Salmonella*. Food may also become contaminated by the unwashed hands of an infected food handler who forgot to wash his or her hands with soap after using the bathroom.

Salmonella may also be found in the feces of some pets, especially those with diarrhea, and people can become infected if they do not wash their hands after contact with these feces. Reptiles are particularly likely to harbor *Salmonella,* and people should always wash their hands immediately after handling a reptile, even if the reptile is healthy. Adults should also be careful that children wash their hands after handling a reptile.

What Can a Person Do to Prevent This Illness?
There is no vaccine to prevent salmonellosis. Since foods of animal origin may be contaminated with *Salmonella,* people should not eat raw or undercooked eggs, poultry, or meat. Raw eggs may be unrecognized in some foods, such as homemade hollandaise sauce, Caesar and other salad dressings, tiramisu, homemade ice cream, homemade mayonnaise, cookie dough, and frostings. Poultry and meat, including hamburgers, should be well-cooked, not pink in the middle. Persons also should not consume raw or unpasteurized milk or other dairy products. Produce should be thoroughly washed before consuming.

Cross-contamination of foods should be avoided. Uncooked meats should be kept separate from produce, cooked foods, and ready-to-eat foods. Hands, cutting boards, counters, knives, and other utensils should be washed thoroughly after handling uncooked foods. Hands should be washed before handling any food, and between handling different food items.

People who have salmonellosis should not prepare food or pour water for others until they have been shown to no longer be carrying the *Salmonella* bacterium.

People should wash their hands after contact with animal feces. Since reptiles are particularly likely to have *Salmonella,* everyone should immediately wash his or her hands after handling reptiles. Reptiles (including turtles) are not appropriate pets for small children and should not be in the same house as an infant.

How Common Is Salmonellosis?
Every year, approximately 40,000 cases of salmonellosis are reported in the United States. Because many milder cases are not diagnosed or reported, the actual number of infections may be thirty or more times greater. Salmonellosis is more common in the summer than winter. Children are the most likely to get salmonellosis. Young children, the elderly, and the immunocompromised are the most likely to have severe infections. It is estimated that approximately 600 persons die each year with acute salmonellosis.

What Else Can Be Done to Prevent Salmonellosis?
It is important for the public health department to know about cases of salmonellosis. It is important for clinical laboratories to send isolates of *Salmonella* to the city, country, or state public health laboratories so the specific

type can be determined and compared with other *Salmonella* cases in the community. If many cases occur at the same time, it may mean that a restaurant, food, or water supply has a problem which needs correction by the public health department.

Some prevention steps occur everyday without your even thinking about it. Pasteurization of milk and treating municipal water supplies are highly effective prevention measures that have been in place for many years. In the 1970s, small pet turtles were a common source of salmonellosis in the United States, and in 1975 the sale of small turtles was halted in this country. Improvements in farm animal hygiene, in slaughter plant practices, and in vegetable and fruit harvesting and packing operations may help prevent salmonellosis caused by contaminated foods. Better education of food industry workers in basic food safety and restaurant inspection procedures may prevent cross-contamination and other food-handling errors that can lead to outbreaks. Wider use of pasteurized egg in restaurants, hospitals, and nursing homes is an important prevention measure. In the future, irradiation or other treatments may greatly reduce contamination of raw meat.

What Is the Government Doing About Salmonellosis?
The Centers for Disease Control and Prevention (CDC) monitors the frequency of *Salmonella* infections in the country and assists the local and state health departments to investigate outbreaks and devise control measures. CDC also conducts research to better identify specific types of *Salmonella.* The Food and Drug Administration inspects imported foods and milk pasteurization plants, promotes better food preparation techniques in restaurants and food processing plants, and regulates the sale of turtles. The FDA also regulates the use of specific antibiotics as growth promotants in food animals. The U.S. Department of Agriculture monitors the health of food animals, inspects egg pasteurization plants, and is responsible for the quality of slaughtered and processed meat. The U.S. Environmental Protection Agency regulates and monitors the safety of our drinking water supplies.

How Can I Learn More About This and Other Public Health Problems?
You can discuss any medical concerns you may have with your doctor or other heath-care provider. Your local city or country health department can provide more information about this and other public health problems that are occurring in your area. General information about the public health of the nation is published every

week in the "Morbidity and Mortality Weekly Report," by the CDC in Atlanta, Georgia. Epidemiologists in your local and state health departments are tracking a number of important public health problems, investigating special problems that arise, and helping to prevent them from occurring in the first place or from spreading if they do occur.

What Can I Do to Prevent Salmonellosis?
- Cook poultry, ground beef, and eggs thoroughly before eating.
- Do not eat or drink foods containing raw eggs or raw unpasteurized milk.
- If you are served undercooked meat, poultry, or eggs in a restaurant, don't hesitate to send it back to the kitchen for further cooking.

- Wash hands, kitchen work surfaces, and utensils with soap and water immediately after they have been in contact with raw meat or poultry.
- Be particularly careful with foods prepared for infants, the elderly, and the immunocompromised.
- Wash hands with soap after handling reptiles or birds, or after contact with pet feces.
- Avoid direct or even indirect contact between reptiles (turtles, iguanas, other lizards, snakes) and infants or immunocompromised persons.
- Don't work with raw poultry or meat and an infant (e.g., feed, change diaper) at the same time.
- Mother's milk is the safest food for young infants. Breast-feeding prevents salmonellosis and many other health problems.

Source: www.cdc.gov

TYPHOID FEVER

For the most current updates about typhoid fever, please visit CDC Travelers' Health at http:// www.cdc.gov/travel/ diseases/ typhoid/htm

Frequently Asked Questions
- How is typhoid fever spread?
- Where in the world do you get typhoid fever?
- How can you avoid typhoid fever?
- Boil it, cook it, peel it, or forget it
- Getting vaccinated
- What are the signs and symptoms of typhoid fever?
- What do you do if you think you have typhoid fever?
- Typhoid fever's danger doesn't end when symptoms disappear

Typhoid fever is a life-threatening illness caused by the bacterium *Salmonella typhi*. In the United States about 400 cases occur each year, and 70 percent of these are acquired while traveling internationally. Typhoid fever is still common in the developing world, where it affects about 12.5 million persons each year.

Typhoid fever can be prevented and can usually be treated with antibiotics. If you are planning to travel outside the United States, you should know about typhoid fever and what steps you can take to protect yourself.

How Is Typhoid Fever Spread?
Salmonella Typhi lives only in humans. Persons with typhoid fever carry the bacteria in their bloodstream and intestinal tract. In addition, a small number of persons, called *carriers*, recover from typhoid fever but continue to carry the bacteria. Both ill persons and carriers shed *S. typhi* in their feces (stool).

You can get typhoid fever if you eat food or drink beverages that have been handled by a person who is shedding *S. typhi* or if sewage contaminated with *S. typhi* bacteria gets into the water you use for drinking or washing food. Therefore, typhoid fever is more common in areas of the world where handwashing is less frequent and water is likely to be contaminated with sewage.

Once *S. typhi* bacteria are eaten or drunk, they multiply and spread into the bloodstream. The body reacts with fever and other signs and symptoms.

Where in the World Do You Get Typhoid Fever?
Typhoid fever is common in most parts of the world except in industrialized regions such as the United States, Canada, western Europe, Australia, and Japan. Therefore, if you are traveling to the developing world, you should consider taking precautions. Over the past 10 years, travelers from the United States to Asia, Africa, and Latin America have been especially at risk.

How Can You Avoid Typhoid Fever?
Two basic actions can protect you from typhoid fever:

1. Avoid risky foods and drinks.
2. Get vaccinated against typhoid fever.

It may surprise you, but watching what you eat and drink when you travel is as important as being vaccinated. This is because the vaccines are not completely effective. Avoiding risky foods will also help protect you from other illnesses, including travelers' diarrhea, cholera, dysentery, and hepatitis A.

"Boil It, Cook It, Peel It, or Forget It"
- If you drink water, buy it bottled or bring it to a rolling boil for 1 minute before you drink it. Bottled carbonated water is safer than uncarbonated water.
- Ask for drinks without ice unless the ice is made from bottled or boiled water. Avoid popsicles and flavored ices that may have been made with contaminated water.
- Eat foods that have been thoroughly cooked and that are still hot and steaming.
- Avoid raw vegetables and fruits that cannot be peeled. Vegetables such as lettuce are easily contaminated and are very hard to wash well.
- When you eat raw fruit or vegetables that can be peeled, peel them yourself. (Wash your hands with soap first.) Do not eat the peelings.
- Avoid foods and beverages from street vendors. It is difficult for food to be kept clean on the street, and many travelers get sick from food bought from street vendors.

Getting Vaccinated
If you are traveling to a country where typhoid is common, you should consider being vaccinated against typhoid. Visit a doctor or travel clinic to discuss your

Vaccine name	How given	Number of doses necessary	Time between doses vaccination	Total time needed to set aside for	Minimum age for vaccination	Booster needed every
Ty21a (Vivotif Berna, Swiss Serum and Vaccine Institute)	1 capsule by mouth	4	2 days	2 weeks	6 years	5 years
ViCPS (Typhim Vi, Pasteur Merieux)	Injection	1	N/A	1 week	2 years	2 years

The parenteral heat-phenol-inactivated vaccine (manufactured by Wyeth-Ayerst) has been discontinued.

vaccination options. Remember that you will need to complete your vaccination at least 1 week before you travel so that the vaccine has time to take effect. Typhoid vaccines lose effectiveness after several years; if you were vaccinated in the past, check with your doctor to see if it is time for a booster vaccination. Taking antibiotics will not prevent typhoid fever; antibiotics only help treat it. The chart above provides basic information on typhoid vaccines that are available in the United States.

What Are the Signs and Symptoms of Typhoid Fever?
Persons with typhoid fever usually have a sustained fever as high as 103° to 104° F (39° to 40° C). They may also feel weak or have stomach pains, headache, or loss of appetite. In some cases, patients have a rash of flat, rose-colored spots. The only way to know for sure if an illness is typhoid fever is to have samples of stool or blood tested for the presence of S. typhi.

What Do You Do if You Think You Have Typhoid Fever?
If you suspect you have typhoid fever, see a doctor immediately. If you are traveling in a foreign country, you can usually call the U.S. consulate for a list of recommended doctors. You will probably be given an antibiotic to treat the disease. Three commonly prescribed

antibiotics are ampicillin, trimethoprim-sulfamethoxazole, and ciprofloxacin. Persons given antibiotics usually begin to feel better within 2 to 3 days, and deaths rarely occur. However, persons who do not get treatment may continue to have fever for weeks or months, and as many as 20 percent may die from complications of the infection.

Typhoid Fever's Danger Doesn't End When Symptoms Disappear
Even if your symptoms seem to go away, you may still be carrying S. typhi. If so, the illness could return, or you could pass the disease to other people. In fact, if you work at a job where you handle food or care for small children, you may be barred legally from going back to work until a doctor has determined that you no longer carry any typhoid bacteria.

If you are being treated for typhoid fever, it is important to do the following:

- Keep taking the prescribed antibiotics for as long as the doctor has asked you to take them.
- Wash your hands carefully with soap and water after using the bathroom, and do not prepare or serve food for other people. This will lower the chance that you will pass the infection on to someone else.
- Have your doctor perform a series of stool cultures to ensure that no S. typhi bacteria remain in your body.

Source: www.cdc.gov

BOTULISM

What Is Botulism?

Botulism is a rare but serious paralytic illness caused by a nerve toxin that is produced by the bacterium *Clostridium botulinum*. There are three main kinds of botulism. Foodborne botulism is caused by eating foods that contain the botulism toxin. Wound botulism is caused by toxin produced from a wound infected with *Clostridium botulinum*. Infant botulism is caused by consuming the spores of the botulinum bacteria, which then grow in the intestines and release toxin. All forms of botulism can be fatal and are considered medical emergencies. Foodborne botulism can be especially dangerous because many people can be poisoned by eating a contaminated food.

What Kind of Germ Is *Clostridium botulinum*?

Clostridium botulinum is the name of a group of bacteria commonly found in soil. These rod-shaped organisms grow best in low oxygen conditions. The bacteria form spores that allow them to survive in a dormant state until exposed to conditions that can support their growth. There are seven types of botulism toxin designated by the letters A through G; only types A, B, E, and F cause illness in humans.

How Common Is Botulism?

In the United States an average of 110 cases of botulism are reported each year. Of these, approximately 25 percent are foodborne, 72 percent are infant botulism, and the rest are wound botulism. Outbreaks of foodborne botulism involving two or more persons occur most years and usually are caused by eating contaminated home-canned foods. The number of cases of foodborne and infant botulism has changed little in recent years, but wound botulism has increased because of the use of black-tar heroin, especially in California.

What Are the Symptoms of Botulism?

The classic symptoms of botulism include double vision, blurred vision, drooping eyelids, slurred speech, difficulty swallowing, dry mouth, and muscle weakness. Infants with botulism appear lethargic, feed poorly, are constipated, and have a weak cry and poor muscle tone. These are all symptoms of the muscle paralysis caused by the bacterial toxin. If untreated, these symptoms may progress to cause paralysis of the arms, legs, trunk, and respiratory muscles. In foodborne botulism, symptoms generally begin 18 to 36 hours after eating a contaminated food, but they can occur as early as 6 hours or as late as 10 days.

How Is Botulism Diagnosed?

Physicians may consider the diagnosis if the patient's history and physical examination suggest botulism. However, these clues are usually not enough to allow a diagnosis of botulism. Other diseases, such as Guillain-Barré syndrome, stroke, and myasthenia gravis, can appear similar to botulism, and special tests may be needed to exclude these other conditions. These tests may include a brain scan, spinal fluid examination, nerve conduction test (electromyography, or EMG), and a tensilon test for myasthenia gravis. The most direct way to confirm the diagnosis is to demonstrate the *botulinum* toxin in the patient's serum or stool by injecting serum or stool into mice and looking for signs of botulism. The bacteria can also be isolated from the stool of persons with foodborne and infant botulism. These tests can be performed at some state health department laboratories and at CDC.

How Can Botulism Be Treated?

The respiratory failure and paralysis that occur with severe botulism may require a patient to be on a breathing machine (ventilator) for weeks, plus intensive medical and nursing care. After several weeks, the paralysis slowly improves. If diagnosed early, foodborne and wound botulism can be treated with an antitoxin that blocks the action of toxin circulating in the blood. This can prevent patients from worsening, but recovery still takes many weeks. Physicians may try to remove contaminated food still in the gut by inducing vomiting or by using enemas. Wounds should be treated, usually surgically, to remove the source of the toxin-producing bacteria. Good supportive care in a hospital is the mainstay of therapy for all forms of botulism. Currently, antitoxin is not routinely given for treatment of infant botulism.

Are There Complications from Botulism?
Botulism can result in death due to respiratory failure. However, in the past 50 years the proportion of patients with botulism who die has fallen from about 50 percent to 8 percent. A patient with severe botulism may require a breathing machine as well as intensive medical and nursing care for several months. Patients who survive an episode of botulism poisoning may have fatigue and shortness of breath for years and long-term therapy may be needed to aid recovery.

How Can Botulism Be Prevented?
Botulism can be prevented. Foodborne botulism has often been from home-canned foods with low acid content, such as asparagus, green beans, beets, and corn. However, outbreaks of botulism have also been linked to more unusual sources, such as chopped garlic in oil, chile peppers, tomatoes, improperly handled baked potatoes wrapped in aluminum foil, and home-canned or fermented fish. Persons who do home canning should follow strict hygienic procedures to reduce contamination of foods. Oils infused with garlic or herbs should be refrigerated. Potatoes that have been baked while wrapped in aluminum foil should be kept hot until served or refrigerated. Because the botulism toxin is destroyed by high temperatures, persons who eat home-canned foods should consider boiling the food for 10 minutes before eating it to ensure safety. Instructions on safe home canning can be obtained from country extension services or from the U.S. Department of Agriculture. Because honey can contain spores of *Clostridium botulinum* and this has been a source of infection for infants, children younger than 12 months of age should not be fed honey. Honey is safe for persons 1 year of age and older. Wound botulism can be prevented by promptly seeking medical care for infected wounds and by not using injectable street drugs.

What Are Public Health Agencies Doing to Prevent or Control Botulism?
Public education about botulism prevention is an ongoing activity. Information about safe canning is widely available for consumers. State health departments and CDC offices have persons knowledgeable about botulism available to consult with physicians 24 hours a day. If antitoxin is needed to treat a patient, it can be quickly delivered to a physician anywhere in the country. Suspected outbreaks of botulism are quickly investigated, and if they involve a commercial product, the appropriate control measures are coordinated among public health and regulatory agencies. Physicians should report suspected cases of botulism to a state health department.

Source: www.cdc.gov

FREQUENTLY ASKED QUESTIONS ABOUT TULAREMIA

What Is Tularemia?

Tularemia is an infectious disease caused by a hardy bacterium, *Francisella tularensis*, found in animals (especially rodents, rabbits, and hares).

How Do People Become Infected with the Tularemia Bacteria?

Typically, persons become infected through the bites of arthropods (most commonly, ticks and deerflies) that have fed on an infected animal, by handling infected animal carcasses, by eating or drinking contaminated food or water, or by inhaling infected aerosols.

Does Tularemia Occur Naturally in the United States?

Yes. It is a widespread disease of animals. Approximately 200 cases of tularemia in humans are reported annually in the United States, mostly in persons living in the south-central and western states. Nearly all cases occur in rural areas and are associated with the bites of infective ticks and biting flies or with the handling of infected rodents, rabbits, or hares. Occasional cases result from inhaling infectious aerosols and from laboratory accidents.

Why Are We Concerned About Tularemia as a Bioweapon?

Francisella tularensis is highly infectious: A small number of bacteria (10 to 50 organisms) can cause disease. If *F. tularensis* were used as a bioweapon, the bacteria would likely be made airborne for exposure by inhalation. Persons who inhale an infectious aerosol would generally experience severe respiratory illness, including life-threatening pneumonia and systemic infection, if they were not treated. The bacteria that cause tularemia occur widely in nature and could be isolated and grown in quantity in a laboratory, although manufacturing an effective aerosol weapon would require considerable sophistication.

Can Someone Become Infected with the Tularemia Bacteria from Another Person?

No. People have not been known to transmit the infection to others, so infected persons do not need to be isolated.

How Quickly Would Someone Become Sick if Exposed to the Tularemia Bacteria?

The incubation period for tularemia is typically 3 to 5 days, with a range of 1 to 14 days.

What Are the Signs and Symptoms of Tularemia?

Depending on the route of exposure, the tularemia bacteria may cause skin ulcers, swollen and painful lymph glands, inflamed eyes, sore throat, oral ulcers, or pneumonia. If the bacteria were inhaled, symptoms would include the abrupt onset of fever, chills, headache, muscle aches, joint pain, dry cough, and progressive weakness. Persons with pneumonia can develop chest pain, difficulty breathing, bloody sputum, and respiratory failure. Forty percent or more of persons with the lung and systemic forms of the disease may die if they are not treated with appropriate antibiotics.

What Should Someone Do if They Suspect They or Others Have Been Exposed to the Tularemia Bacteria?

Seek prompt medical attention. If a person has been exposed to *Francisella tularensis*, treatment with tetracycline antibiotics for 14 days after exposure may be recommended.

Local and state health departments should be immediately notified so an investigation and control activities can begin quickly. If the exposure is thought to be due to criminal activity (bioterrorism), local and state health departments will notify CDC, the FBI, and other appropriate authorities.

How Is Tularemia Diagnosed?

When tularemia is clinically suspected, the health-care worker will collect specimens, such as blood or sputum, from the patient for testing in a diagnostic or reference laboratory. Laboratory test results for tularemia may be presumptive or confirmatory.

Presumptive (preliminary) identification may take less than 2 hours, but confirmatory testing will take longer, usually 24 to 48 hours.

Can Tularemia Be Effectively Treated with Antibiotics?

Yes. After potential exposure or diagnosis, early treatment is recommended with an antibiotic from the tetracycline (such as doxycycline) or fluoroquinolone (such as ciprofloxacin) class, which are taken orally, or the antibiotics streptomycin or gentamicin, which are given intramuscularly or intravenously. Sensitivity testing of the tularemia bacterium can be done in the early stages of a response to determine which antibiotics would be most effective.

How Long Can *Francisella tularensis* Exist in the Environment?

Francisella tularensis can remain alive for weeks in water and soil.

Is There a Vaccine Available for Tularemia?

In the past, a vaccine for tularemia has been used to protect laboratory workers, but it is currently under review by the Food and Drug Administration.

Source: www.cdc.gov

CHEMICAL AGENTS: FACTS ABOUT EVACUATION

Some kinds of chemical accidents or attacks may make staying put dangerous. In such cases, it may be safer for you to evacuate, or leave the immediate area. You may need to go to an emergency shelter after you leave the immediate area.

How to Know if You Need to Evacuate

You will hear from the local police, emergency coordinators, or government on the radio and/or television if you need to evacuate.

If there is a "code red" or "severe" terror alert, you should pay attention to radio and/or television broadcasts so you will know right away if an evacuation order is made for your area.

What to Do

Act quickly and follow the instructions of local emergency coordinators. Every situation is different, so local coordinators may give you special instructions to follow for a particular situation.

Local emergency coordinators may direct people to evacuate homes or offices and go to an emergency shelter. If so, emergency coordinators will tell you how to get to the shelter. If you have children in school, they may be sheltered at the school. You should not try to get to the school if the children are being sheltered there.

The emergency shelter will have most supplies that people need. The emergency coordinators will tell you which supplies to bring with you. Be sure to bring any medications you are taking.

If you have time, call a friend or relative in another state to tell them where you are going and that you are safe. Local telephone lines may be jammed in an emergency, so you should plan ahead to have an out-of-state contact with whom to leave messages. If you do not have private transportation, make plans in advance of an emergency to identify people who can give you a ride.

Evacuating and sheltering in this way should keep you safer than if you stayed at home or at your workplace. You will most likely not be in the shelter for more than a few hours. Emergency coordinators will let you know when it is safe to leave the shelter.

How You Can Get More Information About Evacuation

You can contact one of the following:

- State and local health departments
- Centers for Disease Control and Prevention
    - Public response hotline (CDC)
        - English: 1-888-246-2675
        - Español: 1-888-246-2857
        - TTY: 1-866-874-2646
    - Emergency Preparedness and Response web site
    - E-mail inquiries: cdcresponse@ashastd.org
    - Mail inquiries:
      Public Inquiry c/o BPRP
      Bioterrorism Preparedness and
      Response Planning
      Centers for Disease Control and Prevention
      Mailstop C-18
      1600 Clifton Road
      Atlanta, GA 30333

Source: www.cdc.gov

NUCLEAR TERRORISM AND HEALTH EFFECTS

Q: Is the United States in danger of a terrorist nuclear attack? Is the Centers for Disease Control and Prevention (CDC) prepared to respond to such an attack?

A: CDC is not able to assess the level of threat of a terrorist nuclear attack. However, for many years CDC has participated regularly in emergency-response drills where we have worked closely with other federal, state, and local agencies to develop, test, and implement extensive national radiological emergency-response plans.

Q: What are the potential adverse health consequences from a terrorist nuclear attack?

A: The adverse health consequences of a terrorist nuclear attack vary according to the type of attack and the distance a person is from the attack. Potential terrorist attacks may include a small radioactive source with a limited range of impact or a nuclear detonation involving a wide area of impact.

In the event of a terrorist nuclear attack, people may experience two types of exposure from radioactive materials: external exposure and internal exposure. External exposure occurs when a person comes in contact with radioactive material outside the body. Internal exposure occurs when people eat food or breathe air that is contaminated with radioactive material. Exposure to very large doses of external radiation may cause death within a few days or months. External exposure to lower doses of radiation and internal exposure from breathing or eating radioactive contaminated material may lead to an increased risk of developing cancer and other adverse health effects. These adverse effects range from mild, such as skin reddening, to severe effects, such as cancer and death, depending on the amount of radiation absorbed by the body (the dose), the type of radiation, the route of exposure, and the length of time of the exposure.

If there is a nuclear detonation, bodily injury or death may occur as a result of the blast itself or as a result of debris thrown from the blast. People may experience moderate to severe skin burns, depending on their distance from the blast site. Those who look directly at the blast could experience eye damage ranging from temporary blindness to severe retinal burns.

Q: How can I protect my family and myself from a terrorist nuclear attack?

A: In the event of a terrorist nuclear attack, a national emergency-response plan would be activated and would include federal, state, and local agencies. You should seek shelter in a stable building and listen to local radio or television stations for national emergency-alert information. Your local emergency-response organizations, police agencies, and public health facilities may be able to supply you with additional information. You should follow the protective-action recommendations that are made by your state or local health department in accordance with this plan. As a general rule, you can reduce the potential exposure and subsequent health consequences by limiting your time near the radiation source, increasing your distance from the source, or keeping a physical barrier (such as the wall of a building) between you and the source. You can find out your state radiation control director by contacting the Conference of Radiation Control Program Directors (CRCPD) at (502) 227-4543 or you may visit the CRCPD web site.

Q: What should I do if there is a terrorist attack on a nuclear power plant near my home?

A: A terrorist attack on a nuclear power plant will initiate a national emergency response that has been carefully planned and rehearsed by local, state, and federal agencies for more than 20 years. If you live near a nuclear power plant and you have not received information that describes the emergency plan for that facility, you can contact the plant and ask for a copy of that information. Your local emergency-response organizations, police agencies, and public health facilities have been actively involved in this emergency plan, and they may be able to supply you with additional information. You and your family should study these plans and be prepared to follow the instructions that local and state public health officials provide in the event of a terrorist incident involving the nuclear power plant near your home.

Q: Where can I go to find more information about radiation health effects and emergency response?

- The Environmental Protection Agency counterterrorism programs www.epa.gov
- The Federal Emergency Management Agency (FEMA) can be reached at 1-202-646-4600
- The Radiation Emergency Assistance Center/Training Site (REAC/TS) can be reached at 1-865-576-3131
- The U.S. National Response Team
- The U.S. Department of Energy (DOE) can be reached at 1-800-dial-DOE.

Source: www.cdc.gov

NUCLEAR/RADIOLOGICAL

An interim planning guide for state and local government entitled "Managing the Emergency Consequences of Terrorist Incidents" was prepared by FEMA in July 2002 and states the following concerning nuclear/radiological hazards:

> The difficulty of responding to a nuclear or radiological incident is compounded by the nature of radiation itself. In an explosion, the fact that radioactive material was involved may or may not be obvious, depending upon the nature of the explosive device used. The presence of a radiation hazard is difficult to ascertain, unless the responders have the proper detection equipment and have been trained to use it properly. Although many detection devices exist, most are designed to detect specific types and levels of radiation and may not be appropriate for measuring or ruling out the presence of radiological hazards. [Sidebar 4–6 lists some indicators of a radiological release.]

The scenarios constituting an intentional nuclear/radiological emergency include the following:

1. Use of an improvised nuclear device (IND) includes any explosive device designed to cause a nuclear yield. Depending on the type of trigger device used, either uranium or plutonium isotopes can fuel these devices. While "weapons-grade" material increases the efficiency of a given device, materials of less than weapons grade can still be used.
2. Use of a radiological dispersal device (RDD) includes any explosive device utilized to spread radioactive material upon detonation. Any improvised explosive device could be used by placing it in close proximity to radioactive material.
3. Use of a simple RDD that spreads radiological material without the use of an explosive. Any nuclear material (including medical isotopes or waste) can be used in this manner.

(*Source*: FEMA 2002) (Sidebar 4-7)

A fact sheet developed by the Centers for Disease Control (CDC) on a radiation event is presented in the following pages:

SIDEBAR 4-7 General Indicators of Possible Nuclear Weapon/Radiological Agent Use

- Stated threat to deploy a nuclear or radiological device
- Presence of nuclear or radiological equipment
  - Spent fuel canisters or nuclear transport vehicles
  - Nuclear placards/warning materials along with otherwise unexplained casualties.

Source: Interim Planning Guide for State and Local Government: Managing the Emergency Consequences of Terrorist Incidents, FEMA, July 2002

FREQUENTLY ASKED QUESTIONS (FAQS) ABOUT A RADIATION EMERGENCY

What Is Radiation?
- Radiation is a form of energy that is present all around us.
- Different types of radiation exist, some of which have more energy than others.
- Amounts of radiation released into the environment are measured in units called curies. However, the dose of radiation that a person receives is measured in units called rem.

For more information about radiation, check the following web sites: www.epa.gov/radiation, www. orau.gov/reacts/define.htm

How Can Exposure Occur?
- People are exposed to small amounts of radiation every day, both from naturally occurring sources (such as elements in the soil or cosmic rays from the sun), and man-made sources. Man-made sources include some electronic equipment (such as microwave ovens and television sets), medical sources (such as X-rays, certain diagnostic tests and treatments), and from nuclear weapons testing.
- The amount of radiation from natural or man-made sources to which people are exposed is usually small; a radiation emergency (such as a nuclear power plant accident or a terrorist event) could expose people to small or large doses of radiation, depending on the situation.
- Scientists estimate that the average person in the United States receives a dose of about one third of a rem per year. About 80 percent of human exposure comes from natural sources, and the remaining 20 percent comes from man-made radiation sources—mainly medical X-rays.
- Internal exposure refers to radioactive material that is taken into the body through breathing, eating, or drinking.
- External exposure refers to an exposure to a radioactive source outside of our bodies.
- Contamination refers to particles of radioactive material that are deposited anywhere that they are not supposed to be, such as on an object or on a person's skin.

For more information about radiation, check the following web sites: www.epa.gov/radiation, www. orau.gov/reacts/define.htm

What Happens When People Are Exposed to Radiation?
- Radiation can affect the body in a number of ways, and the adverse health effects of exposure may not be apparent for many years.
- These adverse health effects can range from mild effects, such as skin reddening, to serious effects such as cancer and death, depending on the amount of radiation absorbed by the body (the dose), the type of radiation, the route of exposure, and the length of time a person was exposed.
- Exposure to very large doses of radiation may cause death within a few days or months.
- Exposure to lower doses of radiation may lead to an increased risk of developing cancer or other adverse health effects later in life.

For more information about health effects from radiation exposure, check the following web sites:

- www.epa.gov/radiation
- www.orau.gov/reacts/injury.htm
- www.bt.cdc.gov/radiation/healthfacts.asp

What Types of Terrorist Events Might Involve Radiation?

- Possible terrorist events could involve introducing radioactive material into the food or water supply, using explosives (such as dynamite) to scatter radioactive materials (called a "dirty bomb"), bombing or destroying a nuclear facility, or exploding a small nuclear device.
- Although introducing radioactive material into the food or water supply most likely would cause great concern or fear, it probably would not cause much contamination or increase the danger of adverse health effects.
- Although a dirty bomb could cause serious injuries from the explosion, it most likely would not have enough radioactive material in a form that would cause serious radiation sickness among large numbers of people. However, people who were exposed to radiation scattered by the bomb could have a greater risk of developing cancer later in life, depending on their dose.
- A meltdown or explosion at a nuclear facility could cause a large amount of radioactive material to be

127

released. People at the facility would probably be contaminated with radioactive material and possibly be injured if there was an explosion. Those people who received a large dose might develop acute radiation syndrome. People in the surrounding area could be exposed or contaminated.

- Clearly, an exploded nuclear device could result in a lot of property damage. People would be killed or injured from the blast and might be contaminated by radioactive material. Many people could have symptoms of acute radiation syndrome. After a nuclear explosion, radioactive fallout would extend over a large region far from the point of impact, potentially increasing people's risk of developing cancer over time.

For more information about radiation terrorist events, check the following web sites:

- www.bt.cdc.gov/radiation/terrorismqa.asp
- www.orau.gov/reacts
- www.nrt.org
- www.energy.gov
- www.nrc.gov
- www.epa.gov

What Preparations Can I Make for a Radiation Emergency?

- Your community should have a plan in place in case of a radiation emergency. Check with community leaders to learn more about the plan and possible evacuation routes.
- Check with your child's school, the nursing home of a family member, and your employer to see what their plans are for dealing with a radiation emergency.
- Develop your own family emergency plan so that every family member knows what to do.
- At home, put together an emergency kit that would be appropriate for any emergency. The kit should include the following items:
  - A flashlight with extra batteries
  - A portable radio with extra batteries
  - Bottled water
  - Canned and packaged food
  - A hand-operated can opener
  - A first-aid kit and essential prescription medications
  - Personal items such as paper towels, garbage bags, and toilet paper.

For more information about preparing for a radiation emergency event, check the following web sites:

- www.fema.gov
- www.redcross.org/services/disaster/beprepared/

- www.epa.gov/swercepp/
- www.ojp.usdoj.gov/bja

How Can I Protect Myself During a Radiation Emergency?

- After a release of radioactive materials, local authorities will monitor the levels of radiation and determine what protective actions to take.
- The most appropriate action will depend on the situation. Tune to the local emergency response network or news station for information and instructions during any emergency.
- If a radiation emergency involves the release of large amounts of radioactive materials, you may be advised to "shelter in place," which means to stay in your home or office; or you may be advised to move to another location.
- If you are advised to shelter in place, you should do the following:
  - Close and lock all doors and windows.
  - Turn off fans, air conditioners, and forced-air heating units that bring in fresh air from the outside. Only use units to recirculate air that is already in the building.
  - Close fireplace dampers.
  - If possible, bring pets inside.
  - Move to an inner room or basement.
  - Keep your radio tuned to the emergency response network or local news to find out what else you need to do.
- If you are advised to evacuate, follow the directions that your local officials provide. Leave the area as quickly and orderly as possible. In addition:
  - Take a flashlight, portable radio, batteries, first-aid kit, supply of sealed food and water, hand-operated can opener, essential medicines, and cash and credit cards.
  - Take pets only if you are using your own vehicle and going to a place you know will accept animals. Emergency vehicles and shelters usually will not accept animals.

For more information about emergency response, check the following web sites:

- www.fema.gov
- www.redcross.org/services/disaster/beprepared/
- www.epa.gov/swercepp/
- www.ojp.usdoj.gov/bja

Should I Take Potassium Iodide During a Radiation Emergency?

- Potassium iodide (KI) should only be taken in a radiation emergency that involves the release of radioactive iodine, such as an accident at a nuclear power plant or the explosion of a nuclear bomb. A "dirty bomb" most likely will not contain radioactive iodine.
- A person who is internally exposed to radioactive iodine may experience thyroid disease later in life. The thyroid gland will absorb radioactive iodine and may develop cancer or abnormal growths later on. KI will saturate the thyroid gland with iodine, decreasing the amount of harmful radioactive iodine that can be absorbed.
- KI only protects the thyroid gland and does not provide protection from any other radiation exposure.
- Some people are allergic to iodine and should not take KI. Check with your doctor about any concerns you have about potassium iodide.

For more information about KI, check the following web sites:

- www.bt.cdc.gov/radiation/ki.asp
- www.fda.gov/cder/drugprepare/KI_Q&A.htm
- www.fda.gov/cder/guidance/4825fnl.htm

Source: www.cdc.gov

PREPAREDNESS AND RESPONSE FOR BIOTERROR OR CHEMICAL ATTACK

What Should I Do to Be Prepared?
We continue to hear stories of the public buying gas masks and hoarding medicine in anticipation of a possible bioterrorist or chemical attack. We do not recommend either. As Secretary Thompson said recently, people should not be scared into thinking they need a gas mask. In the event of a public health emergency, local and state health departments will inform the public about the actions individuals need to take.

Does Every City Have an Adequate Emergency Response System, Especially One Geared for a Bioterrorist Attack? How Quickly Can it Be Implemented?
The emergency response system varies from community to community on the basis of each community's investment in its public health infrastructure. Some components of these emergency systems can be implemented very quickly, while others may take longer.

Are Hospitals Prepared to Handle a Sudden Surge in Demand for Health Care?
The preparedness level in hospitals depends on the biological agent used in an attack. Because a sudden surge in demand could overwhelm an individual hospital's resources, hospitals collaborate with other hospitals in their area in order to respond to a bioterrorist attack on a citywide or regional basis. Hospitals are required to maintain disaster response plans and to practice applying them as part of their accreditation process. Many components of such plans are useful in responding to bioterrorism. Specific plans for bioterrorism have been added to the latest accreditation requirements of the Joint Commission on Accreditation of Healthcare Organizations. In an emergency, local medical care capacity will be supplemented with federal resources.

Are Health Department Labs Equipped for/Capable of Doing Testing?
CDC, the Association of Public Health Laboratories, and other officials are working together to ensure that all state health departments are capable of obtaining results of tests on suspected infectious agents. The nation's laboratories are generally classified as Level A, B, C, or D. Level A

laboratories are those typically found in community hospitals and are designated to perform initial testing on all clinical specimens. Public health laboratories are usually Level B; these laboratories can confirm or refute preliminary test results and can usually perform antimicrobial susceptibility tests. Level C laboratories, which are reference facilities and can be public health laboratories, perform more rapid identification tests. Level D laboratories are designed to perform the most sophisticated tests and are located in federal facilities such as CDC. CDC is currently working with public and private laboratory partners to develop a formal national laboratory system linking all four levels.

Every state has a Laboratory Response Network (LRN) contact. The LRN links state and local public health laboratories with advanced-capacity laboratories, including clinical, military, veterinary, agricultural, water, and food-testing laboratories. Laboratorians should contact their state public health laboratory to identify their local LRN representative.

Water Safety
With all this talk about possible biochemical agents, just how safe is our water? Should I be disinfecting my water just in case?

The United States public water supply system is one of the safest in the world. The general public should continue to drink and use water just as they would under normal conditions. Your local water treatment supplier and local governments are on the alert for any unusual activity and will notify you immediately in the event of any public health threat. At this point, we have no reason to believe that additional measures need to be taken.

The U.S. Environmental Protection Agency (EPA) is the lead federal agency that makes recommendations about water utility issues. The EPA is working closely with the CDC and the U.S. Departments of Defense and Energy to help water agencies assess their systems, determine actions that need to be taken to guard against possible attack, and develop emergency response plans. For more information, visit http://www.epa.gov/ safewater.

Source: www.cdc.gov

CHEMICAL AGENTS: FACTS ABOUT SHELTERING IN PLACE

What "Sheltering in Place" Means

Some kinds of chemical accidents or attacks may make going outdoors dangerous. Leaving the area might take too long or put you in harm's way. In such a case it may be safer for you to stay indoors than to go outside.

"Shelter in place" means to make a shelter out of the place you are in. It is a way for you to make the building as safe as possible to protect yourself until help arrives. You should not try to shelter in a vehicle unless you have no other choice. Vehicles are not airtight enough to give you adequate protection from chemicals.

How to Prepare to Shelter in Place

Choose a room in your house or apartment for your shelter. The best room to use for the shelter is a room with as few windows and doors as possible. A large room, preferably with a water supply, is desirable—something like a master bedroom that is connected to a bathroom. For chemical events, this room should be as high in the structure as possible to avoid vapors (gases) that sink. This guideline is different from the sheltering-in-place technique used in tornadoes and other severe weather, when the shelter should be low in the home. You might not be at home if the need to shelter in place ever arises, but if you are at home, the following items would be good to have on hand. (Ideally, all of these items would be stored in the shelter room to save time.)

- First aid kit
- Food and bottled water. Store 1 gallon of water per person in plastic bottles as well as ready-to-eat foods that will keep without refrigeration at the shelter-in-place location. If you do not have bottled water, or if you run out, you can drink water from a toilet tank (not from a toilet bowl).
- Flashlight, battery-powered radio, and extra batteries for both
- Duct tape and scissors
- Towels and plastic sheeting
- A working telephone

How to Know if You Need to Shelter in Place

- You will hear from the local police, emergency coordinators, or government officials on the radio and on television if you need to shelter in place.
- If there is a "code red" or "severe" terror alert, you should pay attention to radio and television broadcasts

to know right away whether a shelter-in-place alert is announced for your area.

- If you are away from your shelter-in-place location when a chemical event occurs, follow the instructions of emergency coordinators to find the nearest shelter. If your children are at school, they will be sheltered there. Unless you are instructed to do so, do not try to get to the school to bring your children home.

What to Do

Act quickly and follow the instructions of your local emergency coordinators. Every situation can be different, so local emergency coordinators might have special instructions for you to follow. In general, do the following:

- Go inside as quickly as possible.
- If there is time, shut and lock all outside doors and windows. Locking them may provide a tighter seal against the chemical. Turn off the air conditioner or heater. Turn off all fans, too. Close the fireplace damper and any other place that air can come in from the outside.
- Go in the shelter-in-place room, and shut the door.
- Tape plastic over any windows in the room. Use duct tape around the windows and doors and make an unbroken seal. Use the tape over any vents into the room and seal any electrical outlets or other openings. Sink and toilet drain traps should have water in them (you can use the sink and toilet as you normally would). If it is necessary to drink water, drink the stored water, not water from the tap.
- Turn on the radio. Keep a telephone close at hand, but don't use it unless there is a serious emergency.

Sheltering in this way should keep you safer than if you are outdoors. Most likely, you will be in the shelter for no more than a few hours. Listen to the radio for an announcement indicating that it is safe to leave the shelter. After you come out of the shelter, emergency coordinators may have additional instructions on how to make the rest of the building safe again.

How You Can Get More Information About Sheltering in Place

You can contact one of the following:

- State and local health departments

- Centers for Disease Control and Prevention Public Response Hotline (CDC)
  - Public response hotline (CDC)
    - English: 1-888-246-2675
    - Español: 1-888-246-2857
    - TTY: 1-866-874-2646
  - Emergency Preparedness and Response web site
  - E-mail inquiries: cdcresponse@ashastd.org
    - Mail inquiries:
    Public Inquiry c/o BPRP
    Bioterrorism Preparedness and Response Planning
    Centers for Disease Control and Prevention
    Mailstop C-18
    1600 Clifton Road
    Atlanta, GA 30333

Source: www.cdc.gov

COMBINED HAZARDS

An interim planning guide for state and local government entitled "Managing the Emergency Consequences of Terrorist Incidents" was prepared by FEMA in July 2002 and states the following concerning combined hazards:

> WMD agents can be combined to achieve a synergistic effect—greater in total effect than the sum of their individual effects. They may be combined to achieve both immediate and delayed consequences. Mixed infections or toxic exposures may occur, thereby complicating or delaying diagnosis. Casualties of multiple agents may exist; casualties may also suffer from multiple effects, such as trauma and burns from an explosion, which exacerbate the likelihood of agent contamination. Attacks may be planned and executed so as to take advantage of the reduced effectiveness of protective measures produced by employment of an initial WMD agent. Finally, the potential exists for multiple incidents in single or multiple municipalities. (Source: FEMA 2002)

One example of a combined hazard is a dirty bomb. Presented in Sidebar 4-8 is information compiled by the Centers for Disease Control (CDC) on dirty bombs.

ROLE OF CDC IN PREPAREDNESS AND RESPONSE

The Centers for Disease and Control (CDC) have become full partners in the nation's emergency management system. With the advent of the new hazards, the CDC has assumed a significant role in defining the characteristics of these hazards and how they may be used as terrorist weapons. This information is critical in preparing first responders, community leaders, business people and individuals to deal with these hazards. This data is also useful in the design and development of protective gear and clothing, mitigation and prevention measures, and response and clean-up protocols and practices.

CDC has developed two fact sheets on preparedness and response and the CDC's role in the event of a radiological event that are presented in Sidebars 4-9 and 4-10.

CONCLUSION

The new hazards of terrorism will require a significant investment in education of the general public, local officials, the media, and our first responders. This will be equaled by the need to invest in training, protective equipment and gear, specialized technical capabilities, and enhancements of our public health networks. The new hazards represent an opportunity to begin to integrate those responsible for mitigating, preparing, responding to, and recovering from any disaster. It is an opportunity to include public health concerns into our disaster planning and to incorporate the private sector, who are prominent players because these new hazards affect financial and communications infrastructures. The R&D efforts connected with these new hazards will surely result in advances across a broad spectrum of human activities from medicine to communications technology to safer fabrics. Most important, these new hazards, and the financial resources connected with addressing them, can provide an opportunity to actually embrace and apply an all-hazards approach to achieving a secure and safe homeland.

FACTS ABOUT DIRTY BOMBS

Because of recent terrorist events, people have expressed concern about the possibility of a terrorist attack involving radioactive materials, possibly through the use of a "dirty bomb" and the harmful effects of radiation from such an event. The Centers for Disease Control and Prevention have prepared this fact sheet to help people understand what a dirty bomb is and how it may affect their health.

What a "Dirty Bomb" Is

A dirty bomb, or radiological dispersion device, is a bomb that combines conventional explosives, such as dynamite, with radioactive materials in the form of powder or pellets. The idea behind a dirty bomb is to blast radioactive material into the area around the explosion. This could possibly cause buildings and people to be exposed to radioactive material. The main purpose of a dirty bomb is to frighten people and make buildings or land unusable for a long period of time.

Dirty Bomb versus Atomic Bombs in Hiroshima and Nagasaki

The atomic explosions that occurred in Hiroshima and Nagasaki were conventional nuclear weapons involving a fission reaction. A dirty bomb is designed to spread radioactive material and contaminate a small area. It does not include the fission products necessary to create a large blast like those seen in Hiroshima and Nagasaki.

Sources of the Radioactive Material

There has been a lot of speculation about where terrorists could get radioactive material to place in a dirty bomb. The most harmful radioactive materials are found in nuclear power plants and nuclear weapons sites. However, increased security at these facilities makes obtaining materials from them more difficult.

Because of the dangerous and difficult aspects of obtaining high-level radioactive materials from a nuclear facility, there is a greater chance that the radioactive materials used in a dirty bomb would come from low-level radioactive sources. Low-level radioactive sources are found in hospitals, on construction sites, and at food irradiation plants. The sources in these areas are used to diagnose and treat illnesses, sterilize equipment, inspect welding seams, and irradiate food to kill harmful microbes.

Dangers of a Dirty Bomb

If low-level radioactive sources were to be used, the primary danger from a dirty bomb would be the blast itself. Gauging how much radiation might be present is difficult when the source of the radiation is unknown. However, at the levels created by most probable sources, not enough radiation would be present in a dirty bomb to cause severe illness from exposure to radiation.

Past Use of Dirty Bombs

According to a United Nations report, Iraq tested a dirty bomb device in 1987 but found that the radiation levels were too low to cause significant damage. Thus, Iraq abandoned any further use of the device.

What People Should Do After an Explosion

Radiation cannot be seen, smelled, felt, or tasted by humans. Therefore, if people are present at the scene of an explosion, they will not know whether radioactive materials were involved at the time of the explosion. If people are not too severely injured by the initial blast, they should attempt the following:

- Leave the immediate area on foot. Do not panic. Do not take public or private transportation such as buses, subways, or cars because if radioactive materials were involved, they may contaminate cars or the public transportation system.
- Go inside the nearest building. Staying inside will reduce your exposure to any radioactive material that may be on dust at the scene.
- Remove your clothes as soon as possible, place them in a plastic bag, and seal it. Removing clothing will remove most of the contamination caused by external exposure to radioactive materials. Saving the contaminated clothing would allow testing for exposure without invasive sampling.
- Take a shower or wash yourself as best you can. Washing will reduce the amount of radioactive contamination on your body and will effectively reduce total exposure.
- Be on the lookout for information. Once emergency personnel can assess the scene and the damage, they will be able to tell people whether radiation was involved.

Even if people do not know whether radioactive materials were present, following these simple steps can help reduce their injury from other chemicals that might have been present in the blast.

Taking Potassium Iodide (KI)

Potassium iodide, also called KI, only protects a person's thyroid gland from exposure to radioactive iodine. KI will not protect a person from other radioactive materials or protect other parts of the body from exposure to radiation. It must be taken prior to exposure (for example, if people hear that a radioactive cloud is coming their way) or immediately after exposure to be effective. Since there is no way to know at the time of an incident whether radioactive iodine was used in the explosive device, taking KI would probably not be beneficial. Also, KI can be dangerous to some people. Taking KI is not recommended unless there is a risk of exposure to radioactive iodine.

If Radioactive Materials Were Involved

Keep televisions or radios tuned to local news networks. If a radioactive material is released, people will be told where to report for radiation monitoring and blood tests to determine whether they were exposed to the radiation as well as what steps to take to protect their health.

Risk of Cancer from a Dirty Bomb

Some cancers can be caused by exposure to radiation. Being at the site where a dirty bomb exploded does not guarantee that people were exposed to the radioactive material. Until doctors are able to check people's skin with sensitive radiation detection devices, it will not be clear whether they were exposed. Just because people are near a radioactive source for a short time or get a small amount of radioactive material on them does not mean that they will get cancer. Doctors will be able to assess risks after the exposure level has been determined.

More Information

For more information about medical response to detonation of a dirty bomb, see the following: *Medical Treatment of Radiological Casualties* (http://www.va.gov/emshg/docs/Radiologic_Medical_Cou ntermeasures_051403.pdf).

For more information about radiation and emergency response, see the Centers for Disease Control and Prevention's web site at http://www.bt.cdc.gov or contact the following organizations:

- The CDC Public Response Source at 1-888-246-2675
- The Conference of Radiation Control Program Directors at 502-227-4543
- The Environmental Protection Agency www. EPA.gov
- The Nuclear Regulatory Commission at 301-415-8200
- The Federal Emergency Management Agency (FEMA) at 202-646-4600.
- The Radiation Emergency Assistance Center/ Training Site at 865-576-3131
- The U.S. National Response Team
- The U.S. Department of Energy (DOE) at 1-800-dial-DOE

Source: CDC, www.cdc.gov

PREPAREDNESS AND RESPONSE

What Should I Do to Be Prepared?

We continue to hear stories of the public buying gas masks and hoarding medicine in anticipation of a possible bioterrorism or chemical attack. We do not recommend either. As Secretary Thompson said recently, people should not be scared into thinking they need a gas mask. In the event of a public health emergency, local and state health departments will inform the public about the actions individuals need to take.

Does Every City Have an Adequate Emergency Response System, Especially One Geared for a Bioterrorist Attack? How Quickly Can It Be Implemented?

The emergency response system varies from community to community on the basis of each community's investment in its public health infrastructure. Some components of these emergency systems can be implemented very quickly, while others may take longer.

Are Hospitals Prepared to Handle a Sudden Surge in Demand for Health Care?

The preparedness level in hospitals depends on the biological agent used in an attack. Because a sudden surge in demand could overwhelm an individual hospital's resources, hospitals collaborate with other hospitals in their area in order to respond to a bioterrorist attack on a citywide or regional basis. Hospitals are required to maintain disaster response plans and to practice applying them as part of their accreditation process. Many components of such plans are useful in responding to bioterrorism. Specific plans for bioterrorism have been added to the latest accreditation requirements of the Joint Commission on Accreditation of Healthcare Organizations. In an emergency, local medical care capacity will be supplemented with federal resources.

Are Health Department Labs Equipped/Capable of Doing Testing?

CDC, the Association of Public Health Laboratories, and other officials are working together to ensure that all state health departments are capable of obtaining results of tests on suspected infectious agents. The nation's laboratories are generally classified as Level A, B, C, or D.

Level A laboratories are those typically found in community hospitals and are designated to perform initial testing on all clinical specimens. Public health laboratories are usually Level B; these laboratories can confirm or refute preliminary test results and can usually perform antimicrobial susceptibility tests. Level C laboratories, which are reference facilities and can be public health laboratories, perform more rapid identification tests. Level D laboratories are designed to perform the most sophisticated tests and are located in federal facilities such as CDC. CDC is currently working with public and private laboratory partners to develop a formal National Laboratory System linking all four levels.

Every state has a Laboratory Response Network (LRN) contact. The LRN links state and local public health laboratories with advanced-capacity laboratories, including clinical, military, veterinary, agricultural, water, and food-testing laboratories. Laboratorians should contact their state public health laboratory to identify their local LRN representative.

With All This Talk About Possible Biochemical Agents, Just How Safe Is Our Water? Should I Be Disinfecting My Water Just in Case?

The United States public water supply system is one of the safest in the world. The general public should continue to drink and use water just as they would under normal conditions. Your local water treatment supplier and local governments are on the alert for any unusual activity and will notify you immediately in the event of any public health threat. At this point, we have no reason to believe that additional measures need to be taken.

The U.S. Environmental Protection Agency (EPA) is the lead federal agency that makes recommendations about water utility issues. The EPA is working closely with the CDC and the U.S. Departments of Defense and Energy to help water agencies assess their systems, determine actions that need to be taken to guard against possible attack, and develop emergency response plans. For more information, visit http://www.epa.gov/safewater.

Source: CDC, www.cdc.gov

CDC'S ROLES IN THE EVENT OF A RADIOLOGICAL TERRORIST EVENT

Last Updated: December 20, 2002

Because of recent terrorist events, people may be concerned about the possibility of a terrorist attack involving radioactive materials. People may wonder what the Centers for Disease Control and Prevention (CDC) would do to protect people's health if such an event were to occur. CDC has prepared this fact sheet to help people understand the roles and responsibilities of CDC during such an incident. (Source: CDC, www.cdc.gov.)

Lead Federal Agencies

In the event of a radiological accident or terrorist attack, the agency that is responsible for the site of the incident also has responsibility for responding to the emergency and protecting the people, property, and environment around the area. For example, if the incident occurs on property owned by the federal government, such as a military base, research facility, or nuclear facility, then the federal government takes responsibility. In areas that are not controlled by the federal government, the state and local governments have the responsibility to respond to the emergency and protect people, property, and the environment.

Regardless of whether the state, local, or federal government is responsible for responding to the emergency, a federal agency would be sent to the terrorist incident site and would act as the lead federal agency (LFA). This agency would work with the state and local government and might be the Nuclear Regulatory Commission (NRC), the Federal Bureau of Investigation (FBI), or another agency, depending on what type of incident occurred (accidental or intentional release of radioactive materials) and where it occurred (nuclear power plant versus a spilled radioactive material in an urban or suburban area). The LFA would implement the Federal Radiological Emergency Response Plan (FRERP); within this plan, the Department of Health and Human Services (HHS) has the major role in protecting people's health through the following measures:

- Monitoring, assessing, and following up on people's health
- Ensuring the safety of workers involved in and responding to the incident
- Ensuring that the food supply is safe
- Providing medical and public health advice

CDC's Roles

As part of HHS, CDC would be the chief public health entity to respond to a radiological incident, whether accidental or intentional. As the chief public health entity, CDC's specific roles and responsibilities would include the following:

- Assessing the health of people affected by the incident
- Assessing the medical effects of radiological exposures on people in the community, emergency responders and other workers, and high-risk populations (such as children, pregnant women, and those with immune deficiencies)
- Advising state and local health departments on how to protect people, animals, and food and water supplies from contamination by radioactive materials
- Providing technical assistance and consultation to state and local health departments on medical treatment, follow-up, and decontamination of victims exposed to radioactive materials
- Establishing and maintaining a registry of people exposed to or contaminated by radioactive materials

CDC's Partners

To carry out its roles, CDC would work with many other agencies to ensure that people's health is protected. These agencies may include the following:

- State and local health departments
- Department of Defense (DoD)
- Department of Energy (DOE)
- Department of Transportation (DOT)
- HHS
  - Food and Drug Administration (FDA)
  - Agency for Toxic Substances and Disease Registry (ATSDR)
  - Office of Emergency Response (OER)
  - Health Resources and Services Administration (HRSA)
  - Substance Abuse and Mental Health Services Administration (SAMHSA)
- Environmental Protection Agency (EPA)
- FBI
- Federal Emergency Management Agency (FEMA)
- NRC
- Department of Agriculture (USDA)

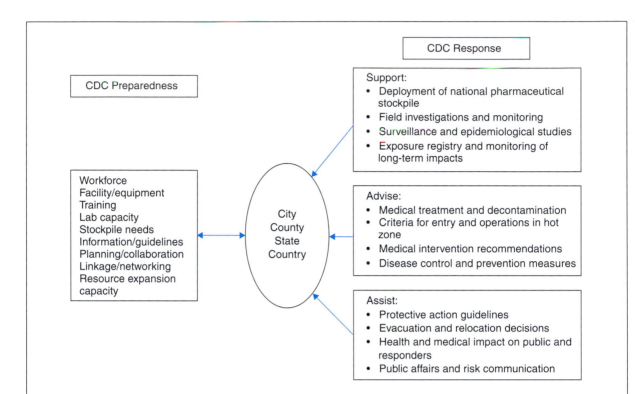

CDC Preparedness

Workforce
Facility/equipment
Training
Lab capacity
Stockpile needs
Information/guidelines
Planning/collaboration
Linkage/networking
Resource expansion
capacity

City
County
State
Country

CDC Response

Support:
• Deployment of national pharmaceutical stockpile
• Field investigations and monitoring
• Surveillance and epidemiological studies
• Exposure registry and monitoring of long-term impacts

Advise:
• Medical treatment and decontamination
• Criteria for entry and operations in hot zone
• Medical intervention recommendations
• Disease control and prevention measures

Assist:
• Protective action guidelines
• Evacuation and relocation decisions
• Health and medical impact on public and responders
• Public affairs and risk communication

CDC's Actions

In the hours and days following a radiological incident, CDC would assist and advise the LFA and the state and local health departments on recommendations that the community would need to accomplish the following:

• Protect people from radioactive fallout
• Protect people from radioactive contamination in the area
• Safely use food and water supplies from the area
• Assess and explain the dangers in the area of the incident

If necessary, CDC would also deploy the National Pharmaceutical Stockpile, a federal store of drugs and medical supplies set aside for emergency situations. In addition, CDC would give workers in the area information on the following:

• The amount of time they can safely work in an area contaminated with radioactive materials

• Equipment needed to protect themselves from radiation and radioactive materials
• Types of respiratory devices needed to work in the contaminated area
• How to use radiation monitoring devices

Radiation Exposure Registry

After an incident involving radioactive materials, CDC would work with ATSDR to establish an exposure registry. The purpose of this registry would be to monitor people's exposure to radiation and perform dose reconstructions to determine the exact amount of radiation to which people were exposed. This registry would help CDC determine the necessary long-term medical follow-up for those who were affected by the incident.

For more information, see CDC's web sites at http://www.cdc.gov, http://www.bt.cdc.gov, and www.bt.cdc.gov/radiation/index.asp.

Source: CDC, www.cdc.gov

REVIEW QUESTIONS

1. Discuss the two major differences between traditional hazards (i.e., hurricanes, floods, tornadoes, earthquakes, hazardous materials incidents) and the new hazards associated with terrorism?
2. What are the five major categories of hazards associated with terrorism?
3. Discuss the appropriate responses to the new hazards associated with terrorism? For each hazard when is it appropriate to shelter in place, evacuate and/or quarantine?
4. Understanding the new hazards associated with terrorism will be critical to reducing the fear among the public of these hazards. This was done very successfully in the past in understanding and dispelling the fear surrounding traditional hazards. How would you design and implement a public education campaign concerning the new hazards? What information would you present and how?
5. As a member of Congress, what role do you perceive for the Federal government in researching these new hazards, identifying appropriate response and preparedness measures and in educating the public? What role would you have if you were a Governor? What role would you have if you were a mayor or County Executive?

REFERENCE

Federal Emergency Management Agency. Managing the Emergency Consequences of Terrorist Incidents—Interim Planning Guide for State and Local Governments, 2002.

Safety and Security

INTRODUCTION

The United States of America experienced the most extensive terrorist attack on its soil on September 11, 2001. This attack precipitated many changes in the American way of life, as well as in the political structure and organization of the American government. Securing the safety of the American people inside the borders of their homeland became a critical priority. On September 20, 2001, President George W. Bush announced the establishment of the Office of Homeland Security within the White House and appointed Tom Ridge, then governor of Pennsylvania, as his homeland security chief. Some months later, after originally rejecting the idea, President Bush proposed the creation of a cabinet-level Department of Homeland Security, whose primary purpose would be to unify those agencies responsible for homeland security missions and achieve greater accountability in the execution of those missions. On November 19, 2002, the U.S. Senate voted overwhelmingly to create a Department of Homeland Security (DHS). The creation of the DHS is the most extensive reorganization of the federal government since the 1940s. (http://post911timeline.org/Timeline/) (http://www.whitehouse.gov/news/releases/2002/06/20020618-5.html)

This chapter will focus on the key components of safety and security in the context of homeland security and identify important stakeholders in charge of these components.

THE INTELLIGENCE COMMUNITY

The information provided in this section is summarized from the "U.S. Espionage and Intelligence, 1947–1996" project performed for the National Security Archive by several researchers including Jeffrey T. Richelson, Jane Gefter, Michael Waters, Michael Evans, Malcolm Byrne, Rubin Rone, John Martinez, Jennifer Grant, Marry Burroughs.

"The United States intelligence community consists of a number of agencies and offices distributed across the military and civilian departments of the government. While the United States government has engaged in various intelligence activities from its inception, it was the Cold War that resulted in the creation of a permanent and extensive intelligence community. That intelligence community would, by the 1980s, comprise over 25 different intelligence collection and analysis organizations, more than 100,000 employees, and a budget of approximately $30 billion.

Even after post-Cold War consolidations (particularly within the military services), significant reductions of civilian personnel (in the neighborhood of 17 to 25 percent), and several years of budget cuts, a substantial intelligence community remains. Currently, intelligence activities reflect a full compliment of operations, including:

- Technical collection: gathering intelligence using technical devices such as satellites, aircraft, and ship- and land-based antenna arrays;
- Human source collection: using agents (recruited foreign nationals) and attaches, and interviewing individuals who have traveled to or reside in areas of interest;
- Open source collection: collecting books, newspapers, and reports, recording radio and television broadcasts, and exploiting computer databases;
- Shared intelligence: meeting with foreign intelligence services and exchanging information;
- Counterintelligence: studying and penetrating foreign intelligence and security services;
- Covert action: attempting to influence foreign political events without the United States role being admitted; and
- Intelligence analysis, production, and dissemination: evaluating information, displaying it in printed, electronic, or video form, and transmitting it to customers.

"The organizations which perform these activities include four national-level organizations, the Central Intelligence Agency (CIA), the National Security Agency (NSA), the National Reconnaissance Office (NRO), the National Imagery and Mapping Agency (NIMA), and several agencies subordinate to the Department of Defense; a number of military service intelligence units, and several smaller civilian intelligence organizations within the federal bureaucracy." (Richelson JT, Gefter J, Waters M, Evans M, Byrne M, Rone R, Martinez J, Grant J, Burroughs M. "U.S. Espionage and Intelligence, 1947–1996," Digital National Security Archive, 2003; http://nsarchive. chadwyck.com/esp_essay.htm)

The next sections will give a brief explanation of the background, duties, and organization of those agencies.

THE CENTRAL INTELLIGENCE AGENCY

"World War II resulted in the creation of America's first central intelligence organization, the Office of Strategic Services (OSS). The OSS performed a variety of functions—traditional espionage, covert action (ranging from propaganda to sabotage), counterintelligence, and intelligence analysis. The OSS represented a revolution in United States intelligence, not only because of the varied functions performed by a single, national agency, but because of the breadth of its intelligence interests and its use of scholars to produce finished intelligence.

"In the aftermath of World War II, the Office of Strategic Services was disbanded, officially closing down on 1 October 1945, as ordered by President Truman. Several of its branches were distributed among other departments of the government. The X-2 (Counterintelligence) and Secret Intelligence branches were transferred to the War Department to comprise the Strategic Services Unit, while the Research and Analysis Branch was relocated in the State Department.

"At virtually the same time that he ordered the termination of the OSS, Truman authorized studies of what intelligence structure the United States would require in the post-World War II world. The result was the creation of the National Intelligence Authority (NIA) and its operational element, the Central Intelligence Group (CIG). CIG's initial responsibility was to coordinate and synthesize the reports produced by the military service intelligence agencies and the FBI. Soon, however, it also assumed the task of clandestine intelligence collection.

"As part of a general consideration of national security needs, the question of intelligence organization was addressed in the National Security Act of 1947. The act established the Central Intelligence Agency (CIA) as an independent agency within the

Executive Office of the President to replace the CIG. According to the act, the CIA was to have five functions:

1. to advise the National Security Council in matters concerning such intelligence activities of the government departments and agencies as relate to national security;

2. to make recommendations to the National Security Council for the coordination of such intelligence activities of the departments and agencies of the government as relate to national security;

3. to correlate and evaluate the intelligence relating to national security, and to provide for the appropriate dissemination of such intelligence within the Government using, where appropriate, existing agencies and facilities;

4. to perform for the benefit of existing intelligence agencies such additional services of common concern as the National Security Council determines can be more effectively accomplished centrally; and

5. to perform other such functions and duties related to intelligence affecting the national security as the National Security Council may from time to time direct.

"The present organizational structure of the CIA began to take shape in the early 1950s under Director Walter Bedell Smith. In 1952, the Office of Policy Coordination was brought under CIA control and merged with the secret intelligence-gathering Office of Special Operations to form the Directorate of Plans. That same year, the offices involved in intelligence research and analysis were placed under a Directorate of Intelligence. A third unit, the Directorate of Administration, was established to perform administrative functions.

"The principal functions of the Directorate of Plans were clandestine collection and covert action (although before the creation of a separate directorate to perform technical collection operations it was heavily involved in the development and operation of overhead collection systems, specifically the U-2 spy plane and CORONA reconnaissance satellite). In 1973, the Directorate of Plans became the Directorate of Operations. Its present functions include clandestine collection, covert action, counter-narcotics and counterterrorism activities, and counterintelligence.

"A fourth directorate, the Directorate of Research was established in 1962, consolidating in one unit agency components involved in technical collection activities. In 1963, it was renamed the Directorate of Science and Technology and assumed control of scientific intelligence analysis. Its present functions include developing technical collection systems, collecting signals intelligence from embassy sites (in cooperation with the National Security Agency), recording foreign radio and television broadcasts (through its Foreign Broadcast Information Service), developing and producing technical devices (such as bugging devices, hidden cameras and weaponry) for agents and officers, and providing research and development in support of intelligence collection and analysis. Until late 1996, the directorate also managed the National Photographic Interpretation Center (NPIC) which interpreted satellite and aerial reconnaissance imagery. NPIC was absorbed by the newly established National Imagery and Mapping Agency.

"The CIA is the best known of the United States intelligence agencies, in part because of its involvement in covert action, and in part because of the central role it and its director play in providing intelligence to the president. However, as noted previously, there are several other U.S. intelligence agencies, some of which rival the CIA in influence and exceed it in budget. The most important are the three other 'national' agencies: the National Security Agency, the National Reconnaissance Office, and the National Imagery and Mapping Agency." (Richelson JT, Gefter J, Waters M, Evans M, Byrne M, Rone R, Martinez J, Grant J, Burroughs M. "U.S. Espionage and Intelligence, 1947–1996," Digital National Security Archive, 2003; http://nsarchive.chadwyck. com/esp_essay.htm)

NATIONAL SECURITY AGENCY

"On 20 May 1949, Secretary of Defense Louis Johnson established the Armed Forces Security Agency (AFSA) and placed it under the command of the Joint Chiefs of Staff. In theory, the AFSA was to direct the communications intelligence and electronic intelligence activities of the military service signals intelligence units (at the time, the Army Security Agency, Naval Security Group, and Air Force Security Service). In practice, the AFSA had little power, its functions being defined in terms of activities not performed by the service units.

"On 24 October 1952—the day that President Truman sent a top secret eight-page memorandum (now declassified) entitled 'Communications Intelligence Activities,' to the secretary of state and secretary of defense—Truman abolished the AFSA and transferred its personnel to the newly created National Security Agency. As its name indicated, the new agency was to have national, not just military, responsibilities. In 1971, NSA became the National Security Agency/Central Security Service (NSA/CSS). The second part of NSA's title (which is rarely used) refers to its role in coordinating the signals intelligence activities of the military services.

"Today's NSA has three basic functions. It conducts or manages, via its Directorate of Operations, and in some instances in conjunction with the Central Intelligence Agency, National Reconnaissance Office, and theater commands, signals intelligence operations on a worldwide basis. In doing so it employs satellites (including the geosynchronous ORION and elliptically orbiting TRUMPET satellites), aircraft (the RC-135, U-2, and others), ships, submarines, and ground stations with a variety of antennae and satellite dishes.

"NSA's Directorate of Information Systems Security is responsible for devising cipher and voice scrambling systems so that United States military, diplomatic, and other sensitive government communications can be transmitted without foreign governments being able to read those communications. The directorate is also responsible for devising means of protecting information, both classified and unclassified, stored in computer data banks or transmitted via computer.

"The Directorate of Technology and Systems (previously known as the Directorate of Research and Engineering) is responsible for developing signals intelligence and information security hardware as well as for developing devices or techniques that can be used to decipher foreign communications or other electronic signals." (Richelson JT, Gefter J, Waters M, Evans M, Byrne M, Rone R, Martinez J, Grant J, Burroughs M. "U.S. Espionage and Intelligence, 1947–1996," Digital National Security Archive, 2003; http://nsarchive.chadwyck.com/esp_essay.htm)

NATIONAL RECONNAISSANCE OFFICE

"The National Reconnaissance Office (NRO) was established on 6 September 1961 to coordinate CIA reconnaissance activities with those of the Department of Defense. NRO's primary function has been to oversee the research and development, procurement, deployment, and operation of imaging, signals intelligence, and ocean surveillance satellites. It awards contracts, oversees the research and development efforts of contractors, supervises the launch of the payloads, and, in conjunction with the CIA and NSA, operates the spacecraft. It has also been involved in the research, development, and procurement of selected aerial reconnaissance systems, such as the SR-71.

"From its inception until 18 September 1992, when its existence was formally acknowledged, the NRO operated as a classified organization. A major restructuring of NRO also began to be implemented in 1992. Prior to that time NRO activities were conducted through three program offices: Program A (the Air Force Office of Special Projects at Los Angeles Air Force Station), Program B (the CIA reconnaissance activity within its Directorate of Science and Technology), and Program C (the U.S. Navy space reconnaissance activity, located in different navy units at different times).

"The CIA and air force elements often competed to develop new systems in both the imaging and signals intelligence areas. As a result of the NRO restructuring, two directorates which combined the personnel from the three program offices were established—one for imagery systems acquisition and operations, the other for signals intelligence systems acquisition and operations." (Richelson JT, Gefter J, Waters M, Evans M, Byrne M, Rone R, Martinez J, Grant J, Burroughs M. "U.S. Espionage and Intelligence, 1947–1996," Digital National Security Archive, 2003; http://nsarchive.chadwyck.com/esp_essay.htm)

NATIONAL IMAGERY AND MAPPING AGENCY

"The National Imagery and Mapping Agency (NIMA), formally proposed by the secretary of defense and the director of central intelligence in November 1995, was established on 1 October 1996. NIMA absorbed four imagery interpretation and mapping organizations (the National Photographic Interpretation Center, the Defense Mapping Agency, the CIA's Office of Imagery Analysis, the DIA's Office of Imagery Analysis), the Central Imagery Office, the Defense Dissemination Program Office, and elements of the Defense Airborne Reconnaissance Office and National Reconnaissance Office that had been doing work in the areas of imagery dissemination and exploitation.

"Initially NIMA will be organized into three main directorates: Operations, Systems and Technology, and Corporate Affairs. Three key units within the Operations Directorate are Imagery Analysis, Geospatial Information and Services, and the Central Imagery Tasking Office. The latter will be responsible for allocating targets to imagery collection systems, and determining when the imagery is obtained.

"The Imagery Analysis unit will combine the activities of NPIC and the CIA and DIA imagery analysis organizations, while Geospatial Information and Services will provide the mapping, charting, and geodesy products formerly provided by the DMA. The unit is responsible for producing strategic and tactical maps, charts, and databases, and specialized products to support current and advanced weapons and navigation systems. The maps, charts, and databases provide information on both undersea and surface terrain for use in military operations and programming cruise missiles. The geodetic information provides data on the impact the earth has on the path of a ballistic missile. Reflecting the increase in computer capabilities, including the creation of virtual reality settings, DMA has produced three-dimensional video maps, such as those used during the Bosnian peace talks to permit negotiators to simulate overlying disputed territory." (Richelson JT, Gefter J, Waters M, Evans M, Byrne M, Rone R, Martinez J, Grant J, Burroughs M. "U.S. Espionage and Intelligence, 1947–1996," Digital National Security Archive, 2003; http://nsarchive.chadwyck.com/esp_essay.htm)

BORDER CONTROL

The borders of any country are strategically important because of the critical role they play in the economic vitality and commerce of the country. Increasing globalization of our economic systems and transportation networks means that virtually every community in America is connected to the outside world through airports, seaports, pipelines, and waterways. Customs are gateways for imported and exported goods to and from the country; therefore their effectiveness and efficiency are important measures for the trade capacity and capability of the country. Borders also have an important role for the international tourism and travel capability of the country. At the same time, they provide major entry points for illegal people and goods into the country. Therefore the security and control of borders is a very important mitigative action for preventing penetration of unwanted or dangerous people and goods into the country. This includes smugglers, drug dealers, criminals, and terrorists. Illegal drugs, conventional weapons, smuggled goods, biological agents, and weapons of mass destruction (WMD) are examples of potential dangerous goods that can penetrate across the borders of countries.

The United States has 5,525 miles of border with Canada and 1,989 miles with Mexico. The maritime border includes 95,000 miles of shoreline and a 3.4 million square mile exclusive economic zone. Each year, more than 500 million people cross the borders into the United States, some 330 million of them are noncitizens. (http://www.whitehouse.gov/deptofhomeland/sect3.html)

Enhanced border and transportation security were a prime focus of the creation of DHS. DHS consolidates the various agencies responsible for the safety, security, and control of the borders. These are as follows: the Immigration and Naturalization Service (INS), the Customs Service (CS), U.S. Coast Guard (USCG), the Animal and Plant Health Inspection Service (APHIS), and the Transportation Security Agency (TSA).

Border and Transportation Security, according to the initial plan draft of the National Response Plan (NRP), refers to activities that promote the efficient and reliable flow of people, goods, and services across borders, while preventing terrorists from using transportation conveyances or systems to deliver implements of destruction. (NRP Initial Plan Draft, pp. 26, 2003)

The Directorate of Border and Transportation Security (DHS-BTS) of the DHS is charged with this mission. The United States Coast Guard (DHS-USCG), the Directorate of Science and Technology (DHS-S&T), the Directorate of Information Analysis and Infrastructure Protection (DHS-IAIP), the Department of Commerce (DOC), the Department of State (DOS), the Department of Defense (DoD), the Department of Energy (DOE), the Department of Justice (DOJ), the Department of Labor (DOL), the Department of Transportation (DOT), the Department of Health and Human Services (HHS), the Director of Central Intelligence (DCI), and the Department of Agriculture (USDA) are mentioned as support agencies for Border and Transportation Security in the National Response Plan Draft. (NRP Initial Plan Draft, 2003)

Table 5-1 presents the main border security operations and the agencies in charge.

The next section will summarize the duties of agencies that have a direct role in border control and security.

DHS/United States Coast Guard

The Coast Guard is the lead federal agency for maritime drug interdiction and shares lead responsibility for air interdiction with the U.S. Customs Service. As such, it is a key player in combating the flow of illegal drugs to the United States. The Coast Guard's mission is to reduce the supply of drugs from the source by denying smugglers the use of air and maritime routes in the Transit Zone, a 6-million square mile area that includes the Caribbean, Gulf of Mexico, and Eastern Pacific. In meeting the challenge of patrolling this vast area, the Coast Guard coordinates closely with other federal agencies and countries within the region to disrupt and deter the flow of illegal drugs. In addition to deterrence, Coast Guard drug interdiction accounts for nearly 52 percent of all U.S. government seizures of cocaine each year. For fiscal year 2002 the rate of Coast Guard cocaine seizures alone had an estimated import value of approximately $3.9 billion. (http://www.uscg.mil/hq/g-o/g-opl/mle/drugs.htm)

As the primary maritime law enforcement agency, the Coast Guard is tasked with enforcing immigration law at sea. The Coast Guard conducts patrols and coordinates with other federal agencies and foreign countries to interdict undocumented migrants at sea, denying them entry via maritime routes to the United States, its territories, and possessions. Interdicting migrants at sea means they can be quickly returned to their countries of origin without the costly processes required if they successfully enter the United States. (http://www.uscg.mil/hq/g-o/g-opl/mle/amio.htm)

DHS/Bureau of Customs and Border Protection

The United States Border Patrol is the mobile uniformed law enforcement arm of the Department of

TABLE 5-1 **Agency Responsibilities by Functional Areas, Functions, and Tasks**

Task	Lead agency	Support agencies
Accomplish border security	DHS-BTS	DHS-USCG, DHS-S&T, DHS-IAIP, DOC, DoD, DOE, DOJ, DOL, DOS, DOT, HSS, DCI, UCDA
Information exchange and intelligence sharing in support of border security operations	DHS-BTS	DOJ, DOS, DCI, DHS-USCG
Conduct deterrence operations	DHS-BTS	DoD, DOJ, DOS, DHS-USCG
Conduct heightened operations to interdict terrorists, terrorist weapons, and other contraband crossing U.S. borders	DHS-BTS	DOJ, DOS, DoD, DHS-USCG, DEA
Apprehend illegal aliens (maritime environment)	DHS-USCG	DOT
Apprehend illegal aliens (on U.S. territory)	DHS-BTS	DOT
Enhance targeted detention/removal of immigration law violators	DHS-BTS	DOJ, DOL, USDA, DOS
Investigate customs and immigration violations	DHS-BTS	DOJ
Prosecute customs/immigration violations	DHS-BTS	DOJ
Coordinate with federal, state, local, and international authorities to secure border infrastructure	DHS-BTS	DOS, DOT
Train, exercise, equip, and evaluate	DHS-BTS	
Conduct contingency planning	DHS-BTS	DOS, HHS
Restore cross-border flow of commerce and trade	DHS-BTS	DOS, Treasury, DOC
Detention and Removal	DHS-BTS	DOJ

Source: NRP Initial Plan Draft, Appendix A, Table 6-2.

Homeland Security. The primary mission of the Border Patrol is the detection and apprehension of illegal aliens and smugglers of aliens at or near the land border. This is accomplished by maintaining surveillance, following up leads, responding to electronic sensor alarms and aircraft sightings, and interpreting and following tracks. Some of the major activities include maintaining traffic checkpoints along highways leading from border areas, conducting city patrol and transportation check, and antismuggling investigations. Since 1994 the Border Patrol has made more than 11.3 million apprehensions nationwide, more than the current combined populations (2000 U.S. Census data) of Iowa, Missouri, and Kansas. In FY2001, Border Patrol agents apprehended almost 1.2 million persons for illegally entering the country. An increase in smuggling activities has pushed the Border Patrol to the front line of the U.S. war on drugs. Its role as the primary drug-interdicting organization along the southwest border continues to expand. The heightened presence of immigration law enforcement officers along the Southwest border has burdened narcotic traffickers and alien smugglers. In FY2001, Border Patrol agents seized more than

18,500 pounds of cocaine and more than 1.1 million pounds of marijuana. The total street value of drugs interdicted in FY2001 was more than $1.4 billion. (http://www.cbp.gov/xp/cgov/enforcement/border_patrol/overview.xml)

DHS/Bureau of Immigration and Customs Enforcement

The immigration enforcement component of the Bureau of Immigration and Customs Enforcement (ICE) promotes public safety and national security by deterring illegal migration, preventing immigration-related crimes, and removing individuals, especially criminals, who are unlawfully present in the United States. This mandate is carried out by the Immigration Investigations, Detention and Removal, and Intelligence programs. (http://www.bice.gov/graphics/immig.htm)

Traditionally the primary mission of the customs enforcement component of ICE has been to combat various forms of smuggling. Over time, however, this mission has been expanded to other violations of law involving terrorist financing, money laundering, arms trafficking (including weapons of mass destruction), technology exports, commercial fraud, and child pornography, to name a few. In fact, Customs enforces more than 400 different laws and regulations, including those of 40 other agencies. For example, the customs component of ICE is charged with investigating violations of the Arms Export Control Act and International Trafficking in Arms Regulations, which includes weapons of mass destruction. (http://www.bice.gov/graphics/customs.htm)

TRANSPORTATION SAFETY AND SECURITY

In its basic definition, transportation is the general term that refers to movement of things or people from one location to another one. Today our domestic transportation systems are intertwined with a global network moving millions of people and products throughout the world on a daily basis. Historically the United States has relied on the private sector to ensure our domestic transportation safety. The events of September 11 illustrated the vulnerabilities of our systems and required a change in the past approach. Transportation security and identifying and reducing the vulnerabilities within the vast transportation networks are a significant challenge. Because of the complexity of these systems as a whole and the complexity of the subsystems included, this is not an easy task.

In the United States of America the Department of Transportation (http://www.dot.gov) and the Directorate of Border and Transportation Security of DHS are the main stakeholders to assure transportation safety and security. The Transportation Security Agency (TSA) is the main agency under the directorate to assure systems security of the transportation infrastructure. The next section will provide information about the agencies that are responsible for safety and security of the various transportation systems and subsystems.

AIR TRANSPORTATION SECURITY

The main agency for aviation safety is the Office of System Safety of the Federal Aviation Administration (FAA) (https://www.nasdac.faa.gov) within the Department of Transportation. The primary function of the office is to develop and implement improved tools and processes, including hazard identification, risk assessment, and risk management tools and processes; to facilitate more effective use of safety data, both inside and outside the agency; and to help improve aviation safety. It also functions as a coordinator within the FAA for safety issues. The mission of the office is to provide international leadership in monitoring safety trends; identify emerging aviation safety issues and concerns as candidates for integrated analysis, study, and response; serve as an independent safety policy advisor; foster innovative aviation safety outreach; and serve as a focal point for aviation safety data and information. The goals of the office are to create an environment that facilitates and encourages sharing aviation safety information; identify appropriate data and analysis techniques and make them readily available to the international aviation community; develop tools to help identify safety issues; promote system safety methodologies within and outside the FAA; maximize impact of safety resource investments; and develop, market, and promote safety information. (http://www.asy.faa.gov/asy_internet/about.htm)

It's the responsibility of the Transportation Security Agency (TSA) under DHS/BTS to protect the nation's transportation systems—aviation, waterways, rails, highways, public transit, and pipelines—to ensure freedom of movement for people and commerce. Because of the events of September 11, aviation security is one of the highest priority responsibilities of TSA, and the agency expends significant budget and human resources to develop strategies and implement necessary technologies to prevent any future terrorist events connected to the abuse of the aviation system and air transportation. (http://www.oig.dot.gov/item_details.php?item=997)

Several new programs were implemented by TSA, including the Known Shipper Program, which allows air carriers to accept cargo only from approved shippers or forwarders who are regular customers and familiar to the carrier. TSA moved to limit the types of cargo that can be transported on passenger aircraft and requires audits of shippers to ensure their credentials. The Federal Air Marshall Program deploys thousands of air marshals to fly on tens of thousands of flights each month on a wide variety of routes and aircraft. Reacting to a February 25, 2003, deadline set by Congress, TSA crafted a program to train volunteer pilots to carry guns in the cockpit. After pilots in April's prototype class assessed their training in an on-the-job setting, TSA took that feedback, made improvements, and launched full-scale training that by next year is expected to have thousands of pilots defending the cockpit. Since September 11 the number of canine teams for explosives detection has doubled to 291 at 64 of the nation's largest airports. A national pilot program that uses explosive detection canines to screen mail is underway at 12 airports. TSA is field-testing potential technologies for a transportation

worker identification credential for transportation workers to limit unescorted physical and/or logistical access to secure areas of transportation facilities. The program will not only enhance security but will generate economic efficiencies by eliminating redundant credentials and background checks. (http://www.tsa.gov/public/display?theme=44&content=680)

The President requested a budget of $4.82 billion for TSA for FY2004, which is over $1 billion than the agency spent in FY2003. The FY2004 budget will be mainly spent by four programs, among which the aviation security program is the largest with a $4.22 billion (86 percent) of the overall budget. The aviation security program consists of a passenger screening program for which $1.80 billion is allocated, a baggage screening program with a budget of $944 million, and a security direction and enforcement program for which $1.47 billion are allocated. [http://www.tsa.gov/public/interweb/assetlibrary/TSA_FY2004_budget_briefing_(public).ppt]

Currently there are about 1,100 electronic detection systems (EDS) and 5,500 electronic trace detectors (ETD) in use by TSA. On September 11, about 5 percent of all checked luggage was screened for explosives; today 100 percent of all checked luggage is screened for explosives. Through August 2003, TSA had intercepted more than 8.1 million prohibited items at checkpoints since assuming responsibility for airport security in February 2002. More than 2.4 million knives and 1,498 firearms and 51,408 box cutters—the weapon of choice for the September 11 terrorists—were among items intercepted. In August alone, 602,913 prohibited items were intercepted. (http://www.tsa.gov/public/display?theme=44&content=680)

TRUCKING SECURITY

Trucking is an important component of transportation security because a significant portion of hazardous materials (HAZMAT) in the United States is being transported by trucks on highways and roads. The Department of Transportation (DOT) has primary responsibility for ensuring the safety and security of

TABLE 5-2 Classification of Serious HAZMAT Incidents in the United States by the Mode of Transportation and Yearly Frequencies

Mode	1993	1994	1995	1996	1997	1998	1999	2000	2001	2002	Total
—											
Air	8	7	8	6	13	23	17	35	36	15	168
Highway	362	349	353	423	409	357	457	463	497	364	4034
Railway	57	82	61	74	61	72	70	75	60	69	681
Water	1	1	1	1	1	4	0	2	1	2	14
Freight forwarder		0	0	0	0	0	0	0	0	0	0
Other	0	0	0	0	0	0	0	0	0	0	0
—											
Total	428	439	423	504	484	456	544	575	594	450	4897

Source: U.S. Department of Transportation, Hazardous Material Information System, http://hazmat.dot.gov/files/hazmat/10year/10yearfrm.htm.

truck traffic. Table 5-2 provides a framework for the importance of safe land transportation of HAZMAT.

A serious HAZMAT incident is defined by the Department of Transportation's (DOT) Research and Special Programs Administration (RISPA) as an incident that involves a fatality or major injury caused by the release of a hazardous material, the evacuation of 25 or more persons as a result of release of a hazardous material or exposure to fire, a release or exposure to fire that results in the closure of a major transportation artery, the alteration of an aircraft flight plan or operation, the release of radioactive materials from Type B packaging, the release of over 11.9 gallons or 88.2 pounds of a severe marine pollutant, or the release of a bulk quantity (over 119 gallons or 882 pounds) of a hazardous material. (http://hazmat.dot.gov/files/hazmat/serious_new_def.htm)

Table 5-2 is important because it shows that the number of HAZMAT incidents that occurred on U.S. highways in the last 10 years constitutes more than 82 percent of all HAZMAT occurrences in the period in United States. And since a significant portion of HAZMAT transportation is done by trucks, trucking becomes an important issue in securing homeland

safety and improving the security of the U.S. transportation systems. The Office of Hazardous Materials Safety of DOT/RISPA is responsible for coordinating a national safety program for the transportation of hazardous materials by air, rail, highway, and water in the United States.

The Code of Federal Regulations (CFR) 49 Part 107 documents the steps being taken to enhance hazardous material transportation security. The subchapter C part 107 specifically discusses regulations for HAZMAT transportation on U.S. highways. The subparts of the document include information about regulations for loading and unloading of HAZMAT transportation vehicles, segregation and separation of HAZMAT, vehicles and shipments in transit, accidents, and regulations applying to hazardous material on motor vehicles carrying passengers for hire. (CFR 49, May 5th 2003, http://www.myregs.com/dotrspa/)

PORTS AND SHIPPING SECURITY

Ports are important facilities of the United States transportation infrastructure. There are 77 U.S. ports that are open to international trade, import, and export, 30 of which account for almost 99 percent of all international maritime trade activity of the United States (Department of Transportation Maritime Administration Statistics, http://www.marad.dot.gov/Marad_Statistics/Con-Pts-02.htm).

Securing maritime transportation is a vital task for the DHS, because a successful terrorist attack on any major U.S. port could result in significant loss of life, tremendous physical damage, and serious disruption to the economy and commerce of the United States and its trade partners.

Two major departments, DOT and DHS, share responsibility for securing the maritime transportation system and the ports.

The DHS/U.S. Coast Guard (USCG) has its own Maritime Strategy for Homeland Security, where duties, responsibilities and strategic missions of the agency are clearly defined. The homeland security mission of the Coast Guard is to protect the U.S. Maritime Domain and the U.S. Marine Transportation System and deny their use and exploitation by terrorists as a means for attacks on U.S. territory, population, and critical infrastructure and to prepare for and, in the event of attack, conduct emergency response operations. When directed as the supported or supporting commander, DHS/USCG conduct military homeland defense operations. In accomplishing its homeland security mission, the strategic goals of the Coast Guard are as follows: to increase maritime domain awareness, conduct enhanced maritime security operations, close port security gaps, build critical security capabilities, leverage partnerships to mitigate security risks, and ensure readiness for homeland defense operations. The Coast Guard is the lead federal agency for Maritime Homeland Security.

DHS/BTS/TSA's main role in maritime and port has been providing grants to support port security and related issues. Of TSA's FY2004 budget, $86 million will be spent on maritime and land safety, and $55 million will be spent for the Transportation Worker Identification Card (TWIC) program, which is a federal program to improve security by establishing a transportation systemwide common credential, used across all modes, for all transportation workers requiring unescorted physical and logical access to secure areas of the transportation system.

The FY2004 budget includes $2.5 million funding for the Safe Commerce Project, which is a pilot program that brings together private businesses, ports, and local, state, and federal representatives to analyze current security procedures for cargo entering the country. The program's objective is to prompt research and development for emerging technology to monitor the movement and ensure the security and integrity of containers through the supply chain. The ports of Seattle and Tacoma, Los Angeles, and Long Beach and the Port Authority of New York/New Jersey are participating in the pilot program. The funding for the project was $58 million in the FY2003.

The Container Security Initiative (CSI), a part of the DHS programs incorporates side-by-side teamwork with foreign port authorities to identify, target, and search high-risk cargo, will be expanded in 2004 to strategic locations beyond the initial 20 major ports to include areas of the Middle East such as Dubai, as well as Turkey and Malaysia. The top 20 ports account for 68 percent of all cargo containers arriving at U.S. seaports. Phase 2 of CSI will enable the DHS to extend port security protection from 68 percent of container traffic to more than 80 percent.

TSA provides specific preparedness grants to state, and local governments and the private sector. In FY2003 TSA provided $170 million for this purpose. (http://www.tsa.gov/public/display?content=85) (http://www.tsa.gov/public/display?theme=39&content=79)

Bus Transportation Security

Bus transportation is an often neglected link in our transportation networks and represents a potential vulnerability to homeland security efforts. The bus transportation system can be one of the next targets of terrorists because the system has comparatively less protection against terrorist attacks, which makes it an easy target for terrorists who are searching for less risky and higher consequence attacks.

The motor coach industry, which includes regularly scheduled point-to-point service and chartered tour operations, carried more than 774 million passengers in the United States in 2000, 28 percent more passengers than carried by domestic commercial airlines and 33 times more passengers than carried by Amtrak. The twelve Class 1 bus companies, defined by the Bureau of Statistics as having revenues of at least $10 million or more annually, carried approximately 33 million passengers in 2000. There are worrisome precedents for the potential for security breaches on buses. In the United States, Greyhound drivers and passengers were the targets of at least four serious assaults in 2002, one killing seven passengers and another injuring 33 passengers, and at least 3 other serious security breaches. These incidents occurred in states throughout the country. Steps have been taken to improve security; however, more has to be done. (TSA Program Announcement 02MLPA 0002, Intercity Bus Security Grants, Attachment A, http://www.tsa.gov/public/interweb/assetlibrary/ ATTACH_A_Background.pdf)

In order to support the intercity bus transportation sector, DHS/BTS/TSA provided $20 million of grants for intercity bus security projects, and more than 60 private bus operators received these grants to complete their proposed projects to improve the security of their staff, customers, and operations. (http://www. buses.org/pressroom/PROutput.cfm?PRID=232)

The priorities that TSA was looking for in the proposals that it reviewed to select the grantees were as follows:

1. Protecting or isolating the driver
2. Monitoring, tracking, and communication technologies for over-the-road buses
3. Implementing and operating passenger and baggage screening programs at terminals and over-the-road buses
4. Developing an effective security assessment/ security plan that identifies critical security needs and vulnerabilities
5. Training drivers, dispatchers, ticket agents, and other personnel in recognizing and responding

to criminal attacks and terrorist threats, evacuation procedures, passenger screening procedures, and baggage inspection.

(TSA Program Announcement 02MLPA0002, Intercity Bus Security Grants, pp.7, http://www.tsa.gov/ public/interweb/assetlibrary/ANNOUNCEMENT_ Intercity_Bus_Security.pdf)

The Senate has included $10 million for bus security in the FY2004 Homeland Security Appropriations bill. (http://www.buses.org/pressroom/ PROutput.cfm?PRID=232)

RAILWAY TRANSPORTATION SECURITY

The railroad system is also another valuable transportation infrastructure that has to be protected against possible vulnerabilities and terrorist attacks.

The DHS made its most noticeable references to the protection of the railway system in the "National Strategy for the Physical Protection of Critical Infrastructure and Key Assets" and in the announcement of the "Operation Liberty Shield."

The National Strategy for the Physical Protection of Critical Infrastructure and Key Assets mentions potential vulnerabilities and talks about possible terrorist attack scenarios to the railroad system, and it identifies four priorities for improvement in the railroad security:

1. The need to develop improved decision-making criteria regarding the shipment of hazardous materials: DHS and DOT, coordinating with other federal agencies, state and local governments, and industry, will facilitate the development of an improved process to assure informed decision making with respect to hazardous materials shipment.
2. The need to develop technologies and procedures to screen intermodal containers and passenger baggage: DHS and DOT will work with sector counterparts to identify and explore technologies and processes to enable efficient and expeditious screening of rail

passengers and baggage, especially at intermodal stations.

3. The need to improve security of intermodal transportation: DHS and DOT will work with sector counterparts to identify and facilitate the development of technologies and procedures to secure intermodal containers and detect threatening content. DHS and DOT will work with the rail industry to devise or enable a hazardous materials identification system that supports the needs of first responders yet avoids providing terrorists with easy identification of a potential weapon.

4. The need to clearly delineate roles and responsibilities regarding surge requirements: DHS and DOT will work with industry to delineate infrastructure protection roles and responsibilities to enable the rail industry to address surge requirements for resources in the case of catastrophic events. Costs and resource allocation remains a contentious issue for the rail sector. DHS and DOT will also convene a working group consisting of government and industry representatives to identify options for the implementation of surge capabilities, including access to federal facilities and capabilities in extreme emergencies.

(The National Strategy for the Protection of Physical Infrastructure and Key Assets, Department of Homeland Security, February 2003, pp. 56–57, http://www.dhs.gov)

The national physical protection strategy clearly identifies the transportation of HAZMAT within the railroad infrastructure as the greatest vulnerability of the system. In response, DOT and DHS released a document regarding the HAZMAT transportation vulnerability and measures to be taken to minimize the terrorist threat to the system.

This document provides background information on the improvements accomplished in the railroad system since September 11. It discusses the security task force established by the Association of American Railroads (AAR) to assess vulnerabilities in several critical areas, such as physical assets, information technology, chemicals and hazardous materials, defense shipments, train operations, and passenger security.

(RSPA-2003-14982, Notice No. 03-7, RSPA, TSA, FRA, Hazardous Materials: Transportation of Explosives by Rail, June 5, 2003)

In March 2003, DHS announced "Operation Liberty Shield" which details the following steps to enhance railway security:

1. To improve rail bridge security: State governors have been asked to provide additional police or National Guard forces at selected bridges.

2. To increase railroad infrastructure security: Railroad companies will be asked to increase security at major facilities and key rail hubs.

3. AMTRAK security measures: AMTRAK will implement security measures consistent with private rail companies.

4. To increase railroad hazardous material (HAZMAT) safety: At the request of the Department of Transportation, private railroad companies will monitor shipments of hazardous material and increase surveillance of trains carrying this material.

(Operation Liberty Shield: Press Briefing by Secretary Ridge, Saturday, Mar 15, 2003, http://www. dhs.gov/dhspublic/display?content−520)

INFORMATION SECURITY AND NATIONAL NETWORK INFRASTRUCTURE SECURITY

Information Security means techniques, technical measures, and administrative measures used to protect information assets from deliberate or inadvertent unauthorized acquisition, damage, disclosure, manipulation, modification, loss, or use. (McDaniel G, editor: *IBM Dictionary of Computing*, New York, 1994, McGraw-Hill.)

The term "network infrastructure security" refers to the protection of the physical infrastructure of data networks and peripherals, such as fiber-optic cables, routers, switches, and servers that allow data in digital format to be transferred from one location to another one or process it to meet user demands.

These two systems are linked because most of the complex systems are digitally controlled, wherein data transfer and processing is done by large telecommunication networks and servers, with clients connected to them in a network fashion.

The fact that complex systems are digitally controlled brings a potential vulnerability to those systems. The possible scenario that proposes terrorists to gain the control of these controlling systems is not an unrealistic one. Once the terrorists gain access to the system, they can abuse it to cause major damage to people and the government, creating major economic disruptions. And in order to do that, the terrorists may not even need to be physically in the facility or system that they are planning to attack. This type of terrorist behavior is called "cyber-terrorism."

The DHS is the main department responsible to secure the cyberspace and the network infrastructure in the United States. The Directorate of Information Analysis & Infrastructure Protection (IAIP) of DHS is the main unit in the department to identify and assess current and future terrorist threats, assess and mitigate risks to the nation's critical infrastructure systems, and disseminate threat information.

Some the information analysis tasks of the directorate are as follows:

1. To identify and assess the nature and scope of terrorist threats, and detect such threats, and administer the five-color coded Homeland Security Advisory System
2. To ensure efficient access by DHS to all related information gathered or analyzed, and disseminate relevant homeland security information externally to DHS
3. Establish and utilize a secure but compatible national security and emergency preparedness communications system for the federal government
4. Conduct training for federal, state, and local governments in information identification, analysis, and sharing

Some infrastructure protection tasks of the directorate are as follows:

1. Conduct a comprehensive risk assessment of U.S. critical infrastructure and develop a comprehensive plan for securing its components
2. Work with other agencies at the federal, state, local, and private levels to recommend protection measures and provide technical assistance and crisis management support upon request
3. Coordinate with other federal government agencies to provide specific warning information to state, local, private, public, and other agencies

The directorate incorporates the Critical Infrastructure Assurance Office, Federal Computer Incident Response Center, National Communications System, National Infrastructure Protection Center, National Infrastructure Simulation and Analysis Center, and Energy Security and Assurance Program. (Coppola, 2003)

The key document from the DHS to assure information security and protect cyberspace is the "National Strategy to Secure Cyberspace." In this document the three strategic objectives to secure the cyberspace are as follows:

1. Prevent cyber attacks against America's critical infrastructures
2. Reduce national vulnerability to cyber attacks
3. Minimize damage and recovery time from cyber attacks that do occur

The National Strategy to Secure Cyberspace articulates five national priorities: Priority 1: A National Cyberspace Security Response System. Rapid identification, information exchange, and remediation can often mitigate the damage caused by malicious cyberspace activity. For those activities to be effective at a national level, the United States needs a partnership between government and industry to perform analyses, issue warnings, and coordinate response efforts. Privacy and civil liberties must be protected in the process. Because no cyber-security plan can be impervious to concerted and intelligent attack, information systems must be able to operate while under attack and have the resilience to restore full operations quickly. The National Strategy to

Secure Cyberspace identifies eight major actions and initiatives cyberspace security response:

1. Establish a public-private architecture responding to national-level cyber incidents
2. Provide for the development of tactical and strategic analysis of cyber attacks vulnerability assessments
3. Encourage the development of a private sector capability to share a synoptic view of the health of cyberspace
4. Expand the Cyber Warning and Information Network to support the DHS in coordinating crisis management for cyberspace security
5. Improve national incident management
6. Coordinate processes for voluntary participation in the development of national public-private continuity and contingency plans
7. Exercise cyber security continuity plans for federal systems
8. Improve and enhance public-private information sharing involving cyber attacks, threats, and vulnerabilities

Priority 2: A National Cyberspace Security Threat and Vulnerability Reduction Program. By exploiting vulnerabilities in our cyber-systems, an organized attack may endanger the security of the United States' critical infrastructures. The vulnerabilities that most threaten cyberspace occur in the information assets of critical infrastructure enterprises themselves and their external supporting structures, such as the mechanisms of the Internet. Lesser-secured sites on the interconnected network of networks also present potentially significant exposures to cyber attacks. Vulnerabilities result from weaknesses in technology and because of improper implementation and oversight of technological products. The National Strategy to Secure Cyberspace identifies eight major actions and initiatives to reduce threats and related vulnerabilities:

1. Enhance law enforcement's capabilities for preventing and prosecuting cyberspace attacks
2. Create a process for national vulnerability assessments to better understand the potential consequences of threats and vulnerabilities

3. Secure the mechanisms of the Internet, improving protocols and routing
4. Foster the use of trusted digital control systems/supervisory control and data acquisition systems
5. Reduce and remediate software vulnerabilities
6. Understand infrastructure interdependencies and improve the physical security of cyber systems and telecommunications
7. Prioritize federal cyber security research and development agendas
8. Assess and secure emerging systems

Priority 3: A National Cyberspace Security Awareness and Training Program. Many cyber vulnerabilities exist because of a lack of cyber security awareness on the part of computer users, systems administrators, technology developers, procurement officials, auditors, chief information officers (CIOs), chief executive officers, and corporate boards. Such awareness-based vulnerabilities present serious risks to critical infrastructures regardless of whether they exist within the infrastructure itself. A lack of trained personnel and the absence of widely accepted, multilevel certification programs for cyber security professionals complicate the task of addressing cyber vulnerabilities. The National Strategy to Secure Cyberspace identifies four major actions and initiatives for awareness, education, and training:

1. Promote a comprehensive national awareness program to empower all Americans, businesses, the general workforce, and the general population to secure their own parts of cyberspace
2. Foster adequate training and education programs to support the nation's cyber security needs
3. Increase the efficiency of existing federal cyber-security training programs
4. Promote private-sector support for well-coordinated, widely recognized professional cyber security certifications

Priority 4: Securing Governments' Cyberspace. Although governments administer only a minority of the nation's critical infrastructure computer systems, governments at all levels perform essential services in the agriculture, food, water, public health, emergency services, defense, social welfare, information and telecommunications, energy, transportation, banking and finance, chemicals, and postal shipping sectors that depend upon cyberspace for their delivery. Governments can lead by example in cyberspace security, including fostering a marketplace for more secure technologies through their procurement. The National Strategy to Secure Cyberspace identifies five major actions and initiatives for the securing of governments' cyberspace:

1. Continuously assess threats and vulnerabilities to federal cyber systems
2. Authenticate and maintain authorized users of federal cyber systems
3. Secure federal wireless local area networks
4. Improve security in government outsourcing and procurement
5. Encourage state and local governments, consider establishing information technology security programs, and participate in information sharing and analysis centers with similar governments

Priority 5: National Security and International Cyberspace Security Cooperation. America's cyberspace links the United States to the rest of the world. A network of networks spans the planet, allowing malicious actors on one continent to act on systems thousands of miles away. Cyber attacks cross borders at light speed, and discerning the source of malicious activity is difficult. America must be capable of safeguarding and defending its critical systems and networks. Enabling the ability to do so requires a system of international cooperation to facilitate information sharing, reduce vulnerabilities, and deter malicious actors. The National Strategy to Secure Cyberspace identifies six major actions and initiatives to strengthen U.S. national security and international cooperation:

1. Strengthen cyber-related counterintelligence efforts
2. Improve capabilities for attack attribution and response

3. Improve coordination for responding to cyber attacks within the U.S. national security community
4. Work with industry and through international organizations to facilitate dialogue and partnerships among international public and private sectors focused on protecting information infrastructures and promoting a global "culture of security"
5. Foster the establishment of national and international watch-and-warning networks to detect and prevent cyber attacks as they emerge
6. Encourage other nations to accede to Council of Europe Convention on Cyber Crime or to ensure that their laws and procedures are at least as comprehensive

(National Strategy to Secure Cyberspace, Department of Homeland Security, February 2003, http://www.dhs.gov)

UTILITIES AND INDUSTRIAL FACILITIES

Utilities are the lifelines of American society. They include essential daily needs such as electricity, energy, water, and telecommunication that are characterized as critical infrastructure. Today's complex terrorist attacks target people and economies, as well as important critical infrastructure such as utilities, in order to cause destruction of property and disruption of society and commerce. For that reason utilities pose an important terrorist target.

Protection of the utilities infrastructure of the United States is an important duty of the DHS. The Directorate of Information Analysis and Infrastructure Protection is the operational branch of the DHS that is responsible for protecting the nation's utility infrastructure. However, this is not an easy task. Almost 85 percent of the utilities infrastructure of the United States is owned or operated by the private sector. Therefore strong relationships and coordination between the DHS and the private sector is essential to successfully protect these infrastructures. A separate section is dedicated for the role of private sector in homeland security, and it will be discussed later on. The next section will talk about federal initiatives to protect the utility infrastructure of the United States.

The main guideline publication for the protection of utilities is again the "National Strategy for the Physical Protection of Critical Infrastructures and Key Assets" from the DHS. The document covers utilities protection in its Water, Energy, and Telecommunication subtitles.

WATER

The nation's water sector is critical from both a public health and an economic standpoint. The water sector consists of two basic, yet vital, components: fresh water supply and wastewater collection and treatment (wastewater treatment will be mentioned later on). Sector infrastructures are diverse, complex, and distributed, ranging from systems that serve a few customers to those that serve millions. On the supply side the primary focus of critical infrastructure protection efforts is the nation's 170,000 public water systems. These utilities depend on reservoirs, dams, wells, and aquifers, as well as treatment facilities, pumping stations, aqueducts, and transmission pipelines.

The water sector has taken great strides to protect its critical facilities and systems. For instance, government and industry have developed vulnerability assessment methodologies for both drinking water and wastewater facilities and trained thousands of utility operators to conduct them. In response to the Public Health Security and Bio-Terrorism Preparedness and Response Act of 2002, the Environmental Protection Agency (EPA) has developed baseline threat information to use in conjunction with vulnerability assessments. EPA has provided assistance to state and local governments for drinking water systems to enable them to undertake vulnerability assessments and develop emergency response plans. To improve the flow of information among water-sector organizations, the industry has begun development of its sector-ISAC. The Water ISAC will provide a secure forum for gathering, analyzing, and sharing security related information. Additionally, several federal agencies are working together to improve the warehousing of information regarding contamination threats, such as the release of biological, chemical, and radiological substances into the water supply, and how to respond to their presence in drinking water. With respect to identifying new technologies, the EPA has an existing program that develops testing protocols and verifies the performance of innovative technologies. It has initiated a new program to verify monitoring technologies that may be useful in detecting or avoiding biological or chemical threats.

The basic human need for water and the concern for maintaining a safe water supply are driving factors for water infrastructure protection. Public perception regarding the safety of the nation's water supply is also significant, as is the safety of people who reside or work near water facilities. In order to set priorities among the wide range of protective measures that should be taken, the water sector is focusing on the types of infrastructure attacks that could result in significant human casualties and property damage or widespread economic consequences. In general, there are four areas of primary concentration:

1. Physical damage or destruction of critical assets, including intentional release of toxic chemicals
2. Actual or threatened contamination of the water supply
3. Cyber attack on information management systems or other electronic systems
4. Interruption of services from another infrastructure

To address these potential threats, the sector requires additional focused threat information in order to direct investments toward enhancement of corresponding protective measures. The water sector also requires increased monitoring and analytic capabilities to enhance detection of biological, chemical, or radiological contaminants that could be intentionally introduced into the water supply. Some enterprises are already in the process of developing advanced monitoring and sampling technologies, but additional resources from the water sector will likely be needed.

Environmental monitoring techniques and technologies and appropriate laboratory capabilities require enhancement to provide adequate and timely analysis of water samples to ensure early warning capabilities and assess the effectiveness of clean-up activities should an incident occur. Specific innovations needed include new broad spectrum analytical methods, monitoring strategies, sampling protocols, and training.

Currently, approaches to emergency response and the handling of security incidents at water facilities vary according to state and local policies and procedures. With regard to the public reaction associated with contamination or perceived contamination, it is essential that local, state, and federal departments and agencies coordinate their protection and response efforts. Maintaining the public's confidence regarding information provided and the timeliness of the message is critical. Suspected events concerning water systems to date have elicited strong responses that involved taking systems out of service until their integrity could be verified, announcing the incident to the public, and issuing "boil water" orders.

The operations of the water sector depend extensively on other sectors. The heaviest dependence is on the energy sector. For example, running pumps to move water and wastewater and operating drinking water and wastewater treatment plants require large amounts of electricity.

Water infrastructure protection initiatives are guided both by the challenges that the water sector faces and by recent legislation. Additional protection initiatives include efforts to do the following:

1. Identify high-priority vulnerabilities and improve site security: EPA, in concert with DHS, state and local governments, and other water sector leaders, will work to identify processes and technologies to better secure key points of storage and distribution, such as dams, pumping stations, chemical storage facilities, and treatment plants. EPA and DHS will also continue to provide tools, training, technical assistance, and limited financial assistance for research on vulnerability-assessment methodologies and risk-management strategies.

2. Improve sector monitoring and analytic capabilities: EPA will continue to work with sector representatives and other federal agencies to improve information on contaminants of concern and to develop appropriate monitoring and analytical technologies and capabilities.

3. Improve sector-wide information exchange and coordinate contingency planning: DHS and EPA will continue to work with the sector coordinator and the water ISAC to coordinate timely information on threats, incidents, and other topics of special interest to the water sector. DHS and EPA will also work with the sector and the states to standardize and coordinate emergency response efforts and communications protocols.

4. Work with other sectors to manage unique risks resulting from interdependencies: DHS and EPA will convene cross-sector working groups to develop models for integrating priorities and emergency response plans in the context of interdependencies between the water sector and other critical infrastructures.

(The National Strategy for the Protection of Physical Infrastructure and Key Assets, Department of Homeland Security, February 2003, pp. 39–40, http://www.dhs.gov)

ENERGY

Energy drives the foundation of many of the sophisticated processes at work in American society today. It is essential to economy, national defense, and quality of life. The energy sector is commonly divided into two segments in the context of critical infrastructure protection: electricity and oil and natural gas.

The electric industry services almost 130 million households and institutions. The United States consumed nearly 3.6 trillion kilowatt hours in 2001. Oil and natural gas facilities and assets are widely distributed, consisting of more than 300,000 producing sites; 4,000 off-shore platforms; more than 600 natural gas processing plants; 153 refineries and more than 1,400 product terminals; and 7,500 bulk stations.

ELECTRICITY

Almost every form of productive activity—whether in businesses, manufacturing plants, schools, hospitals, or homes—requires electricity. Electricity is necessary to produce other forms of energy, such as refined oil. Were a widespread or long-term disruption of the power grid to occur, many of the activities critical to the economy and national defense—including those associated with response and recovery—would be impossible.

The North American electric system is an interconnected, multi-nodal distribution system that accounts for virtually all the electricity supplied to the United States, Canada, and a portion of Baja California Norte, Mexico. The physical system consists of three major parts: generation, transmission and distribution, and control and communications.

Generation assets include fossil fuel plants, hydroelectric dams, and nuclear power plants. Transmission and distribution systems link areas of the national grid. Distribution systems manage and control the distribution of electricity into homes and businesses. Control and communications systems operate and monitor critical infrastructure components.

The North American electric system is the world's most reliable, a fact that can be attributed to industry efforts to identify single points of failure and system interdependencies and to institute appropriate backup processes, systems, and facilities.

North American Electric Reliability Council (NERC), in charge of developing guidelines and procedures for assuring electricity system reliability, is a nonprofit corporation made up of 10 regional reliability councils, whose voluntary membership represents all segments of the electricity industry, including public and private utilities from the United States and Canada. Through NERC, the electricity sector coordinates programs to enhance security for the electricity industry.

The electricity sector is highly regulated even as the industry is being restructured to increase competition. The Federal Energy Regulatory Commission (FERC) and state utility regulatory commissions regulate some of the activities and operations of certain electricity industry participants. The Nuclear Regulatory Commission (NRC) regulates nuclear power reactors and other civilian nuclear facilities, materials, and activities.

The electricity sector is highly complex, and its numerous component assets and systems span the North American continent. The stakeholders in the sector are diverse in size, capabilities, and focus. Currently, individual companies pay for levels of protection that are consistent with their resources and customer expectations. Typically, these companies seek to recover the costs of new security investments through proposed rate or price increases. Under current federal law, however, there is no assurance that electricity industry participants would be allowed to recover the costs of federally mandated security measures through such rate or price increases.

Another challenge for the electricity industry is effective, sector-wide communications. The owners and operators of the electric system are a large and heterogeneous group. Industry associations serve as clearing houses for industry-related information, but not all industry owners and operators belong to such organizations.

Data needed to perform thorough analyses on the infrastructure's interdependencies is not readily available. A focused analysis of time-phased effects of one infrastructure on another, including loss of operations metrics, would help identify dependencies and establish protection priorities and strategies.

For certain transmission and distribution facilities, providing redundancy and increasing generating capacity provide greater reliability of electricity service. However, this approach faces several challenges. Long lead times, possible denials of rights-of-way, state and local siting requirements, "not-in-my-backyard" community perspectives, and uncertain rates of return when compared with competing investment needs are hurdles that may prevent owners and operators of electricity facilities from investing sufficiently in security and service assurance measures.

Building a less vulnerable grid represents another option for protecting the national electricity infrastructure. Work is ongoing to develop a national

R&D strategy for the electricity sector. Additionally, FERC has developed R&D guidelines, and the Department of Energy's (DOE) National Grid Study contains recommendations focused on enhancing physical and cyber security for the transmission system.

The electricity industry has a history of taking proactive measures to assure the reliability and availability of the electricity system. Individual enterprises also work actively in their communities to address public safety issues related to their systems and facilities. Since September 11, 2001, the sector has reviewed its security guidelines and initiated a series of intra-industry working groups to address specific aspects of security.

It has created a utility-sector security committee at the chief executive officer level to enhance planning, awareness, and resource allocation within the industry.

The sector as a whole, with NERC as the sector coordinator, has been working in collaboration with DOE since 1998 to assess its risk posture in light of the new threat environment, particularly with respect to the electric system's dependence on information technology and networks. In the process, the sector has created an awareness program that includes a "Business Case for Action" for industry senior executives, a strategic reference document, "An Approach to Action for the Electric Power Sector," and security guidelines related to physical and cyber security.

With respect to managing security information, the sector has established an indications, analysis, and warning program that trains utilities on incident reporting and alert notification procedures. The sector has also developed threat alert levels for both physical and cyber events, which include action-response guidelines for each alert level. The industry has also established an Information Sharing and Analysis Center (ISAC) to gather incident information, relay alert notices, and coordinate daily briefs between the federal government and electric grid operators around the country.

Power management control rooms are probably the most protected aspect of the electrical network. NERC's guidelines require a backup system and/or

manual workarounds to bypass damaged systems. FERC is also working with the sector to develop a common set of security requirements for all enterprises in the competitive electric supply market.

Additional electricity sector protection initiatives include efforts to do the following:

1. Identify equipment stock pile requirements: DHS and DOE will work with the electricity sector to inventory components and equipment critical to electric-system operations and to identify and assess other approaches to enhance restoration and recovery to include standardizing equipment and increasing component interchangeability.

2. Reevaluate and adjust nationwide protection planning, system restoration, and recovery in response to attacks: The electric power industry has an excellent process and record of reconstitution and recovery from disruptive events. Jointly, industry and government need to evaluate this system and its processes to support the evolution from a local and regional system to an integrated national response system. DHS and DOE will work with the electricity sector to ensure that existing coordination and mutual aid processes can effectively and efficiently support protection, response, and recovery activities as the structure of the electricity sector continues to evolve.

3. Develop strategies to reduce vulnerabilities: DHS and DOE will work with state and local governments and the electric power industry to identify the appropriate levels of redundancy of critical parts of the electric system, as well as requirements for designing and implementing redundancy in view of the industry's realignment and restructuring activities.

4. Develop standardized guidelines for physical security programs: DHS and DOE will work with the sector to define consistent criteria for criticality, standard approaches for vulnerability and risk assessments for critical facilities, and physical security training for electricity sector personnel.

(The National Strategy for the Protection of Physical Infrastructure and Key Assets, Department of

Homeland Security, February 2003, pp. 50–52, http://www.dhs.gov)

OIL AND NATURAL GAS

The oil and natural gas industries are closely integrated. The oil infrastructure consists of five general components: oil production, crude oil transport, refining, product transport and distribution, and control and other external support systems. Oil and natural gas production include exploration, field development, on- and off-shore production, field collection systems, and their supporting infrastructures. Crude oil transport includes pipelines (160,000 miles), storage terminals, ports, and ships. The refinement infrastructure consists of about 150 refineries that range in size and production capabilities from 5,000 to over 500,000 barrels per day. Transport and distribution of oil includes pipelines, trains, ships, ports, terminals and storage, trucks, and retail stations.

The natural gas industry consists of three major components: exploration and production, transmission, and local distribution. The United States produces roughly 20 percent of the world's natural gas supply. There are 278,000 miles of natural gas pipelines and 1,119,000 miles of natural gas distribution lines in the United States Distribution includes storage facilities, gas processing, liquid natural gas facilities, pipelines, city gates, and liquefied petroleum gas storage facilities.

The pipeline and distribution segments of the oil and natural gas industries are highly regulated. Oversight includes financial, safety, and siting regulations. The exploration and production side of the industry is less regulated, but it is affected by safety regulations and restrictions concerning property access.

Protection of critical assets requires both heightened security awareness and investment in protective equipment and systems. One serious issue is the lack of metrics to determine and justify corporate security expenditures. In the case of natural disasters or accidents, there are well-established methods for determining risks and cost-effective levels of investments in protective equipment, systems, and methods for managing risk (e.g., insurance). It is not clear what levels of security and protection are appropriate and cost effective to meet the risks of terrorist attack.

The first government responders to a terrorist attack on most oil and natural gas sector facilities will be local police and fire departments. In general, these responders need to improve their capabilities and preparedness to confront well-planned, sophisticated attacks, particularly those involving CBR weapons. Fortunately, because of public-safety requirements related to their operations and facilities, the oil and natural gas industries have substantial protection programs already in place.

Quick action to repair damaged infrastructure in an emergency can be impeded by a number of hurdles, including the long lead time needed to obtain local, state, and federal construction permits or waivers; requirements for environmental reviews and impact statements; and lengthy processes for obtaining construction rights-of-way for the placement of pipelines on adjoining properties if a new path becomes necessary. The availability of necessary materials and equipment and the uniqueness of such equipment are also impediments to rapid reconstitution of damaged infrastructure.

The current system for locating and distributing replacement parts needs to be enhanced significantly. The components themselves range from state-of-the art systems to mechanisms that are decades old. While newer systems are standardized, many of the older components are unique and must be custom-manufactured. Moreover, there is extensive variation in size, ownership, and security across natural gas facilities. There are also a large number of natural gas facilities scattered over broad geographical areas—a fact that complicates protection.

Oil and natural gas sector protection initiatives include efforts to do the following:

1. Plan and invest in research and development for the oil and gas industry to enhance robustness and reliability: Utilizing the federal government's national scientific and research capabilities, DHS and DOE will

work with oil and natural gas sector stakeholders to develop an appropriate strategy for research and development to support protection, response, and recovery requirements.

2. Develop strategies to reduce vulnerabilities: DHS and DOE will work with state and local governments and industry to identify the appropriate levels of redundancy of critical components and systems, as well as requirements for designing and enhancing reliability.

3. Develop standardized guidelines for physical security programs: DHS and DOE will work with the oil and natural gas industry representatives to define consistent criteria for criticality, standard approaches for vulnerability and risk assessments for various facilities, and physical security training for industry personnel.

4. Develop guidelines for measures to reconstitute capabilities of individual facilities and systems: DHS and DOE will convene an advisory task force of industry representatives from the sector, construction firms, equipment suppliers, oil engineering firms, state and local governments, and federal agencies to identify appropriate planning requirements and approaches.

5. Develop a national system for locating and distributing critical components in support of response and recovery activities: DHS and DOE will work with industry to develop regional and national programs for identifying parts, requirements, notifying parties of their availability, and distributing them in an emergency.

(The National Strategy for the Protection of Physical Infrastructure and Key Assets, Department of Homeland Security, February 2003, pp. 52–53, http://www.dhs.gov)

TELECOMMUNICATIONS

The composition of the telecommunications sector is constantly evolving because of technologic advances, business and competitive pressures, and changes in the regulatory environment. Despite its dynamic nature, the sector has consistently provided robust and reliable communications and processes to meet the needs of businesses and governments. In the new threat environment, the sector faces significant challenges to protect its vast and dispersed critical assets, both cyber and physical. Because the government and critical infrastructure industries rely heavily on the public telecommunications infrastructure for vital communications services, the sector's vulnerabilities and protection initiatives are particularly important.

Every day the sector must contend with traditional natural and human-based threats to its physical infrastructure, such as weather events, unintentional cable cuts, and the insider threat (e.g., physical and cyber sabotage). The September 11 attacks revealed the threat terrorism poses to the telecommunications sector's physical infrastructure. While it was not a direct target of the attacks, the telecommunications sector suffered significant collateral damage. In the future, certain concentrations of key sector assets themselves could become attractive direct targets for terrorists, particularly with the increased use of collocation facilities. The telecommunications infrastructure withstood the September 11 attacks in overall terms and demonstrated remarkable resiliency because damage to telecommunications assets at the attack sites was offset by diverse, redundant, and multifaceted communications capabilities. Priorities for telecommunications carriers are service reliability, cost balancing, security, and effective risk management postures. The government places high priority on the consistent application of security across the infrastructure. Although private- and public-sector stakeholders share similar objectives, they have different perspectives on what constitutes acceptable risk and how to achieve security and reliability. Therefore an agreement on a sustainable security threshold and corresponding security requirements remains elusive.

Because of growing interdependencies among the various critical infrastructures, a direct or indirect attack on any of them could result in cascading effects across the others. Such interdependencies increase the need to identify critical assets and secure them against both physical and cyber threats. Critical infrastructures rely upon a secure and robust telecommunications infrastructure.

Redundancy within the infrastructure is critical to ensure that single points of failure in one infrastructure will not create an adverse impact in others. It is vital that government and industry work together to characterize the state of diversity in the telecommunications architecture. They must also collaborate to understand the topography of the physical components of the architecture to establish a foundation for defining a strategy to ensure physical and logical diversity.

Despite significant challenges, the telecommunications marketplace remains competitive, and customer demand for services is steady, if not increasing. An economic upturn within the industry could rapidly accelerate service demands. The interplay of market forces and FCC oversight will ensure the continuance of service delivery to sustain critical telecommunications functions. Nevertheless, recent economic distress has forced companies to spend their existing resources on basic network operations rather than re-capitalizing, securing, and enhancing the infrastructure, which could amplify the financial impact of necessary infrastructure protection investments.

Given the reality of the physical and cyber threats to the telecommunications sector, government and industry must continue to work together to understand vulnerabilities, develop countermeasures, establish policies and procedures, and raise awareness necessary to mitigate risks. The telecommunications sector has a long, successful history of collaboration with government to address concerns over the reliability and security of the telecommunications infrastructure. The sector has recently undertaken a variety of new initiatives to further ensure both reliability and quick recovery and reconstitution. Within this environment of increasing emphasis on protection issues, public-private partnership can be further leveraged to address a number of key telecommunications initiatives, including efforts to do the following:

1. Define an appropriate threshold for security: DHS will work with industry to define an appropriate security threshold for the sector and develop a set of requirements derived from that definition. DHS will work with industry to close the gap between respective security expectations and requirements. Reaching agreement on a methodology for ensuring physical diversity is a key element of this effort.

2. Expand infrastructure diverse routing capability: DHS will leverage and enhance the government's capabilities to define and map the overall telecommunications architecture. This effort will identify critical intersections among the various infrastructures and lead to strategies that better address security and reliability.

3. Understand the risks associated with vulnerabilities of the telecommunications infrastructure: The telecommunications infrastructure, including the PSTN, the Internet, and enterprise networks, provides essential communications for governments at all levels and other critical infrastructures. DHS will work with the private sector to conduct studies to understand physical vulnerabilities within the telecommunications infrastructure and their associated risks. Studies will focus on facilities where many different types of equipment and multiple carriers are concentrated.

4. Coordinate with key allies and trading partners: More than ever our nation has a common reliance on vital communications circuits and processes with our key allies and trading partners. DHS will work with other nations to consider innovative communications paths that provide priority communications processes to link our governments, global industries, and networks in such a manner that vital communications are assured.

(The National Strategy for the Protection of Physical Infrastructure and Key Assets, Department of Homeland Security, February 2003, pp. 47–49, http://www.dhs.gov)

PIPELINES

The United States has a vast pipeline industry, consisting of many hundreds of thousands of miles of pipelines, many of which are buried underground. These lines move a variety of substances, such as crude oil, refined petroleum products, and natural gas. Pipeline facilities already incorporate a variety of stringent safety precautions that account for the potential effects a disaster could have on surrounding areas. Moreover, most elements of pipeline infrastructures can be quickly repaired or bypassed to mitigate localized disruptions. Destruction of one or even several of its key components would not disrupt the entire system. As a whole, the response and recovery capabilities of the pipeline industry are well proven, and most large control-center operators have established extensive contingency plans and backup protocols.

Pipelines are not independent entities but rather integral parts of industrial and public service networks. Loss of a pipeline could have an impact on a wide array of facilities and industrial factories that depend on reliable fuel delivery to operate.

Several hundred thousand miles of pipeline span the country, and it is not realistic to expect total security for all facilities. As such, protection efforts focus on infrastructure components whose impairment would have significant effects on the energy markets and the economy as a whole. For the pipeline industry, determining what to protect and when to protect it is a factor in cost-effective infrastructure protection. During periods of high demand—such as the winter months—pipeline systems typically operate at peak capacity and are more important to the facilities and functions they serve.

The pipeline industry as a whole has an excellent safety record, as well as in-place crisis management protocols to manage disruptions as they occur. Nevertheless, many of the products that pipelines deliver are inherently volatile. Hence, their protection is a significant issue.

Pipelines cross numerous state and local, as well as international jurisdictions. The number and variety of stakeholders create a confusing, and sometimes conflicting array of regulations and security programs for the industry to manage, especially with respect to the ability of pipeline facilities to recover, reconstitute, and reestablish service quickly after a disruption.

The pipeline industry's increasing interdependencies with the energy and telecommunications sectors necessitate cooperation with other critical infrastructures during protection and response planning. Individually, companies have difficulty assessing the broader implications of an attack on their critical facilities. These interdependencies call for cross-sector coordination for them to be truly responsive to national concerns.

Additionally, some issues concerning recovery or reconstitution will require at least regional planning within the industry, as well as the sharing of sensitive business information that may run into proprietary concerns.

Historically, individual enterprises within this sector have invested in the security of their facilities to protect their ability to deliver oil and gas products. Representatives from major entities within this sector have examined the new terrorist risk environment. As a result, they have developed a plan for action, including industry-wide information sharing. Within the federal sector, DHS and DOT and DOT's Office of Pipeline Safety have major responsibility for enhancing pipeline security. DOT has developed a methodology for determining pipeline facility criticality and a system of recommended protective measures that are synchronized with the threat levels of the Homeland Security Advisory System. Additional pipeline mode protection initiatives include efforts to do the following:

1. Develop standard reconstitution protocols: DHS, in collaboration with DOE, DOT, and industry, will initiate a study to identify, clarify, and establish authorities and procedures as needed to reconstitute facilities as quickly as possible after a disruption.

2. Develop standard security assessment and threat deterrent guidelines: DHS, in collaboration with DOE and DOT, will work with state and local governments and the pipeline industry to develop consensus security guidance on assessing vulnerabilities, improving security plans, implementing specific deterrent and protective actions, and upgrading response and recovery plans for pipelines.

3. Work with other sectors to manage risks resulting from interdependencies: DHS, in collaboration with DOE and DOT, will convene cross-sector working

groups to develop models for integrating protection priorities and emergency response plans.

(The National Strategy for the Protection of Physical Infrastructure and Key Assets, Department of Homeland Security, February 2003, pp. 58–59, http://www. dhs.gov)

Recent publications prove that since September 11 the industry and federal, state, and local government have taken significant steps to secure the nation's critical energy infrastructure—from increasing surveillance of pipelines and conducting more thorough employee background checks to further restricting access to pipeline facilities and Internet mapping systems.

Companies formed task forces with federal, state, and local law enforcement officials to share security information and develop emergency notification and response plans.

Along with issuing new security measures late last year [2002], the DOT developed criteria to evaluate an operator's implementation of those measures. Each operator was asked to submit a statement certifying that he or she had a security plan and had instituted the appropriate security procedures.

Today, 95 percent of oil pipeline operators have already implemented the measures and returned confirmation statements to the DOT. The remaining 5 percent are primarily small operators that are in other businesses but run pipelines between plant facilities.

Some additional steps oil pipeline operators have taken include the following:

- Developing direct relationships with FBI regional field personnel
- Obtaining secret level security clearances for selected operational personnel to ensure that threat information can be communicated directly from federal officials to the company
- Joining government-industry threat information dissemination services
- Installing additional surveillance cameras and physical barriers to entrances at certain facilities
- Conducting response drills using terrorist scenarios as a basis for training personnel and

working with new federal law enforcement officials
- Using guard patrol at certain facilities during certain threat condition levels
- Limiting access to facilities and permitting entrance only after positive identification

(Cooper B: Protecting Pipelines from Terrorist Attack, April 2003, http://www.enewsbuilder.net/aopl/e_article000141902.cfm)

PUBLIC WORKS

The phrase "public works," in its general meaning, refers to all facilities and services provided by the government (usually state and local governments) to meet the basic sanitary needs and comfort of the citizens. Common responsibilities of public works departments include waste management, recycling, street lighting, trash removal, water management, wastewater management, and so on.

Although these facilities are service-localized areas, they represent high vulnerabilities because of the potentially high and widespread health consequences in the case of a successful terrorist attack on those facilities. Water treatment plants, wastewater plants, and landfills are three unique examples of those vulnerable facilities.

WATER TREATMENT PLANTS

When a water supplier takes untreated water from a river or reservoir, the water often contains dirt and tiny pieces of leaves and other organic matter, as well as trace amounts of certain contaminants. When it gets to the treatment plant, water suppliers often add chemicals called coagulants to the water. These act on the water as it flows very slowly through tanks so that the dirt and other contaminants form clumps that settle to the bottom. Usually this water then flows through a filter for removal of the smallest contaminants, such as viruses and *Giardia* protozoa.

The most common drinking water treatment, considered by many to be one of the most important scientific advances of the 20th century, is disinfection. Most water suppliers add chlorine or another disinfectant to kill bacteria and other germs.

Water suppliers use other treatments as needed, according to the quality of their source water. For example, systems whose water is contaminated with organic chemicals can treat their water with activated carbon, which adsorbs or attracts the chemicals dissolved in the water. (http://www.epa.gov/safewater/dwh/treat.html)

The disinfection and purification of water is a rather complex process. It consists of several subprocesses such as prechlorination, coagulation, flocculation, sedimentation, filtration, fluoridation, postchlorination, and corrosion control treatment. These steps are needed in order to produce water that will meet federal and state drinking water standards, that is free of pathogens, and will be suitable for public consumption.

As Figure 5-1 demonstrates, there are several subprocesses the water goes through until its purified, and each of these subprocesses, especially the ones that involve chemical additives, are vulnerable to potential terrorist attacks. The terrorists can secretly change the additives with hazardous materials that they acquired beforehand and therefore change the contents of the city water into a potential chemical weapon against American society. Water with extremely high or low pH can be very dangerous and even poisonous for the body. Extreme chemical changes with the water can usually be detected quickly; however, even so, the panic, stress, and potential psychological effects of such a terrorist attack can be devastating.

The terrorists can also penetrate biological agents that naturally do not exist inside the groundwater for which the water treatment systems do not have any counter measures. The living infectious bacteria can be transported to the city and housing with the water, can get into our bodies once we drink it, and can cause serious infections inside the body, which may be hard to detect because of the long incubation periods of some bacteria. Detecting biological attacks in general is an important issue that is still very much open for research and improvements.

Drinking water utilities today find themselves facing these new responsibilities. While their mission has always been to deliver a dependable and safe supply of water to their customers, the challenges inherent in achieving that mission have expanded to include security and counterterrorism. In the Public Health

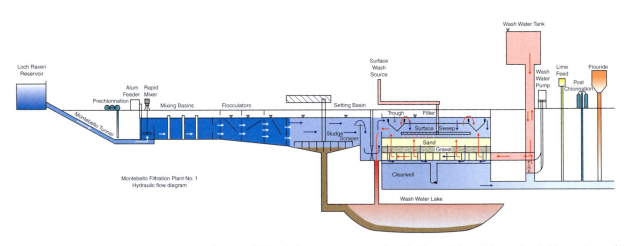

FIGURE 5-1   The Water treatment process diagram of Montebello water treatment plant (Baltimore). (http://cityservices.baltimorecity.gov/dpw/waterwastewater03/waterquality5a.html)

Security and Bioterrorism Preparedness and Response Act of 2002, Congress recognizes the need for drinking water systems to undertake a more comprehensive view of water safety and security. The Act amends the Safe Drinking Water Act and specifies actions community water systems and the U.S. Environmental Protection Agency (EPA) must take to improve the security of the nation's drinking water infrastructure. (http://www.epa.gov/safewater/security/index.html)

In its "Strategic Plan for Homeland Security" EPA has six critical infrastructure protection goals. One of them states, "EPA will work with the states, tribes, drinking water and wastewater utilities (water utilities), and other partners to enhance the security of water and wastewater utilities."

In accomplishing this goal, EPA is planning to use the following approaches:

1. EPA will work with the states, tribes, associations and others to provide tools, training, and technical assistance to assist water utilities in conducting vulnerability assessments, implementing security improvements, and effectively responding to terrorist events. In FY2002, while developing tools and providing training for all utilities, EPA provided direct grants to large drinking water utilities for vulnerability assessments, security enhancement designs, and/or emergency response plans. EPA will work with states, tribes, associations, and water utilities to identify needs and provide assistance for vulnerability assessments for medium and small utilities, and for high-priority security enhancements identified in the water utility vulnerability assessments for all systems. As plans are completed, emphasis on implementation of security enhancements will continue to increase.

By the end of FY 2003, EPA expects all water utility managers to have access to basic information to understand potential water threats, and basic tools to identify security needs. By the end of FY2003, all large community drinking water utilities shall have identified key vulnerabilities and shall be prepared to respond to any emergency. By the end of 2004, all medium community drinking water utilities shall be

similarly positioned. By 2005, unacceptable security risks at water utilities across the country will be significantly reduced through completion of appropriate vulnerability assessments; design of security enhancement plans; development of emergency response plans; and implementation of security enhancements. (EPA Strategic Plan for Homeland Security, pp. 1–2, http://www.epa.gov/epahome/downloads/epa_homeland_security_strategic_plan.pdf)

The 2003 budget of EPA included $3.214 million for safe water that is more than 41% of its total budget. (EPA Budget 2003, pp. xv–2, http://www.epa.gov/ocfo/budget/2003/2003bib.pdf)

2. EPA will work with the DHS, other federal agencies, universities, and the private sector to solicit and review methods to prevent, detect, and respond to chemical, biological, and radiological contaminants that could be intentionally introduced in drinking water systems and wastewater utilities; review methods and means by which terrorists could disrupt the supply of safe drinking water or take other actions against water collection, pretreatment, treatment, storage, and distribution facilities; and review methods and means by which alternative supplies of drinking water could be provided in the event of a disruption.

3. EPA will work with states, tribes, and water utilities to implement water security practices in ongoing water utility operations. EPA will also work with states and tribes to build security concerns into ongoing review systems (e.g., sanitary survey, capacity development, operator certification, and treatment optimization program for drinking water systems and pretreatment program, environmental management systems, and operator certification programs for wastewater).

EPA expects that beginning in FY2003, water utilities will incorporate security measures as a standard aspect of day-to-day operations and EPA, states, and tribes will review security measures at water utilities on a continuous basis. Through ongoing practice and review, water utilities' managers and employees will optimize security measures.

4. EPA will work with other government agencies, utility organizations, and water utilities to establish formal communication mechanisms to facilitate the timely and effective exchange of information on water utility security threats and incidents.

5. EPA and DHS will work together to foster coordination among federal, state, tribal, and local emergency responders, health agencies, environmental and health labs, the medical community, and the law enforcement community at all levels (federal, state, and local) concerning response to potential terrorist actions against water utilities. This will be achieved through training and support of simulations and emergency response exercises.

6. EPA will work with other critical infrastructure sectors to further understand and reduce the impact on water utilities of terrorist attacks on related infrastructure as well as the impacts of attacks on water utilities on other critical infrastructure.

(EPA Strategic Plan for Homeland Security, pp. 2–6, http://www.epa.gov/epahome/downloads/epa_homeland_security_strategic_plan.pdf)

WASTEWATER PLANTS

Wastewater is the spent or used water from homes, communities, farms, and businesses that contains enough harmful material to damage the water's quality. Wastewater includes both domestic sewage and industrial waste from manufacturing sources. Metals, organic pollutants, sediment, bacteria, and viruses may all be found in wastewater. As a result, untreated wastewater can cause serious harm to the environment and threaten human life. EPA regulates the discharge and treatment of wastewater under the Clean Water Act. The National Pollutant Discharge Elimination System (NPDES) issues permits to all wastewater dischargers and treatment facilities. These permits establish specific discharge limits, monitoring and reporting requirements, and may also require these facilities to undertake special measures to protect the

environment from harmful pollutants. (http://www.epa.gov/ebtpages/watewastewater.html)

The basic function of wastewater treatment is to speed up the natural processes by which water is purified. There are two basic stages in the treatment of wastes, primary and secondary. In the primary stage, solids are allowed to settle and removed from wastewater. The secondary stage uses biological processes to further purify wastewater. Sometimes, these stages are combined into one operation. (How Wastewater Treatment Works . . . Basics, EPA, pp. 1)

The nation's wastewater infrastructure consists of approximately 16,000 publicly owned wastewater treatment plants; 100,000 major pumping stations; 600,000 miles of sanitary sewers; and another 200,000 miles of storm sewers, with a total value of more than $2 trillion. Taken together, the sanitary and storm sewers form an extensive network that runs near or beneath key buildings and roads, the heart of business and financial districts, and the downtown areas of major cities and is contiguous to many communication and transportation networks. (http://www.house.gov/transportation/press/press2003/release77.html)

There are several vulnerabilities and risks associated with the wastewater treatment infrastructure. A potential scenario is the abuse of the wastewater collected in wastewater treatment plant by terrorists and its use as a biological or chemical weapon. The terrorists can accomplish this by forwarding the waste into the clean water and making it poisonous. Another scenario would be a direct attack on one of the wastewater facilities where hazardous materials are filtered from the wastewater and stored for further processing. The blast on such a facility (assuming that it contains nuclear waste, such as waste from nuclear power plants) can have the effects of a dirty bomb, which contains radioactive particles that are spread over a large area, making the removal of the debris very difficult and risky for the first responders.

Vulnerability assessments and risk reduction programs are necessary to minimize the potential impacts of terrorist attacks to these facilities.

As mentioned in the previous section, EPA has some programs to improve water security and wastewater security. One of the important programs of EPA, in cooperation with the Association of Metropolitan Sewerage Agencies (AMSA), released two new Vulnerability Self Assessment Tools (VSAT), one for joint water/wastewater utilities and another for small-medium sized water utilities. VSAT™ water/wastewater provides the valuable online vulnerability assessment capabilities to utilities providing both wastewater treatment and water supply services. Its new counterpart, VSAT™ water, will do the same for both public and private water utilities. These new software tools, developed by AMSA for EPA, provide a user-friendly approach to evaluate, prioritize, and remediate vulnerabilities based upon five critical utility assets—physical plant, information technology, knowledge base, employees, and customers. To learn more about the VSAT™ initiative, visit AMSA's web site at http://www.amsa-cleanwater.org. (http://www.epa.gov/safewater/security/)

Another program by EPA to improve safety and security on wastewater plants is the "Wastewater Treatment Plant Operator On-Site Assistance Training Program." The goal of the program is to provide direct on-site assistance to operators at small underserved community wastewater treatment facilities, in order to help the facility achieve and maintain consistent permit compliance, maximizing the community's investment in improved water quality. In a cooperative effort with EPA, states, state coordinators, municipalities, and operators, the assistance endeavor focuses on issues such as wastewater treatment plant capacity, operation training, maintenance, administrative management, financial management, troubleshooting, and laboratory operations. The program identifies any need to repair or build new facilities to meet existing or future permit limits, assists the town during the process of selecting consultants and design review, recommends ways to improve preventive maintenance of equipment and structures, and often reduces energy and chemical costs through more efficient operation techniques. (http://www.epa.gov/owm/mab/smcomm/104g/index.htm#report)

LANDFILLS

Although conservation, reuse, recycling, and composting have reduced municipal waste, most of the waste that is generated still ends up in landfills. At present, there are more than 3,000 landfills in the United States. Many are modern, well-engineered facilities that are located, designed, operated, monitored, and financed to insure compliance with federal regulations. These regulations include restrictions that require landfills to be located away from wetlands, flood plains and other restricted areas; clay reinforced liners; operating practices that reduce odor and control insects and rodents; groundwater monitoring; postclosure care; and corrective action to clean up landfill sites. In addition, the EPA encourages the use of landfill gas as a renewable fuel source through its Landfill Methane Outreach Program. (http://www.epa.gov/ebtpages/wastwastelandfills.html)

Location restrictions ensure that landfills are built in suitable geological areas away from faults, wetlands, flood plains, or other restricted areas. Liners are geo-membrane or plastic sheets reinforced with two feet of clay on the bottom and sides of landfills. Operating practices such as compacting and covering waste frequently with several inches of soil help reduce odor; control litter, insects, and rodents; and protect public health. Groundwater monitoring requires testing groundwater wells to determine whether waste materials have escaped from the landfill. Closure and postclosure care include covering landfills and providing long-term care of closed landfills. Corrective action controls and cleans up landfill releases and achieves groundwater protection standards. Financial assurance provides funding for environmental protection during and after landfill closure (i.e., closure and postclosure care). However, there are still some risks and vulnerabilities associated with landfills. (http://www.epa.gov/epaoswer/non-hw/muncpl/disposal.htm)

More than 40 million tons of hazardous waste is produced in the United States each year. It is produced by large industrial facilities such as chemical manufacturers, electroplating companies, petroleum refineries, and by more common businesses such as dry cleaners, auto repair shops, hospitals, exterminators, and photo processing centers. The EPA has produced a list of more than 500 hazardous wastes and works closely with businesses and state and local authorities to make sure these wastes are properly treated and disposed of. The EPA conducts risk management studies to ascertain the potential health effects of exposure to these wastes and oversees Superfund and other programs that clean-up contaminated waste sites. (http://www.epa.gov/ebtpages/wasthazardouswaste.html)

Radioactive waste is produced by a number of activities, including nuclear power generation, mining, medicine, and industry. Some radioactive waste can remain hazardous for thousands of years. The EPA works with the Nuclear Regulatory Commission (NRC), DOT, DOE, and local authorities to regulate the storage and disposal of radioactive waste. The EPA is responsible for developing environmental standards that apply to radioactive waste disposal facilities. The EPA ensures that waste facilities comply with all federal environmental laws and regulations. (http://www.epa.gov/ebtpages/wastradioactivewaste.html)

The physical security of landfill sites still poses a potential terrorist threat. Recognizing the amount of hazardous toxic waste every year in the United States and the existence of radiological waste, the physical security of landfill sites gets even more important. A scenario in which terrorists attack and blow up a landfill where radiological waste was stored would cause a major disaster. Given that terrorists look for easy targets with the largest potential impact, this scenario is fairly realistic. If physical security of landfills cannot be assured, they can be an easy target of terrorist attacks.

Currently there are a few local and state initiatives to improve physical security of landfills, and federal support, while essential to providing greater physical security, has been limited. EPA, in cooperation with DHS, is the appropriate sources for technical assistance and financial aid. However, because of other competing priorities, there has been limited attention paid to coordinate the initiatives and support state,

local, and publicly held landfill sites for improved physical security.

ROLE OF PRIVATE SECTOR IN HOMELAND SECURITY AND CHANGES IN BUSINESS CONTINUITY AND CONTINGENCY PLANNING

The terrorist attacks of September 11 affected thousands of private businesses; not just businesses in New York or near the Pentagon but businesses as far away as Hawaii and Seattle felt the economic impact of these events. The events killed nearly 3,000 people, most of whom were employees of private corporations that had offices in or near the World Trade Center (WTC). Some companies lost hundreds of employees. In downtown Manhattan, almost 34.5 million square feet of office space was destroyed. Totaling $50 to $70 billion dollars in insured losses, the WTC attack became the most catastrophic economic disaster in U.S. history. Most of these direct economic losses were incurred by the private sector. In addition to the physical resources and systems lost by businesses in the WTC, changes in public behavior following the attacks had a severe impact on travel, tourism, and other businesses. Because the biggest portion of the impact was absorbed by the private sector, September 11 demanded that the private sector focus on understanding the philosophy and implementing programs for corporate crisis management.

The changes in private sector crisis management after September 11 can be analyzed in two perspectives: (1) the changing expectations of the private sector of the new federal role (DHS) in helping achieve greater homeland and (2) the self reassessment of the private sector in terms of corporate crisis management and business continuity. Our reference point in addressing the changing expectations of the federal government from the private sector will be the major federal documents and strategies, such as the "National Strategy for Homeland Security" and official press releases from relevant departments and agencies. While addressing the change of internal processes and procedures among the private sector, we will refer to publications and press releases that address changes in particular companies and try to find general trends between different approaches.

The Expectations of the Department of Homeland Security from the Private Sector

The National Strategy for Homeland Security defines the basic approach of the new Department of Homeland Security and briefly describes the characteristics of the partnership the department is planning to achieve with the private sector. Given the fact that almost 85 percent of the infrastructure of the United States is owned or managed by the private sector, there is no doubt that the private sector should be a major stakeholder in homeland security. Reducing the vulnerabilities and securing the private sector means the same as securing the vast portion of U.S. infrastructure and economic viability.

According to the National Strategy for Homeland Security, a close partnership between the government and private sector is essential to ensuring that existing vulnerabilities to terrorism in the critical infrastructure are identified and eliminated as quickly as possible. The private sector is expected to conduct risk assessments on their holdings and invest in systems to protect key assets. The internalization of these costs is interpreted by the DHS as not only a matter of sound corporate governance and good corporate citizenship but also an essential safeguard of economic assets for shareholders, employees, and the nation. (The National Strategy for Homeland Security, Department of Homeland Security, July 2002, pp. 12, http://www.dhs.gov)

The National Strategy for the Protection of Physical Infrastructure and Key Assets provides more direct clues about what the DHS expects from the private sector as a partner and stakeholder in homeland security.

The strategy defines the private sector as the owner and operator of "the lion's share" of U.S. critical infrastructures and key assets and mentions that private sector firms prudently engage in risk management planning and invest in security as a necessary function of business operations and customer confidence. Moreover, since in the present threat environment the private sector generally remains the first line of defense for its own facilities, the DHS expects private sector owners and operators to reassess and adjust their planning, assurance, and investment programs to better accommodate the increased risk presented by deliberate acts of violence.

Since the events of September 11, many businesses have increased their threshold investments and undertaken enhancements in security in an effort to meet the demands of the new threat environment. For most enterprises the level of investment in security reflects implicit risk-versus-consequence tradeoffs, which are based on: (1) what is known about the risk environment and (2) what is economically justifiable and sustainable in a competitive marketplace or in an environment of limited government resources. Given the dynamic nature of the terrorist threat and the severity of the consequences associated with many potential attack scenarios, the private sector naturally looks to the government for better information to help make its crucial security investment decisions. The private sector is continuing to look for better data, analysis, and assessment from DHS to use in the corporate decision-making process.

Similarly, the private sector looks to the government for assistance when the threat at hand exceeds an enterprise's capability to protect itself beyond a reasonable level of additional investment. In this light the federal government promises to collaborate with the private sector (and state and local governments) to ensure the protection of nationally critical infrastructures and assets; provide timely warning and ensure the protection of infrastructures and assets that face a specific, imminent threat; and promote an environment in which the private sector can better carry out its specific protection responsibilities. (The National Strategy for the Protection of Physical Infrastructure and Key Assets, Department of Homeland Security, February 2003, pp. 11, http://www.dhs.gov)

A good example of partnership between the private sector and the DHS are the sectoral Information Sharing and Analysis Centers (ISAC). ISACs are established by the owners and operators of a national critical infrastructure to better protect their networks, systems, and facilities within the coordination of DHS. ISACs serve as central points to gather, analyze, sanitize, and disseminate private sector information to both industry and the DHS. These centers also analyze and distribute information received from the DHS to the private sector. The objectives of this program are to seek participation from all sector segments/entities, representation of all segments on ISAC Advisory Board in order to establish two-way trusted information-sharing program between ISAC entities and the DHS, and to provide cleared industry expertise to assist DHS in evaluating threats and incidents. Currently ISACs exist and are being created in a variety of critical infrastructure sectors such as electric power (NERC), water supply/wastewater (AMWA), telecommunications (NCS/NCC), information technology (LLC., ISS), financial services (LLC., SAIC), chemicals (ACC/ChemTrec), food (FMI), emergency fire services (USFA), interstate (NASCIO), emergency law enforcement (NIPC/ELES), trucking (ATA), maritime (Coast Guard) (ISAC not yet announced), research and education networks (Indiana University), real estate (Real Estate Roundtable), airports (ACI-NA), surface transportation (LLC., AAR/EWA), and energy [oil and gas] (LLC., SAIC). (DHS: Private Sector Information Sharing: ISAC Program, Harvey Blumenthal, 2003 Government Symposium on Information Sharing and Homeland Security; July 1, 2003)

The Self-reassessment of the Private Sector in Terms of Corporate Crisis Management, Business Continuity, and Contingency Planning

September 11 was the most tragic day in the history of American corporations. The private sector lost

people, expertise, buildings, office space, data, records, and revenue. Some of these losses were permanent and discrete losses, such as people and buildings; however, the companies affected also suffered time-dependent and continuous losses such as business interruption, loss of customer trust, and employee loyalty. The discrete losses could not have been controlled because the private sector itself could not have prevented those hijacked planes from crashing into the twin towers; however, good corporate crisis management and business continuity planning could have minimized the continuous losses.

To put this discussion in perspective, the following statistics and chart will illustrate how the private sector is vulnerable to terrorist actions.

The Department of State report "Patterns of Global Terrorism 2001" shows the total number of facilities struck by international terrorist attacks. The statistic shows attacks with respect to years and the type of facility struck (e.g., private sector, government, diplomat, military). The statistic is important because it shows an unexpectedly different trend in the type of facilities struck by terrorists. There is a common belief that terrorists are more likely to attack military and government facilities, since terrorist attacks usually have a political connotation or reason. However, statistics prove this theory wrong. Statistical data show that private sector facilities have been struck more frequently by terrorists than other types of buildings (Figure 5-2).

This statistic is important because it shows private business executives, owners, and stakeholders that the terrorism risk for the private sector is not as minimal as some people believe. This chart dramatically illustrates that private sector terrorism mitigation and preparedness planning is an important aspect of creating management systems that are robust against all types of hazards, disasters, and crisis.

Another factor that is changing private sector perceptions is insurance and losses. The Insurance Information Institute (Figure 5-3) has charted the distribution of different types of insured damage from the Sept. 11 attacks and it presents some interesting facts.

The important figure in this statistic is the amount of damage from business interruption: $11.0 billion

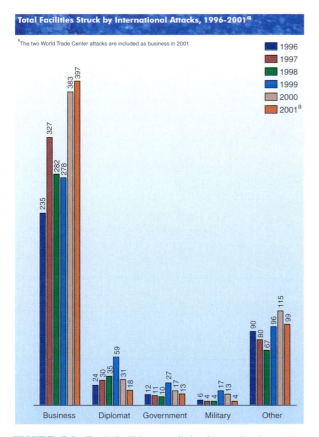

Total Facilities Struck by International Attacks, 1996-2001[a]

[a]The two World Trade Center attacks are included as business in 2001

- 1996
- 1997
- 1998
- 1999
- 2000
- 2001[a]

FIGURE 5-2 Total facilities struck by international terrorist attacks, Department of State, 2001.

(27 percent of all estimated damage) of the total damage. This is a significant portion of the damage, one over which we have some degree of control if adequate preplanning and business impact analysis could be maintained before the crisis. Because of the 1993 WTC bombing and the potential Y2K threat, private sector members located inside the WTC complex were among the most prepared stakeholders; however, there is always space for improvements and things to be learned from each new event.

The WTC attacks have led to a reassessment among the private sector relative to the value and necessity of investing in contingency planning and crisis and disaster management, especially relative to

terrorism. Some of the lessons learned by the private sector from the WTC attacks are proved below and are further evidence of the increased value of these activities to the private sector.

- In the 1990s business continuity and crisis response grew into well-established business disciplines within the corporate world. Large corporations, as well as many business schools, realized that these activities were actually becoming not just separate subrequirements of a business operation but indeed an integral part of the business management process. (Kavanaugh P: Current State of Crisis Management as an Industry in Canada, The Health Canada Emergency Preparedness Forum, October 28, 2002)

The belief "It won't happen to me" in terms of disasters does not seem to be valid because of the random targets of terrorists. Statistics even suggest that the corporate world is more likely to be struck by terrorist attacks than the government or the military facilities.

The events of September 11 will push the private sector to think twice about the physical security of their personnel, facilities, data, and customers under existing security measures and will very likely make them redesign their security system.

The preplanning of backup sites to relocate employees and equipment adds value when disasters cause extensive physical damage to the workplace. The cost-effectiveness of investing in such a spare place to continue operations seems highly questionable from the cost point of view, but the CFO of the New York Board of Trade, Walter Hines, has mentioned the extent to which the spare office the New York Board of Trade rented after the 1993 WTC bombing helped them to return back to business after the September 11 attacks. The spare office cost the board $300,000 annually, including utilities, and was constantly criticized for its high cost and little benefit for the company. However, according to Hines, "We thought we'd use it for four or five days," which justifies the investment after September 11, when

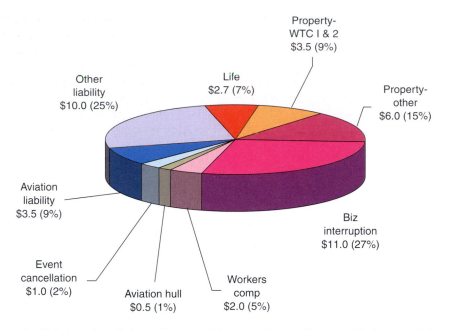

FIGURE 5-3   September 11 Industry Loss Estimates, Insurance Information Institute. Courtesy of the Insurance Information Institute.

the board used the office for several days. (U.S.A. Company—Managing risk in a war zone, The Economist Intelligence Unit Ltd, 2001)

- Ongoing research by Harrald, Shaw, Taha, Coppola, and Yeletaysi identified the relative "recoverers" and "nonrecoverers" of the September 11 terrorist attacks after a structured financial analysis of 23 companies that were selected with respect to predefined criteria. The next step in the research is to identify the best practices of the companies that recovered quickly and at the same time to detect what went wrong among the nonrecoverers. The project will be completed by late 2004, and results will be publicly available. (Assessing the Financial Impacts of the World Trade Center Attacks on Publicly Held Corporations; Harrald, Coppola, Yeletaysi, TIEMS Conference Proceedings, June 2003)

- Crisis Leadership: In a time of crisis, there is something reassuring about hearing the voice of a person in a position of authority, even if the information being provided is scant. Visibility, openness, and communication of leaders with the employees are important for the contribution of the staff to the crisis management process. (Greenberg WJ: September 11, 2001: A CEO's story, *Harvard Business Review*, p. 7)
- Building cross-company relationships inside the sector are important in order to reduce costs associated with mitigation and preparedness activities, as well as creating an environment to share expertise and creative ideas.
- During crisis and disasters that affect your staff and customers, it's very important to prioritize the recovery of the people. According to Jeffrey W. Greenberg, CEO of Marsh & McLennan

Companies, a business that was severely affected by the September 11 attacks,

So many companies acknowledge their people, or at least their intellectual capital, as their greatest strength. But the crucible is a moment like September 11, when we had to make choices fast and instinctively. In the months following that day, our human resource leaders and their teams stayed close to the emerging needs of victim's families and employees and made changes to a wide range of services and benefits. Looking back at the crisis and its aftermath, I believe that our immediate and longer-term assistance gave meaning to our commitment to people. (Greenberg WJ: September 11, 2001: A CEO's story, *Harvard Business Review*, p. 7)

- Another lesson from the WTC attacks is that in building redundancy to our infrastructure, physical location of the backup site is very important. The location of backup sites should be chosen in a way that the probability of a disaster occurring in the primary site to affect the backup site as well is minimized. One strategy to achieve this is to place the backup site physically distant to the primary site; however, different scenarios (natural disaster scenarios, man-made disaster scenarios, as well as terrorism) should be considered before making the decision.

CONCLUSION

Safety and security are two key concepts in the scope of homeland security. However, they are difficult to ensure. The complexity of the systems and infrastructures we deal with today increases our vulnerability and makes it more difficult to mitigate them. In addition to our personal vulnerabilities, we also face much systematic vulnerability, which will affect the society in case the risk becomes a reality.

The public and private sectors are under constant risk from natural, technological, and terrorist threats. In order to deal with those distinct vulnerabilities, the homeland security approach should be an inclusive and interactive one rather than a top-down, exclusive one. Only with the participation of different stakeholders and the public can those systematic vulnerabilities be detected and improved. The interdependency of systems makes it almost impossible to improve safety and security on a subsystem level. In light of this observation, homeland security can only be ensured if it can bring together people from all levels of the public, governmental, and private sectors, as well as academia and NGOs.

REVIEW QUESTIONS

1. What are the key intelligence agencies in the United States? Briefly comment on their roles in terms of Homeland Security?
2. Which are the functional Directorates under the Office of the Deputy Secretary in the Department of Homeland Security? What are the main roles and responsibilities of these Directorates?
3. What's the role of the private sector in Homeland Security? What are your suggestions to improve private sector participation and coordination with the Department of Homeland Security?
4. What are the different transportation modes in the United States? Rank those modes in terms of vulnerability to terrorist attacks, and compare your priority list with the current resource allocations to those modes in the Transportation Security Agency yearly budget. Comment on your findings.
5. a) Consider all possible critical infrastructures for the United States, and define performance measures in terms of vulnerability to terrorism (i.e., accessibility, redundancy, protection, etc.). Assign weights to those performance measures and grade each critical

infrastructure on 1–10 scale. Calculate the weighted average for each infrastructure and rank them.

b) Look to the bottom of your priority list (this should give you the most vulnerable critical infrastructure). How would you attack this type of infrastructure if you intended. (Hint: Don't hesitate to think like a terrorist. It's important to determine potential attack scenarios.)

c) Given the scenario you described in part b) what are your risk intervention measures, and potential mitigation/preparedness activities to prevent or to minimize the impact of such a scenario. If you can acquire cost data for your risk intervention measure.

REFERENCES

Agency Responsibilities by Functional Areas, Functions and Tasks, NRP Initial Plan Draft, Appendix A, Table 6.2.

Blumenthal, H. 2003. "Department of Human Services. Private Sector Information Sharing: ISAC Program." Government Symposium on Information Sharing and Homeland Security, July 1, 2003.

CFR 49, May 5, 2003, http://www.myregs.com/dotrspa/.

Classification of serious HAZMAT incidents in the United States by the mode of transportation and yearly frequencies, http://hazmat.dot.gov/files/hazmat/10year/10yearfrm.htm.

Cooper, B. 2003. Protecting Pipelines from Terrorist Attack, April 2003, http://www.enewsbuilder.net/aopl/e_article 000141902.cfm.

Coppola, D. P. 2003. Annotated Organizational Chart for the Department of Homeland Security. Washington, DC: Bullock & Haddow, LLC.

Department of Transportation Maritime Administration Statistics, http://www.marad.dot.gov/Marad_Statistics/Con-Pts-02.htm.

Environmental Protection Agency. Budget 2003, pp. xv–2, http://www.epa.gov/ocfo/budget/2003/2003bib.pdf.

Environmental Protection Agency. Strategic Plan for Homeland Security, pp. 1–2, http://www.epa.gov/epahome/downloads/epa_homeland_security_strategic_plan.pdf.

Environmental Protection Agency. Strategic Plan for Homeland Security, pp. 2–6, http://www.epa.gov/epahome/downloads/epa_homeland_security_strategic_plan.pdf.

Environmental Protection Agency. "How Wastewater Treatment Works . . . Basics," EPA, p. 1.

Greenberg, W. J. "September 11, 2001: A CEO's Story." *Harvard Business Review*. pp. 7–8.

Harrald, C., Coppola, D. P. and Yeletaysi, S. 2003. "Assessing the Financial Impacts of the World Trade Center Attacks on Publicly Held Corporations." TIEMS Conference Proceedings, June 2003.

http://cityservices.baltimorecity.gov/dpw/waterwastewater03/waterquality5.html

http://hazmat.dot.gov/files/hazmat/serious_new_def.htm

http://nsarchive.chadwyck.com/esp_essay.htm

http://post911timeline.org/Timeline/

http://securitysolutions.com/ar/security_grants_target_wastewater/

http://www.amsa-cleanwater.org

http://www.asy.faa.gov/asy_internet/about.htm

http://www.bice.gov/graphics/customs.htm

http://www.bice.gov/graphics/immig.htm

http://www.buses.org/pressroom/PROutput.cfm?PRID=232

http://www.cbp.gov/xp/cgov/enforcement/border_patrol/overview.xml

http://www.dot.gov

http://www.epa.gov/ebtpages/wasthazardouswaste.html

http://www.epa.gov/ebtpages/wastradioactivewaste.html

http://www.epa.gov/ebtpages/wastwastelandfills.html

http://www.epa.gov/ebtpages/watewastewater.html

http://www.epa.gov/epaoswer/non-hw/muncpl/disposal.htm

http://www.epa.gov/owm/mab/smcomm/104g/index.htm#report

http://www.epa.gov/safewater/dwh/treat.html

http://www.epa.gov/safewater/security/

http://www.epa.gov/safewater/security/index.html

http://www.house.gov/transportation/press/press2003/release77.html

http://www.oig.dot.gov/item_details.php?item=997

http://www.tsa.gov/public/display?content=85

http://www.tsa.gov/public/display?theme=39&content=79

http://www.tsa.gov/public/display?theme=44&content=680

http://www.tsa.gov/public/interweb/assetlibrary/TSA_FY2004_budget_briefing_(public).ppt

http://www.uscg.mil/hq/g-o/g-opl/mle/amio.htm

http://www.uscg.mil/hq/g-o/g-opl/mle/drugs.htm

http://www.whitehouse.gov/deptofhomeland/sect3.html

http://www.whitehouse.gov/news/releases/2002/06/20020618-5.html

https://www.nasdac.faa.gov

Kavanagh, P. 2002. "Current State of Crisis Management as an Industry in Canada." The Health Canada Emergency Preparedness Forum, October 28, 2002.

McDaniel, G., ed., 1994. *IBM Dictionary of Computing*. New York: McGraw-Hill, Inc.

The National Strategy for Homeland Security, Department of Homeland Security, July 2002, p. 12, http://www.dhs.gov.

Ibid, p. 11

Ibid, pp. 39–40

Ibid, pp. 47–49

Ibid, pp. 50–52

Ibid, pp. 52–53

Ibid, pp. 56–57

Ibid, pp. 58–59

National Strategy to Secure Cyberspace, Department of Homeland Security, February 2003, http://www.dhs.gov

NRP Initial Plan Draft, p. 26, 2003.

Operation Liberty Shield: Press Briefing by Secretary Ridge, Saturday, March 15, 2003, http://www.dhs.gov/dhspublic/display?content=520

Richelson, J. T, Gefter, J., Waters, M., Evans, M., Byrne, M., Rone, R., Martinez, J., Grant J., and Burroughs M. 2003. "U.S. Espionage and Intelligence, 1947–1996." Digital National Security Archive.

RSPA-2003-14982, Notice No. 03-7, RSPA, TSA, FRA, Hazardous Materials: Transportation of Explosives by Rail, June 5, 2003.

TSA Program Announcement 02MLPA0002, Intercity Bus Security Grants, Attachment A, http://www.tsa.gov/public/ interweb/assetlibrary/ATTACH_A_Background.pdf.

TSA Program Announcement 02MLPA0002, Intercity Bus Security Grants, p.7, http://www.tsa.gov/public/interweb/assetlibrary/ANNOUNCEMENT_Intercity_Bus_Security.pdf.

"USA Company—Managing Risk in a War Zone." The Economist Intelligence Unit Ltd., 2001.

The Water Treatment Process Diagram of Montebello Water Treatment Plant (Baltimore), http://cityservices.baltimorecity.gov/dpw/waterwastewater03/waterquality5a.html.

6

Mitigation and Preparedness

INTRODUCTION

Mitigation and preparedness are one half of the classic crisis and emergency management life cycle. Both mitigation and preparedness constitute the pre-disaster portion of the process, though some argue that there is also postdisaster mitigation and preparedness, because the aftermath of each disaster often provides an opportunity to implement actions to mitigate and prepare for the next one.

In its classical meaning, "mitigation" refers to a sustained action to reduce or eliminate risk to people and property from hazards and their effects. Preparedness can be defined as a state of readiness to respond to a disaster, crisis or any other type of emergency situation (Figure 6-1).

The concepts of mitigation and preparedness were reviewed after terrorism became a primary threat and we began to hear terms such as "terrorism mitigation" and "terrorism preparedness." So how does the threat of terrorism change those definitions?

DHS/EP&R/FEMA does not directly use the words "terrorism mitigation and preparedness" when it explains its responsibilities regarding antiterrorism or counterterrorism; rather, it states that the philosophy of mitigation does not change from hazard to hazard.

Using the all-hazards approach, DHS/EP&R/FEMA doesn't hesitate to state that whether you mitigate for earthquakes or floods or prepare for a potential terrorist threat the classical mitigation planning process will be your primary guide. DHS/EP&R/FEMA's mitigation planning process consists of four stages: (1) identifying and organizing resources; (2) conducting a risk or threat assessment and estimating losses; (3) identifying mitigation measures that will reduce the effects of the hazards and creating a strategy to deal with the mitigation measures in priority order; and (4) implementing the measures, evaluating the results, and keeping the plan up-to-date. (http://www.fema.gov/fima/antiterrorism/)

MITIGATION PLANS, ACTIONS, AND PROGRAMS

Mitigation activities include different methods and strategies that have the common goal of reducing the risk associated with potential hazards. In order to provide a better understanding of mitigation, it's important to understand the nature of natural, man-made, and terrorism risks.

There are many different definitions of risk, each of which may be appropriate to the circumstances

The four classical phases of disaster management

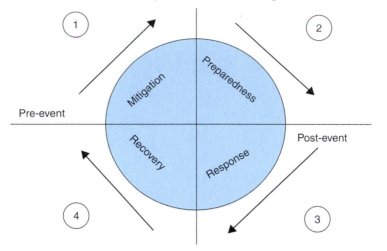

FIGURE 6-1   Life cycle of emergency management

under which it has been defined. Kaplan, rather than providing a full definition of risk, argues the three major questions one has to ask when talking about risk. These questions are as follows: (1) What can happen?; (2) How likely is it?; (3) What are the consequences? (Kaplan, 1997).

This indirect definition really provides a flexible starting point to discuss risk and how to mitigate it. Assuming that there exists a threat that we fear will happen sometime (e.g., natural disasters or terrorist attacks), associated with some degree of uncertainty regarding time and impact, we have already started talking about risk.

The uncertainty component of risk is all about the probability of the disastrous event to happen. It forces us to ask ourselves questions such as the following: What is the probability that a 7.0 Mg earthquake will happen in San Francisco Bay within the next 10 years? What is the probability that terrorists will attack and damage a nuclear power plant in the United States? The probability component of risk is important for us because it is one of the two parameters that help us to quantify and prioritize mitigation actions when dealing with multiple risks. The determination of probabilities for events is often a difficult and complicated process. There are several quantitative methods and tools that can be used to determine probabilities.

The second component of risk, the consequences, applies to the total unwanted impact of the disaster to the community, government, or the interested stakeholders. The consequence is usually an assigned monetary value, but often it has intangible components that have to be considered as well. Interestingly enough, the consequences of disasters also have a probabilistic nature. In practice, it's quite hard to assign a single monetary value to the expected damage; probability distributions are used to model the most likely damage estimates.

Having provided a basic description of the components of risk, let's talk about the mitigation of risk. In applying mitigation, we try to minimize both components of risk, as we defined then as probability and consequence. However, in practice it is not always easy to address both, and since each risk is unique, there are different strategies that must be identified, assessed, and then applied. For example, assume we want to minimize earthquake risk. How can we minimize the probability of it happening? We probably can't. Especially for natural hazards, minimizing the likelihood of the event is usually very limited or impossible. However, we can mitigate earthquake risks by minimizing their impacts. There are several strategies available to minimize the impacts of the earthquake risk, such as adopting and enforcing earthquake building codes, educating the public about earthquakes, and developing robust earthquake response plans.

On the other hand, in dealing with the risk of a potential terrorist attack, the mitigation strategy would be a bit different. This time we have the opportunity to minimize the likelihood of the event as well. Through good intelligence about terrorist activities, the location of terrorists, their networks, and communication strategies we possibly can stop them before they proceed with their actions. Therefore, theoretically, the probability component of terrorism risk can be reduced through mitigation. However, in practice, detecting a potential terrorist attack before it happens is a very complex task, requiring governments to spend large amounts of money to build and manage necessary systems and networks to identify and detain terrorists.

The consequence component of terrorism risk can be mitigated. Since terrorists have many different targets, including facilities, infrastructure, and organizations, different strategies can be employed to minimize the impacts of terrorist attacks to those potential targets. DHS/EP&R/FEMA has a separate manual (FEMA 426), "Reference Manual to Mitigate Potential Terrorist Attacks against Buildings." The manual mainly discusses the importance of minimizing the impacts of potential terrorist attacks against buildings once they happen. To minimize the human impacts of terrorist attacks, potential mitigation strategies are the availability of a robust mass casualty health management system, improved first responder capability, good planning, and training for emergency managers to deal with terrorism incidents (Sidebar 6-1).

Terrorism is not a new issue. Throughout history there have been terrorist organizations and terrorist attacks in many parts of the world, including North America, Europe, and Australia; however, the September 11 attacks produced such serious consequences that terrorism became a major issue for the United States government.

Mitigation against terrorism is important to minimize potential damage that it can cause, but one should not forget that combating terrorism is a hard and long job, one that requires a lot of patience and sacrifice. Therefore all stakeholders, including the government, the public, the private sector, the media and academia, should appreciate mitigation in an all-hazards approach to minimize damage from risks, including terrorism.

DHS/EP&R/FEMA continues to provide funding for predisaster and postdisaster mitigation projects. Although typically applied to natural disasters, the Hazard Mitigation Grant program and the predisaster mitigation programs could support terrorism mitigation through an all-hazards approach. Sidebar 6-2 contains information about these two programs.

PREPAREDNESS ACTIONS AND PROGRAMS

Preparedness within the field of emergency management can best be defined as a state of readiness to respond to a disaster, crisis, or any other type of emergency situation. It includes those activities, programs, and systems that exist before an emergency that are used to support and enhance response to an emergency or disaster (Steve Davis).

Preparedness is an important component of emergency management because it provides for the readiness and testing of all actions and plans before the actual application in a real event or disaster. There is a close connection between mitigation and preparedness. Often, emergency managers argue over whether an action should be considered as mitigation or preparedness. However, preparedness is more about planning for the best response, whereas mitigation includes all the actions that are attempts to prevent the need for a disaster response or to minimize the scope of the needed response.

Examples of preparedness for natural hazards are organizing evacuation drills from buildings in case of fires or other threats, providing first response training to employees so that they can assist each other and their neighbors in small emergencies, and preparing a family disaster plan that covers topics such as the designation of a location where family members will meet if they get separated during an event and what personal papers (e.g., prescriptions, insurance

SIDEBAR 6-1   FEMA 426: Reference Manual to Mitigate Potential Terrorist Attacks against Buildings

The Federal Emergency Management Agency (FEMA) developed the "Reference Manual to Mitigate Potential Terrorist Attacks against Buildings" to provide needed information on how to mitigate the effects of potential terrorist attacks. The intended audience includes the building sciences community of architects and engineers working for private institutions. The manual supports FEMA's mission (to lead America to prepare for, prevent, respond to, and recover from disasters) and the Strategic Plan's Goal 3 (to prepare the nation to address the consequences of terrorism), all of which will be done within the all-hazards framework and the needs of homeland security.

The building science community, as a result of FEMA's efforts, has incorporated extensive building science into designing and constructing buildings against natural hazards (earthquake, fire, flood, and wind). To date, the same level of understanding has not been applied to man-made hazards (terrorism/intentional acts) and technological hazards (accidental events). Since September 11, 2001, terrorism has become a dominant domestic concern. Security can no longer be viewed as a stand-alone capability that can be purchased as an afterthought and put in place. Life, safety, and security issues must become a design goal from the beginning.

The objective of this manual is to reduce physical damage to structural and nonstructural components of buildings and related infrastructure and also to reduce resultant casualties during conventional bomb attacks, as well as attacks using chemical, biological, and radiological agents. Although the process is general in nature and applies to most building uses, this manual is most applicable for six specific types of facilities:

- Commercial office facilities
- Retail commercial facilities
- Light industrial and manufacturing facilities
- Health care facilities
- Local schools (K–12)
- Higher education (university) facilities

Chapter 1 presents selected methodologies to integrate threat/hazard, asset criticality, and vulnerability assessment information. This information becomes the input for determining relative levels of risk. Higher risk hazards require mitigation measures to reduce risk. The chapter also provides an assessment checklist that compiles many best practices to consider during the design of a new building or renovation of an existing building.

Chapter 2 discusses architectural and engineering design considerations (mitigation measures), starting at the perimeter of the property line, and includes the orientation of the building on the site. Therefore this chapter covers issues outside the building envelope.

Chapter 3 provides the same considerations for the building—its envelope, systems and interior layout.

Chapter 4 provides a discussion of blast theory to understand the dynamics of the blast pressure wave, the response of building components and a consistent approach to define levels of protection.

Chapter 5 presents chemical, biological, and radiological measures that can be taken to mitigate vulnerabilities and reduce associated risks for these terrorist tactics or technological hazards.

Appendices A, B, and C contain acronyms, general definitions, and CBR definitions, respectively.

Appendix D describes electronic security systems and design considerations.

Appendices E and F present a comprehensive bibliography of publications and the associations and organizations capturing the building security guidance needed by the building sciences community, respectively.

Source: FEMA 426, June 2003

SIDEBAR 6-2   FEMA Mitigation Grant Program

Mitigation is the cornerstone of emergency management. It's the ongoing effort to lessen the impact disasters have on people and property. Mitigation involves keeping homes away from floodplains, engineering bridges to withstand earthquakes, creating and enforcing effective building codes to protect property from hurricanes—and more.

FEMA currently has three mitigation grant programs: the Hazards Mitigation Grant Program (HGMP), the Pre-Disaster Mitigation program (PDM), and the Flood Mitigation Assistance (FMA) program.

Hazards Mitigation Grant Program (HGMP)

Authorized under Section 404 of the Stafford Act, the Hazard Mitigation Grant Program (HMGP) provides grants to states and local governments to implement long-term hazard mitigation measures after a major disaster declaration. The purpose of the program is to reduce the loss of life and property due to natural disasters and to enable mitigation measures to be implemented during the immediate recovery from a disaster declaration. The purpose of the program is to reduce the loss of life and property due to natural disasters and to enable mitigation measures to be implemented during the immediate recovery from a disaster.

Hazard Mitigation Grant Program funding is only available in states following a presidential disaster declaration. Eligible applicants are as follows:

- State and local governments
- Indian tribes or other tribal organizations
- Certain private nonprofit organizations

Individual homeowners and businesses may not apply directly to the program; however, a community may apply on their behalf. HMGP funds may be used to fund projects that will reduce or eliminate the losses from future disasters. Projects must provide a long-term solution to a problem—for example, elevation of a home to reduce the risk of flood damages as opposed to buying sandbags and pumps to fight the flood. In addition, a project's potential savings must be more than the cost of implementing the project. Funds may be used to protect either public or private property or to purchase property that has been subjected to, or is in danger of, repetitive damage.

Pre-Disaster Mitigation Program

The Pre-Disaster Mitigation (PDM) Program was authorized by §203 of the Robert T. Stafford Disaster Assistance and Emergency Relief Act (Stafford Act), 42 USC, as amended by §102 of the Disaster Mitigation Act of 2000. Funding for the program is provided through the National Pre-Disaster Mitigation Fund to assist states and local governments (to include Indian tribal governments) in implementing cost-effective hazard mitigation activities that complement a comprehensive mitigation program. All applicants must be participating in the National Flood Insurance Program (NFIP) if they have been identified through the NFIP as having a special Flood Hazard Area (a Flood Hazard Boundary Map [FHBM] or Flood Insurance Rate Map [FIRM] has been issued). In addition, the community must not be suspended or on probation from the NFIP.

In 44 CFR Part 201, Hazard Mitigation Planning, criteria are established for state and local hazard mitigation planning authorized by §322 of the Stafford Act, as amended by §104 of the DMA. After November 1, 2003, local governments and Indian tribal governments applying for PDM funds through the states will have to have an approved local mitigation plan prior to the approval of local mitigation project grants. States will also be required to have an approved standard state mitigation plan in order to receive PDM funds for state or local mitigation projects after November 1, 2004. Therefore the

Sidebar 6.2 continued

records) they might need in the aftermath of an event. Other examples would be arranging the logistics of tugboats around oil refineries that are responsible for responding to fire emergencies in the refinery or providing training and relocating necessary HAZMAT teams to areas where the risk of radiological emergencies is higher, such as nuclear power plants.

In the aftermath of September 11, terrorism preparedness became a more pressing issue. The risk of terrorists gaining access to and using weapons of mass destruction, such as biological, chemical, and radiological agents, forces the United States government to establish an adequate response capability, capacity, and expertise to protect American citizens against a potential attack and respond to it, in case these weapons are used.

The Department of Homeland Security's (DHS) Emergency Preparedness and Response Directorate (EP&R) has as its goal "to prepare for and respond to natural and technological disasters and terrorism."

The directorate incorporates Federal Emergency Management Agency (FEMA), Strategic National Stockpile, National Disaster Medical System (NDMS), Nuclear Incident Response Team, Domestic Emergency Support Teams, and National Domestic Preparedness Office (Coppola, 2003).

What are some of the different weapons that are part of the terrorist's arsenal, and how can we prepare or respond to them? The following sections will provide a basic primer of the types of threats/weapons we face and how to prepare for them.

---

development of state and local multihazard mitigation plans is key to maintaining eligibility for future PDM funding.

Flood Mitigation Assistance (FMA) Program

Flood Mitigation Assistance (FMA) provides funding to assist states and communities in implementing measures to reduce or eliminate the long-term risk of flood damage to buildings, manufactured homes, and other structures insurable under the National Flood Insurance Program (NFIP). There are three types of grants available under FMA: planning, project, and technical assistance grants. FMA planning grants are available to states and communities to prepare flood mitigation plans. NFIP–participating communities with approved flood mitigation plans can apply for FMA project grants. FMA project grants are available to states and NFIP–participating communities to implement measures to reduce flood losses. Ten percent of the project grant is made available to states as a technical assistance grant. These funds may be used by the state to help administer the program. Communities receiving FMA planning and project grants must be participating in the NFIP. An example of eligible FMA projects includes the elevation, acquisition, and relocation of NFIP-insured structures.

Funding for the program is provided through the National Flood Insurance Fund, and FMA is funded at $20 million nationally. States are encouraged to prioritize FMA project grant applications that include repetitive loss properties. The FY2001 FMA emphasis encourages states and communities to address target repetitive loss properties identified in the agency's repetitive loss strategy. These include structures with four or more losses and structures with two or more losses in which cumulative payments have exceeded the property value. State and communities are also encouraged to develop plans that address the mitigation of these target repetitive loss properties.

Source: FEMA, www.fema.gov

FIGURE 6-2 Emmitsburg, MD, March 10, 2003—An incident command system course is held at FEMA's National Emergency Training Center, one of dozens of courses offered there each year for first responders, emergency managers, and educators. Photo by Jocelyn Augustino/FEMA News Photo.

CHEMICAL WEAPONS

A chemical attack is the deliberate release of a toxic gas, liquid, or solid that can poison people and the environment. Obvious signs of a chemical attack include people suffering from watery eyes, twitching, choking, respiratory problems, and loss of coordination. Many sick or dead birds, fish, or small animals are also cause for suspicion. If you see signs of chemical attack, quickly attempt to define the source of the chemical and to determine the degree and size of the affected area. Take immediate action to get away from the affected area.

If the chemical is inside a building where you are, try to get out of the building without passing through the contaminated area. Otherwise, it may be better to move as far away from where you suspect the chemical release is and "shelter in place." If you are outside when you see signs of a chemical attack, you must quickly decide on the fastest way to get away from the chemical threat. You must consider evacuating the area or if it would be better to go inside a building and follow "shelter in place." See pages that follow for facts about evacuation and facts about shelter in place prepared by the CDC on preparedness for chemical agents.

BIOLOGICAL ATTACKS

A biological attack is the deliberate release of germs or other biological substances that can make

CHEMICAL AGENTS: FACTS ABOUT EVACUATION

Some kinds of chemical accidents or attacks may make staying put dangerous. In such cases, it may be safer for you to evacuate or leave the immediate area. You may need to go to an emergency shelter after you leave the immediate area.

How to Know if You Need to Evacuate

You will hear from the local police, emergency coordinators, or government on the radio or television if you need to evacuate.

If there is a "code red" or "severe" terror alert, you should pay attention to radio and television broadcasts so that you will know right away if an evacuation order is made for your area.

What to Do

Act quickly and follow the instructions of local emergency coordinators. Every situation can be different, so local coordinators may give you special instructions to follow for a particular situation.

Local emergency coordinators may direct people to evacuate homes or offices and go to an emergency shelter. If so, emergency coordinators will tell you how to get to the shelter. If you have children in school, they may be sheltered at the school. You should not try to get to the school if the children are being sheltered there.

The emergency shelter will have most supplies that people need. The emergency coordinators will tell you which supplies to bring with you. Be sure to bring any medications you are taking.

If you have time, call a friend or relative in another state to tell him or her where you are going and that you are safe. Local telephone lines may be jammed in an emergency, so you should plan ahead to have an out-of-state contact with whom to leave messages. If you do not have private transportation, make plans in advance of an emergency to identify people who can give you a ride.

Evacuating and sheltering in this way should keep you safer than if you stayed at home or at your workplace. You will most likely not be in the shelter for more than a few hours. Emergency coordinators will let you know when it is safe to leave the shelter.

How You Can Get More Information About Evacuation

You can contact one of the following:
- State and local health departments
- Centers for Disease Control and Prevention
  - Public response hotline (CDC)
    - English: 1-888-246-2675
    - Español: 1-888-246-2857
    - TTY (866) 874-2646
  - Emergency Preparedness and Response web site
  - E-mail inquiries: cdcresponse@ashastd.org
  - Mail inquiries:
    Public Inquiry c/o BPRP
    Bioterrorism Preparedness and
    Response Planning
    Centers for Disease Control and Prevention
    Mailstop C-18
    1600 Clifton Road
    Atlanta, GA 30333

CHEMICAL AGENTS: FACTS ABOUT SHELTERING IN PLACE

What "Sheltering in Place" Means

Some kinds of chemical accidents or attacks may make going outdoors dangerous. Leaving the area might take too long or put you in harm's way. In such a case it may be safer for you to stay indoors than to go outside.

"Shelter in place" means to make a shelter out of the place you are in. It is a way for you to make the building as safe as possible to protect yourself until help arrives. You should not try to shelter in a vehicle unless you have no other choice. Vehicles are not airtight enough to give you adequate protection from chemicals.

How to Prepare to Shelter in Place

Choose a room in your house or apartment for your shelter. The best room to use for the shelter is a room with as few windows and doors as possible. A large room, preferably with a water supply, is desirable—something like a master bedroom that is connected to a bathroom. For chemical events, this room should be as high in the structure as possible to avoid vapors (gases) that sink. This guideline is different from the sheltering-in-place technique used in tornadoes and other severe weather, when the shelter should be low in the home.

You might not be at home if the need to shelter in place ever arises, but if you are at home, the following items would be good to have on hand. (Ideally, all of these items would be stored in the shelter room to save time.)

- First aid kit
- Food and bottled water. Store 1 gallon of water per person in plastic bottles as well as ready-to-eat foods that will keep without refrigeration at the shelter-in-place location. If you do not have bottled water, or if you run out, you can drink water from a toilet tank (not from a toilet bowl).
- Flashlight, battery-powered radio, and extra batteries for both
- Duct tape and scissors
- Towels and plastic sheeting
- A working telephone.

How to Know if You Need to Shelter in Place

You will hear from the local police, emergency coordinators, or government on the radio and on television if you need to shelter in place.

If there is a "code red" or "severe" terror alert, you should pay attention to radio and television broadcasts to know right away whether a shelter-in-place alert is announced for your area.

If you are away from your shelter-in-place location when a chemical event occurs, follow the instructions of emergency coordinators to find the nearest shelter. If your children are at school, they will be sheltered there. Unless you are instructed to do so, do not try to get to the school to bring your children home.

What to Do

Act quickly and follow the instructions of your local emergency coordinators. Every situation can be different, so local emergency coordinators might have special instructions for you to follow. In general, do the following:

- Go inside as quickly as possible.
- If there is time, shut and lock all outside doors and windows. Locking them may provide a tighter seal against the chemical. Turn off the air conditioner or heater. Turn off all fans, too. Close the fireplace damper and any other place that air can come in from the outside.
- Go in the shelter-in-place room and shut the door.
- Tape plastic over any windows in the room. Use duct tape around the windows and doors and make an unbroken seal. Use the tape over any vents into the room, and seal any electrical outlets or other openings. Sink and toilet drain traps should have water in them (you can use the sink and toilet as you normally would). If it is necessary to drink water, drink the stored water, not water from the tap.
- Turn on the radio. Keep a telephone close at hand, but don't use it unless there is a serious emergency.

Sheltering in this way should keep you safer than if you were outdoors. Most likely, you will be in the shelter for no more than a few hours. Listen to the radio for an announcement indicating that it is safe to leave the shelter. After you come out of the shelter, emergency coordinators may have additional instructions on how to make the rest of the building safe again.

How You Can Get More Information About Sheltering in Place

You can contact one of the following:

- State and local health departments
- Centers for Disease Control and Prevention public response hotline (CDC)
  - Public response hotline (CDC)
    - English: 1-888-246-2675
    - Español: 1-888-246-2857
    - TTY 1-866-874-2646

- Emergency Preparedness and Response web site
  - E-mail inquiries: cdcresponse@ashastd.org
  - Mail inquiries:
    Public Inquiry c/o BPRP
    Bioterrorism Preparedness and
    Response Planning
    Centers for Disease Control and Prevention
    Mailstop C-18
    1600 Clifton Road
    Atlanta, GA 30333

Source: CDC, www.cdc.gov

you sick. Some agents are inhaled, some enter through a cut in the skin, and some must be ingested to exert an effect. Some biological agents, such as anthrax, do not cause contagious diseases. Others, like the smallpox virus, can result in diseases that you can catch from infected people.

Unlike an explosion, a biological attack may not be immediately obvious. While it is possible that you will see signs of a biological attack, as in the case of the anthrax mailings to the U.S. Congress, it is more likely that local health-care workers will report a pattern of unusual illness or a wave of sick people will seek emergency medical attention. Individuals will probably learn of the danger through an announcement by officials, an emergency radio or TV broadcast, or some other means of warning used in their communities.

In the event of an incident, quickly get away and cover your mouth and nose with something that will filter the air but still allow breathing. Examples include two to three layers of cotton, such as a T-shirt, handkerchief, or towel. Otherwise, several layers of tissue or paper towels may help. Wash with soap and water, and contact authorities. In the event of a biological attack, public health officials will provide information on what you should do as quickly as they can.

However, it can take time for them to determine exactly what the illness is, how it should be treated, and who is in danger. What you can do is watch TV, listen to the radio, or check the Internet for official news, including the following:

- Are you in the group or area authorities consider in danger?
- What are the signs and symptoms of the disease?
- Are medications or vaccines being distributed? Where?
- Who should get them?
- Where should you seek emergency medical care if you become sick?

If a family member becomes sick at the time of a declared biological emergency, it is important to be suspicious. However, do not automatically assume that you should go to a hospital emergency room or that any illness is the result of the biological attack.

Symptoms of many common illnesses may overlap. Use common sense, practice good hygiene and cleanliness to avoid spreading germs, and seek medical advice. (DHS Family Preparedness Guide, DHS 2003, http://www.ready.gov)

RADIOLOGICAL THREATS

A nuclear blast is an explosion with intense light and heat, a damaging pressure wave, and widespread radioactive material that can contaminate the air, water, and ground surfaces for miles around. While experts generally agree that a nuclear attack is less likely than other types of attacks, terrorism by its nature is unpredictable. The following Q&A provides the recommended guidance on preparedness for dealing with nuclear threats.

Q: Is the United States in danger of a terrorist nuclear attack? Are the Centers for Disease Control and Prevention (CDC) prepared to respond to such an attack?

A: CDC is not able to assess the level of threat of a terrorist nuclear attack. However, for many years CDC has participated regularly in emergency-response drills in which we have worked closely with other federal, state, and local agencies to develop, test, and implement extensive national radiological emergency-response plans.

Q: What are the potential adverse health consequences from a terrorist nuclear attack?

A: The adverse health consequences of a terrorist nuclear attack vary according to the type of attack and the distance a person is from the attack. Potential terrorist attacks may include a small radioactive source with a limited range of impact and a nuclear detonation involving a wide area of impact.

In the event of a terrorist nuclear attack, people may experience two types of exposure from radioactive materials: external exposure and internal exposure. External exposure occurs when a person comes in contact with radioactive material outside the body.

Internal exposure occurs when people eat food or breathe air that is contaminated with radioactive material. Exposure to very large doses of external radiation may cause death within a few days or months. External exposure to lower doses of radiation and internal exposure from breathing or eating radioactive-contaminated material may lead to an increased risk of developing cancer and other adverse health effects. These adverse effects range from mild, such as skin reddening, to severe effects such as cancer and death, depending on the amount of radiation absorbed by the body (the dose), the type of radiation, the route of exposure, and the length of time of the exposure.

If there is a nuclear detonation, bodily injury or death may occur as a result of the blast itself or as a result of debris thrown from the blast. People may experience moderate to severe skin burns, depending on their distance from the blast site. Those who look directly at the blast could experience eye damage ranging from temporary blindness to severe retinal burns.

Q: How can I protect my family and myself from a terrorist nuclear attack?

A: In the event of a terrorist nuclear attack, a national emergency-response plan would be activated and would include federal, state, and local agencies. You should seek shelter in a stable building and listen to local radio or television stations for national emergency-alert information. Your local emergency-response organizations, police agencies, and public health facilities may be able to supply you with additional information. You should follow the protective-action recommendations that are made by your state or local health department in accordance with this plan. As a general rule, you can reduce the potential exposure and subsequent health consequences by limiting your time near the radiation source, increasing your distance from the source, or keeping a physical barrier (such as the wall of a building) between you and the source. You can find out your state radiation control director by contacting the Conference of Radiation Control Program Directors (CRCPD) at 1-502- 227-4543 or you may visit the CRCPD web site.

Q: What should I do if there is a terrorist attack on a nuclear power plant near my home?

A: A terrorist attack on a nuclear power plant will initiate a national emergency response that has been carefully planned and rehearsed by local, state, and federal agencies for more than 20 years. If you live near a nuclear power plant and you have not received information that describes the emergency plan for that facility, you can contact the plant and ask for a copy of that information. Your local emergency-response organizations, police agencies, and public health facilities have been actively involved in this emergency plan, and they may be able to supply you with additional information. You and your family should study these plans and be prepared to follow the instructions that local and state public health officials provide in the event of a terrorist incident involving the nuclear power plant near your home.

Q: Where can I go to find more information about radiation health effects and emergency response?

- Environmental Protection Agency counter-terrorism programs
- The Nuclear Regulatory Commission can be reached at 1-301-415-8200.
- The Federal Emergency Management Agency (FEMA) can be reached at 1-202-646-4600.
- The Radiation Emergency Assistance Center/ Training Site (REAC/TS) can be reached at 1-865-576-3131.
- The U.S. National Response Team
- The U.S. Department of Energy (DOE) can be reached at 1-800-dial-DOE.

Source: CDC, www.cdc.gov

CASE STUDY 1
THE TERRORIST ATTACK WITH SARIN IN TOKYO, 1995

In the morning rush hour on March 20, 1995, a group of terrorists placed containers of the nerve gas sarin in five carriages on three of Tokyo's ten underground railway lines. The Tokyo Underground comprises 230 km of track and transports many million people daily.

The sarin containers were put in carriages that were all expected to arrive in one central Tokyo station at approximately the same time. Very soon the Tokyo Emergency Control Centre staff realized that something serious had occurred, for within 15 minutes they received a great number of alarms from fifteen underground stations. Initially a fire or explosion was suspected, but the victims' symptomatology soon indicated a nerve agent. This was verified within a few hours by police chemical experts.

Quite soon there were injured people at fifteen underground stations. They had been exposed to sarin either in the carriages or on the platforms. They reported a strong smell of a solvent (which turned out to be acetonitrile) and intense eye irritation. Soon people also experienced breathing difficulties and muscle weakness, and many lost consciousness. Sarin spread from carriage to carriage, since these were in communication with each other. Only one person died while still in the carriage: All the other exposed victims managed to get out or were exposed to sarin on the platform.

The sarin concentration could not have been very high in any of the carriages except very locally, which is why symptoms appeared slowly in most cases. Although symptoms normally appear very quickly after sarin exposure, there may be a delay of several minutes between exposure and the development of severe symptoms. Several people managed to get out into fresh air before losing consciousness.

Approximately 30 minutes after the first alarm, first aid stations were set up in the street outside the underground stations or in nearby temples. In addition to ambulance personnel (including paramedics), medical teams of doctors and nurses took part in the rescue work. No advanced medical treatment was given on-site, only life-saving procedures. Medical personnel triaged patients for transport to hospitals.

At 8:35 A.M. the first patient was transported by ambulance to St Luke's International Hospital, arriving at 8:40. In all, 550 persons were transported by ambulance to the hospital. Only a few were transported in minibuses provided by the fire brigade. The rest made their way on foot or in private cars to hospitals or private outpatient clinics.

In all 5,000 to 6,000 persons were exposed. Of these, 3,227 went to the hospital, of whom 493 were admitted to 41 of Tokyo's many hospitals. Only 17 developed severe symptoms requiring intensive care. In all, 12 people died from the sarin exposure. During the first 24 hours 10 people died, nine at the accident site and one just after arrival at hospital. Two persons died several weeks later from complications of the hypoxic brain damage suffered during the acute phase. Several other people have permanent brain damage.

Most patients arriving at hospital had rather mild symptoms and could leave the hospital after examination and possible treatment, while most who were admitted could be discharged 24 to 48 hours after the accident. On the third day only a few patients were still in the intensive care unit. Blood samples from the severely injured contained sarin metabolites and a pronounced decrease in plasma cholinesterase activity. The symptomatology of the exposed victims was typical for nerve gas exposure (i.e., a result of overstimulation of those nerves that have acetylcholine as a transmitter substance). In severe cases there were also seizures. The predominant symptom that led to the suspicion of a nerve agent as the toxic substance was pronounced miosis (pin-point pupils).

Source: ttp://www.sos.se/SOS/PUBL/REFERENG/9803020E. htm

COMMUNITY ISSUES

The terrorism threat knows no geographic, social, or economic boundaries. Every citizen and every community is potentially at risk. While DHS focuses on federal and state efforts to prepare for and combat terrorism, local communities are struggling to address the terrorism risk. The next sections will concentrate on initiatives that have been launched to deal with community issues against terrorism (Sidebar 6-3).

CORPORATION FOR NATIONAL AND COMMUNITY SERVICE

The mission of the Corporation for National and Community Service is to provide opportunities for Americans of all ages and backgrounds to engage in service that addresses the nation's educational, public safety, environmental, and other human needs to achieve direct and demonstrable results and to encourage all Americans to engage in such service. In doing so, the corporation fosters civic responsibility, strengthens the ties that bind us together as a people, and provides educational opportunities for those who make a substantial commitment to service.

The Corporation for National and Community Service provides opportunities for Americans of all ages and backgrounds to serve their communities and country through three programs: Senior Corps, AmeriCorps, and Learn and Serve America. Members and volunteers serve with national and community nonprofit organizations, faith-based groups, schools, and local agencies to help meet community needs in education, the environment, public safety, homeland security, and other critical areas. The corporation is

---

SIDEBAR 6-3   DHS Secretary Ridge Cites Neighborhood Security as Instrumental to Homeland Security

In Falcon Heights, Minnesota, a program that trains residents to respond to potential terrorist attacks is becoming a model for other cities and states. Falcon Heights Mayor Sue Gehrz, St. Paul Mayor Randy Kelly, and other officials were joined by Homeland Security Secretary Tom Ridge at a symposium in St. Paul exploring how Americans can protect their food supply, workplaces, and homes. "The potential destruction to life and property from man-made disasters is so large that communities can no longer assume" that agencies in neighboring communities will be available to help, Gehrz said. "That means more individuals need to be trained to assist their families and neighbors until help arrives," she said.

"The only way you can secure the homeland is to make sure the hometowns are secure," Ridge told about 350 people at the symposium. The nation has strengthened security in many ways since the terror attacks of 2001, yet it still needs a greater degree of readiness, he said. "We need to consolidate most of our computer systems and databases in one seamless operation, make it easier for police to communicate with each other, with the rest of federal government, right down to the state and locals," he said.

Since the September 11 attacks, the residents of Falcon Heights have worked together to plan a response to terror attacks, Gehrz said. They have created a community manual on their "intergenerational organizing model" and provided it to more than 70 Minnesota cities and counties. It has been used in Florida, South Carolina, and Washington, DC.

In Falcon Heights, which has a population of 5,600, 65 "neighborhood liaisons" have collected the names, addresses, and phone numbers of people on their blocks, identifying who has medical training or other specialized skills or equipment that might be useful in a disaster, Gehrz said. A neighborhood commission worked with the Red Cross to provide free first-aid training for 62 residents. Police have trained 11 residents how to direct traffic during emergencies. Others will receive 21 hours of training in how to respond to emergencies. "Involving all ages helps reduce fear and protect civil rights," said Gehrz, who is trained as a psychologist. "One of the primary goals of terrorism is to make people feel isolated and vulnerable."

Source: "Falcon Heights security efforts are becoming a national model," *Star Tribune*, June 20, 2003, p.19A

FIGURE 6-3 Sterling, VA., March 7, 2001—Community members review information about the Citizens Corps Neighborhood Watch program after a community meeting. Photo by Elise Moore/FEMA News Photo.

part of U.S.A. Freedom Corps, a White House initiative to foster a culture of citizenship, service, and responsibility and help all Americans answer the president's call to service.

Senior Corps taps the skills, talents, and experience of more than 500,000 Americans 55 years of age and older to meet a wide range of community challenges through three programs: RSVP, Foster Grandparents, and Senior Companions. RSVP volunteers conduct safety patrols for local police departments, participate in environmental projects, provide intensive educational services to children and adults, and respond to natural disasters, among other activities. Foster Grandparents serve one-on-one as tutors and mentors to young people with special needs. Senior Companions help homebound seniors and other adults maintain independence in their own homes.

Fifty thousand Americans are serving their communities 20 to 40 hours a week through AmeriCorps. Most of AmeriCorps' members are selected by and serve with local and national nonprofit organizations such as Habitat for Humanity, the American Red Cross, City Year, Teach for America, and Boys and Girls Clubs of America, as well as with a host of smaller community organizations, both secular and faith-based. AmeriCorps operates in a decentralized manner that gives a significant amount of responsibility to states and local nonprofit groups. Roughly three-quarters of all AmeriCorps grant funding goes to governor-appointed state service commissions, which award grants to nonprofit groups to respond to local needs. Most of the remainder of the grant funding is distributed by the corporation directly to multistate and national organizations through a competitive grants process. AmeriCorps*NCCC (National Civilian Community Corps) is a residential program for more than 1,200 members ages 18 to 24. Based on a military model, it sends members in teams of 10 to 14 to help nonprofit groups provide disaster relief, preserve the environment, build homes for low-income families, tutor children, and meet other challenges. Because members are trained in CPR, first aid, and mass care and can be assigned to new duties on short notice, they are particularly well-suited to meeting the emerging homeland security needs of the nation.

Learn and Serve America provides grants to schools, colleges, and nonprofit groups to support efforts to engage students in community service linked to academic achievement and the development of civic skills. This type of learning, referred to as "service learning," improves communities while preparing young people for a lifetime of responsible citizenship. In addition to providing grants, Learn and Serve America serves as a resource on service and service-learning to teachers, faculty members, schools, and community groups.

The Corporation for National and Community Service is an important initiative for homeland security efforts on the local community level because it provides a significant portion of the total federal funding that goes to volunteer organizations and local communities that are trying to improve their homeland security capabilities.

On July 18, 2002, the corporation announced that it had acquired more than $10.3 million in grants. These grants supported 37,000 volunteers for homeland security in public safety, public health, and disaster mitigation and preparedness. The corporation announced on September 10, 2003, the renewal of 17 of the grants

FIGURE 6-4   Emmitsburg, MD, March 10, 2003—FEMA's National Emergency Training Center is the site for dozens of classes, including sessions that train Community Emergency Response Team (CERT) leaders from across the country. CERT is an important tool for local emergency managers. Photo by Jocelyn Augustino/FEMA News Photo.

from the previous year totaling nearly $4.5 million for homeland security volunteer projects that were developed in the aftermath of the September 11 terrorist attacks. (See Appendix 6 for a full list of corporation grantees and descriptions of their proposed homeland security programs.)

AmeriCorps members and Senior Corps volunteers specially trained in disaster relief have responded to disasters in more than 30 states. The corporation has a long track record of working with DHS/EP&R/FEMA and other relief agencies in helping run emergency shelters, assisting law enforcement, providing food and shelter, managing donations, and helping families and communities rebuild. Hundreds of national ser-

vice volunteers have directly assisted victims of the September 11 terrorist attacks by providing family services, organizing blood drives, raising funds, and counseling victim's families.

(http://www.nationalservice.org/news/factsheets/homeland.html)

(http://www.nationalservice.org/news/homeland.html)

CITIZEN CORPS

Following the tragic events that occurred on September 11, 2001, state and local government officials have increased opportunities for citizens to become an integral part of protecting the homeland and supporting local first responders. Officials agree that the formula for ensuring a more secure and safer homeland consists of preparedness, training, and citizen involvement in supporting first responders. In January 2002, President George W. Bush launched U.S.A. Freedom Corps to capture the spirit of service that has emerged throughout our communities following the terrorist attacks.

Citizen Corps, a vital component of U.S.A. Freedom Corps, was created to help coordinate volunteer activities that will make our communities safer, stronger, and better prepared to respond to any emergency situation. It provides opportunities for people to participate in a range of measures to make their families, their homes, and their communities safer from the threats of crime, terrorism, and disasters of all kinds.

Citizen Corps is coordinated nationally by FEMA. In this capacity, FEMA works closely with other federal entities, state and local governments, first responders and emergency managers, the volunteer community, and the White House Office of the U.S.A. Freedom Corps. (http://www.citizencorps.gov/councils/)

One of the initiatives supported by Citizen Corps is the Community Emergency Response Teams (CERT) (Figure 6-4). The program helps train people to be better prepared to respond to emergency situations in their communities. When emergencies happen, CERT members can give critical support to first responders, provide immediate assistance to victims, and organize spontaneous volunteers at a disaster site. CERT members can also help with nonemergency projects that help improve the safety of the community.

The CERT course is taught in the community by a trained team of first responders who have completed a CERT Train-the-Trainer course conducted by their state training office for emergency management, or DHS/EP&R/FEMA's Emergency Management Institute (EMI), located in Emmitsburg, Maryland. CERT training includes disaster preparedness, disaster fire suppression, basic disaster medical operations, and light search and rescue operations. (http://www. citizencorps.gov/programs/cert.shtm)

Undersecretary of DHS for Emergency Preparedness and Response Mike Brown announced in May 2003 the availability of $19 million in grant money to train citizens to be better prepared to respond to emergency situations in their communities through local CERT.

The grant money represents the FY03 funds made available to expand the CERT program and is in addition to $17 million distributed through the FY02 supplemental appropriation. DHS/EP&R/FEMA will distribute the funds for state and local level CERT programs to each state and territory according to the formula developed through the Patriot Act. The CERT grants will allow states to fund new programs and to expand existing teams. DHS/EP&R/FEMA has a goal of training 400,000 citizens through the CERT program during the next two years throughout the United States.

Another important initiative from the Citizen Corps is the Medical Reserve Corps (MRC) program, which coordinates the skills of practicing and retired physicians, nurses, and other health professionals, as well as other citizens interested in health issues who are eager to volunteer to address their community's ongoing public health needs and to help their community during large-scale emergency situations.

Local community leaders will develop their own Medical Reserve Corps units and identify the duties of the MRC volunteers according to specific community needs. For example, MRC volunteers may deliver necessary public health services during a crisis, assist emergency response teams with patients, and provide care directly to those with less serious injuries and other health-related issues. (http://www.citizencorps. gov/programs/medical.shtm)

During the federal FY2002, $3 million was allocated for MRC. This money was used primarily for the demonstration project small grants program and to fund the technical assistance and support mechanism for the program. The President's budget for FY2003 includes funds for the MRC program, but availability of these funds is pending Congressional action. (http://www.medicalreservecorps.gov/faq.htm)

Neighborhood Watch Program (NWP) and Volunteers in Police Service (VIPS) programs are other homeland security–related projects of the Citizen Corps.

SAFE Conference

The first annual conference on "The Community and Homeland Security," in cooperation with the SAFE project, took place in San Francisco on March 27 to March 28, 2003. The aim of the conference was to bring together local leaders from several states, leaders responsible for shaping homeland security programs and activities in their communities, with representatives from federal, state, local, nonprofit, private, and international organizations working on homeland security–related issues. The conference allowed all these practitioners, participants, and representatives to voice their concerns and to share their experiences and gave them their first opportunity not only to work together to identify existing problems with Homeland Security at the local level but to

---

SIDEBAR 6-4   SAFE Conference: The Community and Homeland Security

The National Council on Crime and Delinquency (NCCD) and the SAFE Project (Securing America's Future for Everyone) hosted the first annual conference on "The Community and Homeland Security" on March 27 and March 28, 2003, in San Francisco, California.

The conference brought over 60 local leaders from around the country, leaders who are responsible for shaping homeland security programs and activities in their communities together with representatives from federal, state, and local government and nonprofit, private, and international organizations working on homeland security–related issues.

The conference allowed participants to voice their concerns and share experiences and gave them their first opportunity not only to work together to identify existing problems with Homeland Security at the local level but also to propose possible solutions.

Four principal areas of concern emerged from these discussions:

- Resources: Greater access to resources to fund homeland security programs and projects at the community level
- Information: Greater access to practical information about application, eligibility, recruitment, retention, and other concerns

- Programming: The need for innovative and effective programming ideas
- Customizing: The need to focus on diverse and special-needs populations

Presented below are some of the comments made by conference participants:

The primary concern of those in attendance was well stated by Carol Lopes (Berkeley, California), who said, "Though there has been a lot of progress, we are willfully unprepared. Community and neighborhood preparedness is the centerpiece of today's work. Our responsibility is to prepare a community before a disaster and assist after a disaster strikes. We must train a cadre of emergency prepared individuals who will interface well with first responders."

Said Chuck Supple (GO SERV): "We must engage citizens to address problems in their own communities to have the greatest possible impact in Community Homeland Security."

Said Valli Wasp (Austin, Texas): "Preparedness must be addressed locally. We need to take this to 'homes'—get rid of the 'land,' get rid of the 'security'—this is about people protecting their homes. If you want people to listen to you, you have to go to where they live."

propose possible solutions to these problems (Sidebar 6-4). A copy of the full conference report on the SAFE Conference is presented in Appendix 9.

Four principal areas of concern on the community level emerged from the discussions in the conference:

1. Resources: Greater access to resources to fund homeland security programs and projects at the community level
2. Information: Greater access to practical information about application, eligibility, recruitment, retention, and other concerns
3. Programming: The need for innovative and effective programming ideas
4. Customizing: The need to focus on diverse and "special needs" populations

To create more resources and to use available resources more effectively, the following ideas were developed in the conference:

- Block grants to communities are an efficient means for providing federal funding for community homeland security efforts.
- Communities should partner with the National Governor's Association, the United States Conference of Mayors, the League of Cities, and other professional associations seeking federal funding for community homeland security efforts.
- Creative funding ideas practiced in communities around the country needs to be identified and widely disseminated among community homeland security officials.

Said Eileen Garry (U.S. Department of Justice): "Every good idea I have ever heard came from the local level."

Resources

One participant expressed concern that "making us fundraisers, in addition to our programmatic [tasks], really stretches municipalities' resources thin. The raw numbers of people required for fundraising exhausts programs."

However, such fundraising actions are recognized as vital to any program's success, echoed by Doris Milldyke (Kansas) who said, "Money is the first goal, volunteers are the second."

Information

Ann Patton (Tulsa, Oklahoma) stated, "An information clearinghouse would be invaluable," while Doris Milldyke (Kansas) noted that information on VIPS, MRS, and other programs is "notoriously difficult to find," adding, "we need a golden key for information on getting grants."

Programming

Chuck Supple (California GO SERV) stated this position well in saying, "We've probably only thought of a 'minutia' of the areas where volunteers would be useful."

Customizing

Ana-Marie Jones (Oakland, California) warned that "special needs communities are often isolated from services," adding that "[programs] must have a trusted leader who either speaks or has access to the languages of all representative groups—you need more than a 'Spanish press release.'" She suggested that participants "involve special needs communities before the disaster" to be effective.

Source: A Report on the First Annual Conference on "The Community and Homeland Security," Coppola, Haddow, Bullock, March 2003 http://www.nccd-crc.org/new/chs_conference_1.pdf

- New partnerships need to be established with the country's business and philanthropic communities to leverage their resources for community homeland security efforts.

Suggestions for improving access to accurate and timely information regarding homeland security issues included the following:

- Establishing an information clearinghouse to catalog homeland security information sources
- Establishing a web-based "chat room" for community officials to exchange ideas and best practices and to discuss current issues
- Establishing a "funding exchange" to share ideas on funding sources and creative funding ideas
- Partnering with the Department of Homeland Security and state homeland security operations to facilitate the flow of information on federal and state programs and funding opportunities to community officials.

In addition to the homeland security programming currently in place (e.g., CERT training, Medical RSVP), conference participants identified a need to design and implement programs that fully leveraged the capabilities of volunteers in the community.

Several ideas were considered, including the following:

- The SAFE Project, designed to develop volunteer programs in support of community emergency management and homeland security operations
- The development of Community Emergency Networks (CEN) designed to facilitate communications between community residents and local homeland security officials before, during, and after a disaster or terrorist incident.

Some of the ideas developed in the conference regarding the "special needs" populations were as follows:

- Reprogramming Community Development Block Grant (CDBG) funding targeted for "special needs" populations to include homeland security efforts

- Establishing "language and culture banks" in communities to facilitate communications and information flow between public safety and emergency officials and "special-needs" populations
- Partnering with national associations and groups that represent the interests of special-needs populations such as the elderly, veterans, minority populations, children, and the disabled
- Partnering with foundations and other philanthropic organizations, such as the Annie E. Casey Foundation, which focuses its efforts and funding in disadvantaged communities
- Partnering with local emergency management/ homeland security and public health operations to help these groups identify and serve special-needs populations in the community.

The existence of voluntary activities for the homeland security, such as the SAFE conference, is important to bring together different stakeholders and provide an opportunity to share expertise and best practices, as well as to create an environment where public-private partnerships can be initiated and brainstorming can occur.

THE AMERICAN RED CROSS

Red Cross has always been one of the most important partners of the federal, state, and local governments in disaster relief operations. Some of the daily community operations of the Red Cross chapters include senior services, caregivers' support, provision of hospital and nursing home volunteers, lifeline (an electronic personal emergency response service), transportation to medical/doctor's appointments and other essential trips, food pantry and hot lunch programs, homeless shelters and transitional housing services, school clubs and community service learning programs and projects, youth programs (violence and substance abuse prevention, peer education and mentoring, leadership development camps), food and rental assistance, language banks, and community information and referral.

Beside its common missions, Red Cross is also trying to find itself an appropriate place in the new homeland security environment. Some of the Red Cross chapters have already developed homeland security programs, in which they provide training for volunteers from local communities.

From the $10.3 million of first federal grants to involve citizen volunteers in homeland security efforts in 2002, the American Red Cross received $1,778, 978, which was distributed among national headquarters and several chapters.

The greater New York chapter received $500,000 of the Red Cross-designated funds for the recruitment, training, and mobilization of 5,000 new disaster volunteers equipped to respond to another terrorist attack on a local level. These volunteers will work with Red Cross service delivery units in New York to train additional volunteers, exponentially increasing the city's force of disaster relief workers.

Another $371,978 was given to the American Red Cross National Headquarters for a nationwide program aimed at increasing volunteers in communities most vulnerable to terrorist attacks. The grant supports a 10-and-a-half–month program with 30 Community Preparedness Corps (CPC) members working in 19 chapters.

Corps members will work in chapters to ensure that all community members—totaling some 27,000,000—have a "family disaster response plan." They will tailor plans for those with language barriers and disabilities and for children and the elderly.

At the same time, CPC volunteers will focus on minimizing intolerance across the country by teaching international humanitarian law and the principles of the International Red Cross Movement (humanity, independence, neutrality, impartiality, voluntary service, unity, and universality).

Corps members will also recruit and train an estimated 400 new volunteers and instructors who will make the educational programs available to additional vulnerable communities. Ultimately, corps members working through Red Cross chapters will create a network of hundreds of skilled volunteers across the country.

Additional grants were awarded to Red Cross chapters nationwide. In California the money will benefit the implementation of homeland security measures in Los Angeles, San Francisco, and Sacramento. The Oregon Trail Chapter was awarded a grant funding 400 new volunteers to dedicate 1,500 hours of service to disaster preparedness.

On the East Coast, the Red Cross will develop "Disaster Resistant Neighborhood" programs across eight wards of Washington, DC. Through the program these communities will create disaster response plans. The southeast Pennsylvania chapter received a grant to create an alliance of more than 100 nonprofits in the Philadelphia area to form the Southeast Pennsylvania Voluntary Organization Active in Disaster (VOAD) to help citizens prevent, prepare for, and respond to disasters.

(http://www.disasterrelief.org/Disasters/020918 security/)

(http://www.redcross.org/faq/0,1096,0_383_,00. html)

THE SALVATION ARMY

The Salvation Army is a voluntary evangelical help organization dedicated to caring for the poor, feeding the hungry, clothing the naked, and befriending the friendless.

Adult rehabilitation centers are among the most widely known of all Salvation Army services and account for the largest resident substance abuse rehabilitation program in the United States. Individuals with identifiable and treatable needs go to these centers for help when they no longer are able to cope with their problems. There they receive adequate housing, nourishing meals, and necessary medical care, and they engage in work therapy, spiritual guidance, and skilled counseling in clean and wholesome surroundings. Residents may be referred or be remanded by the courts.

Donated material, such as furniture, appliances, or clothing, provides both needed work therapy and a source of revenue through the Army's thrift stores. More than 120 adult rehabilitation centers offer these programs in the United States.

Free temporary shelter is available to homeless men and women in severe financial need. Low-cost housing also is available to men and women living on pensions or social security.

On August 28, 2003 the Department of Homeland Security announced a partnership with the Salvation Army. Beginning immediately, the Salvation Army has agreed to distribute "Ready" brochures in its 9,000 retail centers nationwide and to individual homes while collecting donated goods. The Salvation Army will distribute two million "Ready" brochures throughout the United States to support the family preparedness campaign by DHS.

The Salvation Army also supported DHS during the response to Hurricane Isabel that has hit the East Coast in September 2003, causing some damage in a few states such as Maryland, Virginia, the District of Columbia, and North Carolina. The disaster is unique for DHS because it is the first natural disaster that DHS had to manage.

FEMA contacted the Salvation Army on Saturday, September 20, with the request to begin meals at five locations in the District of Columbia on Monday, September 22. The Southern Baptist Convention has provided two mobile kitchens capable of cooking up to 20,000 hot meals per day.

In North Carolina the Salvation Army has established a command center in Greenville to coordinate efforts across the state. The Salvation Army led the way in providing meals to people without power. Sixteen fixed feeding sites have been established, and Salvation Army emergency disaster services vehicles (canteens) continue to rove neighborhoods, delivering meals to residents unable to reach the fixed sites. In the first 36 hours of disaster response, The Salvation Army served more than 28,000 meals.

The Salvation Army's efforts in Maryland included serving 462 meals, sheltering over 100 people, and distributing more than 70 clean-up kits. Local volunteers have been alerted to be on stand-by to help elderly and disabled residents affected by Isabel. (http://www.dhs.gov/dhspublic/display?content = 1395)

(http://www.salvationarmysouth.org/isabel-9-23-03.htm)

ROLE OF PRIVATE SECTOR IN MITIGATION AND PREPAREDNESS ACTIVITIES

The events of September 11 brought home the importance of private sector involvement in crisis, emergency, and disaster management. More private entities are focusing on their needs in this area. This section will discuss the essentials of private sector business continuity planning and disaster management. Most of the components below are learned from natural disasters or man-made accidents; however, the September 11 attacks have proved that those important components of classical crisis management are also important for terrorism risk management.

Business impact analysis (BIA): The management level analysis by which an organization assesses the quantitative (financial) and qualitative (nonfinancial) impacts, effects, and loss that might result if the organization were to suffer a business-interrupting event. Performing BIA as a preparedness measure is important because findings from BIA are used to make decisions concerning business continuity management strategy.

Crisis communications planning: Decision making about how crisis communications will be performed during an emergency is important because communication is a critical success factor for effective crisis management. Preventing rumors about your corporation as well as telling your story before someone else does it for you is only possible via a predefined communication policy.

IT and systems infrastructure redundancy planning: There are different techniques and approaches regarding the enforcement of systems redundancy. Each company is unique, with its own IT and system needs and processes; therefore customized approaches have to be employed to build more reliable systems infrastructure (e.g., backup databases, software, hardware, network redundancy).

Geographic location and backup sites: The selection of the geographic location of headquarters and offices and the distribution of key executives in those buildings are strategically important decisions with regard to minimizing potential losses (both human and physical) during a disaster. The availability of backup sites that allow employees to continue operations in case of physical loss of or damage to a primary facility is a key success factor, one that is, unfortunately, usually difficult to justify in terms of cost and benefit.

Transportation planning: The transportation infrastructure is among the most sensitive infrastructures to emergency and disaster situations. Overloaded transportation infrastructure during crisis is usually a reason for microdisasters in the midst of bigger ones. Therefore realistic transportation planning is important for a successful response.

Crisis leadership: Research and experience has shown that during crisis situations people (e.g., employees, staff, customers) need someone to tell them what is going on and explain what is being done about it, even if the information this person communicates is obsolete or redundant. Strong leadership also helps other people to regain self-esteem and motivates them to commit to the efforts to overcome the crisis.

Insurance: It is important for companies to have a feasible but protective insurance policy. Realistic risk assessments and modeling are necessary to establish this economic feasibility.

There may be other components of private sector risk mitigation and preparedness that are not mentioned in this text (Sidebar 6-5). However, the components mentioned above should be enough to provide a basic understanding of the concept of corporate crisis management.

(Kayyem and Chang, 2002; Smith, 2002)

BEST PRACTICES

The nature of crisis, emergency, and risk management is very complicated: No matter how much you talk about theoretical issues, you cannot appreciate the complexity of the actual environment in which you must try to implement practical applications. The two case studies that follow will document a private

sector company dealing with disaster and a multi-governmental approach to preparedness.

The first case study is about Cantor Fitzgerald, a private company devastated by September 11 attacks. Although the case study mainly concerns response and recovery, it seemed appropriate for the mitigation and preparedness chapter since it clearly shows the importance of mitigation and preparedness to a successful response.

CASE STUDY 2
Cantor Fitzgerald—Forty Seven Hours

(Summarized from original, by Edward Cone and Sean Gallagher)

For Joseph Noviello, September 11 began at 6:30 A.M. with a phone call confirming that an annual fishing trip with colleagues at the Cantor Fitzgerald bond trading firm was still on, despite some foul weather offshore.

Minutes later, the most intense two days of his life would begin. The first plane hijacked by terrorists would hit Cantor's building. Watching on TV from his Manhattan apartment, Noviello had no way of knowing what ultimately lay in store. But clearly a disaster of a proportion he had never had to deal with was unfolding. Fortunately, he had a plan to follow.

That plan may have saved the companies. No firms suffered worse fates on September 11 than Cantor Fitzgerald and its electronic marketplace unit, eSpeed. More than 700 employees of the two companies died in the destruction of the World Trade Center's north tower, where Cantor and eSpeed shared their headquarters and a vital computer center. Yet eSpeed was up and running when the bond market reopened at 8 A.M. on September 13, little more than 47 hours after the disaster.

"The difference for us was the planning we had in place," says Noviello, 36, who was promoted to eSpeed's chief information officer after the disaster. ESpeed's systems were built on a dual architecture that replicated all machines, connections, and functionality at the

World Trade Center and at a Rochelle Park site, with a third facility in London.

ESpeed, which operates as a freestanding business and also serves as the trading engine for its parent company, would lose 180 employees, including about half of its U.S.-based technology staff. But eSpeed had some important assets left. Most of the top technology executives had been out of the office, including Matt Claus, eSpeed's current CTO and Noviello's right-hand man, who had been scheduled to go on the fishing trip.

The atmosphere was tense, with people unsure as to what had happened to their friends or colleagues. "For days, every time a new face came in the door it was an emotional release," says Noviello. "There was a disaster-recovery contact list, but people were seeking to find each other not for work but to find out who was OK."

Beyond the technical questions were operational details such as advising staff on public transportation options to the suburban site, reestablishing shifts, and making sure there were counselors on duty. Conference

---

SIDEBAR 6-5   Private Sector Homeland Security Checklist

The Department of Homeland Security released the following antiterror checklist for the private sector in its May 2003 Homeland Security Information Bulletin:

- Maintain situational awareness of world events and ongoing threats.
- Ensure all levels of personnel are notified via briefings, e-mail, voice mail, and signage of any changes in threat conditions and protective measures.
- Encourage personnel to be alert and immediately report any situation that may constitute a threat or suspicious activity.
- Encourage personnel to avoid routines, vary times and routes, preplan, and keep a low profile, especially during periods of high threat.
- Encourage personnel to take notice and report suspicious packages, devices, unattended briefcases, or other unusual materials immediately; inform them not to handle or attempt to move any such object.
- Encourage personnel to keep their family members and supervisors apprised of their whereabouts.

- Encourage personnel to know emergency exits and stairwells.
- Increase the number of visible security personnel wherever possible.
- Rearrange exterior vehicle barriers, traffic cones, and road blocks to alter traffic patterns near facilities and cover by alert security forces.
- Institute/increase vehicle, foot, and roving security patrols varying in size, timing, and routes.
- Implement random security guard shift changes.
- Arrange for law enforcement vehicles to be parked randomly near entrances and exits.
- Review current contingency plans and, if not already in place, develop and implement procedures for receiving and acting on threat information; alert notification procedures; terrorist incident response procedures; evacuation procedures; bomb threat procedures; hostage and barricade procedures; chemical, biological, radiological, and nuclear (CBRN) procedures; consequence and crisis management procedures; accountability procedures; and media procedures.

calls every two hours kept track of milestones and objectives. "We were talking at 2 A.M., at 4 A.M.," says Noviello. "Who is sleeping during something like this? Work is great therapy."

None of this effort would have succeeded without the duplicate architecture in Rochelle Park. Yet Cantor started moving into the facility only in February. From day one, Rochelle Park was seen as a concurrent system, not a disaster-recovery site.

All that redundancy would be stretched to the limit as eSpeed worked to overcome the technical hurdles between the company and the opening of the bond market Thursday morning. Two of those hurdles were huge: the loss of eSpeed's private network connections and the destruction of the company's ability to handle fulfillment of trades.

The first problem was solved by allowing customers who had overseas offices connected to Cantor's London data center to reroute across their own networks to London. Speed worked with customers to reconfigure their servers to point to London and moved or expanded the permissions on customer accounts to connect to that site. For customers without overseas private networks, eSpeed worked to get them access over the Internet until the customers could get their high-speed connections hooked into the Rochelle Park facility.

To solve the second issue, help arrived in the form of one of eSpeed's competitors. ICI/ADP, another electronic trading company, offered to take care of eSpeed's clearing and settling of transactions through its own connection to banks. By Wednesday night the

- When the aforementioned plans and procedures have been implemented, conduct internal training exercises and invite local emergency responders (fire, rescue, medical, and bomb squads) to participate in joint exercises.
- Coordinate and establish partnerships with local authorities to develop intelligence and information-sharing relationships.
- Place personnel on standby for contingency planning.
- Limit the number of access points, and strictly enforce access control procedures.
- Approach all illegally parked vehicles in and around facilities, question drivers, and direct them to move immediately; if owner cannot be identified, have vehicle towed by law enforcement.
- Consider installing telephone caller I.D.; record phone calls, if necessary.
- Increase perimeter lighting.
- Deploy visible security cameras and motion sensors.
- Remove vegetation in and around perimeters; maintain regularly.
- Institute a robust vehicle inspection program to include checking under the undercarriage of vehicles, under the hood, and in the trunk. Provide vehicle inspection training to security personnel.
- Deploy explosive detection devices and explosive detection canine teams.
- Conduct vulnerability studies focusing on physical security, structural engineering, infrastructure engineering, and power, water, and air infiltration, if feasible.
- Initiate a system to enhance mail and package screening procedures (both announced and unannounced).
- Install special locking devices on manhole covers in and around facilities.
- Implement a counter-surveillance detection program.

Source: Continuity Central 5/21/03

eSpeed team had mapped its financial back-office system to ADP's system and had successfully sent test transactions to J.P. Morgan Chase & Co. and other banks. The cooperation of other companies, including vendors and fellow financial firms, turned out to be essential to Cantor/eSpeed's quick recovery.

The firm was weakened by the loss of so many people and the related shutdown of its voice-broker business. But it survived as a viable business. Thanks to planning, the company can keep operating, even if something should happen to Rochelle Park. Its data center in London will serve as the mirror site going forward.

And going forward, the company's systems should be even more resilient. "We are learning a lot of lessons as we are restoring the system," says Noviello, including how to automate more aspects of bringing systems back up. "And we are not restoring our bad habits." (Source: Case Study summarized from *Baseline Magazine*: http://www.baselinemag.com/print_article/0,3668,a=17022,00.asp)

The second case study is from a governmental preparedness activity, a drill that simulated a radiological and biological terrorist attack to the United States: TOPOFF 2 (Figure 6-6).

FIGURE 6-5   New York, NY, October 13, 2001—Debris removal at Ground Zero continues 24 hours a day. Photo by Andrea Booher/ FEMA News Photo.

CASE STUDY 3
TOPOFF 2

Week-Long National Combating Terrorism Exercise

On Monday, May 12, 2003, a fake dirty bomb was detonated in downtown Seattle, releasing radioactive material throughout the metropolitan area. At the same time in Chicago, hospitals were inundated with patients complaining of flu-like symptoms associated with pneumonic plague.

Fortunately, the mastermind of both scenarios was not a terrorist group but, rather, the federal government. With a price tag of $16 million, TOPOFF 2 has been the most expensive, comprehensive emergency preparedness exercise ever undertaken.

Designed to test and improve the response capacity of "top officials" in the event of a weapons of mass destruction attack, TOPOFF 2 included more than 8,000 participants from 19 federal agencies, such as the Centers for Disease Control and Prevention (CDC) and the Federal Emergency Management Agency (FEMA), as well as state and local emergency responders and the American Red Cross—the only nongovernmental agency included in the exercise.

The goals of TOPOFF 2 were to improve the nation's capacity to manage extreme events; create broader frameworks for the operation of expert crisis and consequence management systems; validate authorities, strategies, plans, policies, procedures, and protocols; and build a sustainable, systematic national exercise program to support the national strategy for homeland security.

The fake crisis began around lunchtime on Monday, with the detonation of a radioactive dirty bomb near a coffee roasting plant in Seattle. Two cars were set afire, releasing plumes of smoke. A small explosion was created. Actors playing victims began to moan and cry. A mock television-news crew broke through a police barrier to get at the action. Some of the first emergency workers on the scene ran through the wreckage. Others ambled.

Emergency response staff at all 17 King County hospitals immediately swung into action, directed by Harborview Medical Center's Emergency Services department. Staff members were able to follow the crisis on a virtual TV network set up exclusively for the drill.

A short time later, Harborview employees learned the explosive device contained radioactive material, although they didn't know what kind of radiation it involved. The decontamination team—designated emergency response medical staff, plus engineering and public safety personnel—was called in and began setting up a heated decontamination tent on the road by the hospital's emergency response wing.

Only six people arrived in the first 90 minutes of the crisis, and the rest trickled in later in the afternoon. In the end, Harborview treated about 30 patients, all of whom "survived."

Just 24 hours later and halfway across the country, the scene was quite different as very sick people began turning up in emergency responses in Chicago and across Illinois. Their devastating symptoms were quickly diagnosed as pneumonic plague, unleashed in a biological attack by the same terrorist group.

Thirty-six people "died" among the more than 300 infected. At hospitals across the state, infected patients—volunteers wearing bright yellow T-shirts printed with "Role Player"—mixed in with real patients to test hospitals' ability to meet the crisis amid business as usual. Every once in a while, a volunteers would produce a card indicating that he or she had died.

Even more victims were represented by faxes pouring into the hospital containing a name, a diagnosis, a brief medical history, and a summary of physical findings. These "paper patients" were triaged and treated as live bodies, subject to the same hospital resource allocations.

Richard Fantus, M.D., Chief of Trauma Services at Advocate Illinois Masonic Medical Center on Chicago's north side, acted as incident commander for his hospital. "We knew early on that something unusual was going on because of what was coming

FIGURE 6-6 Washington, DC, May 13, 2003—FEMA's Emergency Support Team employees were TOPOFF 2 exercise participants as well as assisting with the response and recovery efforts for the tornados that hit the South and Midwest. Photo by Lauren Hobart/FEMA News Photo.

across the mock news network and the communications we received from the public health department," Fantus said.

But he noted that diagnosing all the emergency arrivals was not as straightforward as expected. "Victims came in with various symptoms, many having nothing to do with plague. Some had had heart attacks, some were pregnant, and some had the respiratory symptoms of SARS. Just as in real life, we had to identify who was likely to have been exposed and triage them according to respiratory symptoms," he says. "Staff was gowned and masked and everyone suspected of exposure immediately went into respiratory isolation."

Vivian Chamberlain was an actor who played a passerby when the false bomb exploded. She had to pretend that her eardrums had burst from the force of the bogus blast.

As the first patient to arrive by ambulance at Bellevue's Overlake Hospital Medical Center, Chamberlain screamed and shook, her ears bleeding, her face marked by soot. But before her injuries could be treated, Chamberlain had to be "decontaminated" of radiation.

Her gurney was wheeled into a $30,000 tent set up in the parking lot and manned by hospital staffers wearing "Level C ensembles," sealed jumpsuits with head masks and respirators costing $950 each.

Chamberlain was put on a back board and her T-shirt and shorts were cut off. Four moon-suited workers scrubbed her body with long-handled brushes and hosed her down with unheated water from a nearby fire hydrant.

"It was awful. It was freezing cold," Chamberlain later said of the "decon" shower as she stood shivering in a hospital gown, a white sheet draped over her shoulders.

All did not go smoothly. One male "victim," who was portraying someone with psychiatric problems, refused to put up a fight as instructed by the paper tag on his hand. Prodding by nurses at first could not persuade the shy young man. Finally getting with the program, he "escaped" from the roped-off area. Then hospital guards refused to capture him, saying their jurisdiction was only inside the perimeter.

"You guys need to get him *now*!" bellowed Vickie Nostrant, a veteran emergency-room nurse and one of 70 hospital staffers participating. The guards immediately complied. The incident is a small example of glitches the exercise is designed to reveal, nurses said.

At the same time agencies from around the Puget Sound area responded to the mock crisis in Seattle, and some institutions set up their own simultaneous drills.

At Pacific Lutheran University near Tacoma, students and others acted out a terrorist attack that featured a mock car bomb and a hostage situation.

As part of the overall exercise, events took place in Washington, DC, and Chicago, where a mock bioterror attack was staged at Midway Airport, and a raid was made on a terrorists' lair. City, county, and federal officials proclaimed the drill a success.

For example, County Executive Ron Sims said he and others discovered how much work is involved in rerouting the county's transportation system. Because of the mock radiation, numerous bus lines had to be rerouted, a move that affected mass transit in King, Pierce, and Snohomish counties.

After each day's activities, local and federal officials in each city met to discuss how things went. Within a month, a two-day conference for all participants was planned to review the exercise. By September, a full report was submitted outlining strengths and vulnerabilities.

http://www.dhs.gov/dhspublic/display?content=735
http://www.redcross.org/news/ds/terrorism/
    030512TOPOFF.html
http://www.aamc.org/newsroom/reporter/august03/
    bioterrorism.htm
http://www.emergencypreparednessweek.ca/mr_nr_
    050202_e.shtml
http://seattletimes.nwsource.com/html/localnews/
    134726076_topoff13m.html
http://www.envoyworldwide.com/News/Continuity
    Insights.pdf

Source: Case Study compiled by Sarp Yeletaysi using information from above listed web sites.

SMART PRACTICES

The Federal Emergency Management Agency (FEMA) collects Smart Practices in community preparedness programs. These Smart Practices are published on the FEMA web site. Presented in the following pages are seven examples of Smart Practices endorsed by FEMA.

SMART PRACTICE NO. 1
FEMA Office of National Preparedness
Smart Practices Spotlight
April 23, 2003

Bioterrorism Exercise Vaccinates
5,000 Against the Flu
Baxter County, Arkansas

Summary: In possibly one of the first exercises of its kind, the Baxter County Health Unit, a division of the Arkansas Department of Health, combined an important public health initiative with a bioterrorism preparedness exercise. By using real flu vaccinations in the exercise, the county was able to address a possible flu outbreak while practicing processes for vaccinating large numbers of area residents.

Developing a plan to prevent the spread of a potential flu outbreak, Baxter County, Ark., officials seized the opportunity to provide a valuable public health service and bolster county preparedness through a joint flu inoculation/mock mass vaccination exercise. The county designed a bioterrorism exercise that would test its ability to inoculate a large number of citizens by offering the flu vaccine, free of charge, to local members of the community.

The exercise was designed to be as authentic as possible to replicate a real bioterrorism emergency. Patients entered the complex, staged on the county fairgrounds, and were directed to a mock triage center. Assessed for the likelihood they had been exposed to a biological toxin, they were sent either to the general area or to the "sick" area, where they were given vaccinations. Meanwhile, the local sheriff's office stood guard over the precious stores of vaccine.

More than 5,000 citizens took part in the exercise and were inoculated against the flu. The exercise brought together more than the general public, however. A number of agencies and organizations played critical roles in the exercise, from local government officials to community hospitals and voluntary organizations, media representatives, and even the county judge.

Thinking Locally

- How can you integrate public health initiatives with your preparedness exercises?
- How can you create more public interest in your preparedness initiatives?

The multiagency involvement was one of the exercise's biggest successes, said Baxter County Health Administrator Richard Taffner. "Because of all the entities involved, we were able to identify areas that we need to expand and change," he said. "We had everyone involved, from the garbage disposal services to the National Guard." Most important, he added, the exercise involved a detailed debriefing that highlighted the successes of the vaccination/exercise and also identified specific areas for improvement.

For more information about the mass vaccination exercise, contact Baxter County Health Administrator Richard Taffner at crtaffner@HealthyArkansas.com.

SMART PRACTICE NO. 2
U.S. Department of Homeland Security
FEMA Preparedness
Smart Practices Spotlight
March 12, 2003

A Regional Approach to Terrorism and All-Hazards Preparedness, Pennsylvania Region 13 Working Group

Summary: In 1998, 12 Pennsylvania counties and the city of Pittsburgh together became the first group in the state to try a regional approach to terrorism preparedness. Today, their mutual aid and regional coordination system has been recognized by the FBI and the National Association of Counties as a model approach for intergovernment cooperation in terrorism and all-hazards preparedness.

While attending a Pennsylvania emergency management conference in 1998, a number of county emergency managers began to discuss threats of terrorism and the resources needed to respond effectively should an incident involving weapons of mass destruction occur in their region. In searching for a way to pool their resources, they created the Pennsylvania Region 13 Working Group.

Since formalizing the mutual aid and intergovernment agreements, the Region 13 Working Group has established an incident command system for response operations, created a Metropolitan Medical Response System (MMRS), and developed

plans and procedures for surveillance, notifications, mass immunization, and fatality management. They have organized major training exercises such as "Mall Strike 2001," a simulated nerve agent and radiological incident; a simulated gas attack exercise in the Pittsburgh subway system; and a full-scale exercise testing the ability of 27 hospitals in three of the 13 counties to decontaminate victims of a chemical attack.

When United Airlines Flight 93 crashed in rural Somerset County on September 11, 2001, the chair of the working group was immediately in touch with other members of the group, and emergency teams were deployed swiftly to the site. The group's four years working together and preparing for terrorist events allowed its members to develop and train teams that could work efficiently together during an event of this magnitude.

Meanwhile, work is going forward on the 800 MHz project, an interoperable communications system for emergency response agencies in Region 13 and the rest of western Pennsylvania. Allegheny County has approved the floating of a bond issue for $25 million to build the system infrastructure, while other counties in Region 13 are already using 800 MHz with great success. Other projects include a specialized equipment resource pool specific to WMD responses and specialized WMD training for emergency services personnel and support agencies.

Members of the group include 13 county emergency managers (the 13th county joined the group in 1999), the city of Pittsburgh, the Pittsburgh office of the FBI, and the Pennsylvania Emergency Management Agency (PEMA). The Allegheny County emergency manager serves as chair of the working group, which meets every month at the Allegheny County Emergency Operations Center. Committees focus on communications, training, law enforcement, fire and hazardous materials, and medical issues. On a regular basis various emergency services personnel participate in the meetings, including police, fire, EMS, bomb units, public works, and health and hazardous materials units.

Thinking Locally

- How could you establish a regional emergency management structure?
- Are your current mutual aid agreements truly inclusive of all appropriate agencies and institutions?

For more information about this initiative, contact Chief Robert Full, Chairman, Pennsylvania Region 13 Working Group, at 1-412-473-2550, or rfull@county. allegheny.pa.us.

SMART PRACTICE NO. 3
U.S. Department of Homeland Security FEMA Preparedness Smart Practices Spotlight March 26, 2003

Using GIS to Enhance Emergency Response Operations, Cabarrus County, North Carolina

Summary: Across the nation, state and local personnel are recognizing the need for collaboration and coordination in emergency preparedness and response operations. This week's spotlight focuses on how one county planned a data collection project that will be utilized by multiple departments and will assist in the future planning of emergency and nonemergency situations across the county.

Located in the southwestern part of North Carolina, Cabarrus County is home to a wide range of businesses and industry. In a time where budget constraints are having an impact on jurisdictions at all levels, Cabarrus County has found a way to provide its 911 centers with more accurate information and digital photographs. These functions will aid in the dispatching of emergency services such as fire, EMS, rescue, and law enforcement.

Coordinated by the County Geographic Information Systems (GIS) Department and funded primarily by the sheriff's department, the project involves verifying every address in the county, assigning a longitude/latitude coordinate to each primary structure, verifying street centerlines, and storing an image of each improved property in the county.

The project initially evolved from the need to correct and verify addressing in preparation for implementation of Enhanced 911 (E911) rules, as mandated by the Federal Communications Commission (FCC). E911 rules seek to improve the effectiveness and reliability of wireless 911 service by providing 911 dispatchers with additional information on calls from wireless telephones and improving accuracy in finding the locations of wireless calls, within a 50 to 100 meter radius.

The experience and responsibility of county-wide mapping belongs to the GIS Department, which is spearheading the project initiated by the sheriff's department. In consultation with the sheriff's department, the project was conceived to include the images and geographic coordinates of each property in the county.

When the project was first discussed, the county GIS manager saw the potential for additional benefits and began involving other county departments. Now, what started out as a project for one department has come to involve four departments and a nearby county.

There are additional benefits of the project, as well. For example, the digital photographs will improve the quality of visual data used by county real estate appraisers, allow verification and correction of any addressing discrepancies, and assist emergency management in preparing recovery reports required in the aftermath of disasters and emergencies.

"The inclusion of imaging is very important to law enforcement and EMS," Captain Phil Patterson of the Cabarrus County Sheriff's Department said. "Being able to locate a 911 caller is critical to our emergency service system, because it reduces the amount of time it takes emergency services to locate and arrive at the 911 caller's home or business."

For more information about this initiative, contact Cathy Cole, GIS Manager Cabarrus County, NC, at 704-920-2146 or ccole@co.cabarrus.nc.us.

SMART PRACTICE NO. 4
U.S. Department of Homeland Security
FEMA Preparedness
Smart Practices Spotlight
June 18, 2003

Government and Business Team Up for Emergencies
El Segundo, California

Summary: El Segundo covers just 5.5 square miles and has a resident population of only about 16,000 people. But El Segundo is close to the Los Angeles International Airport and numerous industries that represent national security interests. And during the week, its population expands to include a workforce of more than 90,000. On September 11, 2001, its Emergency Operations Centers (EOCs) were overwhelmed with calls from local businesses and industry.

In the aftermath of the September 11, officials of the City of El Segundo knew they had to do something. When terrorists attacked the World Trade Center and the Pentagon, emergency managers across the country activated their EOCs. This scenario posed a big problem for El Segundo, which has limited personnel resources.

The city's EOC was inundated with calls from local business and industry officials—aerospace and military defense contractors, chemical manufacturers, utility companies, an oil refinery and a range of commercial industries. They wanted to know about potential evacuations, possible bomb threats, road and facility closures, the status of major highways, and whether or not their employees could get to work or leave without being caught in traffic gridlock.

The solution was a government-business partnership in El Segundo. The city established an official business and industry liaison function in its EOC operating plan, with the business community providing personnel to staff the positions. During an emergency at least two private industry staffers work each 12-hour shift on a rotating basis, addressing business community–related issues. Staff would collect information from the city's emergency operations and organization and relay it to the business community, as well as share business sector concerns with emergency management. One person handles telephone calls, and the other manages e-mail communications with business and industry officials. The two staffers would work side-by-side with the city's emergency workers and familiarize themselves with EOC emergency management practices and procedures. The staffers would be part of the emergency management team and a component of the planning and intelligence section of the city EOC.

Liaison personnel are provided through a Business and Industry Emergency Response Committee, which meets monthly to address the range of business community/city emergency operations issues. The committee is made up of about 50 representatives of companies located in the area, and its members have been trained in emergency management systems. They have also participated in an EOC orientation and operations course conducted by El Segundo's emergency services coordinator.

"Before 9/11, a city employee would handle the incoming calls from industry officials and the staff time associated with this task was significant," said David Burns, El Segundo's emergency services coordinator. "There had to be a better way to coordinate the collection and dissemination of information to the business community in an emergency. This process really works for us."

For more information about this initiative, contact David Burns, Coordinator, El Segundo Emergency Services, at 1-310-524-2252 or DBurns@elsegundo.org.

SMART PRACTICE NO. 5
U.S. Department of Homeland Security
FEMA Preparedness
Smart Practices Spotlight
April 9, 2003

F.I.R.E. Educators: Helping Schools Become Better Prepared, Hoover, Alabama, Fire Department

Summary: Increasingly, state and local personnel are recognizing the need to work together to help protect their communities. This week's spotlight focuses on how a local fire department established a program that provides a way to better connect the town's fire department, police department and school system.

When the Hoover, Alabama, Fire Department decided it was time for a better working relationship with the local school system, it developed a program that involved designating a Fire Information Resource Educator (F.I.R.E.) for every school in the community.

Essentially, the fire department was seeking to expand an already successful Police School Resource Officer program at the city's nine elementary schools, three middle schools, and two high schools. To centralize and improve connections with the schools and to identify new ways to serve the more than 10,000 students and faculty members within the school system, the department recruited volunteers from within its ranks to serve as F.I.R.E. educators and principal points of contact for each of the schools.

Having a F.I.R.E. educator certified as a first aid/CPR instructor and responsible for safety and fire code issues at each of the schools has led to a number of useful initiatives:

- F.I.R.E. educators serve as a critical conduit between school nurses and the paramedics at each fire station, and they are involved in fire prevention education and coordination at their respective schools.
- They have provided fire extinguisher training to the schools' nutritionists, kitchen workers, and custodians and helped establish the school system's crisis counseling response network.
- F.I.R.E. educators have provided system-wide training to school administrators in areas such as disaster response and local school mitigation, emergency plan development and implementation, and the Incident Management System (IMS). In fact, this relationship has led to the official adoption of IMS as the school system's crisis management model.

A mobile command unit for the city was a significant result of the partnership between the Hoover Fire Department and the school. A surplus vehicle from the Hoover City Schools and the remodeling efforts of Hoover firefighters and fleet management personnel exemplified this partnership.

Other benefits of this relationship include enhanced communications among all the participants, improved integration of city and school system emergency response plans, and a reduction in the number of safety violations identified during fire inspections of the school campuses.

For more information about this initiative, contact Captain Allan Rice, Hoover Fire Station 2, at ricea@ci.hoover.al.us.

SMART PRACTICE NO. 6
U.S. Department of Homeland Security
FEMA Preparedness
Smart Practices Spotlight
May 21, 2003

Community Emergency Response Network, Howard County, Maryland

Summary: Any disaster situation in the Washington, DC, or Baltimore, Maryland, area could potentially affect residents in neighboring Howard County. That's why the county and its community-based organizations decided to launch a major emergency preparedness effort that would involve as many citizens and sectors of the community as possible.

WASHINGTON—May 21, 2003: The September 11 attacks were a wake-up call for Howard County, Maryland. Located about 25 miles from Washington, DC, and 20 miles from Baltimore, Howard County knows its residents and infrastructure could be affected by a terrorist incident in either of those cities. The Community Emergency Response Network (CERN) was formed to create a network for emergency preparedness that involves both citizens and organizations and is functionally integrated with the county's Emergency Operations Center.

"We now know that as United States citizens, we need to be prepared in the event of a terrorist attack, no matter where we live," said Richard Krieg, CERN chairman and president of the Horizon Foundation, a community-oriented organization based in Howard County. "The missing link has been to mobilize organizations as a way to maximize overall community resilience." CERN is composed of frontline responders and representatives of the nonprofit community, major homeowner associations, the hospital system, the public schools, and others. The group encourages community-wide disaster response planning that includes planning for terrorist incidents. It also encourages organizations without such plans to develop them.

Early this year, CERN and the Howard County Public School System conducted a table-top exercise that provided participants with a realistic experience dealing with a large-scale terrorist event that occurred near, but not directly in, Howard County. The exercise also provided an opportunity to evaluate the schools' emergency plans and organizational structures. Lessons learned: Survivable radio communications are needed to supplement cell and landline telephones, decision making should be decentralized in emergencies to allow maximum flexibility at the school level, and schools need to work with parents to identify individuals to whom their children may be released in the event of an emergency.

More recently, the group organized a tabletop exercise for Howard County Community College, walking participants through a scenario involving a nuclear bomb explosion at Baltimore-Washington International Airport. Lessons learned: The college needs to address liability issues, establish procedures to isolate and assist people arriving from contaminated areas, and ensure that safe areas have enough supplies for sheltering in place.

CERN's web site, located at www.cern.us, is updated frequently with emergency preparedness information and includes links to all-news radio stations as well as local television stations in Washington and Baltimore. It also includes information about family emergency plans and disaster supply kits. The group is now working on a system of public shelters for emergencies and additional simulated disasters for county organizations. CERN was recently designated Howard County's Citizen Corps Council. Citizen Corps, a component of U.S.A. Freedom Corps, creates opportunities for individuals to help their communities prepare for disasters and emergencies of all kinds.

For more information about this initiative, contact Dr. Richard Krieg of The Horizon Foundation at 410-715-0311 or rkrieg@thehorizonfoundation.org.

SMART PRACTICE NO. 7
U.S. Department of Homeland Security
FEMA Preparedness
Smart Practices Spotlight
April 2, 2003

Maine Funds Library of Geospatial Information
State of Maine

Summary: Last year, the people of Maine and their political representatives all voted "yes" to create and fund an initiative designed to provide geospatial information and tools that can be used for a wide range of preparedness applications for emergency planners and first responders throughout the state. Through an outreach and public education effort, project developers were able to overcome legislative and funding challenges.

One of the most important libraries in Maine contains no books. An electronic compendium of geospatial information, the Maine GeoLibrary is designed to support disaster mitigation, preparedness, response, and recovery throughout the state by making precision geographic information available to emergency responders and the general public. The library has numerous applications for emergency preparedness:

- Providing detailed information on terrain elevation, roadways, and watercourses to assist emergency responders during a flood disaster
- Geo-coding outbreaks of a bio-event, such as anthrax, on a map, allowing public health officials

to monitor disease trends, facilitate containment, and possibly pinpoint the disease origin

- Providing precise geographic information about a chemical spill to facilitate the lock-down of perimeters and establishment of evacuation routes.

The Maine GeoLibrary project was approved and funded partly because of the effort project managers put into explaining the need for such a complex and technical initiative to members of the public and their state representatives. By focusing on key legislative committees, project promoters were able to advance a project that would contribute substantially to emergency preparedness in the state. The project team was able to demonstrate that the GeoLibrary was not just a technological tool for experts but also useful to the public at large. In 2002 the team's efforts paid off. The legislature passed the bill creating the library and an oversight

board. After that, residents voted overwhelmingly for the project in a state bond referendum in November.

Building upon the GeoLibrary foundation, the states of Maine, New Hampshire, and Vermont are involved in an effort to build a Regional Incident Management System that will allow emergency officials to track and manage disasters and bioterrorism attacks on a region-wide level. Authorized individuals would be able to enter data in a secure online form to allow a real-time, interactive perspective on the threat.

"This initiative will bring all levels into view in one EOC," said Dan Walters of the Maine Chief Information Officer's office. "There will be one geographic view to allow officials to visually understand what is going on. That's critical for preparedness."

For more information about the Maine GeoLibrary initiative, contact Dan Walters at (207) 624-9435 or dan.walters@maine.gov.

REVIEW QUESTIONS

1. What are the initiatives that help local communities to mitigate/prepare against potential terrorist attacks? Why is community preparedness an important component of Homeland Security?

2. What mitigation/preparedness role does the private sector have in terms of Homeland Security? Do you believe that the private sector learned lessons from 9/11 terrorist attacks?

3. Try to define "terrorism mitigation" using the common definition of mitigation in terms of all hazards approach. (Hint: Define risk as a combination of probability and consequence, and list all potential activities that can reduce both components of the potential terrorist event.)

4. What is the importance of international consensus and cooperation for terrorism mitigation/preparedness?

5. Take a quick look at FEMA Reference Manual to Mitigate Potential Terrorist Attacks in High Occupancy Buildings FEMA 426 (Available at http://www.fema.gov). What are the two most important factors to minimize damage given by car bombs to buildings?

6. Does your family have a disaster plan? If not, start developing one. The preparedness web site of the Department of Homeland Security (http://www.ready.gov) will help you with necessary steps to prepare your plan.

REFERENCES

Cone, E. and Sean, G. "Cantor Fitzgerald—Forty Seven Hours." http://www.baselinemag.com/print_article/0,3668,a=17022,00.asp.

Coppola, D.P. 2003 "Annotated Organizational Chart for the Department of Homeland Security." Washington, DC: Bullock & Haddow, LLC.

Coppola, D.P. 2003. A Report on the First Annual Conference on "The Community and Homeland Security." Haddow and Bullock, LLC. March 2003.

DHS Family Preparedness Guide, DHS 2003, http://www.ready.gov.

FEMA 426: Reference Manual to Mitigate Potential Terrorist Attacks against Buildings. http://www.fema.gov/fima/antiterrorism/

Kaplan, S. 1997. "The Words of Risk Analysis." *Risk Analysis*. vol. 17,no. 4, p. 408.

Kayyem, N.J., and Chang, E.P. 2002. "Beyond Business Continuity: The Role of the Private Sector in Preparedness Planning." August 2002, pp. 3–4.

Smith, J.D. 2002. "Business Continuity Management: Good Practice Guidelines." Business Continuity Institute. p. 231.

The Terrorist Attack with Sarin in Tokyo, 1995, http://www.sos.se/SOS/PUBL/REFERENG/9803020E.htm.

http://www.aamc.org/newsroom/reporter/august03/bioterrorism.htm

http://www.citizencorps.gov/councils/

http://www.citizencorps.gov/programs/cert.shtm

http://www.citizencorps.gov/programs/medical.shtm

http://www.dhs.gov/dhspublic/display?content=735

http://www.dhs.gov/dhspublic/display?content=1395

http://www.disasterrelief.org/Disasters/020918security/

http://www.emergencypreparednessweek.ca/mr_nr_050202_e.shtml

http://www.envoyworldwide.com/News/ContinuityInsights.pdf

http://www.fema.gov/nwz03/nwz03_123.shtm

http://www.medicalreservecorps.gov/faq.htm

http://www.nationalservice.org/news/factsheets/homeland.html

http://www.nationalservice.org/news/homeland.html

http://www.redcross.org/faq/0,1096,0_383_,00.html

http://www.redcross.org/news/ds/terrorism/030512TOPOFF.html

http://www.salvationarmysouth.org/isabel-9-23-03.htm

http://seattletimes.nwsource.com/html/localnews/134726076_topoff13m.html

7

Response and Recovery

INTRODUCTION

When a disaster event such as a flood, earthquake, or hurricane occurs or when an incident such as an oil spill or a terrorist act happens, local police and fire and emergency medical personnel are usually the first to respond. Their job is to rescue and attend those injured, suppress fires, secure and police the disaster area, and begin the process of restoring order. They are supported in this effort by local emergency management personnel and community government officials.

As the saying "practice makes perfect" goes, the past decade has provided an unprecedented number of natural and man-made disasters to test the capacity of the first responders and the nation's response system. In most of these cases, the system and its participants were considered efficient and effective. Unfortunately, the unexpected terrorist attacks of September 11 and the anthrax events shortly thereafter revealed certain weaknesses in this system. Although the immediate response to the World Trade Center attacks actually showed the national system to be working well, there was an unprecedented loss of lives among civilians and first responders (see Figure 7.1). Certain systems in place did not perform as well as expected, and procedures were not followed. As a result, all levels of

government initiated a process to reevaluate response procedures and protocols. The unusual loss of so many first responders to this disaster event has resulted in numerous after-action evaluations that have led to changes in the procedures and protocols for first responders in the future. With the potential for future terrorism events, the reevaluations have focused attention on how best to protect first responders from harm in future attacks.

As a result, the mandate for change in the Initial Draft of the National Response Plan (NRP) states,

> The perception of the inherent dangers and complex threats facing this country and the potential consequences they could have on the American way of life has changed significantly since September 11, 2001. These threats cross a broad spectrum of contingencies from acts of terrorism to natural disasters to other man-made hazards (accidental or intentional). Because all carry the potential for severe consequences, these threats must be addressed with a unified national effort. A new paradigm for incident management is required.

And,

> To make the response and recovery aspects of our nation's readiness system as efficient and effective as possible, a cooperative national effort is essential, one with a unified approach to incident management and with the ultimate goal of a significant reduction in our nation's vulnerability over time.

FIGURE 7-1   New York, NY, September 27, 2001—An aerial view of the rescue and recovery operations underway in lower Manhattan at the site of the collapsed World Trade Center. Photo by Bri Rodriguez/FEMA News Photo.

Although the plan put a clear emphasis on the primary responsibility for initial incident response to remain at the local level with the locally available assets and special capabilities for prevention, it announced a more aggressive integration between agencies in charge and a unified approach to incident management. This task is one of the primary responsibilities of the Department of Homeland Security (DHS).

The changing nature of the threats (i.e. greater population exposure, possible use of weapons of mass destruction, etc.) has been the motivator for developing a new national incident command approach to response operations. The new approach has a significant impact on the response community at state and local level and serves several purposes:

- To unify crisis and consequence management as a single, integrated function, rather than two separate functions, and integrate all existing federal emergency response plans into a single document, the National Response Plan (NRP)
- To provide interoperability and compatibility among federal, state, and local capabilities by developing and implementing a National Incident Management System (NIMS)

- To enhance response and preparedness capabilities of first responders and state and local governments against all kinds of hazards and threats by providing extensive funding for equipment, training, planning and exercises
- To integrate the private sector and the business communities at a greater extent into response activities and responsibilities in order to increase resources in hand

It is the purpose of this chapter to describe how the system in place has worked so far, identify the changes brought by the DHS and discuss their consequences. Some of the highlights of the chapter are legislative issues and budget, local and state response, Volunteer group response, the Incident Command System and the National Incident Management System (NIMS), the Federal Response Plan (FRP) and the National Response Plan (NRP), the recovery function, and the programs available to assist in recovery.

RESPONSE PROCESSES

Whenever the emergency number, 911, is called for assistance for an emergency of any size, whether it be a traffic accident, a tornado sighting, or someone showing signs of a viral disease, the first responders to take the call are always local. But when the size of the disaster or incident is so large that the capabilities of local responders are overwhelmed and the costs of the damage inflicted exceed the capabilities of local government, the mayor or county executive will turn to the governor and state government for assistance in responding to the event and in helping the community to recover. The governor will turn to the state's emergency management agency and possibly the state National Guard and other state resources to provide the assistance to the stricken community.

System in place: Should the governor decide, based on information and damage surveys generated by community and state officials, that the size of the disaster event exceeds the state's capacity to respond,

the governor will make a formal request to the president for a presidential major disaster declaration. The request is prepared by state officials in cooperation with regional staff from the Federal Emergency Management Agency (FEMA). The governor's request is analyzed first by the FEMA Regional Office and then forwarded to FEMA headquarters in Washington, DC. FEMA headquarters staff review and evaluate the governor's request and forward their analysis and recommendation to the president. The president considers FEMA's recommendation and then decides whether to grant the declaration or turn it down.

Changes: The process will remain the same except that, as FEMA is now under the DHS, everything is under the control of the DHS. And it is the Secretary of DHS who makes the recommendation to the President, not the undersecretary for Emergency Preparedness and Response (EP&R) Directorate.

System in place: If the president grants a major disaster declaration, FEMA activates the Federal Response Plan (FRP) and proceeds to direct 27 federal departments and agencies, including the American Red Cross, in support of state and local efforts to respond to and recover from the disaster event. The presidential declaration makes available several disaster assistance programs in FEMA and other federal agencies designed to assist individuals and communities to begin the process of rebuilding their homes, their community infrastructure, and their lives.

Changes: The FRP is still activated after a declaration but it has been revised. It will remain the operating system until the National Response Plan (NRP) is fully implemented. The conceptual and functional differences between these two plans will be discussed in detail later in this chapter but it is enough to know at this point that the updated FRP is currently the plan in use and is composed of 27 Department and Agencies including the American Red Cross.

When a major disaster strikes in the United States, the aforementioned chronology describes how the most sophisticated and advanced emergency management system in the world responds and begins the recovery process. The fundamental pillars on which the

FIGURE 7-2 Denver, CO, March, 7, 2003—Michael Brown, Undersecretary of Homeland Security for Emergency Preparedness and Response and Director of the Federal Emergency Management Agency (FEMA), has a roundtable meeting with Colorado first responders and community leaders about FEMA's entry into the Department of Homeland Security. Photo by Michael D. Rieger/FEMA News Photo.

system is built are, and continue to be, coordination and cooperation among a significant number of federal, state, and local government agencies; volunteer organizations; and, more recently, the business community.

LEGISLATIVE ACTIONS

The establishment of DHS involved several bills and laws, essentially determined by Homeland and National Security Presidential Directives delivered during the two years following the 9/11 attacks. The most significant ones are:

- The U.S.A. PATRIOT Act of 2001
- The Aviation and Transportation Security Act of 2001
- The HR 5005 Homeland Security Act
- The SA 4470 Amendment
- The HR 5710 Homeland Security Act

- The Public Health Security and Bioterrorism Preparedness and Response Act of 2002
- The Enhanced Border Security and Visa Entry Reform Act of 2002
- The Maritime Transportation Security Act of 2002

The main purpose here is to define clearly the mission and organization of the new department and the necessary legislation adjustments to integrate the different agencies. FEMA has been transferred to form one of the 5 directorates, the Directorate of Emergency Preparedness and Response (EP&R). The EP&R will ensure that the Nation is prepared for catastrophes—whether natural or technological disasters or terrorist assaults. It will not only support the first responders' efforts, but also oversee the Federal government's national response and recovery strategy.

DHS emphasizes in its web site that

To fulfill these missions, DHS will build upon the Federal Emergency Management Agency (FEMA), which has a long and solid track record of aiding the nation's recovery from emergency situations. The EP&R Directorate will continue FEMA's efforts to reduce the loss of life and property and to protect our nation's institutions from all types of hazards through a comprehensive, risk-based emergency management program of preparedness, prevention, response, and recovery. And it will further the evolution of the emergency management culture from one that reacts to disasters to one that proactively helps communities and citizens avoid becoming victims. In addition, the directorate will develop and manage a national training and evaluation system to design curriculums, set standards, evaluate, and reward performance in local, state, and federal training efforts.

The directorate will continue FEMA's practice of focusing on risk mitigation in advance of emergencies by promoting the concept of disaster-resistant communities, including providing federal support for local governments that promote structures and communities that reduce the chances of being hit by disasters. EP&R will coordinate with private industry, the insurance sector, mortgage lenders, the real estate industry, homebuilding associations, citizens, and others to create model communities in high-risk areas.

The directorate will lead the DHS response to any sort of biological or radiological attack and coordinate the involvement of other federal response teams, such as the National Guard, in the event of a major incident. Building upon the successes of FEMA, DHS will lead the nation's recovery from catastrophes and help minimize the suffering and disruption caused by disasters.

The HR 5005 describes the responsibilities of the directorate as:

1. Helping to ensure the preparedness of emergency response providers for terrorist attacks, major disasters, and other emergencies
2. Establishing standards, conducting exercises and training, evaluating performance, and providing funds in relation to the Nuclear Incident Response Team (defined in section 504 of the bill)
3. Providing the federal government's response to terrorist attacks and major disasters
4. Aiding the recovery from terrorist attacks and major disasters
5. Working with other federal and nonfederal agencies to build a comprehensive national incident management system
6. Consolidating existing federal government emergency response plans into a single, coordinated national response plan
7. Developing comprehensive programs for developing interoperative communications technology and ensuring that emergency response providers acquire such technology

The responsibility of providing the federal government's response tot terrorist attacks and major disasters—item 3 above—is explained in detail in the HR 5005:

a. Coordinating the overall response
b. Directing the Domestic Emergency Support Team, the Strategic National Stockpile, the National Disaster Medical System, and the Nuclear Incident Response Team
c. Overseeing the Metropolitan Medical Response System and coordinating other federal response resources

It is important to note that the specification of primary responsibilities does not detract from other important functions transferred to the DHS, such as those of the United States Fire Administration (USFA). In all areas, the DHS fully preserves the authority to carry out the functions of FEMA, including support for community initiatives that promote homeland security.

The agencies transferred to the EP&R Directorate are:

1. FEMA, including the functions of the director of FEMA, relating thereto
2. The Integrated Hazard Information System of the National Oceanic and Atmospheric Administration, which shall be renamed "FIRESAT"
3. The National Domestic Preparedness Office of the Federal Bureau of Investigation, including the functions of the attorney general relating thereto
4. The Domestic Emergency Support Teams of the Department of Justice, including the functions of the attorney general relating thereto
5. The Office of Emergency Preparedness, the National Disaster Medical System, and the Metropolitan Medical Response System of the Department of Health and Human Services, including the functions of the secretary of Health and Human Services and the assistant secretary for Public Health Emergency Preparedness relating thereto
6. The Strategic National Stockpile of the Department of Health and Human Services, including the functions of the secretary of Health and Human Services relating thereto.

Other capital changes are as follows:

1. The involvement of the private sector and the citizens in the process of preparedness. This collaboration is announced in the Homeland Security Act as "To the maximum extent practicable, the Secretary [of DHS] shall use national private sector networks and infrastructure for emergency response to chemical, biological, radiological, nuclear, or explosive disasters, and other major disasters."

This topic will be discussed further in the National Response Plan.

2. The response for nuclear incident is thoroughly described, and the secretary of Homeland Security, "in connection with an actual or threatened terrorist attack, major disaster, or other emergency," (HR 5005) is authorized to call certain elements of the Department of Energy (DOE) and the Environmental Protection Agency (EPA) into service as an organizational unit of DHS. These elements are to be, during the operation, subject to the direction, authority, and control of the secretary of DHS, but this grant of authority does not limit the ordinary responsibilities of the secretary of Energy and the administrator of the Environmental Protection Agency.

Other legislations that address local response issues are presented in brief in Table 7-1.

BUDGET

One of the main responsibilities of the new DHS is to provide extensive funding to enhance the response and preparedness capabilities of the first responders. Table 7-2 provides the budget for FEMA for Fiscal Year (FY) 2002, 2003, and the president's requested budget for FY2004.

The U.S. government provided a total of $7.9 billion in grants between 2002 and 2003 to help state and local responders, public health agencies, and emergency managers prepare for terrorist attacks. The president's FY04 budget request included an additional $5.2 billion to ensure first responders and public health and medical personnel are properly trained and equipped. A breakdown of funding for FY03 per state is given in Table 7-3.

Sidebar 7-1 shows how the grants were made available through the period of March to May 2003.

TABLE 7-1   Local Response Related Legislation

Bill	Title	Homeland purpose
HR 3153	State Bioterrorism Preparedness Act of 2001	To assist states in preparing for, and responding to, biological or chemical terrorist attacks.
HR 3435	Empowering Local First Responders To Fight Terrorism Act of 2001	To provide for grants to local first responder agencies to combat terrorism and be a part of homeland defense.
HR 3615	Protecting Our Schools Homeland Defense Act of 2002	To amend the Public Health Service Act to direct the secretary of Health and Human Services to make grants to train school nurses as "first responders" in the event of a biological or chemical attack.
HR 5169	Wastewater Treatment Works Security Act of 2002	To improve the defense and response of publicly owned water treatment plants against terrorist attacks by assessing risks and locating vulnerabilities.
S 1520	State Bioterrorism Preparedness Act of 2002	To assist states in preparing for, and responding to, biological or chemical attack.
S 1602	Chemical Security Act of 2001	To protect the public against the threat of a chemical terrorist attack.
S 1746	Nuclear Security Act of 2001	To strengthen security at sensitive nuclear facilities.
S 2664	First Responder Terrorism Preparedness Act of 2002	To establish an Office of National Preparedness to coordinate terrorism preparedness and response.

Source: http://www.acca.com/infopaks/homeland/legislativechart.pdf

In FY04, much of the funding that was delivered through the EP&R Directorate has been delivered through the DHS Office of Domestic Preparedness (ODP). ODP received $4.446 billion for first responders, including

- $1.9 billion for formula grants to state and local governments
- $510 million for state and local law enforcement terrorism prevention grants
- $500 million for grants to high-threat, high-density urban areas
- $200 million for critical infrastructure grants
- $760 million for firefighter assistance grants that would not have to be used specifically for homeland security purposes
- $168 million for Emergency Management Performance grants
- $125 million for the National Domestic Preparedness Consortium, of which $45 million is for the Center for Domestic Preparedness

These figures include an additional $10 million, coming for the terrorism prevention grants and the firefighter's assistance grants, added by a floor amendment offered by Rep. Lee Terry (NE).

These large numbers are somewhat deceiving as many of these programs already existed and have just been recast as homeland security programs. In addition, the funding approach through the States has restricted the support reaching the local level where the real first responders need it most.

An interesting point is made by ANSER senior analyst Glenn Fiedelholtz:

> Funding also shows a great disparity according to the specific threat it is addressing; for example, President Bush signed in June 2002 the Public Health Security and Bioterrorism Preparedness and Response Act of 2002, authorizing $1.1 billion for bioterrorism preparedness, with the bulk of it, $930 million, to be parceled out among the states for public health improvements. In contrast, the previous year's budget for bioterrorism preparedness was a mere $100,000, most of which came from the CDC. The asymmetric threat of bioterrorism requires dramatic federal funding increases, as well as new emergency management approaches in preparation and response. [Responding to Biological Terrorist Incidents: Upgrading the FEMA Approach, May 2003]

TABLE 7-2 FEMA Budgets

Agencies and offices	Current department	FY02 ($ in millions)	FY03 ($ in millions)
Integrated Hazard Information System of NOAA	Commerce	N/A	N/A
Nuclear Incident Response Team	Energy	N/A	91.0
Office of Emergency Preparedness	Health and Human Services	71.0	107.0
– Metropolitan Medical Response System		10.0	11.0
– National Disaster Medical System		25.0	50.0
Strategic National Stockpile	Health and Human Services	N/A	N/A
Federal Emergency Management Agency	Independent	5,800	6,600
Domestic Emergency Support Teams	Justice		
National Office of Domestic Preparedness (FBI)	Justice	N/A	N/A

N/A: Figure was not available

Source: http://www.armscontrolcenter.org/terrorism/homeland%20security/UpdatedDHS Agencies.pdf

TABLE 7-3   Federal Allocations to States in FY03

State name	Equipment allocation total	Exercise allocation total	Training allocation total	Planning allocation total	Total allocation
Alabama	6,636,000	1,659,000	498,000	664,000	9,457,000
Alaska	3,505,000	876,000	263,000	351,000	4,995,000
Arizona	7,427,000	1,857,000	557,000	743,000	10,584,000
Arkansas	5,189,000	1,297,000	389,000	519,000	7,394,000
California	31,595,000	7,899,000	2,370,000	3,159,000	45,023,000
Colorado	6,653,000	1,663,000	499,000	665,000	9,480,000
Connecticut	5,800,000	1,450,000	435,000	580,000	8,265,000
Delaware	3,638,000	910,000	273,000	364,000	5,185,000
District of Columbia	3,446,000	861,000	258,000	345,000	4,910,000
Florida	16,599,000	4,150,000	1,245,000	1,660,000	23,654,000
Georgia	9,956,000	2,489,000	747,000	996,000	14,188,000
Hawaii	3,995,000	999,000	300,000	399,000	5,693,000
Idaho	4,073,000	1,018,000	305,000	407,000	5,803,000
Illinois	13,248,000	3,312,000	994,000	1,325,000	18,879,000
Indiana	7,999,000	2,000,000	600,000	800,000	11,399,000
Iowa	5,373,500	1,343,000	403,000	537,000	7,656,500
Kansas	5,194,000	1,298,000	390,000	519,000	7,401,000
Kentucky	6,316,000	1,579,000	474,000	632,000	9,001,000
Louisiana	6,633,000	1,658,000	497,000	663,000	9,451,000
Maine	4,035,000	1,009,000	303,000	404,000	5,751,000
Maryland	7,428,000	1,857,000	557,000	743,000	10,585,000
Massachusetts	8,218,000	2,055,000	616,000	822,000	11,711,000
Michigan	11,170,000	2,793,000	838,000	1,117,000	15,918,000
Minnesota	7,071,000	1,768,000	530,000	707,000	10,076,000
Mississippi	5,321,000	1,330,000	399,000	532,000	7,582,000
Missouri	7,603,000	1,901,000	570,000	760,000	10,834,000
Montana	3,722,000	930,000	279,000	372,000	5,303,000
Nebraska	4,389,500	1,097,000	329,000	439,000	6,254,500
Nevada	4,752,000	1,188,000	356,000	475,000	6,771,000
New Hampshire	4,019,000	1,005,000	301,000	402,000	5,727,000
New Jersey	9,980,000	2,495,000	749,000	998,000	14,222,000
New Mexico	4,492,000	1,123,000	337,000	449,000	6,401,000
New York	18,591,000	4,648,000	1,394,000	1,859,000	26,492,000
North Carolina	9,760,000	2,440,000	732,000	976,000	13,908,000
North Dakota	3,497,000	874,000	262,000	350,000	4,983,000

(*continues*)

TABLE 7-3 (*continued*)

State name	Equipment allocation total	Exercise allocation total	Training allocation total	Planning allocation total	Total allocation
Ohio	12,287,000	3,072,000	922,000	1,229,000	17,510,000
Oklahoma	5,827,000	1,457,000	437,000	583,000	8,304,000
Oregon	5,850,000	1,462,000	439,000	585,000	8,336,000
Pennsylvania	13,032,000	3,258,000	977,000	1,303,000	18,570,000
Rhode Island	3,852,000	963,000	289,000	385,000	5,489,000
South Carolina	6,327,000	1,582,000	475,000	633,000	9,017,000
South Dakota	3,601,000	900,000	270,000	360,000	5,131,000
Tennessee	7,704,000	1,926,000	578,000	770,000	10,978,000
Texas	20,728,000	5,182,000	1,555,000	2,073,000	29,538,000
Utah	4,868,000	1,217,000	365,000	487,000	6,937,000
Vermont	3,483,000	871,000	261,000	348,000	4,963,000
Virginia	8,924,000	2,231,000	669,000	892,000	12,716,000
Washington	7,926,000	1,981,000	594,000	793,000	11,294,000
West Virginia	4,449,000	1,112,000	334,000	445,000	6,340,000
Wisconsin	7,414,000	1,854,000	556,000	741,000	10,565,000
Wyoming	3,387,000	847,000	254,000	339,000	4,827,000
Puerto Rico	6,125,000	1,531,000	459,000	612,000	8,727,000
Virgin Islands	1,082,000	271,000	81,000	108,000	1,542,000
American Samoa	1,040,000	260,000	78,000	104,000	1,482,000
Guam	1,120,000	280,000	84,000	112,000	1,596,000
Northern Mariana Islands	1,050,000	262,000	79,000	105,000	1,496,000
Total	397,400,000	99,350,000	29,805,000	39,740,000	566,295,000

Source: DHS. www.dhs.gov

LOCAL RESPONSE

On an operational level, minor disasters occur daily in communities around the United States. Local fire, police, and emergency medical personnel respond to these events in a routine, systematic, and well-planned course of action. Firefighters, police officers, and emergency medical technicians respond to the scene and take immediate actions. Their job is to secure the scene and maintain order, rescue and treat those injured, contain and suppress fire or hazardous conditions, and retrieve the dead. Some notable facts about first responders are:

- There are over 1 million firefighters in the United States, of which approximately 750,000 are volunteers.
- Local police departments have an estimated 556,000 full-time employees, including about 436,000 sworn enforcement personnel.

- Sheriffs' offices reported about 291,000 full-time employees, including about 186,000 sworn personnel.
- There are over 155,000 nationally registered emergency medical technicians (EMT).

Source: DHS

The actions of local first responders are driven by procedures and protocols developed by the responding agency (e.g., fire, police, and emergency medical). Most communities in the United States have developed community-wide emergency plans that incorporate these procedures and protocols. In the aftermath of the September 11 terrorist events, many communities are reviewing and reworking their community emergency plans to include procedures and protocols for responding to all forms of terrorist attacks including bioterrorism and WMD. These changes are most often driven by the funds allocated for specific requirements and the programs that are designed at the federal level.

DHS officials describe the First Responder Initiative (FRI) and the mutual agreement program as follows:

> The FRI has been designed to help the first responders do their jobs better. Building on existing capabilities at the federal, state, and local level, the First Responder Initiative provides an incentive to develop mutually supportive programs that maximize effective response capability. Through joint planning, clear communication, comprehensive coordination, mutual aid at all levels, and increased information sharing, America's first responders can be trained and equipped to save lives in the event of a terrorist attack.

The First Responder Initiative will accomplish the following objectives:

- Provide the first responder community with much-needed funds to conduct important planning and exercises, purchase equipment, and train their personnel

---

SIDEBAR 7-1 Examples of Grants for States, Cities, Urban Areas, and First Responders

- March 7, 2003: $566 million was made available to the states and cities from the FY03 budget to assist first responders in the form of funding for equipment, training, planning, and exercises.
- March 10, 2003: $750 million was made available for firefighter assistance grants from the FY03 budget to help rural, urban, and suburban fire departments better train, prepare, and equip themselves.
- April 8, 2003: $100 million was made available from the FY03 budget to the New York City area, Los Angeles area, San Francisco area, Chicago area, Seattle area, Houston area, and the national Capital region as part of the urban area security initiative to help enhance the local government's ability to secure large population areas and critical infrastructure.
- April 16, 2003: $165 million was awarded from the FY03 budget to help state and local governments plan and prepare for all hazards planning, training, exercising, and facilities.
- April 30, 2003: $1.5 billion was made available to the states and localities from the FY03 supplemental budget to help state and local law enforcement personnel pay for equipment, planning, training, and exercises and to offset costs associated with enhanced security measures deployed during heightened threat periods.
- May 14, 2003: $700 million was allocated from the FY03 supplemental budget as part of the urban area security initiative for 30 cities and their contiguous counties and mutual aid partners to enhance the security of urban areas with high-density populations and critical infrastructure, ports, and mass transit systems.

Source: FEMA, www.fema.gov

- Provide states and localities with the flexibility they require to ensure that the funds are used to address the needs of their local communities
- Establish a consolidated, simple, and quick method for dispersing federal assistance to states and localities
- Encourage mutual aid across the nation so that the entire local, state, federal, and volunteer network can operate together effectively
- Establish a process for evaluating the effort to build response capabilities, in order to validate that effort and direct future resources
- Encourage citizens to participate actively in preparing their communities for the threat of terrorism and other disastrous events.

To achieve these objectives, FEMA will implement a streamlined and simple procedure designed to speed the flow of resources to the states and localities. The funds may be used for the following types of first responder activities:

Planning: The program will support state and local governments in developing comprehensive plans to prepare for and respond to a terrorist attack.

Equipment: The program will allow state and local first responder agencies to purchase a wide range of equipment needed to respond effectively to a terrorist attack, including personal protective equipment, chemical and biological detection systems, and interoperable communications gear.

Training: The First Responder Initiative will also provide resources to train firefighters, police officers, and emergency medical technicians to respond and operate in a chemical or biological environment.

Exercises: The program will support a coordinated, regular exercise program to improve response capabilities, practice mutual aid, and assess operational improvements and deficiencies.

First responders from communities outside major metropolitan areas who must protect large geographic areas with small populations face many response challenges. In fact, over half of the firefighters protect small or rural communities of fewer than 5,000 people. Many of these communities rely upon volunteer departments with scarce resources. Fewer than 10 percent of counties surveyed by the National Association of Counties said they are prepared to respond to a bioterrorist attack.

To build capability in rural communities, first responders from smaller communities need assistance in organizing and developing the unified command and control procedures and protocols necessary for operationally sound mutual aid. These agreements will enable neighboring jurisdictions to share specialized resources rather than duplicate them in every jurisdiction. The FY03 budget provided $140 million to assist rural communities in planning and establishing mutual aid agreements. While mutual cooperation and mutual aid agreements have existed over the years in support of civil defense, fire, and National Guard activities, this is the first time that the federal government has directly supported the establishment of mutual aid agreements with federal resources.

As an established mechanism for sharing or pooling limited resources to augment existing capabilities and supplementing jurisdictions that have exhausted existing resources due to disaster, mutual aid processes will help ensure that jurisdictions across the United States can benefit from each other's efforts to enhance their first response capabilities. Jurisdictions can use the funding provided under this initiative to create or improve their response capabilities, without duplicating their efforts. Many areas have little or no capability to respond to terrorist attack using weapons of mass destruction. Even the best prepared states and localities do not possess adequate resources to respond to the full range of terrorist threats that is faced.

FIRST RESPONDER ROLES AND RESPONSIBILITIES

The roles and responsibilities of first responders are usually detailed in the community emergency plan. Citing the responsibilities of first responders after a terrorist incident provides a useful example of the scope of the changes that first responders are experiencing.

FIGURE 7-3   New York, NY, October 5, 2001—Rescue workers continue their efforts at the World Trade Center. Photo by Andrea Booher/ FEMA News Photo.

The following points are the main objectives for the first responders to a terrorist incident:

- Protect the lives and safety of the citizens and other first responders
- Isolate, contain, and/or limit the spread of any cyber, nuclear, biological, chemical, incendiary, or explosive devices
- Identify the type of agent and/or devices used
- Identify and establish control zones for the suspected agent used
- Ensure emergency responders properly follow protocol and have appropriate protective gear
- Identify the most appropriate decontamination and/or treatment for victims
- Establish victim services
- Notify emergency personnel, including medical facilities, of dangers and anticipated casualties and proper measures to be followed
- Notify appropriate state and federal agencies
- Provide accurate and timely public information
- Preserve as much evidence as possible to aid in the investigation process
- Protect critical infrastructure
- Oversee fatality management
- Develop and enhance medical EMS
- Protect property and environment.

(*Source*: Bullock & Haddow LLC).

LOCAL EMERGENCY MANAGERS

It is usually the responsibility of the designated local emergency manager to develop and maintain the community emergency plans. Often, this individual shares a dual responsibility in local government, such as fire or police chief, and serves only part-time as the community's emergency manager. The profession of local emergency management has been maturing since the 1980s. There are more opportunities for individuals to receive formal training in emergency management in our country. There are currently over 80 junior college, undergraduate, and graduate programs that offer courses and degrees in emergency management and related fields. Additionally, FEMA's Emergency Management Institute (EMI) located in Emmitsburg, Maryland, offers emergency management courses on campus and through distance learning programs. EMI has also worked closely with junior colleges, colleges, universities, and graduate schools to develop coursework and curriculums in emergency management. Details of EMI's Certified Emergency Manager Program are as follows:

- The International Association of Emergency Managers (IAEM) created the Certified Emergency Manager© program to raise and maintain professional standards. It is an internationally recognized program that certifies achievements within the emergency management profession.
- CEM© certification is a peer-review process administered through the International Association of Emergency Managers. You do not have to be an IAEM member to be certified, although IAEM membership does offer you a number of benefits that can assist you through the certification process. Certification is maintained in 5-year cycles.
- The CEM© program is served by a CEM© commission that is composed of emergency management professionals, including representatives from allied fields, education, the military, and private industry.
- Development of the CEM© program was supported by the Federal Emergency Management Agency (FEMA), the National Emergency Management Association (NEMA), and a host of allied organizations.

Source: IAEM, www.iaem.org

More and more communities have designated emergency managers responsible for guiding response and recovery operations. Training and education programs in emergency management are expanding dramatically, resulting in a growing number of professionally trained and certified local emergency managers. The maturing of this profession can only lead to more effective and efficient local responses to future disaster events.

The role and responsibilities of the individual designated as the county emergency manager is also defined by the County Emergency Plan, and they show the same variance as those of the first responders on account of the widening of the incident/threats spectrum. Although there are no specific guidelines given for the new roles of local managers, the essential differences will be based on the following:

- Changes in procedures to handle terrorist incidents
- Changes of response equipment
- Changes of responding agencies and protocols of cooperation
- Changes in local/state/federal operation plans

An example of a local plan for responding to a terrorist event developed by Madison County, North Carolina, is presented on page 228.

STATE RESPONSE

Each of the 50 states and six territories that make up the United States maintains a state government Office of Emergency Management. However, where the emergency management office resides in state government varies from state to state. In California the Office of Emergency Services (OES) is located in the Office of the Governor; in Tennessee the Tennessee Emergency Management Agency (TEMA) reports to the adjunct general. In Florida the emergency management function is located in the Office of Community Affairs. National Guard adjutant generals manage state emergency management offices in more than half of the 56 states and territories. The remaining state emergency management offices are led by civilian employees. A current list of state emergency management directors is presented in Appendix 5. There is no explicit change in most of the state response systems; the procedures remain the same while at the federal level, and the contact with the states is made through DHS instead of FEMA.

Funding for state emergency management offices comes principally from DHS and state budgets. Historically, FEMA has provided up to $175 million annually to the states to fund state and local government emergency management activities. This money is used by state emergency management agencies to hire staff, conduct training and exercises, and purchase equipment. A segment of this funding is targeted for local emergency management operations as designated by the state. State budgets provide funding for emergency management operations, but this funding historically has been inconsistent, especially in those states with minimal annual disaster activity. The principal resource available to governors in responding to a disaster event in their state is the National Guard. The resources of the National Guard that are used for disaster response include personnel, communications systems and equipment, air and road transport, heavy construction and earth-moving equipment, mass care and feeding, equipment, and emergency supplies such as beds, blankets, and medical supplies.

Response capabilities and capacities are strongest in those states and territories that experience high levels of annual disaster activity. But now, all states and territories with critical assets must strive to reinforce their capabilities against the possibility of a terrorist incident. North Carolina is one of the states that regularly faces the risk of hurricanes and floods. How the North Carolina Department of Emergency Management describes its response process on its web site provides a good example state response functions.

The division's emergency response functions are coordinated in a proactive manner from the State Emergency Operations Center located in Raleigh, North Carolina. Proactive response strategies used by the division include the following:

- Area commands that are strategically located in an affected region to assist with local response efforts using state resources
- Central warehousing operations managed by the state that allow for immediate delivery of bottled water, ready-to-eat meals, blankets, tarps, and the like; field deployment teams manned by division and other state agency personnel that assist severely affected counties; coordinate and prioritize response activity
- Incident action planning that identifies response priorities and resource requirements 12 to 24 hours in advance.

The State Emergency Response Team (SERT), which is comprised of top-level management representatives of each state agency involved in response activities, provides the technical expertise and coordinates the delivery of the emergency resources used to support local emergency operations.

When resource needs are beyond the capabilities of state agencies, mutual aid from other unaffected local governments and states may be secured using the Statewide Mutual Aid agreement or Emergency Management Assistance compact. Federal assistance may also be requested through the Federal Emergency Response Team, which collocates with the SERT during major disasters.

Source: North Carolina Department of Emergency Management, http://www.dem.dcc.state.nc.us/

The changes to occur in the role and responsibilities of the state emergency managers will be based on the same principles as the local managers (i.e., changes in procedures to handle terrorist incidents; response equipment; responding agencies and protocols of cooperation; and in local/state/federal operation plans). Described below are the responsibilities of the governor for the public safety and welfare of his or her people as stated in the National Response Plan (NRP).

The Governor:

- Is responsible for coordinating state and local resources to address effectively the full spectrum of actions to prepare for and respond to man-made incidents, including terrorism, natural disasters, and other contingencies
- Has extraordinary powers during a contingency to suspend authority, to seize property, to direct evacuations, and to authorize emergency funds
- Plays a key role in communicating to the public, in requesting federal assistance, when state capabilities have been exceeded or exhausted, and in helping people, businesses, and organizations to cope with disasters
- May also encourage local mutual aid and implement authorities for the state to enter into mutual aid agreements with other states and territories to facilitate resource sharing

(*Source*: The National Response Plan)

VOLUNTEER GROUPS RESPONSE

Volunteer groups are often on the front line of any disaster response. National groups such as the American Red Cross and the Salvation Army maintain rosters of local chapters of volunteers who are trained in emergency response. These organizations work with local, state, and federal authorities to address the immediate needs of disaster victims. These organizations provide shelter, food, and clothing to disaster victims who have had to evacuate or lost their homes to disasters large and small.

In addition to the Red Cross and the Salvation Army, there are numerous volunteer groups across the country that provide aid and comfort to disaster victims. The National Volunteer Organizations Against Disasters (NVOAD) comprises 34 national member organizations, 52 state and territorial VOADs, and a growing number of local VOADs involved in disaster response and recovery operations around the country and abroad. Formed in 1970, NVOAD helps member groups at a disaster location to coordinate and communicate in order to provide the most efficient and effective response. A list of the NVOAD member organizations is as follows:

Adventist Community Services
American Radio Relay League
American Red Cross
America's Second Harvest
Ananda Marga Universal Relief Team
Catholic Charities USA
Christian Disaster Response
Church of the Brethren
Church World Service
Episcopal Relief and Development
Friends Disaster Service
Humane Society of the United States
International Aid
International Relief Friendship Foundation, IRFFint@aol.com
Lutheran Disaster Response
Mennonite Disaster Services
National Emergency Response Team
National Organization for Victim Assistance
Nazarene Disaster Response
Northwest Medical Teams International
The Phoenix Society for Burn Survivors
The Points of Light Foundation
Presbyterian Disaster Assistance
REACT International
The Salvation Army
Society of St. Vincent De Paul
Southern Baptist Disaster Relief
United Jewish Communities
United Methodist Committee on Relief
United States Service Command
Volunteers of America
World Vision

(*Source*: National Volunteer Organizations Against Disasters [NVOAD])

DHS VOLUNTEER PROGRAMS

DHS explains the volunteer programs as follows:

After the terrorist attacks of September 11, 2001, many people have looked for and found many opportunities to help in their communities. U.S.A. Freedom Corps was created in an effort to capture those opportunities and foster a culture of service, citizenship, and responsibility. These volunteers are especially important in smaller communities where resources may be limited.

Citizen Corps is the arm of U.S.A. Freedom Corps that provides opportunities for citizens who want to help make their communities more secure. Since its establishment and President Bush's call for 2 years of volunteer service, almost 24,000 Americans from all 50 states and U.S. territories have volunteered to work with one or more of the Citizen Corps programs. These include the following:

- Citizen Corps Councils
- Community Emergency Response Teams (CERT)
- Citizen Preparedness publications
- Volunteers in Police Service (VIPS)
- Medical Reserve Corps
- Neighborhood Watch

While some of these programs are new, some, such as Neighborhood Watch, have been in place for more than a decade. Brief information about the programs with a response component and a fact sheet are as follows.

THE COMMUNITY EMERGENCY RESPONSE TEAM (CERT)

The Community Emergency Response Team (CERT) program helps train people to be better prepared to respond to emergency situations in their communities. When emergencies occur, CERT members can give critical support to first responders, provide immediate assistance to victims, and organize spontaneous volunteers at a disaster site. CERT members can also help with nonemergency projects that help improve the safety of the community.

The CERT concept was developed and implemented by the Los Angeles City Fire Department in 1985. FEMA made this training available nationally in 1993. Since this time, CERT programs have been established in more than 340 communities in 45 states. CERT teams remain active in the community before a disaster strikes, sponsoring events such as drills, neighborhood clean-up, and disaster-education fairs. Trainers offer periodic refresher sessions to CERT

members to reinforce the basic training and to keep participants involved and practiced in their skills.

VOLUNTEERS IN POLICE SERVICE PROGRAM (VIPS)

Since September 11, 2001, the demands on state and local law enforcement have increased dramatically. As a result, already limited resources are being stretched further at a time when the country needs every available officer out on the beat. Some local police departments are turning to civilian volunteers to supplement their sworn force. These vital efforts will receive new support through the Volunteers in Police Service Program (VIPS). VIPS draws on the time and considerable talents of civilian volunteers and allows law enforcement professionals to better perform their frontline duties.

The program provides resources to assist local law enforcement officials by incorporating community volunteers into the activities of the law enforcement agency, including a series of best practices to help state and local law enforcement design strategies to recruit, train, and utilize citizen volunteers in their departments.

MEDICAL RESERVE CORPS (MRC) PROGRAM

The Medical Reserve Corps (MRC) program coordinates the skills of practicing and retired physicians, nurses, and other health professionals, as well as other citizens interested in health issues who are eager to volunteer to address their community's ongoing public health needs and to help their community during large-scale emergency situations.

Local community leaders will develop their own Medical Reserve Corps units and identify the duties of the MRC volunteers according to specific community needs. For example, MRC volunteers may deliver necessary public health services during a crisis, assist emergency response teams with patients, and provide care directly to those with less serious injuries and other health-related issues. MRC volunteers may also serve a vital role by assisting their communities with ongoing public health needs (e.g., immunizations, screenings, health and nutrition education, and volunteering in community health centers and local hospitals). Once established, how the local MRC unit is utilized will be decided locally. The MRC unit will make decisions, with local officials, including the local Citizen Corps Council, on when the community Medical Reserve Corps is activated during a local emergency.

NEIGHBORHOOD WATCH PROGRAM

The Neighborhood Watch program is a highly successful effort that has been in existence for more than 30 years in cities and counties across America. It provides a unique infrastructure that brings together local officials, law enforcement and citizens to protect our communities.

Around the country, neighbors for three decades have banded together to create Neighborhood Watch programs. Through a willingness to look out for suspicious activity in their neighborhood and report that activity to law enforcement and to each other, residents take a major step toward reclaiming high-crime neighborhoods, as well as making people throughout a community feel more secure and less fearful.

In the aftermath of September 11, the need for strengthening and securing our communities has become even more critical, and Neighborhood Watch groups have taken on greater significance. In addition to serving a crime prevention role, Neighborhood Watch can also be used as the basis for bringing neighborhood residents together to focus on disaster preparedness as well as terrorism awareness; to focus on evacuation drills and exercises; and even to organize group training, such as the Community Emergency Response Team (CERT) training.

More information about the Citizen Corps programs is given in Sidebar 7-2.

SIDEBAR 7-2   Citizen Corps Fact Sheet

- More than 15,000 volunteers are looking to be trained in emergency response skills through FEMA's Community Emergency Response Team program.
- Over the next 2 years, the CERT program aims to double the number of participants, with over 400,000 individuals completing the 20-plus hours of training. Train-the-trainer sessions are being held in all 56 states and territories over the next year to expand the program throughout the United States.
- In FY2003, FEMA will provide over $19 million in grant funds to states and territories to be used to expand the CERT program through additional state-offered train-the-trainer courses as well as to help communities start CERT programs and expand existing teams. The FY2003 grant money is in addition to $17 million distributed through the FY2002 supplemental appropriation.

- Almost 7,000 volunteers have signed up to get involved in Neighborhood Watch activities in their communities.
- More than 15,000 potential volunteers have expressed interest in the new Volunteers in Police Service and Operation (VIPS) programs being developed by the Department of Justice presently.
- The Medical Reserve Corps (MRC) was officially launched in July 2002 by the Health and Human Services secretary. In the program's first year, over 50 MRC units were formed.
- More than 5,000 potential volunteers have expressed an interest in joining a Medical Reserve Corps in their community as part of a program being developed by the Department of Health and Human Services to tap the skills of doctors, nurses, and other health-care professionals in times of community crisis.

Source: DHS. www.dhs.gov

FIGURE 7-4   Arlington, VA, March 7, 2002—A nighttime view of the Pentagon building shows the progress made in the reconstruction of the area damaged by the terrorist attack on the Pentagon on September 11, 2001. Photo by Jocelyn Augustino/FEMA News Photo.

DHS RESPONSE AGENCIES

The different agencies that were brought into DHS and merged to form the EP&R Directorate of DHS are as follows:

- The Federal Emergency Management Agency (FEMA)
- The Integrated Hazard Information System of the National Oceanic and Atmospheric Administration
- The National Domestic Preparedness Office of the Federal Bureau of Investigation
- The Domestic Emergency Support Teams of the Department of Justice,
- The Office of Emergency Preparedness
- The National Disaster Medical System

- The Metropolitan Medical Response System
- The Strategic National Stockpile

FEDERAL EMERGENCY MANAGEMENT AGENCY (FEMA)

The Federal Emergency Management Agency—a former independent agency that became part of the new DHS in March 2003—is tasked with responding to, planning for, recovering from, and mitigating against disasters. Its responsibilities in the new DHS are as follows:

- Coordinate with local and state first responders to manage disasters requiring federal assistance and to recover from their effects

- Administer the Disaster Relief Fund
- Practice a comprehensive, risk-based approach, employing a program of preparedness, prevention, response, and recovery
- Proactively help communities and citizens avoid becoming victims, utilizing public education and volunteerism to achieve this goal
- Maintain administration of the National Flood Insurance Program
- Continue training and responsibilities of the U.S. Fire Administration
- Continue to offer mitigation grant programs, including the Hazards Mitigation Grant Program, the Pre-Disaster Mitigation Programs and the Flood Mitigation Assistance Program
- Administer the Citizen Corps Program

NATIONAL DOMESTIC PREPAREDNESS OFFICE (NDPO)

The National Domestic Preparedness Office (NDPO), within the Department of Justice (DOJ), coordinated all federal efforts, including those of the Department of Defense (DoD), FEMA, the Department of Health and Human Services (DHHS), the Department of Energy (DOE), and the Environmental Protection Agency (EPA), to assist state and local first responders with planning, training, equipment, and exercise necessary to respond to a conventional or nonconventional WMD incident.

The NDPO was transferred into the new DHS and relocated to be part of the EP&R Directorate. Among the functions of the NDPO cited on the DHS web site are the following:

- Serve as a single program and policy office for WMD to ensure that federal efforts are in harmony and represent the most effective and cost-efficient support to the state and local first responder community
- Coordinate the establishment of training curriculum and standards for first responder training to ensure consistency based upon training objectives and to tailor training opportunities to meet the needs of the responder community
- Facilitate the efforts of the federal government to provide the responder community with detection, protection, analysis, and decontamination equipment necessary to prepare for, and respond to, an incident involving WMD
- Provide state and local governments with the resources and expertise necessary to design, conduct, and evaluate exercise scenarios involving WMD
- Communicate information to the state and local emergency response community

OFFICE OF EMERGENCY PREPAREDNESS

The Office of Emergency Preparedness (OEP) was responsible for oversight, coordination, and management of emergency preparedness and response and recovery activities in HHS, prior to its transfer to FEMA.

The Department of Health and Human Services states that

> OEP served as the lead for Emergency Support Function #8 (ESF #8), Health and Medical. In this capacity, it was assigned primary responsibility in the event of a major natural or man-made disaster to coordinate health, medical, and certain social services. To accomplish this responsibility, ESF #8 oversees the emergency management functions of mitigation, preparedness, response, and recovery with all agencies and organizations that carry out health or medical services.

THE NATIONAL DISASTER MEDICAL SYSTEM

The Department of Health and Human Services describes the National Disaster Medical System as follows:

> The National Disaster Medical System (NDMS) is a federally coordinated system that augments the nation's emergency medical response capability. The overall purpose of the NDMS is to establish a single integrated national medical response capability for assisting state and local authorities in dealing with the medical and health effects of major

peacetime disasters and to provide support to the military and the Department of Veterans Affairs medical systems in caring for casualties evacuated back to the United States from overseas armed conventional conflicts.

Federal Coordinating Centers (FCCs) recruit hospitals and maintain local nonfederal hospital participation in the NDMS; coordinate exercise development and emergency plans with participating hospitals and other local authorities in order to develop patient reception, transportation, and communication plans; and, during system activation, coordinate the reception and distribution of patients being evacuated to the area.

The NDMS is a cooperative asset-sharing program among federal government agencies, state and local governments, private businesses, and civilian volunteers to ensure resources are available to provide medical services following a disaster that overwhelms the local health care resources. The way it works is as follows:

Accredited hospitals, usually over 100 beds in size and located in large U.S. metropolitan areas, are encouraged to enter into a voluntary agreement with NDMS. Hospitals agree to commit a number of their acute care beds, subject to availability, for NDMS patients. Because this is a completely voluntary program, hospitals may, upon activation of the system, provide more or fewer beds than the number committed in the agreement. Hospitals that admit NDMS patients will be reimbursed by the federal government.

At the disaster site, patients will be stabilized by DMATs (Disaster Medical Assistance Teams) or Specialty Teams for transport. In most cases, patients will be evacuated by the DoD aeromedical evacuation system. Patients will be regulated to FCC areas. At the airport of the NDMS reception area, patients will be met by a local medical team that will sort, assess, and match those patients to participating hospitals, according to procedures developed by local authorities and the local area's NDMS Federal Coordinating Center. Patients will be transported to participating hospitals using locally organized ground and air transport.

For an overview of how this system works, please refer to Sidebar 7-3.

THE METROPOLITAN MEDICAL RESPONSE SYSTEM

The Department of Health and Human Services states that

The Metropolitan Medical Strike Team (MMST) systems concept began in the Washington Metropolitan area in 1995. Using the combined personnel and equipment resources from Washington, DC; Arlington County, Virginia; and Montgomery and Prince George's County, Maryland; the MMST was the first of its kind in the civilian environment. Primarily a chemical response team, the MMST was capable of providing initial, on-site emergency health and medical services following a terrorist incident involving a weapon of mass destruction (chemical, biological, radiological and/or nuclear). The team can provide emergency medical services, decontamination of victims, mental health services, plans for the disposition of nonsurvivors, and plans for the forward movement of patients to regional health care facilities, as appropriate, via NDMS.

Building from the initial efforts of the Washington Metropolitan Area MMST, OEP sought to develop a similar team in the city of Atlanta in preparation for the 1996 Summer Olympic Games.

As a result of the initial successes of the Washington Metropolitan Area and Atlanta MMSTs, Congress, as part of the Defense Against Weapons of Mass Destruction Act of 1996 (more commonly known as Nunn-Lugar-Domenici), authorized HHS to develop 25 additional MMSTs.

In an effort to show the importance of the system, OEP changed the MMST name to Metropolitan Medical Response System, or MMRS. This name change reflected OEP's ongoing effort to bring together not only the fire, EMS, and HAZMAT communities but also the public, private, and mental health communities. An effective systems response to chemical, biological, radiological, or nuclear incidents will require coordination among hospitals, prehospital providers, laboratories, public health officials, poison control centers, mental health professionals, infectious disease experts, surrounding communities, states, and the federal government.

Contracting with 27 cities in 1997 and additional cities in 1999, HHS/OEP is working to develop a coordinated systems response (fire, police, EMS, hospital, public health, etc.) to WMD incidents. HHS/OEP has approached MMRS development from two perspectives: chemical and biological. Although the two planning approaches focus on different areas, they converge at the same point: greater focus on health systems response.

The current MMRS efforts focus on immediate site-specific response capabilities:

- Enhance existing capabilities
- Develop overall systems plans
- Raise awareness of WMD agents

- Develop enhanced capability to operate in contaminated environments
- Develop specialized treatment protocols for WMD victims

The goals for MMRS enhancement are as follows:

- Integrate biological preparedness into the overall planning process

---

SIDEBAR 7-3   The National Disaster Medical Team

The National Disaster Medical System (NDMS), through the U.S. Public Health Service (PHS), fosters the development of Disaster Medical Assistance Teams (DMATs). A DMAT is a group of professional and paraprofessional medical personnel (supported by a cadre of logistical and administrative staff) designed to provide emergency medical care during a disaster or other event.

- Each team has a sponsoring organization, such as a major medical center; public health or safety agency; nonprofit, public or private organization that signs a Memorandum of Understanding (MOU) with the PHS. The DMAT sponsor organizes the team and recruits members, arranges training, and coordinates the dispatch of the team.
- In addition to the standard DMATs, there are highly specialized DMATs that deal with specific medical conditions such as crush injuries, burns, and mental health emergencies. Other specialty teams include Disaster Mortuary Operational Response Teams (DMORTs) that provide mortuary services, Veterinary Medical Assistance Teams (VMATs) that provide veterinary services, and National Medical Response Teams (NMRTs) that are equipped and trained to provide medical care for victims of weapons of mass destruction.
- DMATs deploy to disaster sites with sufficient supplies and equipment to sustain themselves for a period of 72 hours while providing medical care at a fixed or temporary medical care

site. In mass casualty incidents, their responsibilities include triaging patients, providing austere medical care, and preparing patients for evacuation. In other types of situations, DMATs may provide primary health care and/or may serve to augment overloaded local health-care staffs. Under the rare circumstance that disaster victims are evacuated to a different locale to receive definitive medical care, DMATs may be activated to support patient reception and disposition of patients to hospitals. DMATs are designed to be a rapid-response element to supplement local medical care until other federal or contract resources can be mobilized or the situation is resolved.

- DMATs are principally a community resource available to support local, regional, and state requirements. However, as a national resource they can be federalized to provide interstate aid.

Although the NDMS is designed to respond to major disasters, there are immediate regional benefits to states and local communities that participate in the system. DMATs, specialty teams, and other elements of the NDMS are available to respond to local mass casualty incidents or on an intrastate basis. Thus the NDMS not only enhances nationwide medical response capability; it also improves the ability of participating states and localities to respond to disasters within their own jurisdictions and under their own authorities.

Source: DHHS. www.hhs.gov

- Develop plans for mass prophylaxis of exposed and potentially exposed populations
- Develop plans for mass patient care
- Develop plans for mass fatality management
- Develop plans for environment surety

Sidebar 7-4 gives a more detail description of the MMRS capabilities and the difference it makes at the local level.

THE STRATEGIC NATIONAL STOCKPILE

According to a document prepared by the Centers for Disease Control (CDC):

> In 1999 Congress charged the Department of Health and Human Services (HHS) and the Centers for Disease Control and Prevention (CDC) with the establishment of the National Pharmaceutical Stockpile (NPS). The mission was to provide a resupply of large quantities of essential medical

materiel to states and communities during an emergency within 12 hours of the federal decision to deploy.

The Homeland Security Act of 2002 tasked DHS with defining the goals and performance requirements of the program as well as managing the actual deployment of assets. Effective on March 1, 2003, the NPS became the Strategic National Stockpile (SNS) managed jointly by DHS and HHS. The SNS program works with governmental and non-governmental partners to upgrade the nation's public health capacity to respond to a national emergency. Critical to the success of this initiative is ensuring capacity is developed at federal, state, and local levels to receive, stage, and dispense SNS assets.

The SNS is a national repository of antibiotics, chemical antidotes, antitoxins, life-support medications, IV administration, airway maintenance supplies, and medical/surgical items. The SNS is designed to supplement and resupply state and local public health agencies in the event of a national emergency anywhere and at anytime within the U.S. or its territories.

The SNS is organized for flexible response. If the incident requires additional pharmaceuticals and/or medical supplies, follow-on vendor managed inventory (VMI) supplies

---

SIDEBAR 7-4   MMRS Capabilities

- Initial identification of agents
- Ability to perform operations in OSHA levels A, B, and C personal protective equipment, avoiding secondary responder casualties
- Enhanced triage, treatment, and decontamination capabilities at the incident site and definitive care facilities
- Maintains local caches sufficient to treat 1,000 patients exposed to chemical agents
- Ability to transport uncontaminated/decontaminated patients to area hospitals for definitive care
- Ability to maintain a viable health system
- Ability to transport patients to participating NDMS hospitals throughout the nation
- Mechanisms to activate mutual aid support from local, state, and federal emergency response agencies

- Ability to integrate additional response assets into the ongoing incident command structure

The MMRS impacts at local level are as follows:

- Requires development of response plans unique for each city
- Creates integrated immediate response structure
- Creates additional local and regional support network
- Integrates with local mass casualty plans
- Brings together and encourages city planning agencies to interact where they never interacted before
- Encourages and initiates hospital NBC planning
- Encourages local health-care providers to develop appropriate medical treatment protocols

Source: Department of Health and Human Services. www.hhs.gov

will be shipped to arrive within 24 to 36 hours. If the agent is well defined, VMI can be tailored to provide pharmaceuticals, supplies, and/or products specific to the suspected or confirmed agent(s). In this case, the VMI could act as the first option for immediate response from the SNS.

During a national emergency, state, local, and private stocks of medical materiel will be depleted quickly. State and local first responders and health officials can use the SNS to bolster their response to a national emergency, with a 12-hour Push Package, VMI, or a combination of both, depending on the situation. The SNS is not a first response tool.

Sidebar 7-5 gives an overview of how the process goes when there is a call and how it interacts with the local and state authorities.

URBAN SEARCH AND RESCUE (USAR)

Urban search-and-rescue is considered a "multihazard" discipline because it may be needed for a

---

SIDEBAR 7-5   The Strategic National Stockpile (SNS)

The Strategic National Stockpile (SNS) program is committed to have 12-hour push packages delivered anywhere in the United States or its territories within 12 hours of a federal decision to deploy. The 12-hour push packages have been configured to be immediately loaded onto either trucks or commercial cargo aircraft for the most rapid transportation. Concurrent to SNS transport, the SNS program will deploy its Technical Advisory Response Unit (TARU). The TARU staff will coordinate with state and local officials so that the SNS assets can be efficiently received and distributed upon arrival at the site.

DHS will transfer authority for the SNS materiel to the state and local authorities once it arrives at the designated receiving and storage site. State and local authorities will then begin the breakdown of the 12-hour push package for distribution. SNS TARU members will remain on-site in order to assist and advise state and local officials in putting the SNS assets to prompt and effective use.

The decision to deploy SNS assets may be based on evidence showing the overt release of an agent that might adversely affect public health. It is more likely, however, that subtle indicators, such as unusual morbidity and/or mortality identified through the nation's disease outbreak surveillance and epidemiology network, will alert health officials to the possibility (and confirmation) of a biological or chemical incident or a national emergency. To receive SNS assets, the affected state's governor's office will directly request the deployment of the SNS assets from CDC or DHS. DHS, HHS, CDC, and other federal officials will evaluate the situation and determine a prompt course of action.

The SNS program is part of a nationwide preparedness training and education program for state and local health-care providers, first responders, and governments (to include federal officials, governors' offices, state and local health departments, and emergency management agencies). This training not only explains the SNS program's mission and operations; it alerts state and local emergency response officials to the important issues they must plan for in order to receive, secure, and distribute SNS assets.

To conduct this outreach and training, CDC and SNS program staff are currently working with DHS, HHS agencies, Regional Emergency Response Coordinators at all of the U.S. Public Health Service regional offices, state and local health departments, state emergency management offices, the Metropolitan Medical Response System cities, the Department of Veterans' Affairs, and the Department of Defense.

Source: Centers for Disease Control and Prevention. www.cdc.gov

variety of emergencies or disasters, including earth-quakes, hurricanes, typhoons, storms and tornadoes, floods, dam failures, technological accidents, terrorist activities, and hazardous materials releases. The events may be slow in developing, as in the case of hurri-canes, or sudden, as in the case of earthquakes.

DHS enlarges the definition as follows:

> Urban search-and-rescue (USAR) involves the location, rescue (extrication), and initial medical stabilization of victims trapped in confined spaces. Structural collapse is most often the cause of victims being trapped, but victims may also be trapped in transportation accidents, mines and collapsed trenches.

Some historical background given by FEMA is as follows:

> It is in the early 1980s that the Fairfax County Fire and Rescue and Metro-Dade County Fire Department created elite search-and-rescue teams trained for rescue operations in collapsed buildings. Working with the United States State Department and Office of Foreign Disaster Aid, these teams provided vital search-and-rescue support for catastrophic earthquakes in Mexico City, the Philippines and Armenia.
>
> In 1991, FEMA incorporated this concept into the Federal Response Plan, sponsoring 25 national urban search-and-rescue task forces. Today, in support of DHS, there are 28 national task forces staffed and equipped to conduct round-the-clock search-and-rescue operations following earthquakes, tornadoes, floods, hurricanes, aircraft accidents, hazardous materials spills and catastrophic structure collapses.

Sidebar 7-6 provides information about how the teams are structured and the way they operate.

MARITIME SEARCH AND RESCUE

DHS stated that

> The U.S. Coast Guard remains as an independent entity directly reporting to the Secretary of DHS; however, it works cooperatively with and under the direction of FEMA in the area of maritime search and rescue. It is in charge of the mar-itime search and rescue function, one of the Coast Guard's oldest missions. Minimizing the loss of life, injury, property damage, or loss by rendering aid to persons in distress and property in the maritime environment has always been a Coast Guard priority. Coast Guard SAR response involves multi-mission stations, cutters, aircraft, and boats linked by communications networks. The National SAR Plan divides

> the U.S. area of SAR responsibility into internationally rec-ognized aeronautical and maritime SAR regions. The Coast Guard is the SAR Coordinator for U.S. aeronautical and maritime search and rescue regions that are near America's oceans, including Alaska and Hawaii. To meet this responsi-bility, the Coast Guard maintains SAR facilities on the East, West and Gulf coasts; in Alaska, Hawaii, Guam, and Puerto Rico; as well as on the Great Lakes and inland U.S. water-ways. The Coast Guard is recognized worldwide as a leader in the field of search and rescue.

A brief description of the SAR programs within the agency is given in Sidebar 7-7.

OTHER RESPONSE AGENCIES

The agencies listed in the previous section operate directly under FEMA; besides these agencies, there is another group of agencies that operates in their respective organizations and do not have a day-to-day contact with FEMA but that can be used as a resource if there is need. These departments and agencies are as follows:

DEPARTMENT OF JUSTICE (DOJ)

Web site: www.usdoj.gov

The Federal Bureau of Investigation (FBI) is the lead agency for crisis management and investigation of all terrorism-related matters, including incidents involv-ing a WMD. Within FBI's role as LFA, the FBI federal on-scene commander (OSC) coordinates the overall federal response until the attorney general transfers the LFA role to DHS EP&R. The main concerned units within the FBI are as follows:

- FBI Domestic Terrorism/Counterterrorism Planning Section (DTCTPS): The DTCTPS serves as the point of contact (POC) to the FBI field offices and command structure as well as other federal agencies in incidences of terrorism, the use or suspected use of WMD, and/or the evaluation of threat credibility. If the FBI's Strategic Information and Operations Center

(SIOC) is operational for exercises or actual incidents, the DTCTPS will provide staff personnel to facilitate the operation of SIOC.

- FBI Laboratory Division: Within the FBI's Laboratory Division reside numerous assets,

which can deploy to provide assistance in a terrorism/WMD incident. The Hazardous Materials Response Unit (HMRU) personnel are highly trained and knowledgeable and are equipped to direct and assist in the collection of

---

SIDEBAR 7-6　The Urban Search and Rescue Teams

If a disaster event warrants national Urban Search and Rescue (US&R) support, DHS will deploy the three closest task forces within 6 hours of notification and additional teams as necessary. The role of these task forces is to support state and local emergency responders' efforts to locate victims and manage recovery operations.

- Each task force consists of two 31-person teams, four canines, and a comprehensive equipment cache. For every US&R task force, there are 62 positions. But to be sure, a full team can respond to an emergency; the task forces have at the ready more than 130 highly-trained members.
- A task force is really a partnership between local fire departments, law enforcement agencies, federal and local governmental agencies, and private companies.
- A task force is totally self-sufficient for the first 72 hours of a deployment.
- The equipment cache used to support a task force weighs nearly 60,000 pounds and is worth about $1.4 million. Add the task force members to the cache, and you can completely fill a military C-141 transport or two C-130s.
- US&R task force members work in four areas of specialization: search, to find victims trapped after a disaster; rescue, which includes safely digging victims out of tons of collapsed concrete and metal; technical, made up of structural specialists who make rescues safe for the rescuers; and medical, which cares for the victims before and after a rescue.

- In addition to search-and-rescue support, DHS provides hands-on training in search-and-rescue techniques and equipment, technical assistance to local communities, and in some cases federal grants to help communities better prepare for US&R operations.
- The bottom line in US&R: Someday lives may be saved because of the skills these rescuers gain. These first responders consistently go to the front lines when the nation needs them most.
- Not only are these first responders a national resource that can be deployed to a major disaster or structural collapse anywhere in the country; they are also the local firefighters and paramedics who answer local 911 calls.
- Events such as the 1995 bombing of the Alfred P. Murrah Federal Office Building in Oklahoma City, the Northridge earthquake, the Kansas grain elevator explosion in 1998, and earthquakes in Turkey and Greece in 1999 underscore the need for highly skilled teams to rescue trapped victims.
- What the task force can do: conduct physical search-and-rescue in collapsed buildings; provide emergency medical care to trapped victims; deploy search-and-rescue dogs; assess and control gas, electric service, and hazardous materials; and evaluate and stabilize damaged structures.

Source: FEMA and DHS. www.fema.gov and www.dhs.gov

hazardous and/or toxic evidence in a contaminated environment.

- FBI Critical Incident Response Group (CIRG): The Crisis Management Unit (CMU), which conducts training and exercises for the FBI and has developed the concept of the Joint Operations Center (JOC), is available to provide on-scene assistance to the incident and integrate the concept of the JOC and the Incident Command System (ICS) to create efficient management of the situation.

DEPARTMENT OF DEFENSE (DoD)

Web site: www.defenselink.mil

In the event of a terrorist attack or act of nature on American soil resulting in the release of chemical, biological, radiological, nuclear material or high-yield explosive (CBRNE) devices, the local law enforcement, fire, and emergency medical personnel who are first to respond may become quickly overwhelmed by the magnitude of the attack. The Department of Defense (DoD) has many unique war-fighting support

---

SIDEBAR 7-7   U.S. Coast Guard Search and Rescue Programs

Rescue 21

The Coast Guard currently uses the National Distress and Response System to monitor for maritime distress calls and coordinate response operations. The system consists of a network of VHF-FM antennae high sites and with analog transceivers that are remotely controlled by regional communications centers and rescue boat stations providing coverage out to approximately 20 nautical miles from the shore in most areas.

Salvage Assistance and Technical Support

The Marine Safety Center Salvage Assistance and Response Team provide on-scene technical support at maritime catastrophes in order to predict events and mitigate their impact.

Operational Command, Control, and Communications

The National Strike Force Coordination Center (NSFCC) provides oversight and strategic direction to the strike teams, ensuring enhanced interoperability through a program of standardized operating procedures for response, equipment, training, and qualifications. The NSFCC conducts at least six major government-led spill response exercises each year under the National Preparedness for Response Exercise program; maintains a national logistics network, using the Response Resource Inventory; implements the Coast Guard Oil Spill Removal Organization program; and administers the National Maintenance Contract for the Coast Guard's $30 million inventory of prepositioned spill response equipment.

Amver

Amver is a ship-reporting system for search and rescue. It is a global system that enables identification of other ships in the area of a ship in distress, which could then be sent to its assistance. Amver information is used only for search and rescue and is made available to any rescue coordination center in the world responding to a search and rescue case. The Coast Guard actively seeks to increase participation in this voluntary reporting system. Each year, more vessels participate in the system and

Sidebar 7-7 continued

capabilities, both technical and operational, that could be used in support of state and local authorities, if requested by DHS, as the lead federal agency, to support and manage the consequences of such a domestic event.

When requested, the DoD will provide its unique and extensive resources in accordance with the following principles. First, DoD will ensure an unequivocal chain of responsibility, authority, and accountability for its actions to ensure the American people that the military will follow the basic constructs of lawful action when an emergency occurs. Second, in the event of a catastrophic CBRNE event, DoD will always play a supporting role to the LFA in accordance with all applicable law and plans. Third, DoD support will emphasize its natural role, skills, and structures to mass mobilize and provide logistical support. Fourth, DoD will purchase equipment and provide support in areas that are largely related to its war-fighting mission. Fifth, reserve component forces are DoD's forward-deployed forces for domestic consequence management.

All official requests for DoD support to CBRNE consequence management (CM) incidents are made by the LFA to the executive secretary of the DoD. While the LFA may submit the requests for DoD assistance through other DoD channels, immediately upon receipt, any request that comes to any DoD element shall be forwarded to the executive secretary. In each instance the executive secretary will take the necessary action so that the deputy secretary can determine whether the incident warrants special operational management. In such instances, upon issuance of secretary of Defense guidance to the chairman of the Joint Chiefs of Staff (CJCS), the Joint Staff will translate the secretary's decisions into military orders for these CBRNE-CM events, under the policy oversight of the ATSD(CS). If the deputy secretary of defense

more lives are saved. Currently, ships from more than 143 nations participate.

Amver represents "free" safety insurance during a voyage by improving the chances for aid in an emergency. By regular reporting, someone knows where a ship is at all times on its voyage in the event of an emergency. Amver can reduce the time lost for vessels responding to calls for assistance by orchestrating a rescue response, utilizing ships in the best position or with the best capability to avoid unnecessary diversions in response to a Mayday or SOS call.

Pollution Control

The Response Operations Division develops and maintains policies for marine pollution response. They also coordinate activities with the international community, intelligence agencies, and the federal government in matters concerning threats or acts of terrorism in U.S. ports and territorial waters.

The National Strike Force (NSF)

The National Strike Force (NSF) was established in 1973 as a direct result of the Federal Water Pollution Control Act of 1972. The NSF's mission is to provide highly trained, experienced personnel and specialized equipment to Coast Guard and other federal agencies to facilitate preparedness and response to oil and hazardous substance pollution incidents in order to protect public health and the environment. The NSF's area of responsibility covers all Coast Guard districts and federal response regions.

The strike teams provide rapid response support in incident management, site safety, contractor performance monitoring, resource documentation, response strategies, hazard assessment, oil spill dispersant and operational effectiveness monitoring, and high-capacity lightering and offshore-skimming capabilities.

Source: DHS and U.S. Coast Guard. www.dhs.gov

FIGURE 7-5   New York, NY, September 18, 2001—FBI members look on toward the wreckage at the World Trade Center. Photo by Andrea Booher/FEMA News Photo.

determines that DoD support for a particular CBRNE-CM incident does not require special consequence management procedures, the secretary of the Army will exercise authority as the DoD executive agent through normal director of Military Support, Military Support to Civil Authorities (MSCA) procedures, with policy oversight by the ATSD(CS).

Additionally, DoD has established 10 Weapons of Mass Destruction Civil Support Teams (WMD-CST), each composed of 22 well-trained and equipped full-time National Guard personnel. Upon secretary of Defense certification, one WMD-CST will be stationed in each of the 10 FEMA regions around the

country, ready to provide support when directed by their respective governors. Their mission is to deploy rapidly, assist local responders in determining the precise nature of an attack, provide expert technical advice, and help pave the way for the identification and arrival of follow-on military assets. By congressional direction, DoD is in the process of establishing and training an additional 17 WMD-CSTs to support the U.S. population. Interstate agreements provide a process for the WMD-CST and other National Guard assets to be used by neighboring states. If national security requirements dictate, these units may be transferred to federal service.

DEPARTMENT OF ENERGY (DOE)

Web site: www.dp.doe.gov/emergencyresponse/

Through its Office of Emergency Response, the Department of Energy (DOE) manages radiological emergency response assets that support both crisis and consequence management response in the event of an incident involving a WMD. DOE is prepared to respond immediately to any type of radiological accident or incident with its radiological emergency response assets.

Through its Office of Nonproliferation and National Security, DOE coordinates activities in nonproliferation, international nuclear safety, and communicated threat assessment. DOE maintains the following capabilities that support domestic terrorism preparedness and response:

- Aerial Measuring System (AMS): AMS is an aircraft-operated radiation detection system that uses fixed-wing aircraft and helicopters equipped with state-of-the-art technology instrumentation to track, monitor, and sample airborne radioactive plumes and/or detect and measure radioactive material deposited on the ground.
- Atmospheric Release Advisory Capability (ARAC): ARAC is a computer-based atmospheric dispersion and deposition modeling capability operated by Lawrence Livermore National Laboratory (LLNL) and its role in an emergency begins when a nuclear, chemical, or other hazardous material is, or has the potential of being, released into the atmosphere. ARAC's capability consists of meteorologists and other technical staff using three-dimensional computer models and real-time weather data to project the dispersion and deposition of radioactive material in the environment.
- Accident Response Group (ARG): ARG is DOE's primary emergency response capability for responding to emergencies involving United States nuclear weapons. ARG members will deploy with highly specialized, state-of-the-art equipment for weapons recovery and monitoring operations. ARG advance elements focus on initial assessment and provide preliminary advice to decision makers.
- Federal Radiological Monitoring and Assessment Center (FRMAC): For major radiological emergencies affecting the United States, the DOE establishes a FRMAC. The center is the control point for all federal assets involved in the monitoring and assessment of off-site radiological conditions. FRMAC provides support to the affected states, coordinates federal off-site radiological environmental monitoring and assessment activities, maintains a technical liaison with tribal nations and state and local governments, responds to the assessment needs of the LFA, and meets the statutory responsibilities of the participating federal agency.
- Nuclear Emergency Search Team (NEST): NEST is DOE's program for dealing with the technical aspects of nuclear or radiological terrorism. Response teams vary in size from a five-person technical advisory team to a tailored deployment of dozens of searchers and scientists who can locate and then conduct or support technical operations on a suspected nuclear device.
- Radiological Assistance Program (RAP): Under RAP, DOE provides, upon request, radiological assistance to DOE program elements, other federal agencies, state, tribal, and local governments, private groups, and individuals. RAP provides resources (trained personnel and equipment) to evaluate, assess, advice, and assist in the mitigation of actual or perceived radiation hazards and risks to workers, the public, and the environment.
- Radiation Emergency Assistance Center/ Training Site (REAC/TS): The REAC/TS is managed by DOE's Oak Ridge Institute for Science and Education in Oak Ridge, Tennessee, and it maintains a 24-hour response center staffed with personnel and equipment to support medical aspects of radiological emergencies.

- Communicated Threat Credibility Assessment: DOE is the program manager for the Nuclear Assessment Program (NAP) at LLNL. The NAP is a DOE-funded asset specifically designed to provide technical, operational, and behavioral assessments of the credibility of communicated threats directed against the U.S. government and its interests.
- Nuclear Incident Response: The program provides expert personnel and specialized equipment to a number of federal emergency response entities that deal with nuclear emergencies, nuclear accidents, and nuclear terrorism. The emergency response personnel are experts in such fields as device assessment, device disablement, intelligence analysis, credibility assessment, and health physics.

Department of Health and Human Services (HHS)

Web site: www.hhs.gov

The Department of Health and Human Services (HHS), as the LFA for Emergency Support Function (ESF) #8 (health and medical services), provides coordinated federal assistance to supplement state and local resources in response to public health and medical care needs following a major disaster or emergency. Additionally, HHS provides support during developing or potential medical situations and has the responsibility for federal support of food, drug, and sanitation issues. Resources are furnished when state and local resources are overwhelmed and public health and/or medical assistance is requested from the federal government.

HHS, in its primary agency role for ESF #8, coordinates the provision of federal health and medical assistance to fulfill the requirements identified by the affected state/local authorities having jurisdiction. Included in ESF #8 is overall public health response; triage, treatment, and transportation of victims of the disaster; and evacuation of patients out of the disaster area, as needed, into a network of Military Services, Veterans Affairs, and preenrolled nonfederal hospitals located in the major metropolitan areas of the United States.

ESF #8 utilizes resources primarily available from (1) within HHS, (2) ESF #8 support agencies, (3) the National Disaster Medical System, and (4) specific nonfederal sources (major pharmaceutical suppliers, hospital supply vendors, international disaster response organizations, and international health organizations).

Other than the agencies integrated under FEMA, the Centers for Disease Control and Prevention (CDC) may also be used in response activities. CDC is the federal agency responsible for protecting the public health of the country through prevention and control of diseases and for response to public health emergencies. CDC works with national and international agencies to eradicate or control communicable diseases and other preventable conditions. The CDC's Bioterrorism Preparedness and Response Program oversees the agency's effort to prepare state and local governments to respond to acts of bioterrorism. In addition, CDC has designated emergency response personnel throughout the agency who are responsible for responding to biological, chemical, and radiological terrorism. CDC has epidemiologists trained to investigate and control outbreaks or illnesses, as well as laboratories capable of quantifying an individual's exposure to biological or chemical agents.

Environmental Protection Agency

Web site: www.epa.gov

The Environmental Protection Agency (EPA) is chartered to respond to WMD releases under the National Oil and Hazardous Substances Pollution Contingency Plan (NCP) regardless of the cause of the release. EPA is authorized by the Comprehensive Environmental Response, Compensation, and Liability Act (CERCLA); the Oil Pollution Act; and the Emergency Planning and Community Right-to-Know Act to support federal, state, and local responders in counterterrorism. EPA will provide support to the FBI during crisis management in response to a terrorist incident. In its crisis management role, the EPA on-scene commander (OSC) may provide the FBI special agent in charge (SAC) with technical advice and recommendations, scientific and technical assessments, and assistance (as needed) to state and local responders. The EPA's OSC will support DHS during consequence management for the incident. EPA carries out its response according to the FRP, ESF #10, and Hazardous Materials. The OSC may request an Environmental Response Team that is funded by EPA if the terrorist incident exceeds available local and regional resources. EPA is the chair of the National Response Team (NRT).

DEPARTMENT OF AGRICULTURE

Web site: www.usda.gov

It is the policy of the U.S. Department of Agriculture (USDA) to be prepared to respond swiftly in the event of national security, natural disaster, technological, and other emergencies at the national, regional, state, and county levels to provide support and comfort to the people of the United States. USDA has a major role in ensuring the safety of food for all Americans. One concern is bioterrorism and its effect on agriculture in rural America, namely crops in the field, animals on the hoof, and food-safety issues related to food in the food chain between the slaughterhouse and/or processing facilities and the consumer.

- The Office of Crisis Planning and Management (OCPM): This USDA office coordinates the emergency planning, preparedness, and crisis management functions and the suitability for employment investigations of the department.
- USDA State Emergency Boards (SEBs): The SEBs have responsibility for coordinating USDA emergency activities at the state level.
- The Farm Service Agency: This USDA agency develops and administers emergency plans and controls covering food processing, storage, and wholesale distribution; distribution and use of seed; and manufacture, distribution, and use of livestock and poultry feed.

- The Food and Nutrition Service (FNS): This USDA agency provides food assistance in officially designated disaster areas upon request by the designated state agency. Generally, the food assistance response from FNS includes authorization of Emergency Food Stamp Program benefits and use of USDA-donated foods for emergency mass feeding and household distribution, as necessary. FNS also maintains a current inventory of USDA-donated food held in federal, state, and commercial warehouses and provides leadership to the FRP under ESF #11, Food.
- Food Safety and Inspection Service: This USDA agency inspects meat and meat products, poultry and poultry products, and egg products in slaughtering and processing plants; assists the Food and Drug Administration in the inspection of other food products; develops plans and procedures for radiological emergency response in accordance with the Federal Radiological Emergency Response Plan (FRERP); and provides support, as required, to the FRP at the national and regional levels.
- Natural Resources Conservation Service: This USDA agency provides technical assistance to individuals, communities, and governments relating to proper use of land for agricultural production; provides assistance in determining the extent of damage to agricultural land and water; and provides support to the FRP under ESF #3, Public Works and Engineering.
- Agricultural Research Service (ARS): This USDA agency develops and carries out all necessary research programs related to crop or livestock diseases; provides technical support for emergency programs and activities in the areas of planning, prevention, detection, treatment, and management of consequences; technical support for the development of guidance information on

the effects of radiation, biological, and chemical agents on agriculture; develops and maintains a current inventory of ARS-controlled laboratories that can be mobilized on short notice for emergency testing of food, feed, and water safety; and provides biological, chemical, and radiological safety support for USDA.

- Economic Research Service: This USDA agency, in cooperation with other departmental agencies, analyzes the impacts of the emergency on the U.S. agricultural system, as well as on rural communities, as part of the process of developing strategies to respond to the effects of an emergency.

- Rural Business-Cooperative Service: This USDA agency, in cooperation with other government agencies at all levels, promotes economic development in affected rural areas by developing strategies that respond to the conditions created by an emergency.

- Cooperative State Research, Education, and Extension Service (CSREES): This USDA agency coordinates use of land-grant and other cooperating state college and university services and other relevant research institutions in carrying out all responsibilities for emergency programs.

- Rural Housing Service: This USDA agency will assist the Department of Housing and Urban Development by providing living quarters in unoccupied rural housing in an emergency situation.

- Rural Utilities Service: This USDA agency will provide support to the FRP under ESF #12, Energy, at the national level.

- Office of Inspector General (OIG): This USDA office is the department's principal law enforcement component and liaison with the FBI. OIG, in concert with appropriate federal, state, and local agencies, is prepared to investigate any terrorist attacks relating to the nation's agriculture sector, to identify subjects, interview witnesses, and secure evidence in preparation for federal prosecution. As

necessary, OIG will examine USDA programs regarding counterterrorism-related matters.

- Forest Service (FS): This USDA agency will prevent and control fires in rural areas in cooperation with state, local, and tribal governments and appropriate federal departments and agencies. They will determine and report requirements for equipment, personnel, fuels, chemicals, and other materials needed for carrying out assigned duties.

NUCLEAR REGULATORY COMMISSION

Web site: www.nrc.gov

The Nuclear Regulatory Commission (NRC) is the LFA (in accordance with the Federal Radiological Emergency Response Plan) for facilities or materials regulated by NRC or by an NRC Agreement State. NRC's counterterrorism-specific role, at these facilities or material sites, is to exercise the federal lead for radiological safety while supporting other federal, state, and local agencies in crisis and consequence management.

- Radiological Safety Assessment: NRC will provide the facility (or for materials, the user) technical advice to ensure on-site measures are taken to mitigate off-site consequences; serve as the primary federal source of information regarding on-site radiological conditions and off-site radiological effects; will support the technical needs of other agencies by providing descriptions of devices or facilities containing radiological materials and assessing the safety impact of terrorist actions and of proposed tactical operations of any responders. Safety assessments will be coordinated through NRC liaison at the Domestic Emergency Support Team (DEST), Strategic Information and Operations Center (SIOC), Command Post (CP), and Joint Operations Center (JOC).

FIGURE 7-6 New York, NY, September 21, 2001—Rescue operations continue far into the night at the World Trade Center. Photo by Andrea Booher/FEMA News Photo.

- Protective Action Recommendations: NRC will contact state and local authorities and offer advice and assistance on the technical assessment of the radiological hazard and, if requested, provide advice on protective actions for the public. NRC will coordinate any recommendations for protective actions through NRC liaison at the CP or JOC.
- Responder Radiation Protection: NRC will assess the potential radiological hazards to any responders and coordinate with the facility radiation protection staff to ensure that personnel responding to the scene are observing the appropriate precautions.

- Information Coordination: NRC will supply other responders and government officials with timely information concerning the radiological aspects of the event. NRC will liaison with the Joint Information Center to coordinate information concerning the federal response.

THE NATIONAL INCIDENT MANAGEMENT SYSTEM (NIMS)

A difficult issue in any response operation is determining who is in charge of the overall response effort.

As stated in the introduction of the National Response Plan,

> Most domestic incidents are handled at the local unified command level with government entities (federal, state, and local) participating as appropriate to the incident. In pre-event preparedness and prevention scenarios, the Local Emergency Prevention and Preparedness Councils (LEPPCs) play a vital role in coordinating with the local emergency response, prevention, and preparedness communities. LEPPC(s) are coordinating entities made up of participating local entities.
>
> In the event of the less frequent incident exceeding the local preparedness, response, and/or recovery communities' capabilities, the regional and national incident management organizations will provide support. Working within the State and/or Regional Emergency Operations Centers (SEOC/REOC) and within the Joint Operating Center (JOC) in the case of FBI participation, the multi-agency coordination requirements occur within these frameworks, providing information and resources for the incident commander at the local level.

DHS has been asked by the president in his Homeland Security Presidential Directive-5 (February 28, 2003) to develop a National Incident Management System (NIMS). To see the changes brought by the new system, let's start with a brief description of the ICS.

The Incident Command System (ICS) was developed after the 1970 fires in California, when duplication of efforts and lack of coordination and communication hindered all agencies responding to the expanding fires, and it is still the system in use in many states and localities. The main function of ICS is to establish a set of planning and management systems that would help the agencies responding to a disaster to work together in a coordinated and systematic approach. The step-by-step process enables the numerous responding agencies to effectively use resources and personnel to respond to those in need.

There are multiple functions in the ICS system. They include common use of terminology, integrated communications, a unified command structure, resource management, and action planning. There is a planned set of directives that include assigning one

coordinator to manage the infrastructure of the response and assigning personnel, deploying equipment, obtaining resources, and working with the numerous agencies that respond to the disaster scene. In most instances, it is the local fire chief or fire commissioner who is the incident commander.

For the ICS to be effective, it must provide for effective operations at three levels of incident character: (1) single jurisdiction and/or single agency; (2) single jurisdiction with multiple agency support; and (3) multijurisdictional and/or multiagency support. The organizational structure must be adaptable to a wide variety of emergencies (e.g., fire, flood, earthquake, rescue). The ICS includes agency autonomy, management by objectives, unity integrity, functional clarity, and effective span of control. The logistics, coordination and ability of the multiple agencies to work together must adhere to the ICS so that efficient leadership is maintained during the disaster.

There are five major management systems within the ICS. They include command, operations, planning, logistics, and finance.

1. The command section includes developing, directing, and maintaining communication and collaboration with the multiple agencies on-site, as well as working with local officials, the public, and the media to provide up-to-date information regarding the disaster.
2. The operations section handles the tactical operations, coordinates the command objectives, develops tactical operations, and organizes and directs all resources to the disaster site.
3. The planning section provides the necessary information to the command center to develop the action plan to accomplish the objectives. This section also collects and evaluates information as it is made available.
4. The logistics section provides personnel, equipment, and support for the command center. This section handles the coordination of all services that are involved in the response from locating rescue equipment to coordinating the

response for volunteer organizations such as the Salvation Army and the Red Cross.

5. The finance section is responsible for the accounting for funds used during the response and recovery aspect of the disaster. The finance section monitors costs related to incident and provides accounting procurement time recording cost analyses.

The Unified Command works best when there is a multiagency response. Due to the nature of disasters, multiple government agencies need to work together to monitor the response and manage the large number of personnel responding to the scene. ICS allows for the integration of the agencies to operate under a single response management. It is the same concepts that are the guiding force behind the new National system.

The president has requested in his Homeland Security Presidential Directive-5 that DHS develop a new National Incident Management System (NIMS) to "provide a consistent nationwide approach for federal, state, and local governments to work effectively and efficiently together to prepare for, respond to, and recover from domestic incidents, regardless of cause, size, or complexity." In order to achieve interoperability and compatibility among federal, state, and local capabilities, the NIMS has to include a core set of concepts, principles, terminology, and technologies covering the incident command system; multiagency coordination systems; unified command; training; identification and management of resources (including systems for classifying types of resources); qualifications and certification; and the collection, tracking, and reporting of incident information and incident resources.

In fact, the NRP states that NIMS, just as the ICS,

recognizes the significant benefits of NIIMS (National Interagency Incident Management System) and incorporate many of its principles. The important aspect of this concept is the understanding that there is ongoing preparedness and planning going on at each level. This planning is coordinated through a series of EPPCs, whose members represent the breadth of the incident management community. Within these EPPCs are imbedded information and intelligence management processes. The incident management structures will be rooted in the existing incident management system as explained in the National Interagency Incident Management System (NIIMS), utilizing Joint Information Centers (JICs) to coordinate the passing of information at all levels. The NIMS will focus on the mechanisms to make the proposed incident management structures a reality.

The national structure is shown in Figure 7-7.

As Figure 7-7 shows, NIMS will be a plan to enhance the ability of the United States to manage domestic incidents by establishing a single, comprehensive national incident management system. This proposed system does not exist as an operational model, but will probably surface before the end of 2003. The proposed deadlines by the NRP are:

- By July 1, 2003, in consultation with Federal departments and agencies and with State and local governments, develop a national system of standards, guidelines, and protocols to implement the NIMS and establish a mechanism for ensuring ongoing management and maintenance of the NIMS, including regular consultation with other Federal departments and agencies and with State and local governments.

- By September 1, 2003, in consultation with Federal departments and agencies and the Assistant to the President for Homeland Security, review existing authorities and regulations and prepare recommendations for the President on revisions necessary to implement the NRP fully.

- Beginning in Fiscal Year 2005, Federal departments and agencies shall make adoption of the NIMS a requirement, to the extent permitted by law, for providing Federal preparedness assistance through grants, contracts, or other activities. The Secretary shall develop standards and guidelines for determining whether a State or local entity has adopted the NIMS.

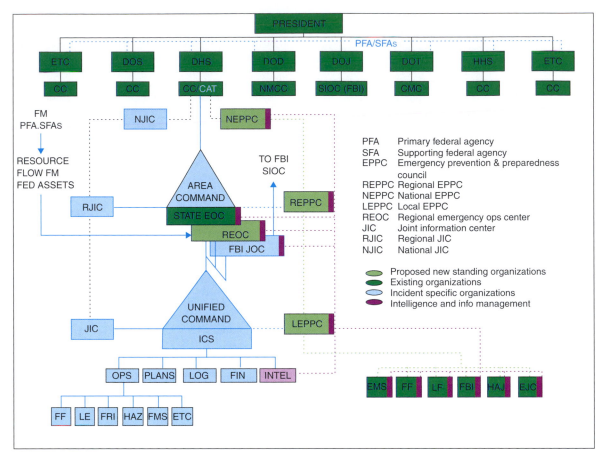

FIGURE 7-7   National structure for NIMS operations

THE FEDERAL RESPONSE

All elements of the Nation's response system have undergone changes as a result of the September 11 events. While some of the more significant changes have occurred at the Federal level, the results seem to reflect a shift toward increased Federal control and direction of disasters, particularly intentional or terrorist driven. The Federal Response Plan (FRP), used successfully during the domestic terrorist event of the

Murray Federal Building bombing, is replaced by the NRP.

The federal response can be initiated in two ways: a governor can request a presidential disaster declaration or the president can declare a presidential emergency upon damage to federal entities (as was the case for the discovery tragedy). This process remains unchanged.

Although a formal declaration does not have to be signed for the federal government to respond, the

FIGURE 7-8   New York, NY, September 27, 2001—Search dogs proved very helpful to the search and rescue teams throughout the cleanup effort at the World Trade Center. Photo by Bri Rodriguez/FEMA News Photo.

governor must make a formal request for assistance and specify in the request the specific needs of the disaster area. The presidential major disaster declaration process is presented in Sidebar 7-8.

The president has the ultimate discretion in making a disaster declaration. There are no set criteria to follow, no government regulations to guide which events are declared disasters by the president and which events are not. FEMA has developed a number of factors it considers in making its recommendation to the president,

including individual property losses per capita, level of damage to existing community infrastructure, level of insurance coverage, repetitive events, and other subjective factors. But in the end, the decision to make the declaration is the president's alone.

A presidential disaster declaration can be made in as short a time as a few hours, as was the case in the 1994 Northridge earthquake, the 1995 Oklahoma City bombing, and the September 11 World Trade Center attacks. Sometimes it takes weeks for damages to be assessed and the capability of state and local jurisdictions to fund response and recovery efforts to be evaluated. Should the governor's request be turned down by the president, the governor has the right to appeal, an appeal that will be considered, especially if new damage data becomes available and is included in the appeal.

Presidential declarations are routinely sought for such events as floods, hurricanes, earthquakes, and tornadoes. In recent years, governors have become more inventive and have requested presidential disaster declarations for snow removal, drought, West Nile virus, and economic losses caused by failing industries, such as the Northwest salmon spawning decline.

From 1976 to September 2003, there have been 1,001 presidential disaster declarations, averaging 36 declarations a year (Table 7-4). As an example of disaster declaration activity in a single year, in 1999 there were 50 major disaster declarations in 38 states, including 18 hurricanes (13 alone for Hurricane Floyd), 11 tornadoes, 7 floods, 6 winter storms, 6 severe storms, 1 flash flood and 1 winter freeze.

In 1992 FEMA developed the Federal Response Plan (FRP). This plan has been revised several times during the course of the years and was the operating bible of the federal government in disasters.

Homeland Security Presidential Directive-5 (February 28, 2003) directs DHS to develop a National Response Plan (NRP) to integrate all existing Federal plans and to serve as a unique guide for the Federal response. The FRP is the foundation of the new NRP, recognizing changes that need to be made to incorporate the specific of the other plans and the new terrorism threat environment. The first draft of the NRP was made public in May 2003 and the last one in June 2004. The last draft is currently under review by the Federal Departments and Agencies involved in

---

SIDEBAR 7-8   Presidential Major Disaster Declaration Process

Listed below are the guidelines that a disaster declaration should include:

- Contact is made between the affected state and the FEMA/EPR regional office. This contact may take place prior to or immediately following the disaster.
- If it appears the situation is beyond state and local capacity, the state requests FEMA/EPR to conduct a joint preliminary damage assessment (PDA). Participants in the PDA will include FEMA/EPR, state and local government representatives, and other federal agencies.
- Based on the PDA findings, the governor submits a request to the president through the FEMA/EPR regional director for either a major disaster or an emergency declaration and identifying the affected counties.
- The FEMA/EPR regional office submits a summary of the event and a recommendation based on the results of the PDA to FEMA/EPR headquarters, along with the governor's request.
- Upon receipt of these documents, the headquarters' senior staff convenes to discuss the request and determine the recommendation to be made to the president.
- FEMA/EPR's recommendation is forwarded to the White House for review.
- The president declares a major disaster or an emergency.

Source: Federal Response Plan, January 2003

TABLE 7-4   **Total Major Disaster Declarations 1976–2003**

Year	Total disaster declarations
1976	30
1977	22
1978	25
1979	42
1980	23
1981	15
1982	24
1983	21
1984	34
1985	27
1986	28
1987	23
1988	11
1989	31
1990	38
1991	43
1992	45
1993	32
1994	36
1995	32
1996	75
1997	44
1998	65
1999	50
2000	45
2001	45
2002	49
2003	46
Total	1001
Average	36

Source: FEMA. www.fema.gov

executing the Plan. As the NRP intends to integrate all existing Federal plans to a single document, here is a brief description of the plans and operation guidelines in place. The federal plans to be integrated under the NRP are as follows:

- The Federal Response Plan (FRP)
- The Federal Radiological Emergency Response Plan (FRERP)
- The Domestic Terrorism Concept of Operations Plan (CONPLAN)
- The Mass Mitigation Emergency Plan (Distant Shore)
- The National Oil Spill and Hazardous Substances Pollution Contingency Plan (NCP)

FEDERAL RESPONSE PLAN

FEMA defines the FRP as follows:

A signed agreement among 26 federal departments and agencies, including the American Red Cross, that: provides the mechanism for coordinating delivery of federal assistance and resources to augment efforts of state and local governments overwhelmed by a major disaster or emergency; supports implementation of the Robert T. Stafford Disaster Relief and Emergency Assistance Act, as amended (42 USC 5121, et seq.), as well as individual agency statutory authorities; and supplements other federal emergency operations plans developed to address specific hazards.

The fundamental goal of the FRP is to maximize available federal resources in support of response and recovery actions taken by state and local emergency officials (Sidebar 7-9).

There are four operating principals that are integral in the successful implementation of the FRP.

1. As stated in the definition of FEMA, the FRP is "the mechanism for coordinating delivery of federal assistance to augment efforts of state and local governments overwhelmed by a major disaster or emergency." So, the FRP does not call for FEMA or any other federal agency to take over direction and control of a disaster relief effort; no governor would allow that to happen. On the contrary and in contrast to public

perception on occasion, the FRP defines how FEMA and its fellow federal agencies and the American Red Cross will support state and local governments in the disaster relief effort. Direction and control of all presidentially declared major disasters remains in the hands of the governor and local officials.

2. The FRP is the only working agreement in existence that involves one federal agency directing the activities of a large number of other federal agencies. This agreement is truly unique in U.S. federal government. Basically, all signatories to the FRP agree to follow the direction of FEMA in providing disaster assistance from their respective agencies. Nowhere else in the federal government are the full resources of 26 federal agencies brought to bear on a single civil problem.

3. The FRP includes a series of agreements between FEMA and the participating federal agencies and the American Red Cross that clearly define the types of services and resources that FEMA

expects each agency to be able to provide in the event of a presidential declaration. In other words, each participating agency agrees to retain the capability to deploy personnel, services, and other resources on a 24-hour on-call basis. Also, agencies are expected to have contract vehicles in place that allow for rapid procurement of contractor services and products. This ensures that when FEMA requests services and resources from a participating agency, they are available and ready to go immediately.

4. What really makes the FRP work is money. FEMA pays for everything out of its annual Disaster Relief Fund (DRF) or from supplemental funding made available for major catastrophes by Congress. FEMA receives approximately $325 million annually for the DRF from Congress and uses these funds to pay for services and products provided by FRP partner agencies. This means that FRP partner agencies do not have to tap existing budgets that are already programmed for disaster spending

---

SIDEBAR 7-9   Types of Federal Disaster Assistance Available

The Federal Response Plan (FRP) makes available to the following types of assistance:

To Deliver Immediate Relief

- Initial response resources, including food, water, emergency generators
- Emergency services to clear debris, open critical transportation routes, provide mass sheltering and feeding

To Speed Return to Normal and Reduce Damage from Future Occurrences

- Loans and grants to repair or replace damaged housing and personal property

- Grants to repair or replace roads and public buildings, incorporating to the extent practical hazard-reduction structural and nonstructural measures
- Technical assistance to identify and implement mitigation opportunities to reduce future losses
- Other assistance, including crisis counseling, tax relief, legal services, job placement

Source: FEMA, Federal Response Plan

and ensures that these agencies will respond quickly to the direction of FEMA to support state and local efforts. FEMA "mission assigns" specific tasks to those agencies capable of completing these tasks, and it is already understood that FEMA will reimburse the FRP partner agencies per a preexisting agreement concerning costs of services. These partners are as follows:

- Department of Agricultures
- Department of Commerce
- Department of Defense
- Department of Education
- Department of Energy
- Department of Health and Human Resources
- Department of Housing and Urban Development
- Department of the Interior
- Department of Justice
- Department of Labor
- Department of State
- Department of Transportation
- Department of the Treasury
- Department of Veterans Affairs
- Agency for International Development
- American Red Cross
- Environmental Protection Agency
- Federal Communications Commission
- Federal Emergency Management Agency (change: replaced by Department of Homeland Security)
- General Services Administration
- National Aeronautics and Space Administration
- National Communications System (change: no longer a partner)
- Nuclear Regulatory Commission
- Office of Personnel Management
- Small Business Administration
- Tennessee Valley Authority
- U.S. Postal Service

(*Source*: FEMA, Federal Response Plan, January 2003).

ESF Primary Agencies

Each of the FRP partners serves as a primary agency or support agency in one or more of the 12 emergency support functions (ESF) in the FRP. Primary and support agencies are defined as follows:

1. Orchestrating the federal agency support within the functional area for an affected state
2. Providing an appropriate level of staffing for operations at FEMA/EPR headquarters, the ROC, DFO, and DRC
3. Activating and subtasking support agencies
4. Managing mission assignments and coordinating tasks with support agencies, as well as appropriate state agencies
5. Supporting and keeping other ESFs and organizational elements informed of ESF operational priorities and activities
6. Executing contracts and procuring goods and services as needed
7. Ensuring financial and property accountability for ESF activities
8. Supporting planning for short- and long-term disaster operations

ESF Support Agencies

When an ESF is activated in response to a disaster, each support agency for the ESF has operational responsibility for the following:

1. Supporting the ESF primary agency when requested by conducting operations using its authorities, cognizant expertise, capabilities, or resources
2. Supporting the primary agency's mission assignments
3. Providing status and resource information to the primary agency
4. Following established financial and property accountability procedures

The 12 ESFs, a brief description of the activities conducted and managed in each ESF, and the identity

FIGURE 7-9   New York, NY, November 7, 2001—FEMA interpreter Richie Park explains teleregistration procedures and disaster assistance options to business owner Betsy Chun at the Disaster Assistance Service Center in New York City. Photo by Larry Lerner/ FEMA News Photo.

of the primary agency in each ESF are provided in Sidebar 7-10 (including changes made to the FRP as of January 2003).

The FRP can be used for all major disasters and emergencies declared under the Stafford Act and (even in response to chemical, biological, or radiological terrorist incidents). DHS is the LFA.

FEDERAL RADIOLOGICAL EMERGENCY RESPONSE PLAN

The Federal Radiological Emergency Response Plan (FRERP) was developed as the operational plan for federal agencies to discharge their responsibilities during peacetime radiological emergencies. The introduction of the plan states that

> the FRERP establishes an organized, integrated capability for participating federal agencies to respond to a wide range of peacetime radiological emergencies. The plan provides a concept of operations, outlines federal policies and planning considerations, and specifies authorities and responsibilities

of each federal agency that has a significant role in such emergencies.

Each participating agency has responsibilities and/or capabilities that pertain to various types of radiological emergencies.

The scope of the plan is:

> The FRERP covers any peacetime radiological emergency that has actual, potential, or perceived radiological consequences within the United States, its territories, possessions, or territorial waters and that could require a response by the federal government. The level of the federal response to a specific emergency is be based on the type and/or amount of radioactive material involved, the location of the emergency, the impact on or the potential for impact on the public and environment, and the size of the affected area. Emergencies occurring at fixed nuclear facilities or during the transportation of radioactive materials, including nuclear weapons, fall within the scope of the plan regardless of whether the facility or radioactive materials are publicly or privately owned, federally regulated, regulated by an agreement state, or not regulated at all.

And as stated in the details about the lead federal agency part

> For any emergency not under the control of a federal agency, the state or local government is responsible for response; the state maintains primary responsibility even if it has requested federal help. If the emergency is at a facility owned or operated by a federal agency, this agency is the LFA responsible for the response. The NRC is the LFA for a licensed nuclear facility under NRC regulatory oversight, as well as for transportation of radioactive materials under NRC oversight. If the facility is owned or operated by, or material is shipped by the DoD or DOE, that agency is the LFA in an emergency. If the facility or shipped material is not licensed, owned, or operated by a federal agency or agreement state, the EPA is the LFA. Satellites containing radioactive materials are to be handled by the agency that has deployed them with technical assistance from DOE and EPA. In the event of radioactive material from a foreign or unknown source, EPA is the LFA with DoD, NASA, DOE, and NRC providing technical assistance. In any other, unforeseen type of emergency, these federal agencies will confer as to which is the LFA: DoD, DOE, NASA, EPA, and NRC. The FBI will manage and direct law enforcement and intelligence aspects of the response.

FRERP partners are as follows:

- Department of Agriculture (USDA)
- Department of Commerce (DOC)
- Department of Defense (DoD)
- Department of Energy (DOE)
- Department of Health and Human Services (HHS)
- Department of Housing and Urban Development (HUD)
- Department of the Interior (DOI)
- Department of Justice (DOJ)
- Department of State (DOS)

- Department of Transportation (DOT)
- Department of Veterans Affairs (VA)
- Environmental Protection Agency (EPA)
- Federal Emergency Management Agency (FEMA)
- General Services Administration (GSA)
- National Aeronautics and Space Administration (NASA)
- National Communications System (NCS) and
- Nuclear Regulatory Commission (NRC).

(*Source*: Federal Radiological Emergency Response Plan)

SIDEBAR 7-10   Emergency Support Functions (ESFs)

The FRP employs a functional approach that groups under 12 Emergency Support Functions (ESFs) the types of direct federal assistance that a state is most likely to need. Each ESF is headed by a primary agency designated on the basis of its authorities, resources, and capability in that functional area. Federal response assistance is provided using some or all ESFs as necessary. Federal ESF representatives coordinate with their counterpart state agencies.

ESF #1, Transportation, Department of Transportation: Assists federal agencies, state and local government entities, and voluntary organizations requiring transportation capacity to perform response missions.

Changes: Department of Treasury is no longer a support agency.

ESF #2, Communications, National Communications System: Ensures the provision of federal telecommunications support to federal, state, and local response efforts.

Changes: DHS is in charge; NCS is no longer a partner.

ESF #3, Public Works and Engineering, U.S. Army Corps of Engineers, Department of Defense:

Provides technical advice and evaluation; engineering services; contracting for construction management, inspection, and emergency repair of water and waste water treatment facilities; potable water and ice, emergency power, and real estate support to assist state(s) in lifesaving and life-protecting needs, damage mitigation, and recovery activities.

ESF #4, Firefighting, Forest Service, Department of Agriculture: Detects and suppresses wild land, rural, and urban fires resulting from, or occurring coincidentally with, a major disaster or emergency.

ESF # 5, Information and Planning, Federal Emergency Management Agency: Collects, analyzes, processes, and disseminates information about a potential or actual disaster or emergency to facilitate the activities of the federal government in providing assistance to affected states.

Changes: FEMA is replaced by the Department of Homeland Security.

ESF #6, Mass Care, American Red Cross: Coordinates federal assistance in support of state and local efforts to meet the mass care needs of victims, including sheltering, feeding, emergency first aid, and bulk distribution of emergency relief supplies.

Sidebar 7-10 continues

DOMESTIC TERRORISM CONCEPT OF OPERATIONS PLAN

The introduction of the plan states it clearly:

The Domestic Terrorism Concept of Operations Plan (CONPLAN) had been established to ensure the policy implemented by the president when he signed the Presidential Decision Directive 39 (PDD-39), the United States' policy on counterterrorism in 1995. This presidential directive built upon previous directives for combating terrorism and further elaborated a strategy and an inter-agency coordination mechanism and management structure to be undertaken by the federal government to combat both domestic and international terrorism in all its forms. This authority includes implementing measures to reduce our vulnerabilities, deterring terrorism through a clear public position, responding rapidly and effectively to threats or actual terrorist acts, and giving the highest priority to developing sufficient capabilities to combat and manage the consequences of terrorist incidents involving weapons of mass destruction (WMD).

The CONPLAN provides overall guidance to federal, state, and local agencies concerning how the federal government would respond to a potential or actual terrorist threat or incident that occurs in the United States, particularly one involving WMD. The CONPLAN outlines an organized and unified capability for a timely, coordinated response by federal agencies to a terrorist threat or act. It establishes conceptual guidance for assessing and monitoring a developing threat, notifying appropriate federal, state, and local agencies of the nature of the threat, and deploying the requisite advisory and technical resources to assist the lead federal agency (LFA) in facilitating interagency/interdepartmental coordination of a crisis and consequence management response. Lastly, it defines the relationships between structures under which the federal government will marshal crisis and consequence management resources to respond to a threatened or actual terrorist incident.

To accomplish its mission, the CONPLAN:

- Establishes a structure for a systematic, coordinated, and effective national response to threats or acts of terrorism in the United States

---

ESF #7, Resource Support, General Services Administration: Coordinates provision of equipment, materials, supplies, and personnel to support disaster operations.
Changes: Department of Treasury is no longer a support agency.

ESF #8, Health and Medical Services, Department of Health and Human Services: Provides coordinated federal assistance to supplement state and local resources in response to public health and medical care needs.

ESF #9, Urban Search and Rescue, Federal Emergency Management Agency: Deploys components of the national Search and Rescue Response System to provide specialized lifesaving assistance to state and local authorities, including locating, extricating, and providing initial medical treatment to victims trapped in collapsed structures.
Changes: FEMA is replaced by the Department of Homeland Security.

ESF #10, Hazardous Materials, Environmental Protection Agency: Provides federal support to state and local governments in response to an actual or potential discharge/release of hazardous substances.
Changes: Department of Homeland Security is now a support agency.

ESF #11, Food, Food and Nutrition Service, Department of Agriculture: Identifies, secures, and arranges for the transportation of food assistance to affected areas requiring federal response and authorizes the issuance of disaster food stamps.

ESF #12, Energy, Department of Energy: Helps restore the nation's energy systems following a major disaster requiring federal assistance and coordinates with federal and state officials to establish priorities for repair of energy systems and to provide emergency fuel and power.
Changes: Department of Homeland Security is now a support agency.

Source: FEMA. www.fema.gov

- Defines procedures for the use of federal resources to augment and support local and state governments
- Encompasses both crisis and consequence management responsibilities, and articulates the coordination relationships between these missions

The federal agencies that provide core federal response are DOJ (lead agency for crisis management) to try to prevent domestic terrorist attacks and to prosecute such attacks that might occur. The FBI will be the LFA and coordinate the emergency response; DoD will provide support to the FBI for crisis management functions. FEMA will be the lead agency for consequence management. DOE, EPA, and DHHS will support the FBI for technical operations and support FEMA/EPR for consequence management.

NATIONAL OIL SPILL AND HAZARDOUS SUBSTANCES POLLUTION CONTINGENCY PLAN (NCP)

The EPA provides the following overview about the plan:

The National Oil and Hazardous Substances Pollution Contingency Plan, more commonly called the National Contingency Plan, or NCP, is the federal government's blueprint for responding to both oil spills and hazardous substance releases.

The purpose of the NCP is to facilitate the federal government's response to both oil spills and hazardous substance releases in the United States and its territories and to ensure overall coordination in the event of such spills among the hierarchy of responders and contingency plans.

FIGURE 7-10   New York, NY, September 27, 2001—The remaining section of the World Trade Center is surrounded by a mountain of rubble following the September 11 terrorist attacks. Photo by Bri Rodriguez/FEMA News Photo.

It describes the basic mechanisms and structures by which the federal government will plan for, prepare for, and respond to oil and hazardous substance releases. The NCP establishes the National Response Team (NRT) to plan and coordinate responses to major discharges of oil and hazardous substances; coordinate a national program of preparedness, planning, and response; and facilitate research to improve response activities. The U.S. Environmental Protection Agency (EPA) serves as the lead agency within the NRT. The plan also establishes regional response teams to coordinate preparedness, planning, and response at the regional level. The NCP requires that spills of oil and hazardous substances be reported to the National Response Center, the central clearinghouse for all pollution incident reporting. The NCP also authorizes the predesignated on-scene coordinator (OSC) to direct all federal, state, local, and private response activities at the site of a discharge. The plan establishes the incident command system for managing responses. Depending on the location of the oil spill, the lead agency will be either the EPA or the U.S. Coast Guard.

For hazardous substance releases, the lead agency may be EPA, U.S. Coast Guard, or DoD, depending on where the spill originates. In addition, the NCP defines the objectives, authority, and scope of other contingency plans, including regional and area contingency plans. For oil spills the NCP establishes the national priorities for responding to such spills.

Under the plan, the OSC determines whether a spill poses a substantial threat to the public health or welfare, and if so directs all federal, state, local and private response and recovery actions. The OSC also may enlist the support of other federal agencies or special teams. In the event of a worst-case discharge, the National Strike Force Coordination Center may assist in coordinating the acquisition of needed response personnel and equipment.

For hazardous substance removals, the NCP authorizes the lead agency or OSC to initiate an appropriate removal or mitigation action. Decisions of action are based on threats to human or animal populations, contamination of drinking water supplies or sensitive ecosystems, high levels of hazardous substances in soils, weather conditions that may cause migration or release of hazardous substances, the threat of fire or

---

SIDEBAR 7-11   What Is Included in the National Response Plan and the Road Ahead

The initial version of the National Response Plan (NRP) sets forth the conceptual structure, key tenets, roles and responsibilities, and main principles of the NRP and the National Incident Management system (NIMS). The final version of the NRP, in conjunction with the NIMS, will:

1. Integrate federal government domestic incident awareness, prevention, preparedness, response, and recovery plans into one all-discipline, all-hazards plan

2. Describe the structure and mechanisms for providing national-level policy guidance and operational direction for federal support to state and local incident management and for exercising direct federal authorities and responsibilities, as appropriate

3. Include protocols for operating under different threats or threat levels

4. Incorporate existing federal emergency and incident management plans (with appropriate modifications and revisions) either as integrated components of the NRP or as supporting operational plans

5. Incorporate additional operational plans or annexes, as appropriate, including public affairs and intergovernmental communications

6. Include a consistent approach to reporting incidents, providing assessments, and making recommendations to the president, the secretary of Homeland Security, and the Homeland Security Council

7. Include rigorous requirements for continuous improvements arising from tests, exercises,

Sidebar 7-11 continues

explosion, or other significant factors affecting the health or welfare of the public or the environment.

THE NATIONAL RESPONSE PLAN

The overview presented in the previous sections provides an indication of the complexity of existing federal plans that are to be merged into the new NRP. The overview presented in the previous sections provides an indication of the complexity of existing Federal plans that are to be merged into the new NRP. The NRP's final draft has been published and is currently under review by the participating Departments and agencies. The section that follows will discuss changes reflected in the draft.

The NRP calls for a change in purpose; scope; planning assumptions and considerations; definition of the life cycle of incident management activities; organization; and concept of operation for events involving a Federal response. Each of these topics is covered as separate sections.

Purpose and Scope

The purpose of the NRP is to provide the nation with a unified, single, comprehensive approach to deal with domestic incidents. The NRP integrates all activities through the "life cycle" of incident management and creates a unique plan to be used in all the possible incident scenarios. It emphasizes coordination between all government levels—local, state, and federal—and cooperation with the private and public sectors. The plan ensures that the federal government works effectively and efficiently with state and local agencies to prevent, prepare for, respond to, and recover from domestic incidents by establishing a common NIMS to be used at all levels. [Source: NRP] (Sidebar 7-11)

Application

The NRP will apply to all domestic incidents occurring within the Unite States. Such incidents may be:

a. An "emergency" or "major disaster"
b. A threat or act of "terrorism" that the secretary, in consultation with the attorney general, determines is of sufficient magnitude to warrant implementation of this plan
c. Any other occasion or instance in which one or more of the following conditions or thresholds applies: (1) A federal department or agency acting under its own authority has requested the assistance of the secretary; (2) the resources of state and local authorities are overwhelmed and federal assistance has been requested by the appropriate state and

---

experience with incidents, and new information and technologies
8. Serve as the foundation for further development of detailed agency, regional, state, and local operational plans and procedures
9. Include guidelines for notification, coordination, and leadership and support of activities necessary for awareness, prevention, preparedness, response, and recovery related to domestic incidents, as well as for the dissemination of emergency public information
10. Acknowledge the unique nature of each incident, the capabilities of local jurisdictions, and the actions necessary to prevent or to mitigate a specific threat or incident
11. Recognize the responsibilities of federal departments and agencies to carry out their responsibilities under the law
12. Illustrate ways in which federal, state, and local governments, with the support of the private sector and the American public, can most effectively unify and synchronize their efforts to prevent or respond to domestic incidents

Source: National Response Plan, First Draft

local authorities; (3) more than one federal department or agency has become substantially involved in responding to the incident; or (4) the secretary has been directed to assume responsibility for managing the incident by the president.

A considerable change has occurred in the definition of who this plan applies to. The NRP applies to all federal departments and agencies; state and local authorities when requesting federal assistance; state and local authorities accepting federal preparedness assistance

---

SIDEBAR 7-12 NRP Assumptions

The NRP reflects certain key tenets as set forth in HSPD-5, namely, that the NRP be:

1. A single plan: The NRP integrates existing federal domestic awareness, prevention, preparedness, response, and recovery plans into one base plan, addressing functional areas common to most contingencies, with annexes to describe unique procedures required under special circumstances.
2. An "all hazards/all disciplines" plan: Current emergency plans are designed to deal with only certain types of contingencies. The NRP is a single plan that is flexible enough to accommodate all hazards and covering all of the disciplines required for conducting activities throughout the life cycle of an incident. Under the NRP, "hazards" refers to the full range of possible contingencies, including:
   a. Natural disasters, such as floods, earthquakes, hurricanes, tornadoes, droughts, and epidemics
   b. Accidents, such as chemical spills, industrial accidents, radiological or nuclear incidents, explosions, and utility outages
   c. Civil or political incidents, including mass migrations, the domestic effects of war, nation-state attacks, and unrest or disorder resulting from riots, public demonstrations, and strikes
   d. Terrorist or criminal incidents, including chemical, biological, radiological, nuclear, explosive, or cyber threats or attacks
   e. Significant events and designated special events requiring security, such as inaugurals,

State of the Union addresses, the Olympics, and international summit conferences

These contingencies are not mutually exclusive and may occur individually, simultaneously, or in combination.

3. A plan that emphasizes unity of effort among all levels of government: The NRP is a national plan that emphasizes unity of effort among all levels of government. Under this plan, federal, state, and local governments, along with private organizations and the American public, work as partners to manage domestic contingencies efficiently and effectively.
4. A plan that integrates crisis and consequence management: In keeping with the presidential directive, the NRP will "treat crisis management and consequence management as a single, integrated function, rather than as two separate functions."
5. A plan that places the same emphasis on awareness, prevention, and preparedness as traditionally has been placed on response and recovery. Traditionally, response plans have been exactly what their name implies—plans for responding to and recovering from an incident or contingency. In the aftermath of September 11, 2001, however, preventing terrorism and reducing our nation's vulnerabilities through preparedness have become top priorities. The NRP sets forth a new concept of a "response" plan by covering five domains: awareness, prevention, preparedness, response, and recovery.

Source: National Response Plan

through grants, contracts, or other activities beginning in FY 2005; and private and nongovernmental entities partnering with the federal government in relation to domestic incident management activities. Sidebar 7-12 shows the assumptions used to make the plan.

"Life Cycle" of Incident Management Activities

The NRP's definition is different from the classic mitigation-preparedness-response-recovery used in the FRP. It can be best described as containing five domains within which domestic incident management activities occur: awareness, prevention, preparedness, response, and recovery.

- **Awareness**

"Awareness" refers to the continual process of collecting, analyzing, and disseminating intelligence, information, and knowledge to allow organizations and individuals to anticipate requirements and to react effectively.

- **Prevention**

"Prevention" refers to actions taken to avoid an incident, to intervene to stop an incident from occurring, or to mitigate an incident's effects.

- **Preparedness**

"Preparedness" refers to the activities necessary to build and sustain performance across all of the other domains.

- **Response**

"Response" refers to the activities necessary to address the immediate and short-term effects of an incident, which focus primarily on the actions necessary to save lives, to protect property, and to meet basic human needs.

- **Recovery**

"Recovery" refers to those actions necessary to restore the community back to normal and to bring the perpetrators of an intentional incident to justice.

Source: National Response Plan

Organization

As described in the organization section of the plan,

The NRP is a base plan that provides the nation with a comprehensive approach to managing all domestic contingencies. When fully developed, the NRP will not be an umbrella for existing federal incident management plans. Rather, it will build upon or incorporate what is best in the current plans of federal, state, and local agencies, as well as those of private voluntary organizations, nongovernmental organizations, and the private sector.

The essential elements of the NRP are shown in Sidebar 7-13.

These essential differences stand out in the concept of operations:

- The NRP indicates incident management operations in "national" terms instead of the usual local-state-federal component division
- The secretary of DHS has a critical role in integrating the operations of various authorities and agencies into a single system
- The use of the NIMS across all levels of government, a single headquarters-level coordination structure, a single framework for preventing and responding to domestic incidents as part of the new national incident management operation system
- NRP partners are all the federal agencies

The plan also redefines entirely the functional areas (or ESF Emergency Support Functions in the FRP). A brief description of the ten functional areas with their respective Principal Function Area (PFA) is given in Sidebar 7-14.

The plan delegates the responsibility for developing the annex of each function area to the respective PFA. The final draft has been sent out to the Federal Departments and Agencies concerned and those should return the plan with their added Functional Annex by August 1, 2004.

Besides the functional areas, the NRP also defines the concept of operations for each of the five domestic incident categories it identifies. This task is necessary, as these categories were previously coordinated using different federal plans (e.g., FRP, NCP), and the coordinating structures used in those plans will be used until the NRP is fully implemented.

Tables 7-5 through 7-8 summarize the PFA for each task in the identified domestic incident as announced in the NRP. The charts contain the four roles defined for the secretary as well.

Sidebar 7-15 shows the calendar ahead for DHS to develop the NRP.

The development timeline for DHS concerning the NRP and the NIMS is depicted in Sidebar 7-16.

Finally, Table 7-10 outlines the response layers according to the different federal emergency plans explained in this section.

SIDEBAR 7-13   Elements of the NRP

1. The Roles and Responsibilities section describes the activities of local, state, and federal authorities and of nongovernmental organizations and the private sector in managing domestic contingencies. A key element in the NRP is the distinction between the ongoing responsibilities of the secretary of Homeland Security and the responsibilities that the secretary assigns to primary federal agencies (PFAs) and supporting agencies (SAs) in the context of a given contingency.

2. The Concept of Operations section describes the principal aspects of the domestic incident management system and makes initial assignments to federal agencies regarding their responsibilities with respect to each of the functional areas and domains that describe the life cycle of an incident. This section also describes how domestic incidents will be managed, using the procedures outlined in this plan in concert with the procedures and coordinating structures contained in existing federal plans, until full implementation of the approved NRP.

3. The Preliminary Framework for the NIMS section provides a description of elements in the NIMS.

4. The Plan for Full Development and Implementation of the NRP section describes the movement from the initial NRP through the development of the NIMS to a fully developed NRP. The NRP is a living document that will constantly be revised in response to new information, new situations, new technology, lessons learned, and refined procedures.

5. Annexes to the NRP will contain supplemental information relevant to selected portions of the NRP. They will describe each of the life cycle domains; special functions managed at the DHS-level in support of all contingencies; special coordination mechanisms pertaining to DHS's engagement with DOJ (including the FBI), DoD, and the Department of State; and the details of the NIMS.

6. Functional area plans will be developed for each functional area by the PFA, in coordination with all of the SAs involved in the functional area. These plans will describe the tasks that will be performed within the functional area, identify potential assignments for each SA, and define the coordination mechanisms by which functional area assessments will be conducted and by which support to awareness, prevention, preparedness, response, and recovery activities will be coordinated.

Source: National Response Plan

RECOVERY

The recovery function is not easy to classify; it often begins in the initial hours and days following a disaster event and can continue for months and in some cases years, depending on the severity of the event. Unlike the response function, where all efforts have a singular focus, the recovery function or process is characterized by a complex set of issues and decisions that must be made by individuals and communities. Those are as follows: actions relative to rebuilding homes, replacing property, resuming

---

SIDEBAR 7-14 NRP Functional Areas

1. Information, Intelligence, and Warning, DHS-IAIP: Intelligence-gathering, information-sharing, and warning system that can detect activities so that appropriate and effective preemptive, preventive, and protective action can be taken

2. International Coordination, Department of State: Activities that relate to cooperative efforts with foreign counterparts on security measures, counterterrorism activities, and other topics relating to incident management, preparedness, and response

3. Terrorism Preparedness, DHS-BTS: A comprehensive national program that encompasses all homeland security systems that plan organizational, operational, and technical measures to achieve full and sustainable performance of various activities

4. Domestic Counterterrorism, DOJ-FBI: The system under which federal, state, and local law enforcement authorities will assign priority to preventing and interdicting terrorist activity within the United States while they continue to carry out their traditional missions to investigate and to prosecute criminal activity

5. Border and Transportation Security, DHS-BTS: Activities that promote the efficient and reliable flow of people, goods, and services across borders, while preventing terrorists from using transportation conveyances or systems to deliver implements of destruction

6. Infrastructure Protection, DHS-IAIP: Activities that improve the protection of the individual pieces and interconnecting systems that makes up our nation's critical infrastructure

7. Homeland Defense, DoD: The protection of U.S. territory, the domestic population, and critical infrastructures against military attacks emanating from outside the United States

8. Emergency Management, DHS-EPR: A comprehensive process to bring together and to coordinate mitigation, preparedness, response, and recovery resources and activities into a comprehensive, all-hazards emergency management system

9. Law Enforcement, DOJ: Traditional law enforcement functions to ensure public safety and security and to bring perpetrators to justice

10. CBRNE Hazard Management, DHS-EPR: Technical structures and systems that prepare for and respond to chemical, biological, radiological, nuclear, and explosive incidents regardless of the cause

Source: National Response Plan

employment, restoring businesses, and permanently repairing and rebuilding infrastructure.

The recovery function has remained essentially the same as it was before the establishment of DHS. Only minor changes affecting the nomenclature and classification of the available assistance, as well as some relief programs and grants, have occurred.

Because the recovery function has such long-lasting impacts and usually high costs, the participants in the process are numerous. They include all levels of government, the business community, political leadership, community activists, and individuals. The major players and programs will be listed here and changes, if any, will be described.

To begin with are some quick facts about recovery (Sidebar 7-17).

Given that the federal government plays the largest role in providing the technical and financial support for recovery, the chapter will focus on the federal role. It will discuss the structure and the various programs available to assist individuals and communities in the postdisaster environment and will briefly reference the various national voluntary organizations that provide some assistance for recovery.

TABLE 7-5   **Natural Disasters: Plan to Be Used in the Interim Federal Response Plan**

Natural disasters					
Secretary's roles	Awareness	Prevention	Preparedness	Response	Recovery
Direction and planning					
Communications and information training and continuous improvement					
Incident management					
Functional areas	Awareness	Prevention	Preparedness	Response	Recovery
Information/intelligence warning	DHS-IAIP	DHS-IAIP	DHS-IAIP	DHS-IAIP	DHS-IAIP
International coordination	DOS		DOS	DOS	DOS
Terrorism preparedness					
Domestic counterterrorism					
Border and transportation security					
Infrastructure protection	DHS-IAIP	DHS-IAIP	DHS-IAIP		
Homeland defense				DoD	DoD
Emergency management			DHS-FEMA	DHS-FEMA	DHS-FEMA
Law enforcement				DOJ	DOJ
CBRNE hazard	DHS-FEMA		DHS-FEMA	DHS-FEMA	DHS-FEMA

TABLE 7-6 Accidents: Plan to Be Used in the Interim: National Contingency Plan

Accidents					
Secretary's roles	Awareness	Prevention	Preparedness	Response	Recovery
Direction and planning					
Communications and information					
Training and continuous improvement					
Incident management					
Functional areas	Awareness	Prevention	Preparedness	Response	Recovery
Information/intelligence warning	DHS-IAIP	DHS-IAIP	DHS-IAIP	DHS-IAIP	DHS-IAIP
International coordination	DOS				
Terrorism preparedness					
Domestic counterterrorism					
Border and transportation security		DHS-BTS	DHS-BTS		
Infrastructure protection	DHS-IAIP	DHS-IAIP	DHS-IAIP		
Homeland defense				DoD	
Emergency management	DHS-FEMA		DHS-FEMA	DHS-FEMA	DHS-FEMA
Law enforcement	DOJ		DOJ	DOJ	
CBRNE hazard	DHS-FEMA			DHS-FEMA	DHS-FEMA

TABLE 7-7 Civil or Political Incidents: Plan to Be Used in the Interim: Mass Migration Emergency Plan (Distant Shore)

Civil or political incidents					
Secretary's roles	Awareness	Prevention	Preparedness	Response	Recovery
Direction and planning					
Communications and information					
Training and continuous improvement					
Incident management					
Functional areas	Awareness	Prevention	Preparedness	Response	Recovery
Information/intelligence warning	DHS-IAIP	DHS-IAIP	DHS-IAIP	DIIS-IAIP	DHS-IAIP

(continues)

TABLE 7-7 (*continued*)

Civil or political incidents					
International coordination	DOS	DOS	DOS	DOS	DOS
Terrorism preparedness					
Domestic counterterrorism					
Border and transportation security		DHS-BTS	DHS-BTS		
Infrastructure protection	DHS-IAIP	DHS-IAIP	DHS-IAIP		
Homeland defense	DoD	DoD	DoD	DoD	
Emergency management			DHS-FEMA	DHS-FEMA	DHS-FEMA
Law enforcement	DOJ	DOJ	DOJ	DOJ	
CBRNE hazard					

TABLE 7-8 Terrorist or Criminal Incidents: Plan to Be Used in the Interim: Domestic Terrorism Concept of Operations Plan

Terrorist or criminal incidents					
Secretary's roles	Awareness	Prevention	Preparedness	Response	Recovery
Direction and planning					
Communications and information					
Training and continuous improvement					
Incident management					
Functional areas	Awareness	Prevention	Preparedness	Response	Recovery
Information/intelligence warning	DOJ-FBI	DOJ-FBI	DOJ-FBI	DOJ-FBI	DOJ-FBI
International coordination	DOS	DOS	DOS	DOS	DOS
Terrorism preparedness			DHS-BTS		
Domestic counterterrorism	DOJ-FBI	DOJ-FBI	DOJ-FBI	DOJ-FBI	DOJ-FBI
Border and transportation security	DHS-BTS	DHS-BTS	DHS-BTS	DHS-BTS	DHS-BTS
Infrastructure protection	DHS-IAIP	DHS-IAIP	DHS-IAIP		
Homeland defense	DoD	DoD	DoD	DoD	
Emergency management			DHS-FEMA	DHS-FEMA	DHS-FEMA
Law enforcement				DOJ	DOJ
CBRNE hazard	DHS-FEMA	DHS-FEMA	DHS-FEMA	DHS-FEMA	DHS-FEMA

TABLE 7-9 Significant Events and Designated Special Events

Significant events and designated special events

Secretary's roles	Awareness	Prevention	Preparedness	Response	
Recovery					
Direction and planning					
Communications and information					
Training and continuous improvement					
Incident management					
Functional areas	Awareness	Prevention	Preparedness	Response	Recovery
Information/intelligence warning	DHS-IAIP	DHS-IAIP	DHS-IAIP	DHS-IAIP	DHS-IAIP
International coordination	DOS	DOS	DOS	DOS	DOS
Terrorism preparedness			DHS-BTS		
Domestic counterterrorism	DOJ-FBI	DOJ-FBI	DOJ-FBI	DOJ-FBI	
Border and transportation security	DHS-BTS	DHS-BTS	DHS-BTS		
Infrastructure protection	DHS-IAIP	DHS-IAIP	DHS-IAIP		
Homeland defense	DoD	DoD	DoD		
Emergency management			DHS-FEMA	DHS-FEMA	DHS-FEMA
Law enforcement	DOJ	DOJ	DOJ	DOJ	
CBRNE Hazard	DHS-FEMA	DHS-FEMA	DHS-FEMA	DHS-FEMA	DHS-FEMA

SIDEBAR 7-15 Tasks Ahead for the NRP

Until the NRP and NIMS are fully developed and implemented, several tasks have to be done during the interim period. These are as follows:

The process for developing an addendum for each of the existing federal interagency plans. This will be led by the respective PFA:

1. Federal Response Plan (FRP): DHS-EPR
2. Domestic Terrorism Concept of Operations Plan (CONPLAN): DOJ (FBI)
3. Federal Radiological Emergency Response Plan (FRERP): DHS-EPR
4. Mass Migration Emergency Plan (Distant Shore): DHS-BTS
5. National Oil Spill and Hazardous Substances Pollution Contingency Plan (NCP): DHS-EPR

Development of NRP Annexes as outlined below:

1. Awareness: DHS-IAIP
2. Prevention: DHS-IAIP
3. Preparedness: DHS-BTS
4. Response: DHS-EPR
5. Recovery: DHS-EPR
6. Public Affairs: DHS-Public Affairs
7. Congressional Relations: DHS-Legislative Affairs
8. Private Sector Liaison: DHS-OPSL
9. State/Local Liaison: DHS-OSLGC
10. Financial Management: DHS-MGT
11. Special Coordination Mechanisms: Task Force Work Group
12. National Incident Management System (NIMS): Task Force Work Group

Source: FEMA, National Response Plan

The Federal Response Plan for Disaster Recovery Operations

Besides addressing the response function, the FRP includes the structure for organizing, coordinating, and mobilizing federal resources for disaster recovery. The Stafford Act assigns to FEMA the principal coordination function—the interactive process by which multiple federal assistance programs are reviewed, initiated, implemented, and delivered to address the unique needs of a particular disaster area.

The fundamental assumption in the FRP is that recovery is a cooperative effort among federal, state, local, voluntary agencies, and the private sector in partnership. A federal coordinating officer (FCO) is appointed by the DHS secretary on behalf of the president and coordinates federal activities from the Disaster Field Office (DFO). The FCO works in partnership with the state coordinating officer (SCO), who is named by the governor. In conjunction with the SCO, the FCO determines the need for Disaster Recovery Centers (DRCs) in the disaster area. State and federal agencies staff the DRCs with knowledgeable officials who provide recovery program information, advice, counseling, and technical assistance. Voluntary organizations are encouraged to provide leadership and coordinate with federal, state, and local governments in recovery planning and program implementation.

The practical work of implementing the recovery process occurs at the DRCs. Two organizational structures, or branches, divide the recovery assistance

---

SIDEBAR 7-16   NRP Development Timeline

Three periods are defined: the Transitional Operational Capability (TOC) from March 2003 to March 2004; the Initial Operating Capability (IOC) from March 2004 to January 2005; and the Full Operating Capability (FOC) after January 2005.

During the first phase (all initial deadlines have been postponed by one month):

- By April 1, 2003, DHS has to come up with an initial version of the NRP, including a plan for its full development and implementation.
- By June 1, 2003, the DHS has to develop a "…national system of standards, guidelines and protocols to implement the NIMS" (HSPD-5).
- By June 1, 2003, each department and agency will revise the existing plans according to the first version of the NRP.
- By August 1, 2003, each department and agency will submit a plan on how to adopt and implement the NIMS.

- By September 1, 2003, DHS will revise the existing plans to fully implement the NRP.
- The first draft of the NRP should be available by December 2003, and the second by March 2004.

During the second phase:

- The third draft of the NRP should be available by June 2004.
- By October 1, 2004, each department and agency will "make adoption of NIMS a requirement . . . for providing federal preparedness assistance."

During the third phase:

- The final version of the NRP should be available by January 2005, and the system should be fully functional.

Source: DHS

TABLE 7-10   **Response Layers**

Name of plan/level	NCP	FRERP	CONPLAN	FRP	NRP
	Lead agency	Lead agency	Lead agency	FEMA	PFA/SFA
National	NRT	LFA/ HQ EOC	CDRG + SIOC	CDRG EST	NJIC/ NEPPC
Regional	RRT	ROC	NRT	RISC ROC	REOC/ SEOC RJIC/ REPPC
Local	AC (FOSC)	JOC, FRMAC (LFA/OSC)	JOC	DFO (FCO)	JOC JIC/ LEPPC

AC (FOSC): Federal on-scene coordinator
CDRG: Catastrophic disaster response group
DFO: Disaster field office
EST: Emergency support team
FRMAC: Federal Radiological Monitoring and Assessing Center
HQ EOC: Headquarters Emergency Operation Center
JIC: Joint Information Center
JOC: Joint Operation Center
LEPPC: Local Emergency Prevention and Preparedness Council
LFA/OSC: Lead Federal Agency/On Scene Coordinator
NEPPC: National Emergency Prevention and Preparedness Council
NJIC: National Joint Information Center
NRT: National Response Team
PFA: Primary Federal Agency
REOC: Regional Emergency Operation Center
REPPC: Regional Emergency Prevention and Preparedness Council
RISC: Regional Interagency Steering Committee
RJIC: Regional Joint Information Center
ROC: Regional Operation Center
RRT: Regional Response Team
SEOC: State Emergency Operation Center
SFA: Support Federal Agency
SIOC: Strategic Information and Operations Center

functions. These branches assess state and local recovery needs at the outset of the disaster and relevant time frames for program delivery. The Human Services branch coordinates assistance programs to help individuals, families, and businesses meet basic needs and return to self-sufficiency. It is responsible for the donations management function. The Infrastructure Support branch coordinates assistance programs to aid state and local governments and eligible private nonprofit organizations to repair or replace damaged public facilities. The two branches assist in identifying appropriate agency assistance programs to meet applicant needs, synchronizing assistance delivery and encouraging incorporation of mitigation measures where possible. In addition to the work of the DRC's, applicant briefings are conducted for local government officials and certain private non-profit organizations to inform them of available recovery assistance and how to apply.

Federal disaster assistance available under a major disaster falls into three general categories: individual assistance, public assistance, and hazard mitigation assistance. Individual assistance is aid to individuals, families, and business owners. Public assistance is aid to public and certain private nonprofit entities for emergency services and the repair or replacement of disaster-damaged public facilities. Hazard mitigation assistance is funding available for measures designed to reduce future losses to public and private property. A detailed description of the first two types of assistance follows, with changes that have occurred in individual assistance.

FEMA's INDIVIDUAL ASSISTANCE RECOVERY PROGRAMS

The "Guide to the Disaster Declaration Process," prepared by FEMA, describes the available programs as follows:

SIDEBAR 7-17   Quick Facts on Recovery

- In the period of 1990 to 1999, FEMA spent more than $25.4 billion for declared disasters and emergencies compared to $3.9 billion in current dollars for 1980–89.
- For the 1990 to 1999 periods, more than $6.3 billion was provided in grants for temporary housing, home repairs, and other disaster-related needs for individuals and families. An additional $14.8 billion went to states and local governments for clean-up and restoration projects, including more than $1.37 billion for mission-assigned work undertaken by other federal agencies.
- In the 1990s, a total of 88 declarations were issued for hurricanes and typhoons, for which FEMA obligated more than $7.78 billion for disaster costs. The most costly to FEMA was Hurricane Georges in 1998, followed closely by Hurricane Andrew in 1992.
- The most frequently declared disaster type was flooding resulting from severe storms, with more than $7.3 billion committed by FEMA for response and recovery costs. The most costly were the Midwest floods in 1993 and the Red River Valley Floods in 1997.
- By November 2002, FEMA had given a total of $306,102,000 in disaster recovery funding for the victims of September 11 attacks. The distribution of different programs is as follows:

  – Temporary home housing: Mortgage and Rental Assistance ($76,275,000), Minimal Home Repair ($1,450,000), Transient Accommodations ($1,225,000), Rental Assistance ($26,150,000)
  – Individual Family Grants ($25,400,000)
  – Crisis Counseling Assistance and Training Program ($162,400,000)
  – Unemployment Assistance ($13,200,000)
  – Legal Services ($2,000)

Source: FEMA

Individual assistance programs are oriented to individuals, families, and small businesses, and the programs include temporary housing assistance, individual and family grants, disaster unemployment assistance, legal services, and crisis counseling. The disaster victim must first register for assistance and establish eligibility. Three national centers provide centralized disaster application services for disaster victims. FEMA's National Processing Service Centers (NPSCs) are located in Denton, Texas; Berryville, Virginia; and Hyattsville, Maryland.

Disaster Housing Program

The Disaster Housing Program ensures that people whose homes are damaged by disaster have a safe place to live until repairs can be completed. These programs are designed to provide funds for expenses that are not covered by insurance and are available to homeowners and renters who are legal residents of the United States and who were displaced by the disaster.

- Lodging expenses reimbursement provides a check for reimbursement for the cost of short-term lodging, such as hotel rooms, incurred because of damage to a home or an official-imposed prohibition against returning to a home.
- Emergency minimal repair assistance provides a check to help repair a home to a habitable condition.
- Temporary rental assistance provides a check to rent a place for the predisaster household to live.
- Mortgage and rental assistance provides a check to pay the rent or mortgage to prevent evictions or foreclosure. In order to qualify, the applicant must be living in the same house before and after the disaster and have a documented disaster-related financial hardship that can be verified by DHS.

FIGURE 7-11 New York, NY, October 30, 2001—FEMA/NY State Disaster Field Office personnel meet to coordinate federal, state, and local disaster assistance programs. Photo by Andrea Booher/FEMA News Photo.

Individual and Family Grants Program

The Individual and Family Grant (IFG) program provides funds for the necessary expenses and serious needs of disaster victims that cannot be met through insurance or other forms of disaster assistance. The state administers the program and pays 25 percent of the grant amount, and the federal government provides the remaining 75 percent. The state also receives up to 5 percent of the federal share of the program for administrative costs. The maximum amount of a grant for each family or individual in fiscal year 2002 is $14,800 and the amount is adjusted annually for inflation.

The average grant, though, tends to be in the range of $2,000 to $4,000. Among the needs that can be met are housing, personal property, medical, dental, funeral, transportation, and required flood insurance premiums. Before an applicant can receive assistance for housing and personal property, the individual may be required to apply to the U.S. Small Business Administration (SBA) for a disaster loan.

Changes in the Individual Assistance Recovery Programs

Disaster Housing Assistance and the IFG program have been repealed and combined into one grant program, the Individuals and Households Program (IHP), under DMA 2000. This new program falls under the federal public benefit standard. It is a combined DHS/EPR and state program. Accordingly, the types of assistance provided under the IHP are given in the "Guide to the Disaster Declaration Process" revised by DHS as follows:

- Temporary housing: Homeowners and renters receive funds to rent a different place to live or a temporary housing unit when rental properties are not available.
- Repair: Homeowners receive grants to repair damage from the disaster that is not covered by insurance. The goal is to make the damaged home safe and sanitary.
- Replacement: Under rare conditions, homeowners receive limited funds to replace their disaster-damaged home.
- Permanent housing construction: Homeowners and renters receive direct assistance or a grant for the construction of a new home. This type of assistance occurs only in very unusual situations, in insular areas, or remote locations specified by FEMA where no other type of housing is possible.
- Other Needs Assistance (ONA): Applicants receive grants for necessary and serious needs caused by the disaster. This includes medical, dental, funeral, personal property, transportation, moving and storage, and other expenses that FEMA approves. The homeowner may need to apply for a SBA loan before receiving assistance.

Another change is that the MRA has been eliminated by the Disaster Mitigation Act of 2000 amendments to the Stafford Act that repealed the MRA program as a component of FEMA's Temporary Housing Assistance for disasters declared on or after May 1, 2002. FEMA received an extension from Congress and has made this effective for all disasters declared on or after October 15, 2002. DMA 2000 also establishes a $25,000 cap on the Individuals and Households Program. These new limitations raise serious issues for addressing economic losses and financial hardships suffered by victims of events similar to the September 11 terrorist attacks. Congressional consideration may be warranted to better position FEMA to address economic issues in future acts of terrorism. (Source: FEMA 2001)

All other federal programs listed here are as provided in the revised "Guide to the Disaster Declaration Process" of DHS.

Small Business Administration Disaster Loans

The SBA can provide three types of disaster loans to qualified homeowners and businesses to repair or replace homes, personal property, or businesses that sustained damages not covered by insurance.

- Home disaster loans provide funds to homeowners and renters to repair or replace disaster-related damages to home or personal property.
- Business physical disaster loans provide funds to business owners to repair or replace disaster-damaged property, including inventory, and supplies.
- Economic injury loans provide capital to small businesses and to small agricultural cooperatives to assist them through the disaster recovery period.

A significant change appears to have occurred relative to the National Flood Insurance program (NFIP). Previously, IFG recipients who live in a Special Flood Hazard Area and receive assistance as a result of flood damages to their home and/or personal property will be provided flood insurance coverage for three years under the National Flood Insurance Program's group flood insurance policy.

The 3-year coverage is part of the grant award. The flood insurance must be kept active for the individual to be eligible to receive federal assistance for any future flood-related losses.

However, with the repeal of the IFG program, nothing has been included to continue the provision of insurance.

Disaster Unemployment Assistance

The Disaster Unemployment Assistance (DUA) program provides unemployment benefits and reemployment services to individuals who have become unemployed because of major disasters and who are not eligible for disaster benefits under regular unemployment insurance programs.

Legal Services

The Young Lawyer's Division of the American Bar Association, through an agreement with FEMA, provides free legal assistance to low-income disaster victims. The assistance that the participating lawyers provide is for insurance claims; counseling on landlord/tenant problems; assistance in consumer protection matters, remedies and procedures; and replacement of wills and other important legal documents destroyed in a major disaster. This assistance is intended for individuals who are unable to secure legal services adequate to meet their needs as a consequence of a major disaster.

Special Tax Considerations

Taxpayers who have sustained a casualty loss from a declared disaster may deduct that loss on the federal income tax return for the year in which the casualty occurred or through an immediate amendment to the previous year's return. Businesses may file claims with the Bureau of Alcohol, Tobacco, and Firearms for payment of federal excise taxes paid on alcoholic beverages or tobacco products lost, rendered unmar-

ketable, or condemned by a duly authorized official under various circumstances, including cases in which a major disaster has been declared by the president.

Crisis Counseling

The Crisis Counseling Assistance and Training program is designed to provide short-term crisis counseling services to people affected by a presidentially declared disaster. The purpose of the crisis counseling is to help relieve any grieving, stress, or mental health problems caused or aggravated by the disaster or its aftermath. These short-term services are provided by FEMA as supplemental funds granted to state and local mental health agencies. The American Red Cross, the Salvation Army, and other voluntary agencies, as well as churches and synagogues, also offer crisis-counseling services.

Cora Brown Fund

Cora C. Brown of Kansas City, Missouri, died in 1977 and left a portion of her estate to the United States to be used as a special fund solely for the relief of human suffering caused by natural disasters. The funds are used to assist surviving victims of presidentially declared major disasters for disaster-related needs that have not or will not be met by government agencies or other organizations.

FEMA's Public Assistance Grant Program

FEMA, under the authority of the Stafford Act, administers the Public Assistance Grant program. The Public Assistance Grant program provides federal assistance to state and local governments and to certain private nonprofit (PNP) organizations. These grants allow them to recover from the impact of disasters and to implement mitigation measures to reduce the impacts from future disasters. The grants are aimed at governments and organizations with the final goal to help a community and its citizens recover from devastating major disasters. The federal share of assistance is not less than 75 percent of the eligible cost for emergency measures and permanent restoration. The state determines how the nonfederal share is split with the applicants.

Eligible applicants include the states, local governments and any other political subdivision of the state, native American tribes, Alaska native villages, and certain PNP organizations. Eligible PNP facilities include educational, utility, irrigation, emergency, medical, rehabilitation, temporary or permanent custodial care facilities, and other PNP facilities that are open to the public and provide essential services of a governmental nature to the general public. The work must be required as the result of the disaster, be located within the designated disaster area, and be the legal responsibility of the applicant. PNPs that provide critical services such as power, water, sewer, wastewater treatment, communications, or emergency medical care may apply directly to FEMA for a disaster grant. All other PNPs must first apply to the SBA for a disaster loan. If the loan is declined or does not cover all eligible damages, the applicant may reapply for FEMA assistance.

Work that is eligible for supplemental federal disaster grant assistance is classified as either emergency work or permanent work.

- Emergency work includes debris removal from public roads and rights-of-way, as well as from private property when determined to be in the public interest. This may also include protective measures performed to eliminate or reduce immediate threats to the public.
- Permanent work is defined as work that is required to restore an eligible damaged facility to its predisaster design. This effort can range from minor repairs to replacement. Some categories for permanent work include roads, bridges, water control facilities, buildings, utility distribution systems, public parks, and recreational facilities. Under extenuating circumstances the deadlines for emergency and permanent work may be extended.

FIGURE 7-12   New York, NY, October 20, 2001—Disaster Field Office staff continue to work with other agencies operating near Ground Zero to provide information about disaster assistance programs. Photo by Andrea Booher/FEMA News Photo.

As soon as possible after the disaster declaration, the state, assisted by DHS/EPR, conducts the applicant briefings for state, local, and PNP officials to inform them of the assistance available and how to apply for it. A Request for Public Assistance form must be filed with the state within 30 days after the area is designated eligible for assistance. A combined federal/state/local team works together to design and deliver the appropriate recovery assistance for the communities. In determining the federal costs for the projects, private or public insurance can play a major role. For insurable buildings within special flood hazard areas (SFHA) that are damaged by floods, the disaster assistance is reduced by the amount of insurance settlement that would have been received had the building and its contents been fully covered by a standard National Flood Insurance Program policy. For structures located outside of a SFHA, the amount is reduced by the actual or anticipated insurance proceeds.

In 1998 FEMA redesigned the Public Assistance program to provide money to applicants more quickly and to make the application process easier. The redesigned program was approved for implementation on disasters declared after October 1, 1998. This redesigned program placed new emphasis on people, policy, process, and performance. The focus of the program was also modified to provide a higher level of customer service for disaster recovery applicants and to change the role of FEMA from inspection and enforcement to an advisory and supportive role.

Other Federal Agency Disaster Recovery Funding

Other federal agencies have programs that contribute to social and economic recovery. Most of these additional programs are triggered by a presidential declaration of a major disaster or emergency under the Stafford Act. However, The secretary of Agriculture and the administrator of the Small Business Administration have specific authority relevant to their constituencies to declare a disaster and provide disaster recovery assistance. All of the agencies are part of the structure of the Federal Response Plan (FRP). This section provides a complete list of all disaster recovery programs available after a disaster declaration. Chapter Appendix 7.11 lists the recovery programs available as they are listed in the revised Federal Response Plan (FRP January 2003).

CONCLUSION

The motives behind the establishment of the Department of Homeland Security are almost as numerous as the number of agencies it involved: politics, power, public relations, or a real need to improve the federal response and recovery systems because of the new spectrum of threats made apparent by the September 11 attacks. For whatever reason or combination of reasons, a system that had demonstrated its operational capabilities in both natural disasters and a domestic terrorism event in Oklahoma City is undergoing significant change. As a result of the integration of different agencies and the need for new procedural system to operate together, the National Response Plan (NRP) has been developed with the National Incident Management System (NIMS). These two documents are now the references and guidelines that determine how the nation's first responders and agencies involved in response operate. The extensive funding provided by the government through DHS has allowed the initiation of training and equipping of the Nation's first responders and this effort will continue for the foreseeable future in order to build a strong, uniform and highly capable response force.

The effort to include citizens and the private sector as active partners is commendable. Programs developed under the Citizen Corps Councils give an opportunity to build strong communities. However, they have been poorly supported by the political leadership and are underfunded. Further collaboration with the business sector will allow for enhanced preparedness and protection of the critical infrastructure and provide a better understanding of its vulnerabilities and how to respond if it is attacked.

As a final point, it is essential to bear in mind that the massive integration of many agencies into one has its drawbacks: the independency is compromised and the overall redundancy of the system decreases. The NRP and NIMS define how different agencies operate together but it should not jeopardize or change the agencies' own integrity and mission. Although redundancy is an attribute that all organizations try to get rid of, it is also what often saves the day during a crisis situation. 'Too efficient' systems with minimal backup, no duplication of function and low flexibility/adaptability have shown to be more vulnerable to unexpected situation; to fail in a worse manner and to be less agile to respond to and deal with the emergency. Thus, an excessive integration to lessen redundancy can cause the involved agencies to depend on each other rather than empower each other. And this might make the way for a catastrophic chain reaction of failure to occur in certain conditions.

CASE STUDY NO. 1
The East Coast Blackout

On August 14, 2003, an estimated 50 million people were affected in what is described as the worst blackout in history. The power went out in the northeastern United States and parts of Canada, affecting large metropolitan areas such as New York, Detroit, Cleveland, Toronto, and Ottawa.

It lasted 29 hours in most places, and research regarding the exact cause for the event continues. The massive blackout has, unfortunately, been described as a "probable" event that could occur again in the future because of the debilitating and degenerating interconnections in the relatively old systems and the overall conditions of the nation's power grid.

As a result of the blackout, the first major event both after the September 11 attacks and of its kind, people across the northeastern part of the country and Canada were plunged into confusion and chaos until authorities from federal and local levels assured them that it was not a terrorist attack. Through the affected regions, six airports (John F. Kennedy and La Guardia in New York, Newark in New Jersey, Cleveland in Ohio, and Toronto and Ottawa in Canada were closed) huge traffic jams occurred as traffic lights went off; subways were nonfunctional, four nuclear power plants were shut down in Ohio and New York State; at least 21 power plants shut down in the affected zone overall; and thousands of people were unable to go home and slept on city streets.

No federal disaster was declared as a result of the blackout, but still the event brought very important issues to light as it was the first emergency of its kind and scale after the establishment of DHS. In New York there were 60 serious fires, up from an average of 10 per night, but all appeared accidental. Approximately 10,000 police patrolled the streets, directing traffic and deterring looters. A total of 40,000 police officers and the entire fire department were mobilized in New York. The 80,000 emergency calls were twice the average. Some actions taken by the local governments include the following: In New York, authorities evacuated an

estimated 350,000 people from the subways within hours; in New Jersey, officials set up receptions centers to assist residents walking home from Manhattan; in Detroit, city officials turned three public schools into "cooling centers" for elderly residents and others in need of relief from the heat; in Ohio and Michigan, firefighters in areas that lost water tapped lakes, swimming pools, and other sources to make sure they had water to put out fires. From the military side, two Air Force F-16 jets were dispatched to patrol the skies between Washington and New York minutes after the power outage.

Some other high points concerning the general organization and response were as follows:

- Quick communications: Within minutes of the electricity shutdown, local authorities spoke with utility officials and informed the public via battery-operated TVs and radios that terrorism was not the reason, a measure that decreased people's panic and anxiety.
- Plans in place: All of the affected major cities had plans in place.
- Effective security: New Yorkers in particular noticed a dramatic increase in police patrols and that gave a sense of security to all residents.
- Reassuring leadership: Many mayors conveyed the message that they were in control of the situation.

On the other hand, the blackout produced some glitches and pointed out some weaknesses of the system:

- Raw sewage washed ashore in Cleveland and New York, where treatment plants failed.
- Detroit was slow in restoring safe drinking water.
- New York City's 911 emergency systems failed. Then the computer-aided dispatch system for its fire department and rescue squads crashed, and the department had to monitor its trucks and personnel manually.
- Detroit also lost its 911 system. The Motor City's government phone network collapsed, as did its brand-new Nextel cell phone system, which had been billed as capable of weathering a terrorist

attack. Homeland Security Secretary Tom Ridge could only talk with Detroit Mayor Kwame Kilpatrick using a consultant as intermediary.

- Some communication-sharing problems were made public when state-level homeland security officials complained that they felt out of the federal loop. On August 14, 40 of them were in Indianapolis for a conference, and the security chiefs first found out about the crisis from colleagues back home, not from the department, even though its No. 2 official for state outreach was attending the gathering.
- Cell phones failed as during September 11, and Senator Schumer blasted cell phone companies for failing to implement a plan that was supposed to give the cell phones of emergency personnel priority during an emergency.

As an aftermath, the federal government announced in August a $5 million payout to help New York state and local governments cover some costs of the blackout. However, the $5 million would not cover the estimated $10 million the city spent for emergency overtime during the outage—let alone business losses the city's controller estimated at $1 billion.

The lack of a presidential declaration limited the amount of money that could be authorized by DHS/EP&R/FEMA. In the absence of evidence of damages and physical devastation, such as destroyed homes or buildings, the hands of DHS officials were tied.

The blackout served to reinforce some of the recurring problems from September 11: poor communications capabilities, resource shortfalls at the local level, and problems with an aging national infrastructure. On the other hand, the quick response and public announcements correctly identifying the cause of the blackout contributed to keeping order, limiting crime, and reducing panic among citizens.

REVIEW QUESTIONS

1. According to your perspective, list the ten most important differences between the NRP and the FRP.
2. As of the publication period of this book, the Metropolitan Medical Response System (MMRS) looks very attractive to the DHS and its large scale implementation is on the table. Can you identify any shortcoming to this system? Do you see any potential obstacle for its implementation?
3. If you were an appointed local emergency manager, what do you think about the information provided in this chapter, what are the pros and cons for you in this emerging structure from a response perspective? Answer the same question from a regional emergency manager officer and a FEMA high level officer point of view.
4. Find an updated version of the National Incident Management System (NIMS) and compare its organization scheme to the ICS organization. Who is involved (personal title and agencies) in the picture, is there anyone left out?
5. The establishment of the Department of Homeland Security is seen by some scholars and experts as a "militarization" of the emergency management field. Do you agree with this view in terms of response? Explain why or why not.

REFERENCES

American Corporate Council Association http://www.acca.com/infopaks/homeland/legislativechart.pdf

American Patriot Friends Network http://www.apfn.org

ANSER Journal of Homeland Security http://www.homelandsecurity.org

Center for Arms Control and Non-Proliferation http://www.armscontrolcenter.org/terrorism/homeland%20security/UpdatedDHSAgencies.pdf

Center for Disease Control and Prevention http://www.cdc.gov

Department of Agriculture http://www.usda.gov

Department of Defense http://www.dod.gov

Department of Energy http://www.doe.gov

Department of Health and Human Services http://www.dhhs.gov

Department of Homeland Security http://www.dhs.gov

Department of Justice http://www.doj.gov

Domestic Terrorism Concept of Operations Plan http://www.fema.gov/pdf/rrr/conplan/conplan.pdf

The Environmental Protection Agency http://www.epa.gov

Federal Emergency Management Agency http://www.fema.gov

Federal Radiological Emergency Response Plan http://www.nrt.org/production/nrt/home.nsf/0/5c23c5d58074d6e48525660c005b56b5?OpenDocument

The Federal Response Plan http://www.fema.gov/pdf/rrr/frp/frp2003.pdf

Federation of American Scientists http://www.fas.org

The International Association of Emergency Managers http://www.iaem.org

National Disaster Medical System http://ndms.dhhs.gov

National Oil and Hazardous Substances Pollution Contingency Plan http://www.epa.gov/oilspill/ncpover.htm

The National Response Plan http://www.nemaweb.org/docs/national_response_plan.pdf

North Carolina Department of Emergency Management http://www.dem.dcc.state.nc.us/

NOVAD http://www.novad.org

Nuclear Regulatory Commission http://www.nrc.gov

Ready.gov http://wwe.ready.gov

Terrorism Annex for North Carolina Counties, D. Coppola, August 2003

U.S. Coast Guard http://www.uscg.mil

White House http://www.whitehouse.gov

APPENDIX 7-1
FRP Disaster Recovery Programs

Program	Agency	Assistance provided	Activating mechanism	Eligibility
Emergency Haying and Grazing	Department of Agriculture (USDA), Farm Service Agency (FSA)	Emergency authority to harvest hay or to graze land devoted to conservation and environmental uses under the Conservation Reserve Program.	AWD	I/B
Emergency Loans	USDA, FSA	Low-interest loans to family farmers and ranchers for production losses and physical damage.	PD: designated by Secretary of Agriculture or Administrator, FSA (physical losses only)	I/B
Noninsured Crop Disaster Assistance Program	USDA, FSA	Direct payments to reduce financial losses resulting from a natural disaster that causes production loss or prevents planting of crops grown commercially for food or fiber, for which Federal crop insurance is not available.	AWD	I

(continues)

APPENDIX 7-1 (*continued*)

Program	Agency	Assistance provided	Activating mechanism	Eligibility
Emergency Conservation Program	USDA, FSA	Cost-share payments to rehabilitate farmlands damaged by natural disasters and to carry out emergency water conservation or water-enhancing measures during times of severe drought, in cases when the damage or drought is so severe that federal assistance is necessary.	AWD	I/B
Agricultural Marketing Transition Act (AMTA) Program	USDA, FSA	Direct payments to eligible producers of program crops that comply with AMTA requirements.	AWD	I/B
Conservation Reserve Program (CRP)	USDA FSA	Voluntary program that offers annual rental payments, incentive payments for certain activities, and cost-share assistance to establish approved cover on eligible cropland.	AWD	I/B
Farm Operation Loans	USDA, FSA	Loans and loan guarantees to be used for farm operating costs.	N/P	I
Farm Ownership Loans	USDA, FSA	Direct loans, guaranteed loans, and technical assistance for farmers in acquiring or enlarging farms or ranches: making capital improvements: promoting soil and water conservation: and paying closing costs.	AWD	I
Emergency Food Assistance (Emergency Food Stamp and Food Commodity Program)	USDA, Food and Nutrition Service (FNS)	Direct payments to states for specified uses.	PD: declaration by the Secretary of Agriculture	S/I
Food Distribution	USDA, FNS	Donations of USDA-purchased food.	PD: declaration by Secretary of Agriculture and compliance with eligibility criteria	F/S/L/N
Emergency Watershed Protection (EWP)	USDA, Natural Resources Conservation Service (NRCS)	Direct payments and technical assistance to install structural and nonstructural measures to relieve imminent threats to life and/or property, and to purchase flood-plain easements. Technical assistance such as site evaluations, design work, and installation inspections also are provided through the program.	AWD; triggered by NRCS State Conservationist	S/L/N/B/I
Water Resources	USDA, NRCS	Project grants for the installation of preventive measures such as dams, channels, flood warning systems, purchasing easements, floodplain delineation, and land treatment. Advisory and counseling services also are available.	N/P	S/L/N

(continues)

APPENDIX 7-1 (*continued*)

Program	Agency	Assistance provided	Activating mechanism	Eligibility
Resource Conservation and Development (RC&D)	USDA, NRCS	Technical assistance and local project costs. Projects may include land and water conservation, resource improvements, recreational development, and waste disposal projects.	AWD loans to finance	L/N
River Basin Project	USDA, NRCS	Technical assistance. Special priority is given to projects designed to solve problems of upstream rural community flooding, water quality improvement that comes from agricultural nonpoint sources, wetlands preservation, and drought management for agricultural and rural communities. Special emphasis is placed on helping state agencies develop strategic water resource plans.	AWD; triggered by NRCS State Conservationist	F/S/L
Soil Survey	USDA, NRCS	Technical assistance. Objective is to maintain up-to-date, published surveys (and soil survey data in other formats) of counties or other areas of comparable size for use by interested agencies, organizations, and individuals; and to assist in the use of this information.	N/P	S/L/N/B/I
Federal Crop Insurance Program	USDA, Risk Management Agency (RMA)	Direct payments of insurance claims. Insurance against unavoidable causes of loss such as adverse weather conditions, fire, insects, or other natural disasters beyond the producer's control.	No activating causes of mechanism is needed, but availability is based on crop-specific sales, closing dates, and the availability of crops in particular counties	I
Business and Industrial Loan Program (B&I)	USDA, Rural Business Service	Guaranteed and direct loans up to $10 million. Possible disaster uses include drilling wells, purchasing water, or tying into other water programs.	AWD	B/N/T and public bodies
Rural Housing Site Loans	USDA, Rural Housing Service (RHS)	Loans for the purchase and development of housing and necessary equipment that becomes a permanent part of the development (e.g., water and server lines).	AWD	N
Rural Rental Housing Loans	USDA, RHS	Loans for the purchase, building, or repair of rental housing. Funds can also be used to provide water and water disposal systems.	AWD	I/S/L/B
Emergency Community Water Assistance Grants (ECWAG)	USDA, Rural Utilities Service (RUS)	Project grants to help rural residents obtain adequate water supplies.	PD	S/L/N

(*continues*)

APPENDIX 7-1 (*continued*)

Program	Agency	Assistance provided	Activating mechanism	Eligibility
Water and Waste Disposal Loans and Grants	USDA, RUS	Project grants and direct and guaranteed loans to develop, replace, or repair water and waste disposal systems in rural areas and towns having populations of 10,000 or less.	AWD	L/N/T
Voluntary Organizations Recovery Assistance	American Red Cross, Mennonite Disaster Service, Salvation Army, and member organizations of the National Voluntary Organization Active in Disaster	Mass care (shelter and feeding), welfare inquiries, health and mental health service, child care, home repairs (labor and funding), emergency communications, debris removal, burn services, cleaning supplies, personal property, distribution of supplies, transportation, loan personnel, and other specialized programs and services.	Disaster event	I
Economic Adjustment Program—Disaster Economic Recovery Assistance	Department of Commerce (DOC), Economic Development Administration (EDA)	Planning and technical assistance grants to State and local governments for strategic recovery planning and implementation to focus on job retention/creation to help offset the economic impacts of a major disaster.	PD: requires supplemental appropriation (S)	S/L/N/T
Economic Adjustment Program—Disaster Economic Recovery Assistance	DOC, EDA	Revolving loan fund grants to state and local governments to provide a source of local financing to support business and economic recovery after a major disaster where other financing is insufficient or unavailable.	PD: SA	S/L/N/T
Economic Adjustment Program—Disaster Economic Recovery Assistance	DOC, EDA	Infrastructure construction grants to address local recovery implementation needs for new or improved publicly owned infrastructure after a major disaster, support job creation and retention, leverage private investment, and help accelerate and safeguard the overall economic recovery of the disaster-impacted area.	PD: SA	S/L/N/T
Corporation for National Service (CNS) Programs	CNS	Volunteers of all ages/backgrounds provide short/long-term response and recovery assistance. They are available through the community or national deployment.	PD	F/S/N/T
Beach Erosion Control Projects	Department of Defense (DoD), U.S. Army Corps of Engineers (USACE)	Specialized services. USACE designs and constructs the project.	Decision of the Chief of Engineers	S/L
Emergency Rehabilitation of Flood Control Works or Federally	DoD, USACE	Specialized services to assist in the repair and restoration of public works damaged by flood, extraordinary wind, wave, or	Approval by HQUSACE	S/L/N/I

(continues)

APPENDIX 7-1 (*continued*)

Program	Agency	Assistance provided	Activating mechanism	Eligibility
Authorized Coastal Protection Works		water action.		
Emergency Water Supply and Drought Assistance Programs	DoD, USACE	Emergence supplies of clean drinking water for human consumption and construction of wells.	Assistant Secretary of the Army for Civil Works designates the area as "drought distressed"	L
Flood and Post-Flood Response, Emergency Operations	DoD, USACE	Specialized services, such as flood fighting and rescue, protection of federally constructed shore or hurricane projects, and postflood response assistance.	Designation by USACE district commander	S/L
Watercourse Navigation: Protecting, Clearing, and Straightening Channels	DoD, USACE	Specialized services, such as clearing or removing unreasonable obstructions to navigation in rivers, harbors, and other waterways or tributaries.	Decision of the Chief of Engineers	S/L
Community Disaster Loan Program	Department of Homeland Security (DHS)	Program provides loans not greater than 25 percent of the local government's annual operating budget.	PD	L
Cora C. Brown Fund	DHS	Grants to disaster victims for unmet disaster-related needs.	PD, designation for individual assistance	I
Crisis Counseling Assistance and Training Program (CCP)	DHS: Department of Health and Human Services (HHS)	Grants to states providing for short-term counseling services to disaster victims.	Governor's request	I, via S
Fire Suppression Assistance Program	DHS	Project grants. DHS approves a grant to a state on the condition that the state takes measures to mitigate natural hazards, including consideration of nonstructural alternatives.	Decision by DHS	S
Hazard Mitigation Grant Program (HMGP)	DHS	Project grants to implement hazard mitigation plans and prevent future loss of lives and property.	PD	L/N, via S
Individual and Family Grant (IFG) Program	DHS	Grants to individuals administered by the state. Objective is to provide funds for the expenses of disaster victims that cannot be met through insurance or other assistance programs.	PD, designation for individual assistance: Requires specific request by State Governor	I, via S
Legal Services	DHS	Free legal advice and referrals. Assistance includes help with insurance claims, counseling on landlord-tenant and mortgage problems, assistance with home repair contracts and consumer protection matters, replacement of legal documents, estate administration, preparation of	PD, designation for individual assistance	I

(continues)

APPENDIX 7-1 (*continued*)

Program	Agency	Assistance provided	Activating mechanism	Eligibility
		guardianships and conservatorships, and referrals.		
National Flood Insurance Program (NFIP)	DHS	Insurance benefits against losses from floods, mudflow, or flood-related erosion.	AWD	I/B/S
NFIP, Community Assistance Program	DHS	Grants to states for technical assistance to resolve floodplain management issues.	AWD	S/L
Public Assistance Program	DHS	Project grants. Funds can be used for clearing debris, emergency measures, and repairing or replacing damaged structures, roads, utilities, public buildings, and infrastructure.	PD, designation for public assistance	L/N, via S
Disaster Housing Program	DHS	Direct-payment grants and services. Grants include transient accommodation reimbursement, and home repair, rental, and mortgage assistance. Services may include a mobile home.	PD, designation for individual assistance	I
Regulatory Relief for Federally Insured Financial Institutions	Federal Deposit Insurance Corporation (FDIC) and other federal regulatory agencies	Specialized services. Supervisory agencies can grant regulatory relief to insured institutions. Regulatory relief includes lending assistance, extensions of reporting and publishing requirements, waivers from appraisal regulations, and implementation of consumer protection laws.	PD: other disaster that affects the ability of a federally insured financial institution to provide normal services	N/B
Donation of Federal Surplus Personal Property	General Services Administration (GSA)	Donation of surplus personal property to eligible recipients.	N/P	S/L/N/ public airports
Disposal of Federal Surplus Real Property	GSA	Sale, exchange, or donations of property and goods.	N/P	S/L/N
Disaster Assistance for Older Americans	HHS, Administration on Aging	Direct payments to state agencies focused on aging-related services.	PD	I, via S
Mental Health Disaster Assistance	HHS, Public Health Service	Project grants to provide emergency mental health and substance abuse counseling to individuals affected by a major disaster.	Supplemental appropriation by Congress relating to PD	I, via S
Community Development Block Grant (CDBG) Program—Entitlement Grants	Department of Housing and Urban Development (HUD), Community Planning and Development (CPD)	Formula grants to entitlement communities. Preferred use of funding is for long-term needs, but funding may also be used for emergency response activities.	Supplemental appropriation by Congress relating to PD	L

(continues)

APPENDIX 7-1 (*continued*)

Program	Agency	Assistance provided	Activating mechanism	Eligibility
CDBG—State's Program	HUD, CPD	Formula grants to states for nonentitlement communities. Preferred use of funding is for long-term needs, but funding may also be used for emergency response activities. States establish methods of fund distribution.	Supplemental appropriation by Congress relating to PD	L, via S
Mortgage Insurance for Disaster Victims Program (Section 203(h))	HUD	Provides mortgage insurance to protect lenders against the risk of default on loans to qualified disaster victims whose homes are located in a presidentially designated disaster area and were destroyed, requiring reconstruction/replacement. Insured loans may be used to finance the purchase or reconstruction of a one-family home that will be the principal residence of the homeowner.	PD	I
Reclamation States Emergency Drought Relief Act of 1991	Department of the Interior (DOI), Bureau of Reclamation	Loans, grants, use of facilities, construction, management and conservation activities, and purchase of water for resale or for fish and wildlife services. Temporary drought assistance may include the drilling of wells, installation of equipment, improved reporting of conditions.	Request for drought assistance and approval by Commissioner of Reclamation	F/S/N/I
Disaster Unemployment Assistance (DUA)	Department of Labor (DOL), DHS	Direct payments of DUA benefits and reemployment assistance services. Objective is to provide assistance to individuals who are ineligible for regular unemployment compensation programs and who are left jobless after a major disaster.	PD, designation for individual assistance. PD maybe limited to DUA only	I, via S
Employment: Job Training Partnership Act (JTPA), National Reserve Emergency Dislocation Grants	DOL, Employment and Training Administration	Program provides states with grant money to provide individuals with temporary jobs and/or employment assistance.	PD	I, via S
Price-Anderson Act	American Nuclear Insurers and Nuclear Regulatory Commission (NRC) (for commercial nuclear power plants); Department of Energy (for DOE facilities)	Payment of liability claims that arise from a nuclear power reactor accident. Insurance-provided assistance may compensate victims for increased living expenses after an evacuation, unemployment, business losses, environmental cleanup, reduced property values, and costs associated from bodily injury.	AWD	I

(continues)

APPENDIX 7-1 (*continued*)

Program	Agency	Assistance provided	Activating mechanism	Eligibility
Price-Anderson Act	NRC	Insurance reimburses states and municipalities for costs necessarily incurred in providing emergence food, shelter, transportation, or police services in evacuating the public after a nuclear power reactor accident.	AWD	S/L
Economic Injury Disaster Loans (EIDLs)	Small Business Administration (SBA)	Direct long-term, low-interest loans to small businesses and agricultural cooperatives. Loans are only available to applicants with no credit available elsewhere, and the maximum amount of an EIDL is $1.5 million.	PD: declaration of a disaster by the Secretary of Agriculture and/or SBA-declared disaster	B
Physical Disaster Loans (Business)	SBA	Direct long-term, low-interest loans to businesses and nonprofit organizations. Loans provided to repair or replace uninsured property damages caused by disasters. Loans limited to $1.5 million.	PD or SBA declaration	N/B
Physical Disaster Loans (Individual)	SBA	Direct long-term, low-interest loans to homeowners and renters to repair or replace uninsured damages caused by disasters to real and personal property. Loan amounts limited to $200,000 to repair or replace real estate, and to $40,000 to repair or replace personal property.	PD or SBA declaration	I
Social Security Assistance	Social Security Administration (SSA)	Advisory and counseling services to process SSA survivor claims, assist in obtaining necessary evidence for claim processing, resolve problems involving lost or destroyed SSA checks, and reprocess lost or destroyed pending claims.	PD: AWD	I
International Donations	Department of State (DOS)	Donations including goods and cash.	Request for international coordination assistance from DHS's Donations Coordinator	I
Transportation: Emergency Relief Program	Department of Transportation (DOT), Federal Highway Administration (FHWA)	Formula and project grants to repair roads. FHWA can provide: (1) up to $100 million in funding to a state for each natural disaster or catastrophic failure; and (2) up to $20 million in funding per year for each U.S. territory. Special legislation may increase the $100 million per state limit.	PD: AWD	F/S

(*continues*)

APPENDIX 7-1 (*continued*)

Program	Agency	Assistance provided	Activating mechanism	Eligibility
Alcohol and Tobacco Tax Refund	Department of the Treasury, Bureau of Alcohol, Tobacco and Firearms	Specialized services to provide federal alcohol and tobacco excise tax refund to business that lost assets in a disaster.	PD	B
Savings Bonds Replacement or Redemption	Treasury, Bureau of Public Debt	Specialized services. Bureau of Public Debt expedites replacement of U.S. Savings Bonds lost or destroyed as a result of a disaster.	PD	I
Taxes: Disaster Assistance Program	Treasury, Internal Revenue Service (IRS)	Advisory and counseling services. IRS provides information about casualty loss deductions, claim procedures, and reconstruction of lost financial records.	PD	I/B
Forbearance on VA Home Loans	Department of Veterans Affairs (VA)	Encourage lenders to extend forbearance to any borrowers who have VA home loans and who are in distress as a result of disaster: provide incentives to such lenders.	PD	I
Coastal Zone Management: Hazards, Environmental Recovery, and Mitigation	DOC, National Oceanic and Atmosphieric Administration (NOAA)	Assistance to state and local governments in mitigation and recovery/restoration planning, postevent permitting assistance, water-level data for storm surge and flooding prediction and mitigation.	PD for postevent: AWD from coastal state(s) for preevent planning	S
Reestablishing Local Survey Networks	DOC, NOAA	Provision of survey mark data to local and state agencies for reestablishing their geodetic control networks: reestablishment of national network if warranted.	PD: AWD depending on funding availability	S/L
Coastal Zone Management Administration Awards	DOC, NOAA	Grants to states for the management of coastal development to protect life and property from coastal hazards.	AWD requires supplemental appropriation by Congress relating to PD for poststorm coastal hazard mitigation and recovery activities	S/L/T via S
Coastal Zone Management Fund	DOC, NOAA	Emergence grants to state coastal zone management agencies to address unforeseen or disaster-related circumstances.	AWD subject to amounts provided in appropriation acts: no funds currently appropriated	S/L/T via S
Technical Support	DOC, NOAA, National Weather Service	Technical assistance for weather, water, and climate warning systems and critical information dissemination systems. Poststorm data acquisition activities.	AWD	F/S/L/N/T

(continues)

APPENDIX 7-1 (*continued*)

Program	Agency	Assistance provided	Activating mechanism	Eligibility
Technical Support	DOC, National Institute of Standards and Technology	Disaster damage surveys, assistance in procurement of consulting services, evaluation of structural and fire performance of buildings and lifelines.	Federally declared disasters to buildings and lifelines, on cost-reimbursable basis	F/S/L

(*Source*: DHS, the Federal Response Plan January 2003)

Abbreviations:

Presidential declaration (PD)   individual/family (I)

available without declaration (AWD)   nonprofit organization (N)

Federal agency (F)   Indian Tribe (T)

state agency (S)   business (B)

locality (L)   not provided (N/P)

8

Communications

INTRODUCTION

Communicating messages to the general public is a critical and underdeveloped aspect of effective emergency management. These messages come in three basic forms: risk, warning, and crisis. Risk communications involves alerting and educating the public to the risks they face and how they can best prepare for and mitigate these risks in order to reduce the impacts of future disaster events. Warning communications involves delivering a warning message in time for individuals and communities to take shelter or evacuate in advance of a disaster event. Crisis communications involves providing timely and accurate information to the public during the response and recovery phases of a disaster event.

The emergency management community has vast experience in practicing risk and warning communications. Preparedness programs have been an active part of emergency management in this country for decades, and public education programs conducted by the Federal Emergency Management Agency (FEMA), the American Red Cross, the Salvation Army, local fire departments, and other public- and private-sector agencies have disseminated millions of brochures and checklists describing the risks of future disaster events

and the steps that individuals and communities can take to reduce and prepare for them. In recent years, these programs have embraced new technologies to disseminate this information, including video and, especially, the Internet. There is a wealth of knowledge supported by scientific research concerning effective means to communicate hazard risk messages for natural disaster and selected technological disaster risks.

The design and implementation of warning systems has similarly advanced in the past decades. From the Civil Defense sirens to the Emergency Broadcast Network to weather radios, warning systems alerting the public to sudden or impending disaster events have become more sophisticated and widely used. Broadcasting timely information that allows individuals to make appropriate shelter and evacuation decisions is at the core of the warning systems designed for natural hazards such as tornados and tsunamis. Watch and warning notices for floods and hurricanes provide individuals and community leaders with valuable information on the path and potential destructiveness of severe storms that could result in flooding events. The public media—television, radio, and most recently the Internet—are the mechanisms most often used by emergency officials to issue watch and warring notices.

The importance of communicating with the public during the response and recovery phases of a natural or technological disaster event has only recently been fully embraced by emergency officials. Too often in the past, little value was placed on communicating with the public during and after a disaster event, and emergency officials had little training and less interest in this area. This changed in the 1990s as FEMA, under the direction of James Lee Witt, made a commitment and marshaled the resources to develop and implement an aggressive public affairs program designed to deliver timely and accurate messages to the public in a time of crisis. The messages focused on what measures government and private sector officials were taking to help a community in responding to and recovering from a disaster event and the methods by which individuals and communities could apply for and receive federal, state, and local disaster relief. FEMA established a working partnership with the media to deliver these messages through press conferences, individual interviews, satellite feeds, radio actualities, and the Internet. Another means of communication is *Recovery Times*, a newspaper supplement published by FEMA and distributed by local newspaper outlets. In time, the FEMA public affairs model has been embraced by state and local emergency officials.

The new terrorist threat has introduced new hazards that are not fully understood, a new risk perception among members of the public concerned about becoming the victim of a terrorist attack (no matter how unlikely that risk may be), new response and recovery (mostly clean-up) procedures and practices, new information uncertainties, new restrictions of releasing information to the public, and new demands for public information. Do the communications models developed in the past for communicating risk, warning, and crisis messages concerning natural and technological hazards apply to terrorism-related communications? Will the traditional delivery systems—television, Internet, radio, and print— adequately disseminate terrorism-related information? Will emergency and government officials find a balance between the need to provide timely and accurate

information to the public and the need to conduct criminal investigations?

These are the types of questions that are addressed in this chapter, which includes sections on risk communications, warning communications, and crisis communications. A case study of the October 2002 sniper attacks in Washington, DC, is also included in the chapter.

RISK COMMUNICATIONS

The Department of Homeland Security (DHS) has initiated several programs to achieve a goal of community and individual resilience to the effects of terrorism and other disasters. One of the primary methods employed to achieve such preparedness is public education.

Public education has long been recognized as an effective method for decreasing the damaging potential of hazards and risks, and the media are often central in such projects (Mullis, 1998). Furthermore, the role of the media in previous risk-related public education endeavors dealing with natural and technological hazards and public health issues has been well documented. From teaching citizens to build tornado-resistant safe rooms to minimizing tsunami drowning and preventing teen pregnancy, public and private agencies have partnered with, cooperated with, or utilized the various players collectively referred to as the mass media to achieve the goal of reducing public risk.

While the news media's reporting on risks has often been blamed for inciting a "culture of fear" (Glassner, 1999) in which people are afraid of a multitude of risks that have only a minute chance of ever occurring, the news media have also been integral in helping to create what could be considered the most risk-free era in recorded history (Walsh, 1996). However, no studies have been conducted to measure the efficacy of the media in informing and educating the public about terrorism and other "intentional" hazards.

The new focus on terrorism within the borders of the United States has brought to question the degree of risk faced by individual Americans. Although the topic has become a daily concern of all media outlets, the effect that this new attention has had on decreasing the vulnerability of the average citizen to that particular hazard is questionable. Citizens have indicated through polls that the threat of terrorist attacks on American soil is one of their primary concerns, and they have looked to their leaders for guidance on personal preparedness for such a threat. The federal government has recognized this concern and has sought to confront the preparedness issue through actions taken by DHS to address national vulnerabilities. DHS has also embarked on a public education campaign the likes of which has not been seen since the Civil Defense drills of the 1950s taught citizens to "duck and cover" during air raids (Waugh, 2000). The media has been involved in this effort from the beginning, and regardless of their goals, intentions, or the level to which they have actually partnered with the federal government in their actions, it is likely that the news media have never before played such a central role in risk communication.

With such a great quantity of headlines, stories, editorials, investigative reports, and briefings related to terrorism, it would seem that all citizens should be able to decode from the barrage of messages relayed by DHS the information they need to protect themselves. However, considering that never before have the media focused on any one subject so intensely, established risk perception and communication models probably do not apply. DHS and the emergency management community in general must ask the following questions now and before planning future activities: Can the news media serve as an effective risk communicator for terrorism in the United States, and do the established risk communications models apply to terrorism and other intentional hazards?

EMERGENCY MANAGEMENT AND RISK COMMUNICATION IN THE UNITED STATES

The most widely practiced form of emergency management in the United States, and the only form practiced by FEMA, is comprehensive emergency management (CEM). This four-phase cyclical system groups actions into the general categories of mitigation, preparedness, response, and recovery. For a given hazard there are generally preevent actions (mitigation and preparedness) and postevent actions (response and recovery) performed. The response phase, includes the immediate period of reaction after a disaster occurs (when critical emergency resources are required). Recovery includes the long-term rebuilding that begins after the emergency functions related to disaster response are no longer required. Mitigation is defined as any activity that prevents or reduces the impact of a disaster, and preparedness involves predisaster planning and training addressing the possibility of future disasters (Waugh, 2000). Like response, disaster preparedness is also always managed at the local level and is considered to be more of a local government responsibility than any of the other phases of CEM.

Preparedness generally consists of training the local first responders and educating the public about ways to prepare for specific hazards within specific communities. A hazard is an event or physical condition that has the potential to cause fatalities, injuries, property damage, infrastructure damage, agricultural loss, damage to the environment, interruption of business, or other types of harm or loss (FEMA, 1997). The risk associated with a hazard is identified as the probability (likelihood) of the hazard occurring, multiplied by the consequence of the hazard should it occur (Ansell and Wharton, 1992). For many hazard risks, public education is seen as the most effective means to reduce both the likelihood and consequence components significantly (Nielsen and Lidstone, 1998). Emergency management public education efforts utilize numerous resources, including in-school education, distribution of pamphlets and fact sheets, and inserts in phone books and utility mailings, among many others (Disaster Management Center, 1995). However, it is the use of the various forms of the news media that has often been seen as the most effective means of public education.

The federal government took a more active role in community preparedness during the Clinton

Administration while FEMA was under the direction of James Lee Witt (a move taken by several governments throughout the world during the same period [Nielsen and Lidstone, 1998]). Director Witt espoused the idea that the emergency response community must shed the view that the media were adversaries and work to form media partnerships in order to be more effective in public disaster preparedness education (Bullock, 2003). Witt worked to institutionalize such tasks as creating media education materials and public service announcements, ensuring availability of "approved" hazard experts, providing training in emergency management terminology and actions for reporters and anchor people, and promoting more responsible reporting by the media. The success of these changes was measured through the increased resilience of communities to hazards in which such changes in individual behavior were known to be the primary means of reducing vulnerability (such as during tsunamis and tornadoes) (Bullock, 2003; Haddow, 2003).

In the wake of the September 11 terrorist attacks and the anthrax mail attacks shortly thereafter, the "all-hazards" approach of the federal government focused its efforts on preparedness and mitigation (prevention) of future terrorist attacks. Although terrorism had been a considered a high-risk hazard by the federal government for some time, it was not necessarily on the minds of the American public. After these events, however, terrorism became an obvious primary concern of both the government and its citizens. Terrorism was no longer seen as something that affected isolated locations known to be at high risk and was instead regarded as a hazard that could affect anyone at any place and any time, a hazard that could result in a mass-casualty event (one that overwhelms the capacity of local health officials to respond). Additionally, the possibility of terrorists employing weapons of mass destruction (WMD)—chemical, biological, radiological, or nuclear—became a reality.

On November 25, 2002, President Bush signed into law the Homeland Security Act of 2002, investing in the new DHS the mission of protecting the United States from further terrorist attacks, reducing the nation's vulnerability to terrorism, and minimizing the damage from potential terrorist attacks and natural disasters. DHS began working to organize the federal response to the consequences of disasters but concentrated its efforts on preparedness and response capabilities to combat terrorism (as is evident by changes in federal funding trends). DHS officials were still operating under the same constraints of the previous administration in terms of what they could do to increase preparedness at the community level. DHS repeatedly acknowledged that, even in the event that a terrorist attack be declared a national disaster, local communities would need to be prepared to be self-sufficient for a minimum of 48 hours. However, public demand for more federal action and information required DHS to address these public education needs.

The Ready.Gov campaign is DHS's primary effort to increase individual citizen preparedness at the community level. It is essentially a web site that offers citizens explicit directions detailing what they can do to prepare themselves and their families for all hazards, including terrorism. Other efforts at informing the public, which are equal components in the larger public education effort, include the five-color-coded Homeland Security Alert system and specific public announcements, such as the well-known "duct tape and plastic" incident (in which DHS Director Tom Ridge made a general appeal to people in the United States to buy those items to protect themselves from the effects of a possible WMD terrorist attack).

Personal preparedness from disasters, as described by the Ready.Gov web site, includes three major components. Specifically, they are "make a kit" (one that contains materials to ensure potable water, food, clean air, first aid, and special-needs items), "make a plan" (in which individuals or families determine actions to be taken in the event of specific disasters), and "be informed" (which involves general information about hazards and their specific personal mitigation and preparedness measures). In order to measure the effectiveness of a citizen's degree of terrorism-hazard preparedness, these three components must be used as performance measures. For the specific case of terrorism, "vigilance" (or actively looking for and reporting suspicious behavior that could be linked to terrorism) is included as a performance measure for personal terrorism preparedness (DHS, 2003).

PAST RESEARCH FOCUSING ON RISK COMMUNICATION

According to acclaimed risk communication experts Baruch Fischhoff, MGranger Morgan, Ann Bostrom, and Cynthia Atman, risk communication is "communication intended to supply laypeople with the information they need to make informed, independent judgments about risks to health, safety, and the environment" (Morgan et al., 2002). Creating messages that satisfy these high ideals requires extensive time, experience, and planning and is therefore more often successful in educating the public about old risks that are well understood than new risks such as terrorism. Although it would seem from a purist's point of view that anything short of the aforementioned definition would not suffice, some authors have defined risk communication to be the mere action of reporting on any existing or proposed hazard regardless of the story's ability to result in any increase in public awareness, knowledge, or preparedness (Willis, 1997).

The news media play a significant role in disaster and emergency management both before and after disasters occur. The media are well recognized for the invaluable service they have consistently performed during the initial critical moments of a disaster, when the emergency response efforts are mobilized. In these events, the media serve to transmit warning messages and alerts and give instructions on where to evacuate, where to seek medical care and shelter, and where to go for more specific information (Mileti, 1999). Jim Willis (1997) writes, "there may be no other area of journalism [than risk communication] where the Fourth Estate has such an awesome responsibility." Furman (2002) contends that the media's ability to educate people during these times is in many cases more likely to save lives than many other components of emergency response, adding that "people will die

if they don't get good information." The emergency response community has embraced the media for their capability in response, recognizing that they will be the primary, if not the only, means of informing large masses of potential victims (McCormick Tribune Foundation, 2002).

With regard to the preparedness phase of emergency management, the primary risk communication tasks that have been assumed by the media include raising citizen awareness to the presence of an existing or future hazard and providing information to those citizens regarding prevention or protection (Burkhart, 1991). The effectiveness of the media as a conduit of educational information has been studied extensively, most notably in the area of public health. A great number of these studies have shown a positive correlation between the use of the media and an increase in the promoted knowledge or behavior. Phyllis Piotrow (1990) and a team of researchers working in Nigeria found that the promotion of family planning and clinic sites on local television played a significant role in the number of people utilizing those services. Charles Westoff and German Rodriguez (1995) found that there was a strong correlation between patients who reported that they had been exposed to family planning messages in the media and the use of contraceptives by those same patients. M. Witzer (1997) writes that "exposure to electronic and print media is associated with later marriage and with greater knowledge and use of family planning among men and women in Sub-Saharan Africa." Jones, Beniger, and Westoff (1980) found that there was a strong correlation between mass media coverage of the adverse affects of the birth-control pill and discontinuation rates among users. Similar results were found relating to sex education among young adults (Brown and Keller, 2000) and early initiation of breast-feeding (McDivitt et al., 1993). Nelken (1987) found in one study that over 60 percent of Americans learn about cancer prevention from the media, whereas less than 20 percent do so from physicians.

With natural and technological hazards, the behavioral modifications and preparatory measures taken by recipients as a result of media risk communication also look promising. Mitigation specialists at FEMA claim that the media's role in community and citizen preparedness is critical if such efforts are to succeed (FEMA, 1998). Dennis Mileti (1999) found that personal preparedness was most likely to be undertaken by those people who are most attentive to the news media but that other attributes are often necessary in conjunction with that attention. Media risk communication has been widely credited as an important supplemental component to official communication in public preparedness to hazards (Burkhart, 1991). Singer and Endreny (1993) contend that there are many factors determining how people view hazards (including personal experience and contact with other people), but with hazards that are extreme in consequence and rare in occurrence (such as terrorism) the media are the most influential source of information. James Walsh (1996) found that several studies indicate that people use the media for obtaining information on hazards more than any other source.

The primary source of the news media's ability to effectively communicate and educate most likely lies in the institutionalized methods of attracting viewers and providing timely information that has been developed and refined over centuries. Burkhart (1991) writes, "in the preparedness phase, the mass media are positioned between the actors who evaluate a threat and decide upon a message, and the media audience." Burkhart adds that it is the media's ability to influence perceived risk and the credibility of the source of information that gives them such power over public behavior. McCombs and Shaw's (1972) research, which found that audiences not only are alerted to important issues by the media but that they learn "how much importance to attach to an issue or topic from the emphasis the media place on it" supports Burkhart's convictions.

This positive view of the media as a successful risk communicator comes not without contention. There are many social scientists who feel that the media, for various reasons, are ineffective at informing the public about the risks they face. Winston (1985) feels that it is the "built-in, organizational, competitive, and institutional biases" that prevent the media from informing citizens about hazards. These biases are coupled with procedural standards that can also make effective communication of risk difficult. For instance, Singer and Endreny (1993) report that the media inform about "events rather than issues, about immediate consequences rather than long-term considerations, about harms rather than risks," and Wenham (1994) describes how the media "tell how bad things are, while [emergency management agencies] make things better." Burkhart (1991) feels that it is a deficiency of knowledge about hazards and disaster management among journalists that makes them unable to effectively communicate due to both a lack of understanding of the most basic concepts and their inability to act as a "surrogate for the layman, to absorb and transform technical information to a public that is often even less well-prepared to grasp technical information and concepts." Such criticisms are repeated by Singer and Endreny (1993). There are other, similar reasons identified by research efforts that sought to explain the media's risk communication deficiencies, including restrictions of time and space that prevent adequate knowledge transfer (Willis, 1997) and the media's insistence on taking control of the selection and presentation of message format that leads to a decrease in message effectiveness (Burkhart, 1991).

There is another subgroup of studies that find the news media to be largely ineffective as a risk communicator but assign less blame to them for such problems. Raphael (1986) turns the focus of the blame onto the public, stating that "citizens often display a magical belief in goodness and protection and a sense of generalized risk, which may explain why people pay less attention to preparedness information provided by the media outside of the context of an emergency." Jerry Hauer from the New York City Office of Emergency Management feels that it is the tendency of the emergency management community to exclude the media from training and drills due to the fear that the media will leak operational plans to terrorists and the fear that the media will cause mass public panic that has prevented them from being able to be effectively inform the public (McCormick Tribune Foundation, 2002). This position is supported by Burkhart (1991), who states, "Media are often limited by the nature of the information they receive," and

Bremer (2002), who states, "Terrorism presents a major dilemma to political leaders in terms of how to get enough attention without bringing too much attention to the problem." Furman (2002) adds, "It is difficult to educate the American people because there's very little we can tell them to do. . . . You're faced with the problem of just how much you want to tell the American people, because, in the end, there's very little we can give them."

There is a third type of research that claims that while the news media are in fact ineffective at educating the public, they still play a vital role in risk communication. McCallum, Hammond, and Morris (1990) state that, "regardless of reservations about their ability to play the role effectively, the media do carry considerable information about certain hazards and risks to most people." This view of the media as informer is fairly widespread. Willis (1997) states that while the media too often avoid contributing to the solution to the problems, they are effective at raising attention to issues and communicating degrees of urgency. Mullis (1998) further promotes this argument, stating that the media are effective at initiating preparedness activities. Burkhart (1991) found that while media warnings were too imprecise to be effective, they "were able to get people talking to other people about the danger mentioned in media warnings." Cohen (1963) succinctly characterized this phenomenon as follows: "The press may not be successful much of the time in telling its readers what to think, but it is stunningly successful in telling them what to think about."

ACCURACY OF INFORMATION

A second area that must be examined when considering the ability of the media to communicate risk is the ability of the media to do so in a way that gives members of the public an accurate perception of their personal risk of victimization. In what is probably one of the earliest descriptions of the media's power to influence public risk perception and, likewise, preparedness and mitigative behavior, Walter Lippmann (1922) writes in his acclaimed Public Opinion that

> We shall assume that what each man does is based not on direct and certain knowledge, but on pictures made by himself or given to him. If his atlas tells him that the world is flat, he will not sail near what he believes to be the edge of our planet for fear of falling off.

Willis (1997) writes that because the media's depiction of public health and safety-related issues has either an indirect or a direct effect on public behavior, the media's responsibility to be as accurate as possible in their presentation of such hazards is vital. In the case of terrorism, DHS has established a five-color-coded Homeland Security Alert system that is intended to inform the public about the current risk of a terrorist attack within the United States. At certain times, the risk is raised in specific locations, such as a city, a landmark, or a building. While the media often refer to this system when it goes up or down in severity, they also provide exhaustive unrelated information that heavily influences public perception. It is this perception that people must use in judging their own risk and, likewise, preparing themselves appropriately. It is important for the media not to understate risks because people will otherwise not expend the time and money needed to adequately prepare themselves, but exaggerating the risk of a hazard can have drastic consequences, including stress-related health problems and financial and economic effects including business and tourism losses.

Thus far, research has found that the media tend to overstate the risk of the hazards on which they focus (which also tend to be those that are the least likely to occur), while they understate commonly occurring hazards (Singer and Endreny, 1993). Altheide (2002) found that almost 80 percent of Americans feel that they are subject to more risk than their parents were 20 years ago, when in fact evidence has shown that we have a "competitive advantage in terms of disease, accidents, nutrition, medical care, and life expectancy" and that the media's portrayal of risk is mainly to blame. One reason this occurs is that the media do not have the time or resources to ensure the accuracy of their reports beyond reasonable doubt. Willis (1997) found that while scientists use elaborate methods of ensuring the validity of their findings, journalists depend on secondary or tertiary sources that confirm

FIGURE 8-1 New York, NY, September 27, 2001—FEMA workers need to stay current with the news in regard to the terrorist attacks on the World Trade Center and the Pentagon. Photo by Bri Rodriguez/FEMA News Photo.

or refute their primary source, all of whom may be incorrect in their assumptions. Warner (1989) feels the problem lies in the media's tendency to use vivid imagery in reporting risk, such as comparing the number of people who die as a result of smoking as equivalent to three fully seated jumbo jets crashing every day. Singer and Endreny (1993) claim that daily reporting of rare hazards, which tend to be more "newsworthy," make these events subject to the availability heuristic. Walsh (1996) notes that over 2 million Americans cancelled travel plans to Europe in 1986 because of fears of terrorism, when their actual risk would have been reduced significantly more if they had lost 10 pounds and traveled to Europe as planned.

Related to this concern that the media do not give the public accurate perceptions of risks is the fear that the public will become emotionally afraid of risks rather than becoming aware of their dangers. This distinction is important because it determines the types of preparedness measures citizens take in response to

the messages they receive and the rationality with which those actions are made. When people are presented with a risk, they are more likely to take preventive and preparatory measures if they are led to believe that the risk is a danger that can be managed rather than one that they should fear (Bullock, 2003). Past research has found that increasing the levels of public fear can actually cause a decrease in public preparedness behavior (Mullis, 1998). Unfortunately, it may be that the nature of media culture promotes and even amplifies fear by attempting to draw viewers through entertainment and framing (Altheide, 2002; Willis, 1997). Walsh (1996) contends that the media pay attention only to issues and situations that frighten viewers, "filling coverage with opinions rather than facts or logical perspective." Furedi (1997) takes a slightly different but related alternative stance on the subject in stating that "the media's preoccupation with risk is a symptom of the problem and not its cause," as the media can only amplify fear that already exists.

ESSENTIAL COMPONENTS OF EFFECTIVE RISK COMMUNICATION

There are numerous components of effective risk communication that have been identified as vital to the success of an effective campaign. Morgan and his colleagues (2002) conclude that effective risk communication requires authoritative and trustworthy sources. They add that if the acting communicators are perceived by the public as having a vested personal interest in the result of such preparedness, they may be skeptical about the communicators' intentions. Dennis Mileti (1999) contends that there are several characteristics that must be considered in creating the messages, including the following: amount of material, speed of presentation, number of arguments, repetition, style, clarity, ordering, forcefulness, specificity, consistency, accuracy, and extremity of the position advocated. These characteristics are adjusted depending on whether the communicators intend to attract attention or enhance the acceptance of their message (Mileti, 1999). Singer and Endreny (1993) claim that in order for a message to be considered comprehensive, it should contain an annual mortality associated with the hazard (if known), the "spatial extent" of the hazard, the time frame associated with the hazard, and the alternatives for mitigating the hazard.

Communicators must also ensure that their messages are understood by those that they are trying to reach (Morgan et al., 2002), which undoubtedly changes from community to community depending on the demographic makeup of each. Mileti (1999) writes, "Most hazard-awareness and education programs have assumed a homogeneous 'public,' and have done little to tailor information materials to different groups." He adds that hazard-awareness programs are more effective if they rely on multiple sources transmitting multiple messages through multiple outlets and that radio and television are best at maintaining hazard awareness, whereas printed materials tend to provide more specific instructions on what should be done (Mileti, 1999).

These are obviously high standards when considering the strict time, length, and content guidelines within which journalists must work. Highlighting the difficulty of both creating and analyzing such endeavors and the need for such a study as this, Morgan (2002) and his colleagues write, "As practiced today, risk communication is often very earnest but also surprisingly ad hoc. Typically, one can find neither a clear analysis of what needs to be communicated nor solid evidence that messages have achieved their impact. Nor can one find tested procedures for ensuring the credibility of information."

FUTURE RESEARCH

The objectives of future research projects should be (1) to determine how effective the news media have been as a conduit of information to citizens as part of a larger terrorism-related public education campaign being conducted by DHS and (2) to develop a risk communications model by which media-provided public education pertaining to terrorism and other intentional hazards can be most effectively applied. Media reports in print, television, and radio formats should be examined for their content to (1) see if they meet the minimum information requirements established by risk communication experts, (2) determine if responsibility for preparedness is focused on the individual or the government, and (3) determine if an accurate portrayal of risk has been made. Surveys should be conducted with a random representative sample of American citizens to determine (1) the levels to which they have prepared for terrorism, (2) by what information they were motivated to do so, and (3) if their perception of risk reflects the level of risk portrayed by DHS and other federal sources. All collected and analyzed data should be used to determine which forms of risk communication are most effective at creating a more informed, prepared citizenry and to generate a list of risk communications' "fundamental requirements" relating to the task of terrorism that builds upon established risk communications models. From these models, strategic recommendations can be targeted to the various agencies and industries that regularly perform risk communication.

EXISTING GOVERNMENT PUBLIC AWARENESS CAMPAIGNS

Ready.gov, with its partners in the public, private, and voluntary sectors, is promoting three basic steps individuals can take to be prepared for a terrorist incident—make a kit, make a plan, and be informed. Presented in "Facts about Guidance" is the guidance provided on the Ready.gov web site (www.ready.gov). This web site also includes basic information on explosives, chemical and biological agents, and nuclear and radiological issues.

WARNING COMMUNICATIONS

In March 2002, the White House Office of Homeland Security unveiled a new terrorist warning system called the Homeland Security Advisory System (HSAS). The system was color-coded with accompanying written descriptions that identified the threat level for a possible terrorist attack at any given time. Currently DHS provides a detailed explanation of how the HSAS works (Sidebar 8-1).

Since its inception, concerns have been raised about the level of information provided through the HSAS. These concerns are shared by both the general public and members of the first responder community (e.g., police, fire, and emergency medical technicians) as well as local officials responsible for ensuring public safety (Sidebar 8-2). Several organizations (*continues on p. 306*)

FACTS ABOUT GUIDANCE

Introduction

Terrorists are working to obtain biological, chemical, nuclear, and radiological weapons, and the threat of an attack is very real. Here at the Department of Homeland Security, throughout the federal government, and at organizations across America, we are working hard to strengthen our nation's security. Whenever possible, we want to stop terrorist attacks before they happen. All Americans should begin a process of learning about potential threats so that we are better prepared to react during an attack. While there is no way to predict what will happen or what your personal circumstances will be, there are simple things you can do now to prepare yourself and your loved ones.

Some of the things you can do to prepare for the unexpected, such as assembling a supply kit and developing a family communications plan, are the same for both a natural or man-made emergency. However, as you will see throughout the pages of Ready.gov, there are important differences among potential terrorist threats that will impact the decisions you make and the actions you take. With a little planning and common sense, you can be better prepared for the unexpected.

Make a Kit

When preparing for a possible emergency situation, it's best to think first about the basics of survival: fresh water, food, clean air and warmth.

- Water and food: Find out how to store and prepare for at least three days of survival.
- Clean air: Learn how to improvise with what you have on hand to protect your mouth, nose, eyes, and cuts in your skin.
- First-aid kit: Knowing how to treat minor injuries can make a difference in an emergency. If you have these basic supplies, you are better prepared to help your loved ones when they are hurt.
- Supply checklists: Assemble clothing and bedding, tools, and other basic supplies.
- Special needs items: Lists for those with special needs—babies, adults, seniors, and people with disabilities.

Make a Plan

You should plan in advance what you will do in an emergency. Be prepared to assess the situation, and use common sense and whatever you have on hand to take care of yourself and your loved ones. Think about the places where your family spends time: school, work, and other places you frequent. Ask about their emergency plans. Find out how they will communicate with families during an emergency. If they do not have an emergency plan, consider helping develop one.

- Creating a family plan: You and your family may not be together when disaster strikes. Be prepared for a variety of situations.
- Deciding to stay or go: Depending on your circumstances and the nature of the attack, the first important decision is whether you stay put or get away. You should understand and plan for both possibilities.
- At work and school: Schools, day-care providers, workplaces, apartment buildings, and neighborhoods should all have site-specific emergency plans. Ask about plans at the places your family frequents.
- In a moving vehicle: You may be in a moving vehicle at the time of an attack. Know what you can do.
- In a high-rise building: You may be in a high-rise building at the time of an attack. Plan for the possibility.

Be Informed

Disaster preparedness is no longer the sole concern of earthquake-prone Californians and those who live in the part of the country known as "Tornado Alley." For Americans, preparedness must now account for man-made disasters as well as natural ones. Knowing what to do during an emergency is an important part of being prepared and may make all the difference when seconds count.

- Biological: If there is a biological threat . . .
- Chemical: If there is a chemical threat . . .
- Explosions: If there is an explosion . . .
  If there is fire . . .
  If you are trapped in debris . . .
- Nuclear Blast: If there is a nuclear blast . . .
- Radiation: If there is a radiation threat or a "dirty bomb" . . .

Source: DHS, www.ready.gov

301

FACTS ABOUT BE INFORMED INFORMATION

Be Informed—Biological Threat

A biological attack is the deliberate release of germs or other biological substances that can make you sick. Many agents must be inhaled, enter through a cut in the skin, or be eaten to make you sick. Some biological agents, such as anthrax, do not cause contagious diseases. Others, like the smallpox virus, can result in diseases you can catch from other people.

If There Is a Biological Threat

Unlike an explosion, a biological attack may or may not be immediately obvious. While it is possible that you will see signs of a biological attack, as was sometimes the case with the anthrax mailings, it is perhaps more likely that local health-care workers will report a pattern of unusual illness or there will be a wave of sick people seeking emergency medical attention. You will probably learn of the danger through an emergency radio or TV broadcast or some other signal used in your community. You might get a telephone call or emergency response workers may come to your door.

In the event of a biological attack, public health officials may not immediately be able to provide information on what you should do. It will take time to determine exactly what the illness is, how it should be treated, and who is in danger. However, you should watch TV, listen to the radio, or check the Internet for official news, including the following:

- Are you in the group or area authorities consider in danger?
- What are the signs and symptoms of the disease?
- Are medications or vaccines being distributed?
- Where?
- Who should get them?
- Where should you seek emergency medical care if you become sick?

Protect Yourself

If you become aware of an unusual and suspicious release of an unknown substance nearby, it doesn't hurt to protect yourself. Quickly get away. Cover your mouth and nose with layers of fabric that can filter the air but still allow breathing. Examples include two to three layers of cotton such as a T-shirt, handkerchief or towel. Otherwise, several layers of tissue or paper towels may help. Wash with soap and water, and contact authorities.

Symptoms and Hygiene

At the time of a declared biological emergency, if a family member becomes sick, it is important to be suspicious. Do not automatically assume, however, that you should go to a hospital emergency room or that any illness is the result of the biological attack. Symptoms of many common illnesses may overlap. Use common sense, practice good hygiene and cleanliness to avoid spreading germs, and seek medical advice.

Be Informed—Chemical Threat

A chemical attack is the deliberate release of a toxic gas, liquid, or solid that can poison people and the environment.

Possible Signs of Chemical Threat

- Many people suffering from watery eyes, twitching, choking, having trouble breathing or losing coordination
- Many sick or dead birds, fish or small animals

If You See Signs of Chemical Attack

- Quickly try to define the impacted area or where the chemical is coming from, if possible.
- Take immediate action to get away.
- If the chemical is inside a building where you are, get out of the building without passing through the contaminated area, if possible.
- Otherwise, it may be better to move as far away from where you suspect the chemical release is and "shelter in place." Read more at Staying Put, www.Ready.gov/text/stay
- If you are outside, quickly decide what is the fastest escape from the chemical threat. Consider if you can get out of the area, or if you should follow plans to "shelter in place."

If You Think You Have Been Exposed to a Chemical

If your eyes are watering, your skin is stinging, and you are having trouble breathing, you may have been exposed to a chemical.

- If you think you may have been exposed to a chemical, strip immediately and wash.
- Look for a hose, fountain, or any source of water, and wash with soap if possible, being sure not to scrub the chemical into your skin.
- Seek emergency medical attention.

For more information, see "Are You Ready?" from Federal Emergency Management Agency. www.fema.gov

Be Informed—Explosions

If There Is an Explosion

- Take shelter against your desk or a sturdy table
- Exit the building ASAP
- Do not use elevators
- Check for fire and other hazards
- Take your emergency supply kit if time allows

If There Is a Fire

- Exit the building ASAP.
- Crawl low if there is smoke.
- Use a wet cloth, if possible, to cover your nose and mouth.
- Use the back of your hand to feel the upper, lower, and middle parts of closed doors.
- If the door is not hot, brace yourself against it, and open slowly.
- If the door is hot, do not open it. Look for another way out.
- Do not use elevators.
- If you catch fire, do not run. Stop-drop-and-roll to put out the fire.
- If you are at home, go to a previously designated meeting place.
- Account for your family members, and carefully supervise small children.
- Never go back into a burning building.

If You Are Trapped in Debris

- If possible, use a flashlight to signal your location to rescuers.
- Avoid unnecessary movement so that you don't kick up dust.
- Cover your nose and mouth with anything you have on hand. (Dense-weave cotton material can act as a good filter. Try to breathe through the material.)
- Tap on a pipe or wall so that rescuers can hear where you are.
- If possible, use a whistle to signal rescuers.
- Shout only as a last resort. Shouting can cause a person to inhale dangerous amounts of dust.

Be Informed—Nuclear Blast

A nuclear blast is an explosion with intense light and heat, a damaging pressure wave, and widespread radioactive material that can contaminate the air, water, and ground surfaces for miles around. While experts may predict at this time that a nuclear attack is less likely than other types, terrorism by its nature is unpredictable.

If There Is a Nuclear Blast

- Take cover immediately, below ground if possible, though any shield or shelter will help protect you from the immediate effects of the blast and the pressure wave.
- Quickly assess the situation.
- Consider if you can get out of the area or if it would be better to go inside a building and follow your plan to "shelter in place."
- In order to limit the amount of radiation you are exposed to, think about shielding, distance, and time.
  - Shielding: If you have a thick shield between yourself and the radioactive materials, more of the radiation will be absorbed and you will be exposed to less.
  - Distance: The farther away you are from the blast and the fallout, the lower your exposure.
  - Time: Minimizing time spent exposed will also reduce your risk.

Use available information to assess the situation. If there is a significant radiation threat, health-care authorities may or may not advise you to take potassium iodide. Potassium iodide is the same stuff added to your table salt to make it iodized. It may or may not protect your thyroid gland, which is particularly vulnerable, from radioactive iodine exposure. Consider keeping potassium iodide in your emergency kit, and learn what the appropriate doses are for each of your family members. Plan to speak with your health-care provider in advance about what makes sense for your family.

For more information, see Potassium Iodide from Centers for Disease Control. www.cdc.gov

For more general information, see "Are You Ready?" from Federal Emergency Management Agency. www.fema.gov

Be Informed—Radiation

A radiation threat, commonly referred to as a "dirty bomb" or "radiological dispersion device" (RDD), is the use of common explosives to spread radioactive materials over a targeted area. It is not a nuclear blast. The force of the explosion and radioactive contamination will be more localized. While the blast will be immediately obvious, the presence of radiation will not be clearly defined until trained personnel with specialized equipment are on the scene. As with any radiation, you want to try to limit exposure.

If There Is a Radiation Threat or "Dirty Bomb"

To limit the amount of radiation you are exposed to, think about shielding, distance, and time.

- Shielding: If you have a thick shield between yourself and the radioactive materials, more of the radiation will be absorbed and you will be exposed to less.
- Distance: The farther away you are away from the blast and the fallout, the lower your exposure.
- Time: Minimizing time spent exposed will also reduce your risk.

As with any emergency, local authorities may not be able to immediately provide information on what is happening and what you should do. However, you should watch TV, listen to the radio, or check the Internet often for official news and information as it becomes available.

For more general information, see "Are You Ready?" from Federal Emergency Management Agency. www.fema.gov

Source: DHS, www.ready.gov

SIDEBAR 8-1   Understanding the Homeland Security Advisory System

The world has changed since September 11, 2001. We remain a nation at risk to terrorist attacks and will remain at risk for the foreseeable future. At all Threat Conditions, we must remain vigilant, prepared, and ready to deter terrorist attacks. The following Threat Conditions each represent an increasing risk of terrorist attacks. Beneath each Threat Condition are some suggested Protective Measures, recognizing that the heads of federal departments and agencies are responsible for developing and implementing appropriate agency-specific Protective Measures:

1. Low Condition (Green): This condition is declared when there is a low risk of terrorist attacks. Federal departments and agencies should consider the following general measures in addition to the agency-specific Protective Measures they develop and implement:

- Refining and exercising as appropriate preplanned Protective Measures
- Ensuring personnel receive proper training on the Homeland Security Advisory System and specific preplanned department or agency Protective Measures

- Institutionalizing a process to assure that all facilities and regulated sectors are regularly assessed for vulnerabilities to terrorist attacks and all reasonable measures are taken to mitigate these vulnerabilities

2. Guarded Condition (Blue): This condition is declared when there is a general risk of terrorist attacks. In addition to the Protective Measures taken in the previous Threat Condition, federal departments and agencies should consider the following general measures in addition to the agency-specific Protective Measures that they will develop and implement:

- Checking communications with designated emergency response or command locations
- Reviewing and updating emergency response procedures
- Providing the public with any information that would strengthen its ability to act appropriately

3. Elevated Condition (Yellow): An Elevated Condition is declared when there is a significant risk of terrorist attacks. In addition to the Protective Measures taken in the previous Threat Conditions, federal departments and agencies should consider the following general measures in addition to the Protective Measures that they will develop and implement:

- Increasing surveillance of critical locations
- Coordinating emergency plans as appropriate with nearby jurisdictions
- Assessing whether the precise characteristics of the threat require the further refinement of preplanned Protective Measures
- Implementing, as appropriate, contingency and emergency response plans

4. High Condition (Orange): A High Condition is declared when there is a high risk of terrorist attacks. In addition to the Protective Measures taken in the previous Threat Conditions, federal

Sidebar 8-1 Continued

have expanded on the information provided by DHS by developing additional guidance on actions that individuals, families, neighborhoods, schools, and businesses should take. Recommendations developed by the American Red Cross and released in August 2003 are presented in Chapter Appendices 8.1–8.5. A copy of "California State Agency Guidance: Homeland Security Advisory System," developed by the Governor's Office for Emergency Services in California, is presented in Appendix 10.

The Partnership for Public Warning (PPW) was formed in January 2002 as a "partnership between the private sector, academia, and government entities at the local, state, and federal levels" (Partnership for Public Warning, 2003). PPW is a nonprofit entity with a stated mission "to develop consensus on processes, standards, and systems that will provide the right information about dangers to life and property to the right people, in the right places and the right times, so that those in harm's way can take timely and appropriate

action to save lives, reduce losses and speed recovery—whether from natural disasters, accidents, or acts of terrorism" (Partnership for Public Warning, 2003).

In May 2003, PPW published "A National Strategy for Integrated for Public Warning Policy and Capability," which examined the current status of public warning systems, practices, and issues across the United States. The report stated,

> Working together in partnership, the stakeholders should assess current warning capability, carry out appropriate research and develop the following:
> - A common terminology for natural and man-made disasters
> - A standard message protocol
> - National metrics and standards
> - National backbone systems for securely collecting and disseminating warnings from all officials sources
> - Pilot projects to test concepts and approaches
> - Training and event-simulation programs
> - A national multimedia education and outreach program
>
> (Partnership for Public Warning, 2003)

departments and agencies should consider the following general measures in addition to the agency-specific Protective Measures that they will develop and implement:
- Coordinating necessary security efforts with federal, state, and local law enforcement agencies or any National Guard or other appropriate armed forces organizations
- Taking additional precautions at public events and possibly considering alternative venues or even cancellation
- Preparing to execute contingency procedures, such as moving to an alternate site or dispersing their workforce
- Restricting threatened facility access to essential personnel only

5. Severe Condition (Red): A Severe Condition reflects a severe risk of terrorist attacks. Under most

circumstances, the Protective Measures for a Severe Condition are not intended to be sustained for substantial periods of time. In addition to the Protective Measures in the previous Threat Conditions, federal departments and agencies also should consider the following general measures in addition to the agency-specific Protective Measures that they will develop and implement:
- Increasing or redirecting personnel to address critical emergency needs
- Assigning emergency response personnel and prepositioning and mobilizing specially trained teams or resources
- Monitoring, redirecting, or constraining transportation systems
- Closing public and government facilities

Source: DHS, www.dhs.gov

| RED | SEVERE – A Severe risk of terrorist attacks |
| BLUE | GUARDED – A general risk of terrorist attacks |

RED	**SEVERE – A Severe risk of terrorist attacks**
ORANGE	**HIGH – A high risk of terrorist attacks**
YELLOW	**ELEVATED – A significant risk of terrorist attacks**
BLUE	**GUARDED – A general risk of terrorist attacks**
GREEN	**LOW – A low risk of terrorist attacks**

CRISIS COMMUNICATIONS

Communications has become an increasingly critical function in emergency management. The dissemination of timely and accurate information to the general public, elected and community officials, and the media plays a major role in the effective management of disaster response and recovery activities. Communicating policies, goals, and priorities to staff, partners, and participants enhances support and promotes a more efficient disaster management operation.

SIDEBAR 8-2   Terror Alerts Could Become More Location Specific

The nation's multicolored terrorism alert system will remain in place, but future alarms could be narrowed to a specific city, state, or region, Homeland Security Secretary Tom Ridge said Monday. "There's enough flexibility in this system as it presently exists to give very specific warnings to a city, a state, a region," Ridge told a gathering of the National Governors Association. But the homeland security secretary also said that singling out a smaller area as the potential attack target would "raise the level of anxiety" for residents of that region

Critics have complained that the warnings are too vague or geographically broad to be of much use. Rarely is an upgraded color code accompanied by any additional information—for the public or for the 700,000 law enforcement officers across the nation, who are asked to step up their vigilance. Before Ridge's arrival at the conference, a survey of the nation's 50 governors indicated that, in the battle against terrorism, the lack of communication was their top concern. (No. 2 was a shortage of federal money to pay for the additional security requirements.)

After a closed, private meeting with governors at the conference, Ridge gave a public address in which he assured them that the flow of information would increase—although perhaps not to the grassroots level that some governors would like. All governors would be asked to designate five staffers to hold top security clearances. They and their governor would have access to a secure web site that would give some details about a specific alert, but they would not be allowed to pass the information on to lower ranks. Ridge also promised the governors flexibility to determine their state's security priorities in heightened alerts, after 150 key locations designated by the federal government had been locked down.

Source: Atlanta Journal and Constitution, 8/19/2003 "Terror Alerts May Become More Localized" p. 12A

During the 1990s, FEMA established a strong communications capability that worked very effectively in numerous natural disasters and during the response to the bombing at the Murrah Federal Office Building in Oklahoma City. There are many similarities between communicating public messages during a terrorist crisis and communicating public messages during a crisis caused by a natural hazard. Former New York Mayor Rudy Giuliani successfully implemented a communications strategy in the aftermath of the World Trade Center attacks that was very similar to the FEMA model.

However, there are significant differences between natural and terrorist events and communications, especially in the area of information collection and dissemination to the public. The anthrax incidents and the sniper attacks in the Washington, DC, metropolitan area clearly highlighted one of the most significant differences—the need to share timely information with the public during an ongoing crisis versus the needs of the criminal investigators to protect and hold close information as they seek to identify and detain the parties responsible for the incident. This very delicate balancing act will likely be repeated time and again in the years to come; how officials, the public, and the media will come to terms with this issue is not especially clear at this time.

In this section we will examine the underlying concepts of the FEMA model and examine some of the research conducted to date on crisis communications during a terrorist crisis.

THE **FEMA** MODEL

The mission of an effective disaster communications strategy is to provide timely and accurate information to the public. The foundation of an effective disaster communications strategy is built on the four critical assumptions:

- Customer focus
- Leadership commitment
- Inclusion of communications in planning and operations
- Media partnership

Customer Focus

An essential element of any effective emergency management system is a focus on customers and customer service. This philosophy should guide any communications with the public and with all partners in emergency management. A customer service approach includes placing the needs and interests of individuals and communities first, being responsive and informative, and managing expectations. The FEMA emergency information field guide illustrates the agency's focus on customer service and its strategy of getting messages out to the public as directly as possible. The introduction to the guide states the following:

> As members of the Emergency Information and Media Affairs team, you are part of the frontline for the agency in times of disaster. We count on you to be ready and able to respond and perform effectively on short notice. Disaster victims need to know their government is working. They need to know where and how to get help. They need to know what to expect and what not to expect. Getting these messages out quickly is your responsibility as members of the Emergency Information and Media Affairs team. (FEMA 1998)

The guide's mission statement reinforces this point further:

> To contribute to the well-being of the community following a disaster by ensuring the dissemination of information that:
>
> - Is timely, accurate, consistent, and easy to understand
> - Explains what people can expect from their government
> - Demonstrates clearly that FEMA and other federal, state, local, and voluntary agencies are working together to provide the services needed to rebuild communities and restore lives.
> FEMA, 1998

The customers for emergency management are diverse. They include internal customers, such as staff, other federal agencies, states, and other disasters partners. External customers include the general public, elected officials at all levels of government, community and business leaders, and the media. Each of these customers has special needs, and a good communications strategy considers and reflects their requirements.

Leadership Commitment

Good communications starts with a commitment by the leadership of the emergency management organization to sharing and disseminating information both internally and externally. The director of any emergency management organization must endorse and promote open lines of communications among the organization's staff, partners, and public in order to effectively communicate. This leader must model this behavior in order to clearly illustrate that communications is a valued function of the organization.

In the 1990s, FEMA Director James Lee Witt embodied FEMA's commitment to communicating with the FEMA staff and partners, the public, and the media. Witt was a very strong advocate for keeping FEMA staff informed of agency plans, priorities, and operations. He characterized a proactive approach in communicating with FEMA's constituents, and his accessibility to the media was a significant departure from that of previous FEMA leaders. Director Witt exhibited his commitment to effective communications in many ways:

- During a disaster response, he held media briefings daily, and sometimes two or three times a day. He would hold special meetings with victims and their families.
- He led the daily briefings among FEMA partners during a disaster response.
- He devoted considerable time to communicating with members of Congress, governors, mayors, and other elected officials, during times of disaster and nondisaster.
- He met four or five times a year with the State Emergency Management Directors, FEMA's principal emergency management partners.
- He gave speeches all over this country and around the world to promote better understanding of emergency management and disaster mitigation.

Through his leadership and commitment to communications, FEMA became an agency with a positive image and reputation. Communications led to increased success in molding public opinion and garnering support for the agency's initiatives in disaster mitigation.

Inclusion of Communications in Planning and Operations

The most important part of leadership's commitment to communications is inclusion of communications in all planning and operations. This means that a communications specialist is included in the senior management team of the emergency management organization. It means that communications issues are considered in the decision-making processes and that a communications element is included in all organizational activities, plans, and operations.

In the past, communicating with external audiences, or customers, and in many cases internal customers was neither valued nor considered critical to a successful emergency management operation. Technology has changed the equation. In today's world of 24-hour television and radio news and the Internet, the demand for information is never-ending, especially in an emergency response situation. Emergency managers must be able to communicate critical information in a timely manner to their staff, partners, the public, and the media.

To do so, the information needs of the various customers and the best methods by which to communicate with these customers must be considered at the same time that planning and operational decisions are being made. For example, a decision process on how to remove debris from a disaster area must include discussion of how to communicate information on the debris removal operation to community officials, the public, and the media.

During the many major disasters that occurred in the 1990s, Director Witt assembled a small group of his senior managers who traveled with him to the sites of disasters and worked closely with him in managing

FIGURE 8-2 Arlington, VA, September 15, 2001—FEMA Director Joe McAllbaugh talks to the media about FEMA's role in the response and recovery operations underway at the Pentagon after Tuesday's terrorist attack. Photo by Jocelyn Augustino/FEMA News Photo.

FEMA's efforts. This group always included FEMA's director of public affairs. Similarly, when planning FEMA's preparedness and mitigation initiatives, Witt always included staff from Public Affairs in the planning and implementation phases. Every FEMA policy, initiative, or operation undertaken during this time included consideration of the information needs of the identified customers, and a communications strategy to address these needs was developed.

Media Partnership

The media plays a primary role in communicating with the public. No government emergency management organization could ever hope to develop a communications network comparable to those networks already established and maintained by television, radio, and newspaper outlets across the country. To effectively provide timely disaster information to the public, emergency managers must establish a partnership with their local media outlets.

The goal of a media partnership is to provide accurate and timely information to the public in both disaster and nondisaster situations. The partnership requires a commitment by both the emergency manager and the media to work together; it also requires a certain degree of trust between both parties.

Traditionally, the relationship between emergency managers and the media has been tenuous. Conflicts have arisen as a result of the emergency manager's need to respond quickly and the media's need to obtain information on the response so it can report it just as quickly. These conflicts sometimes resulted in inaccurate reporting and tension between the emergency manager and the media. The loser in such conflicts is always the public, which relies on the media for its information.

It is important for emergency managers to understand the needs of the media and the value they bring to facilitating response operations. An effective media partnership provides the emergency manager with a communications network to reach the public with vital information. Such a partnership provides the media with access to the disaster site, access to emergency managers and their staff, and access to critical information that informs and ensures the accuracy of the reports before they reach the public.

An effective media partnership helps define the roles of the emergency management organizations, manage public expectations, and boost the morale of the relief workers and the disaster victims. All of these factors can speed the recovery of a community from a disaster event and promote preparedness and mitigation efforts designed to reduce the loss of life and property from the next disaster event.

Communications Infrastructure

FEMA built a substantial communications infrastructure to support these communications objectives. Resources were devoted to hiring and training staff with experience in working with the media and community and providing these employees with the tools they needed to be successful. FEMA built and maintained a television studio with satellite capabilities and an audio studio with radio broadcast capabilities. The agency also established an interactive web site where radio actualities and print information could be posted instantaneously. FEMA hired still and video photographers who were dispatched to the field, filing their photos electronically each night. These photos were then made available to media outlets around the country via the Internet.

Local emergency managers developed similar capabilities on a smaller scale in communities around the country. A research project conducted by graduate students at George Washington University found that many jurisdictions in the Washington, DC, metro area have built varying degrees of communications infrastructure such as communications plans, web and fax communication capabilities and trained staff that served them well during recent natural and man-made events. A copy of the research project is presented in Appendix 11.

Terrorism Application

As noted earlier, Mayor Giuliani was an effective communicator in the aftermath of the World Trade Center attacks. He quickly assumed the role of principal government spokesperson, providing information, solace, and comfort to victims and their families, fellow New Yorkers, the nation, and the world through a series of planned and unplanned media events and interviews over the course of the days and months after September 11. Giuliani has been praised for his candor, his sensitivity, and his availability during these efforts. He has set a standard by which public officials will be judged in future tragedies.

In Washington, DC, a different communications scenario surfaced in the days and weeks after the first anthrax-contaminated letter was discovered in the office of then U.S. Senate Majority Leader Tom Daschle in October 2001. A series of public officials and scientists issued often-conflicting information to the public as both the officials and the public struggled to understand the nature and the reach of the anthrax threat. The failure to communicate accurate and timely information reduced public confidence in the government response and increased the confusion and misinformation surrounding the events.

What factors made Mayor Giuliani's efforts successful and caused the situation in Washington to

worsen? What type of information and infrastructure support did Giuliani have that may or may not have been available to the public officials in Washington? Was the commitment to inform the public different in New York City than it was in Washington, DC?

A study of the anthrax attacks funded by The Century Foundation concluded that "the timely flow of information from experts to the public via the mass media will be the nation's best protection against panic and potential disaster" (Thomas, 2003). To reach this goal, the media and public officials will need to change the way they work together and possibly establish new protocols for determining the methods by which sensitive information is collected and disseminated to the public. These issues must ultimately be balanced against the public's right to know. As the study found, the public is often smarter and better informed than both the media and public officials believe (Thomas, 2003).

A report entitled "What Should We Know? Whom Do We Tell?: Leveraging Communications and Information to Counter Terrorism and Its Consequences" found that the dissemination of information before a terrorist incident is as critical, if not more so, as delivering timely and accurate information during and after a crisis (Chemical and Biological Arms Control Institute, 2002). Preincident planning and coordination and public education and awareness campaigns are critical elements in establishing clear lines of communications among responding agencies, significantly improving the opportunities to collect accurate information and make it available to the public through the mass media. Again, changes in current practices and relationships among responders and with the media must occur to meet the information needs before, during, and after future terrorist attacks (Chemical and Biological Arms Control Institute, 2002).

The Washington sniper attacks provide valuable insight into the difficulties in communicating with the public during an ongoing crisis. The tension between the need to provide timely and complete information when such information was lacking and the need to avoid compromising an ongoing criminal investigation was clearly evident during this nearly month-long crisis. A case study of this event and its media coverage is presented at the close of this chapter.

CONCLUSION

The experience of emergency managers with natural disasters provides at minimum a guide to the development of effective terrorism-related communications strategies. However, there is much work to be done to adapt existing risk, warning, and crisis communications models to the new hazards, the new partners, and the new dynamic between response and recovery and criminal activity associated with the new terrorist threat. One thing will remain constant: Communication with the public about the terrorist threat must receive the same attention and resources that are now going to new technologies, new training programs, and new organizations. It has never been more important that public officials talk to the public, and it has never been more difficult than it is now. If this problem is not addressed properly, it can only compound in the worst way the terrible consequences of any terrorist incident.

CASE STUDY 1
Washington, DC, Sniper Attacks

Introduction

In America's post-911 era of terror-awareness, the extreme actions of groups like al Qaeda are no longer necessary to spark detrimental anxiety-based social reactions. The two "snipers" who placed the nation's capital under a state of siege for 3 weeks with one rifle and a box of bullets confirmed this fact. Washington, DC's latest duct-tape and plastic "panic buying" spree, set off by the Department of Homeland Security's momentary "Terrorism Threat Index" increase, illustrates that the mere hint of a future event can now induce "irrational" behavior. Clearly, the emergency management community can no longer simply blame the media for such strong public sentiments. Controlling public fear is a public safety task that falls squarely upon the shoulders of local government, but

like other terrorism-preparedness and response functions, fear management must be supported by the federal government to be effective. There exists a rapidly growing need for agencies to adopt formal fear management capabilities staffed by appropriately trained, dedicated officials. In many cases of terrorism, fear is the greatest emergency that must be managed, and irresponsible or inadequate attempts to do so can actually increase the public's risk. Using the recent sniper crisis as example, this case study will examine the roots of public fear and the often-distorted reality of risk and will propose methods by which emergency management agencies can successfully manage fear should a terror-based event occur within their jurisdiction.

Background

The residents of the Washington, DC, metropolitan area[1] were confronted with a dramatically heightened sense of personal vulnerability in the $12\frac{1}{2}$ months leading up to the sniper crisis. On September 11, 2001, during the worst terrorist attack to take place on American soil, the city became the target of two hijacked airplanes.[2] Less than 1 month later, several letters containing anthrax were mailed to federal government offices, resulting in the closing of several buildings,[3] a mass prophylaxis with the antibiotic Cipro, and the death of several Washington, DC, postal workers. Ever-increasing security measures became impossible to avoid, with numerous streets surrounding federal buildings closed to the public, military vehicles with mounted machine guns positioned around the Pentagon, and all the while the media reporting that the emergency response capabilities of the Washington, DC, government would be

---

[1]Includes the District of Columbia, Northern Virginia, and several counties in Maryland The population of this region, according to the 2000 census, is 4,922,640 (Fair, 2002b).

[2]While only one plane crashed into a building in the Washington, DC, metropolitan area (the Pentagon), it is believed that the plane that crashed into a Pennsylvania field was heading for either the White House or the United States Capitol (Lochhead, 2002).

[3]As of late November 2002, the Brentwood Postal Facility, where the three postal workers who contracted anthrax worked, remained closed, with no planned reopening in the near future (Fernandez, 2002).

severely deficient should a mass casualty event occur in the near future (Ward, 2001).

It was easy to surmise that, to international and "homegrown" terrorists alike, Washington, DC, was a likely target. Reported levels of stress among area residents were much higher than those observed throughout the rest of the country, as indicated by several polls (Diaz and O'Rourke, 2002). By the time the sniper announced his presence on the morning of October 3 by killing four people, Washingtonians had already been pushed to the limits of their psychological stress tolerance.

Reactions and Actions

To study this case, we must first examine the reactions and actions of the authorities (the police department and other government officials), the media, and the public. These three groups were intimately linked by the virtual dearth of information that was available. The links can be simplified through the understanding that the authorities gathered and analyzed the information, the media broadcast the information, and the public received the information and acted upon it. The information flow diagram (Figure 8-3) depicts these links.

The following pages provide a broader understanding of each of these groups' actions in order to offer insight into why each may have acted as they did.

The Authorities

The individuals considered the "authorities" include the local, state, and federal government officials who were involved with the various aspects related to the response to the Sniper crisis. As this was primarily a law enforcement response to an event that involved only conventional weapons, the local police departments were the lead agencies involved.[4] These authorities, as displayed above, were the sole source of credible information during the crisis.

[4]Presidential Decision Directive-39 (PDD39), signed by President Clinton in 1995, gives the Department of Justice, through the Federal Bureau of Investigation (FBI), lead-agency authority in incidents where weapons of mass destruction are used or if the event is considered terrorism (Watson, 2000). The sniper crisis was never officially classified as such, so Chief Moose remained in command.

The Montgomery County Police Department (MCPD) was the first to become involved in the crisis on the morning of October 3, primarily because the majority of killings had taken place in Montgomery County, Maryland. Having authority in the affected jurisdiction, the MCPD put forth Chief Charles Moose as the official spokesperson for the media.[5] Although Chief Moose could provide only basic information concerning the characteristics of the victims and the locations of the shootings, he was immediately recognized as the leader in the crisis.[6] For the remainder of the crisis, the media (and likewise, the public) continued to look to Chief Moose for information and guidance. In fact, even though FBI agents ultimately arrested the suspects outside of Chief Moose's jurisdiction, it was Chief Moose who officially announced the arrest.

Chief Moose proclaimed that this was one of the greatest challenges he has ever faced (Stockwell, Ruane, and White, 2002). He had never been required to fulfill such an important public-relations role. The crisis quickly escalated to an international scale, and Chief Moose became the one man the world turned to for information so desperately sought. Chief Moose faced a major problem in that he often did not have very much information to give, and when he did, he felt that giving anything specific would jeopardize the investigation.

Chief Moose provided very little information detailing the actual risk people faced. He would regularly assure the public that police were doing their best to keep people safe and that the bulk of police resources were focused on solving the case, but he could not tell people how concerned they should

[5]Initially, MCPD spokeswoman Captain Nancy Demme was issuing statements to the media, but Chief Moose assumed the public-relations role upon further consideration of the severity of the crisis.

[6]Chief Moose, who holds a Ph.D. in Urban Studies, was seen not only as a trustworthy leader but also as the lead decision-maker. It was important that he addressed the media, considering all information passed through his hands—something a spokesperson of a lower rank could not claim. Moose was credited for his on-camera compassion, shedding tears on occasion and uttering comments throughout the crisis that showed his "human" side. At one point, for instance, he urged parents to spend more time with their children (Sun and Ly, 2002).

be about personal safety. On at least one occasion he even stated that "we've not been able to assure anyone their safety in regards to this situation" (Ruane and Stockwell, 2002).

The Washington, DC, Metropolitan Police Department (MPD) publicly issued a list of "Tips for Staying Safe." This list told residents to keep moving when outside, to walk in a rapid zig-zag pattern, and to avoid brightly lit open spaces. It also stated, "Remember that a sniper with the right equipment can shoot accurately from about 500 yards, the equivalent of five football fields" (Hurdle, 2002). These tips did not give any indication to residents of what their actual risk from the sniper might be. Some residents followed the advice they were given in these messages, but it is arguable that the lack of Chief Moose's endorsement of the tips prevented them from being widely observed.

School administrators became major players in the response to the sniper threat. Several schools were closed in the Richmond, Virginia, area after a sniper letter proclaiming that children were not safe was found at a shooting scene. Schools in other areas of Virginia and Maryland were closed as well, though no specific threats were given to the administrators of those schools as in Richmond. These closings were said to have been the result of a fear of liability among school administrators (*Economist*, 2002), and were not based upon solid evidence. While they claimed that "there was no other way to guarantee students' safety" (Gettleman, 2002), the fact remained that they did not want to be held responsible for making a decision to let school stay in session and then have a child shot in their "jurisdiction" during such a high-profile crisis. In fact, none of the schools shut down during the sniper crisis were shut down after the September 11 terrorists attacks or after any other unsolved murders in the area (Reel, 2002). A further explanation could be heard in the words of Henrico County Public School Superintendent Mark Edwards, who stated, "The decision was not based on any specific threats, but on 'the volume of concern'" (Gettleman, 2002). Such statements strengthened arguments that these actions were based on a reaction to fear, not the risk itself. Of course, it is undeniable that there existed a

genuine concern for the safety of the children in the motivation of these decisions, echoed by Montgomery County Superintendent Jerry West, who said, "We have always taken very seriously every day the level of threat to our children We have always consistently done everything we can do to keep our children safe" (Schulte, 2002). The closing of schools became a focus of media attention and undoubtedly affected public opinion about personal safety.[7]

Politicians also become involved in the public reaction to the crisis, and in several cases used the events to further their own agendas. Kathleen Kennedy Townsend, in her gubernatorial campaign, began attacking her opponent's opposition to a federal ban on assault weapons, stating that the gun control would be an answer to the voters' fears (Fineman, 2002). Connie Morella, campaigning for the House of Representatives, said, "I'm still knocking on doors, and when I do that, I think I'm a comfort to the people at home. I mean, if I'm out there doing that, people say, 'Hey, it must be all right'" (Barker, 2002).

There is finally the issue of unnamed authorities passing unreleased information to the media. It is important to stress both the detriment and opportunities presented by these insider "leaks." In numerous instances, the press learned of confidential information that was either never to be shared or not to be released immediately, and they broadcast that information, to the obvious dismay of Chief Moose. While on many occasions these leaks increased the tensions observed between the Sniper Task Force officials and the media, it cannot be overlooked that leaks were directly attributed to the capture of the two suspects.

The Media

The media was virtually the only bridge of information between the authorities and the public (Figure 8-3). Media agencies gleaned information from a myriad of sources, but the only information broadcast that could be deemed "factual" or "credible" almost always came directly from Chief Moose. In addition, that which

---

[7]In a *Washington Post* poll, 82 percent of respondents said that they approved of the way their local schools were handling the situation (*Washington Post* 2, 2002).

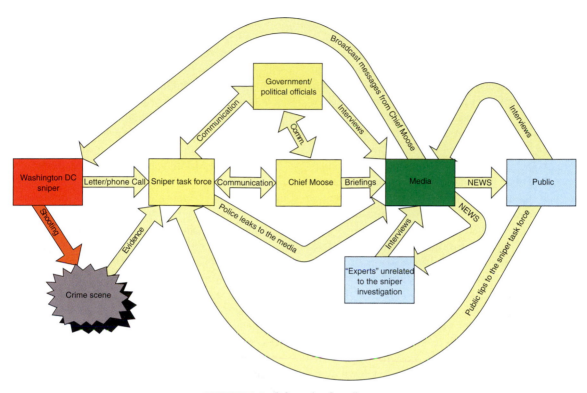

FIGURE 8-3   Information flow diagram

was leaked was usually confirmed or denied by Chief Moose. Media coverage, in regards to air time, was almost total when the crisis began and immediately after each successive victim. Regular news shows became dominated by the case, and there were constant "special reports" with additional information that was considered "related" to the case.

Coverage of the sniper crisis spanned the globe, and early on there were as many international news agencies as national ones camped outside the Montgomery County Police Department. The number of articles seen in the national and international press surged with each successive shooting, peaking immediately after the capture of Muhammad and Malvo. The actual daily number of articles, taken from major national and international newspapers, is displayed in Figure 8-4.

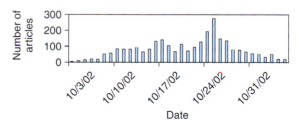

FIGURE 8-4   Number of articles related to the sniper crisis[8] appearing in 47 major international newspapers

[8]Numbers attained by searching for the keyword "sniper," using the Lexis/Nexis "general news search" of 47 major newspapers from throughout the world.

The media had a particularly strong influence in this crisis. Because the events were statistically so rare, and there were so few victims overall, there were startlingly few people outside of the immediate families and close friends of those victims who had any personal experience with "sniping" events.[9] In light of this fact, it is safe to say that members of the public received more than 99 percent of their information concerning the crisis from the media.[10] To put this statistic in perspective, it can be compared to the findings of an *L.A. Times* poll in which respondents claimed their "feelings about crime" were based 65 percent on what they read and saw in the media, and 21 percent on experience[11] (Walsh 1996, p. 9).

The media agencies often looked to alternate sources of information to achieve a competitive edge over one another. It was not uncommon to see "serial killings" experts speaking on news talk shows or to see "geographic profiling" experts doing the same (most notably after Chief Moose announced that geographic profilers were being used in the case). None of these alternate sources could provide any factual information outside of what was already known by the public, as they were not directly connected to the investigation (see Figure 8-3).

---

[9]Many people were affected by the secondary effects of the sniper, such as long traffic jams caused by roadblocks or school closings. However, as the direct consequence of the sniper was death or injury caused by shooting, only a very small group was *directly* affected.

[10]Fear of crime, often cited as being overestimated by the public, is also mainly established through media coverage. In the 1990s, when the murder rate in the United States dropped by 20%, the murder coverage on network newscasts increased by 600%. As a result, 62% of Americans "believed crime was soaring, and described our society as 'truly desperate' about crime" (Jacobson, 2001).

[11]The findings of this poll have been reinforced by other studies on the subject. When Esther Madriz, a professor at Hunter College in New York City, interviewed women in New York City about their fears of crime they frequently responded with the phrase "I saw it in the news." The interviewees identified the news media as both the source of their fears and the reason they believed those fears were valid. Asked in a national poll why they believe the country has a serious crime problem, 76 percent of people cited stories they had seen in the media. Only 22 percent cited personal experience (Glassner, 1999, p. xxi).

As stated earlier, there existed an explicit tension between the media and Chief Moose. This rift was most visible on October 9, when Chief Moose lashed out at the press for publishing information pertaining to a message written on a tarot card found at the school where a 13-year-old boy was shot. In another instance that angered Chief Moose, CNN reported, hours before the information was officially released, that the thirteenth shooting victim had died (Shales, 2002). Chief Moose's public scolding of the media (the result of a combination of sustained high levels of stress and inexperience with such high-profile events), however, was limited after the initial statements made in relation to the tarot card.

A fact that must be noted for its uniqueness is that the media was obviously used by the police as a direct mode of communication with the sniper. Chief Moose would "speak" to the sniper using cryptic messages at regularly scheduled press conferences without giving the media any prior indication that he would be doing this. Chief Moose did acknowledge his recognition of this important role the media played, one they were more than willing to fulfill.

The Public

The general public includes, for the sake of this case study, the people of the Washington, DC, and Richmond, Virginia, Metropolitan Areas. These people were the vulnerable group involved in the crisis—the sniper's targets. They were also the target of the media's and the authorities' information. The public was not only a target of these other players (including the sniper) but also a major source of information and action. The public demand for information fueled the media frenzy that occurred. Their fear of the sniper was the driving force in many of the decisions, rational or irrational, that were made by the authorities. Finally, the public was an integral component in the hunt for the sniper, and it was tips received from several members of the public that eventually led the police to Malvo and Muhammad.

Public action and reaction became the subject of many stories. This exhibited behavior became the focus of countless articles, detailing "newsworthy" actions that were performed in the name of safety.

Examples of such actions, followed by percentages of the affected population who admitted to performing them derived from a *Washington Post* poll (if available), include the following:

- Used different gas stations than one normally used (Morin and Deane, 2002)—36 percent
- Avoided stores/shopping centers close to highways (Morin and Deane, 2002)—32 percent
- Crouched down while pumping gas (Ropeik, 2002a)
- Ran or weaved through parking lots (Walker, 2002)
- Avoided outdoor activities (Irvin and Mattingly, 2002)—44 percent
- Kept constant movement in public places (Eccleston, 2002)
- Stayed at home except when absolutely necessary (Johnson and Finer, 2002)—13 percent
- Drove when one would normally have taken Metro (*Washington Post*, 2002b)—11 percent
- Watched or listened to the news more than usual (*Washington Post*, 2002b)—71 percent

Gas station attendants were witness to much of this fear because so many people believed that the stations were a preferred target location of the sniper. One attendant reported that "some people, when they get out of their cars, they are so scared that their hands shake, and they can't get their [credit] cards into the [gas pumps]" (Nakamura and Davis, 2002).

The public was a responsible recipient of this flood of information, and generally followed any behavioral advice they were given by the authorities. They learned the meaning of terms like "Code Blue" and "Code Red",[12] how to identify .223-firing assault rifles, the meaning of ballistics tests and what government agency conducts them, and how to identify box trucks, Chevy Astro Vans, and ladder racks. The public was told to call in their tips to the FBI tip line, and

[12]School security codes—Code Blue signifies that all outdoor activities are cancelled and positive ID is required to enter the building, and Code Red signifies that students are locked in their classroom in case a threat actually exists within the building (Lambert, 2002).

by the time the sniper was caught, over 90,000 calls had been placed (Whitlock, 2002).

What the public did not do, however, was panic. As much as the media wrote stories detailing the "paralyzing fear" experienced by the average person, life did go on with civility. There were no events where people were pushing each other over to get inside the "safety" of a store, for example. The public was fearful but intelligent, receptive to advice, and obviously able to process information well enough to locate the sniper within 24 hours once they learned the car and license plate information.

So Why Was Everyone So Afraid?

In their article "Rating the Risks," Paul Slovic, Baruch Fischhoff, and Sarah Lichtenstein begin as follows: "People respond to the hazards they perceive" (Slovic, Fischhoff, and Lichtenstein, 1979). The exhibited responses to the sniper at personal, local, regional, and even federal levels would indicate that sources influencing risk perception during the crisis existed at extreme levels. In this section, the sniper crisis will be compared to models developed in recent and historical research in order to better explain the peculiar public risk behavior observed. This examination will be structured according to the four "Risk Perception Fallibility" conclusions of Slovic, Fischhoff, and Lichtenstein found in their article "Rating the Risks" (Slovic, Fischhoff, and Lichtenstein, 1979).

Risk Perception Fallibility Conclusion 1: "Cognitive limitations, coupled with the anxieties generated by facing life as a gamble, cause uncertainty to be denied, risks to be distorted, and statements of fact to be believed with unwarranted confidence."

People tend to fear a risk less as they become better informed, with more specific details of the risk. However, the amount a person can discover about a risk will almost never be complete, as the actual likelihood or consequence most risks pose cannot be quantified in a way that addresses the specific threat faced by individuals (even well-known risks such as cancer or heart disease) (Ropeik, 2002c). The more uncertainty a risk poses, or, as Slovic, Fischhoff, and Lichtenstein state, "the more of a gamble something is," the more people will fear it. The sniper, who could strike anyone, anywhere, at any time, presented citizens in the Washington, DC, metropolitan area with the ultimate in uncertainty.

In the face of uncertainty, people will consciously or subconsciously make personal judgments based upon very imperfect information in order to establish some individual concept of the risk they face (Slovic, Fischhoff, and Lichtenstein, 1979). These judgments based on uncertainties and imperfect information often cause people to wrongly perceive their own risk, more often in a way that overstates reality. There could scarcely have been more uncertainty in regards to the public's knowledge of useful information in the sniper crisis. Members of the public were constantly told by the media that the police had very little to work with, as the sniper was leaving few clues at crime scenes (Patrick, 2002). People had no idea how great of a threat the sniper was in comparison to other public safety threats the police handled during routine action because these statistics were never released. Considering the amount of resources police dedicated, it would appear that the threat to public safety was greater than anything people in the area had ever faced, and considering the ineffectiveness of the actions of the police in catching the sniper (such as the systems of roadblocks),[13] the public could assume only that the police were powerless to combat this "enormous" threat. Many other factors external to the investigation gave an impression of dire seriousness and great uncertainty as well. Every time a media "expert" would attempt to define the sniper's actions, stating that he would likely not strike in place X or at time Y, the sniper would strike in that place or at that time. The great number of white vans in circulation gave the impression that the sniper was

everywhere.[14] The fact that schools were being closed, outdoor activities were regularly cancelled, the government was talking of bringing in the national guard, and the New York-based Guardian Angels were in the area pumping gas only strengthened the public's view that the risk was greater than it actually was. Frequent talk that the crisis may be the result of terrorism propagated the idea that the sniper might be just the first in a series of snipers that could become a regular part of life in America.[15] In a survey that asked citizens of the Washington, DC, metropolitan area how concerned they were that they might personally become a victim of the sniper, 19 percent said a great deal and 31 percent said somewhat scared—a total of 50 percent (*Washington Post*, 2002b).

Risk Perception Fallibility Conclusion 2: "Perceived risk is influenced (and sometimes biased) by the imaginability and memorability of the hazard. People may, therefore, not have valid perceptions even for familiar risks."

People are more afraid of those things that they can imagine or that they can remember. These easily available risks, as they are called, tend to be overestimated in regards to their likelihood of occurrence. Generally, people tend to fear what they hear about repetitively or constantly. This phenomenon is referred to as the "Availability Heuristic," which states that people perceive an event to be likely or frequent if instances of the event are easy to imagine or recall. This is a perception bias that can be correct when considering

---

[13]In one of the most comprehensive roadblock systems set up after the October 22 shooting (which occurred during the morning rush-hour traffic), one person was quoted in the *Washington Post* as saying that, after getting off the highway and onto the back roads, "I didn't see a single police car on the way in [to his job in College Park, MD]. If you're trying to stop someone, you'd have to have a tighter net, and that simply wasn't there. I was a novice trying to make my way through, and it was fairly easy" (Layton and Shaver, 2002).

[14]Mark Warr, a sociology professor at the University of Texas, Austin, writes, "People may experience fear merely in anticipation of possible threats or in reaction to environmental clues (e.g., darkness, graffiti) that imply danger" (Warr, 2000). To many people, the sight of ever-present white vans was a constant reminder that the sniper was still at large. To some, the sight of a white van was influential enough to elicit a physical response; a Connecticut business traveler, working in the area in a white Chevy van, stated "I pull into a gas station, and people jump down. Little kids point and say, 'Look, the sniper'" (Snyder, 2002).

[15]During the sniper crisis, it was reported in several newspapers that an al Qaeda suspect in Belgium had admitted during interrogations that members of al Qaeda had been trained in the terrorist training camps to shoot targets from 50–250 meters. The suspect added that al Qaeda planned to use snipers to kill U.S. senators while they were golfing (Reid, 2002).

events that are, in fact, frequently observed, such as in the case of those who believe that automobile accidents are common because almost everyone they know has been involved in one. However, when a risk that is spectacular but not necessarily common receives constant media attention, such as high-school shootings did in the 1990s (particularly the Columbine attack),[16] people often wrongly assume that similar events are very likely to occur. In the case of the sniper, where coverage in newspapers and on television, radio, and the Internet was constant, receiving front-page placement every day from October 4 until the suspects were captured on October 24,[17] it would follow that people would likely assume their personal risk was greater than it actually was. Again, the omnipresence of white vans and white box-trucks, both intimately associated with the sniper crisis through the police and the media, gave people a constant reminder of the sniper. Many of the decisions by government officials to close schools, restrict the movement of students, and cancel outdoor activities altered people's daily lives in such a way that they were made constantly aware of the crisis around them. In addition, seeing sniper victims on TV who were similar to themselves, doing things they regularly did, made it easy for people to imagine succumbing to the same fate

In an October 13 *Washington Post* poll that asked participants if they felt most threatened by the sniper shootings, the anthrax letters, or the September 11 attacks, 44 percent responded the sniper shootings, 29 percent responded the September 11 attacks, and 13 percent responded the anthrax letters (*Washington Post,* 2002b). Slovic and his colleagues described how events that are "out of sight [are] effectively out of mind." (Slovic, Fischhoff, and Lichtenstein, 1979). It would follow that the opposite was true of the

sniper: that which is always in sight is always on people's minds.

Risk Perception Fallibility Conclusion 3: "[Risk Management] experts' risk perceptions correspond closely to statistical frequencies of death. Laypeople's risk perceptions [are] based in part on frequencies of death, but there [are] some striking discrepancies. It appears that for laypeople, the concept of risk includes qualitative aspects such as dread and the likelihood of a mishap being fatal. Laypeople's risk perceptions were also affected by catastrophic potential."

It can be difficult for people to exactly understand the statistics they are given, and even more difficult for them to conceptualize how those statistics apply to them personally. Furthermore, these statistics tend to do little to affect the way people perceive the risks that are calculated. This is not to say that the average person lacks sufficient intelligence to process numbers; it is just that the numbers are not the sole source of influence on public risk perception. In ranking their risks, people tend to rely more on qualitative factors than on the quantitative likelihood of a hazard resulting in personal consequence (Slovic, Fischhoff, and Lichtenstein, 1979). People are generally more concerned with the consequences than the likelihoods of risks.

In consideration of the statistics provided to the public by the media, it is important to examine their quality and usefulness to the recipients. While it is clear that everyone knew the number of people killed by the sniper, few knew the actual number of people living in the affected area or the actual murder rate in "normal" years within that same area. Without complete information the given statistics were meaningless and likely misleading. In fact, in the absence of complete information, people assumed that their chances of becoming a sniper victim were much greater than they really were. Economists have classified this tendency of people to overestimate unknown or unclear risks as "risk-ambiguity aversion" (*Economist*, 2002). However, even if the statistics were straightforward, it is difficult for people to understand how those numbers affect them as individuals, even if they are risk "experts" (Jardine and Hrudley, 1997).

---

[16]In 1999, two students of Columbine High School in Littleton, CO, shot and killed 13 of their classmates The extensive media coverage led to the public perception that school shootings were on the rise, when in fact, the incidence of school shootings was actually falling that year (Kisken, 2001).

[17]As of November 15, the sniper case was still receiving daily front-page coverage in the *Washington Post*.

Paul Slovic, Baruch Fischhoff, and Sarah Lichtenstein, in their article "Facts and Fears: Understanding Perceived Risk," proposed that there are 18 risk characteristics that influence public risk perception. These qualitative measures have helped to explain what attributes of a risk cause public fear. According to their measures, the risk of being killed by the sniper ranks among the most feared risks, as it is dreaded, has consequences that are fatal, "affects me," is new, is not easily reduced, is uncontrollable, among other reasons. The sniper risk, not surprisingly, falls close to terrorism and crime on the authors' ranking of risks' ability to elicit fear.

Risk Perception Fallibility Conclusion 4: "Disagreements about risk should not be expected to evaporate in the presence of 'evidence.' Definitive evidence, particularly about rare hazards, is difficult to obtain. Weaker information is likely to be interpreted in a way that reinforces existing beliefs."

The sniper announced his presence with a true mass-murder event.[18] The initial news reports described an ensuing crisis that left open the possibility that the murders may continue at an equally high rate of incidence (five killings in 16 hours). By the end of October 3, police had little to work with, and there was little hope that the sniper would be quickly captured. The public had been told from the very beginning that they were dealing with a killer who was a grave threat to public safety. Due to psychological factors described in the previous three Risk Perception Fallibility Conclusions, people were made to believe they were at high risk. This became the frame of reference in which the public was to define the sniper risk, and one that would now be very difficult to alter.

The crisis continued for 3 weeks. Many (often heavily editorialized) articles did try to enlighten people about their actual personal risk, some even giving detailed statistics that illustrated to the public that

their vulnerability to the sniper was extremely low. Unfortunately, not only did these articles rarely (if ever) get front-page coverage but they were greatly outnumbered by articles telling people that their lives were in grave danger from the sniper. In the end, it was not the "long-shot" statistics nor the articles that told people to remain calm that were believed but the fear-mongering and sensational articles given priority coverage by newspapers and news networks. This is not surprising, considering the findings of Slovic, Fischhoff, and Lichtenstein's research. They state that "people's beliefs change slowly and are extraordinarily persistent in the face of contrary evidence. New evidence appears reliable and informative if it is consistent with one's initial belief; contrary evidence is dismissed as unreliable, erroneous, or unrepresentative." They add that "convincing people that the catastrophe they fear is extremely unlikely is difficult under the best conditions. Any mishap could be seen as proof of high risk, whereas demonstrating safety would require a massive amount of evidence" (Slovic, Fischhoff, and Lichtenstein, 1979), evidence that is sometimes impossible to obtain in an accurate or timely manner.

This stoicism is compounded by the fact that once people make their initial judgments, they believe with overwhelming confidence that their beliefs are correct. This phenomenon, called the "Overconfidence Heuristic," suggests that people often are unaware of how little they know about a risk and how much more information they need to make an informed decision. More often than not, people believe that they know much more about risks than they actually do. With regard to the sniper, having overconfidence in incorrect information was inevitable considering the nature of the media coverage. For instance, with "expert" profilers giving descriptions of the killer's "most likely" demographics as a lone young, white male, it is no surprise that everyone was caught off guard when the pair turned out to be two black males (Fears and Thomas-Lester, 2002). However, with no confirmed information provided about the suspects prior to their arrest, there logically should have been no surprise no matter what race or age he, she, or they were.

---

[18]The Sniper was by definition, both a serial killer and a mass murderer. Serial killers are defined as people who kill several people over a period of days, weeks, or years, killing in cycles, shifting between active and "cooling off" periods, while mass murderers kill several people at one time, usually in one location, over a couple of hours without a "cooling off" period (Macalester College, 2002).

This phenomenon has been linked to media coverage of other spectacular events in the past, specifically in regard to the way in which people's rating of risks depends on the amount of media coverage a risk receives. For example, one study showed that the percentage of crimes covered by the media that involve perpetrators and victims of different races is of a greater proportion than occurs in reality. In other words, one is more likely to see a news story describing a white victim of a black attacker than a story depicting a black victim of a black attacker, even though the latter is more common. This inconsistency in coverage is seen as the main reason Caucasians overestimate their likelihood of being a victim of interracial crime by a factor of 3 (Twomey, 2001). Paul Slovic wrote in his article "Informing and Educating the Public About Risk" that "strong beliefs are hard to modify" and "naïve views are easily manipulated by presentation format" (Slovic, 1986).

Often, it is only time that can change people's opinions about the risks they personally face. One major reason people are more scared of a new risk than an old risk is that they have not been able to gather enough information to alter their initial impression. After time has passed, and they realize that their expectations for victimization have not been realized for themselves or anybody that they know, they begin to question the validity of their views. Had the sniper not been caught, the general public would have gained a more accurate appreciation of how small their chance of becoming a victim was, much in the manner that people are no longer as concerned about the child abductions that seemed to plague the United States during 2001.[19] Fortunately, the sniper was caught before this hypothesis could be tested.

Reality—Statistics of the Crisis

"Of all the grim facts surrounding [the] Oklahoma City [bombing], perhaps the grimmest is the one

nobody talks about: against the backdrop of everyday American tragedy, 167 deaths is not many. . . . In a typical year, guns kill 38,000 Americans and about that many die on our roads. These numbers routinely go up or down 2 percent or 3 percent—half a dozen Oklahoma bombings—without making the front page." (Political commentator Robert Wright, *Time*, May 1995—From Walsh, 1996, p. 18.)

In the 3 weeks that the sniper terrorized over 5 million people in the Washington, DC, metropolitan area, shooting 13 people and killing 10, "routine" crime took place virtually unnoticed. In the District of Columbia alone, there were 239 assaults with a deadly weapon, 32 people shot, and 22 people murdered (Barger, 2002). This accounts for just 10 percent of the total area where the sniper operated, so it can be assumed that there were far more of these "routine" murders than 22. However, not one of these crimes merited front-page coverage in the newspapers.

In the previous section it was necessary to put aside statistics in order to understand public risk perception, but now the statistics alone must be analyzed to determine how the real risk people faced during those 3 fearful weeks from the sniper compared to the other risks they face in their daily lives without second thought. Richard Wilson of Harvard University writes in his article "Analyzing the Daily Risks of Life" that "to compare risks we must calculate them" (Wilson, 1979, p. 57). To calculate the statistical risk that the citizens of the Washington, DC, metropolitan area faced, it is necessary to ascertain the population of the area where the sniper operated. These statistics will not be perfect by any means, as they cannot account for the ever-increasing zone in which the sniper operated (*Economist*, 2002). Additionally, although the sniper operated within a large geographic area, there was not an equal distribution of murders across the total area (Montgomery County was the location of seven of these murders, for example). However, these statistics will be more accurate in terms of personal risk (see description in footnotes 24 and 25), because the virtually random selection of victims who were performing a wide range of activities brings the population and personal risk almost to equality.

[19]After a media frenzy followed a series of high-profile child abductions during the early summer of 2001, there was great apprehension reported among parents who began to fear for the safety of their children. Later reports showed that the majority of child abductions were due to child custody disputes and not performed by strangers. The frenzy quickly died down once public knowledge about these facts became more common (STATS, 2002).

To achieve this rough estimate of personal risk, it would be possible to consider the number of victims, divided into the total population of the affected area, spread out over the period in which the sniper was operating. This would not be accurate in projecting future risk, however, because the operating environment changed for the sniper in the early morning of October 3. When the police were not aware of his presence, it was possible for the sniper to repeatedly attack within a short period of time. Shortly after initiation of the crisis, when the sniper's presence was officially recognized, his attacks required more time[20] (presumably for more detailed planning). It is therefore necessary to estimate how the murders would have progressed over the course of a year in the context of a post-awareness scenario. In operating under this assumption, it can be said that the four murders that took place on the morning of October 3 would have likely been only one murder had the police been on alert for the sniper. In that case, the statistics to work with are as follows:

Number of people shot
  (adjusted for post-awareness):   10
Number of people killed
  (adjusted for post-awareness):   7
Population, Washington, DC,
  metropolitan area:[21]   4,922,152
      (83.16% of total sniper-area
      population)
Population, Richmond-Petersburg
  metropolitan area:[22]   996,512
      (16.84% of total sniper-area
      population)
Population, total affected area: 5,919,152
Number of days the sniper operated
  (10/2/02–10/24/02):[23]   23

Multiplier (for 365 day average):   15.870
National murder rate: 5.5/100,000
Washington, DC, metropolitan
  area murder rate: 7.4/100,000
Richmond-Petersburg metropolitan
  area murder rate: 11.1/100,000

Using these numbers, we may derive the following population risk factors for the people living in the area where the sniper operated:

Chance of being shot by the
   sniper in the next 12 mos.:[24] 2.7/100,000
Or   1/37,297
Chance of being killed by the sniper in the next
   12 mos.:[25] 1.9/100,000
Or   1/53,325

Comparing these figures against the risks that people face in their daily lives with little or no concern will put the real risk from the sniper into statistical perspective. Table 8-1 lists the likelihood of death from various causes, listed in order of decreasing risk.

According to these figures, a person was more likely to be accidentally poisoned or to die in a car accident than to be shot and possibly killed by the sniper. As previously noted, the other risks have higher variance between individual and population risk, as more can be done on the personal level to mitigate them (such as wearing a seatbelt or a life-preserver, for example), but the fact remains that for the average of all people these statistics are accurate.

Lessons Learned and Future Implications

Now that the sniper crisis has been compared to risk perception models and the population risk statistics have been calculated, we can ask the question, "Should the public have been so deeply fearful during

---

[20]In addition, the sniper attacks waned in frequency over time, but this factor will not be considered because the sampling period was too short to derive a long-term frequency (*Economist,* 2002).

[21]2000 census information (FAIR, 2002a).

[22]2000 census information (FAIR, 2002b).

[23]The murders that took place before this date were committed for the purposes of robbery or passion and are therefore not included in the analysis of population risk.

[24]The number of people in the affected area (5,919,152) divided by the number of people shot during the sniper crisis (10—adjusted), times the year-adjustment multiplier (15.870).

[25]The number of people in the affected area (5,919,152) divided by the number of people killed during the sniper crisis (7—adjusted), times the year-adjustment multiplier (15.870).

TABLE 8-1 Likelihood of Death from Various Causes

Hazard	Annual risk	Lifetime risk
2000 Murder Rate: Sniper area (weighted)*	1/12,870	1/167
2000 Murder Rate: National	1/18,182	1/236
Car accident**	1/18,752	1/244
Accidental fall	1/20,728	1/270
Accidental poisoning	1/22,388	1/292
Murdered with a gun	1/25,196	1/328
Shot by sniper	1/37,297	1/484
Hit by car while walking	1/45,117	1/588
Killed by sniper	1/53,325	1/693
Drowning (accidental)	1/77,308	1/1,008
Fire/smoke inhalation	1/81,487	1/1,062
Lightning	1/4,262,813	1/55,578

*The combined Washington, DC, metropolitan area (WMA)/Richmond-Petersburg metropolitan area (RPMA) combined crime rate was found by taking the crime rate of the WMA (7.1/100,000) and multiplying it by the WMA percentage of total population area (83.16%), then taking the RPMA crime rate (11.1/100,000) and multiplying it by the RPMA percentage of total population (16.84%), to give a combined crime rate of 7.77/100,000. WMA and RPMA 2000 murder rate data taken from *Crime in the United States*, 2000 (FBI, 2001).

**(Memmott, 2002b)—All figures other than those associated with the sniper are attributed to this source.

the sniper crisis?" The answer, according to these established models is yes, they definitely should have been, considering the information they received. However, according to the statistical data and risk comparison, they did not need to be so afraid, and there are ways in which the media, emergency responders, and other federal, state, and local government officials can limit this type of fear in the future.

1. Respond separately to the event and to the fear

The authorities, namely the police and the government officials, dedicated a vast amount of resources to the sniper investigation because of the high level of public fear and concern, not because of some recognized disproportionate threat to public safety.[26] Conversely, they did little, if anything, to treat the fear itself. When emergency management agencies respond in this way, they can actually amplify the level of anxiety by signaling to the public that their crippling fears are justified[27] and move emergency management and police resources away from routine but necessary public safety work. These actions increase people's susceptibility to other health-related risks by preventing them from exercising and through the damaging physiological effects of fear-induced stress.[28] Variations of the statement "People will never feel safe again until the sniper is caught," repeated in every newspaper, echoed the primary motivation behind this large-scale response.

In the future, police and government officials should treat the event and the fear of the event as two separate problems that need to be addressed separately. This is a need that has already been recognized in past crime and terrorism crises (Warr, 2000). There should be a separate function of emergency management—a "Fear Management Team" consisting of members with backgrounds in sociology, psychology, emergency management, public education, and public relations, among others. This team would have several subfunctions, as follows:

- Measure levels of public fear: There are established ways in which fear can be measured in real-time status, including by conducting

[26]This is not an uncommon action for authorities to take. For instance, the EPA's Science Advisory Board discovered that "agency resources tend to be directed to problems 'perceived' to be the most serious rather than those that actually pose the greatest threat." (Walsh, 1996).

[27]Barry Glassner writes in *The Culture of Fear* that "the turnabout in [American] domestic public spending over the past quarter century, from child welfare and antipoverty programs to incarceration, did not [. . .] produce reductions in *fear* of crime. Increasing the number of cops and jails arguably has the opposite effect: It suggests that the crime problem is all the more out of control" (Glassner, 1999).

[28]James Walsh, author of *True Odds: How Risk Affects Your Everyday Life* writes, "When European terrorism reared up in 1986, 2 million Americans changed their travel plans The reality, of course, was that most of these people could have done a lot more to enhance their life expectancies by losing 10 pounds and going to Europe as planned" (Walsh, 1996).

surveys, recognizing behavioral indicators (what people are doing to avoid what they fear—changes in routine, for example), and establishing recognition-triggers for "transient public episodes of fear" (how a population is acting as a whole in response to fear—drops in the number of public transportation users, for example) (Warr, 2000). Emergency management can only respond to a high level of fear if they know it exists. Not all events will be as obvious as the sniper crisis.

- Develop an informed, educational public relations message: As a part of regular emergency management operations, a trusted leader with decision-making power must be identified and put forth to communicate with the public through the media. The members of the Fear Management Team would process information culled from their monitoring of public fear to create communications through the trusted official in a manner that adequately and accurately addresses public fear. They would develop mental models that give emergency responders a clear understanding of what exactly the public does and does not understand about the risk and what they believe emergency responders are doing and/or are able to do to ensure their security. They would work directly with the emergency response team to inform them about the exact information the public needs to correct or adjust their belief in order to more closely match reality. They would work with government officials as well, helping them to inform the public through reinforcement of the messages given by the emergency response spokesperson.

- Address public fear directly: The Fear Management Team would coordinate the services of mental health specialists in an effort to further reduce public fear to more "healthy" levels. These public health officials would address the public directly, through media outlets, or through community groups.[29] Because they would have information

directly related to the crisis, they would be able to make accurate and informed communications through the media (unlike the uninformed "experts" that were prevalent during the sniper crisis who did not have access to secure information). The information would not be compromised by this team, because it would not be necessary to share the specifics—however, the public would recognize that the team members, as trusted public health officials, were making informed decisions and would more likely invest more faith in these opinions in adjusting their perceptions.

- Assist local government/community authorities in decision making: Both local government and community groups must respond to crises, and their actions often directly affect the public. School superintendents need to know when it is appropriate to cancel school, and community groups need to know when public events must be postponed. Without direction from emergency response (the most "informed" source of information), they will not act with consistency and will likely send a mixed message to the public. In addition, the overreaction by one influential government or community leader can lead to secondary responses from other less organized or less informed groups.[30] This Fear Management Team would serve as an advisory board for government and community groups, ensuring that their leaders are able to make decisions based on the most complete and current information, and allowing the groups to work in consensus rather than as separate entities.

2. Increase responsible reporting by the media

The media have a responsibility to ensure that during crisis events, public safety information reaches a wide audience in a timely and accurate manner, a duty

---

[29]In Loudoun County, MD, a community group formed after 9/11 to help people cope with the stress gave free public seminars to help people cope with the sniper stress (Helderman and Goldenbach, 2002).

[30]Barry Glassner, author of *The Culture of Fear* wrote, "Since the first sniper shooting October 2, a sort of domino effect has spurred decision-makers: School systems have decided, in conference calls with local law enforcement arranged through the Washington Council of Governments, to suspend all outdoor activities. Then day-care centers and youth soccer leagues have followed the lead of their public school systems, and the smaller community groups have fallen into line" (Reel, 2002).

they are recognizing and embracing more each year (Moore, 2002). However, most newspaper and television news employees have never received crisis communications training and therefore have no idea how to fulfill this role. The media operate as a business and are motivated primarily by ratings and viewer and reader numbers, which ensure steady income generation; the media cannot be expected to cease provisions of blanket coverage during extreme events such as the sniper crisis. The industry functions within a time-compressed environment in which editors often must develop stories using incorrect or incomplete information. Journalists will continue to proactively seek information on crises using their own means, and there will always be leaks made to the media by emergency management and public officials.

The media is adroit at using scare tactics and fear-mongering to harness public attention and often does little to calm nerves once that attention is obtained. These agencies must learn as an industry that they can contribute to public safety by providing accurate, responsible, and useful information while still maintaining these traditional "shock" methods to attract viewers, and thereby preserve a competitive edge without sacrificing integrity. For the media to participate in a crisis response constructively, they need to add to the glut of sensationalism a balance of rationality—a reality check for the public to process information and judge individual risk. If they broadcast a message that says, "Four of the victims were shot while pumping gas at local gas stations," for example, they need to qualify this statement by adding, "however, there have been approximately 10.5 million gas transactions made at over 1000 gas stations in the affected area during the crisis so far" (Memmott, 2000b) in order to give adequate perspective to the original statement. Emergency management must recognize the media as willing participants in the process and provide them with this information that may not be readily available otherwise.

The media should recognize and act upon the public's tendency to anchor and adjust[31] in forming perceptions on risk. This cannot be denied. If a story informs citizens that "this is the greatest number of law enforcement officers ever dedicated to a criminal investigation in county history,"[32] readers may incorrectly infer that their lives are at greater risk than ever before,[33] and all future information will be processed within this context. If they are later told in an article that is given proportional emphasis,[34] for instance, that, "although 10 people have been killed by the sniper in the past 3 weeks, there are an average of 38 people killed in traffic accidents alone during the same time period in the Washington DC, metropolitan area," (Memmott, 2002b), they will be able to rank their personal risk more appropriately.

Media agencies must also avoid irresponsible reporting aimed at "creating" stories. Martha Moore of *USA Today* cites as an example of this phenomenon the many cases in which local news stations will make announcements, before a coming storm for example, that "people should prepare by stocking up on batteries and water before the stores run out of these items."

[31]The Anchoring and Adjustment heuristic states that people use a natural starting point as a first approximation in analyzing how a risk affects them. The initial anchoring point is then adjusted as more information is received (Slovic, Fischhoff, and Lichtenstein, 1976). Anchors are generally set according to the first information a person receives about a risk.

[32]In a CNN article titled *Sniper Probe "Unprecedented" for Region*, it was reported that "a conservative estimate would put at 1,000 the number of officers and experts from various federal, state, and local law enforcement officers assigned to the case, and the size of the investigation grows with each new development—and shooting—in the case" (Loughlin, 2002).

[33]Irresponsible reporting has not only caused undue stress on numerous occasions, but has hurt local economies as well. In the 1990s the media widely reported on a crime wave against tourists in Florida, which resulted in ten murders. Barry Glassner, author of *The Culture of Fear*, writes that the event was labeled a crime wave only because the media chose to label it as such. "Objectively speaking, ten murders out of 41 million visitors did not even constitute a ripple, much less a wave, especially considering that at least 97 percent of all victims of crime in Florida are Floridians Although the Miami area had the highest crime rate in the nation during this period, it was not tourists who had most cause for worry. One study showed that British, German, and Canadian tourists who flock to Florida each year to avoid winter weather were more than 70 times more likely to be victimized at home" (Glassner, 1999). This type of reporting made many tourists think twice before traveling to Florida, and the tourism industry suffered as result.

[34]Often, articles that proclaim bad news are given front-page coverage and are in great quantity while those reporting good news are given secondary status and appear less frequently (Johnson, 2002).

Following this statement, the news agency will post teams at local stores to report that people are crowding these local stores in order to get their hands on the few remaining batteries and bottles of water that remain, causing successive waves of panic buying[35] (Moore, 2002). Similar situations occurred during the sniper crisis. The media would report that "gas stations are the preferred location of the sniper," and then run stories showing how people were not going to gas stations, which had the snowball effect of making consumers progressively more afraid to visit gas stations.

The media agencies are not villains. Quite to the contrary, they are a vital component to emergency management without which risk communication would be nearly impossible. Also, not all of today's media reporting is misinformed or irresponsible. There are many news agencies that employ reporters who are trained or knowledgeable in crisis communications and risk perception and who regularly practice the suggestions made above. For example, in a *USA Today* article titled "How to Cope? Keep Guard and Spirits Up," the author suggested that residents of the DC area "take a lesson from people in other nations who confront such fears every day: Get on with life—but be more alert than ever to dangers and more kind than ever to others" (Memmott, 2002a). The knowledge and experience of reporters like this must be shared across the industry. The journalist's goal is to provide the public with timely information; the extent to which that information is both accurate and effective depends largely upon the level of cooperation provided by emergency management.

3. Establish public risk perception and risk communication training standards for emergency management, government officials, and the media

The federal government requires both emergency responders and public officials to complete training and prove competencies in performing many of the tasks associated with their job duties. While many first

responders who communicate directly with the public are trained in public relations and communications, they are often not trained in crisis communications, risk perception, or risk communication. Their support teams, who provide the information on which their public response is based, are just as likely to lack adequate training in these areas. A statement from an ATF agent who described the extensive damage a .223 bullet fired from a rifle does to the human body or the MPD safety tip that reminded residents that a sniper could hit victims from 500 yards are examples of statements that neither provided useful information to the public nor controlled fear. If emergency responders and government officials are to effectively treat the fear associated with a crisis, they must be trained in methods that have proven successful in the past and develop a clear understanding of what drives human fear. Training in these studies will not become institutional unless the need is recognized throughout the emergency management sector. These training opportunities must also be made available to the media in order to ensure a comprehensive approach to fear management. If this training is conducted through a partnership between media and emergency management, interpersonal relationships will likely be created, thus further enhancing fear management.

If training in risk perception and risk communication became a requirement for emergency management public relations-related tasks, fear management would become a routine organizational function. The existence of a Fear Management Team, as proposed above, would be better understood and utilized across all functions of emergency management agencies if management-level employees had a more comprehensive understanding of its purpose. Industry observance of this requirement would be more accepted if the federal or state government covered the costs for this training as they do for many other law enforcement and public safety programs.

Chief Moose did an outstanding job as a crisis manager and leader, but he did little to combat fear directly. Considering the lack of experience among emergency response officials with terrorism in the United States, it is unlikely that many of them would be prepared to take on such a difficult task as fear management. However, if

[35]The phenomenon observed when people irrationally stock up on certain "survival" groceries they believe will be needed but unavailable after a disaster occurs.

the threat of terrorism is growing, as the FBI and the Department of Homeland Security claim it is, then the need for such training is obvious.

4. Seize the opportunity during periods of increased public attention for risk education

Almost every person in the Washington, DC, metropolitan area and likely the entire United States can say with confidence that they know what a .223 caliber bullet is and what it looks like, can identify Bushmaster as a brand of rifle, can tell approximately how far (in meters) a sniper can hit a target, can describe a box truck, and knows what a ladder rack on a Chevy Astro Van looks like. When people are afraid, they pay attention and they learn. It cannot be overlooked that despite the number of police looking for the sniper, it was a truck-driver who located the sniper after learning the make, model, and license plate number of the sniper's vehicle on the news.

People will listen to emergency response and government suggestions if the source of information is trusted and holds decision-making authority.[36] These rare mass-education opportunities must not be wasted. Emergency managers have a moral obligation under such circumstances to inform people of the real risks they face and tell them what it is they need to do to protect themselves from those risks. Telling people to weave while going through a parking lot during the sniper crisis is likely to make people think twice about going to the store, but it is unlikely that the information will save more than a few, if any, lives. Telling people

[36]People tend to heed government suggestions, so they should be rational and helpful, and most importantly, carefully thought out. During the anthrax crisis, when public fear was at epidemic levels, 36 percent of Americans were washing their hands after opening mail as the U.S. Postal Service had instructed them to do. In areas where people had actually contracted anthrax-related sicknesses, hand-washing incidence was higher—45 percent in Washington, DC, and 57 percent in Trenton, NJ—this from an attack that killed only 5 of over 400 million people. People were not acting irrationally, but listening to the advice they had been told by their government (Pelton, 2001). The government warned the public not to hoard the antibiotic Cipro, but the media reported they were stockpiling the drug to such an extreme as to cause pharmacy shortages. Surveys showed that only 4 percent of Americans had bought the antibiotic against the advice of the government.

that if they feel the need to drive long distances to purchase gas in order to feel safe, then they must also be sure to wear their seat belt because car accidents are a much more likely killer than the sniper, instantly contributes to a decrease in thousands of peoples' risk.

Modified Information Flow Diagram— The Road Ahead

On March 1 the emergency management functions of the federal government were officially transferred into the Department of Homeland Security Secretary. Tom Ridge has been given exactly one year to reorganize and improve the functions of 22 absorbed agencies in a way that more effectively prevents, prepares for, responds to, and recovers from future terrorist attacks (and natural and technological disasters). Concurrently, the states have been spending billions of their own dollars to prevent and prepare for terrorist attacks, primarily following the direction of the federal government. This opportunity to improve current emergency management systems must not pass by without a full examination of the vital importance of managing public fear.

The following information flow diagram (Figure 8-5) is provided as a possible solution to managing fear at the local level. The diagram depicts how a Fear Management Team would operate within the overall flow of crisis information and within the range of emergency management activities. Federally funded crisis communications training is displayed in order to indicate the likely recipients of this training. Although this design is simplified, it can be easily adapted to suit the needs of almost any local emergency response to a crisis that captures extensive public attention. Figure 8-5 does not directly address where the additional resources provided in federally declared disasters would apply or how the command structure would accommodate these resources, as it remains to be seen how the DHS reorganization will alter existing response systems.

Conclusion

Fear is irrational only if people have enough information about a hazard to perform a personal risk analysis, find that the likelihood of the hazard affecting them is smaller than or equal to risks they face on a daily

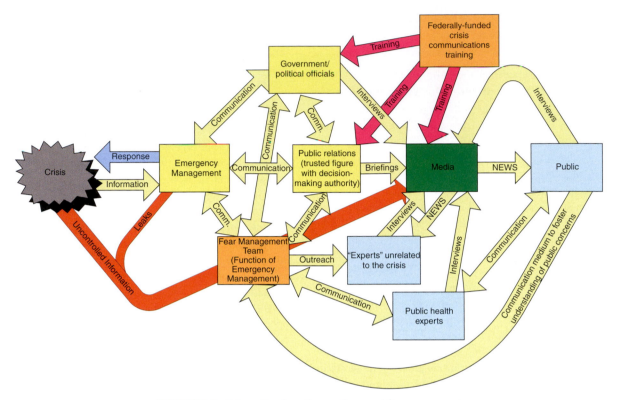

FIGURE 8-5   Information flow diagram: improved fear management

basis with little or no thought, and are still afraid. When there are little or no means for people to gather information to make informed personal risk analyses, they tend to overestimate personal vulnerability because of incomplete and often incorrect information. Only information can combat fear, and only the government (in partnership with the media) can provide for that need.

On November 7, 2002, two people in New York City were hospitalized and confirmed to be infected with bubonic plague—the first cases in that city in over 100 years. Bubonic plague is a disease that is historically one of the greatest killers of man, decimating over a third of the population of Europe during the Middle Ages. To the people of New York City, this disease was dreaded, new, fatal, globally catastrophic, involuntary, and notoriously hard to control. Why did fear not reign in New York when this information hit the newsstands? The answer lies in the way the infor-

mation was first reported by Dr. Thomas Frieden, the health commissioner of New York City (a city that has in recent years experienced two major health crises—the first U.S. outbreak of West Nile virus and the anthrax letters in 2001). After announcing the two cases of the disease, Dr. Frieden made the following statement:

> Bubonic plague does not spread from person to person. There is no risk to New Yorkers from the two individuals who are being evaluated for plague. Those patients became ill within 48 hours of arriving in New York City. Therefore, we are confident that their exposure occurred in New Mexico. More than half of the plague cases in the United States are in New Mexico. A wood rat and fleas from the rodent that were found on the couple's property in Santa Fe, New Mexico, tested positive in July for plague. Bubonic plague is a bacterial disease in rodents transmitted to humans through the bites of infected fleas. (*CNN*, 2002)

The story barely lasted a week.

REVIEW QUESTIONS

1. Identify and discuss the four critical assumptions underlying the crisis communications efforts of the Federal Emergency Management Agency (FEMA) in the 1990s.

2. Discuss the role of the mass media in risk and crisis communications?

3. Review the content and communication delivery mechanisms used in the Department of Homeland Security's Ready.gov campaign.

4. How would you reengineer the Homeland Security Advisory System (HSAS)? How many alert levels would you include, what colors and titles would you associate with each alert level and what preparedness messages designed for individuals and communities would you associate which each alert level?

5. In reviewing the case study of the Washington, DC Sniper Attacks, it is clear that Montgomery County Police Chief Charles Moose was the principal government spokesperson and appeared in front of the media daily. In many of his media appearances, Chief Moose had little information to share with the media and the public principally because of the sensitive nature of the ongoing criminal investigation to identify and comprehend the snipers. These media appearances were a unique opportunity for Chief Moose to deliver preparedness messages to the community. Identify those preparedness messages that Chief Moose did deliver to the community over the course of the sniper crisis and provide suggestions of additional preparedness messages he could have delivered.

REFERENCES

Airline Industry Information (AII). 2002. *BALPA Issues Advice to Concerned Crew Traveling to Washington, DC.* AII. October 18.

Altheide, D. L. 2002. *Creating Fear: News and the Construction of Crisis.* New York: Aldine de Gruyter.

Anderson, P. 2002. *Sniper Suspect Linked to Tacoma Shootings.* Seattlepi.com. October 28. <http://seattlepi.nwsource.com/local/93210_tacoma28ww.shtml>

Ansell, J., and F. Wharton. 1992. *Risk: Analysis, Assessment, and Management.* Chichester, England: John Wiley & Sons.

Atwater, B. F., C. V. Marco, J. Bourgeois, W. C. Dudley, J. W. Hendley II, and P. H. Stauffer. 1999. *Surviving a Tsunami—Lessons Learned from Chile, Hawaii, and Japan.* Washington, DC: USGS Information Services.

The Australian. 2002. "Sniper Search Goes Airborne." *The Australian.* October 17. p. 8.

Barger, B. 2002. "At the Intersection of Bravado and Fear." *The Washington Post.* November 3. p. B2.

Barker, J. 2002. "Montgomery Seeks to Ensure Safety of Voters." *The Baltimore Sun.* October 22. p. 1B.

Bremer, A. L., P. Bremer III. 2002. "The Terrorist Threat." In *Terrorism: Informing the Public.* N. Ethiel (ed.) Chicago: McCormick Tribune Foundation.

Brown, J. D., and S. N. Keller. 2000. "Can the Mass Media Be Healthy Sex Educators?" *Family Planning Perspectives.* vol. 32, no. 5, pp. 255–256.

Bullock, J. 2003. Several interviews over a two-month period with the FEMA Chief of Staff (Fmr.) Washington, DC.

Burkhart, F. N. 1991. *Media, Emergency Warnings, and Citizen Response.* Boulder, CO: Westview Press.

CBS News. 2002. *A Deadly Journey? Crimes and Clues.* n/d. <http://www.cbsnews.com/htdocs/maryland_murders/frame-source.html',540,400>

CDC. 2002. *Suicide in the United States.* National Center for Injury Prevention and Control. <http://www.cdc.gov/ncipc/factsheets/suifacts.htm>

Chemical and Biological Arms Control Institute. 2002. What Should We Know? Whom Should We Tell? Leveraging Communication and Information to Counter Terrorism and Its

Consequences. Michael J. Powers, Project Director. Washingdon, DC. December 2002.

Clines, F. 2002a. "Widening Fears, Few Clues as 6th Death Is Tied to Sniper." *New York Times*. October 5. p. A1.

Clines, F. 2002b. "The Hunt for a Sniper." *New York Times*. October 15. p. A1.

CNN. 2002. *Bubonic Plague Suspected in NYC Visitors*. CNN.com. November 7. <http://www.cnn.com/2002/health/11/07/ny.plague/index.html>

Cohen, B. C. 1963. *The Press and Foreign Policy*. Princeton, NJ: Princeton University Press.

Connor, T., and H. Kennedy. 2002. "Cops Flood Site of VA Shooting." *Daily News* (New York). October 20. p. 3.

Coppola, C. P., MD. Series of Interviews: Dr. Coppola operated on the 13-year old boy who was shot at the middle school in Bowie, MD on October 7.

Coppola, D. 2002. Research on Public Risk Perception in Mexico City, Mexico.

De Morales, L. 2002. "Did on-the-Spot Coverage Put Lawmen on the Spot?" *The Washington Post*. October 24. p. C1.

Department of Homeland Security (DHS). 2003. Ready.Gov website. DHS. Washington, DC. <http://www.ready.gov>

Diaz, K., and L. O'Rourke. 2002. "D.C. Area Breathes Easier, But Not Deeply." *Star Tribune* (Minneapolis). October 25. p. 20A.

Disaster Management Center. 1995. *Disaster Preparedness*. The University of Wisconsin. <http://dmc.engr.wisc.edu/courses/preparedness/BB04-intro.html>

Dishneau, D. 2002. "Virginia Shooting Linked to Sniper Spree." *The Toronto Star*. October 6. p. A9.

Ebner, J., and L. Herring. 2002. *In Disasters, Panic Is Rare; Altruism Dominates*. American Sociological Association. August 7. <www.asanet.org/media/panic.html>

Eccleston, R. 2002. "Killings Have Washington Terrorized." *The Australian*. October 14. p.12.

Economist. 2002. "The Logic of Irrational Fear." *The Economist*. October 19.

Enders, J. 2001. "Measuring Community Awareness and Preparedness for Emergencies." *Australian Journal of Emergency Management*. Spring 2001. pp. 52–59.

FAIR. 2002a. *Washington, D.C. PMSA*. Federation for American Immigration Reform. <http://www.fairus.org/html/msas/042dcwdc.htm>

FAIR. 2002b. *Richmond-Petersburg Metropolitan Area*. Federation for American Immigration Reform. <http://www.fairus.org/html/msas/042varip.htm>

FBI. 2001. *Crime in the United States, 2000*. The Federal Bureau of Investigation (FBI) Uniform Crime Reports. October 22. Washington, DC.

Fears, D., and A. Thomas-Lester. 2002. "Blacks Express Shock at Suspects' Identity." *The Washington Post*. October 26. p. A17.

Federal Emergency Management Agency (FEMA). 1998. "Making Your Community Disaster Resistant: Project Impact Media Partnership Guide." Washington, DC: FEMA.

Federal Emergency Management Agency (FEMA). 1997. *Multi Hazard: Identification and Assessment*. Washington, DC: FEMA.

Fernandez, M. 2002. "Brentwood Postal Plant Fumigation Postponed." *The Washington Post*. November 13. p. B3.

Fineman, H. 2002. "The 'Anxiety Election.'" *National Affairs*. October 21. p. 32.

Furedi, F. 1997. *Culture of Fear: Risk-Taking and the Morality of Low Expectation*. London: Cassell.

Furman, M. 2002. "Good Information Saves Lives." In *Terrorism: Informing the Public*. N. Ethiel (ed.). Chicago: McCormick Tribune Foundation.

Gettleman, J. 2002. "The Hunt for a Sniper: The Scene." *New York Times*. October 21. p. A14.

Glassner, B. 1999. *The Culture of Fear*. New York: Basic Books.

GPO. 2002. *US Code Title 28, Part II, Chapter 33, Section 540B*. Government Printing Office. <http://www.access.gpo.gov/uscode/uscmain.html>

Haddow, G. 2003. Several interviews over a two-month period with the FEMA Deputy Chief of Staff (Fmr.). Washington, DC.

Helderman, R., and A. Goldenbach. 2002. "Autumn's Diversions Disrupted." *The Washington Post*. October 20. p. T3.

Higham, S., and S. Kovaleski. 2002. "Encounters with Sniper Suspects." *The Washington Post*. November 3. p. A1.

Houston Chronicle. 2002. "Sniper's Score: 5 Shots, 5 Dead." *Houston Chronicle* News Services. October 4. p. A1.

Hurdle, J. 2002. "Holidaying in the Line of Fire." *The Daily Telegraph* (London). October 19. p. 4.

ICESI. 2002. *Primera Encuesta Nacional sobre Inseguridad Publica en las Entidades Federativas*. Mexico City: Instituto Ciudadano de Estudios Sobre la Inseguridad A.C. May.

Irvin, C. W., and D. Mattingly. 2002. "Anxiety Becomes Part of Daily Routine." *The Washington Post*. October 17. p. T3.

Jacobson, L. 2001. "Media—The Perception of Panic." *McGill Tribune* via U-Wire. November 14.

Jardine, C. G., and S. E. Hrudey. 1997. "Mixed Messages in Risk Communication," *Risk Analysis*, vol. 17, no. 4, pp. 489–498.

Johnson, D., and J. Finer. 2002. "Sniper Casts Shadow of Fear Over Weekend." *The Washington Post*. October 13. p. C1.

Johnson, P. 2002. "Out in TV Land, 'Local News Is in Bad Shape.'" *USA Today* Online. November 11.

Johnson, P., and M. Moore. 2002. "Media Reports Touch Raw Nerves in Washington." *USA Today*. October 10. p. 2A.

Jones, E. F., J. R. Beniger, and C. F. Westoff. 1980. "Pill and IUD Discontinuation in the United States, 1970–1975: The Influence of the Media." *Family Planning Perspectives*. vol. 12, no. 6, pp. 293–300.

Kennedy, H., M. Mbugua, and R. Pienciak. 2002. "Cops Hunt Two Targets." *The Daily News* (New York). October 24. p. 2.

Kisken, T. 2001. "Climate of Fear Overblown, Sociologist Says." *Ventura County Star*. November 6. p. B1.

Kornblut, A. 2002. "Elusive Sniper Joins DC's Nightmares." *The Boston Globe*. October 20. p. A1.

Kovaleski, S., and M. Ruane. 2002a. "Hundreds of Leads to a Gunman." *The Washington Post*. October 7. p. A1.

Kovaleski, S., and M. Ruane. 2002b. "Boy, 13, Shot by Sniper at School." *The Washington Post*. October 8. p. A1.

Kovaleske, S., and M. Williams. 2002. "Experts Suggest Motive Is Tied to Crafts Store." *The Washington Post*. October 16. p. A13.

Kurtz, H. 2002. "The Leak that Sank the Suspects." *The Washington Post*. October 25. p. C1.

LA Times. 2002. "Americans Fear Sniper More Than Terrorists." *Los Angeles Times*.

Lambert, R. 2002. "The Washington Sniper Is Not the Only Fear Stalking the United States Right Now." *The Times* (London). October 18.

Layton, L., and K. Shaver. 2002. "Experts, Travelers Question Efficacy of Massive Dragnets." *The Washington Post*. October 23. p. A17.

Lichtblau, E., and D. van Natta. 2002. "The Hunt for a Sniper." *New York Times*. October 25. p. A1.

Lochhead, C. 2002. "One Year Later." *San Francisco Chronicle*. September 12. p. A17.

Loughlin, S. 2002. *Sniper Probe "Unprecedented" for Region*. CNN Washington Bureau. October 24.

Macalester College. 2002. *Serial Killers*. <http://www.macalester.edu/~psych/whathap/UBNRP/serialkillers/serialkillers.html>

McCallum, D. B., S. L. Hammond, and L. Morris. 1990. *Public Knowledge of Chemical Risks in Six Communities*. Washington, DC: Georgetown University Medical Center, Institute for Health Policy Analysis.

McCombs, M., and D. Shaw. 1972. "The Agenda-Setting Function of Mass Media." *Public Opinion Quarterly*. vol. 36, pp. 176–187.

McCormick Tribune Foundation. 2002. "Terrorism: Informing the Public." Cantigny Conference Series. N. Ethiel (ed.). Chicago: McCormick Tribune Foundation.

McDivitt, J. A., S. Zimicki, R. Hornik, and A. Abulaban. 1993. "The Impact of the Healthcom Mass Media Campaign on Timely Initiation of Breastfeeding in Jordan." *Studies in Family Planning*. vol. 24, no. 5, pp. 295–309.

Memmott, M. 2002a. "How to Cope? Keep Guard, and Spirits Up." *USA Today*. October 18. p. 6A.

Memmott, M. 2002b. "Fear May Be Overwhelming, But so Are the Odds." *USA Today*. October 18. p. 6A.

METRO. 1998. *Washington Metropolitan Area Transit Authority*. National Transit Database. <http://www.ntdprogram.com/NTD/Profiles.nsf/1998+30+Largest+Agencies/3030/$File/P3030.PDF>

Miga, A. 2002a. "Sniper 'Witness' Arrested." *The Boston Herald*. October 19. p. 3.

Miga, A. 2002b. "Death Penalty Sought for Sniper." *The Boston Herald*. October 26. p. 1.

Miga, A., and K. Rothstein. 2002. "Zeroing In." *The Boston Herald*. October 24. p. 1.

Mileti, D. S. 1999. *Disasters by Design*. Washington, DC: Joseph Henry Press.

Miller, J. 2002. "Who? How? When? What? Where?" In *Terrorism: Informing the Public*. N. Ethiel (ed.). Chicago: McCormick Tribune Foundation.

Morello, C., C. Davenport, and H. Harris. 2002. "Pair Seized in Sniper Attacks." *The Washington Post*. October 25. p. A1.

Morello, C., and J. Stockwell. 2002. "No Attacks, No Arrests, No Shortage of Anxiety." *The Washington Post*. October 14. p. A1.

Morello, C., and J. White. 2002. "8th Killing Linked to Sniper." *The Washington Post*. October 12. p. A1.

Morgan, M. G., B. Fischoff, A. Bostrom, and C. J. Atman. 2002. *Risk Communication: A Mental Models Approach*. Cambridge: Cambridge University Press.

Morin, R., and C. Deane. 2002. "Half of Area Residents in Fear, Post Poll Finds." *The Washington Post*. October 24. p. A1.

Moore, M. T. 2002. *Presentation at the NAS Natural Disasters Roundtable*. National Academy of Sciences. October 31. Washington, DC.

Mullis, J.-P. 1998. "Persuasive Communication Issues in Disaster Management". *Australian Journal of Emergency Management*. Autumn 1998. pp. 51–58.

Nakamura, D., and P. Davis. 2002. "Suddenly, D.C. Gas Looks Cheap Enough." *The Washington Post*. October 15. p. A7.

Naudet, J., and G. Naudet. 2001. *September 11 Documentary*. CBS. Two-hour film shot during the September 11 World Trade Center attack response.

Nelken, D. 1987. *Selling Science: How the Press Covers Science and Technology*. New York: W. H. Freeman.

Nielsen, S., and J. Lidstone. 1998. "Public Education and Disaster Management: Is There Any Guiding Theory?" *Australian Journal of Emergency Management*. Spring 1998. pp. 14–19.

Ottawa Citizen. 2002. "Canadians Told to Avoid Washington." *The Ottawa Citizen*. October 13. p. A8.

Patrick, A. 2002. "Eight Dead, But Still No Real Clues." *Sunday Age* (Melbourne). October 13. p. 1.

Pelton, T. 2001. "36% of Americans Wash Up After Handling Mail." *The Baltimore Sun*. December 18. p. 8A.

Perspectives.org. 2002. *Friend's Apparent Accidental Shot Lodges Near Brain*. Perspectives.com. < http://www.perspectivescs.org/guns/example2.htm>

Phillips, C. 2002. "Malvo Spent Childhood Looking for Father Figure." *The Seattle Times*. November 21. p. A1.

Pienciak, R., and H. Kennedy. 2002. "Sniper's Ransom." *The Daily News* (New York). October 22. p. 3.

Piotrow, P. T., J. G. Rimon, K. Winnard, D. L. Kincaid, D. Huntington, and J. Convisser. 1990. "Mass Media Family Planning Promotion in Three Nigerian Cities." *Studies in Family Planning*. vol. 21, no. 5, pp. 265–274.

Raphael, B. 1986. *When Disaster Strikes: How Individuals and Communities Cope with Catastrophes*. New York: Basic Books.

Rashbaum, W., and K. Flynn. 2002. "Sniper Hits a Teacher at Stuyvesant Town." *New York Times*. October 3. p. B1.

Reel, M. 2002. "A Region Running Scared?" *The Washington Post*. October 19. p. A1.

Reid, T. 2002. "Al Qaeda Trained Snipers for US Attacks." *The Times* (London). October 19. p. 21.

Rennie, D. 2002. "Sniper Stretches City's Nerves to Breaking Point." *The Daily Telegraph* (London). October 22. p. 10.

Ropeik, D. 2002a. *"Fear factors" in an age of terrorism*. MSNBC Online. October 15.

Ropeik, D. 2002b. "We should fear too much fear." *Milwaukee Journal Sentinel*. October 23. p. 23A.

Ropeik, D. 2002c. *Presentation on Risk Perception*. The National Academy of Sciences Roundtable on Natural Disasters. October 31.

Ruane, M., and J. Stockwell. 2002. "Montgomery Bus Driver Fatally Shot." *The Washington Post*. October 23. p. A1.

Schulte, B. 2002. "Schools Shaken by Threat but Won't Shut Down." *The Washington Post*. October 23. p. A1.

Self Knowledge. 2002. *Definition of Fear* <www.selfknowledge.com/35217.htm>

Shales, T. 2002. "TV News Feels Its Way in Dark Times." *The Washington Post*. October 23. p. C1.

Shrader-Frechette, K. S. 1991. *Risk and Rationality*. Berkeley: University of California Press.

Singer, E., and P. M. Endreny. 1993. *Reporting on Risk: How the Mass Media Portray Accidents, Diseases, Disasters, and Other Hazards*. New York: Russell Sage Foundation.

Slovic, P. 1986. "Informing and Educating the Public about Risk." *Risk Analysis*. vol. 6, no. 4, pp. 403–415.

Slovic, P., B. Fischhoff, and S. Lichtenstein. 1996. "Cognitive Processes and Societal Risk Taking." In *Cognition and Social Behavior*. Potomac, M.D.: Lawrence Erlbaum Assoc. pp. 165–184.

Slovic, P., B. Fischhoff, and S. Lichtenstein. 1980. "Facts and Fears: Understanding Perceived Risk." In *Societal Risk Assessment: How Safe Is Safe Enough?* New York: Plenium.

Slovic, P., B. Fischhoff, and S. Lichtenstein. 1979. "Rating the Risks." *Environment*. vol. 21, no. 3, pp. 14–20, 36–39.

Snyder, D. 2002. "Fear Is Traveling the Lanes of I-95." *The Washington Post*. October 21. p. A14.

STATS. 2002. *Abducting the Headlines*. STATS. <http://www.stats.org/newsletters/0208/abduction.htm>

Stephen, A. 2002. *America—Andrew Stephen Reports on Panic in Washington*. New Statesman, Ltd. October 22.

Stockwell, J., M. Ruane, and J. White. 2002. "Man Shot to Death at Pr. William Gas Station." *The Washington Post*. October 10. p. A1.

Sun, L. H., and P. Ly. 2002. "Story 'Not About Me,' Reserved Moose Says." *The Washington Post*. October 28. p. A10.

Thomas, P. 2003. The Anthrax Attacks. The Century Foundation. New York, NY. June 1, 2003.

Timberg, C., and M. Shear. 2002. "Dragnet Comes Up Empty Again." *The Washington Post*. October 21. p. A1.

Tresniowski, A., J. S. Podesta, M. Morehouse, and A. Billups. 2002. "Stalked by Fear." *People* magazine. October 28. p. 58.

Twomey, J. 2001. "Media Fuels Fear About Youth Crime." *The Baltimore Sun*. May 13. p. 1C.

Vulliami, E. 2002. "America Stays Indoors as Sniper Roams Free." *The Observer*. October 13. p.1.

Walker, W. 2002. "Terror Grips D.C. Region." *Toronto Star*. October 23. p. A20.

Wallace, C. 2002. *A New Kind of Killer?* ABC News. October 15.

Walsh, J. 1996. *True Odds: How Risk Affects Your Everyday Life*. Santa Monica, CA: Merritt Publishing.

Ward, B. 2001. "History's Lessons Lost in the Turmoil." *The Ottawa Citizen*. September 18. p. A10.

Warner, K. E. 1989. "The Epidemiology of Coffin Nails." In *Health Risks and the Press: Coverage on Media Coverage of Risk Assessment and Health*. Washington, DC: The Media Institute.

Warr, M. 2000. "Fear of Crime in the United States: Avenues for Research and Policy." In *Measurement and Analysis of Crime and Justice*. pp. 451–489.

Washington Post. 2002a. "Crime and Justice." *The Washington Post*. October 3. p. B2.

Washington Post. 2002b. "Washington Area Sniper Poll." *The Washington Post*. October 24.

Watson, D. 2000. *Statement of Mr. Dale Watson, Asst. Director, FBI Counterterrorism Division, before the Subcommittee on National Security*. U.S. House of Representatives. March 22.

Watson, R. 2002. "Suburbs in Terror of the Beltway Sniper after Boy Is Shot." *The Times* (London). October 8.

Waugh, W. L., Jr. 2000. *Living with Hazards, Dealing with Disasters: An Introduction to Emergency Management*. New York: M.E. Sharpe.

Wenham, B. 1994. "The Media and Disasters: Building a Better Understanding." In *International Disaster Communications: Harnessing the Power of Communications to Avert Disasters and Save Lives*. Washington, DC: The Annenberg Washington Program.

Westoff, C. F., and G. Rodriguez. 1995. "The Mass Media and Family Planning in Kenya." *International Family Planning Perspectives*. vol. 21, no. 1, pp. 26–31, 36.

Whitlock, C. 2002. "The Sniper Case: Out of 90,000 Calls, Just 3 Broke It Open." *Post Gazette* (Pittsburgh). October 25. <http://www.post-gazette.com/nation/20021025probenat2p2.asp>

Wiggins, C. 2002. "Warm Waters Attract People and Sharks." *The Standard* (Baker County). March 27.

Willis, J. 1997. *Reporting on Risks: The Practice and Ethics of Health and Safety Communication*. Westport, CT: Praeger.

Wilson, R. 1979. "Analyzing the Daily Risks of Life." *Technology Review*. vol. 81, no. 4, pp. 41–46.

Winston, J. A. 1985. "Science and the Media: The Boundaries of Truth." *Health Affairs*. vol. 6, pp. 5–23.

Witzer, M. 1997. "In Sub-Saharan Africa, Levels of Knowledge and Use of Contraceptives Are Linked to Media Exposure." *International Family Planning Perspectives*. vol. 23, no. 4, pp. 183–184.

American Red Cross Homeland Security Advisory System Recommendations for Individuals

Risk of Attack	Recommended Actions
SEVERE *(Red)*	• *Complete recommended actions at lower levels* • Listen to radio/TV for current information/instructions • Be alert to suspicious activity and report it to proper authorities immediately • Contact business to determine status of work day • Adhere to any travel restrictions announced by local governmental authorities • Be prepared to shelter in place or evacuate if instructed to do so by local governmental authorities • Provide volunteer services only as requested
HIGH *(Orange)*	• *Complete recommended actions at lower levels* • Be alert to suspicious activity and report it to proper authorities • Review your personal disaster plan • Exercise caution when traveling • Have shelter in place materials on hand and review procedure in *Terrorism: Preparing for the Unexpected* brochure • If a need is announced, donate blood at designated blood collection center • Prior to volunteering, contact agency to determine their needs
ELEVATED *(Yellow)*	• *Complete recommended actions at lower levels* • Be alert to suspicious activity and report it to proper authorities • Ensure disaster supplies kit is stocked and ready • Check telephone numbers and e-mail addresses in your personal communication plan and update as necessary • Develop alternate routes to/from work/school and practice them • Continue to provide volunteer services
GUARDED *(Blue)*	• *Complete recommended actions at lower levels* • Be alert to suspicious activity and report it to proper authorities • Review stored disaster supplies and replace items that are outdated • Develop emergency communication plan with family/neighbors/friends • Provide volunteer services and take advantage of additional volunteer training opportunities
LOW *(Green)*	• Obtain copy of *Terrorism: Preparing for the Unexpected* brochure from your local Red Cross chapter • Develop a personal disaster plan and disaster supplies kit using Red Cross brochures *Your Family Disaster Plan* and *Your Family Disaster Supplies Kit* • Examine volunteer opportunities in you community; choose an agency to volunteer with and receive initial training • Take a Red Cross CPR/AED and first aid course

Red Cross—http://www.redcross.org/article/0,1072,0_1_1418,00.html

APPENDIX 8-2

American Red Cross Homeland Security Advisory System Recommendations for Families

Risk of Attack	**Recommended Actions**
SEVERE *(Red)*	• *Complete recommended actions at lower levels* • Listen to radio/TV for current information/instructions • Be alert to suspicious activity and report it to proper authorities immediately • Contact business/school to determine status of work/school day • Adhere to any travel restrictions announced by local governmental authorities • Be prepared to shelter in place or evacuate if instructed to do so by local governmental authorities • Discuss children's fears concerning possible/actual terrorist attacks
HIGH *(Orange)*	• *Complete recommended actions at lower levels* • Be alert to suspicious activity and report it to proper authorities • Review disaster plan with all family members • Ensure communication plan is understood/practiced by all family members • Exercise caution when traveling • Have shelter in place materials on hand and understand procedure • Discuss children's fears concerning possible terrorist attacks • If a need is announced, donate blood at designated blood collection center
ELEVATED *(Yellow)*	• *Complete recommended actions at lower levels* • Be alert to suspicious activity and report it to proper authorities • Ensure disaster supplies kit is stocked and ready • Check telephone numbers and e-mail addresses in your family emergency communication plan and update as necessary • If not known to you, contact school to determine their emergency notification and evacuation plans for children • Develop alternate routes to/from school/work and practice them
GUARDED *(Blue)*	• *Complete recommended actions at lower levels* • Be alert to suspicious activity and report it to proper authorities • Review stored disaster supplies and replace items that are outdated • Develop an emergency communication plan that all family members understand • Establish an alternate meeting place away from home with family/friends
LOW *(Green)*	• Obtain copy of *Terrorism: Preparing for the Unexpected* brochure from your local Red Cross chapter • Develop a personal disaster plan and disaster supplies kit using Red Cross brochures *Your Family Disaster Plan* and *Your Family Disaster Supplies Kit* • Take a Red Cross CPR/AED and first aid course

Red Cross—http://www.redcross.org/article/0,1072,0_1_1418,00.html

APPENDIX 8-3
American Red Cross Homeland Security Advisory System Recommendations for Neighborhoods

| **Risk of Attack** | **Recommended Actions** |

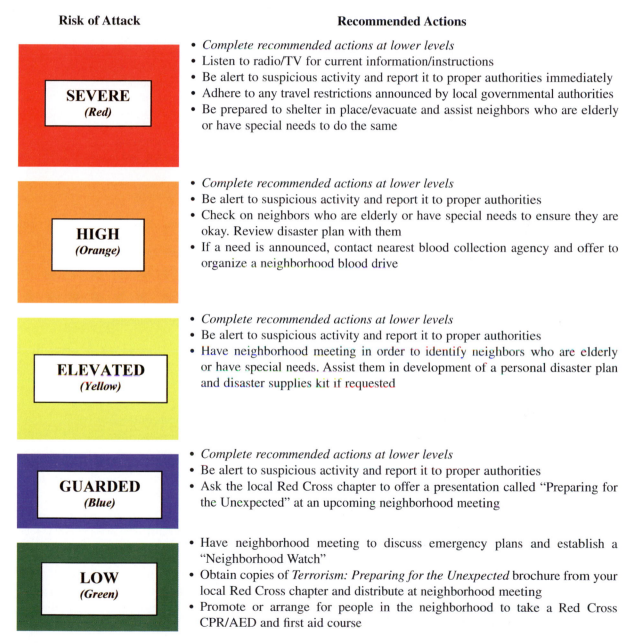

SEVERE (Red)
- *Complete recommended actions at lower levels*
- Listen to radio/TV for current information/instructions
- Be alert to suspicious activity and report it to proper authorities immediately
- Adhere to any travel restrictions announced by local governmental authorities
- Be prepared to shelter in place/evacuate and assist neighbors who are elderly or have special needs to do the same

HIGH (Orange)
- *Complete recommended actions at lower levels*
- Be alert to suspicious activity and report it to proper authorities
- Check on neighbors who are elderly or have special needs to ensure they are okay. Review disaster plan with them
- If a need is announced, contact nearest blood collection agency and offer to organize a neighborhood blood drive

ELEVATED (Yellow)
- *Complete recommended actions at lower levels*
- Be alert to suspicious activity and report it to proper authorities
- Have neighborhood meeting in order to identify neighbors who are elderly or have special needs. Assist them in development of a personal disaster plan and disaster supplies kit if requested

GUARDED (Blue)
- *Complete recommended actions at lower levels*
- Be alert to suspicious activity and report it to proper authorities
- Ask the local Red Cross chapter to offer a presentation called "Preparing for the Unexpected" at an upcoming neighborhood meeting

LOW (Green)
- Have neighborhood meeting to discuss emergency plans and establish a "Neighborhood Watch"
- Obtain copies of *Terrorism: Preparing for the Unexpected* brochure from your local Red Cross chapter and distribute at neighborhood meeting
- Promote or arrange for people in the neighborhood to take a Red Cross CPR/AED and first aid course

Red Cross—http://www.redcross.org/article/0,1072,0_1_1418,00.html

APPENDIX 8-4
American Red Cross Homeland Security Advisory System Recommendations for Schools

Risk of Attack	Recommended Actions
SEVERE *(Red)*	• *Complete recommended actions at lower levels* • Listen to radio/TV for current information/instructions • Be alert to suspicious activity and report it to proper authorities immediately • Close school if recommended to do so by appropriate authorities • 100% identification check (i.e., driver's license retained at front office) and escort of anyone entering school other than students, staff and faculty • Continue offering lessons from Masters of Disaster "Facing Fear: Helping Young People Deal with Terrorism and Tragic Events" curriculum • Ensure mental health counselors available for students, staff, and faculty
HIGH *(Orange)*	• *Complete recommended actions at lower levels* • Be alert to suspicious activity and report it to proper authorities • Review emergency plans • Offer Masters of Disaster "Facing Fear: Helping Young People Deal with Terrorism and Tragic Events" lessons in grades K–12 • Prepare to handle inquiries from anxious parents and media • Discuss children's fears concerning possible terrorist attacks
ELEVATED *(Yellow)*	• *Complete recommended actions at lower levels* • Be alert to suspicious activity and report it to the proper authorities • Ensure all emergency supplies stocked and ready • Obtain copies of *Terrorism: Preparing for the Unexpected* brochure from your local Red Cross chapter and send it home with students in grades K–12, staff, and faculty
GUARDED *(Blue)*	• *Complete recommended actions at lower levels* • Be alert to suspicious activity and report it to proper authorities • Conduct safety training/emergency drills following the school's written emergency plan for all grades • Ensure emergency communication plan updated and needed equipment is purchased • Continue offering lessons from "Masters of Disaster" curriculum for grades K–8 regarding emergency preparedness for natural disasters
LOW *(Green)*	• Use Red Cross *Emergency Management Guide for Business and Industry* to develop written emergency plans to address all hazards including plans to maintain the safety of students, staff, and faculty, as well as an emergency communication plan to notify parents in times of emergency. Disseminate relevant information to families of children, staff, and faculty. • Initiate offering "Masters of Disaster" curriculum for grades K–8 regarding emergency preparedness for natural disasters • Ensure selected staff members take a Red Cross CPR/AED and first aid course

Red Cross—http://www.redcross.org/article/0,1072,0_1_1418,00.html

APPENDIX 8-5
American Red Cross Homeland Security Advisory System Recommendations for Businesses

Risk of Attack	Recommended Actions
SEVERE *(Red)*	• *Complete recommended actions at lower levels* • Listen to radio/TV for current information/instructions • Be alert to suspicious activity and report it to proper authorities immediately • Work with local community leaders, emergency management, government agencies, community organizations, and utilities to meet immediate needs of the community. • Determine need to close business based on circumstances and in accordance with written emergency plan • Be prepared to work with a dispersed or smaller workforce • Ensure mental health counselors available for employees
HIGH *(Orange)*	• *Complete recommended actions at lower levels* • Be alert to suspicious activity and report it to proper authorities • Review emergency plans to include continuity of operations and media materials on hand • Determine need to restrict access to business or provide private security firm support/reinforcement • Contact vendors/suppliers to confirm their emergency response plan procedures • If a need is announced, contact nearest blood collection agency and offer to organize a blood drive
ELEVATED *(Yellow)*	• *Complete recommended actions at lower levels* • Be alert to suspicious activity and report it to proper authorities • Contact private security firm for security risk assessment and to determine availability of support/reinforcement • Contact voluntary organizations you support to determine how you can provide assistance in case of emergency
GUARDED *(Blue)*	• *Complete recommended actions at lower levels* • Be alert to suspicious activity and report it to proper authorities • Dialogue with community leaders, emergency management, government agencies, community organizations and utilities about disaster preparedness • Ensure emergency communication plan updated to include purchase of needed equipment • Ask the local Red Cross chapter to provide a "Terrorism: Preparing for the Unexpected" presentation at your workplace for employees
LOW *(Green)*	• Use Red Cross *Emergency Management Guide for Business and Industry* to develop written emergency plans to address all hazards. Include an emergency communication plan to notify employees of activities; designate an off-site "report to" location in case of evacuation. • Develop continuity of operations plan to include designating alternate work facility/location for business • Arrange for staff to take a Red Cross CPR/AED and first aid course • Obtain copies of *Terrorism: Preparing for the Unexpected and Preparing Your Business for the Unthinkable* brochures from your local Red Cross chapter for distribution to all employees/management as appropriate.

Red Cross—http://www.redcross.org/article/0,1072,0_1_1418,00.html

9

Technology

INTRODUCTION

"If I were asked to describe the Department of Homeland Security (DHS), I would say it's a story about science and technology," said the undersecretary, Charles McQueary, when he addressed the Piedmont Triad Partnership in May 2003. This quotation clearly points out the emphasis that DHS is placing on and investing in technology. Technology is the fastest developing field, incurring major changes as it proceeds. In the case of homeland security, it has brought changes not only in the field of emergency management but throughout governments, national laboratories, research and development facilities and universities, and it is likely to even affect the way scientific work in conducted in the future.

DHS announced from the beginning of its establishment that it "is committed to using cutting-edge technologies and scientific talent" for a safer country and formed the Directorate of Science and Technology (S&T) for this purpose. DHS further states that

The S&T directorate is tasked with researching and organizing the scientific, engineering, and technological resources of the United States and leveraging these existing resources into technological tools to help protect the homeland. Universities, the private sector, and the federal laboratories will be important DHS partners in this endeavor.

An overview of the present situation and future areas of interest was provided in the National Strategy for the Homeland Security, published by the Office of Homeland Security in July 2002. This strategy discusses the goals of the DHS in its technology and science efforts and the objectives underpinning the actions performed by the many different agencies and research facilities involved.

As the S&T Directorate is also responsible for information management, the chapter includes the relevant parts from the National Strategy.

SCIENCE AND TECHNOLOGY

The National Strategy analyzes the current national situation as a "research enterprise, which is vast and complex, with companies, universities, research institutes, and government laboratories of all sizes conducting research and development on a very broad range of issues." The aim of the DHS here is to integrate and use more efficiently all the private and federal entities that have the sufficient knowledge, expertise, and capabilities to develop and produce devices and systems to safeguard and secure the homeland. While some of the concerned private companies have neither worked with nor feel attracted to the federal government; the important issue of not having enough funds dedicated to specific homeland security purposes is another problem. The National Strategy calls for the consolidation of all relevant scientific works under DHS and the eradication of the identified issues that inhibit the national capability. In fact, President Bush's intention and support of such a change is highly visible; he proposed $3.7 billion for homeland security research funds in FY 03, up from $1.4 billion in FY 02.

The national vision is to use the national science and technology base to address catastrophic threats; find and identify terrorists; support research and development efforts in biometric technology; improve accuracy, consistency, and efficiency in biometric systems; and explore bimolecular and other new techniques.

The major initiatives for research and development that are announced in the National Strategy are as follows:

- **Develop chemical, biological, radiological, and nuclear countermeasures** to prioritize efforts to deal with catastrophic threats
- **Develop systems for detecting hostile intent** to highlight criminal behavior and trigger further investigation and analysis of suspected individuals
- **Apply biometric technology** to identification devices and set standards to assist the acquisition decisions of state and local governments and private-sector entities
- **Improve the technical capabilities of first responders** to provide them with technical capabilities for dealing with the effects of catastrophic threats—capabilities that would aid both first responders and victims of the attack
- **Coordinate research and development of the homeland security apparatus** to set the overall direction for our nation's homeland security research and development (R&D), to establish a management structure to oversee its R&D activities, and to guide its inter-agency coordination activities
- **Establish a national laboratory for homeland security** to provide a multidisciplinary environment for developing and demonstrating new

technologies for homeland security and maintain a critical mass of scientific and engineering talent with a deep understanding of the various operational and technical issues associated with homeland security systems
- **Solicit independent and private analysis for science and technology research** to support planning activities
- **Establish a mechanism for rapidly producing prototypes**
- **Conduct demonstrations and pilot deployments** to provide a conduit between the state and local users of technology and the federal developers of that technology
- **Set standards for homeland security technology** to encourage investment in homeland security science and technology efforts
- **Establish a system for high-risk, high-payoff homeland security research** to bring the full force of science to bear on our efforts to secure the homeland.

INFORMATION MANAGEMENT

The National Strategy states,

Information contributes to every aspect of homeland security and is a vital foundation for this effort. Although the U.S. is a leader in information technology, changes to accepted practices and advancements are required to develop a cohesive program to serve the needs of homeland security.

The critical issues are disparate databases dispersed among federal, state, and local entities and systems that cannot share information—either horizontally (across the same level of government) or vertically (between federal, state, and local governments).

Despite spending some $50 billion on information technology per year, two fundamental problems have prevented the federal government from building an efficient government-wide information system:

1. Government acquisition of information systems has not been routinely coordinated, and hundreds of systems have been acquired over time.

2. Legal and cultural barriers often prevent agencies from exchanging and integrating information.

As a result, the national vision announced in the National Strategy for information management is to build a national "system of systems" to share the essential homeland security information horizontally and vertically. And to develop common awareness of threats and vulnerabilities. This task is under the Critical Infrastructure Assurance Office's responsibilities. The five principles the Office relies upon are:

1. To balance the homeland security requirements with citizens' privacy
2. To view the federal, state, and local governments as one entity
3. To capture information once at the source and use it many times to support multiple requirements
4. To create databases of record that will be trusted sources of information
5. To build dynamic information architecture that always evolves

The major initiatives outlined in the National Strategy are as follows:

- Integrate information sharing across the federal government
- Integrate information sharing across state and local governments, private industry, and citizens to enhance the timely dissemination of information from the federal government to state and local homeland security officials. The different efforts under way are:
  - The FBI and other federal agencies are augmenting the information available in their crime and terrorism databases
  - State and local governments should use a secure intranet to increase the flow of classified federal information to state and local entities
  - A secure video conferencing capability connecting officials in Washington, DC. with all government entities in every state will be implemented
  - The expansion of the '.gov' domain on the Internet for use by state governments has already been completed. This will ensure the legitimacy of government websites and enhance searches of all federal and state websites, thereby allowing information to be accessed more quickly
- Adopt common "meta-data" standards for electronic information relevant to homeland security to integrate terrorist-related information from databases of all government agencies responsible for homeland security
- Improve public safety emergency communications to disseminate information about vulnerabilities and protective measures, as well as allow first responders to better manage incidents and minimize damage
- Ensure reliable public health information to assure prompt detection, accurate diagnosis, and timely reporting and investigation of disease epidemics

The purpose of this chapter is to describe the research and development and information management components of the Department of the Homeland Security and the programs they support. The chapter includes relevant information concerning technology in communication; information management; research and development; and personal protective gears. The chapter is organized according to the agencies involved.

OVERVIEW OF INVOLVED AGENCIES AND BUDGET

Different agencies are involved in the creation of the DHS and the related R&D efforts on homeland security remain divided. While DHS is still organizing and needs adjustment time, ongoing research and scientific programs conducted under the various different organizations were given almost instantly new directions and resources to respond to the new threats of terrorism. Table 9.1 contains a description of the Agencies involved in the homeland security R&D field and their recent budgets. Overall, the total federal investment in homeland security R&D is around $3.4 billion in FY04, down 8.7 percent from the FY03 ($3.7 billion). The FY02 budget was, on the other hand, only $1.4 billion.

Overall, the total federal investment in homeland security R&D will be around $3.4 billion in FY 04, down 8.7 percent from FY 03 ($3.7 billion). The FY 02 budget was, on the other hand, only $1.4 billion. The decrease in budget for FY04 year is partly due to discontinued one-time emergency projects and budgetary constraints. Figures 9-1 and 9-2 and Table 9-1 show the distributions of funding by agencies and years.

DEPARTMENT OF HOMELAND SECURITY

Before the establishment of DHS, most R&D efforts dealing with issues relevant to homeland security were dispersed among a wide variety of agencies, and this situation still remains. However, the intent is to make DHS a focus for such R&D. The department is made of four functional and one administrative directorate as well as agencies standing on their own. Although inside DHS, many of them keep their relevant R&D budget and capacities within their jurisdiction; the Directorate of Science and Technology (S&T) has been established in order to coordinate and manage their efforts. A more detailed description of the different directorates and their activities follows.

THE SCIENCE AND TECHNOLOGY (S&T) DIRECTORATE

The purpose of the S&T Directorate, as announced by DHS, "is to use cutting-edge technology to develop

---

SIDEBAR 9-1   Homeland Security R&D Agencies

1. **Department of Homeland Security**
   - *The Science and Technology Directorate.* It makes up approximately 90 percent of the R&D budget devoted to the Department with the majority of funds for development and only about 10 percent each for basic research and applied research. The S&T Directorate has received $147 millions in FY02, $521 million in FY03 and $918.2 millions in FY04.
   - *The Directorate of Border and Transportation Security.* It has an appropriation of $110 million in FY03 rising to $155 million in FY04.
   - *The Directorate for Information Analysis and Infrastructure Protection.* Only $5 million in R&D for this directorate out of a total budget of $839 million.
   - *The Directorate of Emergency Preparedness and Response*: No R&D programs within its $9.1 billion budget in FY04.
   - *The Coast Guard:* The Coast Guard's R&D portfolio became part of DHS in March. DHS takes over responsibility of the Coast Guard from DOT, but the Coast Guard remains an independent entity under the DHS umbrella and retains an independent $16 million R&D portfolio for its science and technology needs.

   The overall funding of R&D for the Department of Homeland Security record over the same years is: (in $ million) 266 in FY02, 669 in FY03 and 1,050 in FY04; showing, thus, the greatest increase in budget (56,9%) among all agencies and departments.

2. **Department of Health and Human Services**
   - *National Institutes of Health*: In FY04, the entire $1.7 billion (nearly one half of the total homeland security R&D funding) goes to biodefense research, both in NIH's own laboratories and through extramural research grants.
   - The Centers for Disease Control and Prevention (CDC), which funds bioterrorism R&D at its own laboratories receives the rest of the related R&D funding allocated to the Department of Health and Human Services.

tools to protect our nation. To successfully implement these technologies requires critical needs such as measurement science, standards for inter-operability and conformity assessment. The directorate intends to tap into resources of the significant capabilities and expertise that exist within the Department of Commerce Technology Administration, specifically at the National Institute of Standards and Technology (NIST)."

Therefore the directorate's mission is to "develop and deliver homeland security technologies by organizing and partnering with the vast homeland security scientific, engineering, and technological resources of the federal laboratory system" (Memorandum of Understanding between the Directorate of Science and Technology and the Technology Administration of the Department of Commerce).

The six key functions for which the S&T Directorate is responsible are stated in the Memorandum of Understanding (MOU) as follows:

- Ensuring the nation has the capability to respond to a weapon of mass destruction
- Setting the homeland security research and development agenda
- Managing the homeland security-related research and development programs, including both intramural and extramural research and development
- Developing and transitioning technology and systems into the field
- Participating in identified threats and incidents
- Providing technical expertise to operational units, regional centers, and other elements of government

3. Department of Defense

The Department of Defense (DoD) sees a decrease in its homeland security R&D of 74 percent, down to $157 million in FY04. The FY03 appropriation contains homeland security-related R&D work, but beginning in FY04 most of this work is funded by DHS, and DoD focuses on its traditional mission of national defense and preventing terrorism overseas.

4. Department of Agriculture

The Department has a small homeland security R&D effort, but counts a portion of its R&D activities as related to homeland security. These security upgrades account for most of the $173 million R&D investment in FY03; because most of these funds were emergency appropriations for construction, the USDA total would fall down to $80 million in FY04 for research only.

5. Environmental Protection Agency

The EPA is another agency with a sharp cut in homeland security R&D funding in FY04. From a small start in FY02 of $4 million, the agency invested $50 million in FY03 for building decontamination research provided as a one-time emergency support to EPA's work in decontaminating congressional office buildings of anthrax. In FY04, EPA homeland security R&D declines to $29 million.

6. National Institutes and Standards and Technology

The National Institute of Standards and Technology (NIST) in Commerce funds R&D on cryptography and computer security and will provide scientific and technical support to DHS in these areas.

7. National Science Foundation

The National Science Foundation (NSF) funds research to combat bioterrorism in the areas of infectious diseases and microbial genome sequencing; these programs increase to $286 million in FY04.

Source: American Association for the Advancement of Science (www.aaas.org)

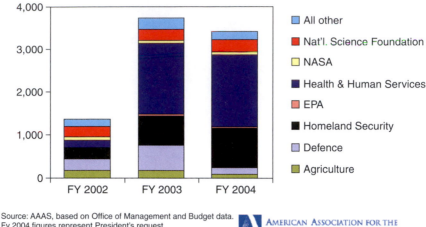

Source: AAAS, based on Office of Management and Budget data.
Fy 2004 figures represent President's request.
SEPTEMBER '03 © 2003 AAAS

AMERICAN ASSOCIATION FOR THE
ADVANCEMENT OF SCIENCE

FIGURE 9-1   Federal homeland security R&D budget authority by agency

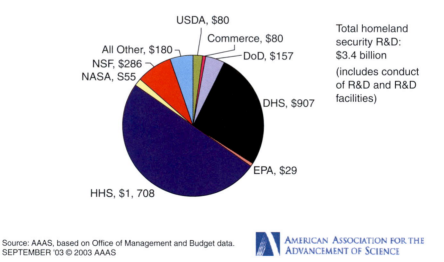

Source: AAAS, based on Office of Management and Budget data.
SEPTEMBER '03 © 2003 AAAS

AMERICAN ASSOCIATION FOR THE
ADVANCEMENT OF SCIENCE

FIGURE 9-2   Distribution of the FY04 federal funds between agencies (as of September 2003)

The S&T Directorate will be responsible for setting the national agenda and giving direction and setting priorities for R&D efforts in other department and agencies, regardless of the funding source.

The S&T directorate has unique features worth mentioning:

- The directorate received a significant increase in its budget (37.2%) because it has to build its capacities from scratch.

TABLE 9-1 Federal Homeland Security R&D Appropriations Based on Data
from the Office Of Management Budget "2003 Report to Congress on
Combating Terrorism," September 2003

| | FY 2002 | FY 2003 | FY 2004 | Change FY2003–2004 | |
				Amount	Percent (%)
Agriculture	175	173	80	−93	−53.8
Commerce	19	16	19	3	18.3
DoD	259	597	157	−440	−73.3
DOE	0	19	0	−19	−100.0
DHS (S&T)	266	669	918	249	37.2
EPA	4	50	29	−21	−41.6
HHS	177	1,651	1,708	57	3.5
NASA	73	65	55	−10	−15.4
NSF	229	269	286	17	6.4
Transportation	55	58	4	−54	−93.2
All Other	104	180	177	−4	−2.1
Total Homeland Security R&D	1,361	3,747	3,422	−325	−8.7
Total DHS spending	32,881	42,909	41,354	−1,566	−3.6

DoD: Department of Defense
DOE: Department of Energy
DHS: Department of Homeland Security Protection Agency
EPA: Environmental
HHS: Health and Human Services
NSF: National Science Foundation
NASA: National Aeronautics and Space Administration

- Unlike many other facilities only responsible for research, the directorate has responsibility for the entire cycle of science and technology (i.e., from product research to bringing the product to the market and deploying it).

The S&T Directorate is in the process of establishing the Homeland Security Advanced Research Project Agency (HSARPA). This agency, based on the existing model of Defense Advanced Research Project Agency (DARPA) in the Department of Defense distributes the resources within the directorate; awards money for the extramural grants; develops and test potential technologies; and; accelerates or prototypes development of technologies for deployment. The new agency has already started hiring people and establishing a grant award procedure. The Directorate is creating a Homeland Security Advisory Committee consisting of 20 members appointed by the Under Secretary representing first responders, citizen groups, researchers, engineers, and businesses to provide science and technology advice to the Under Secretary. A possibility exist that the DHS creates a new federally funded research and development Center (FFRDC), the Homeland Security Institute, to act as a think tank for risk analyses, simulations of threat scenarios, analyses of possible countermeasures, and strategic plans for counterterrorism technology development.

The FY04 budget provides funds for the activities described in Sidebar 9-2.

The S&T Directorate focuses on four areas: weapons of mass destruction; information and infrastructure; laboratories and research facilities; and maritime.

Weapons of Mass Destruction

The DHS web site states, "The S&T Directorate will tap into scientific and technological capabilities to provide the means to detect and deter attacks using weapons of mass destruction. S&T will guide and organize research efforts to meet emerging and predicted needs and will work closely with universities, the private sector, and national and federal laboratories." This effort can be subdivided into two fields: chemical and biological and radiological and nuclear. In both fields, the directorate's aim is to carry research to develop sensors to detect such weapons from production to employment. In the following sections are the different organizations within the federal sector that will support and serve the R&D efforts of S&T. (Note: Most of the information about different agencies and their programs is a summary taken as is from their official web sites.)

SIDEBAR 9-2   FY04 Science & Technology Directorate Programs

- **$88 million for the National Biodefense Analysis and Countermeasures Center** to build a facility that will be the DHS "hub and spoke" system that will further the mission of increasing understanding of potential bioterrorism pathogens and improving protection of human health and agriculture against biological terrorism.
- **$75 million for the Rapid Prototyping Program**, to fund counterterrorism projects selected through last summer's and this fall's Technical Support Working Group solicitations, and to support the rapid adaptation of commercial technologies through the Homeland Security Advanced Research Projects Agency (HSARPA) for use by DHS and state and local first responders.
- **$70 million for the Homeland Security University Programs**. This program will include the Homeland Security Scholars and Fellows program that will provide scholarships to undergraduate and graduate students pursuing scientific studies in homeland security. In addition, it will include the Homeland Security Centers of Excellence (HS-Centers) program that will establish a coordinated, university-based system to enhance the nation's homeland security. The HS-Centers will be a critical component of our nation's defenses by providing a dedicated capability that will enhance our ability to anticipate, prevent, respond to, and recover from terrorist attacks.
- **$66.5 million for critical infrastructure protection**, of which $60 million is provided for the research, development, testing, and evaluation of an antimissile device for commercial aircraft.
- **$39 million for developing a database of homeland security**-related standards from private sector standards development organizations, for certification and accreditation models for products and services, for testing

Chemical and Biological Defense Information and Analysis Center (CBIAC): http://www.cbiac.apgea.army.mil

The CBIAC is operated by Battelle Memorial Institute and supported by Horne Engineering Services, Inc.; Innovative Emergency Management, Inc.; MTS Technologies, Inc.; QuickSilver Analytics, Inc.; and SciTech, Inc. It is a full-service Department of Defense (DoD) Information Analysis Center (IAC) under contract to the Office of the Secretary of Defense and administratively managed by the Defense Technical Information Center (DTIC) under the DoD IAC Program Office and serves as the DoD focal point for information related to Chemical and Biological Defense (CBD) technology.

Its function is to generate, acquire, process, analyze and disseminate CB Science and Technology Information (STI) in support of the combatant commanders, war fighters, the reserve components, the CB defense research, development, and acquisition community, and other federal, state, and local government agencies. The CBIAC accomplishes its mission by the following means:

- Identifying and acquiring relevant data and information from all available sources and in all media
- Processing data and acquisitions into suitable storage and retrieval systems
- Identifying, developing, and applying available analytical tools and techniques for the interpretation and application of stored data and acquisitions
- Disseminating focused information, data sets, and technical analyses to managers, planners, scientists, engineers and military field personnel for the performance of mission related tasks
- Anticipating requirements for CB STI
- Identifying and reaching out to emerging CB defense organizations

and evaluation protocols for commercial radiation detectors, and for developing standard chemical methods of analysis of high explosives, chemical warfare agents, and toxic industrial chemicals.

- **$38 million will be used to continue the deployment of the Urban Monitoring Program**, also known as BioWatch. Through the BioWatch biosurveillance program, DHS, the Environmental Protection Agency and the Centers for Disease Control's Laboratory Response Network provide early detection of biothreats. These partners are working with state and local officials to implement an effective consequence management plan that incorporates the BioWatch system. In addition, these funds are also being applied to develop the next generation of bio-pathogen monitoring sensors.

- **$127 million will be used to develop sensors and other countermeasures** to prevent the illicit transport and use of radiological and nuclear materials within the United States.
- **$199 million for the development of biological countermeasures** to reduce the probability and impacts of a biological terrorist attack.
- **$52 million for chemical countermeasures** to protect U.S. civilians against chemical attacks.
- **$10 million for R&D against explosives attacks.**
- **$94 million for threat and vulnerability assessments** to develop technologies to analyze and evaluate threats, especially in information technologies.
- **$21 million for R&D on emerging threats.**

Source: DHS, www.dhs.gov, and American Association for the Advancement of Science, www.aaas.org

The Defense Threat Reduction Agency (DTRA): http://www.dtra.mil/cb/cb_index.html

The Defense Threat Reduction Agency safeguards national interests from weapons of mass destruction (chemical, biological, radiological, nuclear, and high explosives) by controlling and reducing the threat and providing quality tools and services for the war fighter. DTRA perform four essential functions to reach its mission: combat support, technology development, threat control, and threat reduction. Moreover, the agency's work covers a broad spectrum of activities:

- Shaping the international environment to prevent the spread of weapons of mass destruction
- Responding to requirements to deter the use and reduce the impact of such weapons
- Preparing for the future as WMD threats emerge and evolve

The activities concerning homeland security are as follows:

- The chem-bio defense where DTRA draws upon the disparate chemical and biological weapons defense expertise in the DoD to increase response capabilities
- The Advanced Systems and Concepts Office (ASCO) stimulates, identifies, and executes high-impact seed projects to encourage new thinking, address technology gaps, and improve the operational capabilities of DTRA.

The State Department: http://usembassy.state.gov

The department is a very useful source of information that provides assessment of potential chemical and biological weapons, and analyzes what different countries and groups have as resources.

The Centers for Disease Control (CDC): http://www.cdc.gov

The Centers for Disease Control and Prevention is recognized as the lead federal agency for protecting the health and safety of people by providing credible information to enhance health decisions and promoting health through strong partnerships. CDC serves as the national focus for developing and applying disease prevention and control, environmental health, and health promotion and education activities designed to improve the health of the people of the United States, with the mission to promote health and quality of life by preventing and controlling disease, injury, and disability. CDC provides information about the effects and treatment for exposure to chem-bio weapons and serves as a valuable expert with the 12 centers, institutes, and offices it includes. The most prominent and relevant ones are as follows:

- The National Center for Chronic Disease Prevention and Health Promotion prevents premature death and disability from chronic diseases and promotes healthy personal behaviors.
- The National Center for Health Statistics provides statistical information that will guide actions and policies to improve the health of the American people.
- The National Center for HIV, STD, and TB Prevention provides national leadership in preventing and controlling human immunodeficiency virus infection, sexually transmitted diseases, and tuberculosis.
- The National Center for Infectious Diseases prevents illness, disability, and death caused by infectious diseases in the United States and around the world.
- The National Immunization Program prevents disease, disability, and death from vaccine-preventable diseases in children and adults.
- The Epidemiology Program Office strengthens the public health system by coordinating public health surveillance; providing support in scientific communications, statistics, and epidemiology; and training in surveillance, epidemiology, and prevention effectiveness.
- The Public Health Practice Program Office strengthens community practice of public health by creating an effective workforce, building

information networks, conducting practice research, and ensuring laboratory quality.

Lawrence Livermore National Laboratory

The Lawrence Livermore National Laboratory provides information about nuclear and radiological weapons. Its activities are explained more broadly in the research and development section.

The U.S. Nuclear Regulatory Commission (NRC): http://www.nrc.gov

The U.S. Nuclear Regulatory Commission (NRC) is an independent agency established to regulate civilian use of nuclear materials. The NRC's mission is to regulate the nation's civilian use of by-product, source, and special nuclear materials to ensure adequate protection of public health and safety, to promote the common defense and security, and to protect the environment. The NRC's regulatory mission covers three main areas:

- Reactors: Commercial reactors for generating electric power and nonpower reactors used for research, testing, and training
- Materials: Uses of nuclear materials in medical, industrial, and academic settings and facilities that produce nuclear fuel
- Waste: Transportation, storage, and disposal of nuclear materials and waste, and decommissioning of nuclear facilities from service

The NRC carries out its mission by conducting several activities but most of them are not directly related to the Homeland Security purpose. The Commission performs them as part of its mission to regulate the normal use of radiological material but many of its capabilities and resources can be used during a radiological or nuclear incident. The major contribution fields are: Commission Direction-Setting and Policymaking; Radiation Protection; Establishment of a Regulatory Program; Nuclear Security and Safeguards information on how to promote the common defense and security; Public Affairs; Congressional Affairs; State and Tribal Programs; International Programs.

The Working Group on Radiological Dispersal Device (RDD) Preparedness

The working group on Radiological Dispersal Device within the DHS has also developed a manual on how to protect and treat first responders and civilian against radiological threats. The manual gives incident management guidelines as well as medical countermeasures, decontamination, and patient protection.

Information and Infrastructure

DHS is responsible for the means to detect and deter attacks on the national information systems and critical infrastructures, and the S&T Directorate is developing a national research and development enterprise to support this mission. The three main issues concerning information and infrastructure are as follows: Internet security, telecommunication, and the security systems. The directorate coordinates and integrates several organizations to accomplish its mission:

National Infrastructure Protection Center: http://www.nipc.gov

The National Infrastructure Protection Center operates directly under DHS and gives information about current efforts and possible threats coming from cyberspace. The center produces infrastructure warnings under the titles of assessments, advisories, alerts, and information bulletins (InfoBulletins), which are developed and distributed in a manner that is consistent with the Homeland Security's advisory and information-sharing system.

These threat warning products are based on material that is significant, credible, timely and that address cyber and/or infrastructure dimensions with possibly significant impact. These products will often be based on classified material and include dissemination restrictions, but the center will then seek to develop a sensitive "tear-line" version for distribution to critical sector coordinators, general law enforcement authorities, state and local authorities, and others as appropriate. Some details about each product are as follows.

- An assessment addresses broad, general incident or issue awareness information and analysis that is both significant and current but does not necessarily suggest immediate action.
- Advisories address significant threat or incident information that suggests a change in readiness posture, protective options and/or response.
- Alerts address major threat or incident information addressing imminent or in-progress attacks targeting specific national networks or critical infrastructures.
- And information bulletins. (InfoBulletins) (*Source*: DHS)

Federal Computer Incident Response Center: http://www.fedcirc.gov

The Federal Computer Incident Response Center (FedCIRC) is the federal civilian government's focal point for computer security incident reporting and providing assistance with incident prevention and response. The center became part of DHS's Information Analysis and Infrastructure Protection (IAIP) Directorate beginning March 2003 and focuses on four major activities:

- Incident Prevention: The center provides a Patch Authentication and Dissemination Capability that can assist organizations in identifying and patching known vulnerabilities specific to their systems. The center provides informational notices and advisories about current threats and vulnerabilities.
- Incident Reporting: The center receives incident reports from federal agencies/departments that allow it to identify deliberate targeting efforts and other trends. By sharing sanitized incident information in return, all civilian agencies/ departments can withstand or quickly recover from attacks against US information resources.

- Incident Analysis: the Center has a partnership with CERT/CC and offers Incident and Vulnerability Notes to illustrate the range of adverse events affecting federal agencies/departments as reported.
- Incident Response: The center provides personnel, appropriate remediation, and recovery activities for the aftermath.

The SANS Institute: http://www.sans.org

The SANS (Systems Administration, Audit, Network, Security) Institute is active in the fields of information security research, certification, and education and provides a platform for professionals to share their lessons learned, to conduct research, and teach the information security community. Besides the various training programs and resources aimed at informing its members and the community, the following centers are part of SANS:

- The Internet Storm Center: This center was created to detect rising Internet threats. It uses advanced data correlation and visualization techniques to analyze data from a large number of firewalls and intrusion detection systems in over 60 countries. Experienced analysts constantly monitor the Storm Center data feeds and search for trends and anomalies in order to identify potential threats. When a potential threat is detected, the team immediately begins an intensive investigation to gauge the threat's severity and impact. The Storm Center may request correlating data from an extensive network of security experts from across the globe, and possesses the in-house expertise to analyze captured attack tools quickly and thoroughly. Critical information is then disseminated to the public in the form of alerts and postings.
- The Center for Internet Security (CIS) and SCORE: CIS formalizes the best practice recommendations once consensus between

the SANS Institute and SCORE is reached and the practices are validated. Those latter become minimum standards benchmarks for general use by the industry. Both organizations rely on and have a very broad contact with the field experts.

The CERT Coordination Center:
http://www.cert.org/

The CERT Coordination Center (CERT/CC) is located at the Software Engineering Institute (SEI), a federally funded research and development center at Carnegie Mellon University in Pittsburgh, Pennsylvania. SEI had been charged by DARPA after the Morris worm incident in 1988 to set up a center to coordinate communication among experts during security emergencies and to help prevent future incidents.

The CERT/CC is part of the larger SEI Networked Systems Survivability Program, whose primary goals are to ensure that appropriate technology and systems management practices are used to resist attacks on networked systems and to limit damage and ensure continuity of critical services in spite of successful attacks, accidents, or failures. The areas of work of the center can be summarized as follows:

- Vulnerability Analysis and Incident Handling: Analyze the state of Internet security and convey that information to the system administrators, network managers, and others in the Internet community. In these vulnerability and incident-handling activities, a higher priority is assigned to attacks and vulnerabilities that directly affect the Internet infrastructure (for example, network service providers, Internet service providers, domain name servers, and routers).
- Survivable Enterprise Management: Help organizations protect and defend themselves. To this end, risks assessments that help enterprises identify and characterize critical information assets and then identify risks to those assets have been developed, and the enterprise can use the results of the assessment to develop or refine

their overall strategy for securing their networked systems.

- Education and Training: The center offers training courses to educate technical staff and managers of computer security incident response teams as well as system administrators and other technical personnel within organizations to improve the security and survivability of each system. The center's staff also take part in developing curricula in information security and has compiled a guide, *The CERT® Guide to System and Network Security Practices*, published by Addison-Wesley.
- Survivable Network Technology: The center focuses on the technical basis for identifying and preventing security flaws and for preserving essential services if a system is penetrated and compromised. The center does research for new approaches to secure systems and analysis of how susceptible systems are to sophisticated attacks and finding ways to improve the design of systems. Another focus is on modeling and simulation. The center has developed "Easel," a tool that is being used to study network responses to attacks and attack mitigation strategies. And finally, the center is also developing techniques that will enable the assessment and prediction of current and potential threats to the Internet. These techniques involve examining large sets of network data to identify unauthorized and potentially malicious activity.

The National Communications System:
http://www.ncs.gov/

Through this system, DHS will support the telecommunications critical infrastructure and research and development of tools and technology to prevent disruption or compromise of these services.

The National Communications System (NCS) was established in 1963 as a "single unified communications system to serve the president, Department of Defense, diplomatic and intelligence activities and civilian leaders." The NCS mandate included linking, improving, and extending the communications facilities and components of various federal agencies, focusing on interconnectivity and survivability. The NCS's national security and emergency preparedness (NS/EP) capabilities were broadened in 1984 when it began coordinating and planning NS/EP telecommunications to support crises and disasters.

With the U.S. Information Agency being absorbed into the U.S. State Department in October 2000, the NCS membership currently stands at 23 members. The NCS also participates in joint industry-government planning through its work with the president's National Security Telecommunications Advisory Committee (NSTAC), with the NCC's National Coordinating Center for Telecommunications (NCC), and with the NCC's subordinate Information Sharing and Analysis Center (ISAC).

The NCS comprises numerous programs and committees that represent the majority of the national efforts in the field of communication for national emergencies and crisis.

The President's National Security Telecommunications Advisory Committee (NSTAC) and the Office of the Manager NCS (OMNCS) have been given the tasks of providing access control, priority treatment, user authentication, and other survivability features supporting NS/EP telecommunications to the Advanced Intelligent Network (AIN). The OMNCS has established an AIN Program to address the emerging technology and an associated AIN Program Office to plan, coordinate, and oversee the effort. Two very important examples of initiatives are the following:

- The Alerting and Coordination Network (ACN) provides a stable emergency voice communications network connecting telecommunications service providers' Emergency Operations Centers (EOCs) and Network Operations Centers (NOCs) to support national security and emergency preparedness (NS/EP) telecommunications network restoration coordination, transmission of telecommunications requirements and priorities, and incident reporting when the Public Switched Network is inoperable, stressed, or congested. The

ACN is operational 24 hours a day, 7 days a week, to support the National Coordinating Center (NCC) during normal and emergency operations.
- The Emergency Notification Service (ENS) is a 24×7 service to notify critical government personnel during emergencies using multiple communication channels, including telephone, Short Message Service (SMS), pager, and e-mail. Within minutes of receiving an Activation Order from an authorized representative of an organization, an automated process makes multiple attempts to reach intended recipients until they confirm delivery or until a predetermined number of attempts have been made. After 30 minutes, a report detailing confirmation of delivery is returned to the originator of the notification. Messages can be recorded in advance or when the notification is initiated and can be sent as a general notification or a sensitive notification.

(*Source*: NCS)

In order to initiate, coordinate, restore, and reconstitute national security and emergency preparedness (NS/EP) telecommunications services or facilities, the NCC continues to develop new capabilities and reevaluate or upgrade older ones. The NCC's current capabilities are given in Sidebar 9-3.

The current initiatives going on under the NCC's National Coordination Center for Telecommunications can be summarized as follows:

- In January 2000, the national coordinator for Security, Infrastructure Protection, and Counterterrorism designated the NCC-ISAC as the Information Sharing and Analysis Center for telecommunications. The NCC-ISAC will facilitate voluntary collaboration and information sharing among its participants, gathering information on vulnerabilities, threats, intrusions, and anomalies from telecommunications industry, government, and other sources. The NCC-ISAC will analyze the data with the goal of averting or mitigating impact upon the telecommunications infrastructure.

- The NCC-ISAC uses an Information Sharing and Analysis System (ISAS) to analyze the information provided by the NCC-ISAC participants. The ISAS incorporates capabilities for automated correlation of inputs with other inputs and all-source information. The ISAS provides advanced automation, analysis, modeling, data fusion, and correlation processes to support the near real-time exchange of critical information, assessments, and warning information involving vulnerabilities, threats, and affecting the telecommunications infrastructure.

(*Source*: NCS)

The last issue for emergency communication is wireless communication. Wireless network congestion was widespread on September 11, 2001, and with wireless traffic demand estimated at up to 10 times the normal amount in the affected areas and double nationwide, the need for wireless priority service became critical and urgent. Actually, it has been since the early 1990s that OMNCS works to develop and implement a nationwide cellular priority access capability in support of national security and emergency preparedness (NS/EP) telecommunications. As a result of a petition filed by the NCS in October 1995, the FCC set the wireless Priority Access Service (PAS) as voluntary. For example, the Wireless Priority Service (WPS), the NCS program implementation of the FCC PAS, is the wireless complement to the wire line Government Emergency Telecommunications Service (GETS). GETS utilizes the Public Switched Network (PSN) to provide enhanced wire line priority service to qualified NS/EP personnel.

But as a result of the events of September 11, 2001, the National Security Council issued the following guidance to the Office of the Manager, National Communications System (OMNCS):

- NCS has to move forward on implementing an immediate solution using channel reservation

---

SIDEBAR 9-3   NCC Current Capabilities

- The Communications Resource Information Sharing (CRIS) initiative provides a directory of readily available federal telecommunications assets, services, and capabilities that may be shared with other government agencies to support NS/EP needs. Participation is voluntary and limited to NCS members and their affiliates, and assets are only available if their use does not interfere with departmental or agency missions or operations.
- The Emergency Response Link (ERLink) is a controlled access web site that enables users to access or distribute information about an emergency. Although it is currently a pilot program, ERLink eventually will service all 12 Federal Response Plan (FRP) Emergency Support Functions (ESFs), including national

headquarters, regional offices, and Disaster Field Offices (DFOs).
- The Government Emergency Telecommunications Service (GETS) is a nationwide NS/EP switched voice and voice band data communications service that provides authorized local, state, and federal government users with communications during disasters by using surviving Public Switched Network (PSN) resources. GETS provides access authorization, enhanced routing, and priority treatment in local and long-distance telephone networks and is accessible through a dialing plan and personal identification number (PIN). GETS uses three major types of networks: the major long-distance networks provided by Inter-exchange Carriers (AT&T, MCI WorldCom,

Sidebar 9–3 continued

capability from one vendor for the Washington, DC, area; based on lessons learned in DC, the NCS will make a recommendation on whether to expand the immediate solution to other metro areas.

- In parallel, the NCS will proceed with deploying a priority access queuing system for wireless nationwide.

The two proposed solutions are given in more detail in Sidebar 9-4.

LABORATORIES AND RESEARCH FACILITIES

The Research and Development function is the most important aspect of the S&T Directorate. It will rely on several existing agency programs to accomplish this task: Department of Defense (DoD), Department of Energy (DOE), and Department of Agriculture (USDA) programs, among others. A significant portion of the funding attached to these programs comes from DoD's newly created National

and Sprint); the local networks provided by Local Exchange Carriers (Bell Operating Companies and Independent Companies, cellular carriers, and personal communication services); government-leased networks (including the Federal Telecommunications System and the Defense Information System Network).

- The National Technology Coordination Network (NTCN) connects participating government and industry organizations via a multimodal conferencing bridge. The bridge links disparate communications systems and allows for voice communications including dedicated line, high-frequency radio, satellite telephone, and switched wireline telephone. Telecommunications industry participants are connected to the bridge through the National Telecommunications Alliance's Alerting and Coordination Network (ACN). The ACN is a nonpublic Network (PN) system developed to provide communications and coordination capabilities to industry members during PN outages.
- The Shared Resources (SHARES) High Frequency (HF) Radio Program provides a single interagency emergency message handling system to transmit NS/EP information during disasters by consolidating HF radio resources

belonging to 91 federal and federally affiliated organizations. SHARES stations are in every state and at 20 overseas locations. The network consists of 1,101 HF radio stations located in the United States and abroad, 335 emergency planning and response personnel, and over 250 HF frequencies. It also provides the federal community a forum for addressing issues affecting HF radio operability. The manager of NCC is responsible for day-to-day operations of SHARES, while the manager of NCS is responsible for the overall SHARES program.

- The Federal Communications Commission (FCC) established the Telecommunications Service Priority (TSP) program in 1988 to provide priority provisioning and restoration of NS/EP telecommunication services. Under the TSP program, service vendors are authorized and required to provision and restore services with TSP assignments before services without such assignments. As a result, a telecommunications service with a TSP assignment will receive full attention by the service vendor before any non-TSP service. Nonfederal-government users who request TSP restoration or provisioning must be sponsored by a federal organization.

Source: NCS

Bioweapons Defense Analysis Center, responsible for nearly the entire biological countermeasures portfolio.

DHS intends to establish an Office for National Laboratories that will coordinate DHS interactions with DOE national laboratories with expertise in homeland security. The office has the authority to establish a semi-independent DHS headquarters laboratory within an existing federal laboratory, national lab, or FFRDC to supply scientific and technical

knowledge to DHS; the most recent indications are that DHS plans to do so with at least five national labs. In addition to Livermore, DHS has initial plans to establish four other labs-within-labs at Los Alamos, Sandia, Pacific Northwest, and Oak Ridge National Laboratories. DHS will also establish one or more university-based centers for homeland security.

The National and Federal Lab system possesses significant expertise in the area of weapons of mass

---

SIDEBAR 9-4   NCC Wireless Solutions

• The Immediate Solution: With the White House guidance in October 2001, the NCS began immediate acquisition of service for the Washington metropolitan area and recommended and proceeded with services for New York City as well. The February 2002 Olympics in Salt Lake City also warranted immediate service. The NCS entered into subcontracts with the immediate WPS service providers, T-Mobile (previously VoiceStream), and Globalstar. T-Mobile's implementation of the immediate solution became operational during May 2002 in Washington and New York. By November 2002, T-Mobile supported 2,084 WPS users in Washington and 725 in New York, for a total of 2,809 WPS cellular users. Globalstar also supported 1,506 customers as well.

• The Nationwide Solution: Nationwide WPS is a more comprehensive wireless priority capability. The nationwide initial operational capability (IOC) beginning December 31, 2002, consists of priority radio channel access at call origination, similar to the immediate solution. A full, end-to-end capability—beginning with the NS/EP wireless caller, through the wireless networks, through the interexchange carrier (IXC) and/or local exchange carrier (LEC) wireline networks, and to the wireless or wireline called party—will be realized nationwide full operational capability (FOC) currently planned for

December 31, 2003. This service will offer increased probability of call completion during times of widespread network congestion. The nationwide IOC software development began in July 2002, and installation of this software in commercial mobile radio service provider network switches started in November 2002. The government has contracted with several wireless switch vendors (including Ericsson, Nokia, and Nortel Networks) to include the IOC priority capability features in their switches on an expedited schedule.

As far as concerning the transition from the Immediate Solution to the nationwide solution, the FCC waiver for T-Mobile ended on December 31, 2002, and WPS providers have now implemented a capability to invoke call-by-call WPS NS/EP calls by dialing the WPS prefix *272 before dialing the destination number. WPS will be incrementally developed and deployed over the next several years. Both the Immediate Solution and Nationwide IOC are concentrating on providing priority access to the telecommunications network from the mobile handset to the radio base station. The Immediate Solution has now been displaced by Nationwide IOC and the transition has been successful.

Source: NCS

destruction in addition to massive computing power. These labs include the following:

- DOE National Nuclear Security Administration Labs: Lawrence Livermore Laboratory, Los Alamos National Laboratory, Sandia National Laboratory
- DOE Office of Science Labs: Argonne National Laboratory, Brookhaven National Laboratory, Oak Ridge National Laboratory, Pacific Northwest National Laboratory, other DOE Laboratories
- Department of Homeland Security Labs: Environmental Measurements Laboratory, Plum Island Animal Disease Center
- Department of Health and Human Services Labs: HHS operates several laboratories focused on wide-ranging health and disease prevention issues
- U.S. Customs Laboratory and Scientific Services: The U.S. Customs Laboratory and Scientific Services do testing to determine the origin of agricultural and manufactured products.

This section starts with an overview of the facilities cited above and relevant programs and then discusses other R&D activities, such as university-based center approach, and partnerships between DHS and other agencies. (Note: Most of the information presented is a summary digest taken directly from their official web sites.)

LAWRENCE LIVERMORE LABORATORY:
http://www.llnl.gov

The Homeland Security Organization at Lawrence Livermore National Laboratory (LLNL) will provide comprehensive solutions integrating threat, vulnerability, and trade-off analyses, advanced technologies, field-demonstrated prototypes, and operational capabilities to assist federal, state, local, and private entities in defending against catastrophic terrorism. The center is also dedicated to pursuing partnerships with universities and the private sector to fulfill its

mission. A summary of the programs going on is given in Appendix 9-1 at the end of this chapter.

LOS ALAMOS NATIONAL LABORATORY:
http://www.lanl.gov

Los Alamos National Laboratory is a Department of Energy (DOE) laboratory, managed by the University of California, and is one of the largest multidisciplinary institutions in the world. The Center for Homeland Security (CHS) was established in September 2002 to engage the laboratory's broad capabilities in the areas of counterterrorism and homeland security. It provides a single point of contact for all external organizations.

The organization's emphasis is in the key areas of nuclear and radiological science and technology, critical infrastructure protection, and chemical and biological science and technology. Current Los Alamos projects with a key role in homeland security include the following:

- BASIS (the Biological Aerosol Sentry and Information System), a biological early warning system that was tested and installed at the 2002 Salt Lake City Winter Olympics.
- A novel nuclear detector, the Palm CZT Spectrometer, is also in development and deployment, providing real-time gamma and neutron detection and isotope identification in a handheld device.
- The Los Alamos Laboratory has also been active in the anthrax bacterial DNA analysis and the computerized feature identification tool known as GENIE, for Genetic Image Exploitation.

SANDIA NATIONAL LABORATORY:
http://www.sandia.gov

The Sandia National Laboratories have been developing science-based technologies that support the national security since 1949. Through science and technology, people, infrastructure, and partnerships,

Sandia's mission is to meet national needs in four key areas (given in Appendix 9-2).

ARGONNE NATIONAL LABORATORY BROOKHAVEN NATIONAL LABORATORY: http://www.anl.gov

Argonne is one of the U.S. Department of Energy's largest research centers. It is also the nation's first national laboratory, chartered in 1946. Argonne's research falls into four broad categories: basic science, scientific facilities, energy resources programs, and environmental management.

Industrial technology development is an important activity in moving benefits of Argonne's publicly funded research to industry to help strengthen the nation's technology base. Appendix 9-3 summarizes the homeland security related programs and projects developed by the lab.

OAK RIDGE NATIONAL LABORATORY: http://www.ornl.gov/

The Oak Ridge National Laboratory (ORNL) is a multiprogramming science and technology laboratory managed for the U.S. Department of Energy by UT-Battelle, LLC. Scientists and engineers at ORNL conduct basic and applied research and development to create scientific knowledge and technological solutions that strengthen the nation's leadership in key areas of science; increase the availability of clean, abundant energy; restore and protect the environment; and contribute to national security.

The National Security Directorate's missions are as follows: to provide federal, state, and local government agencies and departments the technology and expertise to support national and homeland security needs; and to develop for, or transfer technology to, industry so it can be used in support of national or homeland security objectives as well as to enhance America's economic competitiveness in world mar-

kets. The different centers and programs of the laboratory are given in Appendix 9-4.

PACIFIC NORTHWEST NATIONAL LABORATORY: http://www.pnl.gov

The Pacific Northwest National Laboratory (PNNL) is one of nine U.S. Department of Energy multiprogramming national laboratories and delivers breakthrough science and technology to meet selected environmental, energy, health, and national security objectives; strengthen the economy; and support the education of future scientists and engineers.

Pacific Northwest's mission in national security supports the U.S. government's objectives against the proliferation of nuclear, chemical, and biological weapons of mass destruction and associated delivery systems. About one third of Pacific Northwest's $600 million annual research and development budget reflects work in national security programs for the Departments of Energy, Defense, and most other federal agencies. The focus is on issues that concern the Air Force, Army, Defense Advanced Research Projects Agency, Defense Threat Reduction Agency, Navy, and nuclear nonproliferation.

Scientists and engineers at Pacific Northwest are finding ways to diagnose the life of the Army's Abrams tank, developing technologies that verify compliance with the Comprehensive Nuclear Test Ban Treaty, helping North Korea secure spent nuclear fuel in proper storage canisters, and training border enforcement officials from the United States and foreign countries. Some National Security projects are given in Appendix 9-5.

OTHER DOE LABORATORIES AND OBJECTIVES: http://www.energy.gov

The Department of Energy also has other affiliated organizations in addition to the ones cited above that focus on the same issues. A quick summary is provided in Appendix 9-6.

ENVIRONMENTAL MEASUREMENTS LABORATORY: http://www.eml.doe.gov

The Environmental Measurements Laboratory (EML), a government-owned, government-operated laboratory, is directly part of the Science and Technology (S&T) Directorate. The laboratory advances and applies the science and technology required for preventing, protecting against, and responding to radiological and nuclear events in the service of homeland and national security.

EML's current programs focus on issues associated with environmental radiation and radioactivity. Specifically, EML provides DHS with environmental radiation and radioactivity measurements in the laboratory or field, technology development and evaluation, personnel training, instrument calibration, performance testing, data management, and data quality assurance. Examples of these programs are given in Appendix 9-7.

The two unique facilities of the lab are as follows:

- Environmental Chamber: A 25-cubic-meter facility, the only one in the United States, that can generate atmospheres with controlled aerosols and gases for calibration and testing of new instruments
- Gamma Spectrometry Laboratory: A fully equipped laboratory with high efficiency and high resolution gamma sensors

PLUM ISLAND ANIMAL DISEASE CENTER: htttp://www.ars.usda.gov/plum/

The Plum Island Animal Disease Center (PIADC) became part of DHS on June 1, 2003. While the center remains an important national asset in which scientists conduct basic and applied research and diagnostic activities to protect the health of livestock on farms across the nation from foreign disease agents, it also has the new mission to help DHS to protect the country from terrorist threats, including those directed against agriculture.

The Department of Agriculture (USDA) is responsible for research and diagnosis to protect the nation's animal industries and exports from catastrophic economic losses caused by foreign animal disease (FAD) agents accidentally or deliberately introduced into the United States While continuing its mission, it will also work closely with DHS personnel to fight agroterrorism. The common goals for the organization are given in Appendix 9-8.

While the island setting and biocontainment facilities of PIADC permit safe and secure research by operating at a Biosafety Level 3, the DHS has no plans in the near or long term for a Biosafety Level 4 facility.

DEPARTMENT OF HEALTH AND HUMAN SERVICES LABS: http://www.hhs.gov

The Department of Health and Human Services operates several laboratories focused on different health and disease prevention issues. The laboratories have extensive programs, and more details can be found in the following sections.

U.S. CUSTOMS LABORATORY AND SCIENTIFIC SERVICES http://www.customs.gov/xp/cgov/import/operations_support/labs_scientific_svcs/

It is one of the principal responsibilities of the Science Officers to manage the Customs Gauger/Laboratory Accreditation program. The program calls for the accreditation of commercial gaugers and laboratories so that their measurements and analytical results can be used by customs for entry and admissibility purposes. The staff edits and publishes the *Customs Laboratory Bulletin* which, as a customs-scientific journal, is circulated internationally and provides a useful forum for technical exchange on subjects of general customs interest. Appendix 9-9 provides an overview of the existing laboratories and their specializations.

ACADEMIC RESEARCH INSTITUTIONS

After looking at the facilities and the different programs available for research and development under the S&T Directorate, it is time to move on to look to the academic world. In fact, universities, their research centers, institutes, and qualified staff represent a very important portion of the scientific research in the United States These facilities represent an estimated one third of the total federal budget available for R&D activities.

The S&T Directorate has already started to show its intent towards universities and institutes. The DHS has released at the end of July 2003 a call for white papers from the academic community to establish the first university-based Homeland Security Center. Although different sources and reports announced the intention of DHS to open one center by the end of the year and plan in the long run for a total of 15 centers nationwide, no official information has been made available at this point.

The call for white papers states that

> These centers are to be an integral part of the effort of DHS to combat terrorism, and their purpose is to provide a focus to attract and retain the nation's best and brightest academic scholars in pursuit of homeland security-related disciplines. The centers will be mission-focused, in close partnership with the other assets of DHS, and be made of several higher education institution as well as private sector partners.

While the first white papers called for a focus on risk-based economic modeling on the impact and consequence of terrorism, behavioral research on terrorism and countermeasures, public safety technology transfer, agroterrorism countermeasures, and research and development of needed response technologies and operations, DHS announced its intent to solicit additional white papers in the coming months. Besides the announced area of work, the HS-centers are also expected to provide policy-informed economic modeling and prediction and to identify the costs and benefits of alternate countermeasures and operation responses aimed at enhancing the security of individuals and systems.

Knowing that the white papers will be evaluated using the following criteria gives valuable information on the intent of the Department about partnerships (source: DHS):

- Innovative and topic-related research directly related to advancing homeland security
- Importance and effectiveness of proposed partnerships
- Established personnel and physical infrastructure that can be leveraged to successfully undertake the proposed research

Although the call for white papers is a very common and frequently used procedure, there are some implications worth emphasizing:

- The initial definition of applicants to form groups and partner with other universities and private organizations is quite different from the standard one. In fact, the National Science Foundation (NSF) supports nearly 50 percent of all nonmedical-based research at colleges and is the lead agency in several fields. While this latter authorizes (and sees a considerable amount of) applications from individuals or groups of individuals, the new style of DHS may affect the entire way work on these areas used to be done.
- Another reason for this change to occur is the phenomenal exiting budget. The NSF budget for homeland security R&D is only $286 million compared with the $1 billion received by the DHS.
- A second important concern is the vague definition of secured work and information and the concern of information security. This ill-defined concept and the need for science to be carried out in an open and international platform risks causing overprecaution in the handling of information as well as the designation of academic staff.
- Along the way, DHS will also have to balance national security interests with academic freedom as certain fields, such as biotechnology, can produce technologies that can be used as weapons if in bad hands.

MARITIME

The scope of the S&T Directorate encompasses the pursuit of a full range of research into the use, preservation and exploitation of the national waterways and oceans. The US Coast Guard Research and Development Center is in charge of conducting research to support defense of this resource and of the homeland.

U.S. COAST GUARD: http://www.uscg.mil

The Research and Development (R&D) Center is the Coast Guard's sole facility performing research, development, test and evaluation (RDT&E) in support of the Coast Guard's major missions of maritime mobility, maritime safety, maritime security, national defense, and protection of natural resources. The center has as its mission "to be the Coast Guard's pathfinder, anticipating and meeting future technological challenges, while partnering with others to shepherd the best ideas into implementable solutions."

The Coast Guard RDT&E program produces two types of products: the development of hardware, procedures, and systems that directly contribute to increasing the quality and productivity of the operations and the expansion of knowledge related to technical support of operating and regulatory programs. Some of the programs are included in Appendix 9-10.

After reviewing all the agencies, laboratories and other facilities that operates under or as a partner of the S&T Directorate, let's have a look at the R&D efforts pursued under the other Directorates of the DHS.

BORDER AND TRANSPORTATION SECURITY (BTS) DIRECTORATE

The Directorate of Border and Transportation Security includes the former Transportation Security Administration's (TSA) R&D programs on aviation security, with an appropriation of $110 million in FY2003 rising to $172 million in FY2004 ($45 million for R&D on next-generation explosive detection technologies in commercial aviation, and $55 million for air cargo security R&D). The S&T Directorate will gradually assume responsibility for these activities over the coming years.

INFORMATION ANALYSIS AND INFRASTRUCTURE PROTECTION (IAIP) DIRECTORATE

The Information Analysis and Infrastructure Protection (IAIP) Directorate has only $5 million in R&D out of a total budget of $839 million. Most of its research and analysis needs on cyber-security will be performed by the S&T Directorate. The Information Directorate will also rely on research performed by other agencies, such as Commerce's National Institute of Standards and Technology (NIST), described later in this chapter.

EMERGENCY PREPAREDNESS AND RESPONSE (EP&R) DIRECTORATE

The Directorate of Emergency Preparedness and Response has no formal R&D programs within its $8.4 billion budget in FY2004. However, Congress and the Bush Administration have agreed to set aside $5.6 billion over the next 10 years to procure biodefense countermeasures from the private sector. So, an additional $4.7 billion between 2005 and 2013 for the program named Project BioShield has been proposed in the president's State of the Union address. Although it is not an R&D program, the program is designed to encourage private-sector R&D investments in biodefense vaccines, therapeutics, and other countermeasures by providing a guaranteed government market for future products. DHS/EP&R will purchase and stockpile these countermeasures using the $5.6 billion total appropriation.

The directorate (FEMA at that time) had announced in April, 2002, that it was partnering with the NIST to work jointly to accomplish the following:

- Reduce loss of life and property and protect the buildings and infrastructure from all types of hazards.

- Aid the development of technology and methods to evaluate first responders and management community equipment.
- Ensure that EP&R/FEMA can call on NIST to help with scientific and technological services in disaster investigations, recovery planning, and support technologies.

DEPARTMENT OF HEALTH AND HUMAN SERVICES (HHS)

THE NATIONAL INSTITUTES OF HEALTH (NIH)

The National Institutes of Health (NIH) most relevant effort in homeland security R&D is in bioterrorism-related research. It has conducted work in the field for years but it became a high priority after the anthrax attacks occurred in 2002. In the FY03 budget, Congress has provided $1.7 billion to support NIH's efforts. The same level has been given in FY04 with $1.708 billion, representing nearly half the whole homeland security R&D funding. Most of these funds would go to the National Institute of Allergy and Infectious Diseases (NIAID). In FY03, roughly $1 billion supported research activities aimed at developing biomedical tools to detect, prevent, and treat infection by biological agents, and $700 million goes to R&D facilities funding for the construction of intramural and extramural biosafety laboratories. In FY04, the entire $1.7 billion supported biodefense research, both in NIH's own laboratories and through extramural research grants.

As stated in the summary of the report,

The NIAID has taken many steps since February 2002 to catalyze the development of vaccines, treatments, and diagnostics for the most threatening bioterror agents. For example, the institute has developed more than 50 initiatives to stimulate biodefense research, three quarters of which are brand new. Through these initiatives, NIAID has greatly expanded its support of investigators in academia and partnerships with industry. It has also created new biodefense resources, taken advantage of genomic research advances, and furthered understanding of how microbes cause disease and how the immune system responds to infection.

Some of these initiatives are given in Appendix 9-11.

THE CENTERS FOR DISEASE CONTROL AND PREVENTION

Another agency of HHS, the Centers for Disease Control and Prevention (CDC), which funds bioterrorism R&D at its own laboratories, receives the rest of the related R&D funding allocated in HHS.

THE DEPARTMENT OF DEFENSE

The Department of Defense (DoD) actually decreased its homeland security R&D by 74 percent, down to $157 million in FY04. This funding is through Defense Advanced Research Projects Agency (DARPA), which works mainly on military applications in areas such as biological warfare defense, but may be relevant to the emergency management field. The FY03 appropriation contains homeland security-related R&D work, but beginning in FY04 most of this work is funded by DHS, and DoD focuses on its traditional mission of national defense and preventing terrorism overseas.

THE U.S. DEPARTMENT OF AGRICULTURE (USDA)

As depicted by the R&D Update of October 1, 2003, prepared by the AAAS, the U.S. Department of Agriculture (USDA) has only a small homeland security R&D effort but counts a portion of its R&D activities in the Agricultural Research Service (ARS), such as biocontainment facilities and upgrades to its laboratory network against terrorist attacks, as related to homeland security. These security upgrades account for most of the $173 million R&D investment in FY03 because most of these funds were emergency appropriations for construction. The USDA total is down to $80 million in FY04 for research only. Details of the work done by the ARS have been previously described under the Plume Island Animal Disease Center.

THE ENVIRONMENTAL PROTECTION AGENCY (EPA)

The EPA has a small but focused R&D effort. From $4 million in FY02, it got to $50 million in FY03 for building decontamination research provided as a one-time emergency support to EPA's work in decontaminating congressional office buildings of anthrax. In FY04, EPA homeland security R&D will decrease to $29 million.

In September 2002, the EPA designated the National Risk Management Research Laboratory (NRMRL) as the new National Homeland Security Research Center. The new Center's goal, over its proposed 3-year life, is to provide appropriate, effective, and rapid risk assessment guidelines and technologies to help decision-makers prepare for, detect, contain, and decontaminate chemical and biological attacks directed against buildings and water treatment systems. Research and development efforts will focus on coordination of three major programs, given in Appendix 9-12.

THE NATIONAL INSTITUTE OF STANDARDS AND TECHNOLOGY (NIST)

The Department of Commerce (DOC) is home to NIST, which funds R&D in many areas and provides scientific and technical support to DHS. Examples of NIST projects are presented in Appendix 9-13.

THE NATIONAL SCIENCE FOUNDATION (NSF)

The National Science Foundation (NSF) funds research to combat bioterrorism in the areas of infectious diseases and microbial genome sequencing. These programs increased to $286 million in FY04.

CONCLUSION

Homeland Security represents an entire new spectrum of issues of R&D and technology and an opportunity to revitalize old issues under the homeland security umbrella. Establishing DHS and the S&T Directorate brought a new, major player into the federally supported R&D efforts. There was much discussion and disgruntlement within the research community concerning the lack of involvement of NSF in the development of the homeland security R&D agenda. In fact, several people questioned the need for the S&T as opposed to just increasing NSF or NIST's portfolios.

With a spectrum of activity varying from research to development and deployment and a span of subjects from bioterrorism to protective gears, communication tools to nonproliferation, and detection devices to mass production of vaccines, the S&T Directorate has been given a huge task. The directorate not only coordinates the R&D facilities of many organizations but also has the authority in setting priority in others. The proposed university-based HS Centers provides a level of new funding that has not been available for some time and provides one of the best funded opportunities for specific R&D to benefit emergency management.

Although the context of change leaves little room for conclusions, the extraordinary budget given to the S&T Directorate either in existing programs or in new ones will provide the emergency management and first responder communities new capabilities never before imagined. It is to be hoped that these technological "toys" do not give a false sense of confidence and overshadow the real requirements of building an improved capacity to mitigate, prepare for, respond to, and recover from the risks of terrorism.

The changes that can be implied with the establishment of the university-based centers should be watched closely. These centers will probably provide the first and most concrete platform for the announced

FIGURE 9-3 New York, NY, September 29, 2001—Lobby of hotel near the World Trade Center site. Photo by Andrea Booher/FEMA News Photo.

partnership, or "integration," of academia, the private sector, and the federal government in support of homeland security. The establishment and progress of these centers should be followed carefully and will answer two fundamental questions:

1. How ready are these sectors to work together? Can the most basic goal of survival and safety of the homeland be a motivation strong enough to overcome the sectors' administrative and functional differences?

2. Will real integration occur? The R&D field may be the place to show if integration at the large scale as proposed by the DHS is really possible or not. This field is probably the most appropriate one because research, development, and deployment are very close functions. But still this task may be more difficult than it seems because it involves many different organizations, whose cooperation, successes, or failures can put the success of the whole organization at risk.

REVIEW QUESTIONS

1. Identify 10 specific areas of research (with their programs) that the DHS encompasses and were previously not included in FEMA or any other existing laboratories/research centers.
2. Explain in your own words the establishment of HSARPA and its scope and objectives.
3. Make a quick search about the missions and goals of the National Science Foundation (NSF) and the National Institute for Science and Technology (NIST). What would be your position in the debate to put the R&D function of homeland security under the DHS or as an extension of NIST or NSF? Why?
4. Develop an agenda as if you were applying on the behalf of your university to be a university based HS center. Who are the partners (academic and private) in your region that you would like to join? What would be the strengths of this team?
5. Develop a basic scheme showing all the research topics under the four major areas that the DHS S&T focuses on. Does it seem consistent to you? Would you add or subtract any topic to adjust it?

REFERENCES

American Association for the Advancement of Science www.aaas.org

Argonne National Laboratory http://www.anl.gov/

Brookhaven National Laboratory http://www.bnl.gov/world/

Centers for Disease Control and Prevention http://www.cdc.gov

CERT Coordination Center http://www.cert.org/

Chemical and Biological Defense Information and Analysis Center http://www.cbiac.apgea.army.mil/

Defense Threat Reduction Agency http://www.dtra.mil/cb/cb_index.html

Department of Agriculture http://www.usda.gov

Department of Defense http://www.dod.gov

Department of Energy http://www.doe.gov

Department of Energy Laboratories, Other http://www.energy.gov

Department of Health and Human Services http://www.dhhs.gov

The Department of Homeland Security http://www.dhs.gov

Department of Justice http://www.doj.gov

Environmental Measurements Laboratory http://www.eml.doe.gov/

Environmental Protection Agency http://www.epa.gov/

Federal Computer Incident Response Center http://www.fedcirc.gov/

The Federal Emergency Management Agency http://www.fema.gov

The Federal Response Plan http://www.fema.gov/pdf/rrr/frp/frp2003.pdf

Health and Human Services http://www.hhs.gov/

Lawrence Livermore National Laboratory http://www.llnl.gov/hso/

Los Alamos National Laboratory http://www.lanl.ov/worldview/

Medical Treatment of Radiological Casualties http://www.appc1.va.gov/emshg/docs/Radiologic_Medical_Countermeasures_051403.pdf

National Communication System http://www.ncs.gov/

National Infrastructure Protection Center http://www.nipc.gov/

National Institute of Standards and Technology http://www.nist.gov/

National Institutes of Health http://www.nih.gov/

National Personal Protective Technology Laboratory http://www.cdc.gov/niosh/npptl/default.html

The National Response Plan http://www.nemaweb.org/docs/national_response_plan.pdf

National Strategy for Homeland Security http://www.whitehouse.gov/homeland/book/

Oak Ridge National Laboratory http://www.ornl.gov/

Pacific Northwest National Laboratory http://www.pnl.gov/

Plum Island Animal Disease Center http://www.ars.usda.gov/plum/

RAND Science and Technology Institute http://www.rand.org

Sandia National Laboratory http://www.sandia.gov/

SANS Institute http://www.sans.org/

State Department http://usembassy.state.gov

U.S. Coast Guard http://www.uscg.mil

U.S. Customs Laboratory and Scientific Services http://www.customs.gov/xp/cgov/import/operations_support/labs_scientific_svcs/

U.S. Nuclear Regulatory Commission http://www.nrc.gov

APPENDIX 9-1
Lawrence Livermore Laboratory Programs

Chemical and Biological Countermeasures

Various efforts are addressing the national need for technologies to quickly detect, identify, and mitigate the use of chemical and biological threat agents against U.S. civilian populations. The principal program is the Chemical and Biological National Security Program (CBNP).

- **Biological Aerosol Sentry and Information System (BASIS)**. This joint Livermore-Los Alamos system uses a network of aerosol collectors and a central deployable field laboratory to provide early warning of biological attack. BASIS has been deployed at the 2002 Winter Olympics and elsewhere.
- **Advanced Biodetection Technology**. Miniaturized PCR technology developed at LLNL forms the basis for today's most advanced commercial biodetectors.
- **Biological Signatures**. Analyses of virulence genes and pathogen pathways to develop targeted DNA and/or protein assays that recognize even engineered organisms are performed.

- **Forensic Science Center**. This center has expertise and instrumentation for the complete chemical and isotopic analysis of nuclear materials, inorganic materials, organic materials (e.g., chemical warfare agents, explosives, illegal drugs), and biological materials (e.g., toxins, DNA).
- ***In-Situ* Chemical Sensors**. These are portable chemical sensors, for both attended and unattended operation, that can variously detect waterborne species, airborne volatiles, and particulates. Also on the way are specialized coatings, based on a range of polymers and novel materials, for improved field sampling and sample concentration.
- **Remote Chemical Sensing**. These are remote sensing systems capable of detecting and identifying a wide range of gases from high overhead and characterizing effluent materials by their spectral fingerprints. The program in chemical signatures analyzes weapons production processes to predict the emissions and other observables indicative of weapons activity.

Nuclear and Radiological Countermeasures

This thrust area focuses on developing technical capabilities aimed at countering the threat of terrorist use of a nuclear or radiological device in or near a U.S. population center.

- **Nuclear Emergency Response**. LLNL scientists and engineers participate in the Nuclear Emergency Search Team (NEST), which responds in the event of a terrorist incident involving nuclear or radiological materials.
- **Cargo Container Security**. The Intermodal Container Evaluation and Experimental Facility provide unbiased testing of commercially available and prototype technologies for detecting nuclear materials inside cargo containers.
- **Radiation Detection**. The center is developing advanced radiation detection technologies, such as the handheld Cryo3, which uses electromechanical cooling instead of liquid nitrogen and thus is well suited for field deployment.
- **Detection and Tracking System**. This rapidly deployable network of correlated radiation detectors and cameras can detect, characterize, and track nuclear or radioactive material carried inside vehicles moving at up to freeway speeds.

Systems Analysis and Studies

This program area focuses on identifying and understanding gaps in U.S. preparedness and response capabilities and the associated opportunities for technology.

- **Homeland Security Analysis**. Systems studies are conducted to evaluate the effectiveness of alternative approaches to early detection, interdiction, and mitigation of damage to the U.S. homeland from a range of possible threats, emphasizing weapons of mass destruction and the disruption of information systems.
- **Vulnerability Assessment**. Ongoing LLNL efforts are assessing vulnerabilities of the U.S. energy infrastructure to physical and cyber attack.

- **Outreach to Operational Entities**. LLNL interacts with representative state, regional, and local agencies to develop, test, and evaluate capabilities for preventing, detecting, and responding to WMD terrorism in real-world settings.

Information Analysis and Infrastructure Protection

This thrust area is aimed at developing tools and capabilities for gathering, manipulating, and mining vast quantities of data and information for the dual purpose of detecting early indications and warnings of terrorist intentions, capabilities, and plans and of identifying and mitigating vulnerabilities to critical U.S. infrastructures.

- **Computer Incident Advisory Center (CIAC)**. CIAC is operated by LLNL as the Department of Energy's cyber alert and warning center. CIAC notifies the complex of vulnerabilities that are being exploited, specifies countermeasures to apply, and provides profiles of attacks. CIAC also develops cyber defense tools and technologies and provides cyber-security training.
- **Information Operations and Assurance**. The Information Operations and Assurance Center provides technologies and expertise to exploit information technology as a defensive strategy and to defend critical infrastructures against attack.
- **International Assessments**. Livermore has one of the strongest capabilities in the United States for all-source analysis of foreign WMD activities by weapons states, proliferators, and terrorists, including early-stage foreign technology development and acquisition as well as patterns of cooperation.
- **Nuclear Threat Assessment**. LLNL's Nuclear Threat Assessment Center is the national center for evaluating nuclear threats and illicit nuclear trafficking cases.

Border and Transportation Security

Activities in this area address opportunities for technology to enhance U.S. border and transportation security, from nuclear detection systems for maritime and air cargo to automated facial screening of airline passengers to integrated data management systems for immigration and border control.

- **Concrete-Penetrating Radar**. Micropower impulse radar (MIR) developed at LLNL can "see" many feet into concrete rubble; it was used at the World Trade Center rubble pile to search for survivors.
- **Baggage Screening Technologies**. Candidate technologies for improved screening of passengers and baggage are in various stages of development, including computed tomography (CT), X-ray scanning, gamma-ray imaging, neutron interrogation, and ultrasonic and thermal imaging.
- **Truck-Stopping Device**. This simple mechanical device attaches to the back of a tanker truck and can be triggered by highway patrol officers to keep a hijacked truck from becoming a motorized missile.

Emergency Preparedness and Response

This program thrust develops technical capabilities for minimizing the damage and recovering from any terrorist attacks that do occur and works with local, regional, state, and federal first responders to ensure that the tools developed meet real-world needs.

- **National Atmospheric Release Advisory Center (NARAC)** NARAC is the premiere capability in the United States for real-time assessments of the atmospheric dispersion of radionuclides, chemical and biological agents, and particulates. In addition to its essential role in emergency response, NARAC can also be used to evaluate specific scenarios for emergency response planning. The LINC (Local Integration of NARAC with Cities) program was recently established to facilitate access to NARAC by local and state agencies to better plan for and respond to toxic releases.
- **Joint Conflict and Tactical Simulation (JCATS)**. JCATS models urban and rural conflicts involving the movement of up to tens of thousands of people, vehicles, weapons, etc., occurring over large areas (up to half the surface of the globe) down to encounters within buildings. In addition to evaluating military tactics, JCATS can be used to assess strategies for protecting cities, industrial sites, and critical U.S. infrastructure against terrorist attack.
- **Homeland Operational Planning System (HOPS)**. HOPS is being developed, in partnership with the California National Guard, specifically for homeland security planning and analysis. HOPS analyses provide insight into the vulnerabilities of elements of U.S. infrastructure and the likely consequences of strikes against potential terrorist targets.

Source: Lawrence Livermore Laboratory

APPENDIX 9-2
Sandia National Laboratory Programs

Nuclear Weapons

The primary mission is to ensure the U.S. nuclear arsenal is safe, secure, reliable, and can fully support the nation's deterrence policy. The initiatives are as follows:

- Enhance the capabilities of radiation-hardened microelectronics to address national security issues

- Develop simulation capabilities to model the entire nuclear weapon life cycle
- Deliver advanced robotics systems to monitor proliferation activities, clean up hazardous sites, and disassemble old munitions
- Improve the methods and practices used to support product delivery

- Incorporate pulsed power technology into defense applications
- Develop Distributed Information Systems for the nuclear weapons complex

Nonproliferation and Assessments

Sandia's Nonproliferation and Assessments program reduces U.S. vulnerability to weapons of mass destruction (WMD). These include nuclear, biological, and chemical weapons, as well as nonconventional WMDs such as the highjacked civilian airlines used to commit acts of war against our nation.

- Develop technologies for early detection of proliferation activities
- Provide leadership for policies and technologies that will bring deterrence, nonproliferation, and nuclear energy into a constructive synergy for the 21st century
- Develop new technologies to protect the United States from chemical and biological threats

Military Technologies and Applications

The Military Technologies and Applications program develops high-impact responses to national security challenges, and the existing integrated science expertise allows developing technologically superior weapons and security systems. The initiatives are as follows:

- Further develop applications of Collectively Intelligent Systems
- Enhance the capabilities of Distributed Information Rich Systems to provide timely and effective solutions to critical national security issues and help divert emerging threats
- Support Sandia's directed energy research efforts
- Enhance technologies to defeat difficult targets
- Continue demilitarization efforts to rid the globe of landmines
- Improve Waste Legacy to dispose of the materials that cannot be reused, to store and recycle the materials that can be put to use, and to clean up contaminated areas

Energy and Infrastructure Assurance

The Energy and Infrastructure Assurance program supports Sandia's core purpose of helping secure the nation through technology. The goal is to enhance the surety (safety, security, and reliability) of energy and other critical infrastructures, and efforts are made in the areas of energy research, earth sciences, transportation systems, risk management technologies, environmental stewardship, and nuclear waste management. Sandia is also actively working to improve the nation's critical infrastructure surety. The focus is on infrastructure elements in the areas of transportation, electric power grid, oil and gas distribution, telecommunications, finance and banking, and vital human services. The initiatives in this matter are as follows:

- Energy Efficiency and Renewable/Fossil Energy, where much of the work centers on partnering with industrial suppliers and users of the technology
- Critical Infrastructure Protection. The Sandia National Laboratories have a number of capabilities that can be applied to assist the nation in improving infrastructure surety as its primary goal is to guarantee the surety of the nuclear weapons stockpile.
- Nuclear Energy. The Nuclear Energy Technology program provides relevant and defensible technical information and effective approaches for making or supporting critical decisions concerning the safety and reliability of nuclear systems. The major program areas are Nuclear Reactor Safety, Light Water Reactor Technology, International Nuclear Safety, DOE Nuclear Facilities Safety, and Risk Assessment.
- Office of Science
- The Water Initiative. Sandia is solving technological challenges innate to water safety, security, and sustainability and thus, enhance national security.

Source: Sandia National Laboratory

APPENDIX 9-3
Argonne Programs

Emergency Preparedness

The mission of the group is to help increase the knowledge, skills, and effectiveness of emergency managers, planners, and responders in the United States and overseas who are dealing with technological and natural disasters. It incorporates a variety of analytical tools and methods, such as exercise planning, evaluation, and review; planning standards and criteria; response planning models; classroom and field training; computer simulations; guidance and policy manuals. The programs are as follows:

1. Consequence Management: The aim is to develop and improve planning, training, exercising, and communication systems that prepare emergency professionals to successfully manage the consequences of high-impact disasters. The program also provides detection and modeling technologies, information systems, and decision support tools that strengthen preparedness and response efforts.

2. Chemical Stockpile Emergency Preparedness Program (CSEP): This program is a national initiative intended to enhance resources, training, public education, and plans for an accidental release of chemical weapons agent from any of the continental U.S. stockpile storage installations. The program involves a unique integrated effort, including not only the eight U.S. Army Soldier and Biological Chemical Command (SBCCOM) storage installations, but also the 10 states and 39 counties that could be affected. The Decision and Information Sciences (DIS) provides a wide variety of scientific and technical support, including the following:

   - Policy and guidance development
   - Training in emergency exercise evaluation, local response methods, emergency risk communications, and planning

   - Emergency exercise scenario preparation, exercise control, and exercise evaluation
   - Emergency planning methods development, modeling support, software development, and site-specific assistance

   DIS collaborates with Oak Ridge National Laboratory and Pacific Northwest National Laboratory in this endeavor. DIS has contributed a number of key products and services to the national CSEP Program such as: developing an installation-based team of emergency planners; initiating the national emergency exercise program; modeling potential agent deposition patterns to enable development of personal protective equipment specifications; developing and implementing a quality assurance program for each installation's meteorological towers; conducting emergency spokesperson training for installation and community leaders to interact with the media during an accident; drafting national guidance on how communities should use memorandums of understanding to enter into mutual aid agreements; developing the Alabama Special Population Planner to enable GIS-based emergency planning for special populations and special facilities; and inventing the Emergency Response Synchronization Matrix to facilitate multijurisdictional emergency planning.

3. The Alabama Special Population Planner (SPP): It is the first geographic information system (GIS)-based software tool designed to facilitate emergency planning for "special populations" and "special facilities." By using its tools and data, SPP allows users to develop specific plans to meet the unusual emergency planning problems posed by special populations and special facilities.

4. Chemical Incident Modeling: Preparedness for the always possible chemical spills from the many industrial chemicals transported requires good science on the likely human impacts of the spread as well as a means of transferring that information in an easy-to-use form for the first responder. The lab has developed a methodology for determining Initial Isolation and Protective Action Distances (PAD) appearing in the 2000 Emergency Response Guidebook. The objective for choosing the PADs specified in the guidebook was to balance the need to adequately protect the public from exposure to potentially harmful substances against the risks and expenses that could result from overreacting to a spill.

5. Policy and Guidance Development: The lab has prepared guidance documents that provide information about hazardous materials, emergency plans, procedures, equipment, training, drills, and exercises needed to prepare for and respond to HAZMAT emergencies.

6. Preparedness Evaluation: Careful review of plans and procedures along with on-site assessments of personnel, equipment, training, and facilities helps provide a complete picture of an organization's ability to react quickly and effectively during a crisis to protect lives, property, and the environment. The organization has assisted different federal, state, and local governments in developing and improving their emergency preparedness and response capabilities.

7. Synchronization Matrix: As the complexity of emergency response planning increases because of expanding interjurisdictional and organizational interactions, it becomes exceedingly more difficult for a person to understand and visualize the interplay of a complete set of response plans, procedures, and checklists and to manage them within a synchronized community response. The lab has a systems-based process solution by which emergency planners and responders can coordinate, integrate, and synchronize their emergency plans. Argonne's emergency response synchronization matrix (ERSM) was developed to organize the increasingly complex interjurisdictional response

necessary to meet the Chemical Stockpile Emergency Preparedness Program (CSEPP) response requirements.

8. Risk Communication: Communicating effectively through the media requires an understanding of the media's role and constraints. As the key decision-makers and public affairs officials lack all the tools they need to anticipate media response and to convey information in a way that ensures it will be correctly interpreted and disseminated, Argonne has developed a full-service, full-cycle approach to planning, training, and exercising.

- Planning services focus on the creation and implementation of strong and effective risk communication plans for all-hazards, specific hazards, and specific emergencies, such as acts of terrorism.
- Training courses build skills and explore the conceptualization and operation of a successful emergency information effort from Joint Information Center/System to spokesperson training.
- Exercise support includes scenario development and preplanning as well as execution of realistic tests of the emergency information program.
- Product development includes multimedia materials to enhance public outreach and education efforts and to enhance public information/affairs programs and staff skills and knowledge.

Environmental Assessment Division (EAD)

EAD develops and applies tools and approaches to help prevent natural and man-made disasters, improve response to ongoing incidents, and address the consequences of incidents. EAD's experience helps analysts, decision-makers, and first responders to:

- Reduce the nation's vulnerability to an attack
- Manage the flow of information during an incident
- Address issues related to recovery after an event.

Efforts to reduce vulnerability to terrorist actions parallel EAD's ongoing activities to safeguard the workplace and the environment from vandalism, human error, and adverse natural events. These efforts include the following: risk mitigation and assessment for critical facilities and systems, hazardous waste management, advanced modeling and analysis, web-based risk management training, and web-based information management.

EAD also has experience modeling the potential effects of attacks on the general population and economy, as well as addressing environmental issues associated with chemical warfare agents, explosives, industrial chemicals, and nuclear materials.

Other activities include the following:

- Integrating information management tools across the entire spectrum of Homeland Security threats is critical to analysts, decision makers, and first responders.
- Conduct real-time threat analysis for determining appropriate emergency response actions (e.g., sheltering, decontamination, evacuation, and addressing the situation of individuals with special needs in times of emergency).
- Address recovery and cleanup efforts including chemical and nuclear damage assessment, gaseous dispersion modeling, surface and groundwater modeling, hazardous material transportation, and public awareness.

Nonproliferation

The mission of the Nonproliferation and National Security Department (NNS) is to carry out research and development, provide technical support, and build prototype systems in order to further U.S. government initiatives and policies in nuclear materials safeguards and security, arms control treaty verification, nonproliferation of weapons of mass destruction, Material Protection Control and Accountability initiatives for nuclear materials in Russia and the NIS, and related national security areas. The lab works were also directed to international safeguards, leading to innovative concepts such as safeguard seals, short-notice random inspections; mail table declarations, and zone approaches. The NNS Department is currently working on establishing capabilities in counterterrorism and critical infrastructure protection.

Source: Argonne National Laboratory

APPENDIX 9-4
Oak Ridge National Laboratory Centers and Programs

Technology Advantage Center

The center functions as a clearinghouse and broker for technologies that can be used in protecting the nation against threats to its safety and security. To identify candidate technologies, the center is developing an automated search engine that uses intelligent software agents to perform tailored, high-speed searches of relevant electronic information. Augmenting the search engine is a network of contacts that spans government, industry, academia, and other sources, ensuring that the latest information in emerging technologies is included.

The center can also assist customers with technology testing, technology roadmap preparation, rapid prototyping, and technology implementation.

The center has assessed the capabilities of a "See Inside Rooms" technology for a DoD agency and orchestrated the vision for Objective Force Warrior, a major U.S. Army science and technology initiative, including a comprehensive review of high-tech solutions that will be available by 2010 and 2018.

The programs that the center is working on are as follows: biological countermeasures, radiological and nuclear countermeasures, chemical and high explosives countermeasures, critical infrastructure protection, information synthesis and analysis, vulnerability/threat assessment, and wireless communication and network.

Technological Capabilities

The various technological capabilities of the Oak Ridge Laboratory are as follows:

- Chemical/Biological Detection: Advanced biosensors, advanced multifunctional biochips, chemical mass spectrometer, calorimetric spectrometer for chem-bio detection, countermeasures to attacks on water supplies, infrared laser array for chem-bio agent detection (LADAR), infrared camera to detect and track chemical plume
- Equipment: Military equipment condition monitoring, technologies for the assessment of heat damage to composite materials and structure
- Mass Spectroscopy: Boarding pass analyzer, calorimetric spectroscopy

- Models and Simulations of: GIS, Landscan, HPAC, SensorNet
- Multipurpose Technologies: Compact high-power light source for LADAR, graphite foam, innovative integration of electronics, micro sensor array platform
- Personal Protection: Advanced ceramic and countermine, biochip, inorganic membranes, microclimate conditioning
- Sensors: DOE industrial wireless program, integrated multichannel sensors, fiber-optic sensor suite of skills, sensor-based tagging and tracking, ultra-weak-signal sensing, nanophotinic sensor materials/systems
- Software: IntelAgents, Total Online Access Data System (TOADS)

Source: Oak Ridge National Laboratory

APPENDIX 9-5
Pacific Northwest National Laboratories Programs

Homeland Security

Pacific Northwest National Laboratories (PNNL) is assessing the vulnerability of critical infrastructures across the nation as well as teaming with organizations to ensure the air and seaports are protected from the threat of terrorist attacks. Around the globe, PNNL is training border enforcement officials to thwart the smuggling of chemical, biological or nuclear materials across foreign borders. The lab works on the following:

- Sensors and electronics for threat detection
- Cyber-security and information assurance
- Information visualization
- Dynamic Information Analysis Laboratory
- Atmospheric monitoring and research

- Center for Coastal Security and Protection
- Weapons of Mass Destruction Emergency Response

High-Tech Crime Fighting

The aim is to develop technological capabilities and tools to investigate crime precisely and rapidly, assess possible risks of consequences, and determine whether incidents of unknown reasons are accidental or voluntary. Some of the programs are as follows:

- Investigating airline crashes for reason of crash
- Getting to the root of the agroterror problem
- Tools for law enforcement agents to access, enter, and transfer large amounts of information at the crime scenes

- Tracking down deadly pathogens with mass spectrometry
- Visualization Software to analyze large amount of compiled data
- Developing methods for assessing accuracy and strength of forensic evidence
- Establishing the Critical Infrastructure Protection and Analysis Center to research and develop tools to safeguard key assets
- Handwriting analysis tool
- Nonintrusive weapon detection

Information Security Resource Center (ISRC)

The center provides support to the Department of Energy Security Policy Staff in the Office of Security by serving as a Center of Excellence for information security issues. The ISRC provides programmatic and technical support in the areas of Information Security, Facility Surveys and Approvals, Foreign Ownership, and Control or Influence and maintains the DOE Incident Tracking and Analysis Center (ITAC). The ISRC also helps to identify and mitigate security threats and vulnerabilities and provides awareness to the DOE complex through the publication of advisory notices and crosstalks.

Pacific Northwest Center for Global Security

The Pacific Northwest Center for Global Security was established in October 1998 by the Department of Energy's Pacific Northwest National Laboratory, with four principal objectives:

- *Coordinate* the arms control, proliferation prevention, emergency response, and regional security activities of the PNNL, serving as Point of Contact on nonproliferation and global security issues, and providing a window to the laboratory's scientific and technical resources
- *Partner* with organizations throughout the Pacific Northwest, particularly universities and nongovernmental organizations, on nonproliferation and global security activities
- *Position* the National Nuclear Security Administration (NNSA) and the Pacific

Northwest National Laboratory to respond to changing conditions of the post-Cold War environment by emphasizing the broader issues of global security and addressing both the traditional and nontraditional aspects of proliferation prevention and regional stability
- *Inform* the laboratory about the current state of global security and nonproliferation, and introduce scholars and policy makers to laboratory programs and staff through a seminar series, workshops, and conferences.

One central purpose of PNNL's global security activities is to help minimize the conditions under which nations or peoples proliferate weapons of mass destruction. A second purpose is to develop a better understanding of the threats posed by environmental, energy, and information security issues and to reduce those threats, especially in regions where the stakes of tension and instability are raised by the presence of weapons of mass destruction. The center combines traditional approaches to global security, such as reducing stockpiles of weapons of mass destruction with nontraditional approaches (such as economic transition, energy, and environmental security) that increase regional stability.

Real-time Engine Diagnostics-Prognostics

Artificial intelligence aims to increase battlefield readiness by diagnosing engine problems in tanks before costly repairs are needed. PNNL is developing REDI-PRO, or Real-time Engine Diagnostics-Prognostics, a prototype system to diagnose and predict failures and abnormal operations in the M1 Abrams main battle tank's turbine engine.

Information Technology

A new software tool known as Starlight being developed at PNNL enables the user to sift through the blizzard of information to discover trends or hidden information. Using Starlight's interactive, investigative tools, it is possible to characterize data, query and search for information, and visualize results using high-fidelity, 3-D graphics.

Source: Pacific Northwest National Laboratories

APPENDIX 9-6
Other DOE Objectives and Laboratories

Nuclear Security

The Department of Energy, through the National Nuclear Security Administration (NNSA), works to enhance national security through the military application of nuclear energy. The NNSA also maintains and enhances the safety, reliability, and performance of the United States' nuclear weapons stockpile, including the ability to design, produce, and test, in order to meet national security requirements.

NNSA has four missions with regard to National Security:

1. To provide the United States Navy with safe, militarily effective nuclear propulsion plants and to ensure the safe and reliable operation of those plants
2. To promote international nuclear safety and nonproliferation
3. To reduce global danger from weapons of mass destruction
4. To support United States leadership in science and technology

Intelligence

The Department of Energy (DOE) has stewardship of vital national security capabilities, from nuclear weapons to leading-edge research and development projects. These capabilities, and related DOE programs, are important not only to the national strength but, within the framework of international cooperation, to the lessening of global threats.

Counterterrorism

Department activities are focused on protecting our nuclear weapons secrets but also place a high priority on protecting the other sensitive scientific endeavors and on combining with other departmental elements in the efforts to defeat terrorism.

Weapons of Mass Destruction

DOE is an integral part of the United States' efforts to reduce global danger from weapons of mass destruction. The Deputy Administrator for Defense Nuclear Nonproliferation within NNSA is responsible for the enhancement of national security through the following four-part strategy:

- Protecting or eliminating weapons and weapons-useable nuclear material or infrastructure and redirecting excess foreign weapons expertise to civilian enterprises
- Preventing and reversing the proliferation of weapons of mass destruction
- Reducing the risk of accidents in nuclear fuel cycle facilities worldwide
- Enhancing the capability to detect weapons of mass destruction, including nuclear, chemical, and biological systems.

Emergency Response

As a high-visibility shipper of radioactive material, the U.S. Department of Energy and its transportation activities have come under intense scrutiny from Congress, states, tribes, local governments, and the public.

An underlying concern is the adequacy of emergency-preparedness along DOE shipping corridors. The Environmental Management program implements the complex-wide Transportation Emergency Preparedness Program (TEPP) to address preparedness issues for nonclassified/nonweapons radioactive material shipments. As an element of the DOE Comprehensive Emergency Management System, TEPP provides support to DOE and other federal, state, tribal, and local authorities to prepare for a response to a transportation incident involving DOE shipments of radioactive material. TEPP is implemented on a regional basis, with a TEPP coordinator designated for each of the eight DOE Regional Coordinating Offices.

Oversight

The Office of Independent Oversight and Performance Assurance (OA) is the independent oversight organization for the Secretary of Energy and for the administrator of the National Nuclear Security Administration. As a corporate resource, it conducts evaluations to verify that the department's safeguards and security interests are protected, that the department can effectively respond to emergencies, and that site workers, the public, and the environment are protected from hazardous operations and materials.

Source: Department of Energy

APPENDIX 9-7
Some EML Programs

Modeling Atmospheric Transport

In collaboration with the World Meteorological Organization (WMO), Global Atmosphere Watch (GAW), the Chinese Academy of Meteorological Sciences, and the Chinese Academy of Sciences measurements are being made using EML's Surface Air Sampling System at Mt. Waliguan in Qinghai Province in central China. The measurements will be used to study the transport process in the atmosphere and will provide unique scientific data for global atmospheric modeling. This collaboration is part of EML's role as a World Calibration Center for Radioactivity in GAW.

International Environmental Sample Archive (IESA)

EML maintains a unique and extensive archive of environmental samples collected throughout the world. Many of these were collected during the period of atmospheric nuclear weapons testing and have unique isotopic compositions. These samples can be used for the following: quality control—test newly developed instruments and techniques; nonproliferation—identify signatures of nuclear proliferation; background—determine global variations of signatures.

Nonproliferation Treaties

As a federal laboratory, EML supports DOE's National Security mission through its detection and deterrence activities for the nonproliferation treaties. EML has been designated as the U.S. Radionuclide Laboratory in support of the International Monitoring System. Development and evaluation of detection systems to aid international weapons inspectors in verification compliance will cross over into counterterrorism applications.

EML's Global Radioactivity Sampling Network

EML has maintained a worldwide network of aerosol and deposition sampling stations for over 40 years. Currently, there are 10 domestic sites. The network serves to identify any new sources of radioactivity released into the environment.

Source: Environmental Measurement Laboratory

APPENDIX 9-8
USDA/DHS Common Activity Goals

- Develop new strategies to prevent and control foreign or emerging animal disease epidemics through a better understanding of the nature of infectious organisms; their pathogenesis in susceptible animals; the host immune responses; the development of novel vaccines; and the development and improvement of diagnostic tests.
- Conduct diagnostic investigations of suspected cases of foreign or emerging animal diseases in the United States or in countries abroad through cooperation with animal-health international organizations.
- Test imported animals and animal products to assure they are free of foreign animal disease agents.
- Assess risks involved in importation of animals and animal products from countries where epidemic foreign animal diseases occur.
- Produce and maintain materials used in diagnostic tests for foreign animal diseases.

- Test and evaluate vaccines for foreign animal diseases and maintain the North American foot-and-mouth disease vaccine bank.
- Train veterinarians and animal health professionals in the diagnosis and recognition of foreign animal diseases through courses at PIADC and at other domestic and international locations.
- Contribute to DHS's biological countermeasures program in the S&T Directorate, which seeks to reduce the probability and potential consequences of a biological attack on the nation's civilian population and its agricultural system.
- Concentrate on high-consequence biological threats, including agricultural diseases such as foot-and-mouth disease and high-volume contamination of food supplies.

Source: Plume Island Animal Disease Center and DHS

APPENDIX 9-9
U.S. Customs Laboratories

1. Research Laboratory: The Research Laboratory is a centralized research facility which provides scientific support to Customs Headquarters and the field laboratories. The laboratory develops new analytical methods and evaluates new instrumentation for application by the field laboratories. Analytical services are also provided to Customs' legal and regulatory functions and to other headquarters offices that may need scientific support, including quality assurance for the Customs Drug Screening Program and technical assistance for the Canine Enforcement Program and for international drug training programs. The Research Laboratory is an important resource in addressing tariff classification issues for high-technology products, in developing statistical data to confirm the country of origin of imported commodities, and in providing a sound technical foundation for Intellectual Property Rights (IPR) enforcement involving copyrights, trademarks, and patents.

2. New York Laboratory: In addition to the analysis of imported merchandise, the New York Laboratory does the following:

- Provides scientific advice for the ruling program and pre-entry assessment of the National Commodity Specialist Division
- Provides technical information on drawback cases
- Responds to request for scientific advice to Assistant Chief Counsel and the Department of Justice on issues before the Court of International Trade
- Provides narcotic test kit training by our forensic chemists to Customs officers and agents
- Manages a computerized database of chemicals entered under the HTS, which as of now consists of 5,000 entries
- Has a strong textile program, and provides training in the use of the textile field kit
- Has on staff the National Petroleum Chemist responsible for the east coast

It also specializes on metals, chemicals, textiles and footwear, building stone, consumer products, polymers and plastics, paper and food products.

3. Chicago Laboratory Customs Service Area: The Laboratory is located in Chicago's Customhouse and is a full-service laboratory, providing technical advice and analytical services to Customs officers and other entities on a wide range of issues and imported commodities. These services assist Customs officers in meeting the primary Customs mission of collecting revenue based on import duties and enforcing Customs and related laws.

The Chicago Laboratory has a Customs-only tensile tester capable of determining certain physical characteristics of industrial fasteners and other steel articles. The laboratory has had a strong involvement in the geological identification of building stones under the harmonized tariff schedule. Because of its northern location, NAFTA issues and Canadian merchandise are prevalent.

In the forensics area, the Chicago laboratory is, at present, the only Customs laboratory with the capability to enhance video and audio tapes for Customs enforcement officers. The laboratory also has a mini photo processor to develop standard color-print film, can provide enlargements, and can process black-and-white film.

4. Savannah Laboratory (including San Juan Branch) Customs Service Area: The laboratory is a full-service analytical laboratory with capabilities for chemical and physical testing of all types of commodities, narcotics and other controlled substances.

The laboratory specializations are generally related to textile and apparel analyses. The laboratory is designated as Customs' testing facility for wool, which includes determining clean content and wool grade. Additionally, the laboratory is uniquely capable of determining if upholstery fabrics meet tariff requirements and for determining tensile strengths of textile products.

5. New Orleans Laboratory Customs Service Area: The services provided by the New Orleans laboratory include analyses of a broad range of imported and exported commodities and merchandise to determine whether said merchandise is properly described by the required documentation or identified as contraband according to its physical and chemical nature. This laboratory is also responsible for providing technical support in areas such as drawback, classification issues, and regulatory audit functions as well as for criminal and civil investigations.

In addition to the normal work of a U.S. Customs Field Laboratory, the New Orleans Laboratory has three areas of specialization:

- Raising fingerprints off of objects is an expertise developed by this laboratory so that the Customs Service would have this capability in-house. State-of-the-art instrumentation is available that can digitize fingerprints and match the prints electronically to known fingerprints in its database. Furthermore, the instrument will be able to match raised prints to the FBI's Automated Fingerprint Identification System (AFIS) database once that system is released.
- One of the three national petroleum chemists is assigned to the New Orleans laboratory. The major

duties of this position include the following: refinery foreign trade zone operations, country-of-origin determination of petroleum, analysis of petroleum products for composition, review of applications for drawback of petroleum products, and review of Public Gauger/ Laboratory facilities for compliance to Customs regulations.

- The only biologist in the Customs Service is on staff at this laboratory. One of the major duties of this position is to introduce new ways of analyzing samples of a biological nature to the laboratory system.

6. Los Angeles Laboratory Customs Service Area: Within its service area, the Los Angeles Laboratory does the following:

- Provides pre-entry technical advice on classification of commodities
- Analyzes entered merchandise for compliance with Customs laws and/or other agency requirements enforced by Customs
- Examines merchandise for technical conformity with copyright, patent, trademark, and marking laws
- Provides Customs officers with advice on sampling and handling of hazardous materials and chemicals
- Supports Customs efforts on technical issues concerned with commercial fraud and drawback enforcement
- Advises the Department of Justice on technical matters related to Customs laws
- Provides forensic support such as analysis of controlled substances and technical advice in forensic areas to Customs officers
- Provides general scientific support to Customs officers in service area

Textiles analysis (mostly finished wearing apparel) and specialized textile analyses such as printed/dyed fabrics and hand/power-loomed fabrics. Intellectual Property Rights analysis, motor testing, hazardous materials handling and analysis.

7. San Francisco Laboratory Customs Service Area: The San Francisco laboratory is a full-service laboratory that provides technical advice and analytical services to the Customs officials and other agencies on a wide range of imported and exported commodities. Available to the technical staff are analytical instruments such as optical spectrophotometers, scanning electron microscope, gas chromatograph-mass spectrometers, gas and liquid chromatograph, and X-ray diffract meters and spectrographs.

Many samples of wearing apparel, footwear, building stone, metal products, foods, beverages, chemicals, and controlled substances are analyzed each year in the laboratory. Expedited services are provided on samples involving intellectual property rights (IPR), textiles that require quota, and visa and forensics. If samples cannot be brought to the laboratory, mobile laboratories are available to conduct on-site examinations.

Because of the laboratory's location on the Pacific Rim, there is an emphasis and greater expertise in that commerce which includes the following: textiles, including intermediates of the manufacturing process as well as finished wearing apparel; oriental food and beverages; and electronics. And because of the very significant value of petroleum importations, the laboratory specializes in petroleum chemistry. A special emphasis of this work targets the country of origin of crude oil and some of its finished products such as aviation fuel.

Source: U.S. Customs and Border Protection

APPENDIX 9-10
Coast Guard Programs

Intelligent Waterway System

- Vessel Traffic Management Research: The present methods, used to gather and distribute vessel traffic and marine safety information, need improvement. New approaches are needed to improve the timeliness of information, increase overall distribution capacity and quality, and conform to the operation of modern navigation systems. This project aims to investigate, develop, test, and demonstrate technologies, methods, and standards useful for providing future vessel traffic management safety and mobility information using fully automated means. Particular emphasis will be placed on information interfaces that automatically gather and deliver safety and mobility information to the marine operator.

- Waterways Information Network: Effective, efficient information exchange with the maritime public and cooperating agencies is the key element to close performance gaps in several areas of marine and navigation safety, but there is no standardized method to exchange and improve the timeliness of waterway relevant information within the larger USCG, federal, state, port, and responsible party "stakeholder" communities. This project aims to develop a low-cost, seamless information infrastructure to exchange security, navigation, marine safety, and other data with other agencies, the maritime industry, and the public.

Risk Competency

- Port State Control Targeting Matrix (PSCTM): Based on a standard statistical analysis, none of the five risk factors associated with the PSCTM were statistically significant in predicting non-compliance. Hence, it does not adequately meet the needs of the Coast Guard to identify those foreign-flagged vessels that pose the greatest risk to our ports. This program aims to produce an improved PSCTM that will adjust the risk factors so that Coast Guard personnel can identify and board vessels that are more likely to pose safety or environmental threats to the nation's ports and waterways.

- Planning and Management: The Coast Guard pursues, under the constraint of limited resources, a multiplicity of risk-based performance goals, including public safety, environmental protection, and marine commerce. Due to the ever-changing demands on the resources and capabilities for effectively managing the safety of ports, waterways, and maritime industry, the Coast Guard needs to develop the guidelines and technical frameworks that will support a marine safety core competency in Coast Guard risk-based decisionmaking (RBDM). This research will develop risk-based approaches that can optimize existing decision-making processes in the field.

Some programs concerning oil spill response are also available, and more detail can be found on the U.S. Coast Guard web site.

Source: The U.S. Coast Guard

APPENDIX 9-11
National Institute of Allergies and Infectious Diseases

Partnerships in Product Development

In addition to awarding contracts for second-generation smallpox and anthrax vaccines, the National Institute of Allergies and Infectious Diseases (NIAID) has expanded other collaborative opportunities with industry. Though the Biodefense Partnerships program, which is a new mechanism that encourages private-sector research and development of countermeasures and a similar initiative that includes academia—cooperative research for the development of vaccines, adjuvant, therapeutics, immunotherapeutic and diagnostics for biodefense and SARS—NIAID is funding 31 grants to companies to develop high-priority biodefense products.

Basic Research

NIAID awarded eight Regional Centers of Excellence for Biodefense and Emerging Infectious Diseases Research. This nationwide network of multidisciplinary academic centers is conducting wide-ranging research on infectious diseases and the development of diagnostics, therapeutics, and vaccines. In addition, through partnerships with other agencies and companies around the world, NIAID has made a significant investment in sequencing pathogen genomes. Finally, dozens of grants made to individual investigators at academic institutions nationwide are opening new avenues for improving the existing ability to prevent, diagnose, and treat diseases caused by potential agents of terrorism.

Biodefense Research Resources and Facilities

NIAID is funding the construction of new biosafety laboratories around the country to address the serious shortage of such facilities to safely conduct research on biodefense and emerging infectious diseases. It also has developed and expanded contracts to screen new drugs; develop new animal models; establish a reagent and specimen repository; and provide researchers with genomic, proteomic, and bioinformatic resources.

Immunology

NIAID is funding research to better understand the body's own protective mechanisms. In particular, one recent large-scale grant is funding sophisticated studies of the human innate immune system. Another new set of grants has established a network of researchers focused on studies of the human immune system and biodefense.

Source: National Institute of Health

APPENDIX 9-12
EPA Programs

The Safe Buildings Program

The Safe Buildings Program activities focus on four areas of building cleanup:

- Detection research includes development of early-warning technologies, methods to protect responders, and information to guide cleanup.
- Containment research deals with isolation of contaminants and protection of building occupants and responders. In this area, scientists are studying the effects of heating, ventilation, and air conditioning on dispersal of contaminants, and evaluating air cleaner and filtration technologies.
- Decontamination research includes studies of interactions of decontaminants with indoor materials.
- Disposal research develops guidance for the safe packaging, transport, and destruction of contaminants or hazardous materials and the assessment of conditions for safe disposal.

The Water Security Research Program

Primary emphasis of the Water Security Research Program is on water supply, treatment, and distribution infrastructures in U.S. communities. Key research areas are as follows:

- Detection and characterization research is creating rapid screening technologies for the identification of unknown contaminants, while verifying the performance of sensors and biomonitors.
- Response and mitigation research includes water decontamination techniques and emergency treatment capacity; validation of field portable monitors, point-of-entry and point-of-use devices; and responses to cyber (computerized) or service (electrical/gas) interruptions.
- Prevention and protection research studies water treatment efficacy, safe transport in distribution systems, and treatment by-products.

A secondary emphasis of the Water Security Research Program is on wastewater treatment and collection infrastructures, which include collection (sanitary and storm sewers or combined sanitary-sewer systems) and impacts on receiving waters such as rivers, estuaries, and lakes.

The Rapid Risk Assessment Program

Rapid Risk Assessment works in the following fields:

- Information systems and tools are being developed that include the compilation of existing—and the development of new—hazard data, exposure models, and risk assessment models that protect first responders and guide final cleanup.
- Risk estimation addresses threats to buildings and water treatment and supply systems to provide guidance for first responders.
- Risk communication research is developing rapid risk assessment tools, methodologies, and products to deliver risk information to the public and to emergency responders. This includes the provision of technical assistance to appropriate emergency managers.

Source: The Environmental Protection Agency

APPENDIX 9-13
NIST Projects

Strengthening Structural and Fire Safety Standards

An essential tool in the fight against terrorism is a solidly built and protected infrastructure. NIST is contributing to this goal on a number of fronts aimed at strengthening structural and fire safety standards in buildings.

- Investigation of the World Trade Center (WTC) buildings' collapse: A 24-month federal building and fire safety investigation to study the structural failure and subsequent progressive collapse of several WTC buildings following the terrorist attacks of September 11, 2001, in New York City.
- On-site survey of Pentagon structural and fire damage: In October 2001, a NIST expert in building and fire research participated in an on-site survey of the Pentagon structural and fire damage as part of a team organized by the American Society of Civil Engineers and led by the U.S. Army Corps of Engineers. The Army Corps of Engineers subsequently funded a team of NIST experts to review and evaluate the performance of the Pentagon's structural system.
- Anthrax air flow study: NIST engineers provided help in understanding how spores may have spread through the buildings. NIST experts in ventilation systems and air quality used a sophisticated NIST-developed computer model to understand different ways in which air flow may have transported spores.
- Coordinated national strategy for protecting critical infrastructures: NIST is actively discussing the development of a coordinated national strategy in this area with the relevant agencies—FEMA, the Department of Defense, the Department of Transportation, and the General Services Administration; state and local building and emergency management officials; and private organizations.

Improved Materials for Structures

NIST is helping the engineering and construction industries improve building materials, enabling stronger, longer-lasting structures, be they bridges, buildings, or off-shore oil rigs.

Cyber-Security Standards and Technologies

NIST helps secure electronic information through programs that develop national and international standards for IT security and improve awareness of and capabilities for security solutions. Sample projects are as follows:

- The development of cryptographic standards and methods to protect the integrity, confidentiality, and authenticity of information resources. In December 2001, NIST and the Department of Commerce announced the newest and strongest-yet encryption standard for the protection of sensitive, nonclassified electronic information.
- Partnership with government and industry to establish more secure systems and networks by developing, managing, and promoting security assessment tools, techniques, services, and supporting programs for testing, evaluation, and validation.
- The development of guidelines to address topics such as risk management, security program management, certification and accreditation, and security training and awareness.

Cyber-Security of Electric Power and Industrial Control Systems

NIST is working with companies and industry organizations to identify the types of vulnerabilities that exist and develop security requirements for the real-time systems that control the power grid and critical industrial production processes. A Process Control Security Requirements Forum has been established to identify and assess threats and risks to process control information and functions, make and promote the adoption of security requirements recommendations, and promote security awareness and integration of security considerations in the life cycle of electric power and industrial process control systems.

Enhanced Threat Detection and Protection

- Ensuring proper doses for irradiation of mail: NIST is a member of a White House task force led by the Office of Science and Technology Policy to ensure that mail intended for Congress and other federal government offices is properly irradiated to kill anthrax bacteria. NIST also is advising federal officials on possible construction of a dedicated radiation source near Washington, DC, for future mail sanitation.
- Weapon detection technologies and standards: With funding from the National Institute of Justice (NIJ), NIST researchers have completed work on new performance standards and operational requirements for both walk-through and handheld metal detectors. The researchers have also created a sophisticated measurement system that uses specialized computer software to evaluate detector effectiveness. Another NIST research group has received funding from the NIJ and the Federal Aviation Administration (FAA) to investigate a new technology for weapons detection based on low-energy, millimeter-size electromagnetic waves.
- Detection of chemical, biological, radiological and other threats: As the primary reference laboratory for the United States, NIST develops standards, protocols, and new test methods to ensure that chemical and biological compounds can be measured accurately. This includes extensive, ongoing programs for the detection of chemical, biological, radiological, nuclear, and explosive threats.

Tools for Law Enforcement

For most of its 100-year history, NIST has worked closely with law enforcement, corrections, and criminal justice agencies to help improve the technologies available for solving and detecting crimes and for protecting law enforcement officers. Some of the projects are as follows:

- Standards for Biometrics: NIST efforts to improve the technologies and standards available for definitive identification of individuals—techniques such as fingerprinting, face recognition, and DNA analysis—have taken on added urgency.
- Standards for forensic DNA typing: Since the development of DNA typing methods more than 10 years ago, NIST has developed a series of Standard Reference Materials (SRMs) that can be used by forensic and commercial laboratories to check the accuracy of their analyses.
- Enhanced surveillance cameras: By mimicking the eye and surrounding the camera with liquid instead of air, NIST researchers (with interagency Technology Support Working Group funding) hope to improve the performance of surveillance cameras substantially. This, in turn, may improve the reliability of other technologies, such as face recognition within airports.
- Protective vests and helmets: At its ballistic research test facility, NIST develops the test methods and conducts the evaluations needed to continually improve standards for testing the performance of bullet- and knife-resistant vests, helmets, and face shields, as well as car windows and body armor, and keep up with changing materials and technologies.
- Standards for bullets and casings: NIST is developing reference material bullets and casings that forensic labs will be able to use with their own instruments and determine whether their analyses produce ballistic signatures that match those supplied by NIST.
- Forensic tools for investigating computer or magnetic data evidence: NIST computer scientists are helping to speed up the detection process dramatically with a new tool, the National Software Reference Library. Working with software manufacturers and others who provided copies of their programs, NIST collected "signature" formats for more than 6 million different computer files.

The library allows law enforcement agencies to eliminate 25 to 95 percent of the total files in a computer, concentrating only on those that really might contain evidence.

- Crimes involving pipe bombs or handguns: NIST chemists, in conjunction with the NIJ, have come up with a reliable way to associate the composition of unfired gunpowder or ammunition with residues collected at handgun or pipe bomb crime scenes. NIST now is preparing a smokeless powder reference material that forensic laboratories will be able to use in checking the accuracy of their bomb and gunpowder residue analyses.

Emergency Response

- Protecting first responders: Existing standards for emergency responders' protective gear were drafted with accidents—not terrorism—in mind. With funding from the NIJ, NIST is facilitating the development of a suite of national chemical and biological protective equipment standards. A standard for a self-contained breathing apparatus to withstand biological and chemical assault was deemed the highest priority and has been developed. Standards for other types of breathing apparatus are in the pipeline, as are standards for personal protective suits. Standards for chemical and biological detectors also have been given a high priority.
- Standardization of communications for first responders: NIST, again with funding from the NIJ, is working with the public safety community to standardize techniques for wireless telecommunications and IT applications. NIST is also working with standards development organizations to have first responder requirements included within the scope of standardization efforts.

- NIST is also working on the development, deployment, and standardization of web-based technologies for integrating sensors, real-time video, smart tags, and embedded microprocessor devices to provide next-generation personnel support for remote monitoring, control, and communications in the field. This technology can enable rapid access to real-time sensor and video information and allow sharing and collaborative use of IT applications.
- Simulation tools: To address the need to provide accurate and thorough simulations, NIST is helping to establish a framework to allow a broad range of simulation systems to share information, including models and results. NIST is working with the response community, industry, and academia to identify information sources, simulation systems, and data requirements; develop an emergency response simulation framework and standard interfaces; and develop and demonstrate distributed simulations using commercial software and the new framework.
- Search and rescue robots: A NIST project aimed initially at protecting emergency personnel by minimizing the amount of time rescuers spend searching earthquake-damaged buildings has helped provide a new tool for rescue workers at the World Trade Center. Since one of NIST's goals is to foster cooperation among robotics researchers around the world, NIST supplies its test arenas to two international robotics conferences, which include competitions to see how well search-and-rescue robots perform on the NIST arena.

Source: National Institute of Standards and Technology

The Future of Homeland Security

INTRODUCTION

The United States had been attacked without warning on its own soil, and more than 2,000 people were killed. For most citizens the brazen act demanded that the nation go to war, primarily to address and redress the wrongs that had been committed but also to prevent the perpetrators from further action against the United States and its allies. Despite the military victories that had occurred overseas, there was still a heartfelt conviction among most that the initial attack could have been prevented and that the government response could have been better organized. Deficiencies, inefficiencies, and barricades to the government's ability to gather information were recognized. The homeland needed to be more secure. Long, heated debates in Congress and throughout the United States followed. The year was 1947, exactly 55 years before the United States Department of Homeland Security (DHS) was created.

On July 26, 1947, President Harry S. Truman signed into law the National Security Act of 1947. In doing so, he effectively reorganized the Army, Navy, and the (newly established) Air Force into a single federal agency that would later become the Department of Defense (DoD). This law also dictated the creation of the Central Intelligence Agency (CIA), the National Security Resources Board (NSRB), and the National Security Council (NSC), thereby increasing the threat assessment powers of the executive office. At the time, the act was seen as fundamental to guaranteeing the security of the citizens of the United States and as a step toward ensuring lasting world peace.

Consideration for this enormous undertaking, which ultimately affected hundreds of thousands of federal employees, began in 1944 in reaction to the attack on Pearl Harbor and the events and lingering aftermath of the American involvement in World War II that followed. Versions of the plans for the reorganization of the armed forces and for the expansion and strengthening of federal foreign policy and intelligence instruments were drawn and redrawn, debated, and eventually refined into a single version and ratified.

Despite two full years of planning, the enactment of such wide-reaching legislation initiated what was to become the "mother of all turf wars" (Peckenpaugh, 2002). The absorbed and established agencies reformed, changed names, dissolved, and expanded considerably in the years and decades that followed. As recently as 1983, when the United States invaded Granada, the continued inability of the armed forces to fully integrate emerged when military operations on the island were simply divided up geographically between Army and Marine forces due to resistance to coordination on the part of military leadership. By 1986, however, nearly 40 years after the act became law, the process of integration was finally seen as being complete when the Goldwater-Nichols Act (which sought to close coordination gaps) was signed. Despite the fact that rivalries, turf issues, and inefficiencies do remain, it is undeniable that the agencies affected by the 1947 legislation are better off for the change.

Like the creation of the DoD, the creation of DHS is an undertaking that challenges the outermost bounds of bureaucratic politics and that requires cooperation among numerous historic rivals. It involves losses of power and authority by many agencies, and likewise the assumption of these powers and authorities by others. Clear lines of leadership and hierarchy will need to be drawn and redrawn, every change affecting hundreds, if not thousands of employees. Tens of thousands of new employees needed to be (and were) hired, and the inevitable growing pains of that increase have and will likely continue to require intense mollification. Despite being smaller in both the number of people and dollars involved than the 1947 reorganization, the scope of this act and the expectation of the American public make it an equally ambitious endeavor.

FIGURE 10-1 New York City, NY, September 11, 2002—Hillcrest, NY, firefighter Chris Agazzi attends a September 11 observance at Ground Zero. Photo by Andrea Booher/FEMA News Photo.

Proposals for such an agency had emerged in several forms before the events of September 11 demanded action to reduce the nation's vulnerability. The terrorist attacks of that day were witnessed live by millions and replayed in the media so often that any who missed them could not escape their horrifying scenes. These tragic events, displayed in horrifying scenes of wanton destruction of property, fire, explosion, death, and suffering, confirmed that great leadership and action were needed. The Bush Administration's initial action was to create the Office of Homeland Security in the White House. As Congress debated legislation to create DHS, the Bush Administration changed positions and endorsed the concept. But unlike the creation of the DoD that was preceded by years of debate and discussion, DHS was approved in a matter of months.

What did happen, as was the case in 1947, was comprehensive in nature, and was to many people astonishing in its sheer magnitude. But DHS was created in the midst of emotional turmoil, within an atmosphere of urgency, and during an upsurge of patriotism unequalled in most Americans' living memory. Such a genesis demands objectives, goals, and deadlines that are ambitious to the point of being unrealistic; instills hopes that are too easily challenged by detractors; creates expectations that easily fall short of target; and requires exceptional leadership of a collective effort that may be unprecedented in the history of government.

In all reality, there is great uncertainty as to whether the act and DHS as it is written today can be fulfilled. DHS is at the heart of our homeland security efforts. In this chapter, we plan to examine the issues facing DHS, its partners at the state and local levels, stakeholders in the private sector, and other forces that will affect the future of homeland security.

THE CREATION OF THE DEPARTMENT

The Homeland Security Act of 2002, signed November 25, 2002, gave Secretary Tom Ridge until March 1 of 2003—just over 3 months—to begin transferring the 22 incorporated federal agencies under the umbrella of DHS. Completion of the full transfer of all agencies from their respective locations into DHS was required by September 1, 2003, and a structural framework for the organization required completion by November 25, 2003 (1 year after the bill's signing). Many critics, including several staff members working within the organization itself, have stated that these goals were unrealistic and in many ways unattainable in functional terms (Mintz, 2003).

Almost 6 months before the Homeland Security Act was ever signed, and in anticipation of what were sure to be impatient goals, Director Ridge began making plans for a new Department by setting forth a "Transition Planning Team" that consisted of representatives from the 22 agencies. To the credit of both Ridge and other DHS leadership, almost all deadlines were met, at least in terms of what the verbiage of the act required. To have done this, however, it is certain that their operational planning must have been rushed (Moscoso, 2003b).

For many of the agencies, meeting these deadlines simply meant changing e-mail addresses, letterheads, web sites, and stationery; little if any physical movement was required. For others, the move was more comprehensive and disruptive. Inefficiencies surfaced almost immediately, and the media quickly took notice. One columnist from the *San Diego Tribune* described the post-transition DHS as a "rudderless, unaccountable organizational morass—incapable of protecting Americans against a bicycle theft, let alone a nuclear

FIGURE 10-2 Arlington, VA, March 7, 2002—A view of the Pentagon building shows the progress made in the reconstruction of the area damaged by the terrorist attack on the Pentagon on September 11, 2001. Photo by Jocelyn Augustino/FEMA News Photo.

attack" (Means, 2003). Assuredly, this was an exaggeration, but the statement emphasized a widespread and growing sentiment that confusion in the department could actually be making the nation less secure (Mintz, 2003; Edmonson, 2003).

Unexpected issues arose during the year that Ridge and his staff were allotted to create the new agency. For instance, 15 possible candidates for the top intelligence office in DHS declined requests to apply for the position, with at least one describing work in the agency as analogous to being "stuck in a government backwater" (Mintz, 2003). The same issue is known to have occurred with other executive positions as well. Staffing "mismatches" also emerged throughout the course of the department's creation, highlighted most significantly by the exodus of the first deputy director, Gordon England, who was quoted during a congressional hearing as being unaware that analyzing terrorism-related intelligence was a core mission of DHS (Mintz, 2003). The lack of a strong team from the outset magnified the organizational challenges.

Not all predictions for the department's creation have been so pessimistic. James Carafano of the Heritage Foundation, for example, publicly stated that "the 22 agencies that merged to form DHS would operate less efficiently at first, until new, more efficient methods could be established" (Simon, 2003). Not all of DHS's efficiencies can be attributed to the organization or its leadership, of course. Legislation has assuredly mandated rushed solutions. For example, a version of the DHS budget that appeared in 2003 would have required the department to develop a strategy for inspecting air cargo with the same vigilance that it did passengers, within a 1-month period, or lose $50 million in funding (Hulse, 2003). This particular requirement has proved to be impossible because appropriate technology did not yet exist. There are numerous other requirements that will not have such an easy solution.

There is an old bureaucratic axiom, about how the first year of reorganization is spent deciding where people will sit, the second what people will do, and the third how they will do it. It is not unrealistic to expect such a transition for DHS. A clear mission, articulation of that mission, and strong leadership, both political and career, can reduce the time frame.

However, it may be several decades or more before such a transition is complete, a sentiment confidently affirmed by many leading policy research institutions (Martin, 2003). In the meantime, as the federal government concentrates on organization, many stakeholders, especially at the local level, feel their needs and concerns are being minimized. Thousands of individuals who volunteered in the wake of September 11 are still waiting to help. Funding for first responders has been sacrificed for other parts of the war on terrorism being fought overseas. As the time between terrorist event lengthens and as the direction and leadership of the new department is slow to materialize, the greater the loss of interest, commitment, and political support from stakeholders and constituencies.

DECISIONS AND TRANSITION OF THE AGENCIES INTO DHS

Policy architects chose for the 22 agencies to be absorbed into DHS because they felt that those agencies' primary missions and objectives related most closely with protecting the nation against and responding to terrorist attacks. The original plans for the department were based upon, among other issues, the belief that the September 11 attacks could have been prevented if the intelligence agencies had shared certain pre-attack information.

As a result of these viewpoints, the initial versions of the department's blueprint included all of the intelligence agencies (CIA, DIA, NSA, and FBI). Fierce resistance fueled by organizational culture ultimately prevented such agencies from being included. Other agencies not associated with intelligence work, such as the Department of Transportation (DOT) and the Department of Health and Human Services (DHHS), were recognized as being closely related but did not warrant sufficiently convincing cases for inclusion; these and others resisted inclusion but lost one or more subagencies to DHS.

Many of those agencies that were absorbed did not have either the political clout or the will to resist inclusion in the new department. Two in particular, the Coast Guard and the Secret Service, maintained a certain degree of autonomy by insisting that they report directly to the DHS Secretary rather than be moved into one of the five directorates. The department's architects ultimately had no choice but to settle with the 22 agencies that appear in the final version of the bill signed by the president.

The result of this inability to bring all related agencies under one umbrella is that DHS must now seek alternative mechanisms to achieve many of its requirements under the act. The following subsections highlight two of the primary issues related to this transition.

SHARING OF INTELLIGENCE

One of the first tests for DHS came through the merging of the 12 terrorist "watch lists" that had drawn widespread attention because some had contained the names of at least 2 of the 19 September 11 hijackers. These lists, which are currently maintained by various agencies throughout the federal government (including the CIA, Department of State [DOS], Department of Justice [DOJ], DHS, Department of Defense [DoD], and others [Hall, 2003]), each serve a different individual purpose and are based upon different and often incompatible design formats.

To solve the problems associated with sharing the information contained within these lists and the sharing of security-related intelligence in general, the Terrorist Threat Information Center (TTIC) was created. TTIC was designed to ensure that "all the 'dots' [will] be connected to avoid another pre-September 11 situation in which vital information was left disassembled in the bowels of various intelligence agencies" (Etzioni, 2003).

The center, instead of residing in DHS, is the responsibility of the FBI, an agency not well known for willingly sharing information. The TTIC has since fallen under harsh criticism. For instance, critics feel that it maintains too small of a staff, and its rules for sharing information remain somewhat restrictive.

Of course, nobody could expect the decades-old cultural difference of these various intelligence agencies to erode so quickly. Steve Cooper, the Department of Homeland Security CIO, presented a realistic outlook on this issue in stating, "There are a lot of new players in town. Changing cultures doesn't occur overnight" (Chabrow, 2003). The greatest challenge likely to emerge in this issue concerns whether or not DHS has the political "muscle" to influence the required adaptation of culture. Interdepartmental cooperation between DHS and DoD, CIA, DOJ, and NSA will ultimately have to improve for the goals of the Homeland Security Act of 2002 to be met. These agencies' abilities to resist joining DHS at its inception are likely an indication of their desire and capacity to stonewall for some time.

Finally, whether this information will ever be extended to the state and local police and fire departments, which are the first responders and the "eyes and ears" of the community, remains to be seen.

LOSS OR CHANGE IN CORE FUNCTION

Several of the absorbed agencies had their core mission either fundamentally or partially altered because of a need to adapt to the overall terrorism mission of DHS. For many of these agencies, tasks they performed in their former capacities were transferred intact into DHS, despite the fact that they did appear to serve the overall goals and mission of DHS. Most of these tasks were important before September 11 and would therefore continue to be so afterwards. How these nonsecurity-related tasks are handled will likely be a test of the ability of DHS leadership to recognize their peripheral value.

A primary concern relating to these tangential functions is that the constituencies for these functions may be seriously diminished or ignored in favor of the more "security-related" functions when budget cuts are required. One need only to consider the Coast Guard to grasp this point. Since its inception the Coast Guard has maintained five historic functional areas that include (1) maritime safety, (2) national defense, (3) maritime security, (4) mobility, and (5) protection of natural resources (e.g., fisheries). In relation to the overall mission of DHS, the task of protecting fisheries could appear somewhat misplaced. Several lawmakers have already voiced concerns that the Coast Guard will slowly draw back their focus on these nonsecurity issues, which also include boating safety and rescue, to accommodate increased demands for the security-related functions of the Coast Guard, such as patrolling ports and waterways. They feel that with no other agency capable of assuming such tasks, these social services could easily disappear until public outcry demanded their return.

FEMA, now merged into DHS/EP&R, is equally at risk of losing the ability to fulfill its former mission responsibilities. To begin, FEMA was formerly a safety-based organization but is now under the direction of a security-based agency. As the security of terrorism takes precedence over earthquake or dam safety, these programs have experienced significant transfer of their budget resources to support DHS organizational activities. Second, FEMA has lost the "president's ear" (as it is called when an agency's director is a member of the president's cabinet) and as a result will have little power or political clout for getting additional revenues, fighting budget cuts, or stopping the cancellation of programs.

Other DHS agencies have and will continue to face similar trials as these, such the former Immigration and Naturalization Service (INS—which is traditionally a function that protects the national economy and jobs market more than one that prevents terrorist attacks), the cyber-security agencies, and Customs, among others. How they will perform will depend upon a range of variables such as changes in budget, public reaction to service losses, and other yet-to-be identified issues. The ability of DHS to maintain these functions will be a testament to the quality of leadership and their ability to meet organizational challenges associated with such a fundamental change in the organization of the federal government.

FULFILLING THE HOMELAND SECURITY GOAL—A "SAFE" NATION?

Regardless of the actual terminology used in defining the DHS mission, it is obvious to most people that its primary goal is to keep the nation safe from terrorist attacks. In fact, many citizens are likely unaware that DHS has any other goals at all, as is indicated by the continued appearance of newspaper articles erroneously defining the department as existing solely for terror prevention. Without a conscious effort by DHS officials to counter these beliefs, it is likely the department will create for itself public expectations that cannot be met.

Ending terrorism, or winning the "Global War against Terrorism" as it is often called, is a fundamentally impossible task. Terrorism, like crime, drugs, and other so-called evils, has always existed in modern times and will likely persist. The September 11 attacks were by no means the first terrorist attacks on American soil, nor will they be the last, although their spectacular nature makes such an event statistically unlikely to be repeated. Minor acts of terrorism, including attacks on abortion clinics, bombings at courthouses and other government facilities, mail bombs, biological attacks (anthrax letters and the Oregon salad bar salmonella attacks), chemical attacks (Tylenol cyanide poisoning), and sniper shootings, are more common. Even threats and hoaxes that instill fear can be correctly categorized as terrorist acts.

The actual threat of terrorism should not be taken lightly, and it is unlikely that it would in light of the gravity of September 11. However, it is possible that we could actually make the nation less secure by devoting so much attention to the terrorism threat.

DHS is responsible for preparing for and mitigating against many hazards besides terrorism that over time have cost much more in terms of life and property. This responsibility was assumed with the incorporation of FEMA into DHS. Effective disaster mitigation practices seek to treat risks proportionally and according to benefit/risk analyses. In practice, mitigation and preparedness decisions are heavily influenced by the perception of risk. Today, the proportional amount of money spent on the prevention of terrorism is astonishing when compared with that being spent on other hazards that traditionally are much more harmful with regard to loss of life and property. For instance, billions are being spent on screening airline passengers (Means, 2003), while less than 200 million is spent on flood, earthquake, tornado, hurricane, and other natural-hazard mitigation programs combined. It is unlikely that the cost of airport screeners or the $10 billion proposed cost of equipping airlines with anti-shoulder-fired missile protection (Burkeman, 2003) would pass this cost-effectiveness test.

It appears that the initial DHS strategy for terrorism prevention and preparedness is to plug "loopholes." However, the terrorist threat is unlike other technological or natural hazards in that it is "intelligent"—it is adaptable, and it learns. Despite the success terrorists had in using commercial airliners as guided missiles in the past, they are unlikely to repeat such success now that the element of surprise is gone. Terrorists tend to look specifically for weaknesses that have yet to be addressed for exploitation.

Plugging loopholes may be an appropriate strategy but will probably not significantly reduce the risk of terrorism in general. Charles McKinley, who shipped himself from New York to Dallas on a cargo plane without being noticed despite elevated airline security, proved there would always be loopholes to find (*Columbus Dispatch*, 2003).

The real test of DHS, then, will not be whether we have won the war and are now safe. The test will be how effectively the nation prevents attacks through improved intelligence and how effectively we respond and minimize damages when another attack occurs. In this context DHS will need to count on its partners for success. It will be the ability of the first responders to initially manage the consequences of the attack and the ability of the federal responders to assist them that will determine the ultimate outcome.

STATE AND LOCAL GOVERNMENT FIRST RESPONSE CAPABILITIES

The value of state and local first responders in making America safe and secure has been repeated throughout this text. These men and women are the first to arrive at the scene of any disaster and must often perform without outside assistance for up to 48 hours afterwards. Even if the federal government can thwart a thousand planned terrorist attacks, the state and local agencies will be needed if just one gets through. Unfortunately, these state and local agencies have been experiencing difficulties in meeting this challenge for a number of reasons.

Ironically, many local-level constraints related to homeland security have caused local police and fire departments to lay off personnel, most noticeably in the smaller communities. Sadly, many have less staff on their payrolls now than they did on September 11, 2001 (Gedan, 2003). These particular localities have become even less "prepared" now then they were before September 11. To compound these problems, many first responders who are military reservists have been called on to fight abroad in the global war against terrorism, leaving police and fire departments even more short-handed. Add these issues to the spending woes related to maintaining increased local vigilance, and one finds the perfect recipe for cuts in staff and programs. This cycle has repeated itself throughout the nation (McGreevy, 2003).

DHS has dedicated a considerable sum of money to equipping and training local first responders. In total, about $4 billion has been disbursed by DHS, but approximately 90 percent of that money is stalled at the state level (Cook, 2003; McGreevy, 2003). These problems stem from cultural and bureaucratic clashes that DHS can do only so much to alleviate. They could, according to many critics, including several prominent members of Congress, devote a greater percentage of overall spending on local preparedness. A survey administered by the *Boston Globe* indicated that a large percentage of police and fire chiefs feel that the government is not doing all it can to support local public safety personnel (Gedan, 2003), nor is it doing enough to encourage states to pass federal funding to the local level (Moscoso, 2003a). Many local agency representatives have stated that they have more of a need for additional public safety and security staff, which they cannot acquire with the current assortment of grants, than they have for equipment and training (Gedan, 2003).

Despite federal, state, and local spending, recent studies have shown that in the event of another attack like September 11, local first responders would be unprepared to deal with the challenges faced (Etzioni, 2003). Senator Warren Rudman, who with Gary Hart described the need for a Department of Homeland Security several months before September 11, believes that the country would be underprepared for a catastrophic attack because of a "lag in equipping the first responders." Rudman believes that up to $98 billion would be needed to reach an adequate level of preparedness at the local level (*Pittsburgh Post Gazette*, 2003b). The fact does remain that many police and fire departments do not have sufficient communications equipment, chemical/biological testing devices, self-contained breathing devices, or other personal protective equipment that would be required. A CDC study found that police officers and firefighters "do not know what they need to be protected against, what form of protection is appropriate, and where to look for such protection" (Means, 2003). Additionally, many local hospitals report that they are not adequately prepared to deal with the victims of such attacks (*Pittsburgh Post Gazette*, 2003a).

Under the federal system of government, DHS will have a difficult time mandating many aspects of safety and security at the local level, but agencies are almost unanimously receptive if such assistance comes without any associated local cost. The amount of federal funding needed to bring all state and local agencies to an adequate level is not available, so these agencies will need to continue supporting such efforts themselves. Because of competing priorities, budget constrictions, and the small risk (but high probability) of a major terrorist attack, local commitment to terrorism preparedness and prevention will suffer. Unless changes to the current resource allocations are made, our first responders and our communities may become the most vulnerable link in our terrorism arsenal.

THE FUTURE OF THE HOMELAND SECURITY ADVISORY SYSTEM

One of the most widely criticized DHS initiatives is the five-color-coded Homeland Security Advisory System. This system, which indicates the level of terror risk within the United States, as analyzed by the intelligence agencies and the president's Homeland Security Council, ranges from green (low risk of attacks) to red (severe risk of attacks). When it was introduced on March 11, 2002 by the former Office of Homeland Security, it was touted as a way to warn "all levels of government, law enforcement, and the general public about the risk of terrorist attacks" (Center for Defense Information, 2002). Since that time, it has never dropped below yellow (significant risk of attacks) but has several times been raised to orange (high risk of attacks).

Without exception, each time the alert system was raised, an accompanying announcement indicated that the increased level of threat was to be considered a general one that affected the entire United States. With these warnings came increased vigilance in almost every large and small city in the country, as well as in many towns. The augmented level of security had been recommended to governors and mayors, and they were hard pressed to neglect their municipality's burden of dedicating scarce resources; not to have done so would surely have been politically disastrous.

Fortunately, no attacks ever materialized from any of these "orange alerts," but the financial costs to the cities that resulted due to increased staff overtime, not to mention the indirect costs such as lost services, increased crime and vulnerability, and lost tourism business have become enormous. The nation's mayors begged repeatedly for DHS to reform this system to address threats in a more targeted manner. Director Ridge heeded their call and pledged to immediately begin working on a solution. Soon after, as the second anniversary of the September 11 attacks came and went, the system surprisingly remained at the yellow level.

In the months and years to come, DHS must decide if the Homeland Security Alert System is of any value to the state and local communities, or to the American people in general. To begin, it should seem apparent to most that the prospect of the Homeland Security Alert System ever being set at "green" does not exist. The terrorism threat, unlike the threat from natural disasters, is not scientific and therefore can never be predicted with any degree of certainty. It is an intelligent threat that adjusts quickly, discovers weaknesses, and strikes without any warning. We know that we could never identify all terrorist organizations that exist now or in the future, and it is certain that there will be individuals who act alone to commit terrorist acts for myriad personal reasons. The Washington, DC, snipers, two "terrorists" who paralyzed the capital region for 22 days in 2002, are a perfect illustration of the unpredictability that cannot be ruled out by the alert system. DHS officials do appear to be accepting this factor realistically. In a recent speech, Ridge said that it would be "decades" before the U.S. Government would be able to lower the threat level to green (Shenon, 2003). Will any future DHS director feel confident enough to make that call?

A second issue is that it is unlikely that the DHS Alert System will ever benefit agencies at the state and local level. The problem exists in that the alerts do not, and likely cannot, provide any location-specific information. As result, the entire nation must be on alert— a great strain on resources.

However, the states, counties, and cities each have a specific jurisdiction that is statistically unlikely to be affected even if an attack occurs. A congressional report addressing these issues stated that the Homeland Security Alert System is currently so vague that "the public may begin to question the authenticity" of reported threats and do nothing when the system level is raised (Shenon, 2003). If this is true, the alerts could actually be causing the opposite of their intended effect.

DHS must decide what value exists in the Homeland Security Alert System, and for whom this value applies. Once that determination has been made, greater and more focused efforts can be placed into redesigning it so that it provides a service of value.

INCREASED INTERNATIONAL COOPERATION AND COORDINATION

The global war on terrorism has necessitated that the United States government cooperate with many governments, in every region of the world. Specific forms of cooperation have ranged from allowing U.S. investigators access to suspected terrorists captured abroad to joining the United States in military action in Afghanistan and Iraq. However, the SARS epidemic served as a wake-up call to the nation and the world alike that cooperation must extend beyond terrorism if national security is to be maintained.

Cooperation in the hunt for terrorists has been very good, despite critics' allegations that the U.S. government has ignored human rights abuses to avoid strained relations. Terror is a universally identifiable problem, and one for which it is easy for countries to comply in hopes of garnering U.S. aid without sacrificing much local political standing. In some countries, this common identifiable problem has led to a general increase in cooperation, such as in Riyadh, where the Saudi government has been working with U.S. FBI and Treasury officials on issues unrelated to the attacks on the housing compounds where Americans were housed (Slavin, 2003; Diamond et al., 2003). Since September 11, 2001, over 170 countries have helped the U.S. seize money labeled as "terrorist funding" (Despeignes, 2003; Diamond et al., 2003).

However, for unknown threats or creeping disasters that are not easily defined (such as a bioterrorist attack), cooperation may be more difficult to achieve. China's withholding of information about SARS, which ultimately led to sickness, death, and great financial strain in several countries around the world, is indicative of the problems DHS will have to address in establishing its standards of preparedness. Cultural differences between the United States and other countries will likely hinder future domestic preparedness and response efforts, especially with public health emergencies like SARS. Laws dictating vaccination, quarantine, and treatment will ultimately affect how natural or bioterror-related diseases affect U.S. citizens.

Every day the interconnectedness of the world's nations expands. Already, the prospect of a disease outbreak in Zambia causing an epidemic in Alabama is very real. DHS will need to expand international cooperation in the future as part of its broader preparedness mission. It will need to address how much the United States must dedicate efforts to increase preparedness and response capabilities abroad to decrease risk levels at home and how to justify to the American people that funds should be dedicated for such endeavors.

POLITICAL SUPPORT—FUNDING

The DHS is a permanent part of the U.S. federal government, merging agencies that have existed for decades or more. However, despite the fact that a Department of Homeland Security was originally an initiative of Congress and resisted by the Bush Administration (Mintz, 2003), it is now intimately linked with President George W. Bush in the minds of the American people. Such a link gives DHS a very political standpoint; not one that is Republican or Democratic but one that is linked to a specific administration. For President Bush, the success of DHS is a major factor in how his effectiveness as a leader will be measured, and it is therefore in his best interest to strongly support the Department (Mintz, 2003). The actual success of DHS under Bush will likely dictate how closely its future is linked to that president when his tenure in office has ended.

With any change in administration comes change in the executive office. If DHS has not established a strong foothold or, worse, if DHS has been unsuccessful in protecting the security of the United States despite the great investment that has been committed, the redesign or complete breakup of the agency could be likely. Unless the terrorist threat goes away soon, which it is unlikely to do, U.S. presidents in the short term will need to place terrorism high on their policy agendas and likewise address the future of DHS as part their commitment to security. On the other hand, as more pressing domestic issues, such as reform of Medicare and prescription drug benefits, dominate the political agenda, the high costs of DHS and whether these costs and benefits are reaching the general public may come under serious question.

"ACADEMICIZATION" OF EMERGENCY MANAGEMENT

Emergency management, and security in general, has been viewed historically as a field that required limited education beyond the high-school level. In many cases,

the local emergency management position was seen as an undesirable one within local fire or police departments. However, since September 11 there has been a sharp increase in emergency management–related university and graduate-level programs that have appeared throughout the country, including several programs that focus specifically on homeland security. Additionally, the position of emergency manager has been elevated in importance. Table 10-1 illustrates the changes that are occurring in the emergency management profession.

The trend toward creating a more educated emergency management employee base is promising in that it will likely help to ensure programmatic success at all levels of government. Emergency management as a profession has taken on new importance since the creation of DHS, but without a local representative with expertise in every community the preparedness and response capabilities of the nation will be lacking.

PRIVATE SECTOR INVOLVEMENT

The September 11 attacks were not only an attack on the people of the United States; they also sought to destroy the American economy. Though it is impossible to measure the actual impacts inflicted due to the complexity of the financial systems involved, there was and continues to be suffering in the business sector as a result of both the attacks and their aftermath. America operates under a capitalist system, and therefore it is the responsibility of the Department of Homeland Security to ensure that it is helping, not harming, business through its actions.

The tourism industry was the obvious victim in the shadow of the 2001 attacks. The airline and hospitality (e.g., hotels, restaurants) industries expressed their anguish at great length in the media and to Congress. The airline industry was able to secure $15 billion in federal funding to help them weather the hard times. Many small businesses failed. Tourism continues to suffer, and many of the actions of DHS have inadvertently contributed. For instance, the U.S. VISIT program, which is criticized as infringing upon civil liberties, has deterred some foreign travelers and

TABLE 10-1   The Emergency Manager

The Stereotype	"New Generation" Emergency Manager
White male with no college education	College educated with many emergency-management degrees
Emergency management second or third career	Professional and knowledgeable
Disaster response planning oriented	Technologically proficient
Job obtained other than with emergency-management knowledge, skills, or abilities	Knowledge base of science and research
Works primarily with emergency services	Emergency management first-choice career
Bureaucratic	Focused on building disaster resistant communities
Has never performed a risk assessment or created a mitigation/strategic plan	Lifelong learner who reads disaster literature
Never reads professional journals or joins professional associations	Plans with jurisdictional stakeholders
Frequently wears other hats	Better paid and better funded for emergency management programs
Poorly funded	Upwardly and geographically mobile
Part-time or volunteer	Maintains a broad range of working contacts

Adapted from Blanchard, 2001

business people from coming to the United States in favor of other destinations where they would not have to be subject to what may be perceived as "demoralizing or demeaning" acts (Hall, 2003b). Many international students, who feel that they are being stalked by the government, are choosing other European destinations for their education, taking away much of the tuition on which American schools have come to depend. But other industries have suffered as well.

For example, commerce and trade, particularly the shipping industries, have been dramatically affected. Roles and responsibilities have changed; new security requirements and systems have stalled tankers and ships in ports and kept them from reaching ports as Customs, INS, and the Coast Guard remain confused about their new priorities (Edmonson, 2003). One journalist commented on the confusion as follows:

In the 23 months since the terrorist attacks, establishing the lines of responsibility for the many phases of security has been an enormous challenge for federal agencies, and a source of constant aggravation for the trade community. Much of the problem stems from the speed with which the agencies were asked to create security systems essentially from scratch. But, as an excuse, that's getting old. More than a year ago, members of the trade community were asking the government, "Who does what?" for cargo security. They are still asking. (Edmonson, 2003)

Private industries are more than just customers of the federal government; they are participants in the maintenance of a secure homeland. Private organizations run a considerable amount of the nation's critical infrastructure; they manage water, energy, fuel, transportation, sewage, and communications-related businesses, among others (Thornton, 2003). Their roles and responsibilities will need to be explicitly defined in the ultimate design of DHS if safety and security is ever to be enjoyed. Such a definition does not yet exist. They will need to be made a greater partner of the government and granted a greater level of trust.

Intelligence information will need to be shared to an extent that has never before been seen.

Tom DiNanno, the director of the DHS Office of Private Sector Coordination, stated in relation to the private industry involvement, "Planning is great, but if you don't exercise, at the time of an event you will not be prepared" (Thornton, 2003). The recognition is obviously there. What remains to be seen is how influential DiNanno's office can be in adapting the DHS culture and outlook to accommodate needed adjustments (Chabrow, 2003).

Businesses have a responsibility to become more active in protecting themselves and the nation. After September 11, there was a great outpouring of financial support and other benefits to help businesses that were affected. It is unlikely that the same level of assistance would appear in a future attack. Businesses need to be engaged in business continuity and crisis-management planning and preparedness for their facilities and their employees. They need to be an active voice and supporter in the homeland security initiatives of their communities. They bring unique and valuable talents, resources, and expertise. The R&D efforts in the private sector can lead to significant advances and efficiencies for the public sector. DHS needs to reach out and engage the private sector as full partners in setting and achieving our goals for homeland security.

FIGURE 10-3 New York City, NY, September 10, 2002—A Ground Zero memorial located in the lobby at Penn Station is visited by people all over the world. Photo by Andrea Booher/FEMA News Photo.

CONCLUSION

September 11 was not the most damaging disaster event to affect the United States. It was not the first terrorist attack. It was not the first time Americans had died on American soil at the hands of a foreign power. It was not the first time that it was recognized that current preparedness and response systems were deficient. It did, however, provide the perfect combination of fear, anger, patriotism, compassion, generosity, ambition, and bravery required to spur great change across the entire federal government and across the entire nation.

This change could be America's greatest test.

Two of the most far-reaching pieces of legislation, the U.S.A. Patriot Act and the Homeland Security Act, dramatically changed the power, organization, and functions of the federal government. The Patriot Act gave the attorney general and DOJ unsurpassed authority over the civil rights and liberties of individuals. The Homeland Security Act combined 22 federal entities with a mandate to establish a safe and secure homeland and represents the largest single reorganization of the federal government since World War II.

As DHS consolidates programs and responsibilities, authorized funding is making its way to the states, but localities complain about being left out of the equation. Funding for the very first line of first responders, local government, is slow in coming. The volunteer effort, championed as a way to help at the local level, has received minimal funds and is still looking for strong support from the leadership.

The window of opportunity opened on September 11, 2001, is wider than anyone has ever seen, but it has already begun to close as months and years pass without another attack to sustain forward motion. Already, people are becoming complacent and are beginning to complain about inconveniences that they only recently saw as necessary (Etzioni, 2003).

Communities are already beginning to question whether or not their money is being well-spent on security-related issues. Terrorists are assuredly planning more sophisticated attacks aimed at weaknesses we have yet to discover. At the same time, we will continue to face a steady barrage of hurricanes, earthquakes, landslides, and other hazards.

With strong leadership, political will, superb management, and the right plan, it will not require another attack to maintain momentum. Change requires time and patience, but also vision, dedication, and skill. Homeland security requires the diligence of each and every institution, community, and individual. Valli Wasp, a local planner working on homeland security issues in Austin, Texas, has set down the challenge from which to measure the success of DHS by saying, "We need to take this (issue down) to homes—get rid of the land, get rid of the security—this is about people protecting their homes and their families. If you want people to listen to you, you have to go where they live" (SAFE Conference, March 27–28, 2003, San Francisco, CA).

REVIEW QUESTIONS

1. Compare and contrast the *Homeland Security Act of 2002* and the *National Security Act of 1947*.
2. How long was Secretary Tom Ridge given to begin transferring the 22 agencies over from their original locations into the Department of Homeland Security? Do you feel this was too ambitious, and if so, why?
3. Choose one of the agencies transferred into the Department of Homeland Security, and describe how its "core functions" have changed.
4. Do you believe that it is possible to win the "war on terrorism"? Why or why not?
5. Choose three challenges experienced during the creation of the Department of Homeland Security and the initial years of its existence. Propose an idealistic solution to each, regardless of whether or not such a solution is economically, logistically, or politically possible.

REFERENCES

Blanchard, W. 2001. "The Emergency Manager." *IAEM Bulletin* (May).

Burkeman, O. 2003. "US to Fit Airliners with Anti-Missile Defenses." *The Guardian*. September 19, p. 15.

Center for Defence Information. 2002. "Terror Alerts: The Homeland Security Advisory." September 1. <http://www.govexec.com/features/0902/0902s4.htm>

Chabrow, E. 2003. "Share and Share Alike—Government Agencies Struggle to Overcome the Many Barriers to Collaboration." *Information Week*. September 1, p. E6.

Cheng, M. 2003. "Homeland Department May Contract Out Jobs." *Newsday* (New York). September 14, p. A17.

Columbus, Dispatch 2003. "Security Risks in the Air." *Editorial.* September 19, p.14A.

Cook, D. T. 2003. "Tom Ridge." *Christian Science Monitor.* September 15, p. 25.

Diamond, J., et. al. 2003. "6 Fronts of the War on Terrorism." *USA Today.* September 11, p. 4A.

Edmonson, R. G. 2003. "Blurring of the Lines." *Journal of Commerce.* August 11, p. 12.

Etzioni, A. 2003. "Our Unfinished Post-9/11 Duty." *Christian Science Monitor.* September 11, p. 9.

Fitzpatrick, D. 2003. "Sounding the Alarm—Again." *Pittsburgh Post Gazette.* September 9, p. C12.

Foster. 2003. "Leave This Patriot Alone." *Milwaukee Journal Sentinel.* September 17, p. 14A.

Gedan, B. 2003. "Local Safety Officials Feel Unprepared Post September 11th Survey Suggests Funds Are Issue." *Boston Globe.* August 29, p. B2.

Hall, M. 2003a. "Terrorist Risk Lists Leave Gap, Even Now." *USA Today.* August 11, p. 1A.

Hall, M. 2003b. "Tracking of Foreign Visitors Hits Snags." *USA Today.* September 22, p. 1A.

Hendrix, A. 2003. "Rights Group Slams Homeland Security Tactics." *San Francisco Chronicle.* May 29, p. A16.

Hulse, C. 2003. "Congress Advances $29.4 Billion Plan for Security Agency." *New York Times.* September 18, p. A25.

Lebihan, R. 2003. "Balancing Security and Privacy." *Australian Financial Review.* September 12, p. 64.

Lichtblau, E. 2003. "Administration Creates Center for Master Terror 'Watch List'." *New York Times.* September 17, p. A20.

Marks, A. 2003. "With 9/11 More Distant, Alertness Wavers." *Christian Science Monitor.* August 5, p. 3.

Martin, G. 2003. "Homeland Defense Mission May Take Decades." *San Antonio Express News.* September 7, p. A12.

McGreevy, P. 2003. "Security Aid Falls Short, Mayors Say." *Los Angeles Times.* September 18, Part 2, p. 3.

Means, M. 2003. "Homeland Security; Desk Shuffling Is Not Enough." *San Diego Union Tribune.* September 7, p. G1.

Mehren, E. 2003. "Latest Trend in Academia: Security." *Los Angeles Times.* September 14, p. 34.

Mintz, J. 2003. "Government's Hobbled Giant; Homeland Security Is Struggling." *Washington Post.* September 7, p. A1.

Moritz, O. 2003. "Ferry Frisk in Riders' Future?" *Daily News* (New York). July 2, p. 25.

Moscoso, E. 2003a. "Cities Await Security Funds." *Atlanta Journal and Constitution.* September 18, p. 8A.

Moscoso, E. 2003b. "September 11, Two Years Later." *Atlanta Journal and Constitution.* September 10, p. 6A.

Occhipinti, J. D. 2002. "Allies at Odds." *Buffalo News.* December 22, p. H1.

Peckenpaugh, J. 2002. "Building a Behemoth." *Government Executive Magazine.*

Pittsburgh Post Gazette. 2003a. "The Age of Insecurity." Editorial. September 21, p. B7.

Pittsburgh Post Gazette. 2003b. "Will They Listen to Rudman This Time?" Editorial. July 7, p. A13.

Sataline, S. 2003. "Democratic Senators Call for Intelligence Reform." *St. Petersburg Times.* p. 6A.

Shapiro, J. S. 2003. "America Risks Repeating a 'Fundamental Injustice'." *Insight on the News.* September 15, p. 51.

Shenon, P. 2003. "High Alerts for Terror Get Harder to Impose." *New York Times.* September 13, p. A9.

Simon, H. 2003. "Emphasis on Illegal Immigrants Could Have Security Tradeoffs." *Aviation Week's Homeland Security and Defense.* September 4, vol. 2, no. 36, p. 5.

Thornton, K. 2003. "Civilians Join Talks on Terror Preparedness." *San Diego Union Tribune.* April 30, p. B1.

USA Today. 2003. "MIA: Terror Database." *USA Today.* August 12, p. 12A.

Walker, L. 2003. "We Have Our Radios. Now What?" *Broadcasting and Cable.* August 18, p. 28.

Appendix 1: List of Acronyms

AAAS	American Association for the Advancement of Science
AAR	Association of American Railroads
ACN	Alerting and Coordination Network
AFIS	FBI's Automated Fingerprint Identification System
AFSA	Armed Forces Security Agency
AIN	Advanced Intelligent Network
AMS	Aerial Measuring System
AMSA	Association of Metropolitan Sewerage Agencies
AMWA	Association of Metropolitan Water Agencies
ARAC	Atmospheric Release Advisory Capability
ARG	Accident Response Group
ARS	Agricultural Research Service
ASCO	Advanced Systems and Concepts Office
ATA	American Trucking Associations
BASIS	Biological Aerosol Sentry and Information System
BIA	Business Impact Analysis
CBD	Chemical and Biological Defense
CBIAC	Chemical and Biological Defense Information and Analysis Center
CBNP	Chemical and Biological National Security Program
CBR	Chemical, Biological, Radiological
CBRNE	Chemical, Biological, Radiological, Nuclear Material or High-Yield Explosive
CDBG	Community Development Block Grant
CDC	Centers for Disease Control and Prevention
CDRG	Catastrophic Disaster Response Team
CEN	Community Emergency Networks
CERCLA	Comprehensive Environmental Response, Compensation, and Liability Act
CERT	Community Emergency Response Teams
CERT/CC	CERT Coordination Center
CFO	Chief Financial Officer
CFR	Code of Federal Regulations
CHS	Center for Homeland Security

CIA	Central Intelligence Agency
CIAC	Computer Incident Advisory Center
CIG	Central Intelligence Group
CIO	Chief Information Officer
CIRG	Critical Incident Response Group
CJCS	Chairman of the Joint Chiefs of Staff
CM	Consequence Management
CMU	Crisis Management Unit
CONPLAN	Domestic Terrorism Concept of Operations Plan
CP	Command Post
CPC	Community Preparedness Corps
CPR	Cardiopulmonary Resuscitation
CRIS	Communications Resource Information Sharing
CSEPP	Chemical Stockpile Emergency Preparedness Program
CSI	Container Security Initiative
CSREES	Cooperative State Research, Education and Extension Service
CSS	Central Security Service
CTO	Chief Technology Officer
DARPA	Defense Advanced Research Project Agency
DCI	Director of Central Intelligence
DEST	Domestic Emergency Support Team
DFO	Disaster Field Office
DHS	Department of Homeland Security
DHS-BTS	Department of Homeland Security—Directorate of Border Transportation Security
DHS-IAIP	Department of Homeland Security—Directorate of Information Analysis and Infrastructure Protection
DHS-OPSL	Department of Homeland Security—Office for Private Sector Liaison
DHS-OSLGC	Department of Homeland Security—Office for State/Local Government Coordination
DHS-S&T	Department of Homeland Security—Directorate of Science and Technology
DHS-USCG	Department of Homeland Security—The United States Coast Guard

DIA	Defense Intelligence Agency	FEMA	Federal Emergency Management Agency
DIS	Decision and Information Sciences	FERC	Federal Energy Regulatory Commission
DMA	Defense Mapping Agency	FFRDC	Federally Funded Research and
DMA 2000	Disaster Mitigation Act 2000		Development Center
DMAT	Disaster Medical Assistance Teams	FNS	Food and Nutrition Service
DMORT	Disaster Mortuary Operational Response	FOC	Nationwide Full Operational Capability
	Teams	FOSC	Federal On-Scene Coordinator
DOC	Department of Commerce	FRERP	Federal Radiological Emergency
DoD	Department of Defense		Response Plan
DOE	Department of Energy	FRMAC	Federal Radiological Monitoring and
DOI	Department of the Interior		Assessment Center
DOJ	Department of Justice	FRP	Federal Response Plan
DOL	Department of Labor	FS	Forest Service
DOS	Department of State	FY	Fiscal Year
DOT	Department of Transportation	GAW	Global Atmosphere Watch
DRC	Disaster Recovery Centers	GETS	Government Emergency
DRF	Disaster Relief Fund		Telecommunications Service
DTCTPS	FBI Domestic	GIS	Geographic Information System
	Terrorism/Counterterrorism Planning	GSA	General Services Administration
	Section	HF	High Frequency
DTIC	Defense Technical Information Center	HHS	Department of Health and Human
DTRA	Defense Threat Reduction Agency		Services
DUA	Disaster Unemployment Assistance	HMRU	Hazardous Materials Response Unit
EAD	Environmental Assessment Division	HOPS	Homeland Operational Planning System
EDS	Electronic Detection Systems	HQ EOC	Headquarters Emergency Operation
ELES	Emergency Law Enforcement Services		Center
EMI	FEMA's Emergency Management	HR	House of Representatives
	Institute	HS-Center	Homeland Security Centers of
EML	Environmental Measurements		Excellence
	Laboratory	HSARPA	Homeland Security Advanced Research
EMT	Emergency Medical Technicians		Project Agency
ENS	Emergency Notification Service	HSPD	Homeland Security Presidential
EOC	Emergency Operations Centers		Directive
EP&R	Directorate of Emergency Preparedness	HUD	Department of Housing and Urban
	and Response		Development
EPA	Environmental Protection Agency	IAC	Information Analysis Center
ERSM	Emergency Response Synchronization	IAEM	International Association of Emergency
	Matrix		Managers
ESF	Emergency Support Function	ICE	Bureau of Immigration & Customs
EST	Emergency Support Team		Enforcement
ETD	Electronic Trace Detectors	ICS	Incident Command System
FAA	Federal Aviation Administration	IESA	International Environmental Sample
FBI	Federal Bureau of Investigation		Archive
FCC	Federal Communications Commission	IFG	Individual and Family Grant
FCC	Federal Coordinating Centers	IHP	Individuals and Households Program
FCO	Federal Coordinating Officer	IOC	Nationwide Initial Operational
FedCIRC	Federal Computer Incident Response		Capability
	Center	IPR	Intellectual Property Rights

ISAC	Information Sharing and Analysis Center	NIAID	National Institute of Allergy and Infectious Diseases
ISAS	Information Sharing and Analysis System	NIH	National Institutes of Health
ISRC	Information Security Resource Center	NIIMS	National Interagency Incident Management System
ITAC	DOE Incident Tracking and Analysis Center	NIJ	National Institute of Justice
IXC	Interexchange Carrier	NIMA	National Imagery and Mapping Agency
JCATS	Joint Conflict and Tactical Simulation	NIMS	National Incident Management System
JIC	Joint Information Centers	NIPC	National Infrastructure Protection Center
JOC	Joint Operations Center	NIST	National Institute of Standards and Technology
LADAR	Laser Array for Chem-Bio Agent Detection	NJIC	National Joint Information Center
LEC	Local Exchange Carrier	NNS	Nonproliferation and National Security Department
LEPPC	Local Emergency Prevention and Preparedness Councils	NNSA	National Nuclear Security Administration
LFA	Lead Federal Agency	NOAA	National Oceanographic and Atmospheric Administration
LINC	Local Integration of NARAC with Cities	NOC	Network Operations Centers
LLNL	Lawrence Livermore National Laboratory	NPDES	National Pollutant Discharge Elimination System
MIR	Micropower Impulse Radar	NPIC	National Photographic Interpretation Center
MMST	Metropolitan Medical Strike Team	NPS	National Pharmaceutical Stockpile
MRA	Mortgage and Rent Assistance	NPSC	National Processing Service Centers
MRC	Medical Reserve Corps	NRC	Nuclear Regulatory Commission
MSCA	Military Support to Civil Authorities	NRMRL	National Risk Management Research Laboratory
NAP	Nuclear Assessment Program	NRO	National Reconnaissance Office
NARAC	National Atmospheric Release Advisory Center	NRP	National Response Plan
NASA	National Aeronautics and Space Administration	NRT	National Response Team
NASCIO	National Association of State Chief Information Officers	NS/EP	NCS's National Security and Emergency Preparedness
NCCC	National Civilian Community Corps	NSA	National Security Agency
NCP	National Oil and Hazardous Substances Pollution Contingency Plan	NSF	National Science Foundation
NCS	National Communications System	NSF	National Strike Force
NDMS	National Disaster Medical System	NSFCC	National Strike Force Coordination Center
NDPO	National Domestic Preparedness Office	NSTAC	President's National Security Telecommunications Advisory Committee
NEMA	National Emergency Management Association		
NEPPC	National Emergency Prevention and Preparedness Council	NCC	National Coordinating Center for Telecommunications
NERC	North American Electric Reliability Council	NTCN	National Technology Coordination Network
NEST	Nuclear Emergency Search Team	NVOAD	National Volunteer Organizations Against Disasters
NHBEM	National Health Bureau of Emergency Management		
NIA	National Intelligence Authority	NWP	Neighborhood Watch Program

OA	Office of Independent Oversight and Performance Assurance	SANS	System, Audit, Network, Security
		SAR	Search and Rescue
OCPM	Office of Crisis Planning and Management	SBA	U.S. Small Business Administration
		SBCCOM	U.S. Army Soldier and Biological Chemical Command
OEP	Office of Emergency Preparedness		
OES	Office of Emergency Services	SCO	State Coordinating Officer
OIG	Office of Inspector General	SEB	State Emergency Boards
OMNCS	Office of the Manager, NCS	SEI	Software Engineering Institute
ONA	Other Needs Assistance	SERT	State Emergency Response Team
ORNL	Oak Ridge National Laboratory	SFA	Support Federal Agency
OSC	FBI Federal On-Scene Commander	SFHA	Special Flood Hazard Areas
OSHA	Occupational Safety and Health Administration	SHARES	Shared Resources
		SIOC	Strategic Information and Operations Center
OSS	Office of Strategic Services		
PAD	Protective Action Distances	SMS	Short Message Service
PAS	ISAS Priority Access Service	SNS	Strategic National Stockpile
PDA	Preliminary Damage Assessment	SPP	Special Population Planner
PFA	Primary Federal Agency	SRM	Standard Reference Materials
PHS	U.S. Public Health Service	STI	Science and Technology Information
PIADC	Plum Island Animal Disease Center	TARU	Technical Advisory Response Unit
PIN	Personal Identification Number	TEMA	Tennessee Emergency Management Agency
PN	Public Network		
PNNL	Pacific Northwest National Laboratory	TEPP	DOE Transportation Emergency Preparedness Program
PNP	Private Non profit		
POC	Point of Contact	TOADS	Total Online Access Data System
PSCTM	Port State Control Targeting Matrix	TOC	Transitional Operational Capability
PSN	Public Switched Network	TSA	Transportation Security Agency
R&D	Research and Development	TSP	Telecommunications Service Priority
RAP	Radiological Assistance Program		
RBDM	(Coast Guard) Risk-Based Decision Making	TWIC	Transportation Worker Identification Card
RDD	Radiological Dispersal Device	US&R	Urban Search & Rescue
RDT&E	Research, Development, Test and Evaluation	USCG	U.S. Coast Guard
		USDA	U.S. Department of Agriculture
REAC/TS	Radiation Emergency Assistance Center/Training Site	USFA	U.S. Fire Administration
		VA	Department of Veterans Affairs
REPPC	Regional Emergency Prevention and Preparedness Council	VIPS	Volunteers in Police Service
		VMI	Vendor Managed Inventory
RISC	Regional Interagency Steering Committee	VOAD	Voluntary Organization Active in Disaster
RJIC	Regional Joint Information Center	VSAT	Vulnerability Self Assessment Tools
ROC	Regional Operation Center		
RRT	Regional Response Team	WMD	Weapons of Mass Destruction
S&T	Science and Technology Directorate	WMD-CST	Weapons of Mass Destruction Civil Support Teams
S/REOC	State and/or Regional Emergency Operations Centers		
		WMO	World Meteorological Organization
SA	Submitted Amendment	WPS	Wireless Priority Service
SAC	FBI Special Agent in Charge	WTC	World Trade Center

Appendix 2: U.S.A. Patriot Act Summary

H.R.3162

Title: To deter and punish terrorist acts in the United States and around the world, to enhance law enforcement investigatory tools, and for other purposes.

Sponsor: Rep Sensenbrenner, F. James, Jr. [WI-9] (introduced 10/23/2001) Cosponsors: 1

Related Bills: H.R.2975, H.R.3004, S.1510

Latest Major Action: 10/26/2001 Became Public Law No: 107-56.

Note: H.R. 3162, the USA PATRIOT Act, incorporated provisions of two earlier anti-terrorism bills: H.R. 2975, which passed the House on 10/12/2001; and S. 1510, which passed the Senate on 10/11/2001. Provisions of H.R. 3004, the Financial Anti-Terrorism Act, were incorporated as Title III in H.R. 3162.

SUMMARY AS OF:

10/24/2001—Passed House, without amendment. (There is 1 other summary)

Uniting and Strengthening America by Providing Appropriate Tools Required to Intercept and Obstruct Terrorism (USA PATRIOT ACT) Act of 2001—Title I: Enhancing Domestic Security Against Terrorism—Establishes in the Treasury the Counterterrorism Fund.

(Sec. 102) Expresses the sense of Congress that: (1) the civil rights and liberties of all Americans, including Arab Americans, must be protected, and that every effort must be taken to preserve their safety; (2) any acts of violence or discrimination against any Americans be condemned; and (3) the Nation is called upon to recognize the patriotism of fellow citizens from all ethnic, racial, and religious backgrounds.

(Sec. 103) Authorizes appropriations for the Federal Bureau of Investigation's (FBI) Technical Support Center.

(Sec. 104) Authorizes the Attorney General to request the Secretary of Defense to provide assistance in support of Department of Justice (DOJ) activities relating to the enforcement of federal criminal code (code) provisions regarding the use of weapons of mass destruction during an emergency situation involving a weapon (currently, chemical weapon) of mass destruction.

(Sec. 105) Requires the Director of the U.S. Secret Service to take actions to develop a national network of electronic crime task forces throughout the United States to prevent, detect, and investigate various forms of electronic crimes, including potential terrorist attacks against critical infrastructure and financial payment systems.

(Sec. 106) Modifies provisions relating to presidential authority under the International Emergency Powers Act to: (1) authorize the President, when the United States is engaged in armed hostilities or has been attacked by a foreign country or foreign nationals, to confiscate any property subject to U.S. jurisdiction of a foreign person, organization, or country that he determines has planned, authorized, aided, or engaged in such hostilities or attacks (the rights to which shall vest in such agency or person as the President may designate); and (2) provide that, in any judicial review of a determination made under such provisions, if the determination was based on classified information such information may be submitted to the reviewing court ex parte and in camera.

Title II: Enhanced Surveillance Procedures—Amends the Federal criminal code to authorize the interception of wire, oral, and electronic communications for the production of evidence of: (1) specified chemical weapons or terrorism offenses; and (2) computer fraud and abuse.

(Sec. 203) Amends rule 6 of the Federal Rules of Criminal Procedure (FRCrP) to permit the sharing of grand jury information that involves foreign intelligence or counterintelligence with Federal law enforcement, intelligence, protective, immigration, national defense, or national security officials (such officials), subject to specified requirements.

Authorizes an investigative or law enforcement officer, or an attorney for the Government, who, by authorized means, has obtained knowledge of the contents of any wire, oral, or electronic communication or evidence derived there from to disclose such contents to such officials to the extent that such contents include foreign intelligence or counterintelligence.

Directs the Attorney General to establish procedures for the disclosure of information (pursuant to the code and the

FRCrP) that identifies a United States person, as defined in the Foreign Intelligence Surveillance Act of 1978 (FISA).

Authorizes the disclosure of foreign intelligence or counter-intelligence obtained as part of a criminal investigation to such officials.

(Sec. 204) Clarifies that nothing in code provisions regarding pen registers shall be deemed to affect the acquisition by the Government of specified foreign intelligence information, and that procedures under FISA shall be the exclusive means by which electronic surveillance and the interception of domestic wire and oral (current law) and electronic communications may be conducted.

(Sec. 205) Authorizes the Director of the FBI to expedite the employment of personnel as translators to support counter-terrorism investigations and operations without regard to applicable Federal personnel requirements. Requires: (1) the Director to establish such security requirements as necessary for such personnel; and (2) the Attorney General to report to the House and Senate Judiciary Committees regarding translators.

(Sec. 206) Grants roving surveillance authority under FISA after requiring a court order approving an electronic surveillance to direct any person to furnish necessary information, facilities, or technical assistance in circumstances where the Court finds that the actions of the surveillance target may have the effect of thwarting the identification of a specified person.

(Sec. 207) Increases the duration of FISA surveillance permitted for non-U.S. persons who are agents of a foreign power.

(Sec. 208) Increases (from seven to 11) the number of district court judges designated to hear applications for and grant orders approving electronic surveillance. Requires that no fewer than three reside within 20 miles of the District of Columbia.

(Sec. 209) Permits the seizure of voice-mail messages under a warrant.

(Sec. 210) Expands the scope of subpoenas for records of electronic communications to include the length and types of service utilized, temporarily assigned network addresses, and the means and source of payment (including any credit card or bank account number).

(Sec. 211) Amends the Communications Act of 1934 to permit specified disclosures to Government entities, except for records revealing cable subscriber selection of video programming from a cable operator.

(Sec. 212) Permits electronic communication and remote computing service providers to make emergency disclosures to a governmental entity of customer electronic communications to protect life and limb.

(Sec. 213) Authorizes Federal district courts to allow a delay of required notices of the execution of a warrant if immediate notice may have an adverse result and under other specified circumstances.

(Sec. 214) Prohibits use of a pen register or trap and trace devices in any investigation to protect against international terrorism or clandestine intelligence activities that is conducted solely on the basis of activities protected by the first amendment to the U.S. Constitution.

(Sec. 215) Authorizes the Director of the FBI (or designee) to apply for a court order requiring production of certain business records for foreign intelligence and international terrorism investigations. Requires the Attorney General to report to the House and Senate Intelligence and Judiciary Committees semi-annually.

(Sec. 216) Amends the code to: (1) require a trap and trace device to restrict recoding or decoding so as not to include the contents of a wire or electronic communication; (2) apply a court order for a pen register or trap and trace devices to any person or entity providing wire or electronic communication service in the United States whose assistance may facilitate execution of the order; (3) require specified records kept on any pen register or trap and trace device on a packet-switched data network of a provider of electronic communication service to the public; and (4) allow a trap and trace device to identify the source (but not the contents) of a wire or electronic communication.

(Sec. 217) Makes it lawful to intercept the wire or electronic communication of a computer trespasser in certain circumstances.

(Sec. 218) Amends FISA to require an application for an electronic surveillance order or search warrant to certify that a significant purpose (currently, the sole or main purpose) of the surveillance is to obtain foreign intelligence information.

(Sec. 219) Amends rule 41 of the FRCrP to permit Federal magistrate judges in any district in which terrorism-related activities may have occurred to issue search warrants for searches within or outside the district.

(Sec. 220) Provides for nationwide service of search warrants for electronic evidence.

(Sec. 221) Amends the Trade Sanctions Reform and Export Enhancement Act of 2000 to extend trade sanctions to the territory of Afghanistan controlled by the Taliban.

(Sec. 222) Specifies that: (1) nothing in this Act shall impose any additional technical obligation or requirement on a provider of a wire or electronic communication service or other person to furnish facilities or technical assistance; and (2) a provider of such service, and a landlord, custodian, or other person who furnishes such facilities or technical assistance, shall be reasonably compensated for such reasonable expenditures incurred in providing such facilities or assistance.

(Sec. 223) Amends the Federal criminal code to provide for administrative discipline of Federal officers or employees who violate prohibitions against unauthorized disclosures of information gathered under this Act. Provides for civil actions against the United States for damages by any person aggrieved by such violations.

(Sec. 224) Terminates this title on December 31, 2005, except with respect to any particular foreign intelligence investigation beginning before that date, or any particular offense or potential offense that began or occurred before it.

(Sec. 225) Amends the Foreign Intelligence Surveillance Act of 1978 to prohibit a cause of action in any court against a provider of a wire or electronic communication service, landlord, custodian, or any other person that furnishes any information, facilities, or technical assistance in accordance with a court order or request for emergency assistance under such Act (for example, with respect to a wiretap).

Title III: International Money Laundering Abatement and Anti-Terrorist Financing Act of 2001—International Money Laundering Abatement and Financial Anti-Terrorism Act of 2001-Sunsets this Act after the first day of FY 2005 if Congress enacts a specified joint resolution to that effect.

Subtitle A: International Counter Money Laundering and Related Measures—Amends Federal law governing monetary transactions to prescribe procedural guidelines under which the Secretary of the Treasury (the Secretary) may require domestic financial institutions and agencies to take specified measures if the Secretary finds that reasonable grounds exist for concluding that jurisdictions, financial institutions, types of accounts, or transactions operating outside or within the United States, are of primary money laundering concern. Includes mandatory disclosure of specified information relating to certain correspondent accounts.

(Sec. 312) Mandates establishment of due diligence mechanisms to detect and report money laundering transactions through private banking accounts and correspondent accounts.

(Sec. 313) Prohibits U.S. correspondent accounts with foreign shell banks.

(Sec. 314) Instructs the Secretary to adopt regulations to encourage further cooperation among financial institutions, their regulatory authorities, and law enforcement authorities, with the specific purpose of encouraging regulatory authorities and law enforcement authorities to share with financial institutions information regarding individuals, entities, and organizations engaged in or reasonably suspected (based on credible evidence) of engaging in terrorist acts or money laundering activities. Authorizes such regulations to create procedures for cooperation and information sharing on matters specifically related to the finances of terrorist groups as well as their relationships with international narcotics traffickers.

Requires the Secretary to distribute annually to financial institutions a detailed analysis identifying patterns of suspicious activity and other investigative insights derived from suspicious activity reports and investigations by Federal, State, and local law enforcement agencies.

(Sec. 315) Amends Federal criminal law to include foreign corruption offenses as money laundering crimes.

(Sec. 316) Establishes the right of property owners to contest confiscation of property under law relating to confiscation of assets of suspected terrorists.

(Sec. 317) Establishes Federal jurisdiction over: (1) foreign money launderers (including their assets held in the United States); and (2) money that is laundered through a foreign bank.

(Sec. 319) Authorizes the forfeiture of money laundering funds from interbank accounts. Requires a covered financial institution, upon request of the appropriate Federal banking agency, to make available within 120 hours all pertinent information related to anti-money laundering compliance by the institution or its customer. Grants the Secretary summons and subpoena powers over foreign banks that maintain a correspondent bank in the United States. Requires a covered financial institution to terminate within ten business days any correspondent relationship with a foreign bank after receipt of written notice that the foreign bank has failed to comply with certain judicial proceedings. Sets forth civil penalties for failure to terminate such relationship.

(Sec. 321) Subjects to record and report requirements for monetary instrument transactions: (1) any credit union; and (2) any futures commission merchant, commodity trading advisor, and commodity pool operator registered, or required to register, under the Commodity Exchange Act.

(Sec. 323) Authorizes Federal application for restraining orders to preserve the availability of property subject to a foreign forfeiture or confiscation judgment.

(Sec. 325) Authorizes the Secretary to issue regulations to ensure that concentration accounts of financial institutions are not used to prevent association of the identity of an individual customer with the movement of funds of which the customer is the direct or beneficial owner.

(Sec. 326) Directs the Secretary to issue regulations prescribing minimum standards for financial institutions regarding customer identity in connection with the opening of accounts.

Requires the Secretary to report to Congress on: (1) the most timely and effective way to require foreign nationals to provide domestic financial institutions and agencies with appropriate and accurate information; (2) whether to require foreign nationals to obtain an identification number (similar to a Social Security or tax identification number) before opening an account with a domestic financial institution; and (3) a system for domestic financial institutions and agencies to review Government agency information to verify the identities of such foreign nationals.

(Sec. 327) Amends the Bank Holding Company Act of 1956 and the Federal Deposit Insurance Act to require consideration of the effectiveness of a company or companies in combating money laundering during reviews of proposed bank shares acquisitions or mergers.

(Sec. 328) Directs the Secretary take reasonable steps to encourage foreign governments to require the inclusion of the name of the originator in wire transfer instructions sent to the United States and other countries, with the information to remain with the transfer from its origination until the point of disbursement. Requires annual progress reports to specified congressional committees.

(Sec. 329) Prescribes criminal penalties for Federal officials or employees who seek or accept bribes in connection with administration of this title.

(Sec. 330) Urges U.S. negotiations for international cooperation in investigations of money laundering, financial crimes, and the finances of terrorist groups, including record sharing by foreign banks with U.S. law enforcement officials and domestic financial institution supervisors.

Subtitle B: Bank Secrecy Act Amendments and Related Improvements—Amends Federal law known as the Bank Secrecy Act to revise requirements for civil liability immunity for voluntary financial institution disclosure of suspicious activities. Authorizes the inclusion of suspicions of illegal activity in written employment references.

(Sec. 352) Authorizes the Secretary to exempt from minimum standards for anti-money laundering programs any financial institution not subject to certain regulations governing financial record keeping and reporting of currency and foreign transactions.

(Sec. 353) Establishes civil penalties for violations of geographic targeting orders and structuring transactions to evade certain record keeping requirements. Lengthens the effective period of geographic targeting orders from 60 to 180 days.

(Sec. 355) Amends the Federal Deposit Insurance Act to permit written employment references to contain suspicions of involvement in illegal activity.

(Sec. 356) Instructs the Secretary to: (1) promulgate regulations requiring registered securities brokers and dealers, futures commission merchants, commodity trading advisors, and commodity pool operators, to file reports of suspicious financial transactions; (2) report to Congress on the role of the Internal Revenue Service in the administration of the Bank Secrecy Act; and (3) share monetary instruments transactions records upon request of a U.S. intelligence agency for use in the conduct of intelligence or counterintelligence activities, including analysis, to protect against international terrorism.

(Sec. 358) Amends the Right to Financial Privacy Act to permit the transfer of financial records to other agencies or departments upon certification that the records are relevant to intelligence or counterintelligence activities related to international terrorism.

Amends the Fair Credit Reporting Act to require a consumer reporting agency to furnish all information in a consumer's file to a government agency upon certification that the records are relevant to intelligence or counterintelligence activities related to international terrorism.

(Sec. 359) Subjects to mandatory records and reports on monetary instruments transactions any licensed sender of money or any other person who engages as a business in the transmission of funds, including through an informal value transfer banking system or network (e.g., hawala) of people facilitating the transfer of money domestically or internationally outside of the conventional financial institutions system.

(Sec. 360) Authorizes the Secretary to instruct the United States Executive Director of each international financial institution to use his or her voice and vote to: (1) support the use of funds for a country (and its institutions) which contributes to U.S. efforts against international terrorism; and (2) require an auditing of disbursements to ensure that no funds are paid to persons who commit or support terrorism.

(Sec. 361) Makes the existing Financial Crimes Enforcement Network a bureau in the Department of the Treasury.

(Sec. 362) Directs the Secretary to establish a highly secure network in the Network that allows financial institutions to file certain reports and receive alerts and other information regarding suspicious activities warranting immediate and enhanced scrutiny.

(Sec. 363) Increases to $1 million the maximum civil penalties (currently $10,000) and criminal fines (currently $250,000) for money laundering. Sets a minimum civil penalty and criminal fine of double the amount of the illegal transaction.

(Sec. 364) Amends the Federal Reserve Act to provide for uniform protection authority for Federal Reserve facilities, including law enforcement officers authorized to carry firearms and make warrant less arrests.

(Sec. 365) Amends Federal law to require reports relating to coins and currency of more than $10,000 received in a non-financial trade or business.

(Sec. 366) Directs the Secretary to study and report to Congress on: (1) the possible expansion of the currency transaction reporting requirements exemption system; and (2) methods for improving financial institution utilization of the system as a way of reducing the submission of currency transaction reports that have little or no value for law enforcement purposes.

Subtitle C: Currency Crimes—Establishes as a bulk cash smuggling felony the knowing concealment and attempted transport (or transfer) across U.S. borders of currency and monetary instruments in excess of $10,000, with intent to evade specified currency reporting requirements.

(Sec. 372) Changes from discretionary to mandatory a court's authority to order, as part of a criminal sentence, forfeiture of all property involved in certain currency reporting offenses. Leaves a court discretion to order civil forfeitures in money laundering cases.

(Sec. 373) Amends the Federal criminal code to revise the prohibition of unlicensed (currently, illegal) money transmitting businesses.

(Sec. 374) Increases the criminal penalties for counterfeiting domestic and foreign currency and obligations.

(Sec. 376) Amends the Federal criminal code to extend the prohibition against the laundering of money instruments to specified proceeds of terrorism.

(Sec. 377) Grants the United States extraterritorial jurisdiction where: (1) an offense committed outside the United States involves an access device issued, owned, managed, or controlled by a financial institution, account issuer, credit card system member, or other entity within U.S. jurisdiction; and (2) the person committing the offense transports, delivers, conveys, transfers to or through, or otherwise stores, secrets, or holds within U.S. jurisdiction any article used to assist in the commission of the offense or the proceeds of such offense or property derived from it.

Title IV: Protecting the Border—Subtitle A: Protecting the Northern Border—Authorizes the Attorney General to waive certain Immigration and Naturalization Service (INS) personnel caps with respect to ensuring security needs on the Northern border.

(Sec. 402) Authorizes appropriations to: (1) triple the number of Border Patrol, Customs Service, and INS personnel (and support facilities) at points of entry and along the Northern border; and (2) INS and Customs for related border monitoring technology and equipment.

(Sec. 403) Amends the Immigration and Nationality Act to require the Attorney General and the Federal Bureau of Investigation (FBI) to provide the Department of State and INS with access to specified criminal history extracts in order to determine whether or not a visa or admissions applicant has a criminal history. Directs the FBI to provide periodic extract updates. Provides for confidentiality.

Directs the Attorney General and the Secretary of State to develop a technology standard to identify visa and admissions applicants, which shall be the basis for an electronic system of law enforcement and intelligence sharing system available to consular, law enforcement, intelligence, and Federal border inspection personnel.

(Sec. 404) Amends the Department of Justice Appropriations Act, 2001 to eliminate certain INS overtime restrictions.

(Sec. 405) Directs the Attorney General to report on the feasibility of enhancing the Integrated Automated Fingerprint Identification System and other identification systems to better identify foreign individuals in connection with U.S. or foreign criminal investigations before issuance of a visa to, or permitting such person's entry or exit from, the United States. Authorizes appropriations.

Subtitle B: Enhanced Immigration Provisions—Amends the Immigration and Nationality Act to broaden the scope of aliens ineligible for admission or deportable due to terrorist activities to include an alien who: (1) is a representative of a political, social, or similar group whose political endorsement of terrorist acts undermines U.S. antiterrorist efforts; (2) has used a position of prominence to endorse terrorist activity, or to persuade others to support such activity in a way that undermines U.S. antiterrorist efforts (or the child or spouse of such an alien under specified circumstances); or (3) has been associated with a terrorist organization and intends to engage in threatening activities while in the United States.

(Sec. 411) Includes within the definition of "terrorist activity" the use of any weapon or dangerous device.

Redefines "engage in terrorist activity" to mean, in an individual capacity or as a member of an organization, to: (1) commit or to incite to commit, under circumstances indicating an intention to cause death or serious bodily injury, a terrorist activity; (2) prepare or plan a terrorist activity; (3) gather information on potential targets for terrorist activity; (4) solicit funds or other things of value for a terrorist activity or a terrorist organization (with an exception for lack of knowledge); (5) solicit any individual to engage in prohibited conduct or for terrorist organization membership (with an exception for lack of knowledge); or (6) commit an act that the actor knows, or reasonably should know, affords material support, including a safe house, transportation, communications, funds, transfer of funds or other material financial benefit, false documentation or identification, weapons (including chemical, biological, or radiological weapons), explosives, or training for the commission of a terrorist activity; to any individual who the actor knows or reasonably should know has committed or plans to commit a terrorist activity; or to a terrorist organization (with an exception for lack of knowledge).

Defines "terrorist organization" as a group: (1) designated under the Immigration and Nationality Act or by the Secretary of State; or (2) a group of two or more individuals, whether related or not, which engages in terrorist-related activities.

Provides for the retroactive application of amendments under this Act. Stipulates that an alien shall not be considered inadmissible or deportable because of a relationship to an organization that was not designated as a terrorist organization prior to enactment of this Act. States that the amendments under this section shall apply to all aliens in exclusion or deportation proceedings on or after the date of enactment of this Act.

Directs the Secretary of State to notify specified congressional leaders seven days prior to designating an organization as a terrorist organization. Provides for organization redesignation or revocation.

(Sec. 412) Provides for mandatory detention until removal from the United States (regardless of any relief from removal) of an alien certified by the Attorney General as a suspected terrorist or threat to national security. Requires release of such alien after seven days if removal proceedings have not commenced, or the alien has not been charged with a criminal offense. Authorizes detention for additional periods of up to six months of an alien not likely to be deported in the reasonably foreseeable future only if release will threaten U.S. national security or the safety of the community or any person. Limits judicial review to habeas corpus proceedings in the U.S. Supreme Court, the U.S. Court of Appeals for the District of Columbia, or any district court with jurisdiction to entertain a habeas corpus petition. Restricts to the U.S. Court of Appeals for the District of Columbia the right of appeal of any final order by a circuit or district judge.

(Sec. 413) Authorizes the Secretary of State, on a reciprocal basis, to share criminal- and terrorist-related visa lookout information with foreign governments.

(Sec. 414) Declares the sense of Congress that the Attorney General should: (1) fully implement the integrated entry and exit data system for airports, seaports, and land border ports of entry with all deliberate speed; and (2) begin immediately establishing the Integrated Entry and Exit Data System Task Force. Authorizes appropriations.

Requires the Attorney General and the Secretary of State, in developing the integrated entry and exit data system, to focus on the use of biometric technology and the development of tamper-resistant documents readable at ports of entry.

(Sec. 415) Amends the Immigration and Naturalization Service Data Management Improvement Act of 2000 to include the Office of Homeland Security in the Integrated Entry and Exit Data System Task Force.

(Sec. 416) Directs the Attorney General to implement fully and expand the foreign student monitoring program to include other approved educational institutions like air flight, language training, or vocational schools.

(Sec. 417) Requires audits and reports on implementation of the mandate for machine readable passports.

(Sec. 418) Directs the Secretary of State to: (1) review how consular officers issue visas to determine if consular shopping is a problem; and (2) if it is a problem, take steps to address it, and report on them to Congress.

Subtitle C: Preservation of Immigration Benefits for Victims of Terrorism—Authorizes the Attorney General to provide permanent resident status through the special immigrant program to an alien (and spouse, child, or grandparent under specified circumstances) who was the beneficiary of a petition filed on or before September 11, 2001, to grant the alien permanent residence as an employer-sponsored immigrant or of an application for labor certification if the petition or application was rendered null because of the disability of the beneficiary or loss of employment due to physical damage to, or destruction of, the business of the petitioner or applicant as a direct result of the terrorist attacks on September 11, 2001 (September attacks), or because of the death of the petitioner or applicant as a direct result of such attacks.

(Sec. 422) States that an alien who was legally in a nonimmigrant status and was disabled as a direct result of the September attacks may remain in the United States until his or her normal status termination date or September, 11, 2002. Includes in such extension the spouse or child of such an alien or of an alien who was killed in such attacks. Authorizes employment during such period.

Extends specified immigration-related deadlines and other filing requirements for an alien (and spouse and child) who was directly prevented from meeting such requirements as a result of the September attacks respecting: (1) nonimmigrant status and status revision; (2) diversity immigrants; (3) immigrant visas; (4) parolees; and (5) voluntary departure.

(Sec. 423) Waives, under specified circumstances, the requirement that an alien spouse (and child) of a U.S. citizen must have been married for at least two years prior to such citizen's death in order to maintain immediate relative status if such citizen died as a direct result of the September attacks. Provides for: (1) continued family-sponsored immigrant eligibility for the spouse, child, or unmarried son or daughter of a permanent resident who died as a direct result of such attacks; and (2) continued eligibility for adjustment

of status for the spouse and child of an employment-based immigrant who died similarly.

(Sec. 424) Amends the Immigration and Nationality Act to extend the visa categorization of "child" for aliens with petitions filed on or before September 11, 2001, for aliens whose 21st birthday is in September 2001 (90 days), or after September 2001 (45 days).

(Sec. 425) Authorizes the Attorney General to provide temporary administrative relief to an alien who, as of September, 10, 2001, was lawfully in the United States and was the spouse, parent, or child of an individual who died or was disabled as a direct result of the September attacks.

(Sec. 426) Directs the Attorney General to establish evidentiary guidelines for death, disability, and loss of employment or destruction of business in connection with the provisions of this subtitle.

(Sec. 427) Prohibits benefits to terrorists or their family members.

Title V: Removing Obstacles to Investigating Terrorism—Authorizes the Attorney General to pay rewards from available funds pursuant to public advertisements for assistance to DOJ to combat terrorism and defend the Nation against terrorist acts, in accordance with procedures and regulations established or issued by the Attorney General, subject to specified conditions, including a prohibition against any such reward of $250,000 or more from being made or offered without the personal approval of either the Attorney General or the President.

(Sec. 502) Amends the State Department Basic Authorities Act of 1956 to modify the Department of State rewards program to authorize rewards for information leading to: (1) the dismantling of a terrorist organization in whole or significant part; and (2) the identification or location of an individual who holds a key leadership position in a terrorist organization. Raises the limit on rewards if the Secretary State determines that a larger sum is necessary to combat terrorism or defend the Nation against terrorist acts.

(Sec. 503) Amends the DNA Analysis Backlog Elimination Act of 2000 to qualify a Federal terrorism offense for collection of DNA for identification.

(Sec. 504) Amends FISA to authorize consultation among Federal law enforcement officers regarding information acquired from an electronic surveillance or physical search in terrorism and related investigations or protective measures.

(Sec. 505) Allows the FBI to request telephone toll and transactional records, financial records, and consumer reports in any investigation to protect against international terrorism or clandestine intelligence activities only if the investigation is not conducted solely on the basis of activities protected by the first amendment to the U.S. Constitution.

(Sec. 506) Revises U.S. Secret Service jurisdiction with respect to fraud and related activity in connection with computers. Grants the FBI primary authority to investigate specified fraud and computer related activity for cases involving espionage, foreign counter-intelligence, information protected against unauthorized disclosure for reasons of national defense or foreign relations, or restricted data, except for offenses affecting Secret Service duties.

(Sec. 507) Amends the General Education Provisions Act and the National Education Statistics Act of 1994 to provide for disclosure of educational records to the Attorney General in a terrorism investigation or prosecution.

Title VI: Providing for Victims of Terrorism, Public Safety Officers, and Their Families—Subtitle A: Aid to Families of Public Safety Officers—Provides for expedited payments for: (1) public safety officers involved in the prevention, investigation, rescue, or recovery efforts related to a terrorist attack; and (2) heroic public safety officers. Increases Public Safety Officers Benefit Program payments.

Subtitle B: Amendments to the Victims of Crime Act of 1984—Amends the Victims of Crime Act of 1984 to: (1) revise provisions regarding the allocation of funds for compensation and assistance, location of compensable crime, and the relationship of crime victim compensation to means-tested Federal benefit programs and to the September 11th victim compensation fund; and (2) establish an antiterrorism emergency reserve in the Victims of Crime Fund.

Title VII: Increased Information Sharing for Critical Infrastructure Protection—Amends the Omnibus Crime Control and Safe Streets Act of 1968 to extend Bureau of Justice Assistance regional information sharing system grants to systems that enhance the investigation and prosecution abilities of participating Federal, State, and local law enforcement agencies in addressing multi-jurisdictional terrorist conspiracies and activities. Authorizes appropriations.

Title VIII: Strengthening the Criminal Laws Against Terrorism—Amends the Federal criminal code to prohibit specific terrorist acts or otherwise destructive, disruptive, or violent acts against mass transportation vehicles, ferries, providers, employees, passengers, or operating systems.

(Sec. 802) Amends the Federal criminal code to: (1) revise the definition of "international terrorism" to include activities that appear to be intended to affect the conduct of government by mass destruction; and (2) define "domestic terrorism" as activities that occur primarily within U.S. jurisdiction, that involve criminal acts dangerous to human life, and that appear to be intended to intimidate or coerce a civilian population, to influence government policy by intimidation or coercion, or to affect government conduct by mass destruction, assassination, or kidnapping.

(Sec. 803) Prohibits harboring any person knowing or having reasonable grounds to believe that such person has committed or to be about to commit a terrorism offense.

(Sec. 804) Establishes Federal jurisdiction over crimes committed at U.S. facilities abroad.

(Sec. 805) Applies the prohibitions against providing material support for terrorism to offenses outside of the United States.

(Sec. 806) Subjects to civil forfeiture all assets, foreign or domestic, of terrorist organizations.

(Sec. 808) Expands: (1) the offenses over which the Attorney General shall have primary investigative jurisdiction under provisions governing acts of terrorism transcending national boundaries; and (2) the offenses included within the definition of the Federal crime of terrorism.

(Sec. 809) Provides that there shall be no statute of limitations for certain terrorism offenses if the commission of such an offense resulted in, or created a foreseeable risk of, death or serious bodily injury to another person.

(Sec. 810) Provides for alternative maximum penalties for specified terrorism crimes.

(Sec. 811) Makes: (1) the penalties for attempts and conspiracies the same as those for terrorism offenses; (2) the supervised release terms for offenses with terrorism predicates any term of years or life; and (3) specified terrorism crimes Racketeer Influenced and Corrupt Organizations statute predicates.

(Sec. 814) Revises prohibitions and penalties regarding fraud and related activity in connection with computers to include specified cyber-terrorism offenses.

(Sec. 816) Directs the Attorney General to establish regional computer forensic laboratories, and to support existing laboratories, to develop specified cyber-security capabilities.

(Sec. 817) Prescribes penalties for knowing possession in certain circumstances of biological agents, toxins, or delivery systems, especially by certain restricted persons.

Title IX: Improved Intelligence—Amends the National Security Act of 1947 to require the Director of Central Intelligence (DCI) to establish requirements and priorities for foreign intelligence collected under the Foreign Intelligence Surveillance Act of 1978 and to provide assistance to the Attorney General (AG) to ensure that information derived from electronic surveillance or physical searches is disseminated for efficient and effective foreign intelligence purposes. Requires the inclusion of international terrorist activities within the scope of foreign intelligence under such Act.

(Sec. 903) Expresses the sense of Congress that officers and employees of the intelligence community should establish and maintain intelligence relationships to acquire information on terrorists and terrorist organizations.

(Sec. 904) Authorizes deferral of the submission to Congress of certain reports on intelligence and intelligence-related matters until: (1) February 1, 2002; or (2) a date after February 1, 2002, if the official involved certifies that preparation and submission on February 1, 2002, will impede the work of officers or employees engaged in counterterrorism activities. Requires congressional notification of any such deferral.

(Sec. 905) Requires the AG or the head of any other Federal department or agency with law enforcement responsibilities to expeditiously disclose to the DCI any foreign intelligence acquired in the course of a criminal investigation.

(Sec. 906) Requires the AG, DCI, and Secretary of the Treasury to jointly report to Congress on the feasibility and desirability of reconfiguring the Foreign Asset Tracking Center and the Office of Foreign Assets Control to provide for the analysis and dissemination of foreign intelligence relating to the financial capabilities and resources of international terrorist organizations.

(Sec. 907) Requires the DCI to report to the appropriate congressional committees on the establishment and maintenance of the National Virtual Translation Center for timely and accurate translation of foreign intelligence for elements of the intelligence community.

(Sec. 908) Requires the AG to provide a program of training to Government officials regarding the identification and use of foreign intelligence.

Title X: Miscellaneous—Directs the Inspector General of the Department of Justice to designate one official to review allegations of abuse of civil rights, civil liberties, and racial and ethnic profiling by government employees and officials.

(Sec. 1002) Expresses the sense of Congress condemning acts of violence or discrimination against any American, including Sikh-Americans. Calls upon local and Federal law enforcement authorities to prosecute to the fullest extent of the law all those who commit crimes.

(Sec. 1004) Amends the Federal criminal code with respect to venue in money laundering cases to allow a prosecution for such an offense to be brought in: (1) any district in which the financial or monetary transaction is conducted; or (2) any district where a prosecution for the underlying specified unlawful activity could be brought, if the defendant participated in the transfer of the proceeds of the specified unlawful activity from that district to the district where the financial or monetary transaction is conducted.

States that: (1) a transfer of funds from one place to another, by wire or any other means, shall constitute a single, continuing transaction; and (2) any person who conducts any portion of the transaction may be charged in any district in which the transaction takes place.

Allows a prosecution for an attempt or conspiracy offense to be brought in the district where venue would lie for the completed offense, or in any other district where an act in furtherance of the attempt or conspiracy took place.

(Sec. 1005) First Responders Assistance Act—Directs the Attorney General to make grants to State and local governments to improve the ability of State and local law enforcement, fire department, and first responders to respond to and prevent acts of terrorism. Authorizes appropriations.

(Sec. 1006) Amends the Immigration and Nationality Act to make inadmissible into the United States any alien engaged in money laundering. Directs the Secretary of State to develop a money laundering watch list which: (1) identifies individuals worldwide who are known or suspected of money laundering; and (2) is readily accessible to, and shall be checked by, a consular or other Federal official before the issuance of a visa or admission to the United States.

(Sec. 1007) Authorizes FY 2002 appropriations for regional antidrug training in Turkey by the Drug Enforcement Administration for police, as well as increased precursor chemical control efforts in South and Central Asia.

(Sec. 1008) Directs the Attorney General to conduct a feasibility study and report to Congress on the use of a biometric identifier scanning system with access to the FBI integrated automated fingerprint identification system at overseas consular posts and points of entry to the United States.

(Sec. 1009) Directs the FBI to study and report to Congress on the feasibility of providing to airlines access via computer to the names of passengers who are suspected of terrorist activity by Federal officials. Authorizes appropriations.

(Sec. 1010) Authorizes the use of Department of Defense funds to contract with local and State governments, during the period of Operation Enduring Freedom, for the performance of security functions at U.S. military installations.

(Sec. 1011) Crimes Against Charitable Americans Act of 2001—Amends the Telemarketing and Consumer Fraud and Abuse Prevention Act to cover fraudulent charitable solicitations. Requires any person engaged in telemarketing for the solicitation of charitable contributions, donations, or gifts to disclose promptly and clearly the purpose of the telephone call.

(Sec. 1012) Amends the Federal transportation code to prohibit States from licensing any individual to operate a motor vehicle transporting hazardous material unless the Secretary of Transportation determines that such individual does not pose a security risk warranting denial of the license. Requires background checks of such license applicants by the Attorney General upon State request.

(Sec. 1013) Expresses the sense of the Senate on substantial new U.S. investment in bioterrorism preparedness and response.

(Sec. 1014) Directs the Office for State and Local Domestic Preparedness Support of the Office of Justice Programs to make grants to enhance State and local capability to prepare for and respond to terrorist acts. Authorizes appropriations for FY 2002 through 2007.

(Sec. 1015) Amends the Crime Identification Technology Act of 1998 to extend it through FY 2007 and provide for antiterrorism grants to States and localities. Authorizes appropriations.

(Sec. 1016) Critical Infrastructures Protection Act of 2001—Declares it is U.S. policy: (1) that any physical or virtual disruption of the operation of the critical infrastructures of the United States be rare, brief, geographically limited in effect, manageable, and minimally detrimental to the economy, human and government services, and U.S. national security; (2) that actions necessary to achieve this policy be carried out in a public-private partnership involving corporate and non-governmental organizations; and (3) to have in place a comprehensive and effective program to ensure the continuity of essential Federal Government functions under all circumstances.

Establishes the National Infrastructure Simulation and Analysis Center to serve as a source of national competence to address critical infrastructure protection and continuity through support for activities related to counterterrorism, threat assessment, and risk mitigation.

Defines critical infrastructure as systems and assets, whether physical or virtual, so vital to the United States that their incapacity or destruction would have a debilitating impact on security, national economic security, national public health or safety, or any combination of those matters.

Authorizes appropriations.

Appendix 3: Homeland Security Act of 2002

SUMMARY AS OF:

11/19/2002—Passed Senate, amended. (There are 3 other summaries)

Homeland Security Act of 2002—Title I: Department of Homeland Security—(Sec. 101) Establishes a Department of Homeland Security (DHS) as an executive department of the United States, headed by a Secretary of Homeland Security (Secretary) appointed by the President, by and with the advice and consent of the Senate, to: (1) prevent terrorist attacks within the United States; (2) reduce the vulnerability of the United States to terrorism; (3) minimize the damage, and assist in the recovery, from terrorist attacks that occur within the United States; (4) carry out all functions of entities transferred to DHS; (5) ensure that the functions of the agencies and subdivisions within DHS that are not related directly to securing the homeland are not diminished or neglected except by a specific Act of Congress; (6) ensure that the overall economic security of the United States is not diminished by efforts, activities, and programs aimed at securing the homeland; and (7) monitor connections between illegal drug trafficking and terrorism, coordinate efforts to sever such connections, and otherwise contribute to efforts to interdict illegal drug trafficking. Vests primary responsibility for investigating and prosecuting acts of terrorism in Federal, State, and local law enforcement agencies with proper jurisdiction except as specifically provided by law with respect to entities transferred to DHS under this Act.

(Sec. 102) Directs the Secretary to appoint a Special Assistant to carry out specified homeland security liaison activities between DHS and the private sector.

(Sec. 103) Creates the following: (1) a Deputy Secretary of Homeland Security; (2) an Under Secretary for Information Analysis and Infrastructure Protection; (3) an Under Secretary for Science and Technology; (4) an Under Secretary for Border and Transportation Security; (5) an Under Secretary for Emergency Preparedness and Response; (6) a Director of the Bureau of Citizenship and Immigration Services; (7) an Under Secretary for Management; (8) not more than 12 Assistant Secretaries; and (9) a General Counsel. Establishes an Inspector General (to be appointed under the Inspector General Act of 1978). Requires the following individuals to assist the Secretary in the performance of the Secretary's functions: (1) the Commandant of the Coast Guard; (2) the Director of the Secret Service; (3) a Chief Information Officer; (4) a Chief Human Capital Officer; (5) a Chief Financial Officer; and (6) an Officer for Civil Rights and Civil Liberties.

Title II: Information Analysis and Infrastructure Protection—Subtitle A: Directorate for Information Analysis and Infrastructure Protection; Access to Information—(Sec. 201) Establishes in the Department: (1) a Directorate for Information Analysis and Infrastructure Protection, headed by an Under Secretary for Information Analysis and Infrastructure Protection; (2) an Assistant Secretary for Information Analysis; and (3) an Assistant Secretary for Infrastructure Protection.

Requires the Under Secretary to: (1) access, receive, and analyze law enforcement and intelligence information from Federal, State, and local agencies and the private sector to identify the nature, scope, and identity of terrorist threats to the United States, as well as potential U.S. vulnerabilities; (2) carry out comprehensive assessments of vulnerabilities of key U.S. resources and critical infrastructures; (3) integrate relevant information, analyses, and vulnerability assessments to identify protection priorities; (4) ensure timely and efficient Department access to necessary information for discharging responsibilities; (5) develop a comprehensive national plan for securing key U.S. resources and critical infrastructures; (6) recommend necessary measures to protect such resources and infrastructure in coordination with other entities; (7) administer the Homeland Security Advisory System; (8) review, analyze, and make recommendations for improvements in policies and procedures governing the sharing of law enforcement, intelligence, and intelligence-related information and other information related to homeland security within the Federal Government and between the Federal Government and State and local government agencies and authorities; (9) disseminate Department homeland security information to other appropriate Federal, State, and local agencies; (10) consult with the Director of Central Intelligence (DCI) and other appropriate Federal intelligence, law enforcement, or other elements to establish collection priorities and strategies for information relating the terrorism threats; (11) consult with State and local governments and private entities to ensure appropriate exchanges of information relating to such threats; (12) ensure the protection from unauthorized disclosure of homeland security and intelligence information; (13) request additional information from appropriate entities relating to threats of terrorism in the United States; (14) establish and utilize a secure communications and information technology infrastructure for receiving and analyzing data; (15) ensure the compatibility and privacy protection of shared information databases and analytical tools; (16) coordinate training and other support to facilitate the identification and sharing of information; (17) coordinate activities with elements of the intelligence community, Federal, State, and local law enforcement agencies, and the private sector; and (18) provide intelligence and information analysis and support to other elements of the Department. Provides for: (1) staffing, including the use of private sector analysts; and (2) cooperative agreements for the detail of appropriate personnel.

Transfers to the Secretary the functions, personnel, assets, and liabilities of the following entities: (1) the National Infrastructure Protection Center of the Federal Bureau of Investigation (other than the Computer Investigations and Operations Section); (2) the National Communications System of the Department of Defense; (3) the Critical Infrastructure Assurance Offices of the Department of Commerce; (4) the National Infrastructure Simulation and Analysis Center of the Department of Energy and its energy security and assurance program; and (5) the Federal Computer Incident Response Center of the General Services Administration.

Amends the National Security Act of 1947 to include as elements of the intelligence community the Department elements concerned with analyses of foreign intelligence information.

(Sec. 202) Gives the Secretary access to all reports, assessments, analyses, and unevaluated intelligence relating to threats of terrorism against the United States, and to all information concerning infrastructure or other vulnerabilities to terrorism, whether or not such information has been analyzed. Requires all Federal agencies to promptly provide to the Secretary: (1) all reports, assessments, and analytical information relating to such threats and to other areas of

responsibility assigned to the Secretary; (2) all information concerning the vulnerability of U.S. infrastructure or other U.S. vulnerabilities to terrorism, whether or not it has been analyzed; (3) all other information relating to significant and credible threats of terrorism, whether or not it has been analyzed; and (4) such other information or material as the President may direct. Requires the Secretary to be provided with certain terrorism-related information from law enforcement agencies that is currently required to be provided to the DCI.

Subtitle B: Critical Infrastructure Information—Critical Infrastructure Information Act of 2002—(Sec. 213) Allows a critical infrastructure protection program to be so designated by either the President or the Secretary.

(Sec. 214) Exempts from the Freedom of Information Act and other Federal and State disclosure requirements any critical infrastructure information that is voluntarily submitted to a covered Federal agency for use in the security of critical infrastructure and protected systems, analysis, warning, interdependency study, recovery, reconstitution, or other informational purpose when accompanied by an express statement that such information is being submitted voluntarily in expectation of such nondisclosure protection. Requires the Secretary to establish specified procedures for the receipt, care, and storage by Federal agencies of critical infrastructure information voluntarily submitted. Provides criminal penalties for the unauthorized disclosure of such information.

Authorizes the Federal Government to issue advisories, alerts, and warnings to relevant companies, targeted sectors, other governmental entities, or the general public regarding potential threats to critical infrastructure.

Subtitle C: Information Security—(Sec. 221) Requires the Secretary to establish procedures on the use of shared information that: (1) limit its re-dissemination to ensure it is not used for an unauthorized purpose; (2) ensure its security and confidentiality; (3) protect the constitutional and statutory rights of individuals who are subjects of such information; and (4) provide data integrity through the timely removal and destruction of obsolete or erroneous names and information.

(Sec. 222) Directs the Secretary to appoint a senior Department official to assume primary responsibility for information privacy policy.

(Sec. 223) Directs the Under Secretary to provide: (1) to State and local government entities and, upon request, to private entities that own or operate critical information systems, analysis and warnings related to threats to and vulnerabilities of such systems, as well as crisis management support in response to threats to or attacks upon such systems; and (2) technical assistance, upon request, to private sector and other government entities with respect to emergency recovery plans to respond to major failures of such systems.

(Sec. 224) Authorizes the Under Secretary to establish a national technology guard (known as NET Guard) to assist local communities to respond to and recover from attacks on information systems and communications networks.

(Sec. 225) Cyber Security Enhancement Act of 2002— Directs the U.S. Sentencing Commission to review and amend Federal sentencing guidelines and otherwise address crimes involving fraud in connection with computers and access to protected information, protected computers, or restricted data in interstate or foreign commerce or involving a computer used by or for the Federal Government. Requires a Commission report to Congress on actions taken and recommendations regarding statutory penalties for violations. Exempts from criminal penalties any disclosure made by an electronic communication service to a Federal, State, or local governmental entity if made in the good faith belief that an emergency involving danger of death or serious physical injury to any person requires disclosure without delay. Requires any government entity receiving such a disclosure to report it to the Attorney General.

Amends the Federal criminal code to: (1) prohibit the dissemination by electronic means of any such protected information; (2) increase criminal penalties for violations which cause death or serious bodily injury; (3) authorize the use by appropriate officials of emergency pen register and trap and trace devices in the case of either an immediate threat to a national security interest or an ongoing attack on a protected computer that constitutes a crime punishable by a prison term of greater than one year; (4) repeal provisions which provide a shorter term of imprisonment for certain offenses involving protection from the unauthorized interception and disclosure of wire, oral, or electronic communications; and (5) increase penalties for repeat offenses in connection with unlawful access to stored communications.

Subtitle D: Office of Science and Technology— (Sec. 231) Establishes within the Department of Justice (DOJ) an Office of Science and Technology whose mission is to: (1) serve as the national focal point for work on law enforcement technology (investigative and forensic technologies, corrections technologies, and technologies that support the judicial process); and (2) carry out programs that improve the safety and effectiveness of such technology and improve technology access by Federal, State, and local law enforcement agencies. Sets forth Office duties, including: (1) establishing and maintaining technology advisory groups and performance standards; (2) carrying out research, development, testing, evaluation, and cost-benefit analyses for improving the safety, effectiveness, and efficiency of technologies used by Federal, State, and local law enforcement agencies; and (3) operating the regional National Law Enforcement and Corrections Technology Centers (established under this Subtitle) and establishing additional centers. Requires the Office Director to report annually on Office activities.

(Sec. 234) Authorizes the Attorney General to transfer to the Office any other DOJ program or activity determined to be consistent with its mission. Requires a report from the Attorney General to the congressional judiciary committees on the implementation of this Subtitle.

(Sec. 235) Requires the Office Director to operate and support National Law Enforcement and Corrections Technology Centers and, to the extent necessary, establish new centers through a merit-based, competitive process. Requires such Centers to: (1) support research and development of law enforcement technology; (2) support the transfer and implementation of such technology; (3) assist in the development and dissemination of guidelines and technological standards; and (4) provide technology assistance, information, and support for law enforcement, corrections, and criminal justice purposes. Requires the Director to: (1) convene an annual meeting of such Centers; and (2) report to Congress assessing the effectiveness of the Centers and identifying the number of Centers necessary to meet the technology needs of Federal, State, and local law enforcement in the United States.

(Sec. 237) Amends the Omnibus Crime Control and Safe Streets Act of 1968 to require the National Institute of Justice to: (1) research and develop tools and technologies relating to prevention, detection, investigation, and prosecution of crime; and (2) support research, development, testing, training, and evaluation of tools and technology for Federal, State, and local law enforcement agencies.

Title III: Science and Technology in Support of Homeland Security—(Sec. 301) Establishes in DHS a Directorate of Science and Technology, headed by an Under Secretary for Science and Technology, to be responsible for: (1) advising the Secretary regarding research and development (R&D) efforts and priorities in support of DHS missions; (2) developing a national policy and strategic plan for, identifying priorities, goals, objectives and policies for, and coordinating the Federal Government's civilian efforts to identify and develop countermeasures to chemical, biological, radiological, nuclear, and other emerging terrorist threats; (3) supporting the Under Secretary for Information Analysis and Infrastructure Protection by assessing and testing homeland security vulnerabilities and possible threats; (4) conducting basic and applied R&D activities relevant to DHS elements, provided that such responsibility does not extend to human health-related R&D activities; (5) establishing priorities for directing, funding, and conducting national R&D and procurement of technology systems for preventing the importation of chemical, biological, radiological, nuclear, and related weapons and material and for detecting, preventing, protecting against, and responding to terrorist attacks; (6) establishing a system for transferring homeland security developments or technologies to Federal, State, and local government and private sector entities; (7) entering into agreements with the Department of Energy (DOE) regarding the use of the national laboratories or sites and support of the science and technology base at those facilities; (8) collaborating with the Secretary of Agriculture and the Attorney General in the regulation of certain biological agents and toxins as provided in the Agricultural Bioterrorism Protection Act of 2002; (9) collaborating with the Secretary of Health and Human Services and the Attorney General in determining new biological agents and toxins that shall be listed as select agents in the Code of Federal Regulations; (10) supporting U.S. leadership in science and technology; (11) establishing and administering the primary R&D activities of DHS; (12) coordinating and integrating all DHS R&D activities; (13) coordinating with other appropriate executive agencies in developing and carrying out the science and technology agenda of DHS to reduce duplication and identify unmet needs; and (14) developing and overseeing the administration of guidelines for merit review of R&D projects throughout DHS and for the dissemination of DHS research.

(Sec. 303) Transfers to the Secretary: (1) specified DOE functions, including functions related to chemical and biological national security programs, nuclear smuggling programs and activities within the proliferation detection program, the nuclear assessment program, designated life sciences activities of the biological and environmental research program related to microbial pathogens, the Environmental Measurements Laboratory, and the advanced scientific computing research program at Lawrence Livermore National Laboratory; and (2) the National Bio-Weapons Defense Analysis Center of DOD.

(Sec. 304) Requires the HHS Secretary, with respect to civilian human health-related R&D activities relating to HHS countermeasures for chemical, biological, radiological, and nuclear and other emerging terrorist threats, to: (1) set priorities, goals, objectives, and policies and develop a coordinated strategy for such activities in collaboration with the Secretary to ensure consistency with the national policy and strategic plan; and (2) collaborate with the Secretary in developing specific benchmarks and outcome measurements for evaluating progress toward achieving such priorities and goals.

Amends the Public Health Service Act to: (1) authorize the HHS Secretary to declare that an actual or potential bioterrorist incident or other public health emergency makes advisable the administration of a covered countermeasure against smallpox to a category or categories of individuals; (2) require the HHS Secretary to specify the substances to be considered countermeasures and the beginning and ending dates of the period of the declaration; and (3) deem a covered person to be an employee of the Public Health Service with respect to liability arising out of administration of such a countermeasure.

Extends liability to the United States (with an exception) with respect to claims arising out of an administration of a covered countermeasure to an individual only if: (1) the countermeasure was administered by a qualified person for the purpose of preventing or treating smallpox during the effective period; (2) the individual was within a covered category; or (3) the qualified person administering the countermeasure had reasonable grounds to believe that such individual was within such category. Provides for a rebuttable presumption of an administration within the scope of a declaration in the case where an individual who is not vaccinated contracts vaccinia. Makes the remedy against the United States provided under such Act exclusive of any other civil action or proceeding against a covered person for any claim or suit arising out of the administration of a covered countermeasure.

(Sec. 305) Authorizes the Secretary, acting through the Under Secretary, to establish or contract with one or more federally funded R&D centers to provide independent analysis of homeland security issues or to carry out other responsibilities under this Act.

(Sec. 306) Directs the President to notify the appropriate congressional committees of any proposed transfer of DOE life sciences activities.

(Sec. 307) Establishes the Homeland Security Advanced Research Projects Agency to be headed by a Director who shall be appointed by the Secretary and who shall report to the Under Secretary. Requires the Director to administer the Acceleration Fund for Research and Development of Homeland Security Technologies (established by this Act) to award competitive, merit-reviewed grants, cooperative agreements, or contracts to public or private entities to: (1) support basic and applied homeland security research to promote revolutionary changes in technologies that would promote homeland security; (2) advance the development, testing and evaluation, and deployment of critical homeland security technologies; and (3) accelerate the prototyping and deployment of technologies that would address homeland security vulnerabilities. Allows the Director to solicit proposals to address specific vulnerabilities. Requires the Director to periodically hold homeland security technology demonstrations to improve contact among technology developers, vendors, and acquisition personnel.

Authorizes appropriations to the Fund. Earmarks ten percent of such funds for each fiscal year through FY 2005 for the Under Secretary, through joint agreement with the Commandant of the Coast Guard, to carry out R&D of improved ports, waterways, and coastal security surveillance and perimeter protection capabilities to minimize the possibility that Coast Guard cutters, aircraft, helicopters, and personnel will be diverted from non-homeland security missions to the ports, waterways, and coastal security mission.

(Sec. 308) Requires the Secretary, acting through the Under Secretary, to: (1) operate extramural R&D programs to ensure that colleges, universities, private research institutes, and companies (and consortia thereof) from as many areas of the United States as practicable participate; and (2) establish a university-based center or centers for homeland security which shall establish a coordinated, university-based system to enhance the Nation's homeland security. Authorizes the Secretary, through the Under Secretary, to: (1) draw upon the expertise of any Government laboratory; and (2) establish a headquarters laboratory for DHS and additional laboratory units.

(Sec. 309) Allows the Secretary, in carrying out DHS missions, to utilize DOE national laboratories and sites through: (1) a joint sponsorship arrangement; (2) a direct contact

between DHS and the applicable DOE laboratory or site; (3) any "work for others" basis made available by that laboratory or site; or (4) any other method provided by law. Allows DHS to be a joint sponsor: (1) with DOE of one or more DOE national laboratories; and (2) of a DOE site in the performance of work as if such site were a federally funded R&D center and the work were performed under a multiple agency sponsorship arrangement with DHS Directs the Secretary and the Secretary of DOE to ensure that direct contracts between DHS and the operator of a DOE national laboratory or site for programs or activities transferred from DOE to DHS are separate from the direct contracts of DOE with such operator.

Establishes within the Directorate of Science and Technology an Office for National Laboratories that shall be responsible for the coordination and utilization of DOE national laboratories and sites in a manner to create a networked laboratory system to support DHS missions.

(Sec. 310) Directs the Secretary of Agriculture to transfer to the Secretary the Plum Island Animal Disease Center of the Department of Agriculture and provides for continued Department of Agriculture access to such Center.

(Sec. 311) Establishes within DHS a Homeland Security Science and Technology Advisory Committee to make recommendations with respect to the activities of the Under Secretary.

(Sec. 312) Directs the Secretary to establish the Homeland Security Institute, a federally funded R&D center. Includes among authorized duties for the Institute: (1) determination of the vulnerabilities of the Nation's critical infrastructures; (2) assessment of the costs and benefits of alternative approaches to enhancing security; and (3) evaluation of the effectiveness of measures deployed to enhance the security of institutions, facilities, and infrastructure that may be terrorist targets.

(Sec. 313) Requires the Secretary to establish and promote a program to encourage technological innovation in facilitating the mission of DHS, to include establishment of: (1) a centralized Federal clearinghouse to further the dissemination of information on technologies; and (2) a technical assistance team to assist in screening submitted proposals.

Title IV: Directorate of Border and Transportation Security—Subtitle A: Under Secretary for Border and Transportation Security—(Sec. 401) Establishes in DHS a Directorate of Border and Transportation Security to be headed by an Under Secretary for Border and Transportation

Security. Makes the Secretary, acting through the Under Secretary for Border and Transportation Security, responsible for: (1) preventing the entry of terrorists and the instruments of terrorism into the United States; (2) securing the borders, territorial waters, ports, terminals, waterways, and air, land, and sea transportation systems of the United States; (3) carrying out the immigration enforcement functions vested by statute in, or performed by, the Commissioner of Immigration and Naturalization immediately before their transfer to the Under Secretary; (4) establishing and administering rules governing the granting of visas or other forms of permission to enter the United States to individuals who are not citizens or aliens lawfully admitted for permanent residence in the United States; (5) establishing national immigration enforcement policies and priorities; (6) administering the customs laws of the United States (with certain exceptions); (7) conducting the inspection and related administrative functions of the Department of Agriculture transferred to the Secretary; and (8) ensuring the speedy, orderly, and efficient flow of lawful traffic and commerce in carrying out the foregoing responsibilities.

(Sec. 403) Transfers to the Secretary the functions, personnel, assets, and liabilities of: (1) the U.S. Customs Service; (2) the Transportation Security Administration; (3) the Federal Protective Service of the General Services Administration (GSA); (4) the Federal Law Enforcement Training Center of the Department of the Treasury; and (5) the Office for Domestic Preparedness of the Office of Justice Programs of the Department of Justice (DOJ).

Subtitle B: United States Customs Service—(Sec. 411) Establishes in DHS the U.S. Customs Service (transferred from the Department of the Treasury, but with certain customs revenue functions remaining with the Secretary of the Treasury). Authorizes the Secretary of the Treasury to appoint up to 20 new personnel to work with DHS personnel in performing customs revenue functions.

(Sec. 414) Requires the President to include a separate budget request for the U.S. Customs Service in the annual budget transmitted to Congress.

(Sec. 416) Directs the Comptroller General to report to Congress on all trade functions performed by the executive branch, specifying each agency that performs each such function.

(Sec. 417) Directs the Secretary to ensure that adequate staffing is provided to assure that levels of current customs revenue services will continue to be provided. Requires the Secretary to notify specified congressional committees prior to taking any action which would: (1) result in any significant reduction in customs revenue services (including hours of operation provided at any office within DHS or any port of entry); (2) eliminate or relocate any office of DHS which provides customs revenue services; or (3) eliminate any port of entry.

(Sec. 419) Amends the Consolidated Omnibus Budget Reconciliation Act of 1985 to create in the Treasury a separate Customs Commercial and Homeland Security Automation Account to contain merchandise processing (customs user) fees. Authorizes appropriations for FY 2003 through 2005 for establishment of the Automated Commercial Environment computer system for the processing of merchandise that is entered or released and for other purposes related to the functions of DHS.

Subtitle C: Miscellaneous Provisions—(Sec. 421) Transfers to the Secretary the functions of the Secretary of Agriculture relating to agricultural import and entry inspection activities under specified animal and plant protection laws.

Requires the Secretary of Agriculture and the Secretary to enter into an agreement to effectuate such transfer and to transfer periodically funds collected pursuant to fee authorities under the Food, Agriculture, Conservation, and Trade Act of 1990 to the Secretary for activities carried out by the Secretary for which such fees were collected.

Directs the Secretary of Agriculture to transfer to the Secretary not more than 3,200 full-time equivalent positions of the Department of Agriculture.

(Sec. 423) Directs the Secretary to establish a liaison office within DHS for the purpose of consulting with the Administrator of the Federal Aviation Administration before taking any action that might affect aviation safety, air carrier operations, aircraft airworthiness, or the use of airspace.

(Sec. 424) Requires the Transportation Security Administration to be maintained as a distinct entity within DHS under the Under Secretary for Border Transportation and Security for two years after enactment of this Act.

(Sec. 425) Amends Federal aviation law to require the Under Secretary of Transportation for Security to take certain action, if, in his discretion or at the request of an airport, he determines that the Transportation Security Administration is not able to deploy explosive detection systems at all airports required to have them by December 31, 2002. Requires the Under Secretary, in such circumstances, to: (1) submit to specified congressional committees a detailed plan for the deployment of explosive detection systems at such airport by December 31, 2003; and (2) take all necessary action to ensure that alternative means of screening all checked baggage is implemented.

(Sec. 426) Replaces the Secretary of Transportation with the Secretary of Homeland Security as chair of the Transportation Security Oversight Board. Requires the Secretary of Transportation to consult with the Secretary before approving airport development project grants relating to security equipment or the installation of bulk explosive detection systems.

(Sec. 427) Directs the Secretary, in coordination with the Secretary of Agriculture, the Secretary of Health and Human Services, and the head of each other department or agency determined to be appropriate by the Secretary, to ensure that appropriate information concerning inspections of articles that are imported or entered into the United States, and are inspected or regulated by one or more affected agencies, is timely and efficiently exchanged between the affected agencies. Requires the Secretary to report to Congress on the progress made in implementing this section.

(Sec. 428) Grants the Secretary exclusive authority to issue regulations with respect to, administer, and enforce the Immigration and Nationality Act (INA) and all other immigration and nationality laws relating to the functions of U.S. diplomatic and consular officers in connection with the granting or refusal of visas, and authority to refuse visas in accordance with law and to develop programs of homeland security training for consular officers, which authorities shall be exercised through the Secretary of State. Denies the Secretary authority, however, to alter or reverse the decision of a consular officer to refuse a visa to an alien.

Grants the Secretary authority also to confer or impose upon any U.S. officer or employee, with the consent of the head of the executive agency under whose jurisdiction such officer or employee is serving, any of these specified functions.

Authorizes the Secretary of State to direct a consular officer to refuse a visa to an alien if the Secretary of State deems such refusal necessary or advisable in the foreign policy or security interests of the United States.

Authorizes the Secretary to assign employees of DHS to any diplomatic and consular posts abroad to review individual visa applications and provide expert advice and training to consular officers regarding specific security threats relating to such applications and to conduct investigations with respect to matters under the Secretary's jurisdiction.

Directs the Secretary to study and report to Congress on the role of foreign nationals in the granting or refusal of visas and other documents authorizing entry of aliens into the United States.

Requires the Director of the Office of Science and Technology Policy to report to Congress on how the provisions of this section will affect procedures for the issuance of student visas.

Terminates after enactment of this Act all third party screening visa issuance programs in Saudi Arabia. Requires on-site personnel of DHS to review all visa applications prior to adjudication.

(Sec. 429) Requires visa denial information to be entered into the electronic data system as provided for in the Enhanced Border Security and Visa Entry Reform Act of 2002. Prohibits an alien denied a visa from being issued a subsequent visa unless the reviewing consular officer makes specified findings concerning waiver of ineligibility.

(Sec. 430) Establishes within the Directorate of Border and Transportation Security the Office for Domestic Preparedness to: (1) coordinate Federal preparedness for acts of terrorism, working with all State, local, tribal, county, parish, and private sector emergency response providers; (2) coordinate or consolidate systems of communications relating to homeland security at all levels of government; (3) direct and supervise Federal terrorism preparedness grant programs for all emergency response providers; and (4) perform specified other related duties.

Subtitle D: Immigration Enforcement Functions—(Sec. 441) Transfers from the Commissioner of Immigration and Naturalization to the Under Secretary for Border and Transportation Security all functions performed under the following programs, and all personnel, assets, and liabilities pertaining to such programs, immediately before such transfer occurs: (1) the Border Patrol program; (2) the detention and removal program; (3) the intelligence program; (4) the investigations program; and (5) the inspections program.

(Sec. 442) Establishes in the Department of Homeland Security (DHS) the Bureau of Border Security, headed by the Assistant Secretary of the Bureau of Border Security who shall: (1) report directly to the Under Secretary; (2) establish and oversee the policies for performing functions transferred to the Under Secretary and delegated to the Assistant Secretary by the Under Secretary; and (3) advise the Under Secretary with respect to any policy or operation of the Bureau that may affect the Bureau of Citizenship and Immigration Services.

Directs the Assistant Secretary to: (1) administer the program to collect information relating to nonimmigrant foreign students and other exchange program participants; and (2) implement a managerial rotation program.

Establishes the position of Chief of Policy and Strategy for the Bureau of Border Security, who shall: (1) make immigration enforcement policy recommendations; and (2) coordinate immigration policy issues with the Chief of Policy and Strategy for the Bureau of Citizenship and Immigration Services.

(Sec. 443) Makes the Under Secretary responsible for: (1) investigating noncriminal allegations of Bureau employee misconduct, corruption, and fraud that are not subject to investigation by the Inspector General for DHS; (2) inspecting and assessing Bureau operations; and (3) analyzing Bureau management.

(Sec. 444) Authorizes the Under Secretary to impose disciplinary action pursuant to policies and procedures applicable to FBI employees.

(Sec. 445) Requires the Secretary of Homeland Security to report on how the Bureau will enforce relevant INA provisions.

(Sec. 446) Expresses the sense of Congress that completing the 14-mile border fence project near San Diego, California, mandated by the Illegal Immigration Reform and Immigrant Responsibility Act of 1996 should be a priority for the Secretary.

Subtitle E: Citizenship and Immigration Services—(Sec. 451) Establishes in DHS a Bureau of Citizenship and Immigration Services, headed by the Director of the Bureau of Citizenship and Immigration Services, who shall: (1) establish the policies for performing and administering transferred functions; (2) establish national immigration services policies and priorities; and (3) implement a managerial rotation program.

Authorizes the Director to implement pilot initiatives to eliminate the backlog of immigration benefit applications.

Transfers all Immigration and Naturalization Service (INS) adjudications and related personnel and funding to the Director.

Establishes for the Bureau positions of: (1) Chief of Policy and Strategy; (2) legal adviser; (3) budget officer; and (4) Chief of the Office of Citizenship to promote citizenship instruction and training for aliens interested in becoming naturalized U.S. citizens.

(Sec. 452) Establishes within the DHS a Citizenship and Immigration Services Ombudsman, with local offices, to:

(1) assist individuals and employers resolve problems with the Bureau; (2) identify problem areas; and (3) propose administrative and legislative changes.

(Sec. 453) Makes the Director responsible for (1) investigating noncriminal allegations of Bureau employee misconduct, corruption, and fraud that are not subject to investigation by the Inspector General of DHS; (2) inspecting and assessing Bureau operations; and (3) analyzing Bureau management.

(Sec. 454) Authorizes the Director to impose disciplinary action pursuant to policies and procedures applicable to FBI employees.

(Sec. 456) Sets forth transfer of authority and transfer and allocation of appropriations and personnel provisions.

(Sec. 457) Amends the INA to repeal the provision permitting fees for adjudication and naturalization services to be set at a level that will ensure recovery of the costs of similar services provided without charge to asylum applicants.

(Sec. 458) Amends the Immigration Services and Infrastructure Improvements Act of 2000 to change the deadline for the Attorney General to eliminate the backlog in the processing of immigration benefit applications to one year after enactment of this Act.

(Sec. 459) Directs the Secretary to report on how the Bureau of Citizenship and Immigration Services will efficiently complete transferred INS adjudications.

(Sec. 460) Directs the Attorney General to report on changes in law needed to ensure an appropriate response to emergent or unforeseen immigration needs.

(Sec. 461) Directs the Secretary to: (1) establish an Internet-based system that will permit online information access to a person, employer, immigrant, or nonimmigrant about the processing status of any filings for any benefit under the INA; (2) conduct a feasibility study for online filing and improved processing; and (3) establish a Technology Advisory Committee.

(Sec. 462) Transfers to the Director of the Office of Refugee Resettlement of the Department of Health and Human Services (HHS) INS functions with respect to the care of unaccompanied alien children (as defined by this Act).

Sets forth the responsibilities of the Office for such children, including: (1) coordinating and implementing the care and placement of unaccompanied alien children who are in Federal custody, including appointment of independent legal counsel to represent the interests of each child; (2) identifying and overseeing individuals, entities, and facilities to house such children; (3) family reunification; (4) compiling, updating, and publishing at least annually a State-by-State list of professionals or other entities qualified to provide guardian and attorney representation services; (5) maintaining related biographical and statistical information; and (6) conducting investigations and inspections of residential facilities.

Directs the Office to: (1) consult with juvenile justice professionals to ensure such children's safety; and (2) not release such children upon their own recognizance.

Subtitle F: General Immigration Provisions—(Sec. 471) Abolishes INS upon completion of all transfers from it as provided for by this Act.

(Sec. 472) Authorizes the Attorney General and the Secretary to make voluntary separation incentive payments, after completion of a strategic restructuring plan, to employees of: (1) INS; (2) the Bureau of Border Security of DHS; and (3) the Bureau of Citizenship and Immigration Services of DHS.

(Sec. 473) Directs the Attorney General and the Secretary to conduct a demonstration project to determine whether policy or procedure revisions for employee discipline would result in improved personnel management.

(Sec. 474) Expresses the sense of Congress that: (1) the missions of the Bureau of Border Security and the Bureau of Citizenship and Immigration Services are equally important and should be adequately funded; and (2) the functions transferred should not operate at levels below those in effect prior to the enactment of this Act.

(Sec. 475) Establishes within the Office of Deputy Secretary a Director of Shared Services who shall be responsible for: (1) information resources management; and (2) records, forms, and file management.

(Sec. 476) Provides for budgetary and funding separation with respect to the Bureau of Citizenship and Immigration Services and the Bureau of Border Security.

(Sec. 477) Sets forth reporting and implementation plan provisions.

(Sec. 478) Directs the Secretary to annually report regarding: (1) the aggregate number of all immigration applications and petitions received, and processed; (2) regional statistics on the aggregate number of denied applications and petitions; (3) application and petition backlogs and a backlog elimination plan; (4) application and petition processing periods; (5) number, types, and disposition of grievances and plans to improve immigration services; and (6) appropriate use of immigration-related fees.

Expresses the sense of Congress that: (1) the quality and efficiency of immigration services should be improved after the transfers made by Act; and (2) the Secretary should undertake efforts to guarantee that such concerns are addressed after such effective date.

Title V: Emergency Preparedness and Response—(Sec. 501) Establishes in DHS a Directorate of Emergency Preparedness and Response, headed by an Under Secretary.

(Sec. 502) Requires the responsibilities of the Secretary, acting through the Under Secretary, to include: (1) helping to ensure the effectiveness of emergency response providers to terrorist attacks, major disasters, and other emergencies; (2) with respect to the Nuclear Incident Response Team, establishing and certifying compliance with standards, conducting joint and other exercises and training, and providing funds to the Department of Energy and the Environmental Protection Agency for homeland security planning, training, and equipment; (3) providing the Federal Government's response to terrorist attacks and major disasters; (4) aiding recovery from terrorist attacks and major disasters; (5) building a comprehensive national incident management system with Federal, State, and local governments to respond to such attacks and disasters; (6) consolidating existing Federal Government emergency response plans into a single, coordinated national response plan; and (7) developing comprehensive programs for developing interoperative communications technology and helping to ensure that emergency response providers acquire such technology.

(Sec. 503) Transfers to the Secretary the functions, personnel, assets, and liabilities of: (1) the Federal Emergency Management Agency (FEMA); (2) the Integrated Hazard Information System of the National Oceanic and Atmospheric Administration, which shall be renamed FIRESAT; (3) the National Domestic Preparedness Office of the FBI; (4) the Domestic Emergency Support Teams of DOJ; (5) the Office of Emergency Preparedness, the National Disaster Medical System, and the Metropolitan Medical Response System of HHS; and (6) the Strategic National Stockpile of HHS.

(Sec. 504) Requires the Nuclear Incident Response Team, at the direction of the Secretary (in connection with an actual or threatened terrorist attack, major disaster, or other emergency in the United States), to operate as an organizational unit of DHS under the Secretary's authority and control.

(Sec. 505) Provides that, with respect to all public health-related activities to improve State, local, and hospital preparedness and response to chemical, biological, radiological, and nuclear and other emerging terrorist threats carried out by HHS (including the Public Health Service), the Secretary of HHS shall set priorities and preparedness goals and further develop a coordinated strategy for such activities in collaboration with the Secretary.

(Sec. 506) Defines the Nuclear Incident Response Team to include: (1) those entities of the Department of Energy that perform nuclear or radiological emergency support functions, radiation exposure functions at the medical assistance facility known as the Radiation Emergency Assistance Center/Training Site (REAC/TS), radiological assistance functions, and related functions; and (2) Environmental Protection Agency entities that perform such support functions and related functions.

(Sec. 507) Includes in the homeland security role of FEMA: (1) all functions and authorities prescribed by the Robert T. Stafford Disaster Relief and Emergency Assistance Act; and (2) a comprehensive, risk-based emergency management program of mitigation, of planning for building the emergency management profession, of response, of recovery, and of increased efficiencies. Maintains FEMA as the lead agency for the Federal Response Plan established under Executive Orders 12148 and 12656. Requires the FEMA Director to revise the Plan to reflect the establishment of and incorporate DHS.

(Sec. 508) Directs the Secretary, to the maximum extent practicable, to use national private sector networks and infrastructure for emergency response to major disasters.

(Sec. 509) Expresses the sense of Congress that the Secretary should: (1) use off-the-shelf commercially developed technologies to allow DHS to collect, manage, share, analyze, and disseminate information securely over multiple channels of communication; and (2) rely on commercial sources to supply goods and services needed by DHS.

Title VI: Treatment of Charitable Trusts for Members of the Armed Forces of the United States and Other Governmental Organizations—(Sec. 601) Sets forth requirements a charitable corporation, fund, foundation, or trust must meet to designate itself as a Johnny Micheal Spann Patriot Trust (a charitable trust for the spouses, dependents, and relatives of military and Federal personnel who lose their lives in the battle against terrorism that is named after the first American to die in such service following the September 11th terrorist attacks). Requires at least 85 percent of each Trust corpus to be distributed to such survivors and prohibits more than 15 percent from being used for administrative purposes. Prohibits: (1) any Trust activities from violating any prohibition against

attempting to influence legislation; and (2) any such Trust from participating in any political campaign on behalf of a candidate for public office. Requires: (1) audits of each Trust that annually receives contributions of more than $1 million; and (2) Trust distributions to be made at least once a year. Provides for the notification of Trust beneficiaries.

Title VII: Management—(Sec. 701) Makes the Secretary, acting through the Under Secretary for Management, responsible for the management and administration of DHS. Details certain responsibilities of the Under Secretary with respect to immigration statistics. Transfers to the Under Secretary functions previously performed by the Statistics Branch of the Office of Policy and Planning of the Immigration and Naturalization Service (INS) with respect to: (1) the Border Patrol program; (2) the detention and removal program; (3) the intelligence program; (4) the investigations program; (5) the inspections program; and (6) INS adjudications.

(Sec. 702) Requires a chief financial officer, a chief information officer, and a chief human capital officer to report to the Secretary. Requires the chief human capital officer to ensure that all DHS employees are informed of their rights and remedies under merit system protection and principle provisions.

(Sec. 705) Requires the Secretary to appoint an Officer for Civil Rights and Civil Liberties who shall: (1) review and assess information alleging abuses of civil rights, civil liberties, and racial and ethnic profiling by employees and officials of DHS; and (2) make public information on the responsibilities and functions of, and how to contact, the Office.

(Sec. 706) Requires the Secretary to develop and submit to Congress a plan for consolidating and co-locating: (1) any regional offices or field offices of agencies that are transferred to DHS under this Act, if their officers are located in the same municipality; and (2) portions of regional and field offices of other Federal agencies, to the extent such offices perform functions that are transferred to the Secretary under this Act.

Title VIII: Coordination With Non-Federal Entities; Inspector General; United States Secret Service; Coast Guard; General Provisions—Subtitle A: Coordination with Non-Federal Entities—(Sec. 801) Establishes within the Office of the Secretary the Office for State and Local Government Coordination to oversee and coordinate Department homeland security programs for and relationships with State and local governments.

Subtitle B: Inspector General—(Sec. 811) Places the DHS Inspector General under the authority, direction, and control of the Secretary with respect to audits or investigations, or the issuance of subpoenas, that require access to sensitive information concerning intelligence, counterintelligence, or counterterrorism matters; criminal investigations or proceedings; undercover operations; the identify of confidential sources; and certain matters of disclosure.

Amends the Inspector General Act of 1978 to: (1) give such Inspector General oversight responsibility for internal investigations performed by the Office of Internal Affairs of the United States Customs Service and the Office of Inspections of the United States Secret Service; and (2) authorize each Inspector General, any Assistant Inspector General for Investigations, and any special agent supervised by such an Assistant Inspector General to carry a firearm, make arrests without warrants, and seek and execute warrants. Allows the latter only upon certain determinations by the Attorney General (exempts the Inspector General offices of various executive agencies from such requirement). Provides for the rescinding of such law enforcement powers. Requires the Inspector General offices exempted from the determinations requirement to collectively enter into a memorandum of understanding to establish an external review process for ensuring that adequate internal safeguards and management procedures continue to exist to ensure the proper utilization of such law enforcement powers within their departments.

Subtitle C: United States Secret Service—(Sec. 821) Transfers to the Secretary the functions of the United States Secret Service, which shall be maintained as a distinct entity within DHS.

Subtitle D: Acquisitions—(Sec. 831) Authorizes the Secretary to carry out a five-year pilot program under which the Secretary may exercise specified authorities in carrying out: (1) basic, applied, and advanced research and development projects for response to existing or emerging terrorist threats; and (2) defense prototype projects. Requires a report from the Comptroller General to specified congressional committees on the use of such authorities.

(Sec. 832) Permits the Secretary to procure temporary or intermittent: (1) services of experts or consultants; and (2) personal services without regard to certain pay limitations when necessary due to an urgent homeland security need.

(Sec. 833) Authorizes the Secretary to use specified micro purchase, simplified acquisition, and commercial item acquisition procedures with respect to any procurement made during the period beginning on the effective date of this Act and ending on September 30, 2007, if the Secretary determines that the mission of DHS would be seriously impaired without the use of such authorities. Requires a report from the Comptroller General.

(Sec. 834) Requires the Federal Acquisition Regulation to be revised to include regulations with regard to unsolicited proposals.

(Sec. 835) Prohibits the Secretary from entering into a contract with a foreign incorporated entity which is treated as an inverted domestic corporation. Sets forth requirements for such treatment. Authorizes the Secretary to waive such prohibition in the interest of homeland security, to prevent the loss of any jobs in the United States, or to prevent the Government from incurring any additional costs.

Subtitle E: Human Resources Management—(Sec. 841) Expresses the sense of Congress calling for the participation of DHS employees in the creation of the DHS human resources management system.

Amends Federal civil service law to authorize the Secretary, in regulations prescribed jointly with the Director of the Office of Personnel Management (OPM), to establish and adjust a human resources management system for organizational units of DHS. Requires the system to ensure that employees may organize, bargain collectively, and participate through labor organizations of their own choosing in decisions which affect them, subject to an exclusion from coverage or limitation on negotiability established by law. Imposes certain requirements upon the Secretary and the OPM Director to ensure the participation of employee representatives in the planning, development, and implementation of any human resources management system or system adjustments.

Declares the sense of Congress that DHS employees are entitled to fair treatment in any appeals that they bring in decisions relating to their employment.

Terminates all authority to issue regulations under this section five years after enactment of this Act.

(Sec. 842) Prohibits any agency or agency subdivision transferred to DHS from being excluded from coverage under labor-management relations requirements as a result of any order issued after June 18, 2002, unless: (1) the mission and responsibilities of the agency or subdivision materially change; and (2) a majority of the employees within the agency or subdivision have as their primary duty intelligence, counterintelligence, or investigative work directly related to terrorism investigation. Declares that collective bargaining units shall continue to be recognized unless such conditions develop. Prohibits exclusion of positions or employees for a bargaining unit unless the primary job duty materially changes or consists of intelligence, counterintelligence, or investigative work directly related to terrorism investigation. Waives these prohibitions and recognitions in circumstances where the President determines that their application would have a substantial adverse impact on the Department's ability to protect homeland security.

Subtitle F: Federal Emergency Procurement Flexibility— (Sec. 852) Provides that the simplified acquisition threshold to be applied for any executive agency procurement of property or services that is to be used to facilitate the defense against or recovery from terrorism or nuclear, biological, chemical, or radiological attack and that is carried out in support of a humanitarian or peacekeeping operation or a contingency operation shall be: (1) $200,000 for a contract to be awarded and performed, or a purchase to be made, inside the United States; or (2) $300,000 for a contract to be awarded and performed, or a purchase to be made, outside the United States.

(Sec. 854) Authorizes the head of each agency to designate certain employees to make such procurements below a micro-purchase threshold of $7,500 (currently $2,500) under the Office of Federal Procurement Policy Act.

(Sec. 855) Permits executive agencies to apply to any such procurement specified provisions of law relating to the procurement of commercial items, without regard to whether the property and services are commercial items. Makes the $5 million limitation on the use of simplified acquisition procedures inapplicable to purchases of property or services to which such provisions apply.

(Sec. 856) Requires executive agencies to use specified streamlined acquisition authorities and procedures for such procurements. Waives certain small business threshold requirements with respect to such procurements.

(Sec. 857) Requires the Comptroller General to review and report to specified congressional committees on the extent to which procurements of property and services have been made in accordance with requirements of this Subtitle.

(Sec. 858) Requires each executive agency to conduct market research to identify the capabilities of small businesses and new entrants into Federal contracting that are available to meet agency requirements in furtherance of defense against

or recovery from terrorism or nuclear, biological, chemical, or radiological attack.

Subtitle G: Support Anti-terrorism by Fostering Effective Technologies Act of 2002—Support Anti-terrorism by Fostering Effective Technologies Act of 2002 or SAFETY Act—(Sec. 862) Authorizes the Secretary to designate anti-terrorism technologies that qualify for protection under a risk management system in accordance with criteria that shall include: (1) prior Government use or demonstrated substantial utility and effectiveness; (2) availability for immediate deployment in public and private settings; (3) substantial likelihood that such technology will not be deployed unless protections under such system are extended; and (4) the magnitude of risk exposure to the public if such technology is not deployed. Makes the Secretary responsible for administration of such protections.

(Sec. 863) Provides a Federal cause of action for sellers suffering a loss from qualified anti-terrorism technologies so deployed. Prohibits punitive damages from being awarded against a seller.

(Sec. 864) Requires sellers of qualified anti-terrorism technologies to obtain liability insurance in amounts certified as satisfactory by the Secretary.

Subtitle H: Miscellaneous Provisions—(Sec. 871) Authorizes the Secretary to establish, appoint members of, and use the services of advisory committees as necessary.

(Sec. 872) Grants the Secretary limited authority to reorganize DHS by allocating or reallocating functions within it and by establishing, consolidating, altering, or discontinuing organizational units.

(Sec. 873) Requires the Secretary to comply with Federal requirements concerning the deposit of proceeds from property sold or transferred by the Secretary. Requires the President to submit to Congress a detailed Department budget request for FY 2004 and thereafter.

(Sec. 874) Requires each such budget request to be accompanied by a Future Years Homeland Security Program structured in the same manner as the annual Future Years Defense Program.

(Sec. 876) Provides that nothing in this Act shall confer upon the Secretary any authority to engage in war fighting, the military defense of the United States, or other military activities or limit the existing authority of the Department of Defense or the armed forces to do so.

(Sec. 878) Directs the Secretary to appoint a senior DHS official to assume primary responsibility for coordinating policy and operations within DHS and between DHS and other Federal departments and agencies with respect to interdicting the entry of illegal drugs into the United States and tracking and severing connections between illegal drug trafficking and terrorism.

(Sec. 879) Establishes within the Office of the Secretary an Office of International Affairs, headed by a Director, to: (1) promote information and education exchange on homeland security best practices and technologies with friendly nations; (2) identify areas for homeland security information and training exchange where the United States has a demonstrated weakness and another friendly nation has a demonstrated expertise; (3) plan and undertake international conferences, exchange programs, and training activities; and (4) manage international activities within DHS in coordination with other Federal officials with responsibility for counter-terrorism matters.

(Sec. 880) Prohibits any Government activity to implement the proposed component program of the Citizen Corps known as Operation TIPS (Terrorism Information and Prevention System).

(Sec. 881) Directs the Secretary to review the pay and benefit plans of each agency whose functions are transferred to DHS under this Act and to submit a plan for ensuring the elimination of disparities in pay and benefits throughout DHS, especially among law enforcement personnel, that are inconsistent with merit system principles.

(Sec. 882) Establishes within the Office of the Secretary the Office of National Capital Region Coordination, headed by a Director, to oversee and coordinate Federal homeland security programs for and relationships with State, local, and regional authorities within the National Capital Region. Requires an annual report from the Office to Congress on: (1) resources needed to fully implement homeland security efforts in the Region; (2) progress made by the Region in implementing such efforts; and (3) recommendations for additional needed resources to fully implement such efforts.

(Sec. 883) Requires DHS to comply with specified laws protecting equal employment opportunity and providing whistle blower protections.

(Sec. 885) Authorizes the Secretary to establish a permanent Joint Interagency Homeland Security Task Force, composed of representatives from military and civilian agencies, for the purpose of anticipating terrorist threats and taking actions to prevent harm to the United States.

(Sec. 886) Reaffirms the continued importance of Federal criminal code proscriptions on the use of the armed forces as posse comitatus and expresses the sense of Congress that nothing in this Act shall be construed to alter the applicability of such proscriptions to any use of the armed forces to execute the laws.

(Sec. 887) Requires the annual Federal response plan developed by DHS to be consistent with public health emergency provisions of the Public Health Service Act. Requires full disclosure of public health emergencies, or potential emergencies, among HHS, DHS, the Department of Justice, and the Federal Bureau of Investigation.

(Sec. 888) Transfers to DHS the authorities, functions, personnel, and assets of the Coast Guard, which shall be maintained as a distinct entity within DHS. Prohibits the Secretary from substantially or significantly reducing current Coast Guard missions or capabilities, with a waiver of such prohibition upon a declaration and certification to Congress that a clear, compelling and immediate need exists. Requires the DHS Inspector General to annually review and report to Congress on performance by the Coast Guard of its mission requirements. Requires the Commandant of the Coast Guard, upon its transfer, to report directly to the Secretary. Prohibits any of the above conditions and restrictions from applying to the Coast Guard when it is operating as a service in the Navy. Directs the Secretary to report to specified congressional committees on the feasibility of accelerating the rate of procurement in the Coast Guard's Integrated Deepwater System from 20 to ten years.

(Sec. 889) Requires the inclusion in the President's annual budget documents of a detailed homeland security funding analysis for the previous, current, and next fiscal years.

(Sec. 890) Amends the Air Transportation Safety and System Stabilization Act, with respect to the September 11th Victim Compensation Fund of 2001, to limit "agents" of an air carrier engaged in the business of providing air transportation security to persons that have contracted directly with the Federal Aviation Administration on or after February 17, 2002, to provide such security and that had not been or are not debarred within six months of that date.

Subtitle I: Information Sharing—Homeland Security Information Sharing Act—(Sec. 891) Expresses the sense of Congress that Federal, State, and local entities should share homeland security information to the maximum extent practicable, with special emphasis on hard-to-reach urban and rural communities.

(Sec. 892) Directs the President to prescribe and implement procedures for Federal agency: (1) sharing of appropriate homeland security information, including with DHS and appropriate State and local personnel; and (2) handling of classified information and sensitive but unclassified information. Authorizes appropriations.

(Sec. 893) Requires an implementation report from the President to the congressional intelligence and judiciary committees.

(Sec. 895) Amends the Federal Rules of Criminal Procedure to treat as contempt of court any knowing violation of guidelines jointly issued by the Attorney General and DCI with respect to disclosure of grand jury matters otherwise prohibited. Allows disclosure to appropriate Federal, State, local, or foreign government officials of grand jury matters involving a threat of grave hostile acts of a foreign power, domestic or international sabotage or terrorism, or clandestine intelligence gathering activities by an intelligence service or network of a foreign power (threat), within the United States or elsewhere. Permits disclosure to appropriate foreign government officials of grand jury matters that may disclose a violation of the law of such government. Requires State, local, and foreign officials to use disclosed information only in conformity with guidelines jointly issued by the Attorney General and the DCI.

(Sec. 896) Amends the Federal criminal code to authorize Federal investigative and law enforcement officers conducting communications interception activities, who have obtained knowledge of the contents of any intercepted communication or derivative evidence, to disclose such contents or evidence to: (1) a foreign investigative or law enforcement officer if the disclosure is appropriate to the performance of the official duties of the officer making or receiving the disclosure; and (2) any appropriate Federal, State, local, or foreign government official if the contents or evidence reveals such a threat, for the purpose of preventing or responding to such threat. Provides guidelines for the use and disclosure of the information.

(Sec. 897) Amends the Uniting and Strengthening America by Providing Appropriate Tools Required to Intercept and Obstruct Terrorism Act (USA PATRIOT ACT) of 2001 to make lawful the disclosure to appropriate Federal, State, local, or foreign government officials of information obtained as part of a criminal investigation that reveals such a threat.

(Sec. 898) Amends the Foreign Intelligence Surveillance Act of 1978 to allow Federal officers who conduct electronic surveillance and physical searches in order to acquire foreign intelligence information to consult with State and local law enforcement personnel to coordinate efforts to investigate or protect against such a threat.

Title IX: National Homeland Security Council—(Sec. 901) Establishes within the Executive Office of the President the Homeland Security Council to advise the President on homeland security matters.

(Sec. 903) Includes as members of the Council: (1) the President; (2) the Vice President; (3) the Secretary; (4) the Attorney General; and (5) the Secretary of Defense.

(Sec. 904) Requires the Council to: (1) assess the objectives, commitments, and risks of the United States in the interest of homeland security and make recommendations to the President; and (2) oversee and review Federal homeland security policies and make policy recommendations to the President.

(Sec. 906) Authorizes the President to convene joint meetings of the Homeland Security Council and the National Security Council.

Title X: Information Security—Federal Information Security Management Act of 2002—(Sec. 1001) Revises Government information security requirements. Requires the head of each agency operating or exercising control of a national security system to ensure that the agency: (1) provides information security protections commensurate with the risk and magnitude of the harm resulting from the unauthorized access, use, disclosure, disruption, modification, or destruction of the information; and (2) implements information security policies and practices as required by standards and guidelines for national security systems. Authorizes appropriations for FY 2003 through 2007.

(Sec. 1002) Transfers from the Secretary of Commerce to the Director of the Office of Management and Budget (OMB) the authority to promulgate information security standards pertaining to Federal information systems.

(Sec. 1003) Amends the National Institute of Standards and Technology Act to revise and expand the mandate of the National Institute of Standards and Technology to develop standards, guidelines, and associated methods and techniques for information systems. Renames the Computer System Security and Privacy Advisory Board as the Information Security and Privacy Board and requires it to advise the Director of OMB (instead of the Secretary of Commerce) on information security and privacy issues pertaining to Federal Government information systems.

Title XI: Department of Justice Divisions—Subtitle A: Executive Office for Immigration Review—(Sec. 1101) Declares that there is in the Department of Justice (DOJ) the Executive Office for Immigration Review (EOIR), which shall be subject to the direction and regulation of the Attorney General under the INA.

(Sec. 1102) Amends the INA to grant the Attorney General such authorities and functions relating to the immigration and naturalization of aliens as were exercised by EOIR, or by the Attorney General with respect to EOIR, on the day before the effective date of the Immigration Reform, Accountability and Security Enhancement Act of 2002.

Subtitle B: Transfer of the Bureau of Alcohol, Tobacco and Firearms to the Department of Justice—(Sec. 1111) Establishes within DOJ, under the Attorney General's authority, the Bureau of Alcohol, Tobacco, Firearms, and Explosives (the Bureau). Transfers to DOJ the authorities, functions, personnel, and assets of the Bureau of Alcohol, Tobacco and Firearms (BATF), which shall be maintained as a distinct entity within DOJ, including the related functions of the Secretary of the Treasury.

Provides that the Bureau shall be headed by a Director and shall be responsible for: (1) investigating criminal and regulatory violations of the Federal firearms, explosives, arson, alcohol, and tobacco smuggling laws; (2) such transferred functions; and (3) any other function related to the investigation of violent crime or domestic terrorism that is delegated to the Bureau by the Attorney General.

Retains within the Department of the Treasury certain authorities, functions, personnel, and assets of BATF relating to the administration and enforcement of the Internal Revenue Code.

Establishes within the Department of the Treasury the Tax and Trade Bureau, which shall retain and administer the authorities, functions, personnel, and assets of BATF that are not transferred to DOJ.

(Sec. 1113) Amends the Federal criminal code to authorize special agents of the Bureau, as well as any other investigator or officer charged by the Attorney General with enforcing criminal, seizure, or forfeiture laws, to carry firearms, serve warrants and subpoenas, and make arrests without warrant for offenses committed in their presence or for felonies on reasonable grounds. Authorizes any special agent to make seizures of property subject to forfeiture to the United States. Sets forth provisions regarding seizure, disposition, and claims pertaining to property.

(Sec. 1114) Establishes within the Bureau an Explosives Training and Research Facility at Fort AP Hill in Fredericksburg, Virginia, to train Federal, State, and local law enforcement officers to: (1) investigate bombings and explosions; (2) properly handle, utilize, and dispose of explosive materials and devices; (3) train canines on explosive detection; and (4) conduct research on explosives. Authorizes appropriations.

(Sec. 1115) Transfers the Personnel Management Demonstration Project to the Attorney General for continued use by the Bureau and to the Secretary of the Treasury for continued use by the Tax and Trade Bureau.

Subtitle C: Explosives—Safe Explosives Act—(Sec. 1122) Rewrites Federal criminal code provisions regarding the purchase of explosives to create a new "limited permit" category. Prohibits a holder of a limited permit: (1) from transporting, shipping, causing to be transported, or receiving in interstate or foreign commerce explosive materials; (2) from receiving explosive materials from a licensee or permittee whose premises are located outside the holder's State of residence; or (3) on more than six separate occasions during the period of the permit, from receiving explosive materials from one or more licensees or permittees whose premises are located within the holder's State of residence.

Requires license, user permit, and limited permit applicants to include the names of and identifying information (including fingerprints and a photograph of each responsible person) regarding all employees who will be authorized by the applicant to possess explosive materials. Caps the fee for limited permits at $50 for each permit. Makes each limited permit valid for not longer than one year.

Modifies criteria for approving licenses and permits. Requires the Secretary of the Treasury to issue to the applicant the appropriate license or permit if, among other conditions: (1) the applicant is not a person who is otherwise prohibited from possessing explosive materials (excluded person); (2) the Secretary verifies by inspection or other appropriate means that the applicant has a place of storage for explosive materials that meets the Secretary's standards of public safety and security against theft (inapplicable to an applicant for renewal of a limited permit if the Secretary has verified such matters by inspection within the preceding three years); (3) none of the applicant's employees who will be authorized to possess explosive materials is an excluded person; and (4) in the case of a limited permit, the applicant has certified that the applicant will not receive explosive materials on more than six separate occasions during the

12-month period for which the limited permit is valid. Authorizes the Secretary to inspect the storage places of an applicant for or holder of a limited permit only as provided under the code. Requires the Secretary of the Treasury to approve or deny an application for licenses and permits within 90 days.

Requires the Secretary: (1) upon receiving from an employer the name and other identifying information with respect to a person or an employee who will be authorized to possess explosive materials, to determine whether such person or employee is an excluded person; (2) upon determining that such person or employee is not an excluded person, to notify the employer and to issue to the person or employee a letter of clearance confirming the determination; and (3) upon determining that such person or employee is an excluded person, to notify the employer and issue to such person or employee a document that confirms the determination, explains the grounds, provides information on how the disability may be relieved, and explains how the determination may be appealed.

(Sec. 1123) Includes among aliens who may lawfully receive or possess explosive materials any alien who is in lawful non-immigrant status, is a refugee admitted under the INA, or i3s in asylum status under the INA and who is: (1) a foreign law enforcement officer of a friendly government; (2) a person having the power to direct the management and policies of a corporation; (3) a member of a North Atlantic Treaty Organization or other friendly foreign military force; or (4) lawfully present in the United States in cooperation with the DCI and the shipment, transportation, receipt, or possession of the explosive materials is in furtherance of such cooperation.

(Sec. 1124) Requires: (1) licensed manufacturers, licensed importers, and those who manufacture or import explosive materials or ammonium nitrate to furnish samples and relevant information when required by the Secretary; and (2) the Secretary to authorize reimbursement of the fair market value of samples furnished, as well as reasonable shipment costs.

(Sec. 1125) Sets penalties for the destruction of property of institutions receiving Federal financial assistance.

(Sec. 1127) Requires a holder of a license or permit to report any theft of explosive materials to the Secretary not later than 24 hours after discovery. Sets penalties for failure to report.

(Sec. 1128) Authorizes appropriations.

Title XII: Airline War Risk Insurance Legislation— (Sec. 1201) Amends Federal aviation law to extend the period during which the Secretary of Transportation may certify an air carrier as a victim of terrorism (and thus subject to the $100 million limit on aggregate third-party claims) for acts of terrorism from September 22, 2001, through December 31, 2003.

(Sec. 1202) Directs the Secretary of Transportation to extend through August 31, 2003, and authorizes the Secretary to extend through December 31, 2003, the termination date of any insurance policy that the Department of Transportation (DOT) issues to an American aircraft or foreign-flag aircraft against loss or damage arising out of any risk from operation, and that is in effect on enactment of this Act, on no less favorable terms to such air carrier than existed on June 19, 2002. Directs the Secretary, however, to amend such policy to add coverage for losses or injuries to aircraft hulls, passengers, and crew at the limits carried by air carriers for such losses and injuries as of such enactment, and at an additional premium comparable to the premium charged for third-party casualty under the policy.

Limits the total premium paid by an air carrier for such a policy to twice the premium it was paying for its third party policy as of June 19, 2002. Declares that coverage in such a policy shall begin with the first dollar of any covered loss incurred.

(Sec. 1204) Directs the Secretary of Transportation to report to specified congressional committees concerning: (1) the availability and cost of commercial war risk insurance for air carriers and other aviation entities for passengers and third parties; (2) the economic effect upon such carriers and entities of available commercial war risk insurance; and (3) the manner in which DOT could provide an alternative means of providing aviation war risk reinsurance covering passengers, crew, and third parties through use of a risk-retention group or by other means.

Title XIII: Federal Workforce Improvement—Subtitle A: Chief Human Capital Officers—Chief Human Capital Officers Act of 2002—(Sec. 1302) Requires the heads of Federal departments and agencies currently required to a have Chief Financial Officer to appoint or designate a Chief Human Capital Officer to: (1) advise and assist agency officials in selecting, developing, training, and managing a high-quality, productive workforce in accordance with merit system principles; and (2) implement the rules and regulations of the President and the Office of OPM and civil service laws.

Requires such Officer's functions to include: (1) setting the agency's workforce development strategy; (2) assessing workforce characteristics and future needs; (3) aligning the agency's human resources policies and programs with organization mission, strategic goals, and performance outcomes; (4) developing and advocating a culture of continuous learning to attract and retain employees with superior abilities; (5) identifying best practices and benchmarking studies; and (6) applying methods for measuring intellectual capital and identifying links of that capital to organizational performance and growth.

(Sec. 1303) Establishes a Chief Human Capital Officers Council (consisting of the Director of OPM, the Deputy Director for Management of the Office of Management and Budget, and the Chief Human Capital Officers of executive departments and other members designated by the Director of OPM) to advise and coordinate the activities of the agencies of its members on such matters as modernization of human resources systems, improved quality of human resources information, and legislation affecting human resources operations and organizations.

(Sec. 1304) Directs OPM to design a set of systems, including metrics, for assessing the management of human capital by Federal agencies.

Subtitle B: Reforms Relating to Federal Human Capital Management—(Sec. 1311) Requires each agency's: (1) performance plan to describe how its performance goals and objectives are to be achieved; and (2) program performance report to include a review of the goals and evaluation of the plan relative to the agency's strategic human capital management.

(Sec. 1312) Authorizes the President to prescribe rules which grant authority for agencies to appoint candidates directly to certain positions for which there exists a severe candidate shortage or a critical hiring need.

Allows OPM to establish quality category rating systems for evaluating applicants for competitive service positions under two or more quality categories based on merit rather than numerical ratings. Requires agencies that establish a quality category rating system to report to Congress on that system, including information on the number of employees hired, the impact that system has had on the hiring of veterans and minorities, and the way in which managers were trained in the administration of it.

(Sec. 1313) Sets forth provisions governing Federal employee voluntary separation incentive payments. Requires each agency, before obligating any resources for such payments, to submit to OPM for modification and approval a plan outlining the intended use of such payments and a proposed organizational chart for the agency once such payments have been completed. Requires such plan to include the positions and functions affected, the categories of employees to be offered such payments, the timing and amounts of payments, and how the agency will subsequently operate. Limits voluntary separation incentive payments to the lesser of: (1) the amount of severance pay to which an employee would be entitled; or (2) an amount determined by the agency head, not to exceed $25,000. Sets forth provisions regarding the repayment and waiver of repayment of such incentive payments upon subsequent employment with the Government. Authorizes the Director of the Administrative Office of the United States Courts to establish a substantially similar program for the judicial branch. Continues existing voluntary separation incentives authority until expiration.

Amends Federal employee early retirement provisions to apply to employees who are: (1) voluntarily separated by an agency undergoing substantial delayering, reorganization, reductions in force, functions transfer, or workforce restructuring; or (2) identified as being in positions that are becoming surplus or excess to the agency's future ability to carry out its mission effectively; and (3) within the scope of the offer of voluntary early retirement on the basis of specific periods or such employee's organizational unit, occupational series, geographical location, and/or skills, knowledge, and other factors related to a position. Expresses the sense of Congress that the implementation of this section is intended to reshape, and not downsize, the Federal workforce.

(Sec. 1314) Includes students who provide voluntary services for the Government as "employees" for purposes of provisions authorizing agency programs to encourage employees to commute by means other than single-occupancy motor vehicles.

Subtitle C: Reforms Relating to the Senior Executive Service—(Sec. 1321) Repeals recertification requirements for senior executives.

(Sec. 1322) Changes the limitation on total annual compensation (basic pay and cash payments) from the annual rate of basic pay payable for level I of the Executive Schedule to the total annual compensation payable to the Vice President for certain senior level executive and judicial employees who hold a position in or under an agency that has been certified as having a performance appraisal system which makes meaningful distinctions based on relative performance.

Subtitle D: Academic Training—(Sec. 1331) Revises agency academic degree training criteria to allow agencies to select and assign employees to academic degree training and to pay and reimburse such training costs if such training: (1) contributes significantly to meeting an agency training need, resolving an agency staffing problem, or accomplishing goals in the agency's strategic plan; (2) is part of a planned, systemic, and coordinated agency employee development program linked to accomplishing such goals; and (3) is accredited and is provided by a college or university that is accredited by a nationally recognized body.

(Sec. 1332) Amends the David L. Boren National Security Education Act of 1991 to modify service agreement requirements for recipients of scholarships and fellowships under the National Security Education Program to provide for recipients to work in other Federal offices or agencies when no national security position is available.

Title XIV: Arming Pilots Against Terrorism—Arming Pilots Against Terrorism Act—(Sec. 1402) Amends Federal law to direct the Under Secretary of Transportation for Security (in the Transportation Security Administration) to establish a two-year pilot program to: (1) deputize volunteer pilots of air carriers as Federal law enforcement officers to defend the flight decks of aircraft against acts of criminal violence or air piracy (Federal flight deck officers); and (2) provide training, supervision, and equipment for such officers.

Requires the Under Secretary to begin the process of training and deputizing qualified pilots to be Federal flight deck officers under the program. Allows the Under Secretary to request another Federal agency to deputize such officers.

Directs the Under Secretary to authorize flight deck officers to carry firearms and to use force, including lethal force, according to standards and circumstances the Under Secretary prescribes. Shields air carriers from liability for damages in Federal or State court arising out of a Federal flight deck officer's use of or failure to use a firearm. Shields flight deck officers from liability for acts or omissions in defending the flight deck of an aircraft against acts of criminal violence or air piracy, except in cases of gross negligence or willful misconduct.

Declares that if an accidental discharge of a firearm results in the injury or death of a passenger or crew member on the aircraft, the Under Secretary: (1) shall revoke the deputization of the responsible Federal flight deck officer if such discharge was attributable to the officer's negligence; and (2) may temporarily suspend the pilot program if the Under Secretary determines that a shortcoming in standards, training, or procedures was responsible for the accidental discharge.

Prohibits an air carrier from prohibiting a pilot from becoming a Federal flight deck officer, or threatening any retaliatory action against the pilot for doing so.

Declares the sense of Congress that the Federal air marshal program is critical to aviation security, and that nothing in this Act shall be construed as preventing the Under Secretary from implementing and training Federal air marshals.

(Sec. 1403) Directs the Under Secretary, in updating the guidance for training flight and cabin crews, to issue a rule to: (1) require both classroom and effective hands-on situational training in specified elements of self-defense; (2) require training in the proper conduct of a cabin search, including the duty time required to conduct it; (3) establish the required number of hours of training and the qualifications for training instructors; (4) establish the intervals, number of hours, and elements of recurrent training; (5) ensure that air carriers provide the initial training within 24 months of the enactment of this Act. Directs the Under Secretary to designate an official in the Transportation Security Administration to be responsible for overseeing the implementation of the training program; and (6) ensure that no person is required to participate in any hands-on training activity that such person believes will have an adverse impact on his or her health or safety.

Amends the Aviation and Transportation Security Act to authorize the Under Secretary to take certain enhanced security measures, including to require that air carriers provide flight attendants with a discreet, hands-free, wireless method of communicating with the pilot of an aircraft.

Directs the Under Secretary to study and report to Congress on the benefits and risks of providing flight attendants with nonlethal weapons to aide in combating air piracy and criminal violence on commercial airlines.

(Sec. 1404) Directs the Secretary of Transportation to study and report within six months to Congress on: (1) the number of armed Federal law enforcement officers (other than Federal air marshals) who travel on commercial airliners annually, and the frequency of their travel; (2) the cost and resources necessary to provide such officers with supplemental aircraft anti-terrorism training comparable to the training that Federal air marshals receive; (3) the cost of establishing a program at a Federal law enforcement training center for the purpose of providing new Federal law enforcement recruits with standardized training comparable to Federal air marshal training; (4) the feasibility of implementing a certification program designed to ensure that Federal law enforcement officers have completed aircraft anti-terrorism training, and track their travel over a six-month period; and (5) the feasibility of staggering the flights of such officers to ensure the maximum amount of flights have a certified trained Federal officer on board.

(Sec. 1405) Amends Federal aviation law to require the Under Secretary to respond within 90 days of receiving a request from an air carrier for authorization to allow pilots of the air carrier to carry less-than-lethal weapons.

Title XV: Transition—Subtitle A: Reorganization Plan— (Sec. 1502) Requires the President, within 60 days after enactment of this Act, to transmit to the appropriate congressional committees a reorganization plan regarding: (1) the transfer of agencies, personnel, assets, and obligations to DHS pursuant to this Act; and (2) any consolidation, reorganization, or streamlining of agencies transferred to DHS pursuant to this Act.

(Sec. 1503) Expresses the sense of Congress that each House of Congress should review its committee structure in light of the reorganization of responsibilities within the executive branch by the establishment of DHS.

Subtitle B: Transitional Provisions—(Sec. 1511) Outlines transitional provisions with regard to assistance from officials having authority before the effective date of this Act; details of personnel and services to assist in the transition; acting officials during the transition period; the transfer of personnel, assets, obligations and functions; and the status of completed administrative actions, pending proceedings and civil actions, and Inspector General oversight. Prohibits DHS use of any funds derived from the Highway Trust Fund, the Airport and Airway Trust Fund, the Inland Waterway Trust Fund, or the Harbor Maintenance Trust Fund, with a specified exception for certain security-related funds provided to the Federal Aviation Administration.

(Sec. 1514) Provides that nothing in this Act shall be construed to authorize the development of a national identification system or card.

(Sec. 1516) Authorizes and directs the Director of OMB to make additional necessary incidental dispositions of personnel, assets, and liabilities in connection with the functions transferred by this Act.

Title XVI: Corrections to Existing Law Relating to Airline Transportation Security—(Sec. 1601) Amends Federal aviation law to require the Administrator of the Federal Aviation Administration (FAA), along with the Under Secretary of Transportation for Security, to each conduct research (including behavioral research) and development activities to develop, modify, test, and evaluate a system, procedure, facility, or device to protect passengers and property against acts of criminal violence, aircraft piracy, and terrorism and to ensure security.

Directs the Secretary of Transportation (currently, the Under Secretary) to prescribe regulations prohibiting disclosure of information obtained or developed in ensuring security under this section if the Secretary of Transportation decides disclosing such information would: (1) be an unwarranted invasion of personal privacy; (2) reveal a trade secret or privileged or confidential commercial or financial information; or (3) be detrimental to the safety of passengers in transportation. Sets forth similar provisions requiring the Under Secretary to prescribe regulations prohibiting the disclosure of information obtained or developed in carrying out security under authority of the Aviation and Transportation Security Act (PL107-71).

(Sec. 1602) Increases the maximum civil penalty to $25,000 for a person who violates certain aviation security requirements while operating an aircraft for the transportation of passengers or property for compensation (except an individual serving as an airman).

(Sec. 1603) Revises certain hiring security screener standards to allow a national (currently, only a citizen) of the United States to become a security screener.

Title XVII: Conforming and Technical Amendments— (Sec. 1701) Sets forth technical and conforming amendments.

(Sec. 1706) Transfers from the Administrator of General Services to the Secretary of Homeland Security law enforcement authority for the protection of Federal property.

(Sec. 1708) Establishes in DOD a National Bio-Weapons Defense Analysis Center to develop countermeasures to potential attacks by terrorists using weapons of mass destruction.

(Sec. 1714) Amends the Public Health Service Act to define "vaccine" to mean any preparation or suspension, including one containing an attenuated or inactive microorganism or toxin, developed or administered to produce or enhance the body's immune response to a disease and to include all components and ingredients listed in the vaccine's product license application and product label.

Appendix 4: List of State Emergency Management Offices

Alabama Emergency Management Agency
5898 County Road 41
P.O. Drawer 2160
Clanton, Alabama 35046-2160
1-205-280-2200
1-205-280-2495 FAX
http://www.aema.state.al.us/

Alaska Division of Emergency Services
P.O. Box 5750
Fort Richardson, Alaska 99505-5750
1-907-428-7000
1-907-428-7009 FAX
http://www.ak-prepared.com

American Samoa Territorial Emergency
   Management Coordination (TEMCO)
American Samoa Government
P.O. Box 1086
Pago Pago, American Samoa 96799
1-011-684-699-6415
1-011-684-699-6414 FAX

Arizona Division of Emergency Management
5636 E. McDowell Road
Phoenix, Arizona 85008
(602) 244-0504 or 1-800-411-2336
http://www.dem.state.az.us

Arkansas Department of Emergency Management
P.O. Box 758
Conway, Arkansas 72033
1-501-730-9750
1-501-730-9754 FAX
http://www.adem.state.ar.us

California Governor's Office of Emergency Services
P.O. Box 419047
Rancho Cordova, California 95741-9047
1-916-845-8510
1-916-845-8511 FAX
http://www.oes.ca.gov/

Colorado Office of Emergency Management
Division of Local Government
Department of Local Affairs
15075 South Golden Road
Golden, Colorado 80401-3979
1-303-273-1622
1-303-273-1795 FAX
www.dola.state.co.us/oem/oemindex.htm

Connecticut Office of Emergency Management
Military Department
360 Broad Street
Hartford, Connecticut 06105
1-860-566-3180
1-860-247-0664 FAX
http://www.mil.state.ct.us/OEM.htm

Delaware Emergency Management Agency
165 Brick Store Landing Road
Smyrna, Delaware 19977
1-302-659-3362
1-302-659-6855 FAX
http://www.state.de.us/dema/index.htm

District of Columbia Emergency Management Agency
2000 14th Street, NW, 8th Floor
Washington, DC 20009
1-202-727-6161
1-202-673-2290 FAX
http://www.dcema.dc.gov

Florida Division of Emergency Management
2555 Shumard Oak Boulevard
Tallahassee, Florida 32399-2100
1-850-413-9969
1-850-488-1016 FAX
www.floridadisaster.org

Georgia Emergency Management Agency
P.O. Box 18055
Atlanta, Georgia 30316-0055
1-404-635-7000

1-404-635-7205 FAX
http://www.State.Ga.US/GEMA/

Office of Civil Defense
Government of Guam
P.O. Box 2877
Hagatna, Guam 96932
1-011-671-475-9600
1-011-671-477-3727 FAX
http://ns.gov.gu

Guam Homeland Security/Office of Civil Defense
221B Chalan Palasyo
Agana Heights, Guam 96910
1-671-475-9600
1-671-477-3727 FAX

Hawaii State Civil Defense
3949 Diamond Head Road
Honolulu, Hawaii 96816-4495
1-808-733-4300
1-808-733-4287 FAX
http://www.scd.state.hi.us

Idaho Bureau of Disaster Services
4040 Guard Street, Building 600
Boise, Idaho 83705-5004
1-208-334-3460
1-208-334-2322 FAX
http://www.state.id.us/bds/bds.html

Illinois Emergency Management Agency
110 East Adams Street
Springfield, Illinois 62701
1-217-782-2700
1-217-524-7967 FAX
http://www.state.il.us/iema

Indiana State Emergency Management Agency
302 West Washington Street
Room E-208 A
Indianapolis, Indiana 46204-2767
1-317-232-3986
1-317-232-3895 FAX
http://www.ai.org/sema/index.html

Iowa Division of Emergency Management
Department of Public Defense
Hoover Office Building
Des Moines, Iowa 50319
1-641-281-3231
1-641-281-7539 FAX
http://www.state.ia.us/government/dpd/emd/index.htm

Kansas Division of Emergency Management
2800 S.W. Topeka Boulevard
Topeka, Kansas 66611-1287
1-785-274-1401
1-785-274-1426 FAX
http://www.ink.org/public/kdem

Kentucky Emergency Management
EOC Building
100 Minuteman Parkway Building. 100
Frankfort, Kentucky 40601-6168
1-502-607-1682
1-502-607-1614 FAX
http://kyem.dma.state.ky.us

Louisiana Office of Emergency Preparedness
7667 Independence Boulevard
Baton Rouge, Louisiana 70806
1-225-925-7500
1-225-925-7501 FAX
http://www.loep.state.la.us

Maine Emergency Management Agency
State Office Building, Station 72
Augusta, Maine 04333
1-207-626-4503
1-207-626-4499 FAX
http://www.state.me.us/mema/memahome.htm

CNMI Emergency Management Office
Office of the Governor
Commonwealth of the Northern Mariana Islands
P.O. Box 10007
Saipan, Mariana Islands 96950
1-670-322-9529
1-670-322-7743 FAX
http://www.cnmiemo.org/

National Disaster Management Office
Office of the Chief Secretary
P.O. Box 15
Majuro, Republic of the Marshall Islands
    96960-0015
1-011-692-625-5181
1-011-692-625-6896 FAX

Maryland Emergency Management Agency
Camp Fretterd Military Reservation
5401 Rue Saint Lo Drive
Reistertown, Maryland 21136
1-410-517-3600
1-877-636-2872 Toll-Free

1-410-517-3610 FAX
http://www.mema.state.md.us

Massachusetts Emergency Management Agency
400 Worcester Road
Framingham, Massachusetts 01702-5399
1-508-820-2000
1-508-820-2030 FAX
http://www.state.ma.us/mema

Michigan Division of Emergency Management
4000 Collins Road
P.O. Box 30636
Lansing, Michigan 48909-8136
1-517-333-5042
1-517-333-4987 FAX
http://www.michigan.gov/msp/1,1607,7-123-1593_
3507—,00.html

National Disaster Control Officer
Federated States of Micronesia
P.O. Box PS-53
Kolonia, Pohnpei—Micronesia 96941
1-011-691-320-8815
1-001-691-320-2785 FAX

Minnesota Division of Emergency Management
Department of Public Safety
Suite 223
444 Cedar Street
St. Paul, Minnesota 55101-6223
1-651-296-2233
1-651-296-0459 FAX
http://www.dps.state.mn.us/emermgt/

Mississippi Emergency Management Agency
P.O. Box 4501—Fondren Station
Jackson, Mississippi 39296-4501
1-601-352-9100
1-800-442-6362 Toll Free
1-601-352-8314 FAX
http://www.mema.state.ms.us
http://www.memaorg.com

Missouri Emergency Management Agency
P.O. Box 16
2302 Militia Drive
Jefferson City, Missouri 65102
1-573-526-9100
1-573-634-7966 FAX
http://www.sema.state.mo.us/semapage.htm

Montana Division of Disaster & Emergency Services
1100 North Main
P.O. Box 4789
Helena, Montana 59604-4789
1-406-841-3911
1-406-444-3965 FAX
http://www.state.mt.us/dma/des/index.shtml

Nebraska Emergency Management Agency
1300 Military Road
Lincoln, Nebraska 68508-1090
1-402-471-7410
1-402-471-7433 FAX
http://www.nebema.org

Nevada Division of Emergency Management
2525 South Carson Street
Carson City, Nevada 89711
1-775-687-4240
1-775-687-6788 FAX
http://dem.state.nv.us/

Governor's Office of Emergency Management
State Office Park South
107 Pleasant Street
Concord, New Hampshire 03301
1-603-271-2231
1-603-225-7341 FAX

New Jersey Office of Emergency Management
Emergency Management Bureau
P.O. Box 7068
West Trenton, New Jersey 08628-0068
1-609-538-6050 Monday–Friday
1-609-882-2000 ext 6311 (24/7)
1-609-538-0345 FAX
http://www.state.nj.us/oem/county

New Mexico Department of Public Safety
Office of Emergency Services & Security
P.O. Box 1628
13 Bataan Boulevard
Santa Fe, New Mexico 87505
1-505-476-9600
1-505-476-9695 FAX
http://www.dps.nm.org/emergency/index.htm

Emergency Management Bureau
Department of Public Safety
P.O. Box 1628
13 Bataan Boulevard
Santa Fe, New Mexico 87505

1-505-476-9606
1-505-476-9650
http://www.dps.nm.org/emc.htm

New York State Emergency Management Office
1220 Washington Avenue
Building 22, Suite 101
Albany, New York 12226-2251
1-518-457-2222
1-518-457-9995 FAX
http://www.nysemo.state.ny.us/

North Carolina Division of Emergency Management
116 West Jones Street
Raleigh, North Carolina 27603
1-919-733-3867
1-919-733-5406 FAX
http://www.dem.dcc.state.nc.us/

North Dakota Division of Emergency Management
P.O. Box 5511
Bismarck, North Dakota 58506-5511
1-701-328-8100
1-701-328-8181 FAX
http://www.state.nd.us/dem

Ohio Emergency Management Agency
2855 W. Dublin Granville Road
Columbus, Ohio 43235-2206
1-614-889-7150
1-614-889-7183 FAX
http://www.state.oh.us/odps/division/ema

Office of Civil Emergency Management
Will Rogers Sequoia Tunnel 2401 N. Lincoln
Oklahoma City, Oklahoma 73152
1-405-521-2481
1-405-521-4053 FAX
http://www.odcem.state.ok.us/

Oregon Emergency Management
Department of State Police
595 Cottage Street, NE
Salem, Oregon 97310
1-503-378-2911 ext. 225
1-503-588-1378
http://www.osp.state.or.us/oem/oem.htm

Palau NEMO Coordinator
Office of the President
P.O. Box 100

Koror, Republic of Palau 96940
1-011-680-488-2422
1-011-680-488-3312

Pennsylvania Emergency Management Agency
P.O. Box 3321
Harrisburg, Pennsylvania 17105-3321
1-717-651-2001
1-717-651-2040 FAX
http://www.pema.state.pa.us

Puerto Rico Emergency Management Agency
P.O. Box 966597
San Juan, Puerto Rico 00906-6597
1-787-724-0124
1-787-725-4244 FAX

Rhode Island Emergency Management Agency
645 New London Avenue
Cranston, Rhode Island 02920-3003
1-401-946-9996
1-401-944-1891 FAX
http://www.state.ri.us/riema/riemaaa.html

South Carolina Emergency Management Division
1100 Fish Hatchery Road
West Columbia South Carolina 29172
1-803-737-8500
1-803-737-8570 FAX
http://www.state.sc.us/epd

South Dakota Division of Emergency Management
500 East Capitol
Pierre, South Dakota 57501-5070
1-605-773-6426
1-605-773-3580 FAX
http://www.state.sd.us/state/executive/military/sddem.htm

Tennessee Emergency Management Agency
3041 Sidco Drive
Nashville, Tennessee 37204-1502
1-615-741-4332
1-615-242-9635 FAX
http://www.tnema.org

Texas Division of Emergency Management
5805 N. Lamar
Austin, Texas 78752
1-512-424-2138
1-512-424-2444 or 7160 FAX
http://www.txdps.state.tx.us/dem/

Utah Division of Emergency Services and
   Homeland Security
1110 State Office Building
P.O. Box 141710
Salt Lake City, Utah 84114-1710
1-801-538-3400
1-801-538-3770 FAX

Vermont Emergency Management Agency
Department of Public Safety
Waterbury State Complex
103 South Main Street
Waterbury, Vermont 05671-2101
1-802-244-8721
1-802-244-8655 FAX
http://www.dps.state.vt.us

Virgin Islands Territorial Emergency Management—
   VITEMA
2-C Contant, A-Q Building
Virgin Islands 00820
1-340-774-2244
1-340-774-1491

Virginia Department of Emergency Management
10501 Trade Court
Richmond, VA 23236-3713
1-804-897-6502
1-804-897-6506
http://www.vdem.state.va.us

State of Washington Emergency Management
   Division
Building 20, M/S: TA-20
Camp Murray, Washington 98430-5122
1-253-512-7000
1-253-512-7200 FAX
http://www.emd.wa.gov

West Virginia Office of Emergency Services
Building 1, Room EB-80, 1900 Kanawha
   Boulevard, East
Charleston, West Virginia 25305-0360
1-304-558-5380
1-304-344-4538 FAX
http://www.state.wv.us/wvoes

Wisconsin Emergency Management
2400 Wright Street
P.O. Box 7865
Madison, Wisconsin 53707-7865
1-608-242-3232
1-608-242-3247 FAX
http://emergencymanagement.wi.gov/

Wyoming Emergency Management Agency
5500 Bishop Boulevard
Cheyenne, Wyoming 82009-3320
1-307-777-4920
1-307-635-6017 FAX
http://wema.state.wy.us

Appendix 5: List of State Homeland Security Contacts

Alabama
James Walker
Homeland Security Director
Alabama Office of Homeland Security
401 Adams Ave., Suite 560
Montgomery, AL 36103-5690
1-334-353-0242
1-334-353-0606 FAX

Alaska
BG Craig Campbell
Box 5800
Ft. Richardson, AK 99505-0800
1-907-428-6003
www.ak-prepared.com/homelandsecurity

Arizona
Frank Navarette, Homeland Security Director
1700 West Washington Street, 3rd Floor
Phoenix, AZ 85007

Arkansas
Jack Dubose
Interim Director
Box 758
Conway, AR 72033
1-501-730-9750
www.adem.state.ar.us

California
George Vinson
Special Advisor on State Security
State Capitol, First Floor
Sacramento, CA 95814
1-916-324-8908

Colorado
Sue Mencer
Executive Director, CO Dept of Public Safety
700 Kipling Street
Denver, CO 80215
1-303-273-1770

Connecticut
Vincent DeRosa
Deputy Commissioner, Division of Protective
  Services
55 West Main St., Suite 500
Waterbury, CT 06702
1-203-805-6600
www.state.ct.us/dps/PS/index.htm
DPS.Feedback@po.state.ct.us

Delaware
Phil Cabaud
Homeland Security Director
Office of the Governor
Tatnall Building 2nd Floor
William Penn Street
Dover, DE 19901
1-302-744-4242

District of Columbia
Margret Nedelkoff Kellems
Deputy Mayor for Public Safety and Justice
1-202-727-4036
http://washintondc.gov

Florida
Daryl McLaughlin
Interim Commissioner, Florida Dept. of Law
  Enforcement
Box 1489
Tallahassee, FL 32302-1489
1-850-410-7233
www.fdle.state.fl.us

Georgia
Bill Hitchens
Director of Homeland Security
P.O. Box 1456
Atlanta, GA 30371
1-404-624-7030
www.gahomelandsecurity.com/

Hawaii
BG Robert Lee
Adjutant General
3949 Diamond Head Rd.
Honolulu, HI 96816-4495
1-808-733-4246
www.scd.state.hi.us

Idaho
MG Jack Kane
Adjutant General
4040 West Guard Street
Boise, ID 83705-5004
1-208-422-5242
www.state.id.us/government/executive.html

Illinois
Carl Hawkinson
Homeland Security Advisor
207 State House
Springfield, IL 62706
1-217-524-1486

Indiana
Clifford Ong
Director, Indiana Counterterrorism and Security
  Council
100 North Senate Avenue
Indianappolis, IN 46204
1-317-232-8303
www.in.gov/c-tasc

Iowa
Ellen Gordon
Administrator, Emergency Management
Hoover State Office Bldg.
1305 E. Walnut
Des Moines, IA 50319
1-515-281-3231
www.iowahomelandsecurity.org

Kansas
MG Gregory Gardner
Adjutant General
2800 SW Topeka
Topeka, KS, 66611-1287
1-785-274-1121-1109

Kentucky
BG D. Allen Youngman
Adjutant General

100 Minutemen Parkway
Frankfurt, KY 40601-6168
1-502-607-1257
http://homeland.state.ky.us

Louisiana
MG Bennett C. Landreneau
Adjutant General and Director
Louisiana Office of Emergency Preparedness
7667 Independence Blvd.
Baton Rouge, LA 70806
1-225-925-7333

Maine
MG Joseph Tinkham, II
Adjutant General
Homeland Security
1 State House Station
Augusta, ME 04333-0001
1-207-626-4440 (normal working hours)

Maryland
Thomas J. Lockwood
Homeland Security Director
State House, 100 State Circle
Annapolis, MD 21401
1-410-974-3901
www.mema.state.md.us

Massachusetts
Richard Swensen
Office of Commonwealth Security
Executive Office of Public Safety
1 Ashburton Place, Rm. 2133
Boston, MA 02108
1-617-727-3600 extension 556

Michigan
COL Tadarial Sturdivant
Director of State Police
Contact: Capt. John Ort
713 South Harrison Rd.
E. Lansing, MI 48823
517-336-6198
www.msp.state.mi.us

Minnesota
Rich Stanek
Commissioner of Public Safety and Homeland
  Security Director
DPS, North Central Life Tower

445 Minnesota St., St. 1000
St. Paul, MN 55101
dps.state.mn.us/homelandsecurity/index.htm

Mississippi
Robert Latham
Executive Director, Mississippi Emergency
  Management Agency
P.O. Box 4501
Jackson, MS 39296-4501
1-601-960-9999
www.homelandsecurity.ms.gov

Missouri
Col. Tim Daniel
Special Adviser for Homeland Security
P.O. Box 809
Jefferson City, MO 65102
1-573-522-3007
www.homelandsecurity.state.mo.us

Montana
Jim Greene
Administrator, Disaster and Emergency Services
Department of Military Affairs HAFRC
Montana Disaster and Emergency Services
1900 Williams Street
P.O. Box 4789
Helena, MT 59604-4789
1-406-841-3911
www.discoveringmontana.com/css/default.asp

Nebraska
Lieutenant Governor Dave Heineman
P.O. Box 94848
Lincoln, NE 68509-4848
1-402-471-2256
dave.heineman@email.state.ne.us

Nevada
Jerry Bussell
Homeland Security Director
2525 S. Carson St.
Carson City, NV 89710
1-775-687-7320

New Hampshire
Donald Bliss
Director, Emergency Management and State
  Fire Marshal
10 Hazen Drive

Concord, NH 03305
1-603-271-3294

New Jersey
Sidney Caspersen, Director
N.J. Office of Counterterrorism
P.O. Box 091
Trenton, NJ 08625
1-609-341-3434
www.njcounterterrorism.org

New Mexico
Annette Sobel M.D., M.S.
Brigadier General
NM Homeland Security Director
P.O. Box 1628
Santa Fe, NM 87507-1628
1-505-476-0267

New York
Mark Cohen
Acting Director, Office of Public Security
Executive Chamber
633 3rd Ave, 38th Floor
NY, NY 10017
1-212-867-7060
info@security.state.ny.us

North Carolina
Bryan Beatty
Secretary, Dept. of Crime Control and
  Public Safety
4701 Mail Service Center
Raleigh, NC 27699
1-919-733-2126
www.ncgov.com/asp.subpages/safety_security.asp

North Dakota
Doug Friez
Homeland Security Coordinator/Emergency
  Management Director
Fraine Barracks Ln., Bldg. 35
Fraine Barracks
Bismark, ND 58504
1-701-328-8100
www.state.nd.us/dem/homesec.html

Ohio
Kenneth L. Morckel
Director of Public Safety
1970 W. Broad St.

Columbus, OH 43223-1102
1-614-466-4344
www.state.oh.us/odps/sos/ohshome.htm

Oklahoma
Bob A. Ricks
Director
Oklahoma Office of Homeland Security
Box 11415
Oklahoma City, OK 73136-0415
Phone: 1-405-425-2001
Fax: 405-425-2324
okohs@dps.state.ok.us
www.youroklahoma.com/homelandsecurity

Oregon
Ronald C. Ruecker
Superintendent of Oregon State Police
400 Public Service Bldg.
Salem, OR 97310
1-503-378-3725

Pennsylvania
Keith Martin
Director, Pennsylvania Office of Homeland Security
2605 Interstate Drive
Harrisburg, PA 17110
1-717-651-2715
www.homelandsecurity.state.pa.us

Puerto Rico
Annabelle Rodriguez
Attorney General
La Fortaleza
P.O. Box 9020082
San Juan, PR 00902-0082
1-787-721-7700

Rhode Island
MG Reginald Centracchio
Adjutant General
222 State House
Providence, RI 02903
1-401-275-4102

South Carolina
Robert M. Stewart
Chief, S.C. Law Enforcement Division (SLED)
P.O. Box 21398
Columbia, SC 29221-1398
1-803-737-9000

South Dakota
John A. Berheim, Director
Division of Emergency Management
500 East Capitol Avenue
Pierre, SD 57501
1-866-homland

Tennessee
MG (Ret.) Jerry Humble
215 Eighth Avenue, North
Nashville, TN 37203
1-615-532-7825

Texas
Jay Kimbrough
Deputy Attorney General for Criminal Justice
P.O. Box 12428
Austin, TX 78711
1-512-936-1882

Utah
Scott Behunin
Division Director, Comprehensive Emergency
    Management
210 State Capitol
Salt Lake City, UT 84114
1-801-538-3400
www.cem.utah.gov

Vermont
Kerry Sleeper
Commissioner, VT State Police
103 South Main Street
Waterbury, VT 05671-2101
1-802-244-8775

Virginia
Assistant to the Governor for Commonwealth Preparedness
John Hager
202 N. 9th Street, 5th Floor
Richmond, VA 23219
1-804-225-3826
http://www.commonwealthpreparedness.state.va.us

Washington
MG Timothy J. Lowenberg
Adjutant General and Director
State Military Department
Washington Military Dept., Bldg. 1
Camp Murray, WA 98430-5000
1-253-512-8201

West Virginia
Joe Martin
Secretary, Dept. of Military Affairs and Public Safety
State Capitol Complex, Bldg. 6, Rm. B-122
Charleston, WV 25305
1-304-558-2930

Wisconsin
Ed Gleason
Administrator, Emergency Management
P.O. Box 7865
Madison, WI 53707-7865
1-608-242-3210
www.wisconsin.gov/state/core/domestic_prep.html

Wyoming
Joe Moore, Director
Governor's Office of Homeland Security
TAG Office—5500 Bishop Blvd.
Cheyenne, WY 82009-3320
1-307-772-5234

Guam
Frank Blas
Homeland Security Advisor
P.O. Box 2950

Hagatna, GU 96932
1-671-475-9600/9602

Northern Mariana Islands
Jerry Crisostomo
Special Advisor for Homeland Security
Caller Box 10007
Saipan, MP 96950
1-670-664-2280

Virgin Islands
MG Cleave A. McBean
Adjutant General
21-22 Kongens Gade
St. Thomas, VI 00802
1-340-712-7711

American Samoa
Leiataua Birdsall V. Ala'ilima
Special Assistant to the Governor
Office of Territory Emergency Mgmt.
American Samoa Government
Pago, Pago, AS 96799
1-011-684-633-4116

Related Link
Map of Homeland Security State Contact List

Appendix 6: List of Corporation for National and Community Service (CNCS) Homeland Security Grantees

CORPORATION FOR NATIONAL AND COMMUNITY SERVICE GRANT RECIPIENTS FROM JULY 18, 2002

GRANT ANNOUNCEMENT—$10.3 MILLION TOTAL

ALABAMA

Colbert County Commission, $75,744
This new RSVP project will serve Colbert County, engaging 200 RSVP volunteers in assisting law enforcement, fire departments, and emergency management services. Volunteers will assist fire and law enforcement with clerical work, neighborhood and business watches, presentations on public safety, meetings on homeland security strategies, and volunteer recruitment. Partners include the County Health Department, the Tennessee Valley Authority, and the Northwest Alabama Regional Airport.

ALASKA

Municipality of Anchorage, $300,000
The Municipality of Anchorage Department of Health and Human Services will assist homebound seniors and an estimated 4,500 physically or developmentally disabled residents of Anchorage prepare to respond to a disaster. Various municipal agencies, the Office of Emergency Management, police and fire departments, American Red Cross, and the Police Chaplains Association will provide training and technical assistance in emergency preparedness and disaster response. Volunteers will act as instructors and will provide education, screening, and supplies to identified residents in need. Department staff will facilitate and coordinate the project by establishing and maintaining a database of the residents in need of these services.

CALIFORNIA

American Red Cross of Greater Los Angeles, $349,125

The American Red Cross, in partnership with the Governor's Office on Service and Volunteerism (GO SERV), will implement homeland security–related projects in Los Angeles, San Francisco, and Sacramento. Twenty-four AmeriCorps members will provide community disaster/emergency-preparedness education and training to individuals, families, and community- and faith-based organizations, including Neighborhood Watch and Citizen Corps groups, with an emphasis on seniors living in the Los Angeles, San Francisco, and Sacramento metropolitan areas. In addition to reaching 24,000 local residents, the AmeriCorps members will provide continuity and contingency planning assistance to 300 community- and faith-based organizations, schools, and businesses to increase their organizational capacity in the event of an emergency or disaster.

COLORADO

Valley Community Fund, $217,400
Valley Community Fund, in conjunction with the San Luis Valley American Red Cross, will develop the capacity of San Luis Valley citizens to become the first line of defense in case of emergencies and disasters. The project will mobilize 5,885 volunteer citizens throughout the San Luis Valley and will recruit and train 200 volunteers to support and sustain activities. The San Luis Valley American Red Cross is the only local volunteer group that, in response to disasters, supports firefighters, search-and-rescue crews, and law enforcement as well as the affected population. The project intends to educate one in four members of the community in order to develop citizens as the first line of defense. The intended outcome will be a community educated in disaster preparedness, schoolchildren educated in disaster preparedness and response, the establishment of trained disaster response teams of at least six people in all six counties, and nurses trained in first aid, CPR, and disaster health service.

CONNECTICUT

The American Radio Relay League, Inc., $181,900

The American Radio Relay League (ARRL) plans to expand its program to 5,200 certified emergency volunteers. ARRL is the national association for Amateur Radio and is the national leader in emergency communications by volunteers who operate their own equipment on their time at no cost to any government, organization, or corporation. The Certified Emergency Radio volunteers serve their local communities and work side by side with emergency medical teams, police and fire departments, and Offices of Emergency Management to stabilize communities with reliable emergency communications service. The Homeland Security Grant will allow the ARRL to train more volunteers by funding the Amateur Radio Emergency Communication Course, which will revise its training curriculum to ensure that new elements of emergency preparedness and homeland security are included.

DISTRICT OF COLUMBIA

Executive Office of the Mayor, $400,000

The Executive Office of the Mayor will recruit, train, and place 2,000 new volunteers in a capacity to support the city in homeland security activities. Placements will be in pre-existing organizations such as Emergency Medical Technician Corps and Volunteers in Police Service and will allow for their expansion. Volunteers will assist or develop local Neighborhood Watch Programs. Neighborhood Citizen Corps teams will be established, with Community Emergency Response Team (CERT) and volunteer management training. The project will strengthen homeland security through community building efforts, volunteer preparation for disaster response, and building and developing volunteer opportunities within the city.

Disaster Resistance Neighborhood Program—Red Cross, $99,174

Eight AmeriCorps members will serve with the Red Cross to develop Disaster Resistant Neighborhood Programs across eight wards encompassing 39 Advisory Neighborhood Commissions in the District. They will promote disaster safety through an organized effort at the neighborhood level, led by neighborhood volunteers. In addition to working with the wards' City Council members, ANC commissioners, and other community-based organizations, the AmeriCorps members will also participate on Disaster Action Teams and present community disaster education to volunteers. The eight members will form four teams of two; each team will be assigned to cover two wards.

FLORIDA

City of Orlando, $400,000

The City of Orlando will engage, train, and empower citizens in volunteer service to protect people and neighborhoods in the event of a disaster. The project will mobilize approximately 3,500 volunteers and will engage 1,400 new volunteers in three years. The city will establish a centralized Homeland Security Volunteer Office to coordinate homeland security training programs and recruit, screen, and track volunteers. Volunteers will partake in a homeland security certification program that will provide them with proficiency in assisting special populations, recruiting volunteers, and collaborating with community leaders on neighborhood disaster preparedness.

Florida Commission on Community Service, $328,000

The Florida Commission on Community Service will subgrant funds to Volunteer Florida. Volunteer Florida empowers volunteer centers throughout Florida to mobilize seniors and veterans to serve in local homeland security initiatives. The volunteer centers have seven program options to implement homeland security programs at the centers. Some programs include: Community Emergency Response Teams, which will be established or expanded according to center needs; Florida Division of Emergency Management's program to help small businesses become more disaster resistant; Event Watch, which will provide additional security for community events that are potential terrorist targets; and Front Porch Florida, which will engage underrepresented populations in implementing improvement programs in their communities.

Florida AmeriCorps Community Emergency Support Initiative, $434,000

Under this grant to the Florida Department of Community Affairs, the AmeriCorps Community Emergency Support Initiative will organize and assign five-member teams to each of the seven emergency management regions in the state. Along with the regional managers for emergency, they will create Citizen Emergency Response Teams. Members will be part of a "train the trainer" model that will multiply the capacity of the emergency management division in each region by training 150 trainers. In addition, members will recruit 1,000 volunteers and implement 70 projects, including weatherizing the homes of senior citizens and economically disadvantaged community residents in areas prone to natural disasters. Senior citizens and people with disabilities are a special target of this program, both as beneficiaries and as prospective volunteers.

Florida Department of Elder Affairs, $235,977
The Department of Elder Affairs will train 20 AmeriCorps members to educate elderly populations in disaster preparedness through community presentations in eight counties in north Florida. In addition, members will train schoolteachers in the use of American Red Cross curricula such as "Facing Fear" and "Masters of Disasters." Members will help to establish three joint volunteer centers working in education for managing disasters. The department will subgrant the program to the local American Red Cross to recruit and train members. The Red Cross plans to involve its community- and school-based partners. The chapter has memorandums of understanding with 25 community- and faith-based agencies, and the proposal states that the chapter plans to utilize its AmeriCorps members and volunteers to work with these agencies.

United Way of Central Florida, $81,772
This new RSVP project will serve Polk County, utilizing 150 RSVP volunteers to focus on disaster preparedness/response and Neighborhood Watch/public safety activities. Volunteers will receive Community Emergency Response Teams (CERT) training to improve community readiness, lead Crime Patrol and Neighborhood Watch patrols, provide administrative support to local deputy and fire offices, and inform neighborhoods on Red Cross Family Disaster Planning. Partners include fire departments, emergency management services, Freedom Corps, the American Red Cross, law enforcement, and public schools.

IOWA
Iowa Commission on Volunteer Service, $136,985
In a project established by the Iowa Commission on Volunteer Service, 16 AmeriCorps members will teach the Red Cross's "Masters of Disaster" and "Facing Fear" programs and other community disaster education materials to students in 28 school districts statewide to help them understand and cope with acts of terrorism and other disasters. The members will also use these materials to educate 320 community groups and will recruit a cadre of 40 volunteers to ensure the program's sustainability. Members will also recruit 200 additional volunteers to assist with service activities.

KENTUCKY
Kentucky Association of Senior Service Corps, $114,330
The Kentucky Association's RSVP project will mobilize 200 RSVP volunteers in five counties (Logan, Simpson, Warren, Calloway, and Graves) that are currently not served by RSVP. The project will focus on crime reduction, Neighborhood

Watch, and school safety, in addition to serving other community needs. Placement of volunteers will be in a variety of community organizations, including police departments, Red Cross chapters, health departments, school systems, and the Salvation Army.

Green River Development District, $123,800
The Green River Development District will operate its program in seven rural counties. AmeriCorps members will be placed in a number of rapid response agencies to educate 1,000 individuals about public safety, public health, and disaster preparedness issues; train 600 volunteers in disaster preparedness and relief; and assist in developing closer collaboration among local agencies in areas of disaster response, health service, and other related areas. Currently, Green River Development District has 18 AmeriCorps members serving who are trained in disaster preparedness and have previously provided disaster relief to the state.

MARYLAND
National Association of Community Health Centers, $434,000
The National Association of Community Health Centers will use its grant to establish the Community Emergency and Disaster Response Initiative at five sites across the country, with a total of 35 AmeriCorps members. The initiative's primary goal is to establish training and resources, disaster and emergency preparedness, and response and recovery strategies for community health center users and other residents in five communities. AmeriCorps members will be trained as trainers and equipped to use the Federal Emergency Management Agency's disaster preparedness curriculum in health centers. The grant will address the concerns revealed by a post-September 11 survey conducted by the association, which reported that 91 percent of the health centers are not adequately prepared for a public health emergency involving bioterrorism. The five sites are: San Francisco Community Clinic Consortium; Grace Hill Neighborhood Health Center, St. Louis, MO; Syracuse Community Health Center, Syracuse, NY; Unity Health Services, Washington, DC; and Michigan Primary Care Association, Okemos, MI.

Volunteer Frederick, Inc., $115,725
This new RSVP project will mobilize 550 volunteers to serve Frederick County, home to Camp David and Fort Detrick. The project's volunteers will work with 52 volunteer stations serving community needs through Neighborhood Watch/Public Safety, Disaster Preparedness/Response, Youth

Education, and Senior Assistance activities. Partners include law enforcement, fire departments, food banks, the YMCA, Big Brothers/Big Sisters, Safe Kids Coalition, the Red Cross, emergency management services, and hospitals. Some volunteers will train to become members of Disaster Action Teams, freeing up trained emergency workers, building disaster response infrastructure, and serving as administrative officers at fire departments. Other programs will include serving in the Sheriff's Office Community Assistance Patrol program and assisting the Frederick Memorial Hospital as liaisons in the Emergency Department.

Civic Works, Inc., $123,948

Civic Works, Inc., will use its grant to train AmeriCorps members in three areas: community outreach and education; volunteer recruitment and management; and disaster response activities. Members will disseminate public health, bioterrorism, and disaster preparedness information to 5,000 residents in Baltimore at community fairs, community association meetings, church groups, schools, and door-to-door. AmeriCorps members will also recruit and train 50 additional volunteers to help meet the program's goal of reaching 20,000 residents in 20 different communities. In the event of an emergency, members can also provide relief to rescue workers, search-and-rescue services, first aid, coordination of supplies, and other support to relief efforts.

MICHIGAN

Detroit Medical Center, $200,000

The Southeast Michigan Weapons of Mass Destruction, Bioterrorism and Disaster Preparedness Consortium will mobilize an estimated 6,000 volunteers. These volunteers will provide local preparedness planning, make Detroit a trauma-ready city by developing a readiness response team for bioterrorism, and focus on all aspects of health care and trauma services that may be needed in the event of a disaster. The strategies of the project include expansion of the community-wide immunization program, development and dissemination of public-health and disaster-preparedness information, and the continued staging of citywide disaster-preparedness trials. The Consortium comprises the fire, police, and EMS teams of Detroit, the Detroit Medical Center, Wayne State University School of Medicine, and the John D. Dingell/Veterans Administration Medical Center.

MINNESOTA

Community Net, $100,000

This new RSVP project, with 400 RSVP volunteers, will serve Olmsted, Goodhue, Rice, and Wabasha counties. Teams of volunteers will be trained to assist with the Public Health Emergency Response Plan and will participate in disaster response exercises to strengthen preparedness and conduct training in other counties. A group of volunteers will assist police, fire, and sheriff's offices with clerical work and ticketing, allowing trained professional personnel to respond to emergencies. Other volunteers will be trained as probation monitors, supervising clients and assisting probation staff with paperwork. Partners include the Olmsted County Public Health Department, the Red Cross, and social services.

MONTANA

Western Montana Area VI Agency on Aging, $104,266

This RSVP project will serve Lake, Mineral, and Ravalli counties, including the Flathead Indian Reservation that lies within Lake County. Some 254 RSVP volunteers will serve with volunteer stations working in Public Safety, Youth Crime, Disaster Response/Preparedness, Public Health, and Health Education activities. Volunteers will assist law enforcement in patrols, expand neighborhood watch groups, provide administrative assistance, develop strategy development plans, and man emergency management office dispatch services, freeing up staff time. The volunteers also will educate the public about the Rocky Mountain Laboratories, a biomedical research lab, to alleviate fear of the facility. Partners include the American Red Cross, Head Start, Kids First, YMCA, and Lake County Youth Court.

Richland County Health Department, $88,718

This new RSVP project will serve the sparsely populated northeastern area of Richland and McCone counties. RSVP will utilize 250 volunteers in homeland security activities through the Richmond Health Network. Volunteer teams will assist the Local Emergency Preparedness Committee in implementation of its emergency plan; work with law enforcement to develop Neighborhood Watch and community policing programs; and staff a Seniors Outreaching to Seniors program that will locate, assess the needs of, educate, and empower seniors and others with special needs related to emergency response. The Richland Health Network is a collaborative effort of the Richland County Health Department, the Sidney Health Center, and the County Commission on Aging.

NEW JERSEY

New Jersey Department of Education, $248,000

New Jersey's location close to New York City, along with the density and diversity of its population, make it a possible target for terrorist attacks. The grant will be used by the New Jersey Department of Education to establish the New Jersey Secure Corps, a statewide initiative with the main objective of creating and activating a Volunteer Organization Active in Disasters (VOAD) in each of the state's 21 counties. Each VOAD will function as the central coordination unit for disasters and emergencies. Members will make at least 20 community presentations to teach residents about bioterrorism and the ways in which they can prepare as a community for a bioterrorist attack. In addition, members will create a statewide database that will link all volunteers who have expressed an interest in becoming involved in disaster preparedness with organizations in the area, according to the volunteer's skills, availability, and geographic location.

NEW YORK

American Red Cross in Greater New York, $500,000

American Red Cross in Greater New York will recruit and train 310 leaders who will mobilize 5,000 coordinated volunteers with the ability to respond quickly, appropriately, and in effective ways should a disaster or another act of terrorism occur. For the training of leaders and mobilization of volunteers, the collaborative project will utilize the New York State Emergency Management Office, New York State Offices for Aging, the New York State Commission on National and Community Service, Retired and Senior Volunteer Programs of New York, Volunteer Organizations Active in Disaster, and the New York State Department of Education. The goal is to strengthen homeland security, log 3,600,000 hours of volunteer service in one year, and create Citizen Corps Councils.

Center for Court Innovation, $484,000

The New York City Public Safety Corps will enhance homeland security by assisting criminal justice officials (police, probation officers, judges) as they perform their duties by working directly with victims and by engaging local residents in solving neighborhood public safety problems. The project expands the New York Red Hook Public Safety Corps into other areas of New York City.

Forty full-time AmeriCorps members will address five principal objectives: to free up police, prosecutors and court staff to focus on pressing duties; to provide critical manpower support in case of an emergency; to address conditions of disorder that, if left unchecked, create a climate where crime would flourish; to build partnerships between criminal justice agencies and neighborhood residents, generating substantial neighborhood volunteers; and to be a visible presence in neighborhoods to communicate that someone who cares and helps is always nearby. Members will help identify community security concerns, develop new solutions to these concerns, and recruit volunteers to participate in projects addressing these concerns.

New York State Corps Collaboration, $293,760

With the New York State Corps Collaboration, 36 AmeriCorps members will serve to develop an infrastructure to address disaster preparation, mitigation, and response in the smaller towns in New York State. Some 36 members will serve in teams of 12 members each in three areas. In Component 1, 12 members assigned to host sites at Red Cross chapters across the state will assist Red Cross personnel and volunteers in emergency preparedness and receive training in Shelter Operations and Mass Care. In Component 2, 12 members will work to develop and strengthen Volunteer Organizations Active in Disaster in 12 areas to be determined by the Red Cross; members will survey existing resources and help build a database for local emergency management. In Component 3, 12 members will serve in one of the group's existing youth corps to identify, recruit, screen, and facilitate the training of 500 local volunteers.

Pace University, $247,973

The Pace University Community and Volunteer Mobilization AmeriCorps program will recruit and train members and volunteers dedicated to the recovery and rehabilitation of the downtown and Chinatown areas of New York City that were devastated on September 11. Members will help build sustainable infrastructure in three areas: Public Health and Public Safety Training Program Infrastructure, in which members will help fire and police departments and local hospitals create a disaster/emergency plan for the downtown area, conduct community asset mapping to determine existing services, and create a public health and public safety manual; Web Volunteer Bulletin Board/Technical and Community Training Network/ Infrastructure, in which members will create a web network that will serve as a clearinghouse to help the downtown community identify volunteers to help with post–September 11 activities and serve as a quick response communication network for future needs; and English as a Second Language activities, in which members will help improve the English language skills of area immigrants so that they can understand when there is an emergency, how to respond, and how to help others who do not speak English. Additionally, this activity will help community residents with job application skills, a particular need as 25 percent of community residents lost jobs due to September 11.

The Valley, $248,087
With the AmeriCorps Public Safety Program, members will be placed within the central administrative office and at firehouses of the New York Fire Department, allowing firefighters to attend to other urgent needs. The members will also promote public and fire safety awareness through community and school presentations, and forge relationships between the fire department and local communities by assisting with the department's minority recruitment efforts and outreach to people of color.

NORTH CAROLINA
North Carolina Commission on Volunteerism and Community Service, $119,900
The Commission on Volunteerism and Community Service will engage 2,000 volunteers to support homeland security and disaster relief activities statewide. The commission will have 100 local volunteer coordinators prepared to serve at disaster sites and will establish a statewide volunteer management database to support the mobilization of volunteers. A public awareness campaign about the volunteer efforts will be utilized to generate public interest in volunteer opportunities throughout North Carolina.

OHIO
Ohio Community Service Council, $450,000
The Ohio Community Service Council will forge statewide and local partnerships with the Ohio Emergency Management Agency, the Ohio Volunteer Center Association, and the Ohio RSVP Directors Association to better facilitate the volunteer needs of emergency systems in Ohio. Pilot Citizen Corps Councils will be developed as part of the State of Ohio Security Task Force for the purpose of supporting and promoting the engagement of citizen volunteers in homeland security roles. Volunteer centers in nine Ohio regions will assess the volunteer needs of the community, train agencies in volunteer management, promote citizen involvement, and mobilize and support volunteers assigned to emergency response roles.

OKLAHOMA
City of Tulsa, $275,000
The City of Tulsa will develop and implement a citywide volunteer mobilization strategy to meet the city's needs in

the event of a disaster. Community units will be created in order to connect people within a community and assist neighborhoods in becoming safe and secure in public safety, public health, and disaster preparedness and relief. The community units will, among other activities, assess vulnerabilities, educate the public about the multiethnic fabric of the community, and fill the volunteer needs of emergency and police response agencies. A Language and Culture Bank will be established, providing language translation required by official first responders. The city will also create a process to mobilize volunteers for disaster response.

OREGON
Oregon Trail Chapter, American Red Cross, $136,392
Serving with the Oregon Trail Chapter of the American Red Cross, 11 AmeriCorps members will respond to disasters, recruit and train disaster responders, teach community disaster preparation and health and safety classes, and mobilize 400 new volunteers who will provide 1,500 hours of service. During the first year of implementation, sites for the AmeriCorps members will be at Oregon Red Cross Chapters, and the plan is to expand outside of the Red Cross in the future. AmeriCorps members will be serving directly with local community- and faith-based organizations.

PENNSYLVANIA
American Red Cross—Southeast Pennsylvania Chapter, $323,000
The American Red Cross—Southeast Pennsylvania Chapter will create an alliance of over 100 nonprofits in the Greater Philadelphia area to form the Southeastern Pennsylvania Voluntary Organizations Active in Disaster. The alliance, joined by United Way, will empower and mobilize citizens of southeastern Pennsylvania to help neighbors prevent, prepare for, and respond to disasters. Initially the alliance will mobilize 400 new volunteers. The goal is to eventually mobilize 7,000 volunteers to attend to victims for the initial 72 hours following a disaster and an additional 1,000 trained volunteers to build a coordinated disaster response system.

SOUTH CAROLINA
South Carolina AmeriCorps Defense Brigade, $297,476
The South Carolina Military Department will support the 25-member South Carolina AmeriCorps Defense Brigade. The AmeriCorps members will identify and prepare 600 volunteers to deliver homeland defense services to individuals and communities in an effort to increase public

awareness about potential threats to homeland security, as well as develop and manage a database of volunteers.

TENNESSEE

Tennessee Commission on National and Community Service, $150,000

The Tennessee Commission will fortify the statewide homeland security infrastructure by developing and strengthening relationships with local councils and statewide disaster agencies. The Tennessee Office of Homeland Security will focus primarily on the mobilization of 1,000 volunteers a year. Partners in the project include the Tennessee Emergency Management Agency. Local homeland security councils and disaster response organizations will assist in identifying opportunities for various kinds of volunteers to support homeland security.

TEXAS

City of Austin, $400,000

The Office of Emergency Management will coordinate 300 volunteers to form the volunteer teams of Disaster Ready Austin, and the Austin Police Department's Civil Defense volunteer program will be expanded by 200 volunteers. The emergency management office will develop a long-term corps of volunteers who will provide direct emergency management services to the community. The Austin Police Department currently has a force of 100 Civil Defense volunteers. The Civil Defense expansion will support airport police by providing supplemental security, assisting in duties that do not require a peace officer's license, and preparing for mobilization in the event of a natural or man-made disaster. Some partners in the project are the American Red Cross, Salvation Army, Senior and Law Enforcement Together, Neighborhood Advocates for Emergency Preparedness, and Austin Area Interreligious Ministries.

VIRGINIA

Mercy Medical Airlift, $253,400

Mercy Medical Airlift's Volunteer Pilot Homeland Security Transportation Network will build on the established volunteer "Angel Flight" pilots program, which serves ten states (Delaware, Kentucky, Maryland, Michigan, North Carolina, Ohio, Pennsylvania, Tennessee, Virginia, West Virginia) and the District of Columbia. The program plans to increase volunteer pilot participation to 400 pilots regionally, with a minimum of 5,000 pilots nationwide. The Angel Flight program currently provides only preplanned charitable long-distance medical transportation for needy patients and their families. The increase in the number of volunteer pilots will decrease the current response time by establishing two pilot groups who can respond on either 1- or 6- hours' notice. In the third year of the grant, the program will be replicated in five other regional volunteer pilot organizations. Examples of the volunteer pilot air transportation system include flying emergency blood shipments to hospitals, key relief agency officials to disaster sites, and "booties" to rescue dogs working at "Ground Zero."

American National Red Cross Rapid Response Corps, $371,978

Thirty AmeriCorps members serving with the American National Red Cross Rapid Response Corps will be placed at American Red Cross chapters across the country. Member activities as will be designed to increase the chapter's capacity to provide integrated community education and outreach efforts focused on homeland security. Specific activities will be determined by each operating site's needs.

WASHINGTON

Pierce County Neighborhood Emergency Teams, $250,000

The Pierce County Department of Emergency Management and Pierce County Sheriff's Department plan to expand the Pierce County Neighborhood Emergency Teams (PC-NET) to over 100 neighborhoods from the existing eight. PC-NET, a local adaptation of the national CERT teams, will expand in scope to include crime prevention and homeland security. The volunteers will be recruited and trained to serve as trainers of neighborhood residents in crime prevention, assessment and reporting of terrorist threats, and emergency response to disaster. The resident training will prepare neighborhoods to be self-sufficient for up to 72 hours without professional emergency response.

WEST VIRGINIA

Council on the Southern Mountains RSVP, $100,000

This new RSVP project will serve the West Virginia counties of McDowell, Wyoming, and Raleigh. The project's 200 RSVP volunteers will be assigned roles in Neighborhood Watch/Public Safety activities, Health Education, Child Literacy, and Disaster Preparedness. Teams of volunteers will work with the Red Cross, National Guard, and FEMA to assist families in a faster recovery from disaster in a flood plain area of McDowell. The volunteers will establish Neighborhood Watches and seek to reduce crime by 40 percent through education and training. Partners include law enforcement agencies, hospitals, rural health-care clinics, physicians, pharmaceutical companies, education systems, AmeriCorps, West Virginia Extension Services, and emergency management services.

WISCONSIN
Housing Authority of the City of Milwaukee, $225,000
The Housing Authority of the City of Milwaukee will recruit and utilize 2,000 multigenerational volunteers for disaster preparedness and response. The Authority's Public Safety Staff, Milwaukee Area Technical College, the Sheriff's Department, American Red Cross, and FEMA will provide training in emergency preparedness, crime prevention, basic responder skills, team organization, risk reduction, and two-way radio communication. Volunteers will establish a Block Watch program, be trained in the rescue and relocation of children, create a school Emergency Response Handbook, organize an intergenerational volunteer network with seniors and youth, and provide CERT training to be utilized in disaster response. The goal of the project is to engage a variety of ages to work together to build a secure community.

Volunteer Center of Racine, $100,000
Racine County will engage 237 community members as RSVP volunteers in order to provide support in areas of public safety, public health, and disaster preparedness and relief. A partial list of partners for the community wide effort include Volunteer Center of Racine, Racine County Emergency Management, Wisconsin Emergency Management Agency, FEMA, Neighborhood Watch, American Red Cross, schools, law enforcement, and the fire department. The volunteers will provide homeland security awareness, assist with food distribution, and focus on transportation in the event of a disaster.

ADVOCAP, Inc., $125,000
The establishment of RSVP in Winnebago and Green Lake Counties will utilize 250 volunteers in homeland security roles. Various teams of trained volunteers will provide recommendations to improve home security through home safety checks for elderly and disabled citizens, serve with TRIAD to provide outreach and safety information to citizens, and become trainers in disaster preparedness. Programs which will utilize the volunteers include TRIAD, Green Lake Sheriff's Office, the American Red Cross chapter, schools, Habitat for Humanity, meal sites, senior centers, and social service departments.

Appendix 7: Centers for Disease Control (CDC) Preparedness and Planning Information Sites

PREPARATION & PLANNING

On this page:
- *General*
- *Businesses*
- *Health-care Facilities*
- *State & Local*
- *National*
- *Legal & Planning Issues*
- *Contacts*
- *Other Resources*

GENERAL INFORMATION

- *Safety in a Power Outage* NEW!
  What to do when the power goes out unexpectedly.
- *Bioterrorism Preparedness FAQ*
- *Chemical Agents: Facts About Sheltering in Place* (*también en español*)
  How to find temporary shelter in an emergency (http://www.bt.cdc.gov/planning/Shelteringfacts.pdf)
- *Chemical Agents: Facts About Evacuation* (*también en español*)
  Knowing when and how to evacuate an area in an emergency (http://www.bt.cdc.gov/planning/evacuationfacts.pdf)
- *Chemical Agents: Facts About Personal Cleaning & Disposal of Contaminated Clothing* (*también en español*)
  What to do if you come in physical contact with dangerous chemicals (http://www.bt.cdc.gov/planning/personalcleaningfacts.pdf)

PREPAREDNESS FOR BUSINESSES

- *Emergency Preparedness for Business*
  Instructions to building occupants, actions to be taken by facility management, and first responder notification procedures. From the National Institute for Occupational Safety and Health (NIOSH)
- *Notice to Readers: Protecting Building Environments from Airborne Chemical, Biologic, or Radiologic Attacks*
  MMWR 2002 Sep 6;51(35):789. (http://www.cdc.gov/mmwr/PDF/wk/mm5135.pdf)
- *Guidance for Protecting Building Environments from Airborne Chemical, Biological, or Radiological Attacks*
  May 2002. From the National Institute for Occupational Safety and Health, CDC (http://www.cdc.gov/niosh/bldvent/pdfs/2002-139.pdf)

PREPAREDNESS FOR HEALTH-CARE FACILITIES

- *Bioterrorism Readiness Plan: A Template for Health-care Facilities* (http://www.cdc.gov/ncidod/hip/Bio/13apr99APICCDCBioterrorism.PDF)
- *Hospital Preparedness for Mass Causalities*
  Provided by the Advancing Health in America Policy Forum.

STATE & LOCAL PREPAREDNESS

- *Continuation Guidance for Cooperative Agreement on Public Health Preparedness and Response for Bioterrorism—Budget Year Four*
  The Centers for Disease Control and Prevention (CDC) announces the availability of FY2003 funding for continuation of the cooperative agreements to upgrade state and local public health jurisdictions' preparedness for and response to bioterrorism, other outbreaks of infectious disease, and other public health threats and emergencies.

- *Public Health Preparedness and Response Capacity Inventories*
  Voluntary assessments of state and local capacity to respond to bioterrorism, infectious disease outbreaks, and other public health threats and emergencies. Includes measures to assess progress toward meeting the benchmarks and critical and enhanced capacities in the Grant Guidance for FY2002 Supplemental Funds for Public Health Preparedness and Response to Bioterrorism (Announcement 99051).

- *Notice to Readers: Protecting Building Environments from Airborne Chemical, Biologic, or Radiologic Attacks*
  MMWR 2002 Sep 6;51(35):789. (http://www. cdc.gov/mmwr/PDF/wk/mm5135.pdf)

- *Guidance for Protecting Building Environments from Airborne Chemical, Biological, or Radiological Attacks*
  May 2002. From the National Institute for Occupational Safety and Health, CDC (http:// www.cdc.gov/niosh/bldvent/pdfs/2002-139.pdf)

- *Notification Procedures for State and Local Public Health Officials*

- *Preparing at the Local Level for Events Involving Weapons of Mass Destruction*
  Emerging Infectious Diseases 2002 Sep;8(9):1006-1007. (http://www.cdc. gov/ncidod/EID/vol8no9/pdf/01-0520.pdf)

- *Public Health Response to Biological & Chemical Terrorism: Interim Planning Guidance for State Public Health Officials*
  (http://www.bt.cdc.gov/file-formats.asp"\l"pdf"

NATIONAL PREPAREDNESS

- *Community Reaction to Bioterrorism: Prospective Study of Simulated Outbreak*
  Emerging Infectious Diseases 2003 June;9(6):708-712.

- *Planning against Biological Terrorism: Lessons from Outbreak Investigations*
  Emerging Infectious Diseases 2003 May;9(5):515-519. (http://www.cdc.gov/ ncidod/EID/vol9no6/pdfs/02-0769.pdf)

- *Fear of Bioterrorism and Implications for Public Health Preparedness*
  Emerging Infectious Diseases 2003 April;9(4):503-505. (http://www.cdc.gov/ ncidod/eid/vol9no4/pdfs/02-0593.pdf)

- *Continuation Guidance for Cooperative Agreement on Public Health Preparedness and Response for Bioterrorism—Budget Year Four*
  The Centers for Disease Control and Prevention (CDC) announces the availability of FY2003 funding for continuation of the cooperative agreements to upgrade state and local public health jurisdictions' preparedness for and response to bioterrorism, other outbreaks of infectious disease, and other public health threats and emergencies.

- *Cooperative Agreement Award Notice and Grant Guidance*
  Guidance for CDC bioterrorism funding for states.

- *Bioterrorism and Public Health Preparedness: The CDC's Program in Brief*
  Brief description of bioterrorism and CDC role.

- *Bioterrorism Preparedness FAQ*

- *Strategic National Stockpile*
  National repository of pharmaceuticals & medical supplies.

- *Epi-X: The Epidemic Information Exchange*
  Secure, web-based communications network
  connecting CDC with state and local health
  departments, poison control centers, and other
  public health professionals.

- *Biological and Chemical Terrorism: Strategic
  Plan for Preparedness and Response*
  Recommendations of the CDC Strategic
  Planning Workgroup.
  MMWR Recommendations and Reports 2000
  Apr 21;49(RR-4);1-14. (http://www.cdc.gov/
  mmwr/PDF/RR/RR4904.pdf)

- *Public Health Assessment of Potential
  Biological Terrorism Agents*
  Emerging Infectious Diseases 2002
  Feb;8(2):225-230. (http://www.cdc.gov/ncidod/
  EID/vol8no2/pdf/01-0164.pdf)

- *Strengthening National Preparedness for
  Smallpox: An Update*
  Emerging Infectious Diseases 2001
  Jan-Feb;7(1):155–157. (http://www.cdc.gov/
  ncidod/eid/vol7no1/pdfs/luduc.pdf)

- *National Bioterrorism Preparedness and
  Response Initiative* (http://www.bt.cdc.gov/
  file-formats.asp"\l"pdf)
  Slide set. Provides an overview and general
  information about the bioterrorism preparedness
  and response activities.

- *Emergency and Environmental Health Services*
  From the National Center for Environmental
  Health. Description of NCEH involvement in
  providing national and international leadership
  for the coordination, delivery, and evaluation of
  emergency and environmental health services.

- *Centers for Public Health Preparedness*
  Program focusing on information technology
  and training in support of bioterrorism
  preparedness and emergency response.

LEGAL AND PLANNING ISSUES

- *Regulations to Control Communicable Diseases*
  42 U.S.C. 264 (From United States Code
  Annotated; Title 42; The Public Health And
  Welfare; Chapter 6a—Public Health Service;
  Subchapter Ii—General Powers And Duties;
  Part G—Quarantine And Inspection).

- *Interstate Quarantine*
  From United States Code Annotated; Title 42;
  The Public Health And Welfare; Part 70. On
  U.S. Government Printing Office site.

- *Foreign Quarantine*
  From United States Code Annotated; Title 42;
  The Public Health And Welfare; Part 71. On
  U.S. Government Printing Office site.

CONTACTS FOR PREPARATION AND PLANNING

- *Bioterrorism Preparedness and Response
  Program*
  Program questions: 404-639-0385

- *Emergency Preparedness and Response
  Branch*
  Provided by the National Center for
  Environmental Health.

- *Health Agency Locator (HAL)*

OTHER RESOURCES

- *Smallpox Preparation & Planning*
- *Anthrax Preparation & Planning*

Appendix 8: Select Web Sites for Additional Information

Americorps—www.americorps.org

Animal and Plant Health Inspection Service—www.aphis.usda.gov

Citizen Corps—www.citizencorps.gov

Corporation for National and Community Service—www.nationalservice.org

Department of Homeland Security—www.dhs.gov

Federal Emergency Management Agency—www.fema.gov

Immigration and Nationalization Service—www.ins.gov

Medical Reserve Corps—www.medicalreservecorps.gov

National Association of Counties—www.naco.org

National Governors Association—www.nga.org

National League of Cities—www.nlc.org

Neighborhood Watch—www.usaonwatch.org

Office for Domestic Preparedness—www.ojp.usdoj.gov/odp

Office for National Preparedness—www.fema.gov/onp

Senior Corps—www.seniorcorps.org

Transportation Security Administration—www.tsa.dot.gov

United States Coast Guard—www.uscg.mil

United States Conference of Mayors—www.usmayors.org

United States Customs Service—www.customs.ustreas.gov

United States Secret Service—www.ustreas.gov/usss/

U.S.A. Freedom Corps—www.usafreedomcorps.gov

Volunteers in Police Service—www.policevolunteers.org

Source: Institute for Crisis, Disaster and Risk Management, George Washington University—http://www.gwu.edu/gelman/guides/sciences/crisis.html

Crisis, Disaster, and Risk Management

Government Information Sources

FEDERAL GOVERNMENT

U.S. Department of Homeland Security

This official site features press releases and other documents that define the role and work of DHS. Emphasis is on these areas: emergencies and disasters, travel and transportation, immigration and borders, research and technology, and threats and protection. Much of the focus is on terrorism, but natural disasters and other emergencies are also addressed. This is a good source for remarks by government officials on issues related to terrorism and national security.

Location: http://www.dhs.gov

Federal Emergency Management Agency (FEMA)

Part of the Department of Homeland Security, the FEMA site includes information about ongoing disaster responses, various response plans, key emergency management officials at the state and local levels, documents, and other resources.

Location: http://www.fema.gov

U.S. Environmental Protection Agency/Chemical Emergency Preparedness and Prevention Office (CEPPO)

EPA's CEPPO site covers prevention, risk management, preparedness, emergency response, and counter-terrorism. Also includes information on regulations, software, publications, and links to related web sites. This is a key site for information dealing with hazardous materials, chemical accidents, and oil spills.

Location: http://www.epa.gov/ceppo

U.S. Geological Survey

This site has sections covering land-based natural hazards (earthquakes, floods, volcanoes).

Location: http://www.usgs.gov

National Oceanographic and Atmospheric Administration/Office of Response and Restoration

This site provides access to tools, information, and software for responders to oil spills, chemical accidents, hazardous materials releases, and ship groundings.
Location: http://response.restoration.noaa.gov/index.html

STATE AND LOCAL EMERGENCY ORGANIZATIONS

National Emergency Management Association (NEMA)
NEMA is an organization of state-level emergency management officials. The NEMA online library provides full-text access to documents and presentations from NEMA committees. This site also includes information on NEMA membership, conferences, job listings, and a directory of emergency management contacts by state.
Location: http://www.nemaweb.org

International Association of Emergency Managers (IAEM)
IAEM is an association of local (city and county) emergency management officials. This site provides information on IAEM activities and membership. Selected issues of the newsletter are available online, as well as a bulletin board and discussion list.
Location: http://www.iaem.com

National Governor's Association (NGA)
The National Governors Association Center for Best Practices (NGAC) provides support to governors in responding to the challenges of homeland security and other emergency management issues. From the NGA homepage, visit the site index and scroll to the homeland security and technology division. This will lead to sections on bioterrorism, emergency management, and homeland security. Within these sections are links to several substantial, full-text publications, including a two-volume governors' guide to emergency management, domestic preparedness checklist, and presentations from the NGA Bioterrorism Summit.
Location: http://www.nga.org/

Center for State Homeland Security
Created to help states fulfill their critical homeland security role, this site provides access to full-text articles, legislation, and reports from government agencies and research institutes in a variety of areas, including counterterrorism, public health, and infrastructure protection. It also provides links to state agencies responsible for homeland security and/or emergency management.
Location: http://www.cshs-us.org

NONGOVERNMENT ORGANIZATIONS

American Red Cross (Disaster Services)
This site gives an overview of the work of the American Red Cross, including reports on Red Cross projects worldwide. It also includes news coverage of disasters and relief efforts.
Location: http://www.redcross.org

Disaster Relief
Sponsored by the American Red Cross, this site features an extensive collection of news stories on disasters back to 1996. The "Library" provides the full text of Red Cross disaster preparedness pamphlets and an extensive collection of disaster statistics. It also includes links to disaster-related sites, including state emergency management offices.
Location: http://www.disasterrelief.org

UNIVERSITY RESEARCH CENTERS

University of Colorado/Natural Hazards Center (NHRAIC)
This site includes links to a number of valuable research sources. These include the full text of articles from newsletters and journals published by the center, working papers, conference papers, and more. The site also provides access to the HazLit Database, an online catalog of over 22,000 items in the center's library.
Location: http://www.colorado.edu/hazards

University of Delaware/Disaster Research Center (DRC)
DRC has studied a broad range of disaster types, including hurricanes, floods, earthquakes, tornadoes, hazardous chemical incidents, plane crashes, civil disturbances, and riots. This site includes descriptions of current projects, as well as extensive bibliographies of DRC publications, including books, articles, preliminary papers, and more. Only some of the publications are available as full-text versions online; others can be purchased through the center.
Location: http://www.udel.edu/DRC/

COMMERCIAL SITES

Disaster Central

Maintained by emergency management researcher, consultant, and educator Claire Rubin, this site provides an extensive set of links to recent research reports and other documents on emergency management, terrorism, homeland security, state and local government, critical infrastructure, health and medicine, policy analysis, and risk management. This site is an excellent source for full-text documents online.

Location: http://www.disaster-central.com/

National Homeland Security Knowledge Base

This site provides an extensive set of links to U.S. and other government agencies as well as international and research organizations. Focus is on various threats to homeland security, including nuclear/radiological, biological, chemical, and explosive incidents, as well as natural disasters.

Location: http://www.twotigersonline.com/resources. html

SPECIALIZED ORGANIZATIONS

Earthquake Engineering Research Institute (EERI)

This site provides information on meetings sponsored by EERI as well as updates on seismic legislation. A catalog of EERI publications is available, but only a few select articles and reports are available in their full-text versions online.

Location: http://www.eeri.org

Association of State Floodplain Managers

ASFPM is involved in floodplain management; flood hazard mitigation; the National Flood Insurance Program; and flood preparedness, warning, and recovery. This site includes information on conferences, publications, grants and fellowships, job listings, and links to related Web sites.

Location: http://www.floods.org

National Hurricane Center/Tropical Prediction Center (NOAA)

The NOAA issues watches, warnings, forecasts, and analyses of hazardous tropical weather. The site includes satellite and radar images, information on hurricane awareness, and historical storm-related data.

Location: http://www.nhc.noaa.gov/

RISK ASSESSMENT AND RISK MANAGEMENT

Risk and Insurance Management Society (RIMS)

This site provides a range of services for society members, including conference announcements, job listings, and a catalog of publications. Several articles from the last few issues of the society's magazine, *Risk Management*, are available online.

Location: http://www.rims.org/

Risk World

Risk World provides extensive coverage of news on risk assessment and management with archives of news stories back to 1995. It also provides abstracts of papers from recent conferences and a collection of research reports, many of which are available online.

Location: http://www.riskworld.com/

Society for Risk Analysis

Highlights of this site include the table of contents of the society's journal, links to sources of specific risk-related resources (data, models, technical reports, etc.), and a glossary of risk analysis terms.

Location: http://www.sra.org/

BUSINESS AND INDUSTRY CRISIS MANAGEMENT/ORGANIZATIONAL CONTINUITY

Disaster Resource Guide

This site consolidates educational, organizational, and vendor resources in the areas of safety/security, emergency/crisis management, and business continuity. It provides an extensive collection of full-text articles, as well as book reviews, descriptions of company programs, and links to related sites.

Location: http://www.disaster-resource.com/

Emergency Management Guide for Business and Industry

This guide provides a step-by-step approach to emergency planning, response, and recovery for companies of all sizes. It requires Adobe Acrobat.

Location: http://www.fema.gov/library/bizindex.htm

Disaster Recovery Institute International (DRII)

The highlight of this site is the complete text of "Professional Practices for Business Continuity Planners," a guide to and standards for developing and implementing business continuity plans. The site also includes information on DRII training and certification programs and links to related sites.

Location: http://www.dr.org

DRI International Glossary of Terms
This site gives definitions of terms commonly used in the industry. It requires Adobe Acrobat.
Location: http://www.dr.org/gloss.htm

Rothstein Associates (Recovery Resources)
This site includes a collection of full-text articles, the Disaster Recovery Forum, the Business Survival Newsletter, and related links. The Rothstein Catalog On Disaster Recovery lists hundreds of books, software, videos, and other materials.
Location: http://www.rothstein.com/

www.ContingencyPlanning.com
This site includes the complete text of articles from *Contingency Planning & Management* magazine. It also includes an extensive collection of "Disruption Defenses," which are prevention, mitigation, response, and recovery recommendations for some of the more common business disruption threats.
Location: http://www.contingencyplanning.com/

Survive: The Business Continuity Group
This site for business continuity professionals features training events and conferences, publications for purchase, news stories, and a directory of disaster recovery and contingency services and products. The complete text of some feature stories and news items are available online.
Location: http://www.survive.com/

The Lukaszewski Group
The Lukaszewski Group is a management consultant firm that offers services in many areas, including crisis and disaster management. The site features an extensive collection of articles, speeches, and presentations by Mr. Lukaszewski.
Location: http://www.e911.com/

Business Continuity Institute
Business Continuity Institute offers a range of services for members, including job postings, conference announcements, links to related sites, and an online bookstore. A highlight of the site is the collection of Business Continuity Planning Guides, the full text of which are available online.
Location: http://www.thebci.org/

Continuity Systems Limited
This UK firm provides a "Recovery Healthcheck" questionnaire online, the full text of a few articles by Ian Charters, disaster statistics, and "myths" about disasters.
Location: http://www.continuity.co.uk/

Business Resumption Planning, Step by Step
From the company Datasure, this is a 13-step plan for business continuity. Other features of this site are a Business Resumption Checklist and guides to computer storage and power protection.
Location: http://datasure.com/stepby.html

MLC and Associates, Inc.
This business continuity consulting firm provides in-depth descriptions of their services, including business continuity programs, simulations and exercises, continuity training, and data security.
Location: http://www.mlc2resq.com/

SunGard Recovery Services—"Getting Started."
This site includes a one-minute risk assessment, ten tips for recovery, frequently asked questions, and case studies of several companies.
Location: http://recovery.sungard.com/home.html

ARTICLE DATABASES

The databases listed here are good sources to search for journal articles and conference papers on crisis, disaster, and risk management.

ABI/Inform
ABI/Inform is the primary database for business and management topics. This database indexes about 800 publications, including research journals, trade journals, and popular business magazines. It provides citations and abstracts for all articles; about half of the articles indexed include the full text.

American Society of Civil Engineers
This database provides full-text access to 29 journals published by ASCE 1999 to present. Of particular interest is the journal *Natural Hazards Review*.

Compendex
This database is a comprehensive index to more than 3,000 journals and conference proceedings from all

areas of engineering. However, it includes only citations and abstracts.

Emerald Library

This database provides full-text articles from over 130 management journals published by MCB University Press. The topics covered go from 1989 to the present.

GEOBASE

GEOBASE is part of the OCLC FirstSearch family of databases; it indexes over 2,000 journals, books, conference proceedings, and reports on geography, geology, and ecology. The coverage is from 1980 to present. Only citations and abstracts are provided. GEOBASE is a good resource for topics dealing with natural and environmental disasters and hazards.

PsycInfo

This database covers over 1,300 journals and books in psychology and related disciplines from 1987 to present. It is a good resource for topics on psychological, organizational, and social aspects of crisis, emergency, disaster, and risk management. It includes only citations and abstracts.

Sociological Abstracts

This database indexes articles from about 800 journals relevant to sociology and related disciplines. It is useful for finding articles on social aspects of crisis, disaster, and risk management. The coverage is from 1963 to present and includes only citations and abstracts.

PERIODICALS

TRADE JOURNALS AND NEWSLETTERS

Disaster Recovery Journal

Both the hard-copy journal and access to the online site are free.

Location: http://www.drj.com

Contingency Planning & Management

Both the hard-copy journal and access to the online site are free. The site includes a searchable archive of past issues.

Location: http://www.contingencyplanning.com

Homeland Protection Professional

Editorial calendar shows articles planned for upcoming issues. No articles are available online, but you can register for a free trial print subscription.

Location: http://www.hppmag.com/

Homeland Security Newsletter

Published monthly by the Anser Institute, this newsletter contains original articles as well as links to articles from government sources, newspapers, and other popular press. Online subscriptions are available with archives back to 2002 available online.

Location: http://www.homelandsecurity.org/ newsletter

RESEARCH JOURNALS

These are professional research journals published in the area of crisis and emergency management. All sites provide instructions for submitting articles, a list of editorial board members, subscription information, and tables of contents and/or abstracts. Except as noted, these journals do not provide full-text articles online. None of these journals are held at WRLC libraries, but GW students, faculty, and staff can request articles through Interlibrary Loan.

International Journal of Emergency Management

This journal began publishing in 2001. Click on "Journals" in the left menu bar, then scroll to the journal title.

Location: http://www.inderscience.com/

Journal of Emergency Management

This journal began publishing in 2003 and has only one issue available online. Table of contents and abstracts are provided, but no full-text articles.

Location: http://www.pnpco.com/pn06001.html

Journal of Homeland Security and Emergency Management

The first issue was published in 2004. Abstracts and full-text articles are available online.

Location: http://www.bepress.com/jhsem/

International Journal of Mass Emergencies and Disasters

This journal began publishing in 1982. The site provides a table of contents and abstracts for 1995 to the present.

Location: http://www.usc.edu/schools/sppd/ijmed/

ONLINE BOOKS

Although most books are still available only in print, some publishers are beginning to make entire books available online at no cost. Listed here are some titles that are available online:

Diasasters by Design: A Reassessment of Natural Hazards in the United States
Dennis Mileti. National Academy Press, 1999.
Location: http://www.nap.edu/books/0309063604/html/

Chemical and Biological Terrorism: Research and Development to Improve Civilian Medical Response
Committee on R&D Needs for Improving Civilian Medical Response to Chemical and Biological Terrorism Incidents, Institute of Medicine, 1999.
Location: http://books.nap.edu/books/0309061954/html/

Disaster Response: Preparation and Coordination
Eric Auf der Heide. Center for Excellence in Disaster Management and Humanitarian Assistance, 1989.
Location: http://www.coe-dmha.org/dr/flash.htm

The Long Road to Recovery: Community Responses to Industrial Disaster
Edited by James K. Mitchell. United Nations University Press, 1996.
Location: http://www.unu.edu/unupress/unupbooks/uu21le/uu21le00.htm

Reducing Disaster Losses Through Better Information
Board on Natural Disasters, Commission on Geosciences, Environment, and Resources, National Research Council. National Academy Press, 1999.
Location: http://books.nap.edu/catalog/6363.html

Visit these publishers' homepages for announcements of new books, some of which may be available online.

- National Academy Press (http://books.nap.edu/)
- United Nations University Press (http://www.unu.edu/unupress/)

HEALTH AND MEDICAL INFORMATION

U.S. Department of Health & Human Services/Office of Emergency Preparedness

This office is responsible for coordinating federal health, medical, and health-related social services and recovery to major emergencies and federally declared disasters, including natural disasters, technological disasters, major transportation accidents, and terrorism. This site includes information on the office's Counterterrorism Program, the National Disaster Medical System (NDMS), and the Metropolitan Medical Response System (MMRS)
Location: http://www.oep.dhhs.gov/

U.S. Centers for Disease Control and Prevention
This extensive site includes health standards and statistics, fact sheets on health information and disease prevention, and health-related news stories. Brochures, software, and other publications are available for download and by order from CDC.
Location: http://www.cdc.gov/

Agency for Toxic Substances and Disease Registry (ATSDR)
This site features many news and information sources on toxic substances. Highlights include ToxFAQs, a series of summaries about hazardous substances; HazDat, the database that provides information on the release of hazardous substances from Superfund sites and from emergency events; and Minimal Risk Levels (MRLs) for hazardous substances. "Science Corner" is a gateway to environmental health information and resources on the web.
Location: http://atsdr1.atsdr.cdc.gov/cx.html

Federal Emergency Management Agency/Rapid Response Information System
Focusing on terrorist incidents, this site provides access to several databases, including characteristics of chemical, biological and radiological materials, first aid measures, federal response capabilities, and information sources on potential weapons of mass destruction.
Location: http://www.rris.fema.gov/

Disaster Mental Health Services
From the Department of Social Work at Walter Reed Army Medical Center, this guidebook is an introduction to the field of disaster mental health (DMH) for clinicians and administrators. Adobe Acrobat is required to view many sections of the book.
Location: http://www.wramc.amedd.army.mil/departments/socialwork/provider/DMHS.htm

INTERNATIONAL DISASTER INFORMATION

United Nations Relief Web

This site covers news and information on humanitarian emergencies and natural disasters, with a focus on improving relief efforts. It includes a searchable database of over 50,000 documents dating to 1981 and an extensive collection of maps.

Location: http://www.reliefweb.int

Volunteers in Technical Assistance (VITA)

VITA is a not-for-profit private volunteer organization that provides technical information as requested by developing countries. The site includes a section on disasters.

Location: http://www.vita.org

United Nations International Strategy for Disaster Reduction (formerly IDNDR)

ISDR focuses on creating disaster prevention strategies and reducing social and economic disruption caused by disasters. This site includes information about ISDR as well as UN documents on disaster reduction.

Location: http://www.unisdr.org

World Health Organization

Part of WHO's mission is to provide aid during emergencies. This site provides extensive information on diseases and health topics and includes links to health-related databases available free on the web.

Location: http://www.who.org

Pan American Health Organization

Regional office for the Americas of the World Health Organization. Includes health statistics, reports on health topics, links to related sources, and news on health issues.

Location: http://www.paho.org

United Nations Development Program

UNDP partners with United Nations relief agencies and helps countries to prepare for, avoid, and manage complex emergencies and disasters. This site provides extensive information and reports on UNDP projects.

Location: http://www.undp.org

European Community Humanitarian Office (ECHO)

ECHO's role is to provide humanitarian aid in response to natural disasters and armed conflict in countries outside the European Union. This site includes statistics, reports, and descriptions of ECHO's operations.

Location: http://europa.eu.int/comm/echo/en/index_en.html

Appendix 9: SAFE Conference Report

Homeland Security at the Community Level

Issues and Opportunities

A Report on the First Annual Conference on The
Community and Homeland Security

San Francisco, CA

March 27–28, 2003

Damon Coppola

George Haddow

Jane Bullock

The SAFE Project

ACKNOWLEDGMENTS

The SAFE Project and NCCD wish to gratefully acknowledge the support of the FAITHS Initiative of the San Francisco Foundation in hosting this conference. We also wish to thank Damon Coppola for his excellent job recording the proceedings and writing this final report.

EXECUTIVE SUMMARY

The National Council on Crime and Delinquency (NCCD) and the SAFE Project (Securing America's Future for Everyone) hosted the First Annual Conference on the Community and Homeland Security on March 27 and 28, 2003, at the San Francisco Foundation in San Francisco, California. The conference brought local leaders, from several states, responsible for shaping homeland security programs and activities in their communities together with representatives from federal, state, local, nonprofit, private, and international organizations working on homeland security–related issues. The conference allowed all of these practitioners, participants, and representatives to voice their concerns and share their experiences, and gave them their first opportunity not only to work together to identify existing problems with homeland security at the local level, but to propose possible solutions to these problems. The conference began with a delivered message from United States Senator Barbara Boxer, who expressed her gratitude for the efforts of participants who had come together to make communities safer. Senator Boxer reaffirmed the need for a conference that addressed homeland security efforts at the community level and stated she was "pleased by [the participants'] commitment to build[ing] a coalition of experts at the local, state, and federal levels."

The primary concern of those in attendance was well stated by Carol Lopes (Berkeley, California), who said, "Though there has been a lot of progress, we are willfully unprepared. Community and neighborhood preparedness is the centerpiece of today's work. Our responsibility is to prepare a community before a disaster and assist after a disaster strikes. We must train a cadre of emergency prepared individuals who will interface well with first responders."

Four principal areas of concern emerged from these discussions, detailed in this report. They include: (1) greater access to resources to fund homeland security programs and projects at the community level; (2) greater access to practical information about application, eligibility, recruitment, retention, and other concerns; (3) the need for innovative and effective programming ideas; and (4) the need to focus on diverse and "special needs" populations. This report will explore these four issues as they were defined by the speakers and the participants, drawing directly from the presentations, panel discussions, and facilitated participant discussions.

INTRODUCTION

The National Council on Crime and Delinquency (NCCD) and the SAFE Project (Securing America's Future for Everyone) hosted the First Annual Conference on the Community and Homeland Security on March 27 and 28, 2003, at the San Francisco Foundation in San Francisco, California.

The conference brought local leaders, from several states, responsible for shaping homeland security programs and activities in their communities together with representatives from federal, state, local, nonprofit, private, and international organizations working on homeland security–related issues. The conference allowed all of these practitioners, participants, and representatives to voice their concerns and share their experiences and gave them their first opportunity not only to work together to identify existing problems with homeland security at the local level, but to propose possible solutions to these problems.

The conference began with a delivered message from United States Senator Barbara Boxer, who expressed her gratitude for the efforts of participants who had come together to make communities safer. Senator Boxer reaffirmed the need for the conference that addressed homeland security efforts at the community level and stated she was "pleased by [the participants'] commitment to build[ing] a coalition of experts at the local, state, and federal levels."

The conference speakers focused their presentations on a multitude of homeland security programs and actions occurring within communities, while exploring a spectrum of topics spanning federal, state, local, private, and nonprofit organizational levels. Over the course of the two-day conference, several common threads emerged, the most significant being how to increase the effectiveness of homeland security efforts at the community level.

This idea was echoed by representatives from all levels of government and private and nonprofit groups and is illustrated through the following sample of statements made throughout the course of the conference:

- Jane Bullock (SAFE project): "The only way to accomplish anything in homeland security preparedness is for it to be grassroots-based. Top-down does not work. It must start neighborhood by neighborhood."
- Chuck Supple (GO SERV): "We must engage citizens to address problems in their own communities to have the greatest possible impact in community homeland security."
- Valli Wasp (Austin, Texas): "Preparedness must be addressed locally. We need to take this to 'homes'—get rid of the 'land,' get rid of the 'security'—this is about people protecting their homes. If you want people to listen to you, you have to go to where they live."
- Eileen Garry (U.S. Department of Justice): "Every good idea I have ever heard came from the local level."

In the process of examining Homeland Security at the community level, the group established that it was necessary to clarify the term "community." Both the speakers and the audience agreed that the "community" concept must be used with the greatest possible flexibility. Limiting the definition

of community will effectively reduce the range of homeland security project options, possible sources of funding, and the pool of available participants in developed programs.

Jane Bullock (SAFE) stated, "The word 'community' can be geographic or organizational, and this conference has shown that the word can mean anything—a church, a mosque. . . . We must consider the word in the broadest way possible. Everyone needs to be a part of the partnership—neighborhoods, churches, unions, senior citizen centers, and many others." A related concern was that the term "homeland security" needed to be defined as it applies to the community level. Monique Morris (NCCD) rhetorically asked participants, "What is homeland security? What is terrorism? Is it a drug dealer? A traditional terrorist? Crime?"

The primary concern of those in attendance was well stated by Carol Lopes (Berkeley, California), who said, "Though there has been a lot of progress, we are willfully unprepared. Community and neighborhood preparedness is the centerpiece of today's work. Our responsibility is to prepare a community before a disaster and assist after a disaster strikes. We must train a cadre of emergency-prepared individuals who will interface well with first responders."

As the attendees primarily consisted of or represented local decision-makers who are seeking preparedness and protection from natural and technological disasters and terrorist attacks in their communities, the sentiments were well received. These attendees exhibited a collective frustration, voiced through their commentary and questions following each of the presentations and during a group discussion that ended the conference.

Four principal areas of concern emerged from these discussions, detailed in this report. They include the following:

- Resources: Greater access to resources to fund homeland security programs and projects at the community level
- Information: Greater access to practical information about application, eligibility, recruitment, retention, and other concerns
- Programming: The need for innovative and effective programming ideas
- Customizing: The need to focus on diverse and "special needs" populations

This report will explore these four issues as they were defined by the speakers and the participants, drawing directly from the presentations, panel discussions, and facilitated participant discussions. Each issue will be defined and placed in context to its source of concern and effect on local communities. The possible remedies identified by participants will be outlined. Finally, a section titled "Conclusions: Where Do We Go from Here?" will offer one viable and potentially effective solution to these issues derived directly from the group discussions.

BACKGROUND

On November 25, 2002, President George W. Bush signed into law the Homeland Security Act of 2002, creating the new Department of Homeland Security (DHS) with a mission of protecting the United States from further terrorist attacks, reducing the nation's vulnerability to terrorism, and minimizing the damage from potential terrorist attacks and natural disasters.

The February 13, 2003, passage of the FY2003 omnibus appropriations bill included significant spending to state and local governments to support first-responder activities. For this purpose, the new DHS received approximately $2 billion in funding, less than the $3.5 billion that had been proposed. Most of this funding will go directly to the states. DHS officials have said that the states must pass along as much as 75 percent of the funding to local governments.

As of the date of the conference, the states had received only a limited amount of this funding, and in reality the states will likely manage to keep a considerable amount of this funding at the state level. If the states do pass the terrorism funding to local governments, they will likely offset these losses by canceling or reducing the amounts of other pass-through funding.

The most direct line funding for communities is through Citizens Corps activities, the Corporation for National and Community Service (CNCS) programs, and other volunteer-driven programs in the Departments of Health and Human Services (HHS) and Justice (DOJ). In FY2004, the new Department of Homeland Security is expected to make funds available to state and local governments through Citizens Corps, the Office of State and Local Government Coordination, the Directorate of Border and Transportation Security, and the Emergency Preparedness and Response Directorate (which is currently overseeing the Federal Emergency Management Agency [FEMA]). The FY2004 budget requests funding levels similar to FY2003 for state and local activities, with a strong emphasis on local support.

In addition, the Bush Administration's $79 billion dollar Supplemental to support the war in Iraq includes additional spending on homeland security. However, the state and local part of this bill is primarily reimbursement for increased security measures, not preparedness or mitigation.

The most promising initiative to support communities is new legislation being proposed in the Senate entitled the "Homeland Security Block Grant Act." This legislation, as written, would provide $3.5 billion directly to communities, each year until 2006, for community homeland security planning and coordination, special projects, development and maintenance of training facilities, best practices clearinghouses, and communication systems.

President Bush created the U.S.A. Freedom Corps in an effort to provide centralized coordination of the various volunteer-based organizations dispersed throughout the federal government, including Peace Corps, Citizen Corps, and the Corporation for National and Community Service. (Peace Corps volunteers work exclusively on international assignments and therefore will not be detailed in this report.) The mission of Freedom Corps is to promote volunteerism as an integral part of citizenship.

CITIZEN CORPS

Citizen Corps was the "new piece," with FEMA tasked as the lead agency, owing to its relevant mission and its existing relationships with local communities. The program was developed to "harness the power of every individual through education, training, and volunteer service to make communities safer, stronger, and better prepared to respond to the threats of terrorism, crime, public health issues, and disasters of all kinds."

To accomplish this mission, Citizen Corps is working to develop a national network of state, local, and tribal Citizen Corps Councils, which will "tailor the activities to the community and build on community strengths to develop and implement a local strategy to have every American participate through personal responsibility, training, and volunteer service."

There are four Citizen Corps programs administered by three federal agencies—the Department of Justice, the Federal Emergency Management Agency, and the Department of Health and Human Services, individually described below.

Department of Justice

- Neighborhood Watch: This crime prevention program, which has a 30-year history, engages volunteer citizen action to enhance security within local communities by encouraging citizens to report suspicious activity in their immediate neighborhoods. Citizen Corps hopes to double the number of neighborhood watch programs to 15,000 by 2005, while incorporating terrorism prevention into the program's mission. The program is partnered by the National Sheriffs' Association.

- Volunteers in Police Service (VIPS): This program provides training for civilian volunteers who assist local police departments by performing "nonsworn" duties, effectively freeing up officers to provide them with more time to spend on critical functions. This program is partnered by the International Association of Chiefs of Police.

Federal Emergency Management Agency

- Community Emergency Response Teams (CERT): This program provides civilians with training in emergency management planning and response functions to bolster the capacity of local communities to respond to disasters. President Bush has proposed a threefold increase in the number people enrolled in CERT to 600,000 by 2005. Since its move into Citizen Corps, the program has added a new module that addresses terrorism preparedness.

Department of Health and Human Services

- Medical Reserve Corps (MRC): This program utilizes the experience and knowledge of active and retired health-care professionals and citizens with an interest in public health issues to augment local health-care capacity in the event of large-scale local emergencies. The volunteers also work throughout the year to promote community public health issues. To date there have been 42 $50,000 grants administered throughout the country. There is expected to be an additional $8 million made available to Medical Reserve Corps in the near future.

CORPORATION FOR NATIONAL AND COMMUNITY SERVICE

CNCS, created by President Bill Clinton, consists of three programs: Senior Corps, AmeriCorps, and Learn and Serve America. CNCS "provides opportunities for Americans of all ages and backgrounds to serve their communities and country." CNCS recruits volunteers to serve with national and community nonprofit organizations, faith-based groups, schools, and local agencies to help meet community needs in education, the environment, public safety, homeland security, and other areas. The three principal CNCS programs are described below.

Senior Corps

This program is described as a network of programs that "tap the experience, skills, and talents of older citizens to meet community challenges." It includes three programs; Foster Grandparents (who serve as tutors and mentors to youths with special needs), Senior Companions (who help homebound seniors and other adults maintain independence in their own homes), and the Retired and Senior Volunteer Program (RSVP—volunteers conduct safety patrols for local police departments, participate in environmental projects, provide intensive educational services, and respond to natural disasters, among other activities). More than half a million Americans, age 55 and over, assist local nonprofits, public agencies, and faith-based organizations in carrying out their missions. The 2004 budget requests funding for 600,000 Senior Corps volunteers ($212 million).

AmeriCorps

This program is described as a network of national service programs that "engage more than 50,000 Americans each year in intensive service to meet critical needs in education, public safety, health, and the environment." AmeriCorps members serve through more than 2,100 nonprofits, public agencies, and faith-based organizations, tutoring and mentoring youth, building affordable housing, teaching computer skills, cleaning parks and streams, running after-school programs, and helping communities respond to disasters. The AmeriCorps program includes AmeriCorps (volunteers serve 20 to 40 hours per week at local and national nonprofit organizations and community-based organizations, both secular and faith-based), AmeriCorps VISTA (focuses on eradicating poverty and helping to meet the needs of people in low-income communities), and AmeriCorps NCCC (National Civilian Community Corps—a residential program that supplies volunteers to nonprofit groups to provide for disaster relief, preserve the environment, build homes for low-income families, tutor children, and meet other challenges). The programs engage more than 55,000 Americans of all ages and backgrounds in service each year. The 2004 budget requests funding for 75,000 AmeriCorps volunteers ($554 million).

Learn and Serve America

This program "supports service-learning programs in schools and community organizations that help nearly 1 million students from kindergarten through college meet community needs, while improving their academic skills and learning the habits of good citizenship." The 2004 budget requests $43 million for programs that could accommodate 1.65 million students.

As of the date of the conference, over 400 Citizen Corps Councils had been established in communities across the country, with more being formed almost every day. Citizen Corps hopes to have fifty-six state and territory Citizen Corps Councils formed by mid-2003.

THE ISSUES

The following four principal areas of concern emerged from the discussions that transpired during the two-day conference.

RESOURCES

Greater access to resources to fund Homeland Security programs and projects at the community level.

Most communities throughout the United States were operating within the constraints of lean fiscal budgets prior to the September 11 attacks. In the aftermath of those events, countless administrative, police, fire, and emergency management staff were called upon to fulfill new or expanded public safety roles. As a result, municipalities were forced to spend funds they could ill afford on these new costs, including overtime pay and expensive prevention and detection equipment. Steve Weston of the California Highway Patrol described how the new requirements created "a tremendous burden" on that law enforcement organization.

Although billions of dollars in federal funding to cover these costs have been promised, few have been granted. Additionally, both state and local governments are finding that many existing programs they have depended on are being cut, such as the Community Oriented Policing Services (COPS) program and the Local Law Enforcement Block Grant, to pay for increasing costs associated with the wars on terrorism and Iraq. Many communities are beginning to feel that "you can't seem to get funding unless you wrap the word 'counterterrorism' around [the project]" (Eileen Garry—DOJ).

Staff involved in initiating and promoting homeland security programs in communities are finding themselves particularly frustrated in their efforts as a result of this severe resource drought. One participant expressed the concern that "making us fundraisers, in addition to our programmatic [tasks], really stretches municipalities' resources thin. The raw numbers of people required for fundraising exhausts programs."

However, such fundraising actions are recognized as vital to any program's success, echoed by Doris Milldyke (Kansas), who said, "Money is the first goal, volunteers are the second." There undeniably exists a fervent desire to promote homeland security programs throughout America's communities, but so many of these project entrepreneurs are finding themselves impotent due to the shortage of available federal resources.

Another related concern of the participants was that funding made available for the local jurisdictions often became "bottlenecked" in the state offices, rarely trickling down to communities. Adam Sutkus, speaking on behalf of then California governor Gray Davis' GO SERV office, stated, "Because of the September 11 environment, there are many new funding streams." However, this came as little consolation to the local representatives.

Valli Wasp of Austin explained during her presentation that "it is very difficult to get local funds from the state, because it is all about control. It is a paternalistic, military-like relationship between the state and local communities." Jane Bullock of the SAFE Project explained, "Money must go to the locals [as required by program rules], but it may not reach them because of 'creative budgeting' at the state level."

Jane Bullock described how "funding can be a huge problem," but added that "additional money in the Homeland Security area is appearing" and that there "should be a 5-year window of increased spending." However, she described these prospects as "shaky."

All participants agreed that funding needs to be an active role of local Citizen Corps and other Homeland Security programs, but most expressed they needed advice and ideas. Speakers and participants alike voiced their frustration and called upon each other for both traditional and alternative means for securing much-needed resources.

The discussions revealed some surprising results, detailed below. These findings are grouped according to whether they apply to the federal government, the business sector, foundations (and other philanthropies), or creative fundraising.

The Federal Government

Karen Marsh, representing the FEMA Citizen Corps program, described how Citizen Corps started after September 11, 2001, without any funding but was later appropriated $20 million that it eventually distributed to the states in August of 2002. Of this amount, 75 percent must be passed directly to the communities. Although these sources of funding "did not fare as well in 2003," $181 million has been requested for 2004. If this money materializes, it would be the primary source of funding for a majority of the programs discussed over the course of the conference.

A community block grant program, such as the one proposed in the "Homeland Security Block Grant Act," that provides funding directly to communities to augment the capabilities of first responders, is desperately needed. Ann Patton of Tulsa, Oklahoma, indicated that "block grants would be invaluable" in accomplishing these community homeland security goals.

In addition, Chuck Supple of GO SERV described how it is possible for Citizen Corps Councils to apply for AmeriCorps grants to bolster their programs, and Kristin Haggins of CNCS stated that with VISTA, you can get "human" grants instead of money.

The Business Community

Business emerged as a vastly underused source for human, material, and financial resources. Participants agreed that local communities need to increase partnerships with the business community but acknowledged that "there [currently] exists no concrete strategy to reach them." Many in attendance stated that one way to increase chances of successfully garnering support from businesses is to ask for merchandise instead of cash donations.

Several participants and speakers relayed successes they had experienced in their own communities, including Ann Patton of Tulsa, Oklahoma, who partnered with several Tulsa McDonalds Restaurants to perform disaster communication through the McDonalds paper [meal] tray liners;

Joseph Bobot from Ohio, who successfully solicited donated Stokes Litters (stretchers) from a local business; and Valli Wasp of Austin, who secured a whole spectrum of donated products and services while working to help her local community prepare for the possible ramifications of the Y2K bug.

One participant suggested that staff involved in community-based homeland security "jump on the homeland security tradeshow bandwagon," referring to the widespread business showcases where homeland security–based products are marketed. Another questioned whether the Fortune 500 companies would, out of recognition of their corporate responsibility in the communities where they operate, endorse community-based homeland security programs. Jane Bullock (SAFE) added that participants should look to local hospitals and the banking and financial community to act as partners.

Foundations

Though discussed in less detail than the preceding two groups, foundations and other philanthropic organizations were also identified as a potential source of funding. One participant stated that "we must create an awareness of both the business and philanthropic communities," referring to a recognition by those groups of both their responsibility to participate in such programs and the potential security and safety benefits of that participation. Chuck Supple stated that the state of California has only recently begun looking into support from foundations and philanthropies and that they have not yet identified a place for philanthropic involvement. He suggested that community foundation networks help in identifying areas for philanthropy involvement.

Creative Fundraising Ideas

The most widely recognized need for communities regarding fundraising resources was that they find creative ways to solve their financial problems. Karen Marsh (Citizen Corps) expressed during her presentation that emergency managers need to focus on volunteer recruitment and donations. Her comments indicated an awareness that these municipal programs require support from nontraditional means for their success.

One participant noted that it has become necessary for the Citizen Corps Councils to reach out to every community "stratum," adding that "waiting for the federal government to offer communities money leads to nothing." Richard

Paige from Mendocino County, California, asserted that local Citizen Corps Councils need to attain 501(c)(3) non-profit status, adding, "This is not just a recommendation!"

The breadth of suggestions for creative fundraising methods was rather impressive and highlighted the need for a platform for sharing ideas among local community programs. In addition to those described above, the following ideas were proposed:

- Give tax breaks to businesses that make donations to Citizen Corps (participant).
- Secure program endorsement from local elected officials to increase the likelihood of consideration for funding (Norma Schroeder, California, EMSA).
- There are many "unofficial" Medical Reserve Corps throughout the community. The classification of "registered unit" can be given to existing MRC-type units if they meet preestablished requirements, therefore "put[ting] them in the loop without the otherwise-required $50,000 grant" (Norma Schroeder).
- Councils must establish close working relationships with police and fire departments, because they are critical partners in getting federal government funding (Jane Bullock, SAFE).
- Resources include more than money. They can be people, space, in-kind, and others (Ken Terao, Aguirre International).
- Communities should try to first establish a local program with which to seek funding, instead of first seeking money to start a nonexistent program (participant).

Summary

The presentations and discussions by conference participants concerning resources identified several critical areas:

- Block grants to communities are an efficient means for providing federal funding for community homeland security efforts. Consideration should be given to expanding the use of Community Development Block Grants for homeland security efforts and passage of the "Homeland Security Block Grant Act."
- Communities should partner with the National Governor's Association, the United States Conference of Mayors, the League of Cities, and other professional associations seeking federal funding for community homeland security efforts.

- Creative funding ideas practiced in communities around the countries need to be identified and widely disseminated among community homeland security officials.
- New partnerships need to be established with the country's business and philanthropic communities to leverage their resources for community homeland security efforts.

INFORMATION

Greater access to practical information about application, eligibility, recruitment, retention, and other concerns.

It was obvious to all of the participants that virtually everyone involved in coordinating homeland security programs at the community level was passionate about initiating or expanding programs in their own communities. However, there exists an overwhelming sense of frustration concerning the lack of access to information to help them pursue these goals.

Although the information they seek often does exist, participants voiced dismay that they had to search for it in what seems to them like countless locations due to a lack of any centralization. Ann Patton (Tulsa, Oklahoma) stated, "An information clearinghouse would be invaluable." Doris Milldyke (Kansas) noted that information on VIPS, MRS, and other programs is "notoriously difficult to find," adding, "We need a golden key for information on getting grants." During the discussion period, participants added that they are frustrated with the application process for Citizen Corps and that, because programs keep changing, they have difficulty "keeping up." One woman exclaimed, while explaining frustration over her inability to retrieve information from the Washington, DC, office of Citizen Corps, said, "Don't tell me to talk to my state!"

Karen Marsh of Citizen Corps explained during her presentation that every community throughout the United States and its territories is different, and therefore the Citizen Corps program was designed to be flexible. She added that Citizen Corps offers guidance to communities for setting up a local Citizen Corps Council. However, a point made by Ana-Marie Jones (Oakland, California) during her presentation on emergency planning described the danger of too much flexibility without sufficient guidance, "When you give 500 agencies money for plans, you get 499 different plans. You must coordinate and standardize."

Ann Patton later added that it would be helpful to have a model Citizen Corps program made available for design and planning purposes. Joanne Burke stated that GO SERV captures and documents best practices for people to draw upon, information of interest to most in attendance. Eileen Garry (DOJ) added that, based upon the participants' discussions, she would add a section to her web site showcasing available counterterrorism training available to state and local first-responders (www.counterterrorismtraining.org) in a section titled "Community Support."

Summary

Access to accurate and timely information was identified by conference participants as critical to their efforts to design and implement community-based homeland security programs. Suggestions for improving access to this information included the following:

- Establishing an information clearinghouse to catalog homeland security information sources
- Establishing a web-based "Chat Room" for community officials to exchange ideas and best practices and to discuss current issues
- Establishing a "Funding Exchange" to share ideas on funding sources and creative funding ideas
- Partnering with the Department of Homeland Security and state homeland security operations to facilitate the flow of information on federal and state programs and funding opportunities to community officials.

PROGRAMMING

The need for new and innovative programming ideas.

Another principal area of concern for the participants involved a wide range of programming issues. Homeland Security program staff in attendance expressed a strong desire to go beyond the traditional "cookie-cutter" approach in designing programs and utilizing volunteers. They agreed that all communities were different and thus had different needs.

Some in attendance felt that more direction from the state and federal levels was necessary ("We cannot just throw people and money at problems and expect to . . . see results," said Chuck Supple), while others felt that the ideas must originate within the community ("New ideas need to surface"). Ana-Marie Jones described how she discovered in Oakland, California, that many teachers were overwhelmed by the thought of their responsibilities in times of disaster. Through her program, children were trained to keep quiet during emergencies, providing the teachers with more "peace of mind." All felt that there needed to be greater exploration to discover additional and improved program areas. Chuck Supple stated this position well in saying, "We've probably only thought of a 'minutia' of the areas where volunteers would be useful."

The speakers and participants were all more than happy to share several original and innovative ideas they had developed in their own communities, and to relay areas of concern they had encountered. Steve Weston of the CHP explained how many new skill sets were needed to handle the increased counterterrorism requirements of homeland security. His organization discovered that they had extensive language capabilities previously unknown to them that were valuable in their investigations.

Ann Patton described how she helped to develop a "Language and Culture Bank" in Tulsa, Oklahoma, that was effective in increasing preparedness and fear management throughout the many diverse communities in that city.

Doris Milldyke said, "We must market to local law enforcement the benefits of Citizen Corps, because many [departments] feel they already have more volunteers than [they] know what to do with." She added that states need to try to encourage the formation of regional Citizen Corps Councils in rural areas where local Citizen Corps Councils are unlikely to form. Jane Bullock (SAFE) expressed concern that public health issues were not adequately addressed by community homeland security programs.

The topic of volunteer training seemed to surface repeatedly throughout these discussions on programming. Adam Sutkus of GO SERV suggested that more courses that "train-the-trainer" were needed. Joanne Burke, also of GO SERV, advised that the twenty-hour CERT training program be built into other larger programs in a way that CERT becomes a required component.

Chuck Supple explained how trained citizens can have a great impact on the community, but insisted that the training must be significant. He added that the training brings people "in the door," thus allowing them to participate in additional programs. Mr. Supple advised participants to "create an opportunity, recruit, and use all volunteers," stating that, "not only those with significant skills are wanted. Training and preparation is part of Citizen Corps."

Even though the specific goals of homeland security programs may differ significantly from community to community, several speakers and participants agreed that the most fundamental driving force behind community Homeland Security programs should be "to knit the community together" (Ann Patton), and "to make neighborhoods where people know each other in the best of times and in the worst of times" (Carol Lopes).

There are literally infinite ways in which communities can tailor these programs to suit the needs of their citizens. The conference participants again expressed the need for a clearinghouse of such experience, advice, and information.

Summary

In addition to the homeland security programming currently in place (i.e., CERT training, Medical RSVP, etc.), conference participants identified a need to design and implement programs that fully leveraged the capabilities of volunteers in the community. Several ideas were considered, including the following:

- The SAFE Project designed to develop volunteer programs in support of community emergency management and homeland security operations
- The development of Community Emergency Networks (CEN) designed to facilitate communications between community residents and local emergency and homeland security officials before, during, and after a disaster or terrorist incident

CUSTOMIZING

The need to focus on diverse populations, including those with "special needs."

A major concern articulated by several of the speakers throughout the two-day conference was the need to address communities' "special needs populations." Presenters stressed the importance of considering these groups in project planning and shared examples of situations in which projects required adaptation to accommodate such groups.

Chuck Supple, who described California as a state where "the majority is a mixed minority," stressed, "National security depends on bringing people in communities of different backgrounds together." Amy Gaver (American Red Cross) said that there are over 100 languages spoken in the San Francisco Bay Area, but stressed that residents "love their diversity."

Valli Wasp (Austin, Texas) explained how the term "special needs" must be considered in multiple ways, describing

one example where the web site "Ready.gov" (DHS) has caused concern for citizens in Texas who don't have underground shelters in their houses to take cover in during certain emergencies as instructed to on the site.

Several speakers offered general advice to participants for working with special-needs populations. Carol Lopes stressed that participants must "ensure that the vulnerable populations are considered" in the planning and execution of programs. Maya Harris-West (Oakland, California) stated that accountability must be a vital component of any homeland security program, "especially in communities with a great distrust of police."

Ana-Marie Jones warned that "special needs communities are often isolated from services," adding that "[programs] must have a trusted leader who either speaks or has access to the languages of all representative groups—you need more than a 'Spanish press release.'" She suggested that participants "involve special needs communities before the disaster" to be effective. George Haddow (SAFE) echoed an earlier presenter's view that in certain special needs communities "people are more likely to respond to those that they know than a person with a gun and a badge."

Specific needs and characteristics of communities can be regarded as a benefit instead of a hindrance. Monique Morris (NCCD) explained how paramedics may be afraid or unwilling to go into more dangerous neighborhoods in times of disaster, but if people from those communities are trained through community homeland security projects, then those communities become safer even outside of disaster events. Ms. Morris also explained how tapping into religious groups that are central to many of these communities could greatly assist both fundraising and recruitment of volunteers. She added, "Design your mission to fit their mission, not the other way around."

Summary

Servicing diverse and "special needs" populations must be a critical component of any community-based homeland security effort. A number of ideas for addressing these needs were discussed by participants, including the following:

- Reprogramming Community Development Block Grant (CDBG) funding targeted for "special needs" populations to include homeland security efforts
- Establishing "Language and Culture Banks" in communities to facilitate communications and information flow between public safety and emergency officials and special-needs populations

- Partnering with national associations and groups that represent the interests of special-needs populations such as the elderly, veterans, minority populations, children and the disabled
- Partnering with foundations and other philanthropic organizations such as the Annie E. Casey Foundation, which focuses its efforts and funding in disadvantaged communities
- Partnering with local emergency management/homeland security and public health operations to help these groups identify and serve "special needs" populations in the community.

CONCLUSIONS

Where do we go from here?

The conference concluded with a general participatory group discussion based on the topics that had been discussed over the 2-day period. This conversation quickly led to suggestions for change and future implications. The range of responses reflected the vast experience, insight, and motivation of the group.

One issue that repeatedly emerged was that there existed no centralized advocacy for funding, information, or programming that communities could turn to for assistance. George Haddow (SAFE) noted, "There has never been a grassroots network for emergency management, but the need is growing." One participant flatly stated that "we must organize at the grassroots level, or we will be having the same conversations next year." Another added, "Unity is the solution. Otherwise, we are just individual sitting ducks."

Ann Patton told the members of the group that they must "recognize it is our problem, and we need to fix it." To illustrate her point, she displayed a map depicting disaster-resistant communities across the nation and said, "We need to connect the dots" (and create a network of communities concerned with Homeland Security issues).

This network of concerned communities could be the "Golden Key" that Doris Milldyke spoke of during her presentation. Karen Marsh (Citizen Corps) described how Citizen Corps captures and documents best practices for communities to draw upon—these experiences need not only to be documented by all communities, but to be shared across all state and territorial borders.

A network would give all communities access to the experiences of the presenters and participants at the conference, and allow them to share their individual expertise as well. Norma Schroeder stated, "Community groups should be able to share lessons and experiences." Given ample access, planners would learn invaluable lessons on volunteer recruitment from people such as Monique Morris (NCCD). They would surely benefit from the programming success stories of groups like, and from other communities such as, Tulsa, Austin, and Oakland.

The tremendous benefits possible from such a "network of practitioners" make the necessity for its existence not only obvious but also immediate. Eileen Garry (DOJ) stated during her presentation that "the solutions to our problems are in this room." Only such a network would allow for the effective sharing of those solutions such that small local achievements can become widespread success stories. Conference participants agreed that such a network could address many of the needs identified over the course of the conference, including the following:

- Improving the flow of information on homeland security funding opportunities at all levels of government and in the business and philanthropic sectors to community officials
- Facilitating the sharing of best practices and ideas on community-based homeland security programs and activities
- Designing and implementing new community-based homeland security programming such as the SAFE Project and the Community Emergency Networks (CEN)
- Ensuring that special-needs populations in communities are identified and helped through programs such as the Language and Culture Bank and partnerships with advocacy groups.

THE NEXT CONFERENCE

The First Annual Conference on Communities and Homeland Security closed with a clear message: Solving the identified problems is a priority for communities. One participant expressed concern that communities "cannot wait a year for the next conference." Others felt that the next conference should focus on additional issues that were only touched upon, such as volunteer liability, the assessment of risk, and mitigation.

One attendee suggested that subgroups be formed to tackle these individual areas of concern. Another stressed that there needs to be greater representation of stakeholders, including a wider representation of communities from across the country and more participation by both foundations and the media.

There was an overwhelming sense among the conference organizers, the speakers, and the attendees that the meeting brought several important issues to the table. Many of these practitioners agreed to work together in the interim via conference calls and online collaboration to develop real solutions. However, the need to address the creation of a formal platform to support a network of communities working together to solve these problems must be foremost in the consideration of any future meeting that is organized.

THE COMMUNITY AND HOMELAND SECURITY CONFERENCE AGENDA

Topic	Speaker
Welcome and Opening Remarks	Barry Krisberg, Ph.D., NCCD
"Homeland Security: A California Perspective"	Chief Dave Wilson, California Highway Patrol
"Citizen Corps and Homeland Security" Corps	Karen Marsh, Citizen
Panel Discussion— "Community-Based Programs and Homeland Security"	Panelists: Ann Patton, Tulsa, OK Carol Lopes, Berkeley, CA
Moderator: Barry Krisberg, Ph.D., NCCD	Ana-Marie Jones, Oakland, CA Maya Harris-West, Oakland, CA
"Integrating Citizen Corps into Statewide Community Response"	Chuck Supple, Executive Director, CA Governor's Office on Service and Volunteerism (GO SERV)
Panel Discussion— "New Approaches to Community-Based Homeland Security Programs"	Panelists: Valli Wasp, Austin, TX Doris Milldyke, Manhattan, KS Adam Sutkus, Sacramento, CA
Moderator: Jane Bullock, SAFE Project	
"National Efforts of the Corporation for National and Community Service (CNCS) and Citizen Corps"	Kristen Haggins, State Director of CNCS
"Volunteer Recruitment and Training"	Monique Morris, NCCD
"Statewide Medical Response Corps Formation, Programs, and Funding"	Norma Schroeder, Emergency Medical Services Authority (EMSA)
"Role of the Red Cross in Homeland Security"	Amy Gaver, American Red Cross
"How to Prepare a Community Homeland Security Plan"	Jane Bullock, SAFE Project
"How to Evaluate Community Homeland Security Programs"	Ken Terao, Aguirre International
"Counter-Terrorism Training and Resources"	Eileen Garry, U.S. Department of Justice
"Building Community Emergency Networks"	George Haddow, SAFE Project
"Next Steps: Forming a National Community NCCD Network" Group discussion and brainstorm	Facilitated by Barry Krisberg,

Appendix 10: California State Agency Guidance: Homeland Security Advisory System

California State Agency Guidance:
Homeland Security Advisory System

March 20, 2003

Purpose

As memorialized in Homeland Security Presidential Directive 3, the Federal Government has implemented the Homeland Security Advisory System to provide a comprehensive and effective means to disseminate information regarding the risk of terrorist acts. The system provides warnings in the form of a set of graduated "Threat Conditions" that would increase as the risk of the threat increases. At each Threat Condition, State departments and agencies would implement a corresponding set of "Protective Measures" to further reduce vulnerability or increase response capability during a period of heightened alert. This document describes the Threat Conditions and provides guidance in creating and implementing the protective measures for State departments and agencies. The content and format were developed from existing, available information and input from the Intelligence and Early Warning Subcommittee of the State Strategic Committee on Terrorism. <u>Each State department and agency is responsible for determining what actions and plans are appropriate to that department or organization.</u>

Federal Homeland Security Advisory System

There are five Threat Conditions, each identified by a description and corresponding color. From lowest to highest, the colors and levels are:

RED	**SEVERE – A Severe risk of terrorist attacks**
ORANGE	**HIGH – A high risk of terrorist attacks**
YELLOW	**ELEVATED – A significant risk of terrorist attacks**
BLUE	**GUARDED – A general risk of terrorist attacks**
GREEN	**LOW – A low risk of terrorist attacks**

The higher the Threat Condition, the greater the risk of a terrorist attack. Risk includes both the probability of an attack occurring and its potential gravity. Threat Conditions may be for the entire State, or may be set for a particular geographic area or industrial sector.

The assignment of a Threat Condition will prompt the implementation of an appropriate set of protective measures. The protective measures are the specific steps an organization should take to reduce its vulnerability or increase its ability to respond during a period of heightened alert. It is recognized that departments and agencies may have several preplanned sets of responses to a particular Threat Condition to facilitate a rapid, appropriate, and tailored response. Department and agency heads are responsible for developing their own protective measures and other antiterrorism or self-protection and continuity plans, as well as resourcing, rehearsing, documenting, and maintaining these plans. Likewise, they retain the authority to respond, as necessary, to risks, threats, incidents, or events at facilities within the specific jurisdiction of their department or agency, and, as authorized by law, to direct agencies and industries to implement their own protective measures. They will continue to be responsible for taking all appropriate proactive steps to reduce the vulnerability of their personnel and facilities to terrorist attack.

Protective Measures

Protective measures and activities for state agencies are recommended actions, not required actions. While each state agency should implement measures/activities appropriate to its own operating environment, the following general guidelines apply:

- The threat/risk goes up with each successive level.

- Responses are additive; each level incorporates all activities from the previous levels.

- Threat information may be general or indicated for different geographical regions of the state.

- Specific implementation must be determined by each agency in light of actual events; protective measures for a higher level than officially designated may be implemented by each agency. For example, if the threat advisory level is elevated from "Yellow" to "Orange" an agency may elect to implement not only "Orange" level suggested protective measures, but also some "Red" level protective measures.

- Measures are numbered for ease of use. For example, an organization may wish to state that it has implemented all measures for YELLOW, but added measures 70 and 73, etc.

The following pages present specific protective measures in response to the Homeland Security Advisory System [HSAS] threat level conditions.

Recommended Protective Measures: GREEN – Low Condition
This condition is declared when there is a *low* risk of terrorist attacks.

Measure 1. Reviewing and revising current Emergency and Business Continuity/ Resumption Plans to include mitigation and contingency planning for conditions that current plans do not address such as biological, nuclear, incindiary, chemical, explosive threats and exposure

Measure 2. Ensure the agency is familiar with all of the requirements of the Standardized Emergency Management System (SEMS). All State agencies must comply with these requirements. Contact the Governor's Office of Emergency Services for further information.

Measure 3. Refining and exercising, as appropriate, preplanned Protective Measures.

Measure 4. Ensuring personnel receive proper training on the Homeland Security Advisory System and specific preplanned department or agency Protective Measures.

Measure 5. Institutionalizing a process to assure that all facilities are regularly assessed for vulnerabilities to terrorist attacks, and all reasonable measures are taken to mitigate these vulnerabilities.

Measure 6. All contractors and visitors must check or sign in and out of designated facilities or areas within the facility that are considered key command, control or communications centers or areas.

Measure 7. Ensure existing security measures are in place and functioning such as fencing, locks, camera surveillance, intruder alarms, and lighting. Identify those additional security measures and resources that can enhance the security at the higher Threat Condition levels (e.g. increased surveillance).

Measure 8. Review procedures for receiving and disseminating information transmitted via the state agency emergency notification system (as required by Management Memo 02-09).

Measure 9. Establish local, regional and system-wide threat and warning dissemination process, emergency communications capability, and contact information with law enforcement and security officials, including CHP and local FBI Field Offices. Emergency communications should have redundancy in both hardware and means to contact security officials, law enforcement agencies, and mobile field command centers.

Measure 10. Develop terrorist and security awareness and provide information and educate employees on security standards and procedures. Caution employees not to talk with outsiders concerning their facility or related issues.

Measure 11. Advise all personnel at each facility to report the presence of unknown personnel, unidentified vehicles, vehicles operated out of the ordinary, abandoned parcels or packages, and any suspicious activities. Report suspicious information immediately to the California Highway Patrol

Measure 12. Develop procedures for shutting down and evacuation, or shelter in place, of facilities. Facilities located near critical community assets should be especially vigilant of security measures.

Measure 13. Incorporate security awareness and information into public education programs and notifications to emergency response organizations.

Measure 14. Survey *surrounding* areas to determine those activities that might increase the security risks that could affect the state facility (e.g. airports, government buildings, industrial facilities, pipelines.)

Measure 15. Ensure contingency and business continuity plans are current and include a response to terrorist threats.

Measure 16. Develop and implement hardware, software, and communications security for computer based operational systems.

Intentionally Blank

Recommended Protective Measures: BLUE – Guarded Condition
This condition is declared when there is a *general* risk of terrorist attacks.

Measure 17. Ensure that a response can be mobilized and review facility security plans and procedures including bomb threat, chemical, biological or radiological threat and evacuation procedures. Ensure plans incorporate EOD and tactical teams as necessary, including accessibility to explosive detection capabilities such as K-9 teams or electronic air sampling devices.

Measure 18. Inspect perimeter fencing and repair all fence breakdowns. In addition, review all outstanding maintenance and capital project work that could affect the security of facilities.

Measure 19. Review all operations plans, personnel details, and logistics requirements that pertain to implementing higher Threat Condition levels.

Measure 20. Inspect all CCTV/Video Camera/VCR equipment and intercom systems where applicable to ensure equipment is operational.

Measure 21. Review and ensure adequacy of personnel and ID issuance and control procedures.

Measure 22. Require each visitor to check in at designated facilities or areas within the facility that are consider key command, control or communications centers or areas and verify their identification. Be especially alert to repeat visitors or outsiders who have no apparent business at the facility and are asking questions about the facility or related issues including the facility's personnel. Be familiar with vendors who service the facility and investigate changes in vendor personnel.

Measure 23. Inspect emergency supplies to ensure equipment is in good working order.

Measure 24. Provide the public with any information that would strengthen its ability to act appropriately.

Measure 25. At regular intervals, remind all personnel to be suspicious and inquisitive about strangers, particularly those carrying suitcases or other containers. Watch for unidentified vehicles on or in the vicinity of facilities. Watch for abandoned parcels or suitcases and any unusual activity.

Measure 26. Consider on-scene emergency medical care in case of delayed outside assistance. (I.e., Basic First Aid and CPR employee training).

Measure 27. Review and familiarize staff with their respective agency Department Operation Centers (DOC's) or Emergency Operation Centers (EOC's) activation criteria and procedures.

Recommended Protective Measures: YELLOW – Elevated Condition
An Elevated Condition is declared when there is a *significant* risk of terrorist attacks.

Measure 28. Inform all security officials, with an operational need to know, of the increased threat. Communicate this information to agency employees who have an operational need to know. Reinforce awareness of responsibilities with employees.

Measure 29. Test security and emergency communications procedures and protocols. Post a Security Alert if appropriate. Check communications with designated emergency response or command locations.

Measure 30. Secure all buildings and storage areas not in regular use. Increase frequency of inspection and patrols within the facility including the interior of buildings and along the facility perimeter. Increase surveillance in areas considered key command, control or communications centers and areas such as truck docks, taxi lanes, and parking lots.

Measure 31. Check designated unmanned and remote sites at more frequent intervals for signs of unauthorized entry, suspicious packages, or unusual activities.

Measure 32. Reduce the number of access points for vehicles and personnel to minimum levels and periodically spot check the contents of vehicles at the access points. Be alert to vehicles parked for an unusual length of time in or near a facility.

Measure 33. Inspect all mail and packages coming into a facility. Do not open suspicious packages. Review the USPS "Suspicious Mail Alert" and the "Bombs by Mail" publications with all personnel involved in receiving mail and packages.

Measure 34. Network with CHP and local law enforcement intelligence units, i.e. FBI field offices, and liaison, as appropriate, with other departments.

Measure 35. Ensure that personnel with access to building plans and area evacuation plans be available at all times. Personnel should be able to seal off an area immediately. The staff required to implement security plans should be on call and readily available.

Measure 36. Increase security spot checks of vehicles and persons entering facilities.

Measure 37. Review and implement security measures for high-risk personnel, as appropriate.

Measure 38. Inform personnel of additional threat information as available. Implement procedures to provide periodic updates on security measures being implemented.

Measure 39. Ensure that an agency or facility response can be mobilized appropriately for the increased security level. Review communications procedures and back-up plans with all concerned.

Measure 40. Review with all facility employees the operations plans; personnel safety, security details, and logistics requirements that pertain to implementing increased security levels. Review notification/recall lists.

Measure 41. Confirm availability of security resources that can assist with 24/7 coverage as applicable.

Measure 42. Step up routine checks of unattended vehicles, scrutiny of packages and vehicles, and monitor critical facilities and key infrastructure to ensure they are properly secured.

Measure 43. Limit visitor access to key security areas and confirm that the visitor has a need to be there and is expected. All unknown visitors should be escorted while in these areas.

Measure 44. Advise CHP and local police agencies that the facility is at Elevated Condition (Yellow) and advise the measures being employed. Coordinate emergency plans as appropriate with nearby jurisdictions.

Measure 45. Resurvey the surrounding area to determine if activities near the facility could create emergencies and other incidents that could affect the facility (e.g. airports, government buildings, industrial facilities, railroads, other pipelines).

Measure 46. Instruct employees working alone at remote locations to check-in on a periodic basis.

Measure 47. Check to ensure all emergency telephone, radio, intercom, and satellite communication devices are in place and operational.

Measure 48. Direct all personnel at the facility to secure vehicles by locking them.

Measure 49. Interface with vendors and contractors to heighten awareness and report suspicious activity. Post signs or make routine public announcements that emphasize the need for all passengers to closely control baggage and packages to avoid transporting items without their knowledge.

Measure 50. Develop and implement a schedule for increasing the frequency of inspection including specific areas and item such as: telephone booths, garbage containers, and all public areas.

Measure 51. Assessing whether the precise characteristics of the threat require further refinement of the preplanned Protective Measures.

Measure 52. Implement, as appropriate, contingency and emergency response plans.

Measure 53. Keep all personnel involved in implementing antiterrorist contingency plans on call.

Measure 54. Secure and regularly inspect all buildings, rooms, and storage areas not in regular use.

Measure 55. At the beginning and end of each workday and at other regular and frequent intervals, inspect the interior and exterior of buildings in regular use for suspicious packages.

Measure 56. Examine mail (above the regular examination process) for letter or parcel bombs.

Measure 57. Check all deliveries to facility and loading docks.

Measure 58. Make staff and dependents aware of the general situation in order to stop rumors and prevent unnecessary alarm.

Measure 59. Operate random patrols to check vehicles, people, and buildings.

Measure 60. Implement additional security measures for high-risk personnel as appropriate.

Intentionally Blank

Recommended Protective Measures: ORANGE – High Condition
A High condition is declared when there is a *high* risk of terrorist attacks.

Measure 61. Move cars and objects (e.g. crates, trash containers) at least 25 meters from buildings (where possible) particularly highly populated, mission related, or high profile buildings. Consider centralized parking. Move automobiles and other non-stationary items from station and terminal perimeters and other sensitive buildings or areas. Identify areas where explosive devices could be hidden.

Measure 62. Close and lock gates and barriers except those needed for immediate entry and egress. Inspect perimeter fences on a regular basis. Ensure that other security systems are functioning and are available.

Measure 63. Increase security manpower for additional surveillance, to act as a deterrent and prevent unauthorized access to secure areas, deploy specialty/technical resources, and enact local tactical plans, if applicable. The areas recommended for additional patrols should include parking areas and loading docks. Increase surveillance of critical locations.

Measure 64. Continue Low, Guarded and Elevated measures or introduce those that have not already been implemented.

Measure 65. Reduce facility access points to the absolute minimum necessary for continued operation. Restrict threatened facility access to essential personnel only.

Measure 66. Advise CHP and local police agencies that the facility is at a High Condition (Orange) and advise the measures being employed.

Measure 67. Consult with CHP and local authorities about control of public roads and accesses that might make the facility more vulnerable to terrorist attack if they were to remain open. Take additional precautions at public events and possibly consider alternative venues or even cancellation.

Measure 68. Implement centralized parking and shuttle bus service where feasible.

Measure 69. Schedule more frequent visits to remote sites and other locations that are potentially impacted.

Measure 70. Increase the frequency of call-ins from remote locations. Employees should not work alone in remote areas.

Measure 71. Check all security systems such as lighting and intruder alarms to ensure they are functioning. Install additional, temporary lighting if necessary to adequately light all suspect areas or decrease lighting to detract from the area.

Measure 72. Identify the owner of all vehicles parked at key command, control, or communications areas or other critical areas/facilities/ and have all vehicles removed which are not identified.

Measure 73. Strictly enforce control of entry. Inspect all vehicles entering key areas/facilities including the vehicle's cargo areas, undercarriage, glove boxes, and other areas where dangerous items could be concealed.

Measure 74. Limit access to designated facilities to those personnel who have a legitimate and verifiable need to enter the facility. Implement a procedure for positive identification of all personnel, allowing no exceptions. Evacuate all non-essential personnel.

Measure 75. Implement frequent inspection of key areas or facilities including the exterior and roof of all buildings and parking areas. Increase patrolling at night and ensure all vulnerable critical points are fully illuminated and secure.

Measure 76. Review procedures and make necessary preparations to activate Command Center(s) where applicable. Prepare to execute contingency procedures, such as moving to an alternate site or dispersing the workforce.

Measure 77. Coordinate security efforts with the California Highway Patrol. This should include enhancements to security efforts with Federal, State, and local law enforcement agencies or any National Guard or other appropriate armed forces organizations. **NOTE:** Any resource taskings will be in accordance with current policies and procedures.

Measure 78. Keep all personnel responsible for implementing antiterrorist plans on call.

Measure 79. Enforce centralized parking of vehicles away from buildings.

Measure 80. Increase patrolling of the facilities.

Measure 81. Protect all designated vulnerable points.

Recommended Protective Measures: RED – Severe Condition
A Severe Condition reflects a *severe* risk of terrorist attacks.

Measure 82. Increase security patrol activity to the maximum level sustainable. Increase perimeter patrols and inspections of facility.

Measure 83. Postpone or cancel all non-vital facility work conducted by contractors, or continuously monitor their work as applicable.

Measure 84. Continue all Low, Guarded, Elevated and High Condition measures or introduce those that have not already been implemented.

Measure 85. Implement emergency and continuity plans as appropriate. Reduce restricted area access points to an operational minimum.

Measure 86. Augment security forces to ensure absolute control of key command, control or communications centers or areas and other potential target areas. Establish surveillance points and reporting criteria and procedures.

Measure 87. Remove unattended, unauthorized vehicles parked within 300 feet of a terminal building or station where passengers load or unload.

Measure 88. Increase or redirect personnel to address critical emergency needs.

Measure 89. Identify all vehicles within operational or mission support areas.

Measure 90. Search all vehicles and their contents before allowing entrance to facilities.

Measure 91. Control access and implement positive identification of all personnel.

Measure 92. Search all suitcases, briefcases, packages, etc., brought into the facility.

Measure 93. Conduct frequent checks of building exteriors and parking areas.

Measure 94. Minimize all administrative journeys and visits.

Measure 95. Coordinate the possible closing of public access roads and/or facilities with CHP and local authorities.

Conclusion

Each State department and agency is responsible for determining what actions and plans are appropriate to that department or organization. Along with emergency response preparation, each state department and agency should ensure Continuity of Government and Continuity of Operations. The above guidelines should be used as a catalyst for the review, refinement, and modification of existing emergency and business resumption plans, as needed. Contact the Governor's Office of Emergency Services for further assistance on emergency planning issues, or the California Highway Patrol for physical security issues.

Appendix 11: Communicating During Emergencies

By Jane A. Bullock, George D. Haddow, and Richard Bell

(NOTE: Research support for this paper was provided by Lauren Block, Tracy R. Bolo, Amina Chaudary, Brain D. Cogert, David DeCicco, Aspasia Papadopoulos, Robert Paxton, and Michael Stinziano.)

INTRODUCTION

Communicating with the public is one of the critical tasks facing emergency management agencies (EMAs). Reaching the widest possible audience with the most up-to-date, credible information can save lives and property, reduce public fears and anxiety, and maintain the public's trust in the integrity of government officials.

We recently conducted a survey of how EMA communicators had fared during a number of national disasters and terrorist attacks. Our concern about the adequacy of EMA communications planning has been heightened by a striking change in the intensity of media coverage. In describing their work with the press, our respondents used imagery very much like that which they applied to the emergency event itself. They found themselves swamped by a veritable "tidal wave" of reporters almost literally beating down their doors.

In this article we review the findings of our survey and interviews and lay out the principal suggestions we received from a cross-section of EMAs on putting the personnel and infrastructure in place to execute robust, flexible communications plans.

METHODOLOGY

This article is based on responses to a questionnaire that we received from communicators involved in the following recent natural disasters or terrorist attack, including interviews in most cases with the principal spokesperson involved:

- Tropical Storm Allison, Harris County Texas, Office of Emergency Management, Mayor's Office, June 5–10, 2001
- The Hayman forest fire, Colorado, Public Affairs, U.S. Forest Service, Rocky Mountain Region, Summer 2000
- Attack on the Pentagon, northern Virginia, Office of the Assistant Secretary of Public Affairs and Media Relations, U.S. Department of Defense, September 11, 2001
- Attack on the Pentagon, northern Virginia, Capitol Police, September 11, 2001
- Sniper attacks, Washington, DC, metro area, Media Services, Montgomery County Police Department, Fall 2002
- Anthrax attack on Hart Senate Office Building, Washington, DC, October, 2001
- Anthrax attacks, Office of Communications, Division of Media Relations, Centers for Disease Control and Prevention, Fall 2001
- F4 level tornado, La Plata, Maryland, Maryland Emergency Management Agency, April 28, 2002

PLANNING

Creating a communications plan on the fly during a crisis is an extremely daunting task. The absence of a plan virtually guarantees that communicators will not be able to reach the public as effectively as they would if they had a plan in place.

Producing a workable written plan is inherently an agency-by-agency process, contingent on available personnel, budget limitations, etc. By soliciting critical review of the plan from all the affected participants—the public, the press, other government agencies—EMAs have the opportunity to produce the best possible plan under the circumstances.

Some of the EMAs with whom we talked had highly elaborate communications plans. But regardless of length, they all agreed that their plans made them more effective during emergencies. And the EMAs who had been through a trial by fire without a written communications plan were equally adamant about putting such a plan in place as soon as possible.

PEOPLE

The most well-written communications plan is not worth much without a strong commitment from elected officials and department managers to put the infrastructure in place to carry out the plan.

The spokesperson's credibility is a key to his/her effectiveness at representing the government, reassuring the public, and keeping the media happy. In some jurisdictions, the highest ranking elected official or the head of the department managing the crisis will be the lead communicator, giving them a kind of automatic credibility at the onset of an event (like New York Mayor Rudy Guiliani after 9/11).

Given the increasing intensity of media coverage, the media spokesperson plays an increasingly important role in ensuring the overall effectiveness of an EMA. In order to maintain the spokesperson's credibility as a source with the media, the spokesperson needs to be "at the table" for all senior management decisions. If reporters believe that a spokesperson is not fully integrated into the decision-making process, they will inevitably be more suspicious of the information they do receive.

By participating in decision making, the spokesperson can also play a vital internal role by making sure that decision-makers have fully considered how their decisions may play out in the media, giving them a better chance of avoiding public relations blunders.

After the terrorist attack on the Pentagon on September 11, 2001, Arlington County officials significantly upgraded its top public communications official. The change was more than just a title change (from Assistant County Manager for Public Information to Director of Communications and Public Affairs). The county also raised the position's salary and provided that the new director would report directly to the county manager. The job description for this new position includes the development of "a comprehensive communications program that will provide a cohesive image, identity, and brand message both externally and internally by optimizing the use of existing electronic resources (Internet, intranet, and cable television) and nonelectronic sources (print media) as well as developing new communications venues."

If possible, one person should be the principal spokesperson (the single voice/single face model). Nothing is likely to be more confusing to the media or the public than dealing with a constantly changing array of talking heads. (There's a reason almost all the daily White House press briefings are handled by one person!)

MEDIA TRAINING

Learning to be a media spokesperson in the middle of a crisis is risky. There is no substitute for practical media training before a crisis arrives. In Harris County, Texas, the three authorized spokespeople had all been through a FEMA-approved 32-hour public information officer (PIO) course offered through the Texas Department of Public Safety's Office of Emergency Management. The Forest Service spokesperson during the 2002 Hayman forest fire had roughly 50 hours of formal media training.

In addition, the agency's public affairs staff worked with him on "war game" crises, creating what he called "murder boards" to put him through the kind of tough questioning he would encounter in a real crisis. And the Capitol Police officer who handled the anthrax attack on the Senate Hart Building was a media trainer himself with over 160 hours of training.

INFRASTRUCTURE

BUILDING AN EMERGENCY OPERATIONS CENTER

Just as some jurisdictions had no written EM plan, some did not have an Emergency Operations Center (EOC), although there was broad agreement that having a well-equipped EOC was the physical foundation for an effective communications effort.

For planning purposes, the EOC should have redundant communications capabilities, both internally and with the outside. No communications technology works every time. Land lines can fail; during the attack on the Pentagon, there were frequent problems with cell phones.

Without a well-equipped EOC, crisis managers face difficult hurdles staying on top of what is happening. After the September 11 attack on the Pentagon, local officials found that their EOC was ill equipped for the emergency management team to communicate with first responders or to receive accurate information from the scene. Phone lines were down, and the room was not equipped with radios or televisions. They were forced to delay press briefings until they could verify facts with first responders and people on-site.

EOCs should be designed with the media in mind. The Harris County, Texas, EOC has an on-site press room with telephone and computer access. EOCs can make life easier for television reporters by preparing video footage (called "B-roll") of scenes that reporters could use, like the interior of the Emergency Operations Center. EOCs can also prepare fact sheets and other printed background materials on the major threats that the agency has identified.

Communicators can also provide the press with special support if necessary. During the Hayman forest fire, the Forest Service gave out personal protective equipment to reporters (hard hats, fire clothes, etc.).

CARVING THROUGH THE JURISDICTIONAL JUNGLE

The communications plan provides a framework for mapping and, where possible, negotiating communications procedures about how to handle one of the most common problems of the EMA universe, overlapping jurisdictions. Such overlaps are inherent in the nature of almost every large-scale emergency event. A comprehensive plan must include not only local, state, and federal law enforcement and emergency management agencies but also the spectrum of veterinary and public health agencies (in light of the threat of the use of biological, chemical, or radiological weapons by terrorists).

In the aftermath of the anthrax attacks, the Centers for Disease Control and Prevention has published a useful analysis of the similarities and differences in public health and law enforcement investigations and the steep learning curves for both sets of agencies in their collaborations. ("Collaboration Between Public Health and Law Enforcement: New Paradigms and Partnerships for Bioterrorism Planning and Response," Jay C. Butler et al., http://www.cdc.gov/ncidod/EID/vol8no10/02 0400.htm). The authors emphasis the importance of pre-existing relationships between law enforcement and public health agencies and the need for practice exercises, and call for adding liaisons who are cross-trained in the public health aspects of communicable diseases and in law enforcement and criminal investigations.

Even without a written communications plan, an informal prior agreement can be helpful in reducing confusion. In the case of the anthrax attack on the Hart Senate Office Building, there was no written plan. But the Capitol Police Board and the House and Senate leadership had previously determined that the Capitol Police would be the designated agency to handle media inquiries after any terrorist or criminal incidents within the Capitol complex. Members of

Congress—a group not known for being media-shy—conferred with the police spokesperson before holding their own press conferences, and the spokesperson attended these events, off camera, to provide guidance as needed.

In our study, several communicators highlighted the importance of maintaining clear channels of communications with all of the government agencies involved, regardless of which agency had been designated the lead communications agency. This cross-agency communications is essential for keeping everyone "on the same page" so that reporters do not get confusing or conflicting information from their contacts at other agencies. Up-to-date e-mail and fax lists are a relatively cheap way to distribute breaking information to other agencies in a timely way.

The Office of Emergency Management in Harris County used an Internet e-mail and pager software they developed to reach more than 140 media outlets in the region, 125 law-enforcement agencies, 54 fire departments, 29 cities, and selected individuals throughout the surrounding 41 counties. After Tropical Storm Allison, the office expanded the list of individuals requesting real-time information, adding more elected federal, state, and local officials and media outlets. (Copies of the Harris County plans can be downloaded from http://www.hcoem.org.)

WORKING WITH THE MEDIA

BUILDING PRIOR RELATIONSHIPS

The media play an integral part in EMA outreach efforts to keep the public informed and up-to-date. But without preexisting relationships with reporters, it's not uncommon or unexpected that in the heat of the moment, EMAs might come to look upon the press in a crisis as adversaries engaged in a "feeding frenzy" for new facts.

Planning is essential to building relationships with the media, so that EMAs and the media understand each other's needs and operating styles and how to work together as much as possible as allies. Both EMAs and

the press share a deep concern about protecting the health and welfare of the public. Far from being adversaries, reporters can be valuable allies, particularly in devising an effective communications plan in the first place.

Harris County's Office of Emergency Management had a policy of inviting reporters in twice a year to talk about how the agency could better meet the needs of the press. Such conversations are no guarantee, of course, against future disagreements. But such meetings do allow for EMAs and reporters to share each others' perspectives in a nonstressful environment, reducing the possibility of misunderstandings later on during crises. And such exchanges also allow EMAs to plan to meet the media's needs where possible. Another useful technique for improving media relations is to schedule meetings with the editorial boards of local media outlets.

CONSERVING CREDIBILITY WITH THE MEDIA

Credibility is a dynamic asset in a crisis; a spokesperson can lose credibility quickly if the media and the public come to believe they're being misinformed or under-informed. Every effort should be made to ensure that whatever information is released to the public is accurate and up-to-date. As one PIO told us, his goal was to be "the first and best source of information, especially if it's bad news."

Misinformation only compounds one of the other common communications problems during crisis, the rapid spread of unfounded rumors, the rebutting of which can take up valuable time. During the Capitol Hill anthrax attack, many Capitol Hill reporters—who were used to covering policy debates, not terrorist attacks—were anxious about their own medical conditions, having been in the "hot zone" at some point. Congressional staffers, their usual sources of information, were also anxious about their own health and provided information often based on rumor, outside their areas of legislative expertise. Reporters, frustrated with what seemed to them to be the slow release of information, would go with these rumor sources and end up being forced to back-track later. Many of the communications managers in our survey said that combating such rumors was one of the most difficult tasks they faced during a crisis.

Limiting the amount of information that reaches the public poses a different kind of challenge. It is not uncommon for government or corporate managers to use the control of the release of information as a way of gaining or preserving bureaucratic power. But in a crisis, this withholding tendency can aggravate the public's anxieties. In Arlington County, Virginia, after the September 11 attack on the Pentagon, officials found that although they might not have any new, more specific information about what might happen next, citizens still wanted frequent updates and reassurances from their county government.

In a crisis management setting, withholding information may very well result in a loss of power and control. Our respondents agreed that one should lean in the direction of making more, rather than less, information available, consistent with law enforcement and public safety considerations.

In a full-blown media circus, even a vigorous attempt at openness may not be enough to halt a media feeding frenzy. One of the more striking examples of this press intensity came from the Montgomery County, Maryland, police during the Fall 2002 Washington, DC area sniper attacks. The department was already providing frequent media releases, one-on-one interviews, web updates, and as many as four press briefings a day.

But reporters wanted more. Some went so far as to peer through a half-inch opening in the window shades at the operations center, stealing a look at text on a dry erase board. Within seconds, they were questioning Montgomery County police chief Charles Moss about the information they had gleaned, showing little concern about whether their questions might endanger public safety.

KEEPING ALTERNATIVE MEDIA CHANNELS OPEN

In addition to the traditional media (TV, radio, newspapers), EMAs have access to newer media like e-mail, web sites, and local cable TV, which can be used to reach the public directly. Because these tools also do not reach as wide an audience as traditional mass media, they should be seen as adjuncts, not substitutes.

These unmediated channels can be very effective tools for providing the public with a great deal of information without tying up large numbers of EMA staff. However, if an EMA is using a web site, it is essential that staff updates the site on a frequent basis; stale information drives users away.

The agencies we surveyed reported a wide range of satisfaction in using new media tools. In some cases, results were disappointing because too few people were aware of the local cable TV channel or did not know the agency had a web site. On the other hand, one agency reported over 1.6 million contacts on its web site from press, first responders, and the public and regarded the web site as a valuable component of its overall communications strategy.

CONCLUSION

Communicating during emergencies is necessarily fraught with uncertainty: The unexpected is most likely to happen. No emergency communications plan can fully encompass all of the scenarios that may arise. But the findings from our survey show that EMAs can take steps to create a robust communications plans, train spokespeople, and build the infrastructure that will allow EMAs to roll with the punches and maximize their effectiveness at getting their messages to the press, the public, and other government agencies.

Glossary of Hazard Terms

GENERAL TERMS

Aerosol   Fine liquid or solid particles suspended in a gas (for example, fog or smoke).

Biological agents   Living organisms or the materials derived from them that cause disease in or harm to humans, animals, or plants or cause deterioration of material. Biological agents may be used as liquid droplets, aerosols, or dry powders.

Chemical agent   A chemical substance that is intended to kill, seriously injure, or incapacitate people through physiological effects. Generally separated by severity of effect: lethal, blister, and incapacitating.

Consequence management   Measures to protect public health and safety, restore essential government services, and provide emergency relief to governments, businesses, and individuals affected by the consequences of terrorism. State and local governments exercise primary authority to respond to the consequences of terrorism (Source: Federal Response Plan [FRP] Terrorism Incident Annex, page TI-2, April 1999). The Federal Emergency Management Agency (FEMA) has been designated the lead agency for consequence management to ensure that the FRP is adequate to respond to terrorism. Additionally, FEMA supports the Federal Bureau of Investigation (FBI) in crisis management.

Crisis management   This is the law enforcement aspect of an incident that involves measures to identify, acquire, and plan the resources needed to anticipate, prevent, and/or resolve a threat of terrorism. The FBI is the lead agency for crisis management for such an incident (Source: FBI). During crisis management, the FBI coordinates closely with local law enforcement authorities to provide successful law enforcement resolution to the incident. The FBI also coordinates with other federal authorities, including FEMA (Source: Federal Response Plan Terrorism Incident Annex, April 1999).

Cyber-terrorism   Malicious conduct in cyber-space to commit or threaten to commit acts dangerous to human life or against a nation's critical infrastructures, such as energy, transportation, or government operations in order to intimidate or coerce a government or civilian population, or any sequence thereof, in furtherance of political or social objectives.

Decontamination   The process of making people, objects, or areas safe by absorbing, destroying, neutralizing, making harmless, or removing the hazardous material.

Federal Response Plan (FRP)   The FRP establishes a process and structure for the systematic, coordinated, and effective delivery of federal assistance to address the consequences of any major disaster or emergency declared under the Robert T. Stafford Disaster Relief and Emergency Assistance Act, as amended (42 U.S. Code [USC] et seq.). The FRP Terrorism Incident Annex defines the organizational structures used to coordinate crisis management with consequence management (Source: FRP Terrorism Incident Annex, April 1999).

Infrastructure Protection   Proactive risk management actions intended to prevent a threat from attempting to or succeeding at destroying or incapacitating critical infrastructures (for instance, threat deterrence and vulnerability defense).

Lead agency The federal department or agency assigned lead responsibility under U.S. law to manage and coordinate the federal response in a specific functional area. The FBI is the lead agency for crisis management, and FEMA is the lead agency for consequence management. Lead agencies support the overall lead Federal agency (LFA) during all phases of the response.

Lead federal agency (LFA) The agency designated by the president to lead and coordinate the overall federal response is referred to as the LFA and is determined by the type of emergency. In general, an LFA establishes operational structures and procedures to assemble and work with agencies providing direct support to the LFA in order to provide an initial assessment of the situation, develop an action plan, monitor and update operational priorities, and ensure each agency exercises its concurrent and distinct authorities under U.S. law and supports the LFA in carrying out the president's relevant policy. Specific responsibilities of an LFA vary according to the agency's unique statutory authorities.

Mitigation Those actions (including threat and vulnerability assessments) taken to reduce the exposure to and detrimental effects of a WMD incident.

Nonpersistent agent An agent that, upon release, loses its ability to cause casualties after 10 to 15 minutes. It has a high evaporation rate, is lighter than air, and will disperse rapidly. It is considered to be a short-term hazard; however, in small, unventilated areas, the agent will be more persistent.

Persistent agent An agent that, upon release, retains its casualty-producing effects for an extended period of time, usually anywhere from 30 minutes to several days. A persistent agent usually has a low evaporation rate and its vapor is heavier than air; therefore, its vapor cloud tends to hug the ground. It is considered to be a long-term hazard. Although inhalation hazards are still a concern, extreme caution should be taken to avoid skin contact as well.

Plume Airborne material spreading from a particular source; the dispersal of particles, gases, vapors, and aerosols into the atmosphere.

Preparedness Establishing the plans, training, exercises, and resources necessary to achieve readiness for all hazards, including WMD incidents.

Radiation High-energy particles or gamma rays that are emitted by an atom as the substance undergoes radioactive decay. Particles can be either charged alpha or beta particles or neutral neutron or gamma rays.

Recovery Recovery, in this document, includes all types of emergency actions dedicated to the continued protection of the public or promoting the resumption of normal activities in the affected area.

Response Executing the plan and resources identified to perform those duties and services to preserve and protect life and property as well as provide services to the surviving population.

Terrorism The unlawful use of force or violence against persons or property to intimidate or coerce a government, the civilian population, or any segment thereof, in furtherance of political or social objectives. Domestic terrorism involves groups or individuals who are based and operate entirely within the United States and U.S. territories without foreign direction and whose acts are directed at elements of the U.S. government or population.

Toxicity A measure of the harmful effects produced by a given amount of a toxin on a living organism.

Weapons-grade material Nuclear material considered most suitable for a nuclear weapon. It usually connotes uranium enriched to above 90 percent uranium-235 or plutonium with greater than approximately 90 percent plutonium-239.

Weapon of mass destruction Any destructive device as defined in 18 USC 921; any weapon that is designed or intended to cause death or serious bodily injury through the release, dissemination, or impact of toxic or poisonous chemicals or their precursors; any weapon involving a disease organism; or any weapon that is designed to release radiation or radioactivity at a level dangerous to human life (Source: 18 USC 2332a). In 18 USC 921, a destructive device is defined, with certain exceptions, to mean any explosive, incendiary, or poison gas, bomb, grenade, or rocket having a propellant charge of more than 4 ounces, or a missile having an explosive incendiary charge of more than 0.25 ounce, or a mine, or a device similar to the above; any type of weapon by whatever name known that will, or that may be readily converted to, expel a projectile by the action of an explosive or other propellant and that has any barrel with a bore of more 0.5 inch in diameter; any combination of parts either designed or intended for use in converting any device into any destructive device described above and from which a destructive device may be readily assembled.

Source: CDC, www.cdc.gov

BIOLOGICAL

Adventive   Arrived in the geographical area specified from somewhere else by any means; not native (nonindigenous) to the area in which it has arrived.

Alien   Native somewhere else. Same as exotic and foreign.

Anorexia   Loss of appetite.

Ataxia   Lack of muscular coordination.

Augmentative biological control   Release of large numbers of a biological control agent to supplement the small numbers already present, in expectation of a greatly increased effect.

Autochthonous   Native; indigenous; this arcane word means the same as native and indigenous, and those are older and well-accepted expressions.

Biological control   The use of living natural enemies to control pests *or:* the active manipulation of antagonistic organisms to reduce pest population densities, either animal or plant, to noneconomically important levels.

Biopesticide   A living organism applied as an inundative biological control agent or augmentative biological control agent.

Biorational pesticide   A chemical such as a toxin or growth regulator derived from a living organism and applied either as the entire dead organism or as an extract from the organism; alternatively, the chemical or an analog of it synthesized in vitro. Use of biorational pesticides is usually considered to be chemical control not biological control.

Carnivore   An organism that feeds on animals.

Classical biological control   A form of inoculative biological control in which specialist natural enemies are imported from the supposed homeland of an adventive pest and released in small numbers in attempt to establish a permanent population. A variant form of classical biological control uses biological control agents imported from a third area, inhabited by a close relative of the target pest.

Cleptoparasitism   A form of multiple parasitism in which a parasite preferentially attacks a host that is already parasitized by another species.

Coagulopathy   Disorder of blood clot formation.

Commensalism   A situation in which two or more organisms of distant phylogeny use the same food resource without competition.

Cyanosis   Bluish discoloration of skin suggesting lack of oxygen to tissues.

Dementia   Mental deterioration.

Detritivore   An organism that feeds on detritus (decaying material).

Diaphoresis   Perspiration.

Direct pest   Said of a pest that damages the marketable part of a plant (e.g., the fruit).

Dysarthria   Difficulty of speech suggesting a neurological cause.

Dyspepsia   Epigastric discomfort secondary to indigestion.

Dysphagia   Difficulty in swallowing.

Dysphasia   Difficulty in arranging words in proper order due to a neurological lesion.

Dysphonia   Vocal impairment.

Dyspnea   Difficulty breathing.

Ecchymosis   Hemorrhagic discoloration of the skin.

Ectoparasite   A parasite that lives on the external surface of its host; examples include lice and fleas.

Ectoparasitoid   A parasitoid that lives on the external surface of its host, feeding on it and killing it in the process.

Enanthem   An eruption on the mucosal surface.

Encapsulation   A cellular defense strategy used by hosts of an endoparasitoid (or any other invading organism) to isolate it and deprive it of resources (oxygen and/or nutrients), so as to kill it.

Encephalitis   Inflammation of the brain.

Endemic   Occurring constantly in an area in small numbers, but allowing a switch to large numbers, at which time the population or species is said to be epidemic; the antonym of *endemic*.

Endemism   The condition of being native to and restricted to a specified area.

Endocarditis   An inflammation within the heart.

Endoparasite   A parasite that lives in another organism, feeding on it but not usually killing it (noun).

Endoparasitoid   A parasitoid that lives in another organism, feeding on it and killing it in the process.

Endophage   An organism that feeds inside another animal; the corresponding adjective is *endophagous*.

Entomogenous   Reproducing within insects; used mainly to describe habits of some nematodes.

Epidemic   Occurring in unusually large numbers; said of a population or species.

Epistaxis   Nosebleed.

Erythema   Redness of the skin from various causes.

Exotic   Native somewhere else. Kangaroos are exotic species as far as inhabitants of North America are concerned, but they are not exotic in Australia.

Facultative parasitism   A condition in which a free-living organism may exist by parasitism (parasitoidism) but does not rely upon this way of life.

Facultative parasitoidism   The condition of existing by parasitoidism but not relying upon this way of life.

Gregarious parasitoid   A parasitoid whose nutritional requirements are such that several can exist in the body of the host.

Hematemesis   Bloody vomitus.

Hemifacial   Involving one side of the face.

Hemoptysis   Bloody sputum.

Hepatomegaly   Enlargement of the liver.

Host   The living organism that serves as food for a parasite, parasitoid, or pathogen.

Host-discrimination   The selection of an appropriate host by a parasite or parasitoid, according to the species, developmental stage, and physiological condition (including absence of existing parasites/parasitoids) of that host.

Host-specific   A parasite, parasitoid, or pathogen that, at least in the area specified, is monophagous.

Hyperparasite   A parasite that lives on another parasite.

Idiobiont   A parasitoid whose host is rendered immobile by the parent of the idiobiont, and the said host is consumed in the location and stage it is in when attacked, or at least in a nearby location to which the parent of the idiobiont has moved it.

Indirect pest   Said of a pest that damages the unmarketed part of a plant (e.g., the leaves, when it is the fruit that is marketed).

Inoculative biological control   Importation and release of biological control agents in an area in which they are not already present, with intent to establish a permanent population.

Inundative biological control   Release of large numbers of a biological control agent relative to the numbers of a target species, in expectation of a rapid effect. There is no implication that the released biological control agent will establish a permanent population.

Invasive   A population or species that is expanding its range.

Koinobiont   A parasitoid developing in a host that continues to be mobile and able to defend itself; hosts that are larvae often are not killed until they have prepared cryptic pupation retreats.

Lethality   The ratio of the number of deaths to the number of afflicted patients.

Leukopenia   A decrease in the number of white blood cells.

Macule   A flat discoloration on the skin.

Malaise   A perception of physical distress.

Melena   Stools blackened by blood pigment.

Meningitis   Inflammation of the membranes that envelop the brain.

Myalgia   Muscular pain.

Mydriasis   Markedly dilated pupil.

Nuchal   Pertaining to the back of the neck.

Osteomyelitis   Inflammation of the bone, usually due to a bacterial infection.

Pancytopenia   A marked decrease of all blood cells.

Papule   A small, raised lesion on the skin.

Parasite   An organism that lives in or on the body of its host without killing the host, but usually debilitating it.

Peritonitis   Inflammation of the membrane lining the abdominopelvic compartment.

Persistence   The ability of a biological agent to remain in the environment while still retaining its capacity to cause casualties.

Pest   An animal or plant that is deemed by mankind to be too numerous [this includes weeds].

Petecchia   A tiny, hemorrhagic spot on the skin.

Phoresy   The habit of gaining transport from one place to another on an animal (i.e., "hitching a ride").

Photophobia   Abnormal intolerance to light.

Predator   An organism that, during its development, consumes more than one prey individual.

Prey   The living organism that serves as food for a predator.

Prostration   Extreme exhaustion.

Ptosis   Drooping of the upper eyelid.

Pustule   Small collection of pus on the skin.

Pyelonephritis   Inflammation of the kidneys, usually due to an infection.

Rhinorrhea   Mucousy nasal discharge.

Rigor   Exaggerated stiffening of the body.

Sacroiliitis   Inflammation of the sacroiliac joint.

Splenomegaly   Enlargement of the spleen.

Spore   An inactive, resistant form of a bacterium.

Synchronous   Occurring at the same time.

Thrombocytopenia   A decrease in the absolute number of platelets.

Vector   An animal that transmits a pathogen to plants or animals.

Vesicle   A small, raised collection of clear, serous fluid on the skin.

Sources:

1. The Florida Integrated Pest Management and Biocontrol
2. http://biocontrol.ifas.ufl.edu/glossary.htm
3. http://www.bioterry.com/Manual/Appendix/ Glossary.asp

CHEMICAL

Abiotic   An abiotic system is one that is free of biological organisms. Abiotic transformations are those brought about by a nonbiological mechanism. Thus the modification of a chemical through heating or by the absorption of radiation is, strictly, an abiotic transformation or process.

Absolute risk   Absolute Risk is the excess risk due to an exposure to a hazard.

Acceptable Daily Intake   The Acceptable Daily Intake (ADI) is a measure of the quantity of a particular chemical in food that, it is believed, can be consumed on a daily basis over a lifetime without harm. Data for the calculation of an ADI may be derived from a variety of sources; often direct observation of human eating habits is used, but laboratory tests may also be appropriate. The concept of an ADI is most valuable when applied to chemicals which are not usually found in foods, such as additives or the residues of pesticides or veterinary drugs. ADIs may be defined both for humans and for animals and are widely used by organizations such as the World Health Organization.

Acceptable risk   The concept of acceptable risk is not particular easy to define. It is essentially a measure of the risk of harm, injury, or disease arising from a chemical or process that will be tolerated by a person or group. Whether a risk is "acceptable" will depend upon the advantages that the person or group perceives to be obtainable in return for taking the risk, whether they accept whatever scientific and other advice is offered about the magnitude of the risk, and numerous other factors, both political and social.

ACGIH   The American Conference of Governmental Industrial Hygienists.

Acid   Chemists use a variety of ways to define what they mean by an acid. The definition which is most readily understood, due to Arrhenius, is that an acid is a chemical which produces hydrogen ions when dissolved in water. The strength of an acidic solution is usually measured in terms of its pH (a logarithmic function of the H^+ ion concentration). Strongly acidic solutions have low pHs (typically around 0–3), while weakly acidic solutions have pHs in the range 3–6.

Acidic solution   See **Acid.**

Action level   The action level is the exposure level at which (USA) OSHA regulations take effect. This is generally one-half of the PEL.

Acute effect   An acute effect is one that involves severe symptoms that develop rapidly and may quickly reach a crisis.

Acute hazard   An acute hazard is one to which a single exposure may cause harm, but which is unlikely to lead to permanent damage.

Acute toxicity   See **Toxicity.**

ADI   See **Acceptable Daily Intake.**

AIHA   American Industrial Hygiene Association.

Allergen   An allergen is any material which produces an allergic reaction in an individual.

Allergic contact dermatitis   Allergic contact dermatitis is a type of skin hypersensitivity. Its onset may be delayed by several days to as much as several years for weaker sensitizers. Once sensitized, fresh exposure to the sensitizing material can trigger itching and dermatitis within a few hours.

Allergy   An allergy is the appearance of symptoms of disease, irritation, or discomfort upon exposure to a material, often one that has little effect on other people. Development of allergies is essentially an unwanted (or faulty) reaction of the immune system.

All-or-none effect   See **Quantal effect.**

AMA   The American Medical Association.

Ambient standard   See **Environmental quality standard.**

Ames test   The Ames test is used to assess whether a chemical might be a carcinogen. It assumes that carcinogens possess mutagenic activity and uses bacteria and mammalian microsomes to determine whether a chemical is a mutagen. Approximately 85 percent of known carcinogens are mutagens. The Ames test, therefore, is a helpful but not perfect predictor of carcinogenic potential.

Analgesic   An analgesic, such as aspirin, is a chemical that reduces the body's sensitivity to pain.

Anoxia   Anoxia is the absence of oxygen in blood, gases or human (or animal) tissues. It can be thought of as an extreme case of hypoxia, the lowering of oxygen levels.

Argyria   See **Argyrism.**

Argyrism   Argyria or argyrism is an irreversible bluish-black discoloration of the skin, mucous membranes, or internal organs caused by ingestion of, or contact with, various silver compounds.

Asphyxiant   An asphyxiant is a material capable of reducing the level of oxygen in the body to dangerous levels. Most commonly, asphyxiants work by merely displaying air in an enclosed environment. This reduces the concentration of oxygen below the normal level of around 19 percent, which can lead to breathing difficulties, unconciousness, or even death.

Asphyxiation   See **Asphyxiant.**

Atmosphere   See **Units of pressure.**

Auto-ignition temperature   The auto-ignition temperature of a chemical is the lowest temperature at which a material will ignite without an external source of ignition.

Base   Chemists define the word *base* in a variety of ways. The simplest (though perhaps most limited) is that a base generates hydroxide ions (OH⁻) when dissolved in water. Typical bases according to this definition are the alkali hydroxides, such as sodium hydroxide or potassium hydroxide. The pH of a strongly basic solution will be in the range 11 to 14. Basic solutions are caustic and corrosive, but the most serious hazard they present is damage to the eyes. A strongly basic solution will attack the cornea very rapidly and may create sufficient damage to cause blindness. Safety glasses must therefore always be worn when handling bases.

Basic solution   See **Base.**

Binary effect   See **Quantal effect.**

Biohazard   A biohazard (biological hazard) is one which is posed to humans by a biological organism or by a material produced by such an organism.

Breakthrough   Breakthrough is the movement of a chemical through a protective material, such as a rubber glove. This may be due to gradual permeation of the chemical into and through the material or as a result of chemical or physical degradation of the material.

Breakthrough time   The breakthrough time is the time taken in standard tests for permeation of a chemical through a protective barrier (such as a rubber glove) to be detected.

Carcinogen   A carcinogen is a chemical known or believed to cause cancer in humans. The number of proven carcinogens is comparatively small, but many more chemicals are suspected to be carcinogenic.

Carcinogenic   A carcinogenic chemical is one which is believed to be capable of causing cancer; that is, acting as a carcinogen.

CAS number   The CAS registry number is a unique number assigned to a chemical by the Chemical Abstracts Service.

Ceiling level   The ceiling level, or ceiling value, is the maximum permissible concentration of a hazardous material in the working environment. This level should not be exceeded at any time. It is usually (but not invariably) set somewhat above the relevant time-weighted average for the chemical.

Ceiling value (CV)   See **Ceiling level.**

Chronic hazard   A chronic hazard is presented by a chemical that has the potential to cause long-term damage to health, often as a consequence of repeated or prolonged exposure to it.

Chronic toxicity   See **Toxicity.**

Chrysiasis   Chrysiasis is the development of a blue-grey pigmentation in skin and mucous membranes. May be caused by exposure to gold compounds.

Clastogen   A clastogen is a material which is capable of causing chromosomal breaks.

CNS   CNS is an acronym for *central nervous system.* A wide variety of chemicals may damage or depress the CNS, from relatively innocuous materials such as ethyl alcohol, which is a depressant when consumed in large amounts, to nerve gases and organomercury compounds, such as methylmercury hydroxide, which may be fatal if inhaled or absorbed through the skin in even tiny amounts.

Combustible substances   A combustible substance is any material that will burn.

Copolymer   A copolymer is a material created by polymerizing a mixture of two (or more) starting compounds. The resultant polymer molecules contain the monomers in a proportion that is related both to the mole fraction of the monomers in the starting mixture and to the reaction mechanism.

Corrosive   A corrosive material is one that causes damage to skin, eyes, or other parts of the body on contact. The technical definition is written in terms of "destruction, or irreversible damage to living tissue at the site of contact." Often this damage is caused directly by the chemical, but the action of some corrosive materials is a consequence of inflammation that they may cause. Concentrated acids are obvious examples of corrosive materials, but even dilute solutions of bases such as sodium or ammonium hydroxide may also be very corrosive, particularly in contact with the eyes.

CTDs See **Repetitive strain injury.**

Cumulative trauma disorders See **Repetitive strain injury.**

Cutaneous hazard A cutaneous hazard is a chemical that may cause harm to the skin, such as defatting, irritation, skin rashes, or dermatitis.

Cytotoxic A cytotoxic material is one that is harmful to cell structure and function and that may ultimately cause cell death.

Degradation Degradation is the term generally used to describe the loss of resilience of material used for protective gloves. Degradation may cause the material to soften, swell, become hard and brittle, or in severe cases, disintegrate.

Dermatitis Dermatitis is an inflammation of the skin that may be brought about by repeated contact with chemicals. A wide variety of chemicals may be responsible, especially those which can cause defatting of the skin, such as chlorinated solvents. Irritation, cracked skin, and blisters are common symptoms. Dermatitis may also arise if a person is susceptible to sensitization and is allergic to butyl rubber, latex, or other types of gloves designed to protect the skin from contact with chemicals. Dermatitis may seem a comparatively minor problem compared to the other hazards posed by chemicals but should be regarded as a potentially serious condition and not ignored.

Desquamation Desquamation is the detachment of cells from the surface of an epithelium.

Detoxify The word *detoxify* is used in at least two senses in safety. Detoxify is often used to indicate the treatment of a patient who has ingested or been exposed to a harmful chemical, in such a way as to lessen the effects of exposure. It is also used to

indicate the process by which a harmful material may be treated to render it harmless or less toxic.

ECn ECn is a commonly used abbreviation that refers to the (exposure) concentration of a toxic material that has a defined effect upon n% of a test population.

ED50 The ED50 (Effective Dose 50) is the amount of material required to produce a specified effect in 50 percent of an animal population. (See qualification in the definition of **LD50**).

EDn EDn is the usual abbreviation for the dose of a chemical which will have the expected effect upon n% of a test population.

Embryotoxic An embryotoxic material is anything that can adversely affect the growth or development of the embryo.

Embryotoxins Embryotoxins, such as aflatoxin, are naturally produced chemicals that retard the growth or affect the development of the unborn child. In serious cases they can cause deformities or death.

Emetic An emetic is a substance that induces vomiting (emesis).

Emission standard An emission standard is a regulatory limit on the amount of a toxic (or potentially toxic) chemical that may be emitted from a source (often but not necessarily some sort of industrial plant). Various forms of emission standard exist; the simplest is the so-called Uniform Emissions Standard (UES) which places the same limit on all emissions of a particular product.

Environmental quality objective An environmental quality objective (or EQO) is typically a nonenforceable goal, which specifies a target for environmental quality that, it is hoped, will be met in some particular environment, such as a river, beach, or industrial site. EQOs are generally not set by regulation (unlike "Environmental Quality Standards") and often are cast in the rather vague form of generally desirable objectives, rather than as more concrete quantitative measures.

Environmental quality standard An environmental quality standard is a value, generally defined by regulation, that specifies the maximum permissible concentration of a potentially hazardous chemical in an environmental sample, generally of air or water. (Sometimes also known as an ambient standard.)

Epidemiology Epidemiology is a scientific process that attempts to link the effects of factors such as lifestyle (for example, level of smoking or drinking) or exposure to toxic chemicals to disease and, if relevant, mortality. Statistical correlations are developed whose purpose is ultimately to indicate the degree of risk that someone with a particular exposure pattern, lifestyle, or genetic profile has of contracting a specific disease.

ET50 ET50 is an abbreviation for the exposure time required for a defined effect to be observed among 50 percent of a population when that population is treated with a known amount or concentration of a toxicant.

Etiologic agents Microscopic organisms, such as bacteria or viruses, that can cause disease.

Explosion limits See **Flammability limits.**

f/cc f/cc or fcc is an abbreviation for fibers per cubic centimeter of air. (In crystallography, it is an abbreviation for face-centered cubic.)

Flammable limits The flammable limits refer to the conditions under which a mixture of a flammable material and air may catch fire or explode. If the percentage of flammable material in the air is between the minimum and maximum limits, the presence of a flame or a source of ignition is likely to lead to rapid combustion or explosion. Flammable limits for many materials are in the range 2 percent to 10 percent, but for some materials the limits are much wider. Ether, for example, has flammable limits of 1.7 percent to 48 percent, which is an unusually wide range. This, coupled with the low boiling point of ether (34.6°C) and high vapor pressure at room temperature (400 mm Hg at 18°) means that it is easy to create a potentially explosive mixture of ether in air and renders this compound an extreme fire hazard.

Flashback Flashback occurs when the flame in a gas torch burns back into the torch or hose; this is often accompanied by a hissing or squealing sound and a pointed or smoky flame.

Flash point The flash point of a chemical is the lowest temperature at which a flame will propagate through the vapor of a combustible material to the liquid surface. It is determined by the vapor pressure of the liquid, since only when a sufficiently high vapor concentration is reached can it support combustion. It should be noted that the source of ignition need not be an open flame but could equally be, for example, the surface of a hot plate or a steam pipe.

Foreign matter Foreign matter most commonly refers to the presence of unwanted or undesirable material present in foods or chemicals. When used in connection with foods, foreign matter may include packing materials inadvertently (or deliberately) included in the product, plant, or meat products that should have been removed in manufacture or processing; and vermin remains, stones, grit, sand, and so forth. Chemicals may be contaminated by a range of foreign matter, most commonly packing materials, such as glass or polystyrene chips.

Genotoxic Genotoxic chemicals are those that are capable of causing damage to DNA. Such damage can potentially lead to the formation of a malignant tumor, but DNA damage does not lead inevitably to the creation of cancerous cells.

Graded effect A graded effect is one whose severity is related continuously to dose. Increases in dose rate or exposure level thus have a steadily increasing (sometimes linear) effect upon the severity of symptoms.

Guinea pig maximization test The guinea pig maximization test is a widely-used test in the screening of contact allergens for the possibility that they may act as sensitizers in humans.

Hematopoietic agent A hematopoietic agent is a chemical that interferes with the blood system by decreasing the oxygen-carrying ability of hemoglobin. This can lead to cyanosis and unconsiousness. Carbon monoxide is one such agent, familiar to smokers.

Hepatotoxin   A hepatotoxin is a naturally-produced chemical capable of causing liver damage.

Highly toxic   The term *highly toxic* is to some extent imprecise, and exactly how it is defined varies from one regulatory or standards body to another. A typical (and widely-used) definition follows:

Highly toxic—A chemical falling within any of the following categories:

(a) A chemical with a median lethal dose (LD50) of 50 milligrams or less per kilogram of bodyweight when administered orally to albino rats weighing between 200 and 300 grams each.

(b) A chemical with a median lethal dose (LD50) of 200 milligrams or less per kilogram of body weight when administered by continuous contact for 24 hours (or less if death occurs within 24 hours) with the bare skin of albino rabbits weighing between 2 and 3 kilograms each.

(c) A chemical that has a median lethal concentration (LD50) in air of 200 parts per million by volume or less of gas or vapor, or 2 milligrams per liter or less of mist, fume or dust, when administered by continuous inhalation for 1 hour (or less if death occurs within 1 hour) to albino rats weighing between 200 and 300 grams each.

Hypersensitivity   See **Allergy.**

Hypertonic   A hypertonic solution contains a higher concentration of electrolytes than that found in body cells. If such a solution is allowed to enter the blood stream, the osmotic pressure difference between the blood and the cells will cause water to flow out of the cells, which will then shrink. This may cause serious harm or even be fatal. Consequently, it is essential when blood transfusions are given or blood replacement products are used that the electrolyte concentration in the material to be given to a patient matches that of the body.

Hypotonic   A hypotonic solution is one in which the concentration of electrolytes is below that in cells. In this situation, osmotic pressure leads to the migration of water into the cells in an attempt to equalize the electrolyte concentration inside and outside the cell walls. If the difference in concentration is significant, the cell walls may rupture, leading to the death of the cell. Consequently, it is vital that the electrolyte concentration of liquids used during blood transfusions be equal to that in cells.

Hypoxia   Hypoxia is a condition defined by a low supply of oxygen.

Immunotoxic   An immunotoxic chemical is one that is potentially harmful to the immune system.

Inhibitor   An inhibitor is a material that is added to a chemical to prevent an unwanted reaction. For example, 2,6-di-t-butyl-p-cresol may be added to tetrahydrofuran (THF) to prevent potentially dangerous polymerization. Inhibitors are often added to chemicals that tend to undergo self-induced free-radical polymerization.

Insoluble   An insoluble material is one that is incapable of dissolving to any significant extent in a specified solvent.

Intraperitoneal   Intraperitoneal is the term used when a chemical is contained within or administered through the peritoneum (the thin, transparent membrane that lines the walls of the abdomen). It may be abbreviated IP, IPN, or IPR on safety data sheets.

Intravenous   Intravenous indicates the introduction of a material into or through a vein. This is frequently abbreviated IV or IVN in LD50 values quoted on Material Safety Data Sheets.

In vitro   An in vitro biological study is one that is carried out in isolation from a living organism.

In vivo   An in vivo biological study is one that takes places within a living biological organism.

Irritant   An irritant is a chemical that may cause reversible inflammation on contact.

Ketosis   Ketosis is an excess of ketones in the body. This can be brought about by exposure to certain types of chemicals.

LC50 (Lethal Concentration 50) is the concentration of a chemical that kills 50 percent of a sample population. This measure is generally used when exposure to a chemical is through the animal breathing it in, while the LD50 is the measure generally used when exposure is by swallowing, through skin contact, or by injection.

LD50 (Lethal Dose 50) is the dose of a chemical that kills 50 percent of a sample population. In full reporting, the dose, treatment, and observation period should be given. Further, LD50, LC50, ED50 and similar figures are strictly only comparable when the age, sex, and nutritional state of the animals is specified. Nevertheless, such values are widely reported and used as an effective measure of the potential toxicity of chemicals.

Level A Level A is an EPA designation for the highest level of PPE required during an emergency response. This generally includes a totally encapsulated layer of clothing, together with self-contained respiratory equipment.

Logistic effect See **Quantal effect.**

Median lethal concentration The median lethal concentration is the concentration of a harmful chemical, generally in aqueous solution, that can be expected to cause the death of 50 percent of a specified population of organisms under a defined set of experimental conditions.

MSDS MSDS is a very widely used abbreviation for Material Safety Data Sheet. A MSDS contains details of the hazards associated with a chemical and gives information on its safe use.

Multigeneration study In a multigeneration study, several generations of animals (usually at least three generations) are exposed to a toxic chemical to test its effect. Exposure is typically continuous, rather than repeated dose.

Mutagen A mutagen is an agent that changes the hereditary genetic material that is a part of every living cell. Such a mutation is probably an early step in the sequence of events that ultimately leads to the development of cancer.

Mutagenic A mutagenic agent is one that is capable of causing mutations. It may also (but does not necessarily) act as a carcinogen.

Mutation A mutation is a heritable change in genetic material—in other words, a change that can potentially be passed from parent to child. This change may occur in a gene or in a chromosome and may take the form of a chemical rearrangement or a partial loss or gain of genetic material.

Nephrotoxic See **Nephrotoxin.**

Nephrotoxin A nephrotoxin is a naturally produced chemical that may cause kidney damage.

Neurotoxin A neurotoxin is a chemical whose primary action is on the CNS (central nervous system). Many neurotoxins are extremely toxic and must only be used under carefully controlled conditions.

Nuisance material A nuisance material is one that can cause transient irritation or discomfort but that has no long-term or systemic effects.

Nystagmus Nystagmus is an involuntary rapid motion of the eyes. It can be caused by exposure to a variety of chemicals, such as barbiturates, or may be a congenital condition. Any risk that chemical exposure may lead to this condition must be noted clearly on the MSDS.

Occlusion Occlusion is the trapping of hazardous material next to the skin. This keeps the material in contact with the skin for long periods of time, increasing the chance that dermal damage will occur.

Occupational hygiene Occupational hygiene is an applied science that is concerned with ensuring that standards of health in the workplace are maintained. It deals with the chemical, environmental, and physical factors that may affect the health of workers. The practice of occupational hygiene is increasingly dominated by regulatory standards designed to protect the workplace environment.

Occupational overuse injuries See **Repetitive strain injuries.**

Odor threshold The odor threshold is the lowest concentration of a vapor in air that can be detected by smell.

Oxidizing agent An oxidizing agent may be defined in various ways, depending on the context in which the phrase is used. In broad terms it is often taken to mean a chemical that can act as an electron acceptor.

Oxygen deficient atmosphere An oxygen deficient atmosphere is one in which the level of oxygen is below that of normal air, around 19.5 percent.

Packing group The packing group for a chemical indicates the degree of hazard associated with its transportation. The highest group is Group I (great danger); Group II is next (medium danger), while Group III chemicals present the lowest hazard (minor danger). Packing groups are often shown on MSDS data sheets for chemicals under the heading "Transport Information."

Pascal see **Units of pressure.**

PEC See **Predicted Environmental Concentration.**

Permeability Permeability is the ability of a chemical to pass through a material, such as a protective glove.

Permeation rate The Permeation rate is a measure of the rate at which a chemical will pass through protective material, such as that used for gloves. It is generally specified as the mass of material passing through unit area in unit time. For this value to be meaningful, the thickness of the protective material must also be specified.

Peroxidizable materials Peroxidizable materials can form peroxides in storage, generally when in contact with the air. These peroxides present their most serious risk when the peroxide-contaminated material is heated or distilled, but they may also be sensitive to mechanical shock. The quantity of peroxides in a sample may be determined using a simple peroxide test strip.

Photoallergic contact dermatitis Photoallergic contact dermatitis is a skin condition brought on by exposure to light following skin contact with certain types of chemicals, such as sulphonamides.

Physical hazard A physical hazard arises when use of a chemical is potentially dangerous due, for example, to the possibility of explosion, fire, or violent reaction with water. Peroxides, sulfuric acid, diethyl ether, and phosphorus pentachloride are examples of materials that present physical hazards. Often, of course, such materials will also present health hazards due to their toxicity.

Pictographs Pictographs are widely-used pictorial representations of the hazards presented by chemicals.

P.O. Abbreviation for *per os*, meaning oral administration.

Poison Class A or B Poison Class A or B poisons are classified by the DOT into two classes. Those in Class A are highly toxic materials that, even in very small quantities, present a hazard to life. Examples are cyanogen, phosgene, and hydrocyanic acid. Class B poisons, though less toxic, are presumed to present a serious threat to health during transportation.

Potentiation Potentiation is the enhancement of the action of one chemical by the presence of a second.

ppb Parts per billion. Used to specify the concentration (by volume) of a gas or vapor at very low concentration or a dissolved material at high dilution.

PPE An abbreviation for personal protective equipment, PPE refers to whatever protective equipment may be used to insulate an individual from the chemical, thermal, explosive, or other hazards presented by the environment in which he or she is working. In most instances, the PPE will comprise such items as safety glasses, laboratory coat, protective shoes, and chemical-resistant gloves.

ppm Parts per million. Used to specify the concentration (by volume) of a gas or vapor at low concentration or a dissolved material at high dilution.

Predicted Environmental Concentration The Predicted Environmental Concentration is an indication of the expected concentration of a material in the environment, taking into account the amount initially present (or added to) the environment, its distribution, and the probable methods and rates of environmental degradation and removal, either forced or natural.

Pulmonary Relating to the lungs.

PVA Abbreviation for polyvinyl alcohol. This material has excellent resistance to organic solvents (though is somewhat water-soluble) so is widely used in protective clothing. PVA is a trademark of Ansell Edmont Co.

Pyrophoric materials Pyrophoric materials ignite spontaneously in air. Since a wide variety of chemicals will burn if heated sufficiently, it is usual to define a pyrophoric material as one that will ignite spontaneously at temperatures below about 45°C.

QSAR See **Structure-activity relationship.**

Quantal effect A quantal effect is one for which there are only two possible outcomes; the effect thus occurs or does not. In the field of safety, the context in which the term quantal effect is most widely used (and the most dramatic) is death.

Quantitative structure-activity relationship See **Structure-activity relationship.**

REACH Acronym for Registration, Evaluation, and Authorization of Chemicals. This is a new system to regulate chemical use in the EU, which will replace a large quantity of existing legislation and place controls on some chemicals that are not currently covered by regulation. As of summer 2003 this is a proposal, but it seems clear that new regulations will be promulgated in due course. The effect of the legislation will be to force companies to show that the chemicals they produce are safe for humans and for the environment.

Recommended limit For chemicals which are believed to be toxic, a recommended limit is often specified. This is the maximum quantity or concentration that is believed to be safe. It may be backed up by regulation or simply be an advisory limit.

Reducing agent A reducing agent may be defined in various ways, depending on the context in which the phrase is used. In broad terms it is often taken to mean a chemical which can act as an electron donor.

Renal The term *renal* describes an effect or process that relates to the kidneys.

Repetitive strain injury The term *repetitive strain injury (RSI)* refers to a wide range of musculoskeletal injuries, such as carpal tunnel syndrome, bursitis, or tendonitis. Such injuries are often also referred to as *work-related upper limb disorders, occupational overuse injuries*, or *cumulative trauma disorders*, but there is no suggestion that such problems can arise only in the workplace—they can equally well arise through activities performed in the home. RSI has become much more prominent with the rapid rise in computer use, which has resulted in many people complaining of hand, neck, and arm problems. However, other activities, such as repetitive use of a pipette or the playing of a musical instrument may also give rise to symptoms. RSI is potentially a very serious problem, and employers are under a legal obligation to minimize the risk of employees developing RSI.

Reproductive toxin A reproductive toxin is a naturally produced chemical that may cause birth defects or sterility.

Respirable dust Respirable dust is airborne material that is capable of penetrating to the gas-exchange region of the lungs.

Rodenticide A rodenticide is a term applied to any chemical used to kill rodents.

Routes of entry The routes of entry are the ways in which a toxic chemical can enter the body. Chemicals are easily swallowed or inhaled, and many chemicals are readily absorbed through the skin upon contact. The fourth route of entry is deliberate or accidental injection of the chemical under the skin through use of a hypodermic or as a result of an accident.

RSI See **Repetitive strain injury.**

SAR See **Structure-activity relationship.**

SCBA Abbreviation for self-contained breathing apparatus. Such an apparatus consists of a suitable face mask, combined with a hose and source of fresh air, generally in the form of a tank of compressed air. The SCBA may be incorporated into a full-body protection suit. It is important to recognize that use of a SCBA is not trivial, and they are not designed to be worn by those without training.

Sensitizer   A sensitizer is a chemical that may lead to the development of allergic reactions after repeated exposure.

Short-term exposure limit (STEL) This is the maximum permissible concentration of a material, generally expressed in ppm in air, for a defined short period of time (typically 5 or 15 minutes, depending upon the country). This "concentration" is generally a time-weighted average over the period of exposure. These values, which may differ from country to country, are often backed up by regulation and therefore may be legally enforceable.

Stochastic   A phenomenon is stochastic (random) in nature if it obeys the laws of probability.

Structure-activity relationship   The structure-activity relationship (SAR) is a means by which the effect of a drug or toxic chemical on an animal, plant, or the environment can be related to its molecular structure. This type of relationship may be assessed by considering a series of molecules and making gradual changes to them, noting the effect upon their biological activity of each change. Alternatively, it may be possible to assess a large body of toxicity data using intelligent tools such as neural networks to try to establish a relationship.

Subacute toxicity   See **Toxicity.**

Subcutaneous   *Subcutaneous* means below the skin. The subcutaneous toxicity of a chemical is important if the chemical is injected (deliberately or accidentally) or is forced through the skin by injury.

Surfactant   A surfactant lowers the surface tension of a liquid. Soaps and some components of detergents are typical surfactants.

Synergistic effect   It is not uncommon for the effect of two chemicals on an organism to be greater than the effect of each chemical individually or the sum of the individual effects. The presence of one chemical enhances the effects of the second. This is called a synergistic effect or synergy, and the chemicals are sometimes described as showing synergism.

Synergy   See **Synergistic effect.**

Systemic poison   Systemic poisons have an effect that is remote from the site of entry into the body.

TDI   See **Tolerable Daily Intake.**

Teflon   Teflon is a polymer that is widely used in safety clothing because of its excellent resistance to chemicals and heat. However, it has poor mechanical properties, so is generally combined with other materials to provide the required mechanical durability.

Temperature rating   The temperature rating is a measure of the highest (or occasionally lowest) temperature at which it is safe to use a product for a particular purpose. For example, temperature ratings are often quoted for electrical insulators, specifying the maximum temperature at which they provide adequate protection against electrical breakdown.

Temporary safe reference action level   The temporary safe reference action level of a potentially hazardous chemical is the maximum inhalation level at which, over a short period of time, the chemical is supposed not to present a significant hazard. The level of the chemical in the environment should nevertheless be reduced as rapidly as possible by improvements in ventilation, for example, or ameliorated through the use of suitable protection, such as breathing apparatus.

Teratogen   A teratogen is a chemical that may cause nonheritable genetic mutations or malformations in the developing foetus.

Teratogenesis   Teratogenesis is the production of nonheritable reproductive defects.

TLV   TLV (Threshold Limit Value) is the maximum permissible concentration of a material, generally expressed in parts per million in air for some defined period of time (often 8 hours, but sometimes for 40 hours per week over an assumed working lifetime). These values, which may differ from country to country, are often backed up by regulation and therefore may be legally enforceable.

TLV-C TLV-C ceiling exposure limit; an exposure limit that should not be exceeded under any circumstances.

Tolerable Daily Intake The Tolerable Daily Intake (TDI) is an estimate of the quantity of a chemical contaminant in food or water that can be ingested daily over a lifetime without posing a significant risk to health. "Contaminants" are different from "residues" in this context a contaminant is a chemical whose presence in food or water does not serve, and never has served, any useful purpose. TDIs are thus distinct from ADIs (the Acceptable Daily Intake), which relate to residues of chemicals that have been deliberately added to a product (for example, residues of pesticide sprays or antifungal agents).

Tolerance Tolerance is the ability of an animal or plant to withstand single or repeated doses of a potentially harmful chemical without adverse effect.

Torr See **Units of pressure.**

Toxicant *Toxicant* is a comparatively rarely used term that describes any material that is potentially toxic.

Toxicity The term *toxicity* is very widely used in a safety context, for obvious reasons. It is used in two contrasting senses: to denote the capacity to cause harm to a living organism and to indicate the adverse effects caused by a chemical. The degree of harm caused to an organism by exposure to a toxic chemical generally increases with exposure level but is also dependent upon the type of organism, the length of exposure, the physiological status of the organism (essentially its fitness) and its developmental stage. For example, some toxic chemicals have a more serious effect upon a developing fetus than upon an adult organism. Toxicity is often subdivided into:

– **Acute toxicity** Adverse effects are observed within a short time of exposure to the chemical.

This exposure may be a single dose, or a short continuous exposure, or multiple doses administered over 24 hours or less.

– **Subacute (subchronic) toxicity** Adverse effects are observed following repeated daily exposure to a chemical, or exposure for a significant part of an organism's lifespan (usually not exceeding 10 percent). With experimental animals, the period of exposure may range from a few days to 6 months.

– **Chronic toxicity** Adverse effects are observed following repeated exposure to a chemical during a substantial fraction of an organism's lifespan (usually more than 50 percent). For humans, chronic exposure typically means several decades; for experimental animals, it is typically more than 3 months. Chronic exposure to chemicals over periods of 2 years using rats or mice may be used to assess the carcinogenic potential of chemicals.

Trohoc Trohoc is a type of epidemiological study in which one identifies certain outcomes and then looks for possible causes. This backwards design has lead to the coining of the term trohoc (cohort spelled backwards).

TSCA Toxic Substances Control Act. This regulates the manufacture, transport, and use of toxic substances.

TSRAL See **Temporary safe reference action level.**

Tumorigenic Tumorigenic is a description that can be applied to any material or phenomenon (a chemical, a radiochemical, radiation, etc.) capable of generating tumors.

TWA (Time Weighted Average) This term is used in the specification of Occupational Exposure Limits (OELs) to define the average concentration of a chemical to which it is permissible to expose a worker over a period of time, typically 8 hours.

Uniform emission standard See **Emission standard.**

Units of pressure Units of pressure are often somewhat confusing, because of the different systems in use. A Torr (named after Torricelli) is the pressure produced by a column of mercury 1 mm high, so it equals 1/760th of an atmosphere. The Pascal is now widely used. This is the S.I. unit, and equals a force of one Newton per square meter (in turn, a Newton is the force required to give a 1 kilogram mass an acceleration of 1 meter per second). The Pascal is quite a small pressure, so we often use KiloPascals (kPa), equal to one thousand Pascals. 101.325 kPa equals one atmosphere. Pounds per square inch (psi) used to be common in the UK but has now been supplanted in virtually every country other than the United States by the S.I. unit. One atmosphere is approximately 15 psi.

VDU   See **Display screen equipment.**

Vesicant   A vesicant is a chemical that, if it can escape from the vein, causes extensive tissue damage, with vesicle formation or blistering.

Very toxic   The designation of a chemical as being very toxic is to some extent arbitrary. It is most commonly applied to chemicals whose ORL-RAT LD50 value is <25 mg kg^{-1}, but this should be taken as providing guidance only.

Viton   Viton is a hexafluoropropylene-vinylidene fluoride co-polymer that is widely used in protective clothing. Viton is a trademark of the DuPont Company.

VOCs   Volatile organic compounds.

Work-related upper limb disorder   See **Repetitive strain injury.**

WULD   See **Repetitive strain injury.**

Xenobiotic   A xenobiotic is a chemical (or, more generally, a chemical mix) that is not a normal component of the organism that is exposed to it. Xenbiotics, therefore, include most drugs (other than those compounds that naturally occur in the organism), as well as other foreign substances.

Sources:

1. The Physical and Theoretical Chemistry Laboratory, Oxford University, England
2. Chemical Safety Information—Glossary
3. http://physchem.ox.ac.uk/MSDS/glossary.html

RADIOLOGICAL/NUCLEAR

Absolute risk   The proportion of a population expected to get a disease over a specified time period.

Absorbed dose   The amount of energy deposited by ionizing radiation in a unit mass of tissue. It is expressed in units of joule per kilogram (J/kg), and called "gray" (Gy).

Activity (radioactivity)   The rate of decay of radioactive material expressed as the number of atoms breaking down per second measured in units called becquerels or curies.

Acute exposure   An exposure to radiation that occurred in a matter of minutes rather than in longer, continuing exposure over a period of time.

Acute radiation syndrome (ARS)   A serious illness caused by receiving a dose greater than 50 rads of penetrating radiation to the body in a short time (usually minutes). The earliest symptoms are nausea, fatigue, vomiting, and diarrhea. Hair loss, bleeding, swelling of the mouth and throat, and general loss of energy may follow. If the exposure has been approximately 1,000 rads or more, death may occur within 2 to 4 weeks.

Air burst   A nuclear weapon explosion that is high enough in the air to keep the fireball from touching the ground. Because the fireball does not reach the ground and does not pick up any surface material, the radioactivity in the fallout from an airburst is relatively insignificant compared with a surface burst.

Alpha particle   The nucleus of a helium atom, made up of two neutrons and two protons with a charge of +2. Certain radioactive nuclei emit alpha particles. Alpha particles generally carry more energy than gamma or beta particles and deposit that energy very quickly while passing through tissue. Alpha particles can be stopped by a thin layer of light material, such as a sheet of paper, and cannot penetrate the outer, dead layer of skin. Therefore they do not damage living tissue when outside the body. When alpha-emitting atoms are inhaled or swallowed, however, they are especially damaging because they transfer relatively large amounts of ionizing energy to living cells.

Americium (Am)   A silvery metal, it is a man-made element whose isotopes Am-237 through Am-246 are all radioactive. Am-241 is formed spontaneously by the beta decay of plutonium-241. Trace quantities of americium are widely used in smoke detectors and as neutron sources in neutron moisture gauges.

Background radiation   Ionizing radiation from natural sources, such as terrestrial radiation due to radionuclides in the soil or cosmic radiation originating in outer space.

Becquerel (Bq)   The amount of a radioactive material that will undergo one decay (disintegration) per second.

Carcinogen   A cancer-causing substance.

Chain reaction   A process that initiates its own repetition. In a fission chain reaction, a fissile nucleus absorbs a neutron and fissions (splits) spontaneously, releasing additional neutrons. These, in turn, can be absorbed by other fissile nuclei, releasing still more neutrons. A fission chain reaction is self-sustaining when the number of neutrons released in a given time equals or exceeds the number of neutrons lost by absorption in nonfissile material or by escape from the system.

Chronic exposure   Exposure to a substance over a long period of time, possibly resulting in adverse health effects.

Cobalt (Co)   A gray, hard, magnetic, and somewhat malleable metal, cobalt is relatively rare and generally obtained as a by-product of other metals, such as copper. Its most common radioisotope, cobalt-60 (Co-60), is used in radiography and medical applications. Cobalt-60 emits beta particles and gamma rays during radioactive decay.

Collective dose   The estimated dose for an area or region multiplied by the estimated population in that area or region.

Committed dose   A dose that accounts for continuing exposures expected to be received

over a long period of time (such as 30, 50, or 70 years) from radioactive materials that were deposited inside the body.

Conference of Radiation Control Program Directors (CRCPD)   An organization whose members represent state radiation protection programs.

Contamination (radioactive)   The deposition of unwanted radioactive material on the surfaces of structures, areas, objects, or people where it may be external or internal.

Criticality   A fission process in which the neutron production rate equals the neutron loss rate to absorption or leakage. A nuclear reactor is "critical" when it is operating.

Cumulative dose   The total dose resulting from repeated or continuous exposures of the same portion of the body, or of the whole body, to ionizing radiation.

Curie (Ci)   The traditional measure of radioactivity based on the observed decay rate of 1 gram of radium. One curie of radioactive material will have 37 billion disintegrations in 1 second.

Cutaneous radiation syndrome (CRS)   The complex syndrome resulting from radiation exposure of more than 200 rads to the skin. The immediate effects can be reddening and swelling of the exposed area (like a severe burn), blisters, ulcers on the skin, hair loss, and severe pain. Very large doses can result in permanent hair loss, scarring, altered skin color, deterioration of the affected body part, and death of the affected tissue (requiring surgery).

Decontamination   The reduction or removal of radioactive contamination from a structure, object, or person.

Depleted uranium   Uranium containing less than 0.7% uranium-235, the amount found in natural uranium.

Deposition density   The activity of a radionuclide per unit area of ground. Reported as becquerels per square meter or curies per square meter.

Deterministic effects   Effects that can be related directly to the radiation dose received. The severity increases as the dose increases. A deterministic effect typically has a threshold below which the effect will not occur.

Deuterium   A nonradioactive isotope of the hydrogen atom that contains a neutron in its nucleus in addition to the one proton normally seen in hydrogen. A deuterium atom is twice as heavy as normal hydrogen.

Dirty bomb   A device designed to spread radioactive material by conventional explosives when the bomb explodes. A dirty bomb kills or injures people through the initial blast of the conventional explosive and spreads radioactive contamination over possibly a large area—hence the term "dirty." Such bombs could be miniature devices or large truck bombs. A dirty bomb is much simpler to make than a true nuclear weapon.

Dose (radiation)   Radiation absorbed by person's body. Several different terms describe radiation dose.

Dosimeter   A small portable instrument (such as a film badge, thermoluminescent dosimeter [TLD], or pocket dosimeter) for measuring and recording the total accumulated dose of ionizing radiation a person receives.

Enriched uranium   Uranium in which the proportion of the isotope uranium-235 has been increased by removing uranium-238 mechanically.

Epidemiology   The study of the distribution and determinants of health-related states or events in specified populations and the application of this study to the control of health problems.

Exposure (radiation)   A measure of ionization in air caused by X-rays or gamma rays only. The unit of exposure most often used is the roentgen.

Fallout, nuclear   Minute particles of radioactive debris that descend slowly from the atmosphere after a nuclear explosion.

Fissile material   Any material in which neutrons can cause a fission reaction. The three primary fissile materials are uranium-233, uranium-235, and plutonium-239.

Fission (fissioning)   The splitting of a nucleus into at least two other nuclei that releases a large amount of energy. Two or three neutrons are usually released during this transformation.

Fusion   A reaction in which at least one heavier, more stable nucleus is produced from two lighter, less stable nuclei. Reactions of this type are responsible for the release of energy in stars or in thermonuclear weapons.

Gamma rays   High-energy electromagnetic radiation emitted by certain radionuclides when their nuclei transition from a higher to a lower energy state. These rays have high energy and a short wave length. All gamma rays emitted from a given isotope have the same energy, a characteristic that enables scientists to identify which gamma emitters are present in a sample. Gamma rays penetrate tissue farther than do beta or alpha particles but leave a lower concentration of ions in their path to potentially cause cell damage. Gamma rays are very similar to X-rays.

Gray (Gy)   A unit of measurement for absorbed dose. It measures the amount of energy absorbed in a material. The unit Gy can be used for any type of radiation, but it does not describe the biological effects of the different radiations.

High-level radioactive waste   The radioactive material resulting from spent nuclear fuel reprocessing. This can include liquid waste directly produced in reprocessing or any solid material derived from the liquid wastes having a sufficient concentration of fission products. Other radioactive materials can be designated as high-level waste, if they require permanent isolation. This determination is made by the U.S. Nuclear Regulatory Commission on the basis of criteria established in U.S. law.

Hot spot   Any place where the level of radioactive contamination is considerably greater than the area around it.

Ingestion   (1) The act of swallowing; (2) in the case of radionuclides or chemicals, swallowing radionuclides or chemicals by eating or drinking.

Inhalation   (1) The act of breathing in; (2) in the case of radionuclides or chemicals, breathing in radionuclides or chemicals.

Internal exposure Exposure to radioactive material taken into the body.

Iodine A nonmetallic solid element. There are both radioactive and nonradioactive isotopes of iodine. Radioactive isotopes of iodine are widely used in medical applications. Radioactive iodine is a fission product and is the largest contributor to people's radiation dose after an accident at a nuclear reactor.

Isotope A nuclide of an element having the same number of protons but a different number of neutrons.

Kiloton (Kt) The energy of an explosion that is equivalent to an explosion of 1,000 tons of TNT. One kiloton equals 1 trillion (1,012) calories.

Lead (Pb) A heavy metal. Several isotopes of lead, such as Pb-210, which emits beta radiation, are in the uranium decay chain.

Low-level waste (LLW) Radioactively contaminated industrial or research waste such as paper, rags, plastic bags, medical waste, and water-treatment residues. It is waste that does not meet the criteria for any of three other categories of radioactive waste spent nuclear fuel and high-level radioactive waste; transuranic radioactive waste; or uranium mill tailings. Its categorization does not depend on the level of radioactivity it contains.

Megaton (Mt) The energy of an explosion that is equivalent to an explosion of 1 million tons of TNT. One megaton is equal to a quintillion (1,018) calories.

Nuclear energy The heat energy produced by the process of nuclear fission within a nuclear reactor or by radioactive decay.

Penetrating radiation Radiation that can penetrate the skin and reach internal organs and tissues. Photons (gamma rays and X-rays), neutrons, and protons are penetrating radiations. However, alpha particles and all but extremely high-energy beta particles are not considered penetrating radiation.

Pitchblende A brown to black mineral that has a distinctive luster. It consists mainly of urananite (UO2) but also contains radium (Ra). It is the main source of uranium (U) ore.

Plume The material spreading from a particular source and traveling through environmental media, such as air or groundwater. For example, a plume could describe the dispersal of particles, gases, vapors, and aerosols in the atmosphere or the movement of contamination through an aquifer (for example, dilution, mixing, or adsorption onto soil).

Plutonium (Pu) A heavy, man-made, radioactive metallic element. The most important isotope is Pu-239, which has a half-life of 24,000 years. Pu-239 can be used in reactor fuel and is the primary isotope in weapons. One kilogram is equivalent to about 22 million kilowatt-hours of heat energy. The complete detonation of a kilogram of plutonium produces an explosion equal to about 20,000 tons of chemical explosive. All isotopes of plutonium are readily absorbed by the bones and can be lethal depending on the dose and exposure time.

Polonium (Po) A radioactive chemical element and a product of radium (Ra) decay. Polonium is found in uranium (U) ores.

Radiation Energy moving in the form of particles or waves. Familiar radiations are heat, light, radio waves, and microwaves. Ionizing radiation is a very high-energy form of electromagnetic radiation.

Radioactive contamination The deposition of unwanted radioactive material on the surfaces of structures, areas, objects, or people. It can be airborne, external, or internal.

Radioactive decay The spontaneous disintegration of the nucleus of an atom.

Radioactive material Material that contains unstable (radioactive) atoms that give off radiation as they decay.

Radiological dispersal device (RDD) A device that disperses radioactive material by conventional explosive or other mechanical means, such as a spray.

Radium (Ra) A naturally occurring radioactive metal. Radium is a radionuclide formed by the decay of uranium (U) and thorium (Th) in the environment. It occurs at low levels in virtually all rock, soil, water, plants, and animals. Radon (Rn) is a decay product of radium.

Radon (Rn)   A naturally occurring radioactive gas found in soils, rock, and water throughout the United States. Radon causes lung cancer and is a threat to health because it tends to collect in homes, sometimes to very high concentrations. As a result, radon is the largest source of exposure to people from naturally occurring radiation.

Rem (roentgen equivalent, man)   A unit of equivalent dose. Not all radiation has the same biological effect, even for the same amount of absorbed dose. Rem relates the absorbed dose in human tissue to the effective biological damage of the radiation. It is determined by multiplying the number of rads by the quality factor, a number reflecting the potential damage caused by the particular type of radiation. The rem is the traditional unit of equivalent dose, but it is being replaced by the sievert (Sv), which is equal to 100 rem.

Roentgen (R)   A unit of exposure to X-rays or gamma rays. One roentgen is the amount of gamma or X-rays needed to produce ions carrying 1 electrostatic unit of electrical charge in 1 cubic centimeter of dry air under standard conditions.

Shielding   The material between a radiation source and a potentially exposed person that reduces exposure.

Sievert (Sv)   A unit used to derive a quantity called *dose equivalent*. This relates the absorbed dose in human tissue to the effective biological damage of the radiation. Not all radiation has the same biological effect, even for the same amount of absorbed dose. Dose equivalent is often expressed as millionths of a sievert, or micro-sieverts (μSv). One sievert is equivalent to 100 rem.

Somatic effects   Effects of radiation that are limited to the exposed person, as distinguished from genetic effects, which may also affect subsequent generations.

Strontium (Sr)   A silvery, soft metal that rapidly turns yellow in air. Sr-90 is one of the radioactive fission materials created within a nuclear reactor during its operation. Stronium-90 emits beta particles during radioactive decay.

Surface burst   A nuclear weapon explosion that is close enough to the ground for the radius of the fireball to vaporize surface material. Fallout from a surface burst contains very high levels of radioactivity.

Tailings   Waste rock from mining operations that contains concentrations of mineral ore that are too low to make typical extraction methods economical.

Thermonuclear device   A "hydrogen bomb." A device with explosive energy that comes from fusion of small nuclei, as well as fission.

Thorium (Th)   A naturally occurring radioactive metal found in small amounts in soil, rocks, water, plants, and animals. The most common isotopes of thorium are thorium-232 (Th-232), thorium-230 (Th-230), and thorium-238 (Th-238).

Tritium (chemical symbol H-3)   A radioactive isotope of the element hydrogen (chemical symbol H).

Uranium (U)   A naturally occurring radioactive element whose principal isotopes are uranium-238 (U-238) and uranium-235 (U-235). Natural uranium is a hard, silvery-white, shiny metallic ore that contains a minute amount of uranium-234 (U-234).

Source:

1. Centers for Disease Control and Prevention
   http://cdc.gov

References

Altheide, David L. 2002. *Creating Fear: News and the Construction of Crisis*. New York: Aldine de Gruyter.

Ansell, Jake, and Frank Wharton. 1992. *Risk: Analysis, Assessment, and Management*. Chichester: John Wiley & Sons.

Atwater, Brian F., Marco Cisternas V., Joanne Bourgeois, Walter C. Dudley, James W. Hendley II, and Peter H. Stauffer. 1999. *Surviving a Tsunami: Lessons learned from Chile, Hawaii, and Japan*. Washington, DC: USGS Information Services.

Baldwin, Thomas E. 2003. *Historical Chronology of FEMA Consequence Management Preparedness and Response to Terrorism*. Argonne, Illinois: Argonne National Laboratory.

Blanchard, Wayne. 2001. "The Emergency Manager." *IAEM Bulletin* (May).

Bohn, Kevin. 2003. "ACLU Files Lawsuit Against Patriot Act." *CNN* (July 30).

Bremer, Ambassador L., and Paul Bremer III. 2002. "The Terrorist Threat." In *Terrorism: Informing the Public*, edited by Nancy Ethiel. Chicago: McCormick Tribune Foundation.

Brookings Institution. 2003. "Protecting the American Homeland: One Year On." Washington, DC. January.

Brookings Institution. 2002. "Homeland Security: The White House Plan Explained and Examined." *A Brookings Forum* (September 4).

Brown, Jane D., and Sarah N. Keller. 2000. "Can the Mass Media Be Healthy Sex Educators?" *Family Planning Perspectives*. vol. 32. no. 5. pp. 255–256.

Brunker, Mike. 2002. "Sea Change for the Coast Guard." MSNBC (December 19).

Bullock, Jane. 2003. Several interviews over a two-month period with the FEMA Chief of Staff (Fmr.) Washington, DC. Unpublished Damon Coppola Intexvelnee.

Burkeman, Oliver. 2003. "U.S. to Fit Airliners with Anti-Missile Defenses." *The Guardian* (September 19).

Burkhart, Ford N. 1991. *Media, Emergency Warnings, and Citizen Response*. Boulder, Colorado: Westview Press.

Center for Defense Information. 2002. "Terror Alerts: The Homeland Security Advisory." September 1. <http://www.govexec.com/features/0902/0902s4.htm>

Central Intelligence Agency. 2002. "Terrorism: Guide to Chemical, Biological, Radiological and Nuclear Weapons Indicators." November.

Chabrow, Eric. 2003. "Share and Share Alike: Government Agencies Struggle to Overcome the Many Barriers to Collaboration." *Information Week* (September 1).

Cheng, Mae M. 2003. "Homeland Department May Contract Out Jobs." *Newsday* (September 14).

Citizen Corps web site <www.citizencorps.gov>

The City of Oklahoma. 1996. *Alfred P. Murrah Federal Building Bombing April 19, 1995*. Stillwater, Oklahoma: Fire Protection Publications. Oklahoma State University.

CNCS. 2003. "President Calls for More Americorps and Senior Corps Volunteers in 2004 Budget" (February 3). <http://www.nationalservice.org/news/pr/020303.html>

CNCS. 2002. "White House and CNCS Announce New Grants to Involve Volunteers in Homeland Security" (July 18). <http://www.nationalservice.org/news/pr/071802.html>

Cohen, Bernard C. 1963. *The Press and Foreign Policy*. Princeton, New Jersey: Princeton University Press.

Columbus Dispatch. 2003. "Security Risks in the Air." Editorial. (September 19).

Cook, David T. 2003. "Tom Ridge." *Christian Science Monitor* (September 15).

Coppola, Damon P. 2003. *Annotated Organizational Chart for the Department of Homeland Security*. Washington, DC: Bullock & Haddow, LLC.

Davis, Lance. 2003. "City Officials Respond to Orange Alert." *The National League of Cities* (February 17).

Department of Homeland Security (DHS). 2003. Ready. Gov web site. Washington, DC: DHS. <http://www.ready.gov>

Department of Homeland Security web site <http://www.dhs.gov>

Department of Homeland Security. 2003. "2004 Budget in Brief." <http://www.dhs.gov/interweb/assetlibrary/FY_2004_BUDGET_IN_BRIEF.pdf>

Department of Homeland Security. 2003. The National Strategy for the Protection of Physical Infrastructure and Key Assets, pp. 39–40. <www.dhs.gov>.

Department of Homeland Security. 2002. "The Department of Homeland Security" (June). <http://www.dhs.gov/interweb/assetlibrary/book.pdf>

Diamond, John, et al. 2003. "6 Fronts of the War on Terrorism." *USA Today* (September 11).

Disaster Management Center. 1995. *Disaster Preparedness.* Madison, Wisconsin: The University of Wisconsin. <http://dmc.engr.wisc.edu/courses/preparedness/BB04-intro.html>

Edmonson, R.G. 2003. "Blurring of the Lines." *Journal of Commerce* (August 11), p. 12.

Enders, Jessica. 2001. "Measuring Community Awareness and Preparedness for Emergencies." *Australian Journal of Emergency Management* (Spring), pp. 52–59.

Etzioni, Amitai. 2003. "Our Unfinished Post-9/11 Duty." *Christian Science Monitor* (September 11), p. 9.

Federal Emergency Management Agency. 2003. *A Nation Remembers, A Nation Mourns* (September). Washington, DC. FEMA.

Federal Emergency Management Agency. 2002. *Managing the Emergency Consequences of Terrorist Incidents— Interim Planning Guide for State and Local Government.* Washington, DC: FEMA.

Federal Emergency Management Agency. 2002. "Allbaugh Announces Citizen Corps' First Official Affiliate Program During National Fire Prevention Week" (October 10). FEMA Press Release.

Federal Emergency Management Agency. 2001. *Delivery of Individual Assistance Programs.* New York: FEMA, Office of Inspector General (September).

Federal Emergency Management Agency (FEMA). 1998. "Making Your Community Disaster Resistant: Project Impact Media Partnership Guide." Washington, DC: FEMA.

Federal Emergency Management Agency (FEMA). 1997. *Multi Hazard: Identification and Assessment.* Washington, DC: FEMA.

FFIS. 2003. "Federal Actions Affecting States." Federal Funds Information for States web site (February 14). <www.ffis.org/misc/sum.htm>

FindLaw. 2002. "Homeland Security Act of 2002" (November 19). <http://news.findlaw.com/wp/docs/terrorism/hsa2002.pdf>

Fitzpatrick, Dan. 2003. "Sounding the Alarm—Again." *Pittsburgh Post Gazette* (September 9). p. C12.

Foster. 2003. "Leave This Patriot Alone." *Milwaukee Journal Sentinel* (September 17) p.14A.

Furedi, Frank. 1997. *Culture of Fear: Risk-Taking and the Morality of Low Expectation.* London: Cassell.

Furman, Matt. 2002. "Good Information Saves Lives." In *Terrorism: Informing the Public,* edited by Nancy Ethiel. Chicago: McCormick Tribune Foundation.

Fusco, Anthony L. 1993. "The World Trade Center Bombing: Report and Analysis." U.S. Fire Administration. Washington, DC.

Gay, Lance. 2001. "How the New Antiterrorism Bill Could Affect You." *Scripps Howard News Service* (October 26).

Gedan, Benjamin. 2003. "Local Safety Officials Feel Unprepared Post September 11th Survey Suggests Funds Are Issue." *Boston Globe* (August 29) p. B2.

Ghent, Bill. 2003. "Senate Dems fault Bush over Homeland Security Funds." *Government Executive Magazine* (February 13).

Ghent, Bill. 2003. "White House Threatens Veto as Omnibus Deal Nears Hill." *Government Executive Magazine* (February 5).

Glassner, Barry. 1999. *The Culture of Fear.* New York: Basic Books.

Haddow, George. 2003. Several interviews over a two-month period with the FEMA Deputy Chief of Staff (Fmr.) Washington, DC. Damon Coppola.

Hall, Mimi. 2003. "Tracking of Foreign Visitors Hits Snags." *USA Today* (September 22) p. 1A.

Hall, Mimi. 2003. "Terrorist Risk Lists Leave Gap, Even Now." *USA Today* (August 11) p. 1A.

Hendrix, Anastasia. 2003. "Rights Group Slams Homeland Security Tactics." *San Francisco Chronicle* (May 29) p. A16.

Hughes, Amy C. 2003. "Summit tackles tough issues." *State Government News.* The Council of State Governments (August).

Hulse, Carl. 2003. "Congress Advances $29.4 Billion Plan for Security Agency." *New York Times* (September 18) p. A25.

Jones, Elise F., James R. Beniger, and Charles F. Westoff. 1980. "Pill and IUD Discontinuation in the United States, 1970–1975: The Influence of the Media." *Family Planning Perspectives.* vol. 12. no. 6. pp. 293–300.

Kaplan, Stan. 1997. "The Words of Risk Analysis." *Risk Analysis.* vol. 17 no. 4, p. 408.

Kayyem, N. Juliette, Chang E. Patricia. 2002. *Beyond Business Continuity: The Role of the Private Sector in Preparedness Planning.* pp. 3–4, August 2002 Business Continuity Institute.

Lebihan, Rachel. 2003. "Balancing Security and Privacy." *Australian Financial Review* (September 12) p. 64.

Lichtblau, Eric. 2003. "Administration Creates Center for Master Terror 'Watch List'." *New York Times* (September 17) p. A20.

Lumpkin, John J. 2003. "Bush Seeks $41.3B for Homeland Security." Newsday.com (January 31).

Marks, Alexandra. 2003. "With 9/11 More Distant, Alertness Wavers." *Christian Science Monitor* (August 5) p. 3.

Martin, Gary. 2003. "Homeland Defense Mission May Take Decades." *San Antonio Express News* (September 7) p. A12.

McCallum, D. B., S. L. Hammond, and L. Morris. 1990. *Public Knowledge of Chemical Risks in Six Communities.* Washington, DC: Georgetown University Medical Center, Institute for Health Policy Analysis.

McCombs, M., and D. Shaw. 1972. "The Agenda-Setting Function of Mass Media." *Public Opinion Quarterly.* vol. 36. pp. 176–187.

McCormick Tribune Foundation. 2002. "Terrorism: Informing the Public." In *Cantigny Conference Series,* edited by Nancy Ethiel. Chicago: McCormick Tribune Foundation.

McDivitt, Judith A., Susan Zimicki, Robert Hornik, and Ayman Abulaban. 1993. "The Impact of the Healthcom Mass Media Campaign on Timely Initiation of Breastfeeding in Jordan." *Studies in Family Planning.* vol. 24. no 5. pp. 295–309.

McGreevy, Patrick. 2003. "Security Aid Falls Short, Mayors Say." *Los Angeles Times* (September 18) Part 2, p. 3.

Means, Marianne. 2003. "Homeland Security; Desk Shuffling Is Not Enough." *San Diego Union Tribune* (September 7) p. G1.

Mehren, Elizabeth. 2003. "Latest Trend in Academia: Security." *Los Angeles Times* (September 14) p. 34.

Mileti, Dennis S. 1999. *Disasters by Design.* Washington, DC: Joseph Henry Press.

Miller, Judith. 2002. "Who? How? When? What? Where?" In *Terrorism: Informing the Public,* edited by Nancy Ethiel. Chicago: McCormick Tribune Foundation.

Mintz, John. 2003. "Government's Hobbled Giant; Homeland Security Is Struggling." *Washington Post* (September 7) p. A1.

Moretti, M. Mindy. 2003. "Homeland Security Task Force Presses Congress to Act." *NACo County News* (January 27).

Morgan, M. Granger, Baruch Fischoff, Ann Bostrom, and Cynthia J Atman. 2002. *Risk Communication: A Mental Models Approach.* Cambridge: Cambridge University Press.

Moritz, Owen. 2003. "Ferry Frisk in Riders' Future?" *Daily News* (July 2) p. 25.

Moscoso, Eunice. 2003. "Cities Await Security Funds." *Atlanta Journal and Constitution* (September 18) p. 8A.

Moscoso, Eunice. 2003. "September 11, Two Years Later." *Atlanta Journal and Constitution* (September 10) p. 6A.

Mullis, John-Paul. 1998. "Persuasive Communication Issues in Disaster Management." *Australian Journal of Emergency Management* (Autumn) pp. 51–58.

National Association of Counties. 2003. "Policy Agency to Secure the People of America's Counties." NACo homepage. <http://www.naco.org/programs/homesecurity/homelandpolicy.pdf>

National Governors Association. 2002. "States' Homeland Security Priorities." *NGA Center for Best Practices* (August 19).

National League of Cities. 2002. "Homeland Security: Practical Tools for Local Governments" (November). <http://www.nlc.org/nlc_org/site/files/reports/terrorism.pdf>

Nelken, D. 1987. *Selling Science: How the Press Covers Science and Technology.* New York: W. H. Freeman.

Nielsen, Samuel, and John Lidstone. 1998. "Public Education and Disaster Management: Is There Any Guiding Theory?" *Australian Journal of Emergency Management* (Spring) pp. 14–19.

Occhipinti, John D. 2002. "Allies at Odds." *Buffalo News* (December 22) p. H1.

Office of Management and Budget. 2003. "Department of Homeland Security." <http://www.whitehouse.gov/omb/budget/fy2004/homeland.html>

Patten, Wendy. 2002. "U.S. Homeland Security Bill: Civil Rights Vulnerable and Immigrant Children Not Protected." *Human Rights Watch* (November 21).

Peckenpaugh, Jason. 2002. "Building a Behemoth." *Government Executive Magazine.*

Physical Infrastructure and Key Assets, pp. 39–40, <http://www.dhs.gov>

Piotrow, Phyllis T., Jose G. Rimon, Kim Winnard, D. Lawrence Kincaid, Dale Huntington, and Julie Convisser. 1990. "Mass Media Family Planning Promotion in Three Nigerian Cities." *Studies in Family Planning.* vol. 21. no. 5. pp. 265–274.

Pittsburgh Post Gazette. 2003. "The Age of Insecurity." Editorial. (September 21) p. B7.

Pittsburgh Post Gazette. 2003. "Will They Listen to Rudman This Time?" Editorial. (July 7) p. A13.

Raphael, B. 1986. *When Disaster Strikes: How Individuals and Communities Cope with Catastrophes.* New York: Basic Books.

Richelson J. T., J. Gefter, M. Waters, M. Evans, M. Byrne, R. Rone, J. Martinez, J. Grant, M. Burroughs, 2003. "U.S. Espionage and Intelligence, 1947–1996," *Digital National Security Archive.* <http://nsarchive.chadwyck.com/esp_essay.htm>

Sataline, Suzanne. 2003. "Democratic Senators Call for Intelligence Reform." *St. Petersburg Times* p.6A

Shapiro, Jeffrey Scott. 2003. "America Risks Repeating a 'Fundamental Injustice.'" *Insight on the News* (September 15) p. 51.

Shenon, Philip. 2003. "High Alerts for Terror Get Harder to Impose." *New York Times* (September 13) p. A9.

Simon, Harvey. 2003. "Emphasis on Illegal Immigrants Could Have Security Tradeoffs." *Aviation Week's Homeland Security and Defense* (September 4) vol. 2. no. 36. p. 5.

Singer, Eleanor, and Phyllis M. Endreny. 1993. *Reporting on Risk: How the Mass Media Portray Accidents, Diseases, Disasters, and Other Hazards.* New York: Russell Sage Foundation.

Smith J. David. 2002. "Business Continuity Management: Good Practice Guidelines, System." CDI web site. <http://www.cdi.org/terrorism/alerts.cfm>.

Taylor, Gus. 2003. "Communities Shun Patriot Act." *The Washington Times.* July 21, 2003.

The United States Conference of Mayors. 2003. "Statement of Boston Mayor Thomas M. Menino, President, U.S. Conference of Mayors, on FY 2003 Omnibus Appropriations Bill." Report by *USCM* (February 13).

The United States Conference of Mayors. 2002. "One Year Later: A Status Report on the Federal-Local Partnership on Homeland Security." Report by *USCM* (September 9).

The United States Conference of Mayors. 2001. "A National Action Plan for Safety and Security in America's Cities." Report by *USCM* (December).

Thornton, Kelly. 2003. "Civilians Join Talks on Terror Preparedness." *San Diego Union Tribune* (April 30) p. B1.

USA Today. 2003. "MIA: Terror Database." (August 12) p. 12A.

Walker, Laura. 2003. "We Have Our Radios. Now What?" *Broadcasting and Cable* (August 18) p. 28.

Walsh, James. 1996. *True Odds: How Risk Affects Your Everyday Life.* Santa Monica: Merritt Publishing.

Warner, Kenneth E. 1989. "The Epidemiology of Coffin Nails." In *Health Risks and the Press: Coverage on Media Coverage of Risk Assessment and Health.* Washington, DC: The Media Institute.

Waugh, William L., Jr. 2000. *Living with Hazards, Dealing with Disasters: An Introduction to Emergency Management.* New York: M.E. Sharpe.

Wenham, Brian. 1994. "The Media and Disasters: Building a Better Understanding." In *International Disaster Communications: Harnessing the Power of Communications to Avert Disasters and Save Lives.* Washington, DC: The Annenberg Washington Program.

Westoff, Charles F., and German Rodriguez. 1995. "The Mass Media and Family Planning in Kenya." *International Family Planning Perspectives.* vol. 21. no. 1. pp. 26–31, 36.

The White House. 2002. "Department of Homeland Security Reorganization Plan" (November 25). <http://www.whitehouse.gov/news/releases/2002/11/reorganization_plan.pdf>

The White House. 2002. "Fact Sheet: Homeland Security Council." (October 29). <http://www.whitehouse.gov/news/releases/2001/10/20011029-16.html>

The White House. 1997. "50th Anniversary of the National Security Act of 1947." Office of the Press Secretary. <http://clinton4.nara.gov/WH/EOP/NSC/html/50thanniv.html>

Willis, Jim. 1997. *Reporting on Risks: The Practice and Ethics of Health and Safety Communication.* Westport, Connecticut: Praeger.

Winston, J. A. 1985. "Science and the Media: The Boundaries of Truth." *Health Affairs.* vol. 6. pp. 5–23.

Witwer, M. 1997. "In Sub-Saharan Africa, Levels of Knowledge and Use of Contraceptives Are Linked to Media Exposure." *International Family Planning Perspectives.* vol. 23. no. 4. pp. 183–184.

Index